E-COMMERCE
An Indian Perspective

E-COMMERCE
An Indian Perspective

SEVENTH EDITION

P.T. JOSEPH, S.J.
Professor
Information Systems at XLRI, Delhi–NCR Campus
and
Former Director of Xavier Institute of Management, Bhubaneswar
and
Former Professor of Information Systems at XLRI, Jamshedpur

PHI Learning Private Limited

Delhi-110092
2025

In fond memory of ***Shri Asoke K. Ghosh*** *(October 1942–February 2024), Founder Chairman and Managing Director of PHI Learning, whose vision endlessly inspires.*

The Legacy Continues....

Published by Pushpita Ghosh, PHI Learning Private Limited, Rimjhim House, 111, Patparganj Industrial Estate, Delhi-110092 and Printed by Star Print-O-Bind, F-31, Okhla Industrial Area Phase I, New Delhi-110020.

₹695.00

E-COMMERCE AN INDIAN PERSPECTIVE, Seventh Edition
P.T. Joseph, S.J.

ISBN-978-93-91818-92-0 (Print Book)
ISBN-978-93-91818-91-3 (e-Book)

Contents

Preface

Recent developments in Artificial Intelligence and Business Analytics are transforming electronic commerce. We are in the age of knowledge management and instant communication and consequently in the midst of an electronic revolution, the impact of which on the economy is much more profound than that caused by the industrial revolution. With the inception of the Web, organizations and individuals are more and more making use of it to create new business ventures. The WWW is not only a definitive source of information, but an astounding business opportunity as well. People throughout the world are venturing out onto the Web for buying and selling goods and services. The Web has indeed proved to be a boon to business, drawing its power from the flow of easy and instantaneous transactions, worldwide. Online business is thriving.

Presently, with more than 5 billion internet users worldwide and 2.87 million apps in the play store, smartphones are transforming our day-to-day life in amazing ways. In a span of 35 years since its inception, smartphones have transformed communication among humankind.

E-commerce refers to the aspects of online business involving exchanges among customers, business partners and vendors. It has increased the speed and ease with which business can be transacted today, resulting in intense competitions between enterprises. Companies are at the crossroads, with just two vistas ahead of them—either go online or go out of business. Once the choice of online business is made, further roadblocks are encountered—"which business model to adopt?" "which management strategies and tactics will make business successful?" and "how to explore opportunities, understands limitations, and issues?" The solution is to gain a deeper insight into the e-commerce strategies.

This is the aim of my revised **seventh edition** of the book, i.e., to provide students with a thorough overview of e-commerce. Through this book, students will be able to learn the whole gamut of e-commerce from developing online strategies for launching and organizing a site to planning and overseeing the transaction systems. From the business strategy perspective, the book also describes the technologies that help businessmen in their e-commerce endeavors.

The book contains 13 chapters. Chapter 1 describes the history of e-commerce and, in particular, focuses on e-transaction challenges for Indian corporates. The recent as well as the projected statistics concerning the growth of the Internet are described. Some case studies emphasize the crucial issues that Indian corporates face while e-transforming themselves.

Chapter 2 is an analysis of different business transaction models based on transaction types and parties. Such an analysis is critical for creating the underlying e-business infrastructure.

The business models of a few Indian corporates are described in case studies. The focus of Chapter 3 is on Web enabled technologies and their growing relevance to e-business. The terms related to networking such as routers, protocols, servers, search engines and methods of networking and usage of networking languages have been thoroughly elucidated with sufficient examples, tables, and figures.

Chapter 4 defines and discusses the concepts and strategies of e-marketing. Real-world examples of popular websites, the techniques involved in Web-browsing and conducting business on the Internet are included to enhance the reader's interest in e-commerce.

An important issue of concern is internet security. There is a definitive requirement to conduct secure and safe transactions over the Web. Chapters 5 and 6 throw light on e-security and e-payment, respectively. Features related to e-security such as firewall protection and virus attacks, and those related to e-payment techniques, including electronic tokens, digital currencies, and digital signature are all analyzed in great detail.

Chapters 7 and 8 are directed towards corporations. How to create customers and maintain a good relationship with them should be the prime concern of any enterprise conducting online business. Chapter 7 discusses the tactics for creating and maintaining customer relations. It focuses on the provisions required for maintaining the quality of service for customers. Customer satisfaction, being the key to business success, requires innovative strategies for the establishment of personal relationship with customers. It is important to keep the online business alive by maintaining an easy and smooth flow of goods and information. Chapter 8 provides a deep insight into this aspect of e-business, i.e., e-supply chain management.

Chapter 9 is an overview of the e-strategies and knowledge management. This chapter highlights the importance of data warehousing and data mining in an organization. Procedures for implementing e-business and strengthening value chain have also been clearly discussed. A case study on knowledge management is included as well.

Chapter 10 is exclusively devoted to 'mobile–commerce', the upcoming e-commerce trend enables by wireless communications. Mobile computing technologies and Web-based applications, which enable mobile business, are clearly explained in this chapter.

Having a gained good knowledge about e-commerce, we reach the final step—the art of Web designing. Chapter 11 describes the features of Web designing and offers useful tips on creating a good e-commerce site. It further goes on to describe about incorporating e-commerce analytics.

The realm of digital transmission is not limited by geography, i.e., cyberspace, is posing significant challenges to the legal system. These issues are explored in Chapter 12, which deals with legal and ethical issues involving the use of the Internet.

E-commerce has challenged the taxation structures all over the world. Traditional transaction laws cannot be applied to e-commerce. So, nations all over the world have been grappling with taxation issues. Chapter 13 looks into these issues.

This book is suitable for the students of management and business administration, computer applications, and information technology. It will also be useful to managers, corporate planners and technical professionals in their endeavors to set up online business processes.

I wish to thank various people at PHI Learning, who devoted their precious time and energy and supervised the overall project and managed excellently to bring the seventh edition on time.

P.T. JOSEPH, S.J.

CHAPTER 1

History of E-commerce and Indian Business Context

LEARNING OBJECTIVES

After reading this chapter, you should be able to:

- Know the impact of internet on the culture of our civilization.
- Explain the birth and growth of the internet revolution.
- Describe how world wide web has changed the business scenario.
- Understand what is meant by e-commerce.
- Appreciate the effects of internet and e-commerce.
- Ascertain the importance of e-commerce for Indian business.

ITC's e-Choupal[1]

The e-Choupal is a multilingual, web-based e-procurement solution providing comprehensive information targeted at the farmer. It is a pioneering techno-business initiative of ITC Ltd and is part of **ITC's rural development initiatives**[2]. Launched in June 2000, 'e-Choupal', has already become the largest initiative among all Internet-based interventions in rural India. 'e-Choupal' services today reach out to over 4 million farmers growing a range of crops—soyabean, coffee, wheat, rice, pulses, shrimp—in over 40,000 villages through 6,500 kiosks across ten states (Madhya Pradesh, Haryana, Uttarakhand, Karnataka, Andhra Pradesh, Uttar Pradesh, Rajasthan, Maharashtra, Kerala and Tamil Nadu).

The existing supply chain was typically "Village->Mandi->ITC Factory/Warehouse".

1. Case prepared by A.Vijayshankar, PM&IR student of XLRI
2. Case prepared by A.Vijayshankar, PM&IR student of XLRI

Some of the irregularities in this scheme were:

- Farmers had only one option to sell their produce—The Mandi. The Mandi was disorganized and run by middlemen, who often cheated the farmers in terms of weight and in terms of price.
- Farmers were usually in the dark about the meteorological information that is so crucial during the sowing time. The available information was usually too generic in nature.
- Farmers were unaware of the latest techniques in farming, soil analysis, fertilizer application, etc. As a result, crop yields were much lower than in other developed countries.

Most importantly, they were unaware of the actual prices at which middlemen sold their produce. As a result, they had to accept whatever prices were offered to them. In May 1999, the e-Choupal plan took concrete shape. The Choupal is a common place in a village where farmers and villagers gather after a day's work to discuss their activities and share knowledge. ITC decided to launch a revolution at the grass roots level, based on this age-old knowledge sharing concept of the Choupal.

Soya bean and soya-related products formed the basis of the IBD's business in 1999. Madhya Pradesh was the state producing the largest quantities of soya bean. The e-Choupal was rolled out, as part of the initiative called *www.soyachoupal.com.*

As per this concept, each village was provided with a computer kiosk containing the following:

- A PC
- Connection lines—telephone-based modems, or VSAT terminals
- A UPS powered by solar energy
- A printer

Technology and Logistics[3]

Challenges. The challenges posed are:

- Low availability of electric power and lots of fluctuations in supply
- Transportation issues—reaching equipment and technicians into remote areas
- Telecom infrastructure—very poor quality. Designed only for voice, not data
- An alien customer base—almost 100 per cent computer illiterate consumer base

System specification. A four-layered IT infrastructure model was conceived. It consisted of:

- Organizational—training, support, planning, people, and processes
- Information—data gathered and managed
- Application—application, goals, resources occupied, performance metrics
- Technical—servers, clients, network, system software

ITC set up a special telecom infrastructure using tweaked C-DOT RNS kits to get a data throughput of 40 kbps and used a modem. In places where the telephone connectivity was absent, VSATs were used for data communication. Spike suppressors and isolation transformers were used along with the UPS to provide smooth, uninterrupted power.

3. www.digitaldividend.org/pdf/e-Choupal_case.pdf

The software consisted of a multilingual word processor called *Ankur* to provide a vernacular graphical interface for farmers. The PC also had video clips on soil testing.

To overcome logistical issues, mobile vans were used to demonstrate and popularize the system through road shows. They also carried technicians to install and support the system.

System Software Development

The system was developed by ITC Infotech India Ltd., a 100 per cent subsidiary of ITC, using. Microsoft technologies—primarily ASP and VB components on an IIS server. HTML is used for presentation and an RDBMS is used at the backend.

The system is linked to ITC IBD's ERP so that transactions can be updated into the system on a real-time basis.

Of the Farmer, by the Farmer, for the Farmer

A literate member of the farming community is chosen as the **Sanchalak**, or coordinator, on behalf of the village. The Sanchalak accesses the site on behalf of the farmers and explains the features of the site and provides them with the relevant information that they want.

Each such Sanchalak is given a user name and password to access the system. Besides serving as an authentication, the user name-location mapping ensures that information is location-specific, making the process more relevant and specific.

ITC pays for the installation cost, the equipment, support and equipment maintenance, while the Sanchalak pays for the day-to-day charges such as electricity and internet. Sanchalaks make a commission of 0.5 per cent per ton of processed product that they get the farmers to sell to ITC.[4]

Before the eChoupal came up, there were commission agents who used to pick up grains from the farmer at the mandis on behalf of ITC. They were given the new role of **Samyojaks**, or facilitators. The Samyojaks help establish e-Choupal kiosks in villages falling within their geographical area. They help in selecting and training Sanchalaks in the villages. They also organize activities at the ITC hubs and warehouses and sell ITC products directly to the farmers when they come to sell their produce. Samyojaks get a commission for this from ITC. In this way, ITC has appeased their older commission agents as well. Sanchalaks and Samyojaks in particular regions are called for meetings/workshops on a regular basis.

The e-Choupal concept is **a big hit with the farmers** for the following reasons:

- ITC puts up its offer prices on the site. Farmers can obtain information about other offers and make an independent decision about where they want to sell their produce.
- In the traditional system, the farmer is obliged to go to the Mandi whenever the sales/auctions take place. The e-Choupal system gave the farmer an option to sell his produce to ITC anytime he wanted.
- The transparency in the system was there for farmers to see. There was no word-of-mouth communication of prices. The prices were on the site in writing.
- The system is multilingual, so the farmers can actually read what is presented on the screen. Hence the system is used rather comfortably by farmers.

4. http://poverty.worldbank.org/files/14647_e-Choupal-web.pdf

- The entire system is used by the villagers with the sanchalak himself being another villager, so the degree of ownership is very high.

ITC has thus provided the farmer an option which he never had before. By directly interacting with the farmer, ITC now has the opportunity to obtain the quality produce that it desires. ITC set up a well-connected network of warehouses and hubs to receive and store the produce and paid the farmer on the spot for his produce. A **very effective e-procurement model** as depicted in Figure 1.1 was thus created.

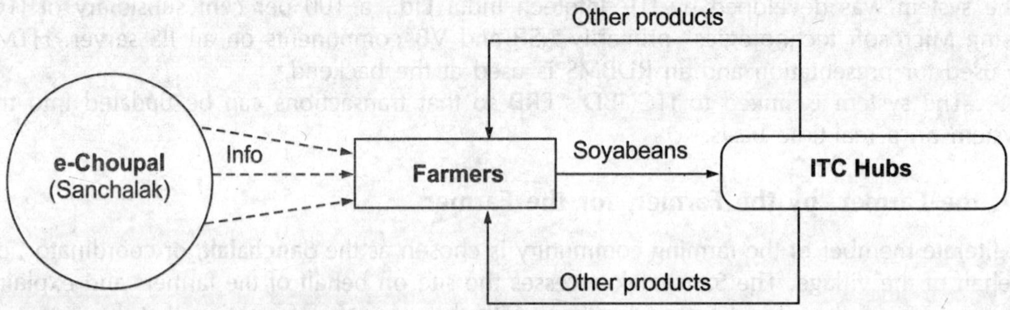

Figure 1.1 An e-procurement model.

A Wealth of Information

The e-Choupal gives farmers a lot of relevant information. This includes the following[5]:

- Weather information
- Best farming practices
- Market information
- Crop information
- Questions and answers and answers to frequently asked questions (FAQ)
- Soil testing
- Feedback
- Farmer information
- Information on state and central government schemes
- News

Extending the Internet

After the success of *www.soyachoupal.com*, ITC decided to venture into pruning the supply chain of other commodity exports. As a result, *www.aquachoupal.com* for aquaculture and *www.plantersnet.com* for coffee were started. Similar initiatives have been considered for optimizing the procurement of wheat[6] and horticultural products.

Marketing Goes Rural

In addition to acting as an e-Procurement model, ITC has started leveraging this e-Choupal infrastructure to broaden its distribution network into the rural heartland as well.

5. http://www.eChoupal.com/home/Sitemap.asp
6. http://www.itcportal.com/newsroom/press_jan16.htm

ITC is in a position to sell products allied with agriculture such as fertilizers, agrichemicals and seeds. ITC's subsidiary, Megatop, sells insurance to the farmers. Credit schemes for farmers are also on the anvil for those who feel exploited by banks.

In addition, ITC has started using the e-Choupal as a network for marketing their range of goods in the Food and FMCG sector, such as edible oils (from soya), salt, biscuits, confectionary, etc.

It is also in a position to auction its infrastructure to other companies that desire to penetrate the rural markets. For example, BPCL has started using the e-Choupal to sell LPG cylinders in Madhya Pradesh and Uttar Pradesh.[7]

The e-Choupal initiative offers the following important lessons for any e-business initiative:

- ***Leverage existing assets and relationships.*** ITC's tobacco and agribusiness divisions own a distribution and collection system with unparalleled reach into rural India. It also has strong relationships with farmers and intermediaries in the agricultural supply chain. These assets and relationships allowed ITC to create a unique and defensible online franchise.
- ***Define a clear value proposition for everyone.*** The e-Choupal venture benefits ITC by reducing procurement costs, improving quality of produce procured and creating a lucrative information franchise. For farmers, it reduces transaction costs, gets them better prices and empowers them with information, and the Sanchalaks get the opportunity to run their own business.
- ***Adapt solutions to the business context.*** ITC creatively overcame the lack of computing and communications infrastructure by creating appropriate technology solutions, including a human interface to overcome literacy and Internet access limitations.
- ***Re-intermediate, do not disintermediate.*** Instead of eliminating the middlemen, ITC redefined their role by decoupling information flows from physical flows in the supply chain. In this way, ITC mitigated any channel conflict.
- ***Co-opt customers in designing solutions.*** ITC recognized that getting farmers to adopt technology would pose a huge challenge. By recruiting the *Sanchalaks* from within the villages, ITC was able to get buy-in from the farmers. ITC also made the Sanchalaks take a public oath of office, recognizing that a social contract was far more effective than a formal contract.
- ***Think big, but start small.*** ITC's long-term vision for e-choupal is grand. But the company started with a modest and focused value proposition—helping farmers get better prices for their crops. This phased approach allows ITC to gain credibility through early successes and to learn from its mistakes.

Case Discussion

The following need to be discussed:

1. Discuss the impact ITC can make for the rural sections of the country through e-Choupal.

7. http://www.eChoupal.com/NewsRoom/Press/news2.htm

2. What is innovative about e-Choupal?
3. Identify the difficulties that e-Choupal may face.
4. What are the other areas where the e-Choupal concept may be applied in rural India?

Electronic Commerce

The cutting edge for business today is electronic commerce (e-commerce). Broadly defined, *electronic commerce* is a modern business methodology that addresses the needs of organizations, merchants, and consumers to cut costs while improving the quality of goods and services and increasing the speed of service delivery. The term also applies to the use of computer networks to search and retrieve information in support of human and corporate decision making.

More commonly, e-commerce is associated with the buying and selling of information, products, and services via computer networks today and in the future via any one of the myriad of networks that make up the *Information Superhighway*. Combining a range of processes, such as Electronic Data Interchange (EDI), electronic mail (e-mail), World Wide Web (WWW), and Internet applications, e-commerce provides ways to exchange information between individuals, companies, and countries, but most important of all, between computers. More simply put, e-commerce is the movement of business onto the World Wide Web. This movement has been broken up into two main sectors: **business-to-business (B2B)** and **business-to-consumer (B2C)**. E-commerce comprises core business processes of buying, selling goods, services, and information over the Internet. The e-commerce information available on the Internet is huge and still growing.

Unfortunately, the political structures of the world have not kept up with the Internet technology, and thus business internationally presents a number of challenges. Currency conversions, tariffs, import and export restrictions, local business customs, and the laws of each country in which a trading partner resides can make international electronic commerce difficult.

Many of the international issues that arise, relate to legal, tax, and privacy concerns. Each country has the right to pass laws and levy taxes on businesses that operate within its jurisdiction. European countries have strict laws that limit the collection and use of personal information that companies gather in the course of doing business with consumers. Even within the United States, the individual states and countries have the power to levy sales taxes on goods and services. In other countries, national sales and value-added taxes are imposed on an even broader list of business activities.

E-commerce is already very big and it is going to get much bigger. But the actual value of transactions currently concluded online is dwarfed by the extraordinary influence the Internet is exerting over purchases carried out in the offline world. That influence is becoming an integral part of e-commerce.

When the technology bubble burst in 2000, the crazy valuations for online companies vanished with it, and many businesses folded up. The survivors plugged on as best they could, encouraged by the growing number of Internet users. Now valuations are rising again and some of the dotcoms are making real profits, but the business world has become much more cautious about the Internet's potential. An astonishing thing is that the wild predictions made at the height of the boom, namely that vast chunks of the world economy would move into cyberspace, are in one way or the other coming true.

People seem to enjoy shopping on the internet, if high customer-satisfaction scores are any guide. Websites are doing ever more and cleverer things to serve and entertain their customers, and seem set to take a much bigger share of people's overall spending in the future. This has enormous implications for business. A company that neglects its website may be committing commercial suicide. A website is increasingly becoming the gateway to a company's brand, products and services—even if the firm does not sell online. A useless website suggests a useless company, and a rival is only a mouse-click away. But even the coolest website will be lost in cyberspace if people cannot find it, so companies have to ensure that they appear high up in internet search results.

The other way to get noticed online is to offer goods and services through one of the big sites that already get a lot of traffic. Ebay, Yahoo! and Amazon are becoming huge trading platforms for other companies. But to take part, a company's products have to stand up to intense price competition. People check online prices, compare them with those in their local high street and may well take a peek at what customers in other countries are paying. Even if websites are prevented from shipping their goods abroad, there are plenty of web-based entrepreneurs ready to oblige.

The effects of e-commerce are already appearing in all areas of business, from customer service to new product design. It facilitates new types of information-based business processes for reaching and interacting with customers—online advertising and marketing, online order taking, and online customer service, to name a few. It can also reduce costs in managing orders and interacting with a wide range of suppliers and trading partners, areas that typically add significant overhead to the cost of products and services. Finally, e-commerce enables the formation of new types of information-based products such as interactive games, electronic books, and information on demand that can be very profitable for content providers and useful for consumers. In sum, companies believe that e-commerce can result in improved efficiency in finding and interacting with customers, in communicating with trading partners, and in developing new products and markets.

Clearly, a key element of e-commerce is information processing. All steps of commerce, except for production, distribution, and delivery of physical goods, are forms of information gathering, processing, manipulation, and distribution, which computers and networks are perfectly suited to handle.

E-commerce vs E-business

IBM was among the first to use e-Business when it launched a thematic campaign built around the term in 1997. Until then, the widely used buzzword was e-Commerce. The shift in terms also meant a shift in paradigm; selling and selling support were the only experiences that companies could reproduce on the Web. Broadening the approach to allow more types of business on the Web created the new term e-Business. E-Business can be defined as the conduct of automated business transactions by means of electronic communications networks (e.g., via the Internet and/or possibly private networks) end-to-end.

The term *end-to-end business transaction* signifies that a succession of automated business processes and information systems of different companies, which are involved in an inter-company business transaction, are successfully integrated. The aim is to provide seamless inter-operation and interactive links between all the relevant members of an extended demand and supply chain—ranging from product designers, suppliers and their partners to end-customers. An end-to-end process involves integrating designers, suppliers, and buyers, trading partners, logistics providers and end-customers in the entire planning and execution process. In simple terms, it promotes inter-enterprise business relationships. Note that this definition of e-Business subsumes the term *collaborative business*.

E-Business encompasses sophisticated business-to-business interactions and collaboration activities at a level of enterprise applications and business processes, enabling business partners to share in-depth business intelligence, which leads, in turn, to the management and optimization of inter-enterprise processes such as supply chain management. More specifically, electronic business enables companies to link their internal and external processes more efficiently and flexibly, work more closely with suppliers and better satisfy the needs and expectations of their customers. Internal or *back-office processes* include distribution, manufacturing, and accounting while external or *front-office processes* include these processes that connect an organization to its customers and suppliers.

Early Business Information Interchange Efforts

The emergence of large business organizations in the late 1800s and early 1900s triggered the need to create and maintain formal records of business transactions. In the 1950s, companies began to use computers to store and process internal transaction records, but the information flows between businesses continued to be on paper. Purchase orders, invoices, bills of lading, cheques, remittance advices, and other standard forms were used to document transactions.

The process of using a person or a computer to generate a paper form, mailing that form, and then having another person enter the data into the trading partner's computer was slow, inefficient, expensive, redundant, and unreliable. By the 1960s, businesses that engaged in large volumes of transactions had begun exchanging transaction information on punched cards or magnetic tape. Advances in data communications technology eventually allowed trading partners to transfer data over telephone lines instead of shipping punched cards or magnetic tapes to each other.

Although these information transfer agreements between trading partners increased efficiency and reduced errors, they were not an ideal solution. Since the translation programs that one trading partner wrote usually would not work for other trading partners, each company participating in this information exchange had to make a substantial investment in computing infrastructure. Only large trading partners could afford this investment, and even those companies had to have a significant number of transactions to justify the cost.

Smaller- or lower-volume trading partners could not afford to participate in the benefits of these paper-free exchanges.

In 1968, a number of freight and shipping companies joined together to form the Transportation Data Coordinating Committee (TDCC), which was charged with exploring ways to reduce the paperwork burden that shippers and carriers faced. The TDCC created a standardized information set that included all the data elements that shippers commonly included in bills of lading, freight invoices, shipping manifests, and other paper forms. Instead of printing a paper form, shippers could transform information about shipments into a computer file that conformed to the TDCC standard format. The shipper could electronically transmit that computer file to any freight company that had adopted the TDCC format. The freight company translated the TDCC format into data it could use in its own information systems. The savings from not printing and handling forms, not entering the data twice, and not having to worry about error-correction procedures were significant for most shippers and freight carriers.

After a decade of fragmented attempts at setting broader EDI standards, a number of industry groups and several large companies decided to make a major effort to create a set of cross-industry standards for electronic components, mechanical equipment, and other widely used items. The American National Standards Institute (ANSI) has been the coordinating body for standards in the United States since 1918. ANSI does not set standards, though it creates procedures and organizational standards for the development of national standards and accredites committees that follow those procedures.

In 1979, American National Standard Institute (ANSI) chartered a new committee to develop uniform EDI standards. This committee is called the *Accredited Standards Committee X12* (ASC X12). The committee meets three times a year to develop and maintain EDI standards. The committee and its subcommittees include information technology professionals from over 800 businesses and other organizations. Membership is open to organizations and individuals who have an interest in the standards. The ASC X12 standard has benefitted from the participation of members from a wide variety of industries. This standard currently includes specifications for several hundred transaction sets, which are the names of the formats for specific business data interchanges.

In 1987, the United Nations published its first standards under the title *EDI for Administration, Commerce, and Transport* (EDIFACT, or UN/EDIFACT). As the Internet gained prominence as a tool for conducting business, the trading partners who had been using EDI began to view the Internet as a potential replacement for the expensive leased lines and dial-up connections they had been using. Companies that were unable to afford EDI began to look at the Internet as an enabling technology that might get them back in the game of selling to a large number of customers who demanded EDI capabilities of their suppliers.

The major hurdles to conducting EDI over the Internet initially were general concerns about security and the Internet's general inability to provide audit logs and third-party verification of message transmission and delivery. The lack of third-party verification continues to be an issue, since the Internet has no built-in facility for that. Because EDI transactions are business contracts and often involve large amounts of money, the issue of non-repudiation causes significant concern.

Emergence of the Internet

The role of the Internet in the evolution of e-commerce has been so crucial that the history of e-commerce will remain incomplete without the inclusion of the history of the Internet.

Using the Internet, you can communicate with other people throughout the world by means of e-mail, read online versions of newspapers, magazines, academic journals, and books, join discussion groups on almost any conceivable topic, participate in games and simulations, and obtain free computer software. In recent years, the Internet has allowed commercial enterprises to connect with one another and with customers. Today, all kinds of businesses provide information about their products and services on the Internet. Many of these businesses use the Internet to market and sell their products and services. The part of the Internet known as the World Wide Web, or, more simply, the Web, is a subset of the computers on the Internet that are connected to each other in a specific way that makes those computers and their contents easily accessible to each other. The most important thing about the Web is that it includes an easy-to-use standard interface. This interface makes it possible for people who are not computer experts to use the World Wide Web to access a variety of Internet resources.

In the early 1960s, the US Department of Defense became very much concerned about the possible effects of a nuclear attack on its computing facilities. The Defense Department realized the need for powerful computers for coordination and control. The powerful computers of that time were all large mainframe computers. So the Defense Department began examining ways to connect these computers to each other and also to weapon installations that were distributed all over the world. The Defense Department agency, charged with this task, hired many of the best communications technology researchers and funded research at leading universities and institutes to explore the task of creating a worldwide network that could remain operational even if parts of the network were destroyed by enemy military action or sabotage. These researchers worked to devise ways to build networks that could operate independently—that is, networks that would not require a central computer to control network operations.

The world's telephone companies were the early models for networked computers, because early networks of computers used leased telephone company lines for their connections. Telephone company systems of that time established a single connection between sender and receiver for each telephone call, and that connection carried all the data along a single path. When a company wanted to connect computers it owned at two different locations, it placed a telephone call to establish the connection and then connected one computer to each end of that single connection.

The Defense Department was concerned about the inherent risk of this single-channel method for connecting computers. So its researchers developed a different method of sending information through multiple channels. In this method, files and messages are broken into packets and labelled electronically with codes about their origin and destination. The packets travel from computer to computer along the network until they reach their destination. The destination computer collects the packets and reassembles the original data from the pieces in each packet. Each computer that an individual packet encounters on its trip through the network, determines the best way to move the packet forward to its destination.

In 1969, these Defense Department researchers used this network model to connect four computers—one each at the University of California at Los Angeles, SRI International, the University of California at Santa Barbara, and the University of Utah. During the subsequent years, many researchers in the academic community connected to this network and contributed to technological developments that increased the speed and efficiency with which the network operated. At the same time, researchers at other universities were creating their own networks using similar technologies.

The upshot was the Internet Protocol (IP), which enabled any number of computer networks to link up and act as one—and eventually it was given the name, the Internet. This meant that the communication network among the computers was not dependent on any single computer to operate, and so could not be shut down by destroying one or even several of the computers. Thus, the Defense Department got what it wanted. And a new, growing system of computer networks was spawned.

Although the goals of the Defense Department network were still to control weapons systems and transfer research files, other uses of this vast network began to appear in the early 1970s. In 1972, a researcher wrote a program that could send and receive messages over the network. Thus was born the e-mail which came to be widely used very quickly. The number of network users in the military and education research communities continued to grow. Many of these new participants used the networking technology to transfer files and access remote computers. The network software included two tools for performing these tasks. File Transfer Protocol (FTP) enabled users to transfer files between computers, and Telnet let users log on to their computer accounts from remote sites. Both FTP and Telnet are still widely used on the Internet for file transfers and remote logins, even though more advanced techniques are now available that allow multimedia transmissions such as real-time audio and video clips.

The first e-mail mailing lists also appeared on these networks. In 1979, a group of students and programmers at the Duke University and the University of North Carolina started Usenet, an abbreviation for Users News Network. Usenet allows anyone who connects to the network to read and post articles on a variety of subjects. The Defense Department's networking software became more widely used as academic and research institutes realized the benefits of having a common communications network. The explosion of personal computer use during that time also helped more people become comfortable with computing. In the late 1980s, these independent academic and research networks merged into one infrastructure—the *Internet* that links today hundreds and thousands of networks to one another.

Commercial Use of the Internet

As personal computers became more powerful, affordable, and available during the 1980s, companies increasingly used them to construct their own internal networks. Although these networks included e-mail software that enabled the employees to send messages, businesses wanted their employees to be able to communicate with people outside their corporate networks for promoting business. The Defense Department network and most of the other academic networks that had teamed up with it were receiving funding from the National

Science Foundation (NSF). The NSF prohibited commercial network traffic on its networks and so businesses turned to commercial e-mail service providers to handle their e-mail needs. Larger firms built their own networks that used leased telephone lines to connect field offices to corporate headquarters.

In 1989, the NSF permitted two commercial e-mail services, MCI Mail and CompuServe to establish limited connections to the Internet for the sole purpose of exchanging e-mail transmissions with users of the Internet. These connections allowed commercial enterprises to send e-mail directly to Internet addresses and allowed members of the research and education communities on the Internet to send e-mail directly to MCI Mail and CompuServe addresses. The NSF justified this limited commercial use of the Internet as a service that would primarily benefit the Internet's non-commercial users.

Growth of the Internet

In 1991, the NSF further eased its restrictions on Internet commercial activity and began implementing plans to privatize the Internet. The privatization of the Internet was substantially completed in 1995, when the NSF turned over the operation of the main Internet connections to a group of privately owned companies. The new structure of the Internet was based on four Network Access Points (NAPs), each operated by a separate company. These companies, which are known as *network-access providers*, sell Internet access rights directly to larger customers and indirectly to smaller firms through other companies, called *Internet Service Providers* (ISPs).

The Internet was a phenomenon that truly sneaked into an unsuspecting world. The researchers who had been so involved in the creation and growth of the Internet just accepted it as a part of their working environment. People outside the research community were largely unaware of the potential offered by a large interconnected set of computer networks.

Within 30 years, the Internet became one of the most amazing technological and social accomplishments of the 20th century. Millions of people are using today this complex, inter-connected network of computers. These computers run thousands of different software packages. The computers are located in almost every country of the world. Every year, billions of dollars change hands over the Internet in exchange for all kinds of products and services. All of this activity occurs with no central coordination point or control, which is especially interesting, given that the Internet began as a way for the military to maintain control while under attack.

The opening of the Internet to business activities helped increase the Internet's growth dramatically; however, there was another development that worked hand in hand with the commercialization of the Internet to spur its growth. That development was the World Wide Web (WWW).

Emergence of the World Wide Web

The web is more a way of thinking about and organizing information storage and retrieval than a technology. As such, its history goes back to many years. Two important innovations played key roles in making the Internet easier to use and more accessible to people who were not research scientists. These two innovations were *Hypertext* and *Graphical User Interfaces* (GUIs).

In 1945, Vannevar Bush, who was director of the US Office of Scientific Research and Development, wrote an Atlantic Monthly article about ways that scientists could apply the skills they learned during World War II to peacetime activities. The article included a number of visionary ideas about future uses of technology to organize and facilitate efficient access to information. Bush speculated that engineers would eventually build a machine that he called the *Memex* (a memory extension device), that would store all—a person's books, records, letters, and research results—on microfilm. Vannevar Bush described a system for associatively linking information in his July 1945 article in *The Atlantic Monthly*, 'As We May Think'.[8]

Hypertext, as implemented on the Web, however, has its origins in the start of the electronic computer age, when ideas about associative linking could be married with the possibilities of automated storage-and-retrieval systems. Douglas Engelbart, who also invented the computer mouse, created the first experimental hypertext system on one of the largest computers of the 1960s. In 1965, Ted Nelson coined the term *hypertext* to describe a text that is not constrained to be sequential. Hypertext, as described by Nelson, links documents to form a web of relationships that draws on the possibilities for extending and augmenting the meaning of a 'flat' piece of text with links to other texts. Hypertext therefore is more than just footnotes that serve as commentary or further information in a text. Instead, it extends the structure of ideas by making 'chunks' of ideas available for inclusion in many parts of multiple texts. Nelson also coined the term *hypermedia*, which is a hypertext not constrained to be text. It can include the combination of text, pictures, graphics, sound, and movies.

The ideas of Vannevar Bush, Ted Nelson and others, about information systems, showed up in another project in the late 1980s. In March 1989, Tim Berners-Lee, a researcher at the *Conseil Europeen pour la Recherche Nucleaire* (CERN), the European Laboratory for Particle Physics in Geneva, Switzerland, proposed a hypertext system to enable efficient information sharing for members of the high-energy physics community. This proposal, called *HyperText* and *CERN*, was circulated for comments. The important components of the proposal follow:

- A user interface that would be consistent with all platforms and that would allow users to access information from many different computers.
- A scheme for this interface to access a variety of document types and information protocols.
- A provision for universal access, which would allow any user on the network to access any information.

In October of 1991, a gateway from the Web to Wide Area Information Server (WAIS) software was completed. On 15 January 1991, the WWW interface became publicly available from CERN, and the CERN team demonstrated the Web to researchers internationally throughout the rest of the year.

---

8. http://www.isg.sfu.ca/~duchier/misc/vbush

By 1993, there were about 50 Web servers in existence, and the first graphical interfaces (called *clients* or *browsers*) for the X Window System and the Macintosh became available in Switzerland. Until 1993, most of the development of Web technologies came out of CERN. In early 1993, however, a young undergraduate, Marc Andreessen, at the University of Illinois at Urbana-Champaign shifted the stage to the United States. Working on a project for the National Center for Supercomputing Applications (NCSA), Andreessen led a team that developed an X Window System browser for the Web and called it *Mosaic*. Marc Andreessen and his colleagues then left NCSA in March 1994 to form a company that later came to be known as Netscape Communications Corporation. By May 1994, the interest in the Web was so intense that the first international conference on the WWW, held in Geneva, overflowed with attendees. By mid 1994, it was clear to the original developers at CERN that the stable development of the Web should fall under the guidance of an international organization. In July, the Massachusetts Institute of Technology (MIT) and CERN announced the World Wide Web Organization (which was later known as the World Wide Web Consortium, or W3C). Today, the W3C guides the technical development and standards for the evolution of the Web.

In 1995, the Web development was marked by rapid commercialization and technical change. Netscape Communication's browser, called *Netscape Navigator* (nicknamed *Mozilla*) continued to include more extensions of the Hypertext Markup Language (HTML), and at the same time the issues of security for commercial cash transactions garnered much attention. By May 1995, there were more than 15,000 known public Web servers—a ten-fold increase over the number that existed only a year before.

Hypertext Transfer Protocol (HTTP) is the Internet protocol responsible for transferring and displaying Web pages. HTTP runs in the application layer of the Transmission Control Protocol/Internet Protocol (TCP/IP) model. Like the other Internet protocols, HTTP employs the client-server model in which a user's Web browser opens an HTTP session and sends a request to the remote server for a Web page. In response, the server creates an HTTP response message that is sent back to the user's Web browser. The response contains the page displayed by the client's browser. After the client determines that the message it received is correct, the TCP/IP connection is closed and the HTTP session ends. The process is demonstrated in Figure 1.2.

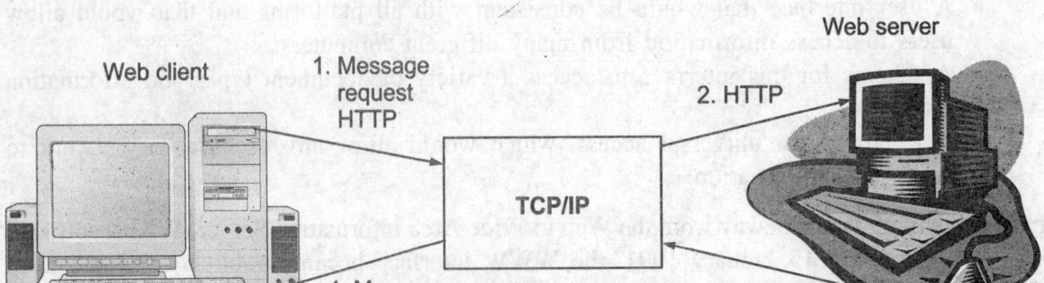

Figure 1.2 Client-server architecture using HTTP.

The Milestones[9]

1988 — The number of hosts on the net became over 60,000.
1989 — Over 10,000 hosts on the net were registered.
1991 — The World Wide Web (WWW) was created by CERN in Switzerland.

The number of World Wide Web users continues to double in size about every 12 to 15 months. All of these have had an impact. Perhaps the most significant factor, though, is that the Internet offers a range of messaging techniques, all of which work rapidly. The standards used to make it work are not all ratified by international standards bodies, but they do work. The factor of not having to wait for standards to be agreed has surely accelerated the growth in the number of Internet users.

The growth of websites and users exploded dramatically as shown in Table 1.1. The first website, info.cern.ch, has been online for the past 30 years and is still running. Since then, billions of new websites had been created. Of today's 1.8 billion+ websites on the world wide web[10], below 200 million are active. A total of 5 billion people around the world use the internet today.

TABLE 1.1 Growth of the Number of Web Hosts Over the Years

Year	*Web hosts*	*Internet users*
1991	1	0
1995	23,500	44,838,900
2000	17,087,182	413,425,190
2005	64,780,617	1,027,580,990
2014	861,379,000	2,925,249,355
2021	1,829,268,586	5,000,000,000

Source: Excerpts from Netcraft's public websites may be reproduced if Netcraft and the url http://www.netcraft.com/ are attributed.

Advantages of E-commerce

Some of the key strengths of using the Internet for businesses include the following:

1. ***24×7 operation.*** Round-the-clock operation is an expensive proposition in the 'brick-and-mortar' world, while it is natural in the 'click-and-conquer' world.
2. ***Global reach.*** The net being inherently global, reaching global customers is relatively easy on the net compared to the world of bricks.
3. ***Cost of acquiring, serving and retaining customers.*** It is relatively cheaper to acquire new customers over the net; thanks to 24 × 7 operation and its global reach. Through

9. http://www.w3.org/History
10. (https://financesonline.com/30-essential-web-hosting-statistics-2019-analysis-of-trends-data-and-market-share/#:~:text=As%20of%20January%202021%2C%20the,growing%20at%20a%20steady%20rate.)

innovative tools of 'push' technology, it is also possible to retain customers' loyalty with minimal investments.

4. ***An extended enterprise is easy to build.*** In today's world every enterprise is part of the 'connected economy'; as such, you need to extend your enterprise all the way to your suppliers and business partners like distributors, retailers and ultimately your end-customers. The Internet provides an effective (often less expensive) way to extend your enterprise beyond the narrow confines of your own organization. Tools like enterprise resource planning (ERP), supply chain management (SCM) and customer relationship management (CRM), can easily be deployed over the Internet, permitting amazing efficiency in time needed to market, customer loyalty, on-time delivery and eventually profitability.
5. ***Disintermediation.*** Using the Internet, one can directly approach the customers and suppliers, cutting down on the number of levels and in the process, cutting down the costs.
6. ***Improved customer service to your clients.*** It results in higher satisfaction and more sales.
7. ***Power to provide the 'best of both the worlds'.*** It benefits the traditional business side-by-side with the Internet tools.
8. ***A technology-based customer interface.*** In a brick-and-mortar business, customers conduct transactions either face-to-face or over the phone with store clerks, account managers, or other individuals. In contrast, the customer interface in the electronic environment is a 'screen-to-face' interaction. This includes PC-based monitors, ATM machines, PDAs, smart phones, or other electronic devices. Operationally, these types of interfaces place an enormous responsibility on the organization to capture and represent the customer experience because there is often no opportunity for direct human intervention during the encounter. If the interface is designed correctly, the customer will have no need for a simultaneous or follow-up phone conversation. Thus, the 'screen-to-customer' interface has the potential to both increase sales and decrease costs. In fact, a number of innovators are entering the e-commerce markets with solutions that reintroduce humans into the process, such as the service representatives available on demand for Web users at www.liveperson.com. When the interface does not work, not only is the revenue lost but the organization also incurs the technology costs. Thus, a poorly designed customer interface has both negative revenue and cost implications.
9. ***The customer controls the interaction.*** At most websites, the customer is in control during screen-to-face interaction, in that the Web largely employs a 'self service' model for managing commerce or community-based interaction. The customer controls the search process, the time spent on various sites, the degree of price/product comparison, the people with whom he or she comes in contact, and the decision to buy. In a face-to-face interchange, the control can rest with either the

buyer/seller or the community member. At a minimum, the seller attempts to influence the buying process by directing the potential buyer to different products or locations in the store, overcoming price objections and reacting in real item to competitive offering. The virtual store can attempt to shape the customer experience with uniquely targeted promotions, reconfiguration of storefronts to reflect past search behaviour, recommendations based on previous behaviour of other similar users, and access to proprietary information. However, the seller has much less power in the online environment due to the control and information flows that the online world puts in customer's hands.

10. ***Knowledge of customer behaviour.*** While the customer controls the interaction, the firm has unprecedented access to observe and track individual consumer behaviour. Companies, through a third-party measurement firm such as Vividence and Accrue, can track a host of behaviours on websites visited, length of stays on a site, page views on a site, contents of wish lists and shopping carts, purchases, dollar amounts of purchases, repeat purchases behaviour, conversion rates of visitors who have completed transactions and other metrics. This level of customer behaviour tracking, in contrast with tracking consumer attitudes, knowledge or behavioural intentions, is not possible in the brick-and-mortar world. Armed with this information, companies can provide one-to-one customization of their offerings. In addition, companies can dynamically publish their storefronts on the Web to configure offerings to individual customers. In a tactical embellishment, electronic retailers can welcome a user back by name. In more strategic terms, an online business can actually position offers and merchandise in ways that uniquely appeal to specific customers.

11. ***Network economics.*** In information intensive industries, a key competitive battleground centres on the emergence of industry-standard products, services, components, and or architecture. Network effects, as described by Metcalfe's law, can best be expressed as the situation where the value of a product or service rises as a function of the number of other users who are using the product. A key characteristic of network's economic is positive feedback, that is, as the installed base grows, more and more users are likely to adopt the technology because of the installed base. Many commercial wares in the digital economy revolve around setting a standard, growing the installed base and attempting to 'lock-in' customers to the standard because of rising switching costs. This applies to both hardware and software (e.g. MP3 versus streaming audio). A key result of network effects and positive feedback is 'increasing return' economies as compared to the traditional decreasing-returns model often associated with the brick-and-mortar world. It also means that the traditional realities of marketing such as the importance of word-of-mouth (WOM) among potential customers, become greatly magnified in this new environment. It is this turbocharged WOM phenomenon that makes viral marketing a reality for consumer-oriented e-commerce business as seen in the use of WhatsApp by consumers.

Disadvantages of E-commerce

Some business processes may never lend themselves to electronic commerce. For example, perishable foods, and high-cost items (such as jewellery, antiques, and the like), may be difficult to inspect from a remote location, regardless of any technologies that might be devised in the future. Most of the disadvantages of electronic commerce today, however, stem from the newness and rapidly developing pace of the underlying technologies. These disadvantages will disappear as e-commerce matures and becomes more and more available to and gets accepted by the general population. Many products and services require a critical mass of potential buyers who are well-equipped and willing to buy through the Internet.

Businesses often calculate the return-on-investment before committing to any new technology. This has been difficult to do with e-commerce, since the costs and benefits have been hard to quantify. Costs, which are a function of technology, can change dramatically even during short-lived e-commerce implementation projects, because the underlying technologies are changing rapidly. Many firms have had trouble in recruiting and retaining employees with technological, design, and business process skills needed to create an effective e-commerce atmosphere. Another problem facing firms that want to do business on the Internet is the difficulty of integrating existing databases and transaction-processing software designed for traditional commerce into a software that enables e-commerce.

In addition to technology and software issues, many businesses face cultural and legal obstacles in conducting e-commerce. Some consumers are still somewhat fearful of sending their credit card numbers over the Internet. Other consumers are simply resistant to change and are uncomfortable viewing merchandise on a computer screen rather than in person. The legal environment in which e-commerce is conducted is full of unclear and conflicting laws. In many cases, government regulators have not kept up with the trends in technologies.

Online Extension of a BAM Model

Since most conventional brick-and-mortar (BAM) organizations have established processes, people, structures and supply chains, they can become strong competitors to the *dot-coms* (that have no offline presence) by e-enabling their supply chains. Most BAM organizations will gain competitive advantage by creating more value for the customers at the same cost or delivering the same goods at a lower cost by using the Internet. For example, an automobile manufacturer can pass on the cost savings achieved by e-procurement, a bank can reduce the need for physical branches by making use of e-banking. So leveraging the supply chain by making use of information, relationships, and commerce and squeezing out more value out of it, would enable BAM organizations to have a level of efficiency, unparalleled by pure dotcoms. Besides, dot coms without any offline presence would have to set up their supply chains from scratch. In this respect, they are greatly disadvantaged in comparison to their offline counterparts.

Transition to E-commerce in India

The potential for e-commerce is enormous in India, owing to the rapid growth of the number of Internet users. The enormous savings in time and money achieved by both buyers and sellers is the principal advantage.

The Internet has undergone a steady evolution from being a source of instant communication in the early 90s to a rich source of infotainment and education. This evolution has been driven by the growing customer expectations with the content of Internet. Thus, newer segments of Internet usage have emerged and there lie potential user segments that are still unexplored and may emerge in the future[11].

Ten years ago, there was limited Internet access but only in few major cities, all in the hands of government. VSNL, the agency responsible for Internet activities, and the DOT (Department of Telecommunications) provided an agonizingly erratic connectivity, with miserly bandwidth and far too few phone lines. Connection rates ran as low as 5% and users were frequently cut off, and the rates for this pathetic level of service were among the highest in the world.

The potential for e-commerce is enormous in India, owing to the rapid growth of the number of Internet users. The enormous savings in time and money by both buyers and sellers is the principal advantage.

According to the Internet and Mobile Association of India (IAMAI), the Internet user base in the country stood at 213 million in 2013 and 658 million at the end of 2022. See Table 1.2.

TABLE 1.2 Growth of Internet Users in India

Year	*Internet users*
1997	25,000
2001	1,130,000
2005	6,000,000
2009	13,540,000
2013	213,000,000
2017	437,000,000
2022	658,000,000

The growth of Internet users has also led to a substantial growth of other digital industries such as e-commerce and digital advertising. Digital commerce market stood at ₹5,79,699 crores at the beginning of 2023. This growth is depicted in Table 1.3.

11. http://data.worldbank.org/indicator/IT>NET>USER?cid=GPD_58

TABLE 1.3 Growth of E-commerce Revenues in India[12]

Year	*E-commerce revenues (₹ in crores)*
2001	450
2007	7,080
2013	47,349
2019	188,646
2023	579,699

E-commerce Opportunities[13] for Industries

Following are some of the areas where e-commerce is witnessing rapid growth in the global markets. Indian software and services companies need to tap into some of these vertical segments to gain the maximum advantage in the e-commerce solution sector.

1. ***Financial services.*** A large number of users use the Internet for some form of financial guidance.
2. ***Stock trading.*** Online stock trading is nowadays one of the most demanding e-commerce utilities. The ability to offer market access at competitive prices is a key advantage of online stock broking companies and this is slowly happening in India too.
3. ***Banking.*** Internet banking is now growing. Many banks like ICICI and HDFC are making inroads into this area.
4. ***Legal and professional services.*** Opportunities also exist for Indian companies in legal and other professional services. There are significant legal and regulatory implications of implementing an Internet business or in migrating from a traditional off-line business. In terms of opportunities for Indian legal service providers, the requirement for professional, legal and regulatory advice is expected to increase as e-commerce volumes increase.
5. ***Tour and travel.*** The travel industry has readily adapted to e-commerce. There has been a growing emphasis on the search for alternative distribution channels within the sector, particularly with the airlines, as they seek to reduce costs. These sectors have adapted well because of their online reservation system.
6. ***Healthcare.*** Healthcare represents one of the biggest expenditures of governments worldwide. The Internet has the potential to enhance communications, streamline processes and create new business opportunities, by providing high-quality administrative services and integrating information systems.

12. https://www.statista.com/outlook
13. NASSCOM Strategic Review, 2001, p. 144.

Tata Motors—Managing Supply Chain on the Internet

India's largest commercial vehicle manufacturer, Tata Motors started connecting its existing 130-strong dealer network online with the company's Internet-based system. It also has plans to bring all its dealers for commercial vehicles and passenger cars on the company's network. Group Company Tata Technologies Limited is developing interfaces with its back-end ERP systems. The Internet-based system currently covers the company's major manufacturing locations in Pune, Jamshedpur and Lucknow and its headquarters in Mumbai. It is also negotiating with a few banks to establish payment gateways between the value chain at the company-end and the banks. The effort, which has taken ₹ 3 crores worth of investment in infrastructure and eight man-years of system development and implementation, is expected to help Tata Motors cut down conventional delays in transactions. Tata Motors is also expecting to cut down the existing transaction time at the dealer-end by 50 per cent. The initiative will also result in more accurate and secured information and eliminate chaos and confusion. The dealers will be able to book according to their requirements and receive supplies much faster. The initiative will help both the company and the dealers to keep inventories under control. The company will also be in a better position to customize products according to specific dealer requirements at a short notice.

Hindustan Lever—Getting the E-advantage

As a part of the Internet initiative, Hindustan Lever has put in place a network, connecting all its suppliers and has launched a pilot project to wire up its 7500 distributors. In the second phase, it will attempt the mammoth task of connecting its top retailers. Finally, it also wants to use the Internet for transactions. Lever sees the e-tailing opportunity not only for its own product categories but also for a larger universe of products. With its formidable distribution system, which covers nearly two million retail outlets, Lever already has in place the back-end infrastructure that other e-tailers could kill for and is uniquely positioned to create India's most widespread, robust and efficient clicks-and-bricks company. Lever's e-gameplan is to build a number of market-leading B2B and B2C businesses in high-potential areas. And in doing this, it will leverage its strong consumer and supplier relationships and its cache of human talent.

Asian Paints—E-transforming the Organization

Asian Paints, India's largest paint company, is reaping the benefits of its investments in Internet-enabling its organization. Information Technology has been made use of efficient data collection, demand forecasting, reduction in working capital and online information about material flows across factories and other locations. Given the complexity of the demand chain and the logistics and the seasonal nature of the demand, the use of the Internet in connecting the 15,000 dealers and the 55 branch offices has improved the efficiency of the supply chain. It has also increased the service levels and has cut down the working capital in the chain. The company is also planning to do bulk transactions for its products through its website by making it a one-stop virtual storefront. The use of a comprehensive database of customers for e-relationship management is also being mulled.

CRISIL—Cost-effective Distribution Channels

CRISIL, the largest credit-rating agency in India, has already made its presence felt in the new economy sector for online dissemination of its research products. CRISIL has built up a large database on Indian corporates and research products over the years and is currently using the Web to enhance its reach as well as establish a cost-effective distribution channel for its products. It plans to use its website for quick delivery of quality research products for its customers as well as develop interactive tools based on what-if scenarios.

ICICI Bank—Comprehensive Transactions

ICICI Bank is using the Internet to acquire more customers by offering them a host of services. Its idea is to become a one-stop site where the account holders can do all their money transactions. On other sites one can trade online but all other transactions still have to be done physically. ICICI offers the entire chain, from the Demat account in which a customer's shares are credited to the savings account from which the money is debited to settle the transaction for access.

The bank has also launched an electronic bill payment service through its Internet banking service. The new payment system will do away with any paperwork since the biller will be presenting his bills to customers through the bank's website, while the customer will pay through the Internet. For this, the customers will have to register for an Internet banking account with the bank. Thus the bank will be able to target both the B2B and B2C markets.

E-transition Challenges for Indian Corporates

Some issues that Indian corporates face while e-transforming themselves are worth delving into, in the following manner.

Internal Resisting Issues

Bureaucratic wrangles. With organizations e-transforming themselves, the old ways of doing things are being replaced by new ways which destabilize the existing power equations. The fear of this among the staff is a significant barrier to the organizational transformation.

Cultural changes. The e-biz team spearheading the e-com initiatives in an organization, mostly consists of young, externally recruited, tech savvy populace who maintain a 'skunkwork' like culture. This open culture may be in direct conflict with the already established culture in the organization and may force the old-timers to oppose any change.

Not many are prepared. A survey by the GIIC found out that only 20 per cent of the organizations covered under the CIO segment are trying to use e-commerce at least to some extent. Eighty per cent of the industry is in the process of gearing up for the show, such as banks and sectors like IT, courier, travel and transport.

Lack of skill and training. Lack of skill and training within a company (28 per cent) and lack of funds (24 per cent) are other factors impeding the implementation of IT in companies. Most of these companies are from traditional businesses like manufacturing, travel, transport and education.

External Driving Factors

Sheer necessity. No one will dispute the argument that any business will benefit if it cuts down the processing time for a transaction. E-commerce does exactly this—it increases process efficiency by reducing transaction time and this can have a significant impact on cash flows and the bottom line.

Big business, the driving factor. Business entities will themselves be the key drivers. The big bosses of the industries will be the guiding and forcing factor for SMEs to adopt the Internet. A good example is that of Cisco which has mandated that it will deal with its suppliers, dealers and partners only if they are Web-enabled. The partners, whether they like it or not, have been forced to make the change. If the same happens in India and companies like HLL, Maruti, TELCO, Reliance Industries and other major players in their respective segments make it mandatory to have their dealers, suppliers and others linked to their supply chain on the Internet, one can imagine the stampede that will ensue. Sooner or later, these companies must have their supply chain e-driven, if they are to compete in the global market, and this again will lead to growth in the B2B segment.

Global market. If you are looking at 'the world as your market', e-commerce will fit in neatly with your plans. Globalization is forcing organizations to achieve new competitive levels in order to enter the world market. So if we are late to react, we shall lose the early-entrant advantage and a whole lot of market share. It is imperative that we get on to the e-commerce bandwagon for the sheer efficiencies that it can generate.

Value for money. Purely from the customer's perspective, e-commerce will be one of the key factors in propelling B2C growth in the Indian market. The driving factors for the B2C segment will be convenience, low cost to end-consumers and a wider choice. If you take a look at the products available on *rediff.com*, this point will be clear. Most products are available at discounts of 20–50 per cent over the price in the physical world. Besides, the opportunity of comparing prices on two different sites is just a click away and you will then avail the best option available.

No-entry barriers. The good thing about the Internet is that one does not need deep pockets to be successful. The Internet is an upstart's paradise. Even if you have a flourishing business in the physical world, it will not take much resource or time for a new entrant to compete with you. Remember how the innovative *amazon.com* grew from nothing to become the largest bookseller 'in the universe'. All this while, Barnes & Noble, the dominant player with huge financial resources, watched its market share being eroded by the upstart, forcing it finally to get on the e-commerce bandwagon. If this can happen with Barnes & Noble, it can happen with your business too. Alternatively, if *amazon.com* can give Barnes & Noble a run for its money, so can you to your established competitor.

Other factors. With the private ISPs becoming aggressive and also looking at the huge cable market to provide Internet connections, it is only a matter of time before subscriber numbers start looking up.

Smart Phone Apps

The recent success stories of Flipkart and Amazon India in e-commerce and their use of mobile applications have been a game changer. Suddenly, e-commerce companies are becoming profitable and the logistics for India is becoming a manageable aspect of e-commerce.

Now, we shall discuss some of the factors that could hinder the success of e-commerce.

Doubts and Difficulties

Households are shaky about buying over the Internet. A very high proportion among PC owners and PC non-owners opine that they would not like to buy through the Internet. The reasons are they are not sure of the quality and the delivery of the products. They need to feel the products and bargain before they buy them. Many do not understand the new method of buying and selling in a digital environment. This reluctance among households prevents e-commerce from achieving the critical mass, and forces the corporates to adopt a 'wait and watch' policy.

Computers are not bought for browsing the Internet. Browsing the Internet and purchasing through the Internet are among the least important perceived benefits of owning a computer. Business, learning (self) and education for children are so far given as the main reasons for purchasing a computer.

Lack of proper commercial and legal system. Security, lack of proper and secure payment structures, legal issues: a clear fix on contracts and liabilities in the digital economy, and trust and assurance are the main concerns.

EXERCISES

1. Describe the advances in technology which has facilitated e-commerce
2. Define e-commerce and e-business.
3. List the advantages and disadvantages of e-commerce.
4. Find recent information on *amazon.com* and comment on its battle with Barnes & Noble.
   (a) Enter the Amazon's site and print a list of current books on e-commerce.
   (b) Find a review of one of these books.
   (c) Review the services you can get from Amazon and describe all the benefits you can receive.
   (d) Enter Barnes & Noble website (*www.bn.com*) and compare it with *amazon.com.*
5. What are the key differences between traditional commerce and e-commerce?
6. What are the developments that have contributed to the emergence of the Internet as an electronic commerce infrastructure?
7. Go to *sify.com* and find out all the information that you can get on this website.
8. What is the difference between EDI and e-commerce?
9. For each of the following items, locate two websites in India that sell them:
   (a) airline tickets
   (b) personal computers
10. Make a study of HDFC banking services on the Internet. A brief summary is given in the following paragraph:

    HDFC BANK—E-broking through the Internet

    HDFC Bank is said to be looking at Internet banking as the medium between the bank and the consumer. The bank's services can be split into two areas. One is the area where people need to access data about their accounts and the other area concerns transactions. The bank intends to secure more and more transactions like issuing cheques or opening accounts via the Internet so that its staff will be free to do more value-added work.

    To get more account holders to bank online, HDFC Bank is setting up a shopping mall. The users will access these malls through the bank site, the money will be debited directly from their account. Thus, it will cut out the security aspect which such shopping malls face. It also plans to offer e-broking services online which is expected to bring in more customers. HDFC Bank has already picked up well since it started these services in September 2000 with 1000 users. It currently has about 20,000 users out of its 2.75 lakh savings account holders. It is now targeting to 100,000 customers. It is now targeting about 1,00,000 customers before the end of this year.

11. Make a study of Elbee Services and Blue Dart and find from their websites the success and popularity of their business. A brief summary of their respective business is given below:

1. *ELBEE SERVICES—End-to-End Solutions*

A major player in the courier industry, Elbee Services has also launched *elbeenet.com*, a customized product providing end-to-end solutions for e-business for both B2B and B2C transactions. Elbee collects consignments from the vendors and delivers them to the addressees. The company also collects the value of the consignment from the receiver if required. The customers can track their consignments through the Elbee website.

The company intends to offer single-point interface and increased geographical and market reach. Customers will also benefit through reduced overheads, a virtual inventory, a standardized distribution cost and high levels of service and recoveries.

Elbee had aimed to corner about 55 per cent of ₹ 500 crore logistics market which in value terms worked out to an incremental turnover of ₹ 275 crore by 2002.

2. *BLUE DART—Rapid Delivery through the Internet*

Recognizing the business opportunities of the future, Blue Dart has prepared a comprehensive plan to maximize the potential which e-commerce will offer to a courier service. The company is largely banking on the delivery side.

The company believes that e-commerce is opening up more opportunities on the B2C side. In the B2C segment, the capacity to deliver to the residence is critical. To cash in on this, the company is increasing its warehousing capacity and has recently opened a 10,000 sq. feet warehouse in Chennai. It has an intranet in place which connects over 1000 terminals through Vsat, interfaced together by communication systems. This is to help a customer track his shipment.

Blue Dart now wants the customer to use the technology it has set up. "Instead of just adding an edge within the company and adding exponential growth we want our customers to use it by putting it on the Internet", so says a company spokesman. Blue Dart is already doing business with portals like Rediff and Fabmart among others. Here again the company intends to interface its own system with that of its customers.

CHAPTER 2

Business Models for E-commerce

LEARNING OBJECTIVES

After reading this chapter, you should be able to:

- Explain the features of the Internet that has created so much business potential.
- Understand the role of strategy in e-business and how an opportunistic approach to e-business can be effective.
- Describe the components of business models and where e-business can be used effectively.
- Explain how e-marketplaces are changing supply chains.
- Describe and explain a range of e-business concepts relating to planning and strategy.
- Know how KM becomes important in new business models.

Social Networking and Facebook

Social networking is the way the 21st century communicates now. To be more specific, Social networking is the grouping of individuals into specific groups, like small rural communities or a neighbourhood subdivision, if you will. In 1995, Stewart Brand and Larry Brilliant founded a company called WELL, which could be considered as the first social networking site. Although social networking is possible in person, especially in the workplace, universities, and high schools, it is most popular online. This is because unlike most high schools, colleges, or workplaces, the internet is filled with millions of individuals who are looking to meet other people, to gather and share first-hand information and experiences about any number of topics ranging from golfing, gardening to developing friendships, professional alliances, etc. Social networking services are changing the ways in which people use and engage with the Internet and with each other. Young people, particularly, are quick to use the new technology in ways that increasingly blur the boundaries between online and offline activities. When it comes to online social networking, websites are commonly used. These websites are known as social sites. Social networking websites function like an online community of internet users. Depending on the website in question, many of these online community members share common interests in hobbies, religion, or politics.

Once you are granted access to a social networking website, you can begin to socialize. This socialization may include reading the profile pages of other members and possibly even contacting them. The friends that you can make are just one of the many benefits to social networking online. Another one of those benefits includes diversity because the internet gives individuals from all around the world access to social networking sites. This means that although you are in India, you could develop an online friendship with someone in Denmark or in the United states. Not only will you make new friends, but you just might learn a thing or two about new cultures or new languages and learning is always a good thing. As mentioned, social networking often involves grouping specific individuals or organizations together. While there are a number of social networking websites that focus on particular interests, there are others that do not. The websites without a main focus are often referred to as "traditional" social networking websites and usually have open memberships. This means that anyone can become a member, no matter what their hobbies, beliefs, or views are. However, once you are inside this online community, you can begin to create your own network of friends and eliminate members that do not share common interests or goals. Social media is a medium designed to be disseminated through social interaction, created using highly accessible and scalable publishing techniques. Social media has modernized the reach consumers in a new way; through the internet. Social media has become appealing to big business. Credible brands are utilizing social media to reach old customers, gain new ones and build or maintain credibility and reputation among consumers.

In recent years social mediums have drastically grown. This has tremendously increased the number of consumers that producers are able to reach. Social mediums have not only grown in popularity with the increase in consumer participants, but social mediums have also expanded globally. Social media describes websites that allow users to share content, media, etc. Common examples are the popular social networking sites like Orkut, Twitter, LinkedIn, Friendster, Facebook, MySpace, etc. Social media also includes YouTube, Photobucket, Flickr, and other sites aimed at photo and video sharing. News aggregation and online reference sources, examples of which are Digg and Wikipedia, are also counted in the social media bucket.

The logos of various social networking sites are shown in Figure 2.1 and Table 2.1 shows the trends in technology use as of December 2018.

Figure 2.1 Logos of various social networking companies.

TABLE 2.1 Trends in technology use as of December 2018[1]

Number of Internet users	3.896 billion
Number of social media users	3.25 billion
Facebook users	900 million

Facebook is a social networking service and website launched in February 2004, operated and privately owned by Facebook, Inc. As of July 2015, Facebook has more than one billion active users. Users may create a personal profile, add other users as friends, and exchange messages, including automatic notifications when they update their profile. Facebook users must register before using the site. Additionally, users may join common-interest user groups, organized by workplace, school or college, or other characteristics. The name of the service stems from the colloquial name for the book given to students at the start of the academic year by university administrations in the United States to help students get to know each other better. Facebook allows any users who declare themselves to be at least 13 years old to become registered users of the website.

Facebook was founded by Mark Zuckerberg with his college roommates and fellow computer science students Eduardo Saverin, Dustin Moskovitz and Chris Hughes. The website's membership was initially limited by the founders to Harvard students, but was expanded to other colleges in the Boston area, the Ivy League, and Stanford University.

On October 24, 2007, Microsoft announced that it had purchased a 1.6 per cent share of Facebook for $240 million, giving Facebook a total implied value of around $15 billion. Microsoft's purchase included rights to place international ads on Facebook. In October 2008, Facebook announced that it would set up its international headquarters in Dublin, Ireland. In September 2009, Facebook said that it had turned cash-flow positive for the first time. In June 2015, Facebook's valuation was more than 230 billion.

Most of Facebook's revenue comes from advertising (Table 2.2).

TABLE 2.2 Facebook Advertising Revenues (estimated, in millions US$)[2]

Year	*Revenue (estimated in millions US$)*
2006	52
2008	280
2010	2,000
2018	3,384
2022	1,13,000

Case Discussion

1. Identify the business model used in the Facebook.
2. What are the various ways in which revenue is generated by the Facebook.
3. Compare and contrast the Facebook with other social networking sites like Twitter.

1. https://datareportal.com/reports/digital-2019-global-digital-overview
2. https://www.statista.com

Business Model

Electronic commerce has reached new heights in the recent years. The growth around this area has been great. There have been many technological advances that have been added to the growth of e-commerce businesses, resulting in many types of e-commerce business models. According to statistics, e-commerce sales are expected to reach $4.5 trillion by 2021. In a competitive environment, who will succeed depends on the viability of the business model.

A business model is the method of doing business by which a company can sustain itself, i.e. generate revenue. The business model spells out how a company makes money by specifying where it is positioned in the value chain. Some models are quite simple. A company produces goods or services and sells it to the customers. If all goes well, the revenues from sales exceed the cost of operation and the company realises profit. Other models can be more intricately woven. Radio and television broadcasting is a good example. The broadcaster is a part of a complex network of distributors, content creators, advertisers, and listeners or viewers. Who makes money and how much, it is not always clear at the outset. The bottom line depends on many competing factors such as value proposition, distribution channels, revenue earning, customer segments, key activities, costs, customer relationships, key resources and partners. Figure 2.2 shows a business model.

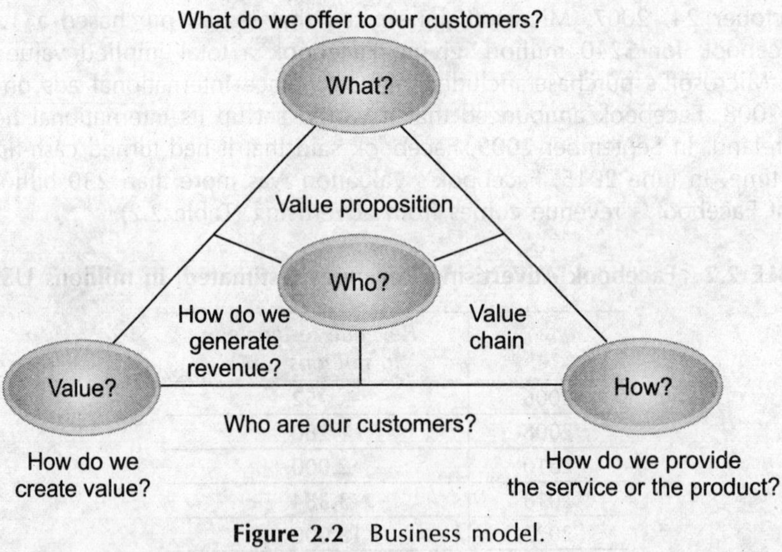

Figure 2.2 Business model.

A business model answers the following questions:

1. What do we offer to our customers?
2. How do we provide the service or the product?
3. How do we create value to all the stakeholders?
4. How do we generate revenue?
5. What is our value proposition?

However, a business model does not discuss how the business mission of the company will be realised. The marketing strategy of the company is needed to assess the commercial viability of a business model and to answer questions such as the following:

1. How is competitive advantage being built?
2. What is the positioning?
3. What is the marketing mix?
4. Which product-market strategy is followed?

E-commerce Business Model

For our understanding, e-commerce can be defined as any form of business transaction in which the parties interact electronically[3]. A transaction in an electronic market represents a number of interactions between parties. For instance, it could involve several trading steps such as marketing, ordering, payment, and support for delivery. An electronic market allows the participating sellers and buyers to exchange goods and services with the aid of information technology. Electronic markets have three main functions—(i) matching buyers and sellers, (ii) facilitating commercial transactions, and (iii) providing legal infrastructure. Information technology permeates all the three functions and also helps in increasing market efficiency and reducing transaction costs. The interaction between participants is supported by electronic trade processes that are basically search, valuation, payment and settlement, logistics, authentication, etc. The Internet and the World Wide Web allow companies to efficiently implement these key trading processes. For instance, many search services and brokers are available to help buyers find information, products, and merchants in electronic markets.

E-commerce can be formally defined as technology-mediated exchanges between parties (individuals, organizations, or both) as well as the electronically-based intra- or inter-organizational activities that facilitate such exchanges[4]. It is global. It favours intangible things—ideas, information, and relationships. And it is intensely interlinked. These three attributes produce a new type of marketplace and society, one that is rooted in ubiquitous electronic networks.

The effectiveness of an e-commerce website is measured through the various parameters that constitute the Web usage analysis for e-commerce. The return on investment is a major cause of worry for the Web merchants. The Web channel provides new opportunities and challenges for analysis. It collects a large amount of detailed information on every user action. There is little experience and knowledge of the end-to-end process—from identifying what usage analysis is interesting to an organization, and what needs to be tracked down and measured—for acting on analysis for revising Web content, and updating advertising and promotion strategies.

An e-business model can be defined as an architecture for product, service, and information flow, including a description of business players, their roles, and revenue sources. For example,

3. Menasce D.A., *Scaling for E-business*, Prentice Hall PTR, NJ, 2000.
4. Jeffrey F. Rayport and Bernard J. Jaworski, *E-Commerce*, Tata McGraw Hill, 2002, p. 3.

some of the most popular revenue-generating models adopted by companies are: (i) charge fees for advertising, (ii) sell goods and services, (iii) sell digital contents, and (iv) charge for processing the transactions that occur between two parties on the Web. E-commerce models can be perceived in the form of relationship between two entities such as:

- Direct marketing versus indirect marketing
- Fully cybermarketing versus partial cybermarketing
- Electronic distributor versus electronic broker
- Electronic store versus shopping mall
- Generalized e-malls versus specialized e-malls
- Proactive versus strategic cybermarketing
- Global versus regional marketing
- Sales versus customer service.

And the list will go on. However, it is possible to classify e-business models according to this criteria.

To develop a successful business model in any arena, the model should effectively address the eight elements listed in Figure 2.3. These elements are as follows:

1. Value proposition
2. Revenue model
3. Business opportunity
4. Innovation
5. Competitive advantage
6. Marketing strategy
7. Innovative human resource management
8. Return on investment.

These are described below:

Value Proposition

A value proposition defines how a company's product or service fulfills the needs of customers. It has several key elements. The main one is the opportunity. What's the issue you are going to solve? What is the new idea that is going to make a difference? The problem also has to align with a specific audience. Who are the people that have this problem or who will jump on this opportunity? Are they unique sets of people one can reach in various ways?

Uber's value proposition is to the passengers as well as to the drivers. For riders, the value propositions are that it is the best way to get around, to be able to call a ride with one tap 24×7 and track the driver arriving. The other side of that value proposition is the value proposition that causes there to be Uber drivers. If you have a car and a smartphone and a little spare time, you can make some extra money. That is a value proposition for becoming a driver.

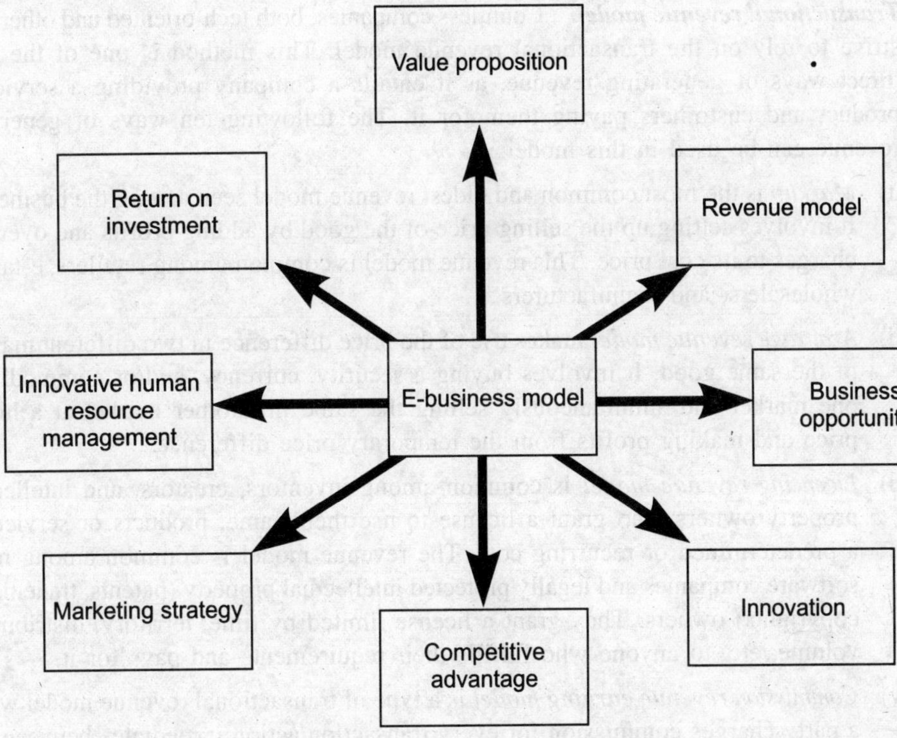

Figure 2.3 E-business model.

Revenue Model

An e-commerce revenue model is a plan for generating revenue for an online business. While e-commerce revenue models share many similarities with brick-and-mortar businesses, they also enable you to reach customers around the globe and offer more diverse methods of generating sales.

A revenue model is a conceptual structure that states and explains the revenue earning strategy of the business. It includes the product and/or service of value, the revenue generation techniques, the revenue sources, and the target consumer of the product offered.

Revenue can be generated from a myriad of sources, can be in the form of commission, markup, arbitrage, rent, bids, etc. and can include recurring payments or just a one-time payment. A revenue model includes every aspect of the revenue generation strategy of the business. Some of the possible models are described below:

1. ***Ad-based revenue model.*** Ad-based revenue models entail creating ads for a specific website, service, app, or other product, and placing them on strategic, high-traffic channels.
2. ***Affiliate revenue model.*** Another popular web-based revenue model is the affiliate revenue model, which works by promoting links to relevant products and collecting commission on the sales of those products, and can even work in conjunction with ads or separately.

3. ***Transactional revenue model.*** Countless companies, both tech-oriented and otherwise, strive to rely on the transactional revenue model. This method is one of the most direct ways of generating revenue, as it entails a company providing a service or product and customers paying them for it. The following ten ways of generating revenue can be used in this model:

(i) *Markup* is the most common and oldest revenue model seen among the businesses. It involves setting up the selling price of the good by adding profits and overhead charges to its cost price. This revenue model is common among retailers, e-tailers, wholesalers, and manufacturers.

(ii) *Arbitrage revenue model* makes use of the price difference in two different markets of the same good. It involves buying a security, currency, and/or commodity in one market and simultaneously selling the same in another market at a higher price and making profits from the temporary price difference.

(iii) *Licencing revenue model* is common among inventors, creators, and intellectual property owners who grant a license to use their name, products or services at a predetermined or recurring cost. The revenue model is common among many software companies and legally protected intellectual property (patents, trademarks, copyrights) owners. They grant a license limited by time, territory, distribution, volume, etc. to anyone who fulfills their requirements and pays for it.

(iv) *Commission revenue earning model* is a type of transactional revenue model where a party charges commission for every transaction/action it mediates between two parties or any lead it provides to the other party. It is one of the most common revenue-earning strategy among the online marketplaces and aggregators where they provide a platform for selling items digitally and charge a commission as a percentage or fixed price on every item sold. Affiliates, brokers, and auctioneers are also seen working on a commission-based revenue model.

(v) *Rent/lease revenue model* is common where a physical asset is involved. This revenue-earning strategy involves recurring (rent) or one time (lease) payment for a temporary use of the asset.

(vi) *Subscription model* is a great example of recurring revenue strategy. This strategy is common in entertainment services, and online hosting companies like Netflix, Youtube, etc. where they provide the specified service for a pre-determined periodic cost.

(vii) *Advertising revenue model* is usually adopted by media houses and information providers, which usually earn money by including advertisements in the content provided. This revenue model is widespread in both offline and online businesses and the company makes money by charging the advertiser per size of the space offered, thousand impressions or per click on the advertisement.

(viii) *Fee-for-service model* charges the customers for the type of and times the service is provided. This is a pay-as-you-go or pay-per-usage revenue model where the customer pays only for the services he actually used. This revenue model is common in telecom and cloud-based services industries.

(ix) *Interest-based revenue strategy* or an *investment-based revenue strategy* is common among banks and prepaid wallet service providers. Banks usually generate revenue in the form of interest on their offerings (loans) and prepaid-wallet service providers like Paytm and PayPal generate their revenue by depositing the money kept in their e-wallets in escrow bank accounts.

(x) *Donation* is the method some companies like Wikipedia uses to sustain. However, they do not make profits.

4. ***Subscription revenue model.*** The subscription revenue model entails offering your customers a product or service that customers can pay for over a longer period of time, usually month to month, or even year to year.
5. ***Web sales.*** This is an offshoot of the transactional revenue model, in which a customer pays directly for a product or service, except that customers must first come to your company via a Web search or outbound marketing, and conduct transactions solely over the Internet.
6. ***Product is free, but services are not.*** This model is unique compared to others, in that you have to give your product for free, yet require customers to pay for installation, customisation, training or other additional services.
7. ***Freemium model.*** The freemium model is one in which a company's basic services are free, yet users must pay for additional premium features, extensions, functions, etc. One of the biggest companies to use this model is Linkedin, the most popular business/social media platform.

Business Opportunity

A competitive business opportunity is the dynamic external system in which a business competes and functions. The more sellers of a similar product or service, the more competitive the environment in which they compete. Look at fast food restaurants—there are so many to choose from; the competition is high.

In business, being good is not good enough unless it comes from your customers and is supported by sales and market growth. The meaning of factors in the macro-environment and the competitive nature of business is that the business and market position can easily be affected if the trends and movements within the economy, global community and in the industry and market segment are not predicted. Doing a competitive business environment analysis involves an analysis of three aspects—(i) Industry analysis, (ii) Industry competitiveness, and (iii) Competitor analysis.

1. ***Industry analysis.*** In analysing the industry and market sector, we are interested in answering two questions:

   (i) What are the major trends affecting the growth of the industry in the future?

   (ii) In summary, will this industry grow faster or slower than the average?

2. ***Industry competitiveness.*** The model of the five competitive forces was developed by Michael E. Porter in the 1980s. Since that time, it has become an important tool

for analysing the industry structure of an organization in strategic processes. Porter's model is based on the insight that a corporate strategy should meet the opportunities and threats in the organization's external environment. Especially, competitive strategy should be based on an understanding of industry structures and the way they change. Porter has identified five competitive forces that shape every industry and every market. These forces determine the intensity of competition, and hence, the profitability and attractiveness of an industry too. The objective of corporate strategy should be to modify these competitive forces in a way that improves the position of the organization.

3. ***Competitor analysis.*** Now, we have looked at the competitive nature of your industry/market, it is time to focus on the actual competitors themselves. This subsection of your analysis will require some research about various aspects of your competitor's business such as
   - description of key competitors and their market positioning
   - size of key competitors in units/dollars
   - market shares of key competitors
   - sales trends of key competitors
   - strengths and weaknesses of key competitors compared to your organization's goods or services
   - perceived marketing strategies of key competitors and their probable impact on your organization

Innovation

We have heard of many major businesses and brands of the recent past now reduced to non-entities. Hindustan Motors (HM) had monopoly in passenger cars till the 1980s with its classic Ambassador reigning supreme on Indian roads. With the arrival of Maruti car and later on several new generation cars, HM lost out miserably. Likewise, Hindustan Lever dominated the washing powder market with its premium brand, but Nirma came along with a more affordable product capturing the mass market and Hindustan Lever had to follow suit with a few lower-priced offerings.

Nokia dethroned Motorola and other mobile phone manufacturers to number one position in 1998, but it lost out miserably to iPhone and Samsung. In today's fast changing market where new entrants come with innovative technologies, market dominance is not for eternity for any company and they need to constantly innovate to retain their existing position.

One of the keys to any successful business is being able to come up with new ideas to keep operations, products and services fresh. The process of bringing those ideas to reality is called *innovation*. While thinking up new ideas is one step of the process, businesses have a much greater task in trying to turn that into an actual product or service that will benefit customers.

In order to successfully innovate, businesses need to install the strategies that best fit their needs and goals. When trying to be innovative, businesses can choose from a variety of different strategies. Each offers advantages and disadvantages. Among the different types of innovation processes, business can employ the following:

Open. Open innovation is when companies use internal and external ideas to help advance their operations.

Disruptive. Disruptive innovation is when new products or services start out at the bottom of the marketplace, but end up eventually moving up and displacing their competitors. An example of disruptive technology was mobile phones being developed as a replacement for home phones.

Reverse. Reverse innovation is when products or services are developed first for use in developing nations. Examples of reverse innovation include dried noodles that Nestle developed for use in India that eventually became popular in Australia and New Zealand.

Incremental. Incremental innovation is when companies make small changes to products and services to ensure they keep their spot in the marketplace. Examples of incremental innovation include men's razor blades, which started with one blade and now have three or four, and the automobile, which is consistently being updated with new features and technology.

Breakthrough. Breakthrough innovation, also commonly referred to as *radical innovation*, is developing completely new ideas and concepts that do not build off any existing products, servicers or operations. Often developed by research and development teams, breakthrough innovations use new technology as a way to quickly climb to the top of new markets. Examples of the breakthrough innovations include the Internet and transistors.

Competitive Advantage

A competitive advantage is the unique ability of a firm to utilize its resources effectively, managing to improve customer value and position itself ahead of the competition. In other words, it is something that a company does better than its competitors because of some proprietary process, service, or brand.

It is an attribute that allows a company to outperform its competitors. If it is easily copied or imitated, it is not considered a competitive advantage.

Examples of competitive advantage are given below:

1. Access to natural resources that are restricted to competitors
2. Highly skilled labour
3. A unique geographic location
4. Access to new or proprietary technology
5. Ability to manufacture products at the lowest cost
6. Brand image recognition

To construct a competitive advantage, a company must be able to detail the benefit that it provides to its target market in ways that other competitors cannot. However, real markets are imperfect, and asymmetries leading to competitive advantages do exist, at least in the short term. Most competitive advantages are short term, although some can be sustained for very long periods, but not forever. In fact, many respected brands fail every year. Companies are said to leverage their competitive assets when they use their competitive advantages to achieve more advantage in surrounding markets. The main challenge for business strategy is to find a way of achieving a sustainable competitive advantage over the other competing products and firms in a market.

Porter suggested four 'generic' business strategies that could be adopted in order to gain competitive advantage. The strategies relate to the extent to which the scope of a business activities are narrow versus broad and the extent to which a business seeks to differentiate its products.

There are several great examples of differentiation comparative advantage such as Nike, Google, and Honda. All these brands achieve important economies of scale by their strong brand name, which increases customer loyalty and customer satisfaction.

Google is the number one search engine and the best website for optimization searches that returns the most accurate results in no time. Google has achieved a competitive advantage by offering innovative services such as Google Search, Gmail, Google Finance, Google Docs, and more; it maintains an incredibly powerful infrastructure and occupies 70% of the Internet market.

Marketing Strategy

A marketing strategy is the overall game plan of a business for reaching people and turning them into customers of the product or service that the business provides. The marketing strategy of a company contains the company's value proposition, key marketing messages, information on the target customer and other high-level elements. No matter how tremendous a firm's qualities, its marketing strategy and execution are often just as important. The best business concept, or idea, will fail if it is not properly marketed to the potential customers. Everything you do to promote your company's products and services to the potential customers is known as *marketing*. Market strategy is the plan you put together that details exactly how you intend to enter a new market and attract new customers. For instance, Twitter, YouTube, and Pinterest have a social network marketing strategy that encourages users to post their content on the sites for free, build personal profile pages, contact their friends, and build a community.

Though there is no template for the perfect digital marketing strategy, there are a few elements that should be present in the marketing strategy. Here are a few marketing strategy examples of what is often present in a winning plan:

- Market research
- Target customers
- Marketing tools

Social media marketing is one of the best marketing strategy examples for businesses of all sizes. Many consumers are using social media channels on a daily basis to communicate with friends, stay current on what is happening in the world, and even get news and updates from their favorite brands. If your business is not on social media, you are missing out on a powerful opportunity to reach your target customers.

There are a lot of different elements to social media marketing. The first is posting quality content. This content can be updates from your business, including promotions, special offers, sales, or other deals. Another element of social media marketing is engagement. Social media marketing is a strategy that can be used by any business that wants to engage its audience and start a conversation with the target buyers online. Most consumers are active on at least one social media channel. Many will even follow their favourite brands to engage with their content and posts over time.

Airbnb, a community marketplace for people to list and book accommodations around the world, was founded in 2008 out of San Francisco, California. Since then, Airbnb has grown to 1,500,000+ listings in 34,000+ cities worldwide. A large contributor to the company's explosive global success was social media. In January 2015, Airbnb launched a social media campaign around the hashtag #OneLessStranger. The company referred to the campaign as a 'global, social experiment,' in which Airbnb asked the community to perform random acts of hospitality for strangers, and then take a video or photo with the person and share it using the hashtag. And it was a great success.

Innovative Human Resource Management

Although many entrepreneurial ventures are started by one visionary individual, it is rare that one person alone can grow an idea into a multi-million dollar company. In most cases, fast-growth companies, especially e-commerce businesses, need employees and a set of business procedures. In short, all firms—new ones in particular—need an organization to efficiently implement their business plans and strategies. Many e-commerce firms and many traditional firms that attempt an e-commerce strategy have failed because they lacked the organizational structures and supportive cultural values required to support new forms of commerce. Companies that hope to grow and thrive need to have a plan for organizational development, which describes how the company will organize the work that needs to be accomplished. Typically, work is divided into functional departments such as production, shipping, marketing, customer support, and finance. Jobs within these functional areas are defined, and then recruitment begins for specific job titles and responsibilities. Typically, in the beginning, generalists who can perform multiple tasks are hired. As the company grows, recruiting becomes more specialized. For instance, at the outset, a business may have one marketing manager.

Historically, Human Resources (HR) professionals were primarily concerned with the efficient management of the employment process (from recruitment to termination). HR also focused on helping the organization comply with the governmental regulations and in mitigating employment-related risks. Thus, HR professionals found themselves acting in a support role to the other business units. Organizational development (OD), on the other hand, was created as a way of applying behavioral science to help organizations improve individuals and systems. The goal of OD is to help people function better within an organizational context. At its heart, OD is supposed to represent purposeful and meaningful change for the better. Put together, the role of HR is to

- Manage the hiring, retention, and performance processes
- Mitigate employment-related risks
- Ensure legal compliance
- Confirm there is 'enough' equity and diversity
- Enforce policies and procedures
- Reduce labor costs

- Promote workplace health and safety
- Increase organizational effectiveness
  - Maximize employees' potential and help them amplify their contributions
  - Assess to try and create positive change
  - Align human behavior with the organization's strategy and structures
  - Help promote the organization's values throughout the workplace

Leadership team also plays a vital role in organizational development. Very often, investors would look at the quality of the leadership team to decide on funding the business.

Return on Investment

A new company may not be generating enough revenue to cover operating costs, and so, additional capital will be needed. Traditional sources of capital include incubators, commercial banks, angel investors, venture capital firms, and strategic partners. The Return on Investment (ROI) metric is a popular method for evaluating the financial consequences of investments and actions. The calculated ROI is a ratio or percentage, comparing net gains to net costs.

Investors and decision-makers use the ROI metric to compare the magnitude and timing of expected gains with the scale and timing of costs. Businesses are in the business to make money. But, calculating the true value of any project with respect to its impact on margin has always been challenging, mainly due to the ambiguity of turning notions into dollar values.

The advantages of knowing the ROI are given below:

1. ***It quantifies project value.*** Perhaps, the most important aspect of ROI is its ability to show business leaders dollar figures of a project's worth. ROI turns the subjective into the objective, which can often turn uncertainty into support.
2. ***It can build stakeholder support.*** Tying a dollar value to a project may help with a 'go/no-go' decision. Many times, stakeholders want to see what the dollar value is to them if they are to support a particular project. Without an ROI, that is very difficult to do.
3. ***It can uncover additional benefits.*** The process of calculating ROI forces practitioners to investigate benefits that might not have seemed obvious at project inception.
4. ***It can lead to project prioritization.*** Once the decision has been made to launch a project, ROI helps determine the project's ranking among other priorities; usually, projects with greater ROI are ranked higher and gain resource support more quickly.

Different Kinds of E-business Models

Reading the literature, we find business models categorized in different ways. Presently, there is no single, comprehensive and cogent taxonomy of e-business models that one can point to. Although there are many different ways to categorize e-business models, they can be broadly classified as follows:

1. E-business model based on the relationship of transaction parties (described in the subsequent section).

2. E-business model based on the relationship of transaction types (described later).
3. Classification by revenue model [A revenue model may comprise (a) product sales model that charges customers directly for the products or services they buy; (b) subscription model that charges a fixed monthly or annual rental for the service; (c) transaction fee model that charges a service fee based on volume and value of the transactions offered; (d) advertising support model that charges advertisers instead of charging users; and (e) sponsorship model that provides sponsorship by companies for non-financial reasons.]
4. Classification by distribution channel [A distribution channel may comprise (a) direct marketing where manufacturers such as Dell, Nike, Lego or Sony market directly from company sites to individual customers; (b) pure play e-tailers who have no physical stores, only an online sales presence; *amazon.com* is an example of such a model; and (c) click-and-mortar retailers who are traditional retailers with a supplementary Web site like *Walmart.com.*]

E-business Models Based on the Relationship of Transaction Parties

Electronic markets are emerging in various fields. Different industries have markets with different characteristics. For example, an information B2C market differs in many respects from the automotive B2B market. The former represents companies that sell digital information goods, such as news, articles, music, books, or digital videos. In the information B2C market, the electronic infrastructure not only helps match customers and sellers, but also acts as the distribution channel, delivering products to customers. In this case, the infrastructure, such as servers and networks, must support the delivery of large files, streaming media and other types of digital goods in an efficient way. This B2C market over the Internet can be viewed as an open system, where the number of participants is unknown. In the automotive B2B market, the products traded, such as parts and components of cars, have a high degree of specificity. The market infrastructure used is to be mainly based on Electronic Data Interchange (EDI) over expensive VAN services. EDI involves the exchange of standardized, structured information between organizations, permitting direct communication between computer systems. At the heart of B2B applications is the strong integration of different applications. Servers, networks, and software should provide the infrastructure to integrate Web-based applications with mainframe and legacy systems. B2B is also a closed market in the sense that the number of participants involved in trading is limited and known a priori.

Understanding the nature of the market's requirements is critical for creating the underlying e-business infrastructure. The relation between B2B and B2C models is clearly shown in Figure 2.4. B2B covers business transactions along the various interactions existing in the value chain from producers of raw materials to retailers and consumers including manufacturers and distributors. On the contrary, B2C reflects only the interactions between a customer and a retailer. Basically, B2C transactions include the following steps: (i) account acquisition, (ii) product discovery through search and browse, (iii) price negotiation, (iv) payment, and (v) product delivery. In some cases, dispute resolution and customer services may also exist.

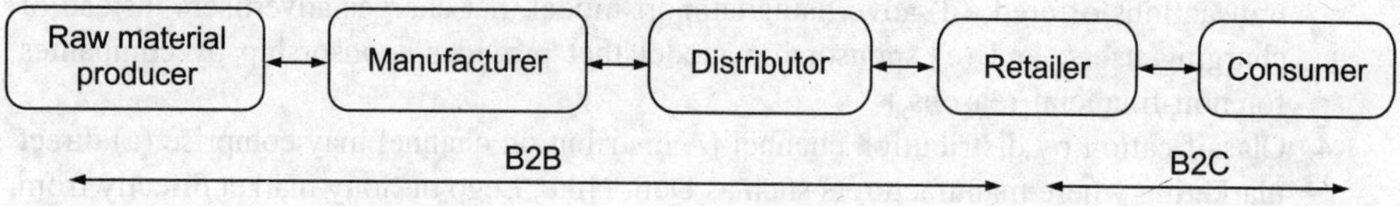

Figure 2.4 Relation between B2B and B2C models.

E-commerce can be classified according to the transaction partners such as **business-to-consumer (B2C)**, **business-to-business (B2B)**, **business-to-government (B2G)**, **consumer-to-consumer** (C2C), and **consumer-to-business (C2B)**. Within these broad categories, there are a number of variations in the way the models are implemented. Table 2.3 summarizes some of the current e-business models. The contents of this table are illustrated in the form of a diagram in Figure 2.5.

TABLE 2.3 Summary of e-business Transaction Models

Model	*Description*	*Examples*
B2C	Sells products or services directly to consumers.	*amazon.com, autobytel.com, eDiets.com, Pets.com*
B2B	Sells products or services to other businesses or brings multiple buyers and sellers together in a central marketplace.	*MetalSite.com, VerticalNet.com, SHOP2gether.com*
B2G	Businesses selling to local, state, and federal agencies.	*iGov.com*
C2C	Consumers sell directly to other consumers.	*ebay.com, InfoRocket.com*
C2B	Consumers fix price on their own, which businesses accept or decline.	*Priceline.com*
B2E	Business-to-employee (B2E) electronic commerce uses an intrabusiness network which allows companies to provide products and/or services to their employees. Typically,companies use B2E networks to automate employee-related corporate processes.	*Online insurance policy management. Corporate announcement dissemination. Online supply requests. Special employee offers. Employee benefits reporting.*

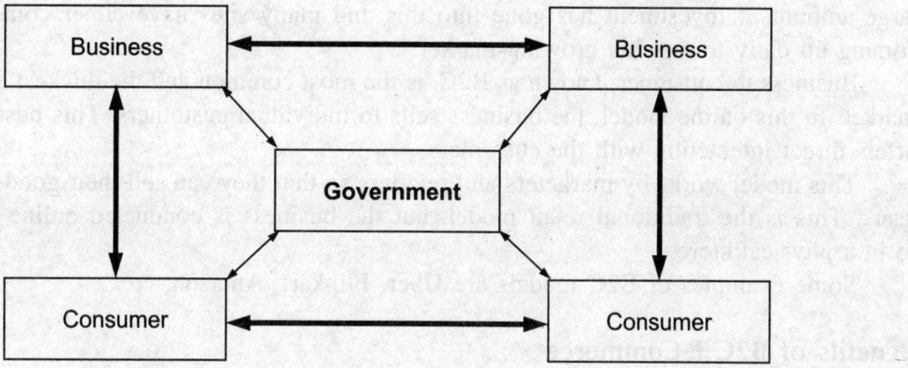

Figure 2.5 E-business transaction model.

Business-to-Consumer (B2C)

Consumers are increasingly going online to shop for and purchase products, arrange financing, arrange shipment or take delivery of digital products such as software, and get service after the sale. B2C e-business includes retail sales, often called e-retail (or e-tail), and other online purchases such as airline tickets, entertainment venue tickets, hotel rooms, and shares of stock.

Many traditional brick-and-mortar retailers such as Barnes & Noble are now e-tailers with a Web storefront. These combined brick-and-mortar/online businesses are also known as *brick-and-click* companies.

Some B2C e-businesses provide high-value content to consumers for a subscription fee. Examples of e-business following this subscription model include the *Wall Street Journal* (financial news and articles), *Consumer Reports* (product reviews and evaluations), and *eDiets.com* (nutritional counselling).

B2C e-business models include virtual malls, which are websites that host many online merchants. Virtual malls typically charge setup, listing, or transaction fees to online merchants, and may include transaction handling services and marketing options. Examples of virtual malls include *excite.com, choicemall, women.com, networkweb.com, amazon.com, Zshops.com,* and *yahoo.com*.

E-tailers that offer traditional or Web-specific products or services only over the Internet are sometimes called *virtual merchants*, and provide another variation on the B2C model. Examples of virtual merchants include *amazon.com* (books, electronics, toys, and music), *eToys.com* (children's books and toys), and *ashford.com* (personal accessories).

Some businesses supplement a successful traditional mail-order business with an online shopping site, or move completely to Web-based ordering. These businesses are sometimes called *catalogue merchants*. Examples include *avon.com* (cosmetics and fragrances), chefs (cookware and kitchen accessories), Omaha Steaks (premium steaks, meats, and other gourmet food), and Harry and David (gourmet food gifts).

Many people were very excited about the use of B2C on the Internet, because this new communication medium allowed businesses and consumers to get connected in entirely new ways. The opportunities and the challenges posed by the B2C e-commerce are enormous. A large amount of investment has gone into this and many sites have either come up or are coming up daily to tap this growing market.

Business to consumer, known as B2C, is the most common and the thickest e-commerce market. In this online model, the business sells to individual customers. This business model offers direct interaction with the customers.

This model works by marketers and retailers so that they can sell their goods to internet users. This is the traditional retail model, but the business is conducted online as opposed to in a physical store.

Some examples of B2C models are Uber, Flipkart, Amazon, etc.

Benefits of B2C E-Commerce

- Global reach
- No physical overheads
- More data to profile customers
- Trackable marketing

B2C Dropshipping

Running an online store through dropshipping means holding no inventory, and only placing product orders as they come in from your customers. There is no need to worry about packaging, shipping, and storage costs as these fall on your supplier, who ships products straight to your customers. B2C dropshipping is a great business solution as it allows small business to make bigger profits and scale accordingly. With the potential customers located across the globe, B2C dropshipping enables businesses to save money on packaging and delivery while still building a strong brand that customers can rely on.

B2C marketing aims to invoke an emotional response and capitalize on the value of the brand. B2C marketers know that their customers are prone to making impulse purchases and typically making buying decisions independently. They can be swayed by various factors, including a trendy brand, quality customer service, convenience, and social proof. However, not all buyers respond to the same marketing methods, hence why good B2C marketing is based on market segmentation and targeted messaging. In order to craft effective promotional campaigns, marketers need to consider the best practices for each channel and target audience and tailor their efforts to achieve the highest possible return on investment.

Features of B2C

- Easy to understand
- Short sales cycle
- Clear target market
- Lower risk and costs of entry
- Potential for emotional and impulse purchases
- Mass/consumer media marketing strategy
- Price-sensitive customers

Some of the reasons why one should opt for B2C are:

1. ***Inexpensive costs, big opportunities.*** Once on the Internet, opportunities are immense as companies can market their products to the whole world without much additional cost.

2. ***Globalization.*** Even being in a small company, the Web can make you appear to be a big player which simply means that the playing field has been levelled by e-business. The Internet is accessed by millions of people around the world, and definitely, they are all potential customers.

3. ***Reduced operational costs.*** Selling through the Web means cutting down on paper costs, customer support costs, advertising costs, and order processing costs.

4. ***Customer convenience.*** Searchable content, shopping carts, promotions, and interactive and user-friendly interfaces facilitate customer convenience, thus generating more business. Customers can also see order status, delivery status, and get their receipts online.

5. ***Knowledge management.*** Through database systems and information management, you can find out who visited your site, and how to create, better value for customers.

How Does B2C Work?

B2C e-commerce is more than just an online store. It really is about managing the entire process, but just using technology as a tool for order processing and customer support. Figure 2.6 depicts the processes in B2C. The B2C process is now explained in greater detail.

1. ***Visiting the virtual mall.*** The customer 'visits' the mall by browsing the online catalogue—a very organized manner of displaying products and their related information such as price, description, and availability. Finding the right product becomes easy by using a keyword search engine. Virtual malls may include a basic to an advanced search engine, product rating system, content management, customer support systems, bulletin boards, newsletters and other components which make shopping convenient for shoppers.

2. ***Customer registers.*** The customer has to register to become part of the site's shopper registry. This allows the customer to avail of the shop's complete services. The customer becomes a part of the company's growing database and can use the same for knowledge management and data mining.

3. ***Customer buys products.*** Through a shopping cart system, order details, shipping charges, taxes, additional charges and price totals are presented in an organized manner. The customer can even change the quantity of a certain product. Virtual malls have a very comprehensive shopping system, complete with check-out forms.

4. ***Merchant processes the order.*** The merchant then processes the order that is received from the previous stage and fills up the necessary forms.

5. ***Credit card is processed.*** The credit card of the customer is authenticated through a payment gateway or a bank. Other payment methods can be used as well, such as debit cards, prepaid cards, or bank-to-bank transfers.

6. ***Operations management.*** When the order is passed on to the logistics people, the traditional business operations will still be used. Things like inventory management, total quality management, warehousing, optimization and project management should still be incorporated even though it is an e-business. Getting the product to the customer is still the most important aspect of e-commerce.

7. ***Shipment and delivery.*** The product is then shipped to the customer. The customer can track the order/delivery as virtual malls have a delivery tracking module on the website which allows a customer to check the status of a particular order.

8. ***Customer receives.*** The product is received by the customer, and is verified. The system should then tell the firm that the order has been fulfilled.

9. ***After-sales service.*** After the sale has been made, the firm has to make sure that it maintains a good relationship with its customers. This is done through customer relationship management or CRM.

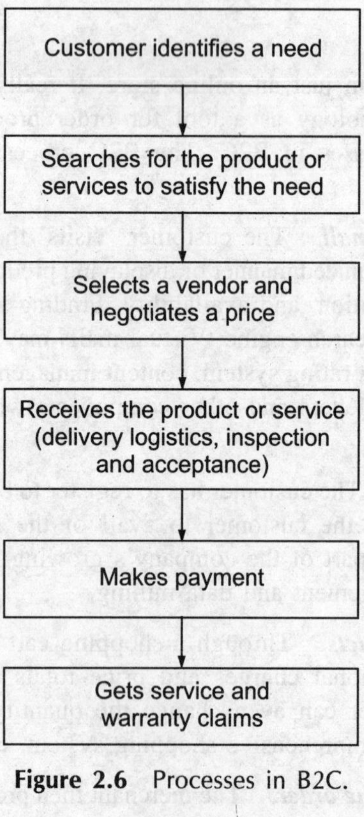

Figure 2.6 Processes in B2C.

Business-to-Business (B2B)

B2B is that model of e-commerce whereby a company conducts its trading and other commercial activity through the Internet and the customer is another business itself. This essentially means commercial activity between companies through the Internet as a medium.

This is supposed to be a huge opportunity area on the Web. Companies have by and large computerized all the operations worldwide and now they need to go into the next stage by linking their customers and vendors. This is done by supply chain software, which is an integral part of your ERP application. Companies need to set up a backbone of B2B applications, which will support the customer requirements on the Web. Many B2B sites are company and industry specific, catering to a community of users, or are a combination of forward and backward integration. Companies have achieved huge savings in distribution-related costs due to their B2B applications.

Major Advantages of B2B[5]

1. ***Direct interaction with customers.*** This is the greatest advantage of e-business. The unknown and faceless customer including other businesses, buying the products of a large MNC like say HLL or Procter & Gamble through distributors, channels, shops and the like, now has a name, face, and a profile. Large MNCs pay a fortune for this information on customer buying patterns.

2. ***Focussed sales promotion.*** This information gives authentic data about the likes, dislikes and preferences of clients and thus helps the company bring out focussed sales promotion drives which are aimed at the right audience.

3. ***Building customer loyalty.*** It has been observed that online customers can be more loyal than other customers if they are made to feel special and their distinct identity is recognized and their concerns about privacy are respected. It has also been found that once the customers develop a binding relationship with a site and its product, they do not like to shift loyalties to another site or product.

4. ***Scalability.*** This means that the Web is open and offers round-the-clock access. This provides an access never known before, to the customer. This access is across locations and time zones. Thus a company is able to handle many more customers on a much wider geographical spread if it uses an e-business model. The company can set up a generic parent site for all locations and make regional domains to suit such requirements. Microsoft is using this model very successfully. The additional cost of serving a larger segment of customers comes down drastically once a critical mass is reached.

5. ***Savings in distribution costs.*** A company can make huge savings in distribution, logistical and after-sales support costs by using e-business models. Typical examples are of computer companies, airlines, and telecom companies. This is because the

5. http://www.indiainfoline.com/cyva/repo/ecom/

e-business models involve the customer in the business interaction to such a level that companies are able to avoid setting up the huge backbone of sales and support force, which ordinarily would have to be set up.

Tools and Techniques at the Disposal of B2B Enterprises

It is important to know the right marketing strategies, which would be required to sell successfully and profitably over the Web. The Web as a medium provides you with a unique platform to enable various strategies, which would not have been possible to execute in a conventional scenario. Some of these are:

1. ***Use of pricing as a tool.*** There is a wealth of research on pricing used as a tool to generate sales on the Internet. The biggest e-tailer of them all, *amazon.com,* made it big by giving substantial discounts. Part of these heavy discounts is attributed to the distributor level commissions, which are now being passed on to the customer. Apart from this, companies have started giving things free on the Internet in order to get a critical mass of subscribers, which helps in getting advertising revenues. The best example is the Apple IMac computer machine being given free if the buyer agrees to make a certain amount of purchase using the Apple's e-commerce website.
2. ***Use of application service provider model.*** This is an old model of the 1970s, which was used among mainframes, and dumb terminals, and which is being revisited with a vengeance. Software companies are offering their packages not in CDs and boxes but through the Web. The customer can log in over the Internet and access the software from the web server of the company and need not download it into his PC. This goes one step further in the age of the networked PCs where one need not use even a hard disk and all critical application data is kept on the Web and can be accessed from anywhere in the world. These services (which are not products) are being offered at, say, \$5 an hour.
3. ***Use of generic models which are known for efficiency as well as personalized attention to various business customers.*** The Web has given rise to a new partnership between brick-and-mortar manufacturers, e-tailers, and express delivery companies like FedEx. These organizations take care of the individual elements of the customer, the order fulfillment and the post sale complaints, if any.
4. ***Use of comparison shopping.*** The Internet has brought in a whole new concept of price matching and comparison-shopping. Today there are sites, which will take you to hundreds of sites to find the cheapest product to suit your specifications. This would never have been possible without the Internet.

Business activities between companies can be transacted over an extranet. An extranet consists of two or more intranets connected via the Internet, where participating companies can view each other's data and complete business transactions such as purchasing.

Like B2C models, B2B models take a variety of forms. There are basic B2B Internet storefronts, such as Staples and Office Depot, that provide business customers with purchase, order fulfilment, and other value added services. Another B2B model is a business trading community, also called a *vertical Web community*, that acts as a central source of information for a *vertical market*. A vertical market is a specific industry in which similar products or services are developed and sold using similar methods. Examples of broad vertical markets include insurance, real estate, banking, heavy manufacturing, and transportation. The information available at a vertical Web community can include buyer's guides, supplier and product directories, industry news and articles, schedules for industry trade shows and events, and classified advertisements. *MediSpeciality.com* (healthcare), *HotelResource* (hospitality), and *NetPossibilities* (building trades) are examples of virtual vertical marketspaces. B2B exchanges are websites that bring multiple buyers and sellers together in a virtual centralized marketspace. In this marketspace, buyers and sellers can buy from and sell to each other at dynamic prices determined by the exchange rules. Table 2.4 illustrates some common elements of B2B exchanges. B2B exchanges can be further categorized into several ways as aggregators, trading hubs, post and browse markets, auction markets, and fully automated exchanges.

B2B aggregators provide a single marketspace for company purchasing by providing many like-formatted supplier product catalogues in one place. Examples of B2B aggregators include *e-chemicals* (industrial chemicals), *Chemdex* (chemicals), *MetalSite* (steel and other metals), and *freightquote.com* (shipping services).

TABLE 2.4 Common Elements of B2B Exchanges

Element	*Benefit*
Centralized marketspace	Neutral and nonaligned with either sellers or buyers.
Standardized documentation	Users are prequalified and regulated.
Price quotes, price history, and after-the-sale information provided	Pricing mechanism is self-regulating.
Confidential transactions between businesses.	Clearing and settlement services provided.

Trading hubs are B2B sites that provide a marketspace for multiple vertical markets. Horizontal trading hubs support buyers and sellers from many different industries. *VerticalNet* is an example of a horizontal trading hub. A pioneer in providing virtual vertical marketspaces, it maintains business trading communities for many different industries, including communications, energy, health care, food service, and manufacturing. Diagonal trading hubs support specific types of buyers or sellers, or specific types of products across multiple industries. *SHOP2gether.com* is an example of a diagonal trading hub.

Post and browse markets such as *CATEX* (insurance, reinsurance, and risk management), *CreditTrade* (credit derivatives), and *TechEx* (life sciences intellectual property) enable participants to post buy or sell opportunities on an electronic bulletin board. Interested parties meet through the postings and negotiate transactions for themselves.

B2B auction markets enable multiple buyers or sellers to enter competitive bids on a contract. Examples of B2B auction markets include *e-STEEL* (steel and other metals), *HoustonStrect.com* (energy), *Altra* (energy), and *Manheim Online* (auto dealer auctions).

Auction markets may include reverse auctions or "name your price" auctions. In a reverse auction, a product's selling price continues to decline until the product is purchased. "Name your price" auctions, which allow buyers to enter a bid for a product or service that a seller can then provide at the bid price, are also called reverse auctions. *FreeMarkets* is an example of a B2B site conducting reverse auctions.

Business-to-Business Transactions and Models

B2B interactions involve much more complexity than B2C. For instance, typical B2B transactions include, among others, the following steps: (i) review catalogues, (ii) identify specifications, (iii) define requirements, (iv) post request for proposals (REP), (v) review vendor reputation, (vi) select vendor, (vii) fill out purchase orders (PO), (viii) send PO to vendor, (ix) prepare invoice, (x) make payment, (xi) arrange shipment, and (xii) organize product inspection and reception. Due to the large number of transactions involved, business-to-business operations can be too risky if e-business sites cannot guarantee adequate quality of service in terms of performance, availability, and security.

Several models and classifications have been proposed for B2B commerce. Figure 2.7 illustrates an electronic marketplace for B2B trading. The model could be oriented to a vertical market (e.g. wholesale trade, chemicals, construction, and electronics) or to a horizontal approach (e.g. office supply, and logistics).

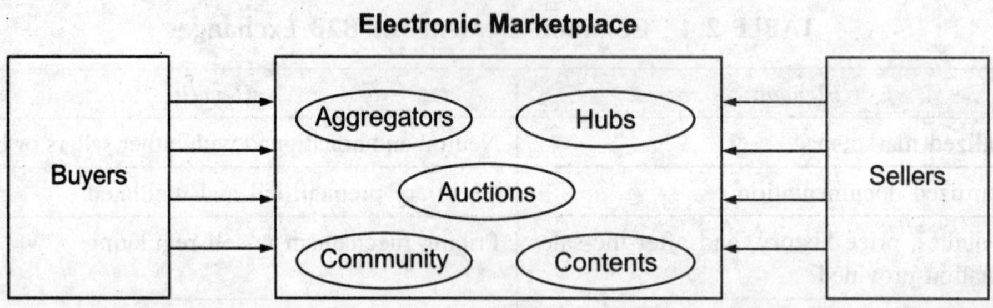

Figure 2.7 Business-to-Business (B2B) marketplace.

The models can now be described as follows:

1. ***Aggregators.*** In the aggregation model, one company aggregates buyers to form a virtual buying entity and/or aggregates suppliers to constitute a virtual distributor. For example, in the science marketplace, one company became the central buying location for thousands of buyers to implement their own purchasing rules and obtain volume discounts. The aggregator takes the responsibility for selection and fulfilment, pricing, and marketing segmentation. Another example is an electronic company that offers a total home buying service, from search to financing, under one site.
2. ***Hubs or process integration.*** Hubs or process integration focusses on producing a highly integrated value proposition through a managed process. Hubs have been defined as *neutral Internet-based intermediaries* that focus on a specific industry or a specific business process. Hubs host electronic markets and create value by reducing the costs of transactions between sellers and buyers. There are examples

of vertical hubs that serve a vertical market or a specific industry, such as energy, steel, telecommunications, and plastic. On the contrary, functional hubs specialize in horizontal markets across different industries. Functional hubs focus on business processes such as project management and MRO (Maintenance, Repair and Operating, and procurement). An electronic business company that provides office supplies to many industries is a good example of a functional hub in B2B commerce.

3. ***Community or alliance.*** In the community model, alliances are used to achieve high value integration without hierarchical control. Members and end-users play key roles as contributors and customers. Basically, communities produce knowledge with economic value, such as Linux, MP3, and Open Source.

4. ***Content.*** Content is the end product of this model of B2B commerce. It has the purpose of facilitating trading. Revenue can be generated from subscriptions, membership, or advertising. For example, there are e-companies that sell information about contracts to bid market intelligence and analysis, and jobs by industry.

5. ***Auctions or dynamic pricing markets.*** Auctions or dynamic pricing markets handle complex exchanges between buyers and sellers in B2B commerce. Auctions (e.g. English, Dutch, Vickrey, Reverse) are dynamic and efficient mechanisms for mediating and brokering in complex marketplaces, like supply-chain and procurement systems. Bundle auctions allow agents to bid for bundles of items and are useful for B2B applications such as automatic supply-chain or procurement.

In a fully automated B2B exchange, multiple buyers and sellers competitively bid on commodities or standardized products, and the buy and sell orders are matched automatically. *PaperExchange.com* is a fully automated B2B exchange. A summary of B2B models is given in Table 2.5.

TABLE 2.5 B2B Summary

Type	*Description*	*Examples*
B2B storefronts	Provide businesses with purchase, order fulfillment, and other value-added services	*Staples.com* *OfficeDepot.com*
B2B vertical markets	Provide a trading community for a specific industry	*HotelResource.com*
B2B aggregators	Provide a single marketspace for business purchasing from multiple suppliers	*MetalSite.com*
B2B trading hubs	Provide a marketspace for multiple vertical markets	*VerticalNet.com*
B2B post and browse markets	Provide a marketspace where participants post buy and sell opportunities	*CATEX.com* *CreditTrade.com* *TechEx.com*
B2B auction markets	Provide a marketspace for buyers and sellers to enter competitive bids on contracts	*e-STEEL.com* *HoustonStreet.com* *Altra.com* *FreeMarkets.com*
B2B fully automated exchanges	Provide a marketspace for the automatic matching of standardized buy and sell contracts	*PaperExchange.com*

Another business model similar to the B2B exchange model is the business-to-government, or B2G procurement model. B2G e-businesses such as *eFederal.com* and *Gov.com* in the US are hoping to tap the $18 billion per year market for government procurements that do not require a bid.

Not only do businesses sell directly to consumers and other businesses online, but consumers are now interacting with each other to buy, sell, or trade products, personal services, or information.

Consumer-to-Consumer (C2C)

With the C2C e-business model, consumers sell directly to other consumers via online classified ads and auctions, or by selling personal services or expertise online. Examples of consumers selling directly to consumers are *ebay.com* (auction) and *TraderOnline.com* (classified ads).

There are also a number of new consumer-to-consumer expert information exchanges that are expected to generate $6 billion in revenue by 2005. Some of these exchanges, such as *AskMe.com* and abuzz, are free, and some allow their experts to negotiate fees with clients. *InfoRocket.com*, one of the first question-and-answer marketplaces, is driven by a person-to-person auction format. The *InfoRocket.com* bidding system allows a person who submits a question to review the profiles of the "experts" who offer to answer the question. When the person asking the question accepts an "expert" offer, *InfoRocket.com* bills the person's credit card, delivers the answer, and takes a 20 per cent commission.

Consumer-to-Business (C2B)

The C2B model, also called a *reverse auction* or *demand collection model*, enables buyers to name their own price, often binding, for a specific good or service generating demand. The website collects the "demand bids" and then offers the bids to the participating sellers. *ReverseAuction.com* (travel, autos, consumer electronics) and *priceline.com* (travel, telephone, mortgages) are examples of C2B e-business models.

E-government Classification

The classification of e-government is as follows:

1. ***Government-to-citizen (G2C).*** The online non-commercial interaction between the local and Central Governments and private individuals, e.g. IRS, FirstGov, etc.
2. ***Government-to-government (G2G).*** The online interaction between government organizations, departments, and authorities and with other Government organizations, departments, and authorities. An example of a successful G2G project is the Northeast Gang Information System (NEGIS).
3. ***Government-to-employees (G2E).*** The online interaction between government organizations and its employees, e.g. egovonline.com.

4. ***Business-to-government (B2G) or government-to-business (G2B).*** On the Internet, business-to-government (B2G) is the concept that businesses and government agencies can use central websites to exchange information and do business with each other more efficiently than they usually can off the Web, e.g. Gov.com.

E-business Models Based on the Relationship of Transaction Types

This business model is essentially ruled by the following two parameters:

On the basis of value addition. Value addition is the addition of value to a product or service because of the opportunities that it offers on the Web.

On the basis of control. At the high end of control there is hierarchical control and at the low end there is no control, so that it is self-organizing. Normally, the control is done through the policies of the website.

Based on these, nine types of transactions can be identified as listed below:

1. Brokerage
2. Aggregator
3. Info-mediary
4. Community
5. Value chain
6. Subscription
7. Manufacturer
8. Advertising
9. Affiliate

These transaction types take place in a variety of ways. Moreover, any given firm may combine one or two of these as part of its Web business strategy (see Figure 2.8).

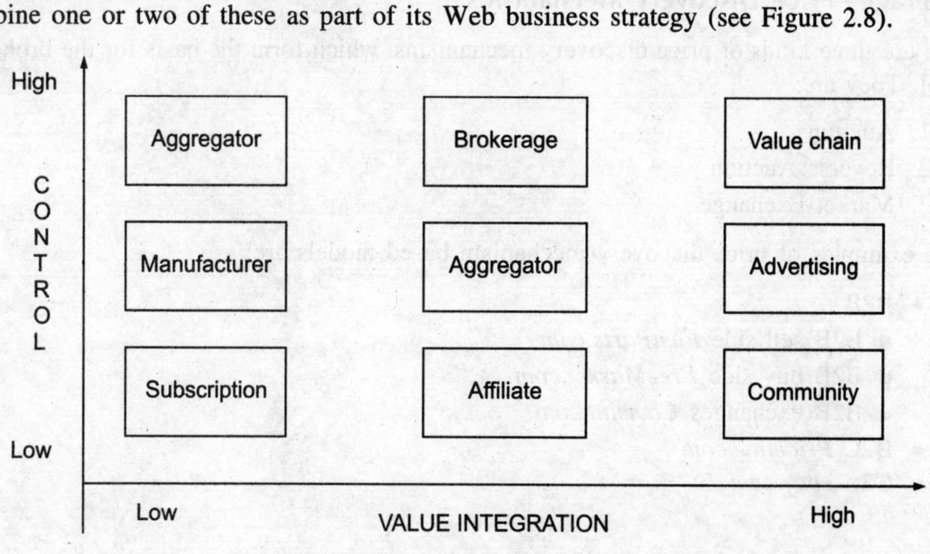

Figure 2.8 Transaction model.

1. *Brokerage Model*

The characteristics of the brokerage model are as follows:

- The price-discovery mechanism is its key-principle.
- It is a meeting point for sellers and buyers.
- auctions and exchanges are the modes of transactions.
- It is a 'Free Market'.
- It consists of Global Network of Buyers and Sellers.
- It is a Virtual Marketspace enabled by the Internet.
- It encompasses all types of organizations now.

Advantages of the Brokerage Model

Following are the advantages of the brokerage model:

- C2C trading
  (a) allows buyers and sellers to trade directly bypassing intermediaries, and
  (b) reduces cost for both the parties.
- Global reach
- Trading convenience, which
  (a) allows trading at all hours, and
  (b) provides continually updated information.
- Sense of community through direct buyer and seller communication
- Efficient access to information
- Alleviation of the risks of anonymous trading.

Brokerage—Price Discovery Mechanisms

There are three kinds of price discovery mechanisms, which form the basis for the brokerage model. They are:

1. Auction
2. Reverse Auction
3. Market Exchange

Some examples of price discovery mechanism based models are:

- B2B
  - B2B sell side *FastParts.com*
  - B2B buy side *FreeMarket.com*
  - B2B exchanges *Covisint.com*
- B2C *Priceline.com*
- C2C *ebay.com*

Some Indian brokerage sites are:

www.ebay.in
www.mahindrafirstchoice.com
www.indiacar.com
www.steelexchangeindia.com

Of the three mechanisms listed, the first two—auction and reverse auction—can be discussed now.

Auction broker. Many different auction formats have emerged since the first auction occurred in Babylon in about 500 B.C. Today, different auction formats are aggregated on certain common attributes. There are open and sealed-bid auctions. There are auctions where the auction price ascends as the auction proceeds and there are auctions where the price descends at regular intervals. There are single auctions and double auctions.

English auction. The English auction is one of the most common auction formats. It is also known as the open-outcry auction or the ascending-price auction. It is frequently used for selling art, wine, and other physical goods, which do not have a limited lifetime.

The English auction is defined in the following way: The auctioneer starts off the auction with the lowest acceptable price or the reserve price. He then receives bids from the bidders until the point from which there is no raise in the bid. At that point, the auctioneer 'knocks down' the item, which indicates that the highest bidder will receive the item in exchange for the sum of money he bid for. Sometimes, the reserve price will not be made known to the public. This may happen when the auctioneer is uncertain about the price expectation of the bidders and when he wishes the bidders to totally set the price level. As a consequence of not giving the reserve price, the item will never be sold if the highest bid is lower than the reserve price.

The bidders are often anonymous, especially if the bidding occurs through electronic means. This is done to preserve the identity of the bidders. A well-known bidder may increase the price expectation of the product just because a person known to him has entered a bid. He may be his business rival. Therefore this kind of bidding will not be beneficial for the bidders. The seller might benefit from a 'non-anonymous' bidding process, if he wants to acquire the highest price possible. We must nevertheless keep in mind that some bidders might not join this bidding process, which can result in a lower final price for the seller.

In a traditional physical auction, the auctioneer can highly influence the bidding process. He can manipulate bidders with his voice, his gestures, and his personality. Manipulation can also occur within an electronic English auction. Sometimes the auction site may provide the bidders with alert messages if their bids are too low. If this function is just a service function or a manipulative function, it depends on how the messages are formatted. It is always up to the actual bidder to decide if he feels manipulated or not.

Winner's curses is a widespread phenomenon within the English auction format. This occurs when the bidder gets too excited in an auction and pays more for an item than his actual valuation. On the other hand, the bidder might come away paying less for an item than his maximum valuation since he only needs to increase his bidding price by small incremental steps.

Dutch auction. The Dutch auction was developed in the Netherlands to auction flowers and other products with a limited life. It is also known as the descending-price auction. In a Dutch auction, the opening price is set extremely high. The price then descends with a predefined amount, at predefined time intervals, until a buyer claims the product to be *mine*. When many items of the same product are auctioned at the same time, many bidders may claim the product as mine at different points of time until no more items of the product are left. This process results in different prices for different bidders, with the first person claiming the product as mine being the one who pays the highest price.

The auction time period is often very short. This auction format is normally used for products that will perish in a short time. Besides the flower auctions in Holland, it has been used to sell fish in England and in Israel. A dispose Dutch auction is often practised in department stores during the sales season to dispose off excess inventory accumulated over a period of time. Therefore, the discount rate increases. Thus, we have a time period and a descending price (increasing discount rate)—the two main ingredients in a Dutch auction.

From a bidder's perspective, the Dutch auction forces the bidder to make a bidding decision earlier if he really wants the product, compared to the English auction where the buyer has the possibility to bid at a lower price. This means that the bidder may bid at or near his actual valuation of the item.

First-price sealed-bid auction. The first-price sealed-bid auction has the main characteristic of not being an open-cry auction, like the English or Dutch auction, and thus the individual bids are hidden from other bidders.

This auction has two different phases—a bidding phase, in which all the bids are collected, and a resolution phase, in which the bids are opened and the winner is determined. During the bidding phase, each bidder submits his bid, which is based on his own valuation. The bidder is thus totally ignorant of all the other bids that have been submitted. The resolution phase works like this: all the bids are opened and sorted from the highest to the lowest bid. If it is only one item that is auctioned, the highest bid will be the winning bid. If multiple items of the same product are auctioned, the items are awarded to the highest bids until no more items are left. This is called a Discriminatory Sealed-Bid Auction, since not all the bidders pay the same price. The first-price sealed-bid auction is often used for refinancing credit and foreign exchange. Until 1993, this auction format was used by the US Treasury to issue debt securities. From a bidder's perspective, a high bid (compared to the expected market valuation) raises the probability of winning. To avoid the winner's curse, the bidder might therefore lower his bid to reflect his own (and probably the market's) valuation.

Vickrey auction. William Vickrey, the winner of the 1996 Nobel Prize in Economics, developed the Vickrey auction. It is also called the *uniformed second-price auction*.

In a Vickrey auction the bids are sealed and each bidder bids from his own intuitive knowledge ignorant of all the other bids. What is different in this auction format compared to the first-price sealed-bid auction is that, the winning bidder will pay the price of the second highest bid, which is the same as the highest unsuccessful bid. Thus, the winner pays less than what he has bidden. When the Vickrey auction is applied to include multiple units of the same item, all the winning bidders will pay the same price. This price will be the highest unsuccessful bid.

From a seller's perspective, one might wonder why anybody would like to use the Vickrey auction format. Why should the Vickrey auction with the second-price rule generate more income for the seller than the first-price sealed-bid auction? Theoretical literature has shown that, under the assumption of private value (i.e. when an item is wanted for personal consumption), the Vickrey and the first-price sealed-bid auction will both yield the same expected price. This can be explained with the fact that in a Vickrey auction the bidder will adjust his bids as he increases the price upwards, since he knows that he needs only to pay the second highest bid. Therefore, the actual bids will better reflect the bidder's valuation of the item in a Vickrey auction than in a first-price sealed-bid auction.

Economic Rationality Behind Auctions

From a market microstructure perspective, auctions are basically trading processes which bring buyers and sellers together. Auctions may be used when other trading procedures fail to work or when a price discovery process is needed. Two main motives for auctions are identified from an economical point of view:

- Auctions as a mechanism to determine a price
- Auctions as a distribution allocation mechanism.

Auctions as a mechanism to determine a price identifies auction as a procedure to establish an equilibrium market price. This may be done for products that are not traded on the traditional markets, like rare antique items, or for products with highly fluctuating prices, like stocks, currencies, and commodities. The common identifier for these auctions is that buyers and sellers are brought together to provide purchase and sale orders and hence liquidity.

Auctions as a distribution allocation mechanism identifies auctions for consumer products which are difficult to sell through the ordinary market channels because they are:

- Products with limited life, such as airplane seats (which are worthless after the plane has taken off);
- Overstocked products which need to be separated from the new incoming products.

In this case, the auction is a new separate distribution channel which is created to attract a large audience. In return, the sold products will often have a large discount. The auctioneer's main goal is to attract as many customers as possible, so that the market will be liquid without forcing the auctioneer to do major price reductions. These kinds of auctions will often attract bargain hunters who are well-informed customers and who know what specific products they are looking for.

Buyers and sellers are attracted to the price discovery mechanism and the distribution allocation mechanism for different reasons. Table 2.6 shows a comparison between the two mechanisms.

TABLE 2.6 Role of Buyer, Seller and Auctioneer

Auction group	*Price discovery mechanism*	*Distribution allocation mechanism*
Buyer	To determine an equilibrium price, to acquire rare items at a reasonable price.	To make a bargain, to acquire products at a low price.
Seller	To determine an equilibrium price, to find a customer base for rare items.	To off load excess inventory, to sell products with limited life.
Auctioneer/ Intermediary	To achieve high trading volumes, which will lead to high returns.	To achieve high trading volumes, which will lead to high returns.

Impact of the Web on Electronic Auctions

The electronic auction process is illustrated in Figure 2.9. The auctioneer brings together the suppliers (sellers) and the customers (buyers or bidders) within the auction process. During the process of transaction, trade objects and a rule base are needed. The entire auction process can be executed on the World Wide Web.

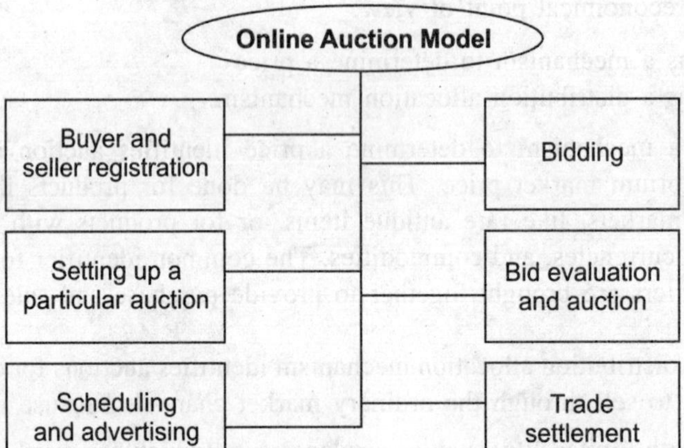

Figure 2.9 Functional model of an online auction.

The impact of the Web on the electronic auction is significant. The electronic auction can benefit from the following Web-related features:

1. Common infrastructure with millions of potential users, which increases the possibility of an auction to occur between potential suppliers and customers.
2. Standardized hypertext protocol for displaying the trade objects (i.e. items to be auctioned), which increases the economic feasibility of the electronic auctions.
3. Development of standardized search functions, which help suppliers and customers to find each other.
4. Standards for secure payments (e.g. SSL and SET), which encourage suppliers and customers to actually use the Web medium for trading.

Critical factors. There are four main factors that characterize electronic auctions. At least one of these factors will be present where an electronic auction appears. The four factors are:

- Perishability
- Scarcity
- Goods that may be moved electronically
- Goods that are geographically constrained.

Perishability. This is a valid factor, if the value of the products to be sold at a given point in time is zero. An example of a perishable product is an airplane ticket. Each flight travel has a fixed cost to cover the fuel, maintenance, and the salaries bill. Each sold ticket will generate revenue to cover part of these elements of cost. When the airplane leaves the airport, the unsold tickets go waste. If these tickets can be sold at an auction site at a price which more than covers the marginal cost of the ticket, the company would make a greater profit than it would do without the said auction. This is valid, assuming that the cost of the auction process will be less than the revenue that the actual auction will generate.

Scarcity. This occurs when there is an excess demand, compared to the actual supply of a particular product. An auction market can be used to provide a price discovery mechanism for the product. The price of the product will increase to reflect the excess demand until an equilibrium price is reached where supply equals demand. Some product examples where an Internet auction may be used for price discovery are:

- New computer parts (e.g. the Intel Pentium III processor)
- Domain names
- IP addresses
- Collectibles: stamps, coins, wine, and so on
- Communication frequencies

Goods that may be moved electronically. These goods have a great possibility of appearing in the electronic markets. In terms of electronic auctions, securities are one of the most promising areas where an electronic auction may occur. The largest entry barriers that an electronic auction site for securities must overcome are the regulations set up by various Securities Exchange Commissions (SECs) around the world. These Commissions have been established by different governments to protect the public interest in terms of company reporting criteria, inside trading rules, and so on. Therefore, it can take longer time than one may think, before the electronic security auction sites are widely available to the public.

Goods that are geographically constrained. These goods have better chances to be part of a successful electronic auction. This is due to the fact that if the transportation cost exceeds the customer's local search cost, the customer will not engage in an electronic auction. Therefore, a global market for physically constrained goods makes little sense. It has to be kept in mind that the goods that can be moved electronically are on the other hand excellent for electronic auctions.

Electronic auction seller-buyer perspective. From a seller-buyer perspective, there are three different pairs of buyers and sellers that appear in electronic auctions. These different pairs are:

- Consumer-to-Consumer (C2C)
- Business-to-Consumer (B2C)
- Business-to-Business (B2B)

Consumer-to-Consumer represents in an electronic auction, the modern version of classified advertisements. This auction will require the two persons to be located somewhat near each other, so that the transportation cost does not exceed the local search cost.

Business-to-Consumer can be identified with companies trying to sell off excess stock or fixing prices for new products. Thus, the B2C auction will have at least one of the perishability and scarcity market factors.

Business-to-Business auctions are mainly used by companies and governments to sell public contracts and surplus property. B2B auctions are to some extent privately held since, only business companies can qualify as potential buyers. Therefore, B2B auction sites tend not to be as vigorously promoted to the general public as C2C and B2C auction sites are. The graphical representation of C2B vs. B2C is shown in Figure 2.10.

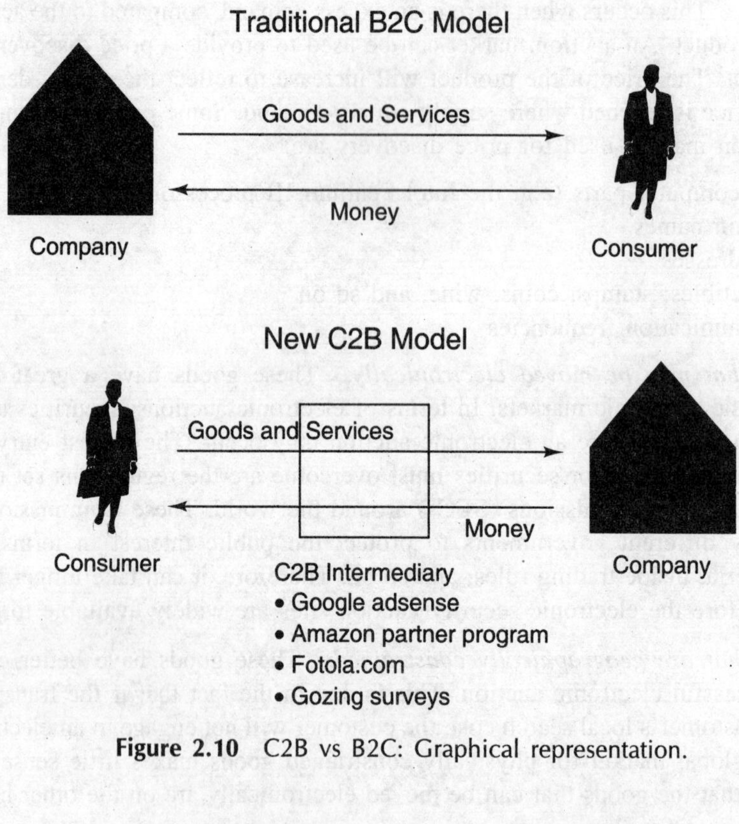

Figure 2.10 C2B vs B2C: Graphical representation.

eBay

eBay is the world's largest personal online trading community. eBay created a new market, an efficient one-to-one trading system in an auction format on the Web. Individuals—not big businesses—use eBay to buy and sell items in more than 4320 categories, including automobiles, collectibles, antiques, sports memorabilia, computers, toys, Beanie Babies, dolls, figures, coins, stamps, books, magazines, music, pottery, glass, photography, electronics, jewellery, gemstones, and much more. Users can find the unique and the interesting—everything from chintz china to chairs, teddy bears to trains, and furniture to figurines on eBay.

As the leading person-to-person trading site, buyers are compelled to trade on eBay due to a wide variety of items available. Similarly, sellers are attracted to eBay to conduct business. eBay provides over 4 million new auctions and 450,000 new items every day.

The eBay community is made up of individual buyers and sellers who visit the site to do more than just buy or sell—they have fun, shop around, and get to know each other (by chatting at the eBay Café) and much more. Through the bulletin boards, users meet and get to know each other, discuss topics of mutual interest, and petition one another for information. These bulletin boards are public forums that encourage open communication between users. eBay also encourages open and honest communication between the community and the company. Frequently, the members of the community organize grass-root movements to improve the environment in which they work and play. More than 60 million auctions have been completed on eBay since its inception. Figure 2.11 describes the eBay model.

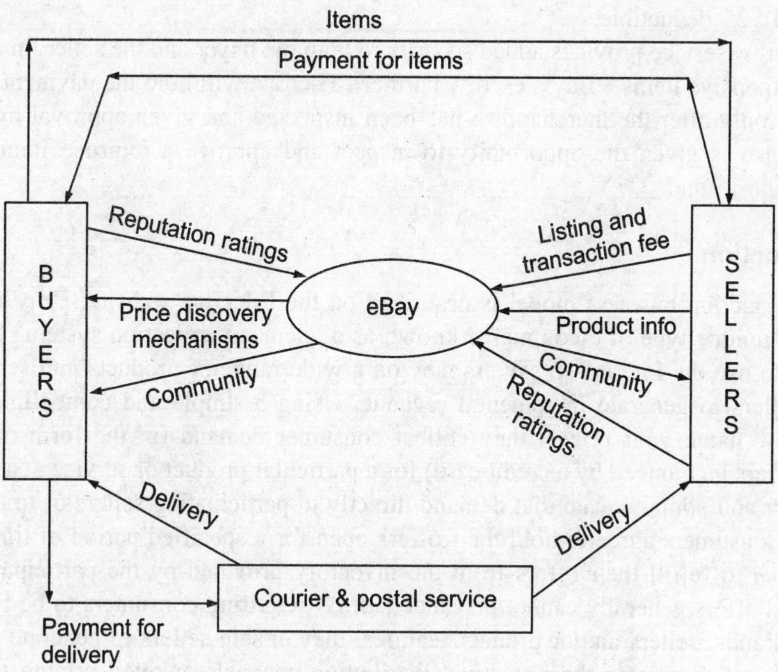

Figure 2.11 eBay model.

The key to eBay's success is the trust between the buyers and sellers who make up the eBay community, and the trust between the user and eBay, the company. To overcome hesitancy sometimes associated with Internet commerce, eBay invented the industry's first electronic information exchange exclusive to one-to-one trading, the Feedback Forum.

How Does One Bid?

First, the user needs to register as an eBay member. The registration is free and takes only a couple of minutes. The user can then enter the auction field using his id and password. The person has to carefully look for what he is bidding on. Consider, for example, an item which costs $20.00. Enter the maximum bid in the bid box at the bottom of the page. Then, click on the "Review Bid" button. eBay will now bid on behalf of the person, up to his maximum bid. The credit card should be placed on file with eBay. The seller, for his part, can sit back (after entering his id and password) and watch the auction.

Security. You can instantly check the reputation or business practices of anyone at eBay. The Feedback Forum is a place where users leave comments about each other's buying and selling experiences at eBay. A bidder checks his seller's Feedback Profile, before he places a bid, to learn about the other person's reputation with the previous buyers. If a person is a seller, he follows the same procedure with the bidders.

Every eBay purchase is covered by insurance, free of charge under the terms of eBay's program. If a person paid for an item and did not receive it (or if he has received the item in a form unlike what was described earlier), eBay will reimburse buyers up to $200, less the standard $25 deductible.

An escrow service provides added security to both the buyer and the seller, in transactions involving expensive items. eBay's escrow partner i-Escrow, will hold the payment and send it to the seller only after the merchandise has been inspected and given approval by the buyer. The seller also is given the opportunity to inspect and approve a returned item before the buyer gets the refund.

Reverse Auction

The reverse auction business model is described on the Priceline website. *Priceline.com* has pioneered a unique type of e-commerce known as a "demand collection system" that enables consumers to use the Internet to save money on a wide range of products and services while enabling sellers to generate incremental revenue. Using a simple and compelling consumer proposition—"name your price", they collect consumer demand (in the form of individual customer offers guaranteed by a credit card) for a particular product or service at a price set by the customer and communicate that demand directly to participating sellers or to their private databases. Consumers agree to hold their offers open for a specified period of time to enable *Priceline.com* to fulfill their offers from the inventory provided by the participating sellers. The fulfilled offers generally cannot be cancelled. By requiring consumers to be flexible with respect to brands, sellers and/or product features, they enable sellers to generate incremental revenue without disrupting their existing distribution channels or retail pricing structures.

Priceline.com was founded in October 1997. It launched its website in April 1998, trumpeting the idea of buyer-driven commerce as a way to use the Internet to secure the lowest possible price on airline fares. Patent claims have been a key factor in driving *Priceline's* remarkable value. *Priceline.com* has succeeded in part due to alliances formed with customers in areas of airline service industry, automobile industry, hotel reservation services industry, home financing services industry, adaptive marketing programs, and through website banner referral.

By creating these alliances, *Priceline.com* has been able to capture the market in these various service areas, using their patented "name your price" business model as already explained above. With competition growing, such alliances have merely given *Priceline.com* an advantage. Alliances formed in the automobile industry are with both new and used car dealers and with car rentals. Ford, Honda, Nissan are a few brands available on *Priceline.com.* Some firms have allied with *Priceline.com* for their rental car business. The Affiliate Network Program enables the qualified independent websites to place the *Priceline.com* hyperlink on their site. Any referral from an independent website to *Priceline.com* that results in business for *Priceline.com*, receives $10 for first time qualified user and $1 for subsequent users.

Priceline.com has adaptive marketing programs with numerous companies. These programs facilitate a revenue stream based on a referral basis. There are also third-party participators who enable *Priceline.com* to thrive. These third parties are indirect alliances. *Priceline.com* depends on the use of the third party's computer systems. Some of these computer systems include: the central computer system for hotel and airline reservations, Lending Tree Inc. for home financing, Exodus Communication for infrastructure, Web and database servers, and CallTech Communications Inc. for call centre. *Priceline.com's* major sources of revenue are derived from the following areas:

- Airline ticket reservation services
- Hotel ticket reservation services
- New auto purchasing
- Home financing, including mortgages, refinancing, and equity loans
- Adaptive marketing programs
- Licensing patents

Priceline's competitive advantage lies in its "name your price" business model. It is the world's first buyer-driven commerce system, and benefits both consumers and sellers by providing a unique platform where demand and supply meet. The model is fundamentally different from any other form of electronic commerce and it seems to revolutionize the way people shop for products.

2. *Aggregator Model*

Classic wholesalers and retailers of goods and services are increasingly referred to as "e-tailers". Sales can be made based on list prices or through auctions. In some cases, the goods and services are unique to the Web and do not have a traditional "brick-and-mortar" storefront (see Figure 2.12).

Following are some of the aggregator models:

1. ***Virtual merchant.*** This is a business that operates only from the Web and offers either traditional or Web-specific goods and services. The method of selling may be by list price or auction. An example of a service merchant is *Facetime*, which calls itself an "application service provider". It offers live customer support for e-commerce websites (e.g. Amazon, eToys, Eyewire and OnSale).

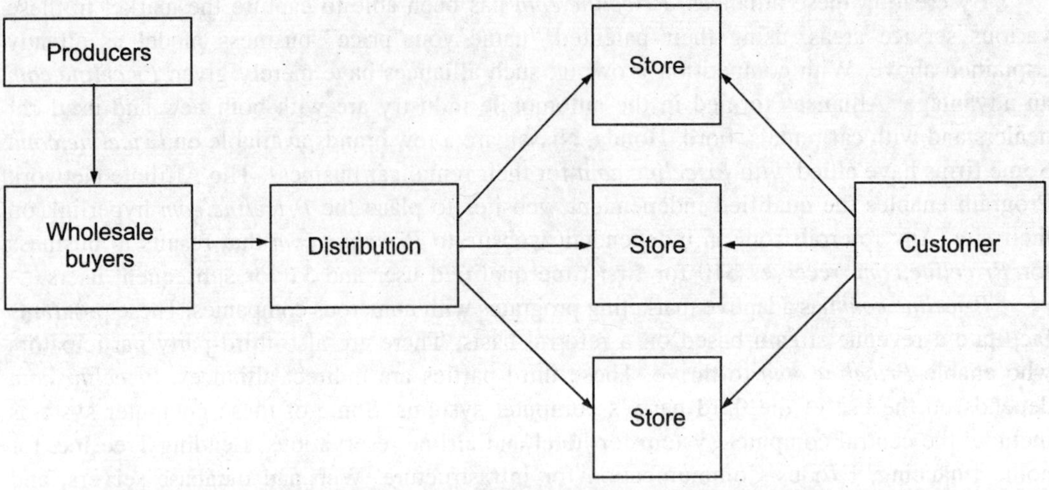

Figure 2.12 Traditional business model.

2. ***Catalogue merchant.*** Catalogue merchant is the migration of mail order to a Web-based order business (e.g. Levenger).
3. ***Surf-and-turf.*** This is a traditional brick-and-mortar establishment with Web storefront. The model has the potential for channel conflict.
4. ***Bit vendor.*** This is a merchant that deals strictly in digital products and services and, in its purest form, conducts both sales and distribution over the Web.
5. ***Subscription model.*** In this, the users pay for access to the site. High value-added content is essential (e.g. *WallSt. Journal*, *ConsumerReports*). Generic news content, viable on the news-stand, has proven less successful as a subscription model on the Web [e.g. *Slate*].

What Do Aggregators Do?

Based on the electronic marketplace, the aggregator model bypasses distributors so that the buyers and sellers come together. Figure 2.13 can help you form an idea about the model.

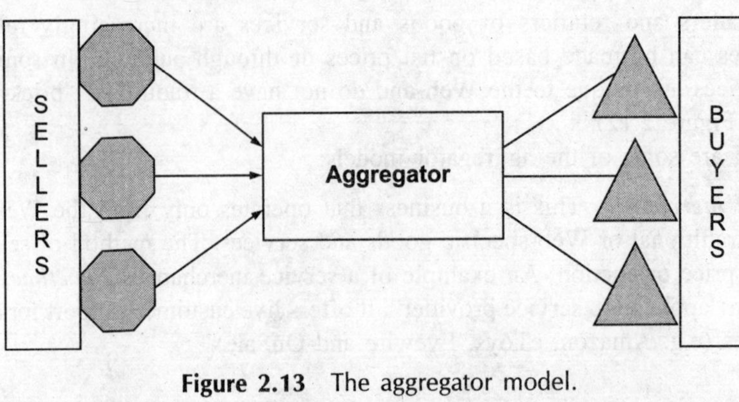

Figure 2.13 The aggregator model.

To be more precise, the aggregators are the connectors between the buyers and the sellers. They are involved in the overall process of selection, organization, matching the buyers' requirement with the particulars of the available goods, fulfillment of the orders and enabling the customers to create a value about the sellers.

There are four types of aggregators such as the following:

1. ***Content aggregators.*** They are among the first large-scale sites on the Web and mostly represent large publishing companies, e.g. *Pathfinder.com*. Their basic challenge is that content has to be attractive enough to make the site viable. For example, CANOE and Hockeyplus, that provide extensive statistics, analysis, pool information or *cricinfo.com*.

2. ***Mainstream aggregators.*** These include sites like Yahoo providing a Web directory and a search engine, along with a bunch of attractive tools like e-mail addresses, home pages, reminders, and many others. The most attractive feature of these sites is that they have an 'easy-to-remember' URL which is one of the reasons for them to be the top traffic sites on the Web.

3. ***Event aggregators.*** These are sites that provide in-depth content and tools tailored to the needs of a particular group, which doubles as a clearly defined customer base, for example, mortgages—build tools, rates, advise, and the ability to purchase a mortgage online in the same place (Microsoft's *HomeAdvisor* or *HomeShark*).

4. ***Shopping aggregators.*** Shopping aggregators let consumers roam through hundreds of sites and catalogues and find the best price in seconds. They help consumers sift through dozens of e-commerce sites. For example, *compare.com* and *bizrate.com* evaluate their quality on independent basis as in the case of consumer reports.

E-commerce is forcing changes in the distribution channels that require all parties—manufacturers, distributors, retailers, consumers and logistics companies—to evaluate their value proposition and develop capabilities that will meet the evolving demands of the Internet age.

Implications for manufacturers, other challenges and opportunities of e-commerce are that, it:

1. Requires investment in marketing directly related to the consumers so as to sustain customer loyalty to their brands.
2. Relies on consumers' support for the sale of products.
3. Requires brick-and-mortar enablers to function as a distribution centre for local delivery and returns, and for regular retail activity.

The distribution channel and logistics infrastructure remains largely unchanged for products that are either perishable or require contact with the product prior to selection.

The changes generated by e-commerce represent equally significant opportunities and challenges for logistics and transportation companies such as GATX, ASD Systems, Logistix, *Clickship.com*, and a host of others that have sprung up to leverage the capabilities of the Internet.

The implications of the model are that, for the growth of the ability to realize the potential for Internet-generated demand for delivery from local brick-and-mortar enablers, the same-day pickup and delivery infrastructure, will need to evolve rapidly. The fragmented nature of the same-day pickup and delivery service has limited achievement of delivery density, productivity and proper marketing to reduce the cost of service.

Logistics and transportation enablers who can use the same level of technology, marketing, operational planning, management talent to same-day service that has fuelled the growth of the express market, will find that the pent-up demand for this service with e-commerce models can be greater than what Frederick Smith envisioned for overnight service when he launched Federal Express.

The capabilities needed for this model are:

- Greater investment in the brick-and-mortar infrastructure.
- Handling of inbound freight for finished goods.
- Management of a more traditional distribution network with truckload and less-than-truckload deliveries to local distribution centres.
- Optimization of stores to support customer visits to view new products and to handle exchanges and returns.
- Integration of the existing retailers with the online channel for sales to e-consumers.
- Handling the same-day delivery of goods and pickup returns.

3. *Info-mediary Model*

An organizer of virtual community is called an *information intermediary* or *info-mediary*, who helps sellers to collect, manage, and maximize the value of information about consumers. Data about consumers and their buying habits are extremely valuable, especially when that information is carefully analyzed and used to target marketing campaigns. Some firms are able to function as info-mediaries by collecting and selling information to other businesses. An info-mediary may offer users free Internet access (e.g. NetZero) or free hardware (e.g. *eMachines.com*) in exchange for detailed information about their surfing and purchasing habits. This is more likely to succeed than the pure advertising model (see Figure 2.14).

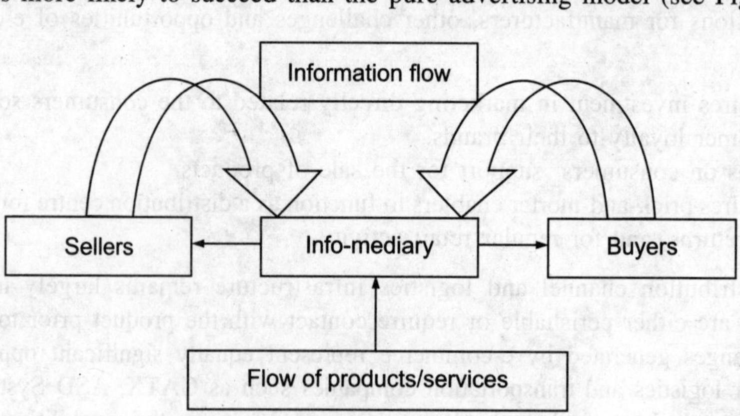

Figure 2.14 Info-mediary model.

The info-mediary model can also work in the other direction, i.e. providing consumers with useful information about the websites in a market segment that competes for their dollar. Info-mediaries are in information business, implying that they competes on their ability to capture and manipulate information in a manner that adds value for their clients, who could be sellers or buyers. A real info-mediary provides information services by capturing information from both sides of a transaction. They do not own the products or services that are shipped directly from suppliers to customers. Many info-mediaries today follow business models that generate revenue from the deeper pockets on the seller side. These models could be in the form of exclusive contractual arrangements whereby the info-mediary is the leader in finding customers for a seller. Membership fees for participating in an electronic market could be another source of revenue. However, more common models involve advertising revenue, whereby the info-mediary accepts payments from suppliers based on advertising (screen) space, number of user page views, and transactional revenue, whereby a certain per cent of sales goes to the info-mediary.

Buyer-based revenue sources are relatively rare but can be expected to increase over the next few years as info-mediary services become valued in online shopping environments characterized by increasing choice, complexity, and information overload. Such sources could include membership or subscription fees, allowing access to valued information or services, a transactional percentage, or fees based on services, such as connecting a seller to a buyer and ensuring privacy protection. An info-mediary front end to the Web could help protect consumers from unsolicited mailings and confusing product selection.

Value Addition

An analysis of the general info-mediary business model reveals that info-mediaries create and add value for the customer during several critical phases from the initial search of the supplier and product comparison (as to whether it fulfils the requirements) to the actual transaction and ultimate product or service delivery (sales fulfilment). To support the initial phase, info-mediaries leverage the potential of the Internet to provide almost unlimited expansion of search space for consumers, thus overcoming the limitation of physical space inherent in traditional brick-and-mortar operations. While the conventional stores carry only the most popular items, *amazon.com* offers millions of items, most of which are sought only by a relatively few customers with specialized tastes. Buyers can certainly expand their search space through search engines, but a more organized universe provided by info-mediaries is generally preferable. For example, at *Yahoo.com's* shopping area and *amazon.com's zShops.com*, buyers can search thousands of stores and millions of products. Aggregating a large number of suppliers, these info-mediaries save buyers' invaluable hours on tedious piecemeal searches through direct use of search engines. Ironically, the bringing together of buyers and sellers becomes increasingly necessary as the search space grows larger. In this sense, info-mediaries create and perpetuate their own demand.

Finally, info-mediaries also provide valuable assistance to buyers to make their purchasing decisions, by offering "suitable" suggestions. This function is supported by technology for one-to-one marketing based on online customer profiling. *amazon.com* not only anticipates book-buyers' demands, but also facilitates the purchase decision by presenting the previous buyers' comments about the books on sale.

This analysis reveals how info-mediaries help buyers expand, organize, and optimize their search spaces with information and information technologies. For some products, including books, CDs, and flowers that are small in size and relatively easy to ship, info-mediaries provide support through both the requirements and the acquisition phases. Thus, we identify two dimensions—vertical and horizontal—underlying the manner in which info-mediaries add and create value, as represented in the form of an info-mediary value grid: the vertical dimension is the potential to increase navigational value; the horizontal dimension is the acquisition cost.[6]

The text 'products' in Figure 2.14 (the bottom-most block) refers to typically information-intensive items such as books, CDs, and houses. Flowers are not information-intensive, but info-mediaries like 1-800-*Flowers.com* expand buyers' search spaces by locating a florist to deliver flowers anywhere in the world on their behalf. Similarly, the search space for PCs is also enlarged, since buyers readily specify any desired PC configuration, often impossible to work out in a brick-and-mortar store. Home buyers can also benefit from info-mediaries such as *Realtor.com*, to navigate the range of selections. To complete an acquisition however, they need to work with local realtors collaborating with *Realtor.com*. For certain segments of the population (such as people who are just too busy), frequent trips to local stores to buy common household items and other daily necessities are inconvenient. Start-up info-mediaries like *Kozmo.com* and *Webvan.com* provide value to busy people by helping them save time in doing their daily chores. *Kozmo.com* advertises itself by saying: "Delivery to you in under an hour."

Classification of Info-mediaries[7]

Info-mediaries can be classified, in terms of their relationships with sellers and buyers, into four types based on whether these relationships are open (non-proprietary, giving anyone free access) or closed (proprietary, restricting access). Closed relationships imply a certain relationship-specific investment (such as membership fee), and parties making that investment expect a return. The four types of relationships are:

1. ***Specialized agents.*** The related proprietary networks are sectioned off the broader Internet by having closed relationships with both buyers and suppliers. Entering the info-mediary's domain requires incurring cost on the part of buyers and sellers alike, usually in the form of a fee or a certificate that they satisfy a certain membership profile. These info-mediaries usually manage a specialized market; their business performance depends on their ability to deliver value through scope (sufficient numbers of sellers and buyers), specialization (a well-defined and lucrative niche), and infrastructure (a platform for transactions).
2. ***Generic agents.*** These info-mediaries maintain open relationships with both buyers and suppliers and involve no relationship-specific investment. Examples include search engines *Hotbot.com* and *Google.com* that provide open search capabilities to

6. www.superprofile.com/paper1/introduction.html
7. www.superprofile.com/paper1/introduction.html

any buyer looking for a supplier. The info-mediaries create value through their comprehensive and unbiased service, often generating revenue from advertising, which is priced based on eyeballs or number of unique user clicks, and the value of screen real estate. Some info-mediaries like *Yahoo.com* attempt to create additional stickiness by providing community and personalization services. Others like *Bizrate.com* provide customers a rating system on various e-tailers' ability to deliver promised service.

3. ***Supplier agents.*** Many info-mediaries start off in this quadrant, sponsored either by specific companies with a vested interest in selling their products or by close affiliation to the core group of sellers. Thus, they do not provide unbiased options for buyers. Major auto manufacturers, for example, host their own websites. Prior to offering other stock and mutual funds from a number of direct competitors, the Charles Schwab website started off as a supplier agent providing access to only its own products. The sustainability of these info-mediaries depends on the quality of suppliers they include, provision of benefits to buyers, and the ability to maintain a good infrastructure and seamless exchange platforms.
4. ***Buyer agents.*** These info-mediaries establish relationships with a core set of buyers, working on their behalf and any number of suppliers. To succeed, they must build a large base of clients, at the same time, winning their trust. However, extracting valuable information and constructing information profiles, deep and broad enough, to create substantial value for clients is a slow process. The value of each client increases as more and more clients join the service. Since trust is often correlated with branding, and the ability to build profile (the strength of some pure-play Internet companies), we can see alliances between branded companies like Disney and pure-plays like *Infoseek.com* in order to create info-mediaries like *Go2Net.com*.

Evolution of Info-mediaries

Many early info-mediaries were sponsored by a seller or a group of sellers wanting to participate in the e-commerce environment, where it is in the agent's best interest to sell the supplier's products. Their affiliations with suppliers are strong but weak with buyers, who may not value a biased market of limited scope. The negative spiral could force such info-mediaries to disappear. However, an info-mediary, effective in providing value-added services, establishing partnerships that extend its product line, and promoting its website, could generate a critical mass of both consumers and suppliers sufficient to reverse the cycle of network effects from negative to positive. Positive network effects feed on themselves; greater product and service scope attracts more buyers, and in turn more suppliers.

A larger supplier base naturally reduces the affiliation of the info-mediary vis-à-vis the few original sponsors. In contrast, the info-mediary does not compete on margin but on its ability to deliver information and provide navigation and other value added services to buyers. It might therefore be expected that info-mediary evolution will be towards greater buyer affiliation and buyer sources of revenue.

Some Examples of Info-mediaries

1. Typical of generic agents, *Yahoo.com* provides comprehensive search facilities for both suppliers and buyers. However, such services eventually favour buyers. For example, if you search for the Prudential Insurance Co. from *Yahoo.com*, you will find the company's web address. Also, you will also be linked to Yahoo's "Insurance Center" where you can fill out a form to get quotes from insurance companies other than Prudential. The extent to which the process for obtaining quotes is truly competitive is the extent to which Yahoo acts as a buyer's agent. To be truly effective in helping clients expand, organize, and optimize their search spaces, info-mediaries inevitably evolve to be the buyer agent.
2. In response to the information explosion challenge for the chain-pharmacy industry, *ChainDrugStore.net* entered the B2B marketplace as a state-of-the-art "info-mediary" hub and the wholly-owned subsidiary of the NACDS. Through the *ChainDrugStore.net*, retailers and manufacturers will be able to streamline and target the flow of communications, saving time and money in the current way they do business. For product buyers, this means being able to analyze better and manage information and make more effective purchasing decisions. They can instantly receive the product information they require when they ask for it. Suppliers can also reach the right person with the right message at the right time.

4. *Community Model*

"Community" is an Internet buzzword these days. The dictionary[8] defines it as

(a) *a unified body of individuals….*
(b) *the people with common interests living in a particular area, broadly, the area itself.*
(c) *an interacting population of various kinds of individuals in a common location….*

E-communities (or electronic communities) are formed when groups of people meet online to fulfil certain needs, which include personal interests, relationships, entertainment and transactions. Of course, e-communities are not confined to just individuals but businesses as well. E-communities cater to groups of people who come online to serve their common interests and needs, exchange information, share interests, trade goods and services, entertain and, seek help. The viability of the community model is based on user loyalty (as opposed to high traffic volume). Customer loyalty can be achieved by building e-communities. First, visitors come and look for information. Then, they start to contribute to the website by, for instance, suggesting ways to improve the site or its services. Finally, they work inside the website by, for instance, volunteering as editors for a message board or by serving on a customer advisory board. Users make a high investment in both time and emotion on the site. In some cases, users are regular contributors of content and/or money. Having regular visitors contributes to advertising on info-mediary or specialized portal opportunities. The community model may also run on a subscription fee for premium services.

8. *Merriam Webster's Collegiate Dictionary*. 10th Edition, p. 233.

Functions of Communities on the Web

1. Most people long to be accepted and loved and concerned about. These along with a desire to learn cause online communities to attract people. Word goes around about a discussion going on or about a place to make personal or business contacts, and visitors thus are attracted. They may end up joining the community.
2. Communities on the Internet provide information. Since they tend to revolve around a particular interest or common task or hobby, they can be the sources for sharing information, and can become deep reservoirs of technical information.
3. Communities also beget loyalty. Members develop the habit of visiting one particular site again and again. They get so used to the site, that they develop a sense of ownership, especially if they are involved in online communication.
4. Communities also build your business. Once people become used to a site, they are quite comfortable making a purchase through it rather than going into unknown territory. Communities build "stickiness" (the tendency to spend a long session at a particular site), and that in turn builds loyalty, which in return builds traffic and trust, and trust is the common currency of business.

Community Structures

The Internet communities can be found structured in several predictable ways as follows:

Newsletters. Newsletters, by definition, are one-way communication. They generally use listserver software that sends the same message to an entire list of people, and handles new subscribers and those who wish to unsubscribe. Listserver software (sometimes called a "listserv") is also the backbone for e-mail discussion lists.

Discussion lists. One of the best ways to build a sense of community is by e-mail discussion lists. In a typical discussion list, the listserver software allows a member to send a message to the list address, and then sends that message to all the list members, all within a few minutes.

There are three types of discussion lists:

E-mail discussion list. All messages from the members are forwarded to other members as soon as they are received. If a particular list is not active, several hundred messages could be on such a list. But a larger list with lots of discussion can easily generate 50 to 100 e-mails per day and swamp many users. Lists can be configured so that a moderator approves a message before it is sent to the members. The larger lists usually offer a digest option.

E-mail discussion list digest. The digest collects all the messages sent to the list, bundles them, and e-mails them in one e-mail to subscribers, either daily or when the accumulation reaches a certain size, depending on how the list is set up. A digest helps control the level of e-mail, but tends to inhibit spontaneous interactions among members on the list.

Moderated discussion list digest. Large discussion lists are eventually forced to limit the quantity and screen the quality of messages that go out to the list members. When people receive e-mail from the discussion list nearly every day, they begin to get acquainted with other list subscribers and recognize them by their comments and hobby-horses and idiosyncrasies. These various points of view make for a rich sense of community and commonality. If one member shares a problem, another will jump in with a solution that may work out well for the member.

Discussion lists on the Internet number in hundreds of thousands, on every conceivable kind of topic. They are often used for product support and troubleshooting. They can also become support groups. If you sell orthopedic equipment, for example, your discussion list could be very valuable to people who share the same need and encounter similar problems. If you sell hobby items, a discussion list could be a magnet for hobbyists who are happy to share their stories about radio-controlled airplane models, dollhouse collectables, antiques. Training groups and online class discussions are another use.

Bulletin Boards

One of the struggles of e-mail-based communities is keeping "threads" (different topics of conversation) separate. Sure, the subject line usually includes the topic, but if you are reading 15 messages a day that are not sorted by topic, things will look disjointed. One solution to this is a Web-based bulletin board system. Their great strengths are:

1. Keeping threads separate
2. Allowing posts to be read, searched, and researched later by individuals who may not have been part of the original conversation.

Chat Rooms

Another significant type of community building tool is the chat room. This is a useful source of knowledge and information for any user. As for business people, it has a great utility value. Sometimes even people from Public relations schedule chats and interviews with famous personalities. Such chats may have overwhelming responses and may also gear up businesses. For nearly every business, it is preferred that the chats are scheduled ahead of time so that enough people gather around for the same topic and have a meaningful discussion. This may give fruitful results for business starters. If a small business needs a chat room, web hosting services often have no-or-low-cost rooms available. *eGroups* has a Java-based chat room built into their online list areas, if there is a need for occasional facility, but all participants need to register as group members to use the chat room. This gives additional security for the participants.

- **Open source**: Software developed collaboratively by a global community of programmers who share code openly. Instead of licensing code for a fee, open source relies on revenue generated from related services like systems integration, product support, tutorials and user documentation. [Red Hat]
- **Open content**: Openly accessible content developed collaboratively by a global community of contributors who work voluntarily. [Wikipedia]
- **Public broadcasting**: User-supported model used by not-for-profit radio and television broadcasting extended to the web. A community of users support the site through voluntary donations. [The Classical Station WCPE.org.]

- **Social networking services:** Sites that provide individuals with the ability to connect to other individuals along a defined common interest (professional, hobby, romance). Social networking services can provide opportunities for contextual advertising and subscriptions for premium services. [Flicker, Facebook, Orkut]

Necessary Elements for the Community Model

What is really necessary to build a successful community? A lot of care and planning are involved. But be sure to have:

1. A clear focus for the community that makes sense to prospective members.
2. The requisite technical capability through your own software and hardware or a free service.
3. A proper structure, guidelines, and parameters for the discussion to keep the group on target.
4. A moderator responsible for each group or list.
5. A clear strategy on how the community will benefit your business. Since communities care a lot for maintenance, it has to achieve something to make it worth your while.

The Bottom Line

What effects can you expect a community to have on your business's profit and loss statement? Let us list them out as follows:

1. Customer satisfaction through effective customer support is difficult to reckon with, although the availability of customer support will make the product or service more attractive, and therefore enhance sales.
2. Increased traffic leads to increased publicity. Participants or visitors to the site will circulate the word around, and news media will write stories about the site.
3. Repeated use will develop loyalty among the users towards the site.
4. Moderating or sponsoring a group puts you in the role of an expert in the industry, and gives you and your business high visibility.
5. Narrowly focussed groups you sponsor (those who have a clear interest in your product or service).
6. When your list is well developed you can earn some advertising revenue from e-mail ads or banner ads, but do not start a list expecting this to be your primary revenue stream—it probably will not develop this way for at least a year or two, if at all.

Building a community can be an extremely valuable strategy in developing your online business. But one warning: if you treat communities as a tool of publicity and betray them later, they will soon become a negative force rather than a positive one. Make sure your community building strategy is part of a carefully designed business plan that you are committed to maintain over the long-term.

The viability of the community model is based on user loyalty (as opposed to high traffic volume). Users make high investments of both time and emotion on the site. In some cases, users are regular contributors of content and/or money. Having users who visit continuously offers advertising, info-mediary, or specialized portal opportunities. The community model may also run on a subscription fee for premium services.

WhatsApp program as well as social networking sites like Facebook and Twitter have been game changer in building communities.

E-communities—An Indian Overview

For Indian surfers, the starting point to community is served by the portals. By building community features into their sites, portals hope to increase retention, stickiness, and transactions. Rediff and Sify are the most active in this regard, either building community 'channels' or outsourcing them. The idea is to build a community around something Indian. Sify, a typical example, has a carnatic music channel and language portals. They are also moving into the city-community area. However, horizontal communities tend to be loose-knit while the vertical ones tend not to be.

Another major sub-category is general interest communities, focussed on sports, music, medicine, finance, and the like. A plethora of cricket-driven sport sites have been launched. Of these, it is sure that only a few will survive, and they will be the ones with the strongest content alliances. And while there are specialized sites on, say, carnatic music, online medical resources have just got off the starting blocks. The bottom line is that there are few general interest communities that have made a mark with Indian surfers.

5. *Value Chain Model*

Value chain moves businesses away from discrete streams of data about the product being made to one unified pool of information—one that even extends outside the company to suppliers and customers. The goal is to develop full and seamless interaction among all members of the chain, resulting in lower inventories, higher customer satisfaction, and shorter time to the market.

Generalized Portal: AltaVista as a Value Chain Model

AltaVista Company is the premier knowledge resource on the Internet. With its strong search engine tool and patented technology, AltaVista opens up avenues in the maze of Internet to the richest and the most relevant information on any subject from any nook of the Web world, Web pages, shopping, up-to-the-minute news, live audio and video, and community resources.

By capitalizing on the unique Web-wide features and services, the AltaVista network provides a distinct Internet experience through multiple integrated platforms, as in the following:

1. ***AltaVista search.*** The world's fastest, most comprehensive search service available in 25 languages with 8 distinct search dimensions.
2. ***AltaVista shopping.com.*** The first Web-wide comparison shopping service on the Internet, providing objective price and product comparison features to help users make intelligent purchasing decisions.

3. ***AltaVista live!*** The only real-time, customizable content source on the Web, linking content channels on topics such as money, news, sports, entertainment, and more.

4. ***AltaVista raging bull.*** The Web's stickiest site, which has the Web's most active community of message boards, with an emphasis on finance.

5. ***AltaVista free access.*** One of the fastest growing ISP services in the world, with over 2 million registered users in the US and Canada.

6. ***AltaVista international.*** Currently over half of its traffic comes from outside the US. To further encourage this growth, AltaVista has recently created local sites in France, Germany, Italy, the Netherlands, Sweden, and the UK.

The portal gives the website owner access to online traffic reporting through *Reporting.net* site. With reports available at any time, the owner can assess how effectively his affiliate network site is marketing AltaVista's products.

The following are just a few of the things that can be done with the latest AltaVista search technology:

1. Search catalogues, inventory databases, auctions, classifieds, job listings, and even suppliers.
2. Improve the success rate of incoming searches—new linguistic query processing tools let customers find products even when they do not know exact product names or model numbers.
3. Allow users to sort results by brand, price, availability, or any method.

With these, we can tailor the search to fulfil specific requirements. They build communities on deep and rich topics and region-specific contents. They also present search results with the help of a customized interface. Added to all these, they leverage AltaVista's global index of images, new articles, and audio and video clips.

These create a central knowledge source to help make your enterprise more competitive. The company could link business partners, suppliers and others to the network.

Personalized Portal: My Yahoo! as a Value Chain Model

My Yahoo! is the user's own personalized version of *Yahoo!* After the user gives his personal information, *My Yahoo!* allows him to collect all his favourite sections of *Yahoo!* in one place. He can choose what he wants to surf, such as news, weather, stock prices, sports scores, TV and movie listings, horoscopes, and much more. It is like having a personal secretary who would collect the favourite sections of the newspaper, give information about mail and appointments for the day, and so on.

My Yahoo! is absolutely free. To register, just click 'Get your Own *My Yahoo!*' on the *My Yahoo!* home page and feed in your favourite sections. *My Yahoo* is also completely portable, which means, a person can check *My Yahoo!* from work, home, school, a friend's house, or a cyber cafe. These are just some of the things that makes *My Yahoo!* a great home page. *My Yahoo!* allows a user to have two pages—a home page, and another page. The important and frequently accessed information may be stored here. All secondary information may be stored on the other page.

Some of the topics that *Yahoo*! offers are:

- Pick your weather cities
- Track your stock quotes
- Read your choice of news
- Find local movie showtimes
- Follow your favourite sports teams

6. *Manufacturer Model*

The manufacturer or "direct model", is predicated on the power of the Web to allow a manufacturer (i.e. a company that creates a product or service) to reach buyers directly and thereby compress the distribution channel. The manufacturer model can be based on efficiency, improved customer service, and a better understanding of customer preferences. In this model, the manufacturer sells its products through the use of its website.

Purchase. The sale of a product in which the right of ownership is transferred to the buyer.

Lease. In exchange for a rental fee, the buyer receives the right to use the product under a "terms of use" agreement. The product is returned to the seller upon expiration or default of the lease agreement. One type of agreement may include a right-of-purchase upon expiration of the lease.

Licence. The sale of a product that involves only the transfer of usage rights to the buyer, in accordance with a "terms of use" agreement. The ownership rights remain with the manufacturer (e.g. in case of software licensing).

Brand integrated content. In contrast to the sponsored-content approach (i.e. the advertising model), brand-integrated content is created by the manufacturer itself for the sole basis of product placement.

Tata Steel[9]

Established in 1907 at Jamshedpur, the company is one of India's best known symbols of industrial growth. It represents the country's single largest, integrated steel works in the private sector, with a market share of about 13 per cent. The company is India's single largest exporter of high-quality, value-added steel products. It is the producer of one of the cheapest HR coils in the world. A blue-chip company, Tata Steel Ltd has successfully raised $100 million through Euro bonds.

The company offers a diverse range of products and services. These include HR/CR coils and sheets, tubes, construction bars, forging quality steel, rods, structural strips and bearings, steel plant and material handling equipment, Ferro alloys and other minerals, software for process controls, and cargo handling services. Sister companies offer tinplate, wires, rolls, refractories, project management services, and material handling equipment.

9. www.tatasteel.com

The Company has technological and strategic tie-ups with world leaders such as Thyssen, Nippon Steel, Hitachi, Posdata, SMS, Krupp Stahl, and McKinsey.

E-business

Tata Steel establishes e-business through its website *www.tatasteel.co.in*

E-sales

Building a trusting, long lasting, and mutually beneficial relationship with their customers has been Tata Steel's fundamental belief and driving force. This has formed the cornerstone of all their initiatives. In line with this, their latest offering is the self-help customer service.

Their site offers you a collection of reports on an online basis anywhere—anytime, easy to read directly from their SAP R/3 system. As a valued customer, you can now access information ranging from your order status to delivery status, invoices to credit notes, payment dues to credit status, and many more, through exclusively tailored reports.

E-procurement

The e-procurement site is Tata Steel's Business-to-Business (B2B) procurement platform. Among the many forward looking initiatives being undertaken by Tata Steel to tap the tremendous opportunities offered by Information Technology, especially the Web, e-procurement is one of them being used to conduct business with the suppliers.

The suppliers of Tata Steel, who would become e-partners, are expected to reap lot of benefits through this system.

E-auction and Tenders

The Tata Iron & Steel Company was founded by the visionary Indian industrialist Jamshedji Nusserwanji Tata in 1907. Today, the company consists of steel works at Jamshedpur with its own captive collieries at Jharia and West Bokaro and ore mines and quarries at Noamundi and Joda. It has a wide product range that includes billets, structural bars, strips, tubes and bearings, H-R coil, C-R coil, GP sheets and plates.

The Secondary Products Profit Centre focusses its attention on marketing of products which are secondary to the company's main business. It encompasses selling of steel scrap, used and rejected material, by-products, raw materials from works, under size and extra generation from their collieries, and obsolete capital equipment and spares. The division has its headquarters at Jamshedpur and the marketing office at Kolkata.

In order to meet the customer's demand in the best possible manner, this site has been launched for Tender Information and online quoting, which is the quickest method to serve the customers.

Case Discussion

1. What are the advantages of having a website for e-sales?
2. What are the advantages of having a website for e-procurement?
3. Find out the difference between the Tata Steel website and the Sail website. Which site is more professional?

7. *Advertising Model*

The Web advertising model is an extension of the traditional media broadcast model. The broadcaster, in this case a website, provides content (usually, but not necessarily, for free) and services (like e-mail, chat, forums), together with advertising messages in the form of banner ads. The banner ads may be the major or sole source of revenue for the broadcaster. The broadcaster may be a content creator or a distributor of content created elsewhere. The advertising model only works when the volume of viewer traffic is large or highly specialized.

Advertising-driven sites are currently one of the cornerstones of e-commerce. The principle is simple and well known. A site offers free access to something and shows advertisements on every page. When a user clicks on an advertisement, he goes to an advertiser's page. The advertiser pays the site operator for showing his advertisement (eyeballs) or for every time someone clicks on the advertisement (click-through).

The same idea is popular in computer programs. Users can download and use the program for free but advertisements are shown during operation or start-up of the program. In particular, advertisements can be shown when the user needs to wait for some time-consuming operation, such as printing or scanning (US 5,781,894).

It is well known that an advertisement related to the topic at hand on the site will get higher exposure and click-through since such advertisements are targeted to the site visitors. So, the site operator earns more money if he places on the site such targeted advertisements. When displaying advertisements in a computer program, it is possible to target the advertisements to the purpose of the program, e.g. a spreadsheet shows advertisements for a stock brokering service.

Search engines use this idea as well, but relate the advertisements to the keywords entered in a query. For instance, if someone searches information on holidays, an advertisement is shown for a hotel chain on the page with search results. The advertisement can further be targeted based on the user profile for the user doing the search.

The existence of advertising-driven sites created a business opportunity for companies such as DoubleClick, which collects advertisements from many sources and arranges for placements on different sites. The sources pay DoubleClick for placing their advertisements, and this revenue is then shared with the site owners. Additionally, DoubleClick tracks the users that view all the advertisements, which allows it to build a user profile. This profile can then be used to more accurately target advertisements to these users.

Web Pricing Models

1. CPM or impression only (sets cost-per-thousand of guaranteed ad views)
2. Click-through (the advertiser pays based on the number of times the banner is clicked by a user)
3. Sponsorships (package deals of impressions and click-throughs)
4. Cost-per-lead (the advertiser pays when a viewer registers or submits personal information)
5. Cost-per-sale (agreed upon charge for the viewers who actually purchase a product or service based on the ad)

6. Straight revenue sharing deals (the publisher receives a commission which is paid upon sale from an ad)[10]

Types of Advertising on the Internet

1. ***Portals.*** A search engine that may include varied content or services. A high volume of user traffic makes advertising profitable, and permits further diversification of site services. A personalized portal allows customization of the interface and content to user. Example: *Yahoo*![11]
2. ***Classifieds.*** Lists items for sale or wanted for purchase. Listing fees are common but there also may be a membership fee. Example: *Monster.com*[12]
3. ***User-based registration.*** Content-based sites that provide free access to users but require the user to submit demographic details by registration. Example: *NYTimes Digital*[13].
4. ***Query-based paid placement.*** Sells favourable link positioning (i.e. sponsored links) or advertising keyed to particular search terms in a user query. Example: *Google*[14].
5. ***Contextual advertising.*** Freeware developers who bundle ads with their product. For example, a browser extension that automates authentication and form fill, installs delivers advertising links or pop-ups as the user surfs the Web. Example: eZula[15].

Different Web Advertising Formats[16]

1. ***Banners.*** An ad appearing at the top of a Web page.
2. ***Vertical columns.*** On a frame Web page positions alongside requested content (often as form of sponsorship).
3. ***Pop-up windows.*** Java script opens a browser window with an ad.
4. ***Interstitials.*** Full screen ads that appear on a Web browser while a page is loading.
5. ***Advertorials.*** Content-based advertising related to an article or other site content.
6. ***Intromercials.*** Animated full-screen ads placed at entry of a site before a user reaches the intended content (CBS Market watch)[17].
7. ***Ultramercials.*** Interactive online ads that require the user to respond intermittently in order to wade through the message before reaching the intended content.[18]

Formats that permit more effective online ads[19]:

1. Richer ad content through sight, sound, and motion
2. More information (larger files)

10. www.pwcglobal.com
11. www.digitalenterprise.org
12. www.digitalenterprise.org
13. www.digitalenterprise.org
14. www.digitalenterprise.org
15. www.digitalenterprise.org
16. www.broadcastpapers.com
17. www.digitalenterprise.org
18. www.digitalenterprise.org
19. www.broadcastpapers.com

3. More interactivity
4. Larger screen size
5. More prominent screen positions
6. Less content competition
7. Reliable measurement and reporting to enable each advertiser to determine its ad ROI—impressions, interactivity, brand sell
8. Accurate audience measurement
9. Meaningful user targeting
10. Cost-effective advertising model with rates reflecting advertiser value

8. *Subscription Model*

Users are charged a periodic—daily, monthly, or annual—fee to subscribe to a service. It is not uncommon for sites to combine free content with "premium" (i.e. subscriber or member-only) content. Subscription fees are incurred irrespective of actual usage rates. Subscription and advertising models are frequently combined.

Content Services provide text, audio, or video content to users who subscribe for a fee to gain access to the service. Example: *Netflix.com*

Person-to-Person Networking Services are conduits for the distribution of user-submitted information, such as individuals searching for former schoolmates. Example: *Classmates.com*

Trust Services come in the form of membership associations that abide by an explicit code of conduct, and in which members pay a subscription fee. Example: *Truste.com*

Internet Services Providers offer network connectivity and related services on a monthly subscription. Example: *America Online*.

The organization makes money on the basis of membership/subscription.

Some popular topics of Subscription model are:

- Existing newsletter topics
- Trade associations

eGurucool.com

NIIT's vast experience in the field of education and eGurucool's expertise and in-depth understanding of the curricula have come together to make this a good site for e-education. Students are assured of a holistic learning experience that ensures a rewarding performance in school and board examinations, apart from the building up of a strong conceptual foundation for later life.

The salient features and benefits of the eGurucool way of learning are:

- Well-structured lesson plans that generate interest, curiosity, and provide clarity about the objectives that should be achieved through the lessons. This ensures that students are drawn towards the lesson and derive maximum benefit from it.

- The lesson is not overloading, and is administered step-by-step. It is built around sub-topics that highlight principles. At all times, each lesson is not just textual. It incorporates the attributes of a very good teacher who asks, stimulates, prods, cajoles, and inspires.
- Technology is used wherever necessary—not to dazzle or distract but to provide greater insight through interactivity—without disrupting the flow of the lesson.

Courses Offered

An array of courses from eGurucool for students and teachers, course help and test preparation modules plus value-added services that enhance the quality of education.

- CBSE Programs
- ICSE Programs
- Maharashtra Board Programs
- IIT JEE Programs

eConnect

This is a service that empowers schools by connecting students, teachers and parents 24 hours a day and 7 days a week! It includes creation and maintenance of school websites, online classnotes and assignments, and performance tracking. Through eConnect, eGurucool has tie-ups with over 1600 schools across the country and is here to change the way schools look at education.

Course Structure

The program is designed to cover the entire syllabus prescribed for a class:

- The theory and concepts of each chapter are covered in detail in the class. Illustrative examples are used to reinforce concepts.
- Regular assignments and tests with 'ideal' solutions.
- Mid-course assessment is done through a set of section tests.
- A set of full length tests that closely simulate the board pattern. A minimum of 7 tests.
- In addition to lectures, students also get printed booklets as study material.

E-services

This is a Web-based service that connects students, teachers and parents round-the-clock, 7 days a week. It allows students to access classnotes and assignments prepared by teachers and track their academic performance. Besides, eConnect provides an online marking tool for multiple choice questions.

Within an year of its launch, the eConnect network has spread in schools across India. Here is a quick glimpse at what all eConnect offers:

1. ***eAssignments.*** Homework gets exciting. eAssignments give students access to their assignments wherever they are.
2. ***eClassnotes.*** Notes are just a click away. eClassnotes provide value-based synopsis and insight into the forthcoming topics.

3. ***Online MCQ test.*** Allows students to take MCQ tests online and gauge their performance instantly.
4. ***Performance tracker.*** This allows students and their parents to access their performance graphs.
5. ***Online quizzes.*** Subject and chapter-specific quizzes are available for all students from Class IX to Class XII.

eAssignments

eAssignments allow teachers to put up their assignments for the class on the Web. So students can access it anytime ... wherever there is a computer. This makes learning exciting, and helps students learn beyond the confines of their classrooms.

In short, eAssignments are an extension of value added information that teachers provide in classrooms. It increases pace of learning, integrates concept learning and test preparation, and undoubtedly gives a better forum for discussion.

eAssignments are supported by objective type questions which the students can answer online and get an instant evaluation. The subjective assignments can be submitted online or in class.

Benefits for Students

- Assignments provide theoretical and conceptual clarity.
- Assignments integrate concept understanding and test preparation.
- Assignments facilitate avenues for self-assessment by providing instant evaluation of objective questions.

Benefits for Teachers

- Assignments facilitate effective classroom discussions.
- Assignments allow closer interaction among the teachers and students.
- Automated checking of objective questions saves time.

Benefits for Parents

- Makes it easy for their wards to access reference material.
- Objective and subjective questions provide easy testing facility at home.
- Parents can keep track of what is taught in the class and also follow up on their wards' performance.

eClassnotes

eClassnotes are a compilation of notes. A value-based synopsis, eClassnotes also offer students an insight into the forthcoming topics. The notes are also archived to facilitate revision. Prepared by school teachers, these notes are password protected and can be accessed at a convenient time.

eClassnotes provide an extension of value added information that teachers give in classrooms. It increases the pace of learning, integrates concept understanding and test preparation, and undoubtedly provides a better forum for discussions and interaction amongst teachers and students.

Online MCQ Test

This allows students to take MCQ tests online. Not only this, an automated in-built tool does an instant evaluation. Students get a fair idea of their preparation as both the questions and the answers are provided by their school teachers.

An extension of value added information that teachers provide in classrooms, MCQ tests provide ease of accessibility, besides increasing the pace of learning while integrating concept internalization and test preparation.

Performance Tracker

An automated, user-friendly and efficient online system, the Performance Tracker keeps track of a student's academic performance throughout the year.

It generates descriptive report cards—class, student, test and subject-wise—and provides information on a student's individual performance. Besides, it provides a comparative analysis vis-à-vis the class for all the exams and class tests conducted in a year. The Performance Tracker archives all the marks saved.

Moreover, teachers are saved from all the laborious calculations that are associated with the preparation of report cards. The teacher simply has to login and feed in the marks for every exam and test conducted. The in-built tool in the Performance Tracker automatically makes new calculations for grand total, aggregate percentage, and class average, and accordingly updates the report card. While making calculations, it even takes into account the weightages awarded to class tests and term-exams. Teachers can subsequently take printouts of the results for reference and qualitative feedback to the parents.

Performance Tracker, being online, can be referred to without the constraints of time. Separate login IDs are provided to teachers, students and parents to access the same.

Course Activation

Course activation is a one-time process. Once you have activated your course, you can access it straightaway from the 'My Account' area.

Enter the Order Number and Course Code for the course given in your Starter kit. Enter Course Activation Pin and then click SUBMIT.

Case Discussion

1. How does eGurucool fit into the subscription model?
2. Why would anyone subscribe to eGurucool?
3. What is unique about the services provided by eGurucool?
4. Why is eGurucool a success?

9. *Affiliate Model*

In contrast to the generalized portal, which seeks to drive a high volume of traffic to one site, the affiliate model provides purchase opportunities wherever people may be surfing. It does this by offering financial incentives (in the form of a percentage of revenue) to affiliated partner sites. The affiliates provide purchase-point click-through to the merchant. It is a pay-for-performance model—if an affiliate does not generate sales, it represents no cost to the merchant. The affiliate model is inherently well-suited to the Web, which explains its popularity. Variations include banner exchange, pay-per-click, and revenue-sharing programs.

Banner exchange. It trades banner placement among a network of affiliated sites.

Pay-per-click. It is the site that pays affiliates for a user click-through.

Revenue sharing. It offers a per cent-of-sale commission based on a user click-through in which the user subsequently purchases a product.

The affiliate saves the expense of handling inventory, advertising and promoting the product, and processing the transaction. In fact, the affiliate risks no funds whatever. *Cdnow.com* and *amazon.com* were two of the first companies to create successful affiliate programs on the Web. CDnow's Web Buy program, which includes more than 250,000 affiliates, is one of CDnow's main sources for new customers. The *amazon.com* program has over 400,000 affiliate sites. Most of these affiliate sites are devoted to a specific issue, hobby, or other interest. Affiliate sites choose books or other items that are related to their visitors' interests and include links to the seller's site on their Web pages. Books and CDs are natural for this type of shared promotional activity, but sellers of other products and services also have successful affiliate marketing programs. One of the more interesting marketing tactics made possible by the Web is cause marketing, which is an affiliate marketing program that benefits a charitable organization (and, thus, supports a "cause"). In cause marketing, the affiliate site is created to benefit the charitable organization. When visitors click a link on the affiliate's Web page, a donation is made by a sponsoring company. The page that loads after the visitor clicks the donation link, carries advertising for the sponsoring companies. Many companies have found that the click-through rates on these ads are much higher than the typical banner ad click-through rates. A leading retail Web florist, *proflowers.com,* has had excellent results advertising on *The Hunger Site* page. When a visitor clicks the button on this page, a group of sponsoring advertisers donates food to a hungry person and a page appears in the visitor's browser with ads for the sponsors.

EXERCISES

1. What is the current and prospective size of the electronic market?
2. Visit *Priceline.com* site and write a report on the way they have implemented their model.

3. Explain the features required of a B2B platform for e-commerce.
4. What sort of details could a hotel chain provide to assist potential clients in booking a hotel that matches their travel plans?
5. Select a product that a computer retailer might sell, such as printers, scanners, and zip drives. What sort of details about this product could an online computer company provide to their clients?
6. What advantages do you see in web ordering to a company?
7. What are the factors attributed to the success of eBay and bazzee.com?
8. Define dynamic pricing.
9. Distinguish between forward and reverse auctions.
10. What are the major business models for e-tailing?
11. Why do some consumers prefer online transactions while others do not?
12. Visit *bazzee.com* and see how you can bid for an item.
13. Visit Sahara airline's site (*www.airsahara.net*) and Jet airline's site (*www.jetairlines.com*), and compare them.
14. Study the site of eDeal and derive their business model. The summary of eDeal site is given below:

    eDeal is a C2C trading community. Individual consumers can buy and sell personal items using different auction formats. eDeal has profiled itself as the world's trading community with the possibility of making trades in 300 different currencies. The company encourages international customers to post objects for sale in their own currencies to encourage trading communities in their own countries. To facilitate trading at eDeal, like eBay, it categorizes the different items to be sold. eDeal has 15 different categories, which is much less than eBay's more than 1000 categories.
15. Study the ICICI bank's site. What is the three-in-one concept? How is the Web made use of for enhancing the business? A summary of their site is given as follows:

    ICICIDirect is the first service in India to provide complete end-to-end integration for seamless electronic trading on the stock exchanges. The service will enable the user to tie-in his trading bank account and his demat account to your brokerage account electronically. This integration of brokerage, demat and bank accounts ensures that money is transferred to/from the user bank account and the shares are transferred from/to his demat account automatically without any paperwork. *ICICIDirect* keeps track of the transactions, the settlement dates, and stock exchange rules. This relieves the user of the inconvenience of tracking his transactions, issuing cheques, or writing out Demat Transfer Instructions, as the case may be, and ensuring timely delivery of these documents.

    Product Features

    ICICIDirect brings Indian customers the international experience of online investing. Buying and selling of shares is just a click away. The powerful 3-in-1 concept ensures that the user is relieved of the inconvenience of tracking stock exchange trading calendars, settlement dates, writing cheques, and Transfer Instructions For Debit (TIFD). ICICI not only provides the type of account to fit the customer's investment/trading style but also a host of tools to allow him to make the best use of the online investing. A multitude of resources like online quotes, charts, news, research, fundamental database and detailed analysis is just a click away to help customers make smarter and better decisions. A few product offerings are:

- Exchanges
- List of stocks
- Online order confirmation and trades
- View positions
- View transaction history
- Online news analysis
- Follow the markets

CHAPTER 3

Enabling Technologies of the World Wide Web

LEARNING OBJECTIVES

After reading this chapter, you should be able to:

- Identify the technologies supporting the world wide web.
- Understand client server applications.
- Describe the difference between digital and analog information.
- Explain the difference between circuit and packet switching.
- Understand what is meant by the term 'protocol' and give suitable examples of local and wide area network protocol.
- Understand the use of 'software agents'.
- Learn the basics of 'hypertext'.

Akshaya Project

Malappuram district in Kerala has become the first e-district in India through the implementation of the Akshaya project which envisions the creation of a 'knowledge society' by providing training in basic computer skills and internet connectivity to the people. In order to realize the vision of the 'knowledge society', the Government of Kerala has set up 634 Akshaya Tele-centres in the district to provide ICT facilities and through these centres, at least one member in every family is provided with training in basic computing skills. The Akshaya centres are connected to the Internet and also to an intranet. Important government offices including Police Stations and educational institutions have also been made part of the network by integrating them though the Internet and the Intranet. Over half a million people have already been trained under the e-literacy programme and provided with certificates out of which 65 per cent were women.

Akshaya centres also offer computer courses and programmes and, on an average, yearly 7000–10,000 students attend various programmes. Moreover, data entry work for various departments, private companies and banks are being processed through Akshaya centres. Many companies and service providers have tie-ups with Akshaya centres to offer their products and services. These centres are also offering content services including agriculture, health, education, career, law, etc. Government application forms and schemes are also available through these centres. 100 Akshaya centres are selected to offer e-krishi[1] service to provide ICT-enabled agriculture practices to the farmers.

'Internet for All' is a project that aims to enable at least 100,000 people to use modern communication technologies available on the Internet. Connectivity usage of the public through the Akshaya centres is increasing steadily and many people are now using these centres to communicate with their relatives abroad. Since a very large population is working outside the state, the government claims that the use of the Internet as a communication channel will help people to have cost-effective ways of interaction. The course in which internet training is provided to people has been structured as a 15-hour package and at the end of the training, the person attending the programme will be given an email ID. During 2006 November, 144,372 people visited *www.google.co.in* and 139,351 people visited *www.manoramaonline.com*, the website of the leading newspaper in Kerala. 126,986 people have used Google mail service. Students have started using the centres for e-tuition and more than 10,000 students are undergoing training in IT tuition programmes (School Syllabus) in 400 Akshaya centres per month. Furthermore, more than 12,000 students are using Akshaya centres for Games, Multimedia Contents, etc. a month.

The computer training programmes include a Certificate Course in Basic Computer literacy. The programme is divided into ten lessons, which can be completed in ten classes of two hours. The course syllabus of the course includes computer fundamentals, Windows/ Linux operating systems, word processing, Internet and email. Another course run by the project is called e-Vidhya, a Certificate Course in Office Management which aims to develop computer usage skills of the people. The syllabus of the course includes Microsoft Word, Microsoft Excel, details of Internet, Malayalam Word Processor, and the World Wide Web. Considering the Muslim population in the district, the project has introduced a computer-based Arabic typing tutor-Al-Tadreeb- which is developed by the Keltron, a public sector company. The software and its course contents are designed to enable computer literate users to learn Arabic typing.

For providing e-payment facility to people, the government has introduced a project called FRIENDS (Fast Reliable Instant Efficient Network for Disbursement of Services) which provide opportunity to pay utility payments to the government. FRIENDS has been extended to 150 Akshaya centres in Malappuram and people can remit taxes and fees due to the government. They can also pay electricity and telephone bills through FRIENDS.

A Public Grievance Redressal System has been introduced at the district level under which people can access the District Collector through the internet. Complaints are received through software called 'e-parathi'. The District Collector will be available online on all Wednesdays at all Akshaya centres and people can log on to register complaints. The Collector, after talking to the person and receiving the complaint through e-parathi, will take appropriate action and will publish the results in the website. People can also e-mail

1. Krishi means agriculture.

complaints to various ministers and officials through Akshaya centres. The project has also taken up data digitization and 3 million birth, marriage, and death registration digitization works are at the processing stage. Manuscript digitization, health mapping, water resource mapping, biodiversity mapping, and campaign against epidemics are also done under the project.

Regarding computer penetration, 3150 computers were purchased for 630 centres initially and accessories like printers, scanners, webcams, and UPS were also purchased for centre set-up. Furthermore, Akshaya centres have sold an average of 10 computers in the district in the first two years of operation. It is claimed that the project indirectly impacted the computer penetration in the district by speeding up the computerization of cooperative banks and societies, business establishments and shops and schools and other educational institutions. The elected village bodies had played an important role in the selection of the private entrepreneurs to set up Akshaya centres and they continue to monitor, e.g. the tariff and kind of service provided.

The government of Kerala is to provide legal, institutional and resource support to the programme and the IT mission designs the Akshaya structure and systems, including the business model and development of software support. The Akshaya team in Malappuram represents the IT mission in the district and carries forward the mission's work at district level, and also liaises with other stakeholders. Malappuram District Administration selects and oversees Akshaya franchisees and helps them to get loans, etc. and also organizes meetings of the local Panchayats. Village Panchayats oversee the Akshaya centres in their jurisdiction; and develop ICT-based services/activities along with franchisees. The responsibility of the franchisees is to set-up the centres with their own capital and maintain it. Ultimately, the communities make use of ICT services, give input to elected representatives about services, operational and physical conditions at the centres, and also provide suggestions for new services.

According to the government of Kerala[2], the uniqueness of the project has been the concept of social entrepreneurship where entrepreneurs with a social attitude are promoted to start small ICT enterprises especially in the rural areas where people are not exposed to the new technology. Another uniqueness of the project is the e-literacy component which intends to take ICT to every household through a massive campaign and helping the common man to overcome mental barriers to adopting new technology. The people are then given e-literacy training through Akshaya centres with financial support from local self-governing bodies. Continuous training has also been given to entrepreneurs on enterprise management, marketing skills, technology, data digitalization, etc.

Development of locally relevant content is another distinctiveness of the project. The content set is being developed through handholding of domain expert and technologists. The content is structured in a manner that would empower the users with information that will affect their lives in a positive manner. A wide range of topics including those on education, career development, agriculture, health, information technology, and law and justice have already been developed. In addition, self-development modules covering spoken English, vocational training, personality development, career planning, accounting for small businesses have also been developed. A distinct feature of this project is that it has got rid of the language barrier for getting information online, by developing all the content in the local language Malayalam.

2. http://210.212.236.212/akshaya/uniqueness.html

The intervention of Internet technology into everyday life of the people raises important questions about its impact on the behaviour of the people and their domestic as well as communal relationships. The Internet use by ordinary people will be impacting their access to resources, social interaction, and commitment to community. Internet as a communication medium would provide new means of connectivity and opens new channels for keeping in touch and hence new channels for community building. Internet access may allow people to participate in public policy development and political process. Internet users may be forming a networked society by socializing on cyberspace. Many communities are strengthened through online interaction.

Case Discussion

1. What is the uniqueness of the Akshaya project?
2. What are the resources needed to implement this in other parts of India?

World Wide Web

The World Wide Web (abbreviated Web, WWW, or W3) is a system of Internet servers that supports hypertext to access several Internet protocols on a single interface. Almost every protocol type available on the Internet is accessible on the Web. This includes e-mail, File Transfer Protocol (FTP), Gopher, Telnet, and the like. In addition to these, the World Wide Web has its own protocol, the HyperText Transfer Protocol (HTTP).

The World Wide Web provides a single interface for accessing all these protocols. This creates a convenient and a user-friendly environment. It is no longer necessary to be conversant with these protocols within separate, command level environments. The Web gathers together these protocols into a single system. Because of this feature, and because of the Web's ability to work with multimedia and advanced programming languages, the World Wide Web is the fastest growing component of the Internet.

The operation of the Web relies primarily on hypertext as its means of information retrieval. HyperText is a document containing words that connect to other documents. These words are called *links*, and open on a single click. A single hypertext document can contain links to many documents. In the context of the Web, words or graphics may serve as links to other documents, images, video and sound. Links may or may not follow a logical path and it depends on how the source document is programmed. On the whole, the WWW contains a complex virtual web of connections among a vast number of documents, graphics, videos, and sounds.

HyperText for the Web is created by documents written in HyperText Markup Language (HTML) or its various offshoots. With HTML, tags are placed within the text to accomplish document formatting such as font size, font style, and visual features like images, animations and creation of hypertext links. The World Wide Web consists of files, called pages, created in HTML and opened with any program which can read the language. Generally, it is comprised of a home page which links to other pages accessed with just a mouse-click.

The Web provides a vast array of experiences including multimedia presentations, real-time collaborations, interactive pages, radio and television broadcasts, and the automatic 'push' of information to a client computer. New programming languages such as Java and JavaScript are expanding these capabilities of the Web.

Internet Client-Server Applications

The users of the Internet interact through one of the several client-server applications. As the name suggests, in a client-server application there are two major classes of software—the client software, which usually exists on an end-user's desktop and provides navigation and display. The other software is the server software, which usually exists on a workstation or a server-class machine and provides back-end data access services, where the data can be something simple like a file or complex like a relational database. The most widely used client-server applications are listed in Table 3.1.

TABLE 3.1 Client-server Applications

Application	*Protocol*	*Purpose*
World Wide Web	HyperText Transport Protocol (HTTP)	Offers access to hypertext documents, executable programs, and other Internet resources.
E-mail	Simple Mail Transport Protocol (SMTP) Post Office Protocol version 3 (POP3) Multipurpose Internet Mail Extensions (MIME)	Allows the transmission of text messages and binary attachments across the Internet.
File Transfer	File Transfer Protocol (FTP)	Enables files to be uploaded and downloaded across the Internet.
Chat	Internet Relay Chat Protocol (IRC)	Provides a way for users to talk to one another in real-time over the Internet. The real-time chat groups are called channels.
UseNet Newsgroups	Network News Transfer Protocol (NNTP)	Discussions forums where users can asynchronously post messages and read messages posted by others.
Interactive text-oriented communications	Remote login Sessions (Telnet)	Offers users the capability of running programs remotely and facilitates remote administration.
Network management systems	Simple Network Management Protocol (SNM)	Allows for remote and local management of items on the network including servers, workstations, routers, switches and other managed devices.
Library	Wide Area Information Servers (WAIS)	Allows users of computers to share information using a common computer-to-computer protocol.

E-mail allows computer users to exchange messages worldwide. Each user of e-mail has a mailbox address or user account identity, with which all main transactions are done. Messages sent via e-mail reach their destination within a matter of seconds. A powerful aspect of e-mail is the option to send electronic files to a person's e-mail address. Non-ASCII files, known as binary files, may be attached to e-mail messages. For example, a document created in Microsoft Word can be attached to an e-mail message and retrieved by the recipient in any e-mail program such as Pine, Netscape messenger or Outlook Express.

Networks and Internets

A computer network consists of two or more computers that are connected to each other using cables and other network devices that handle the flow of data. When you connect two or more computers together, you form a network. Later, if you connect one network to another, you form an Internetwork or an Internet, for short. Network technology enables employees to use resources located in computers of different networks, without being influenced by the technology difference behind each of these networks. Figure 3.1 shows the relationship between networks and Internetworks (Internets).

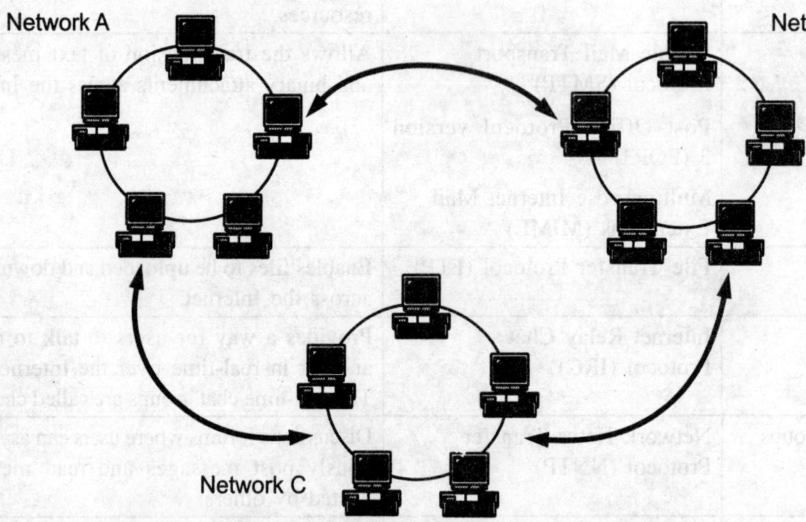

Figure 3.1 Relationship between networks and Internets.

Communication Switching

Through the use of communication switching, computer networks allow computers to transfer data using shared lines of communication such as a cable. Communication switching works similar to telephone switching networks. A telephone switching network eliminates the need to connect a wire between your telephone and every telephone you may ever call. Instead, the phone company connects your phone (and everyone else's phone) to a set of switches. When you place a phone call, the switches create the connection between the two phones. Without a telephone switching network, if you needed to call 1000 different people, you would need to connect 1000 lines to your phone. In a similar way, computer networks rely on communication switches. Networks use two common methods of communication switching to transfer data—circuit switching and packet switching. In circuit switching, the switches create a single, unbroken path between devices that want to communicate.

Most computer networks, including the Internet, do not use circuit switching. They use a technique called **packet switching**. In a typical terminal-to-host data connection, the line remains idle for most of the time. Thus, with data connections, a circuit-switched approach is inefficient. In a circuit-switched network, the connection provides for transmission at a constant data rate. Thus, each of the two devices that are connected must transmit and receive at the same data rate as the other. This limits the utility of the network in interconnecting host computers and terminals.

In packet switching, data are transmitted in short packets. A typical upper limit on packet length is 1 kilobyte. If a source has a longer message to send, the message is broken up into a series of packets. Each packet contains a portion (or all for a short message) of the user's data, plus some control information. The control information, at a minimum, includes the information that the network requires in order to be able to route the packet through the network and deliver it to the intended destination. At each node on the route, the packet is received, stored briefly, and passed on to the next node. In packet switching, programs break data into small pieces, called *packets*, and then transmit the packets between computers. Packets are pieces of data that adhere to a standard set of rules (protocols) that define their size and format. Unlike circuit switching, in a packet-switched network, data can flow along multiple paths, as shown in Figure 3.2.

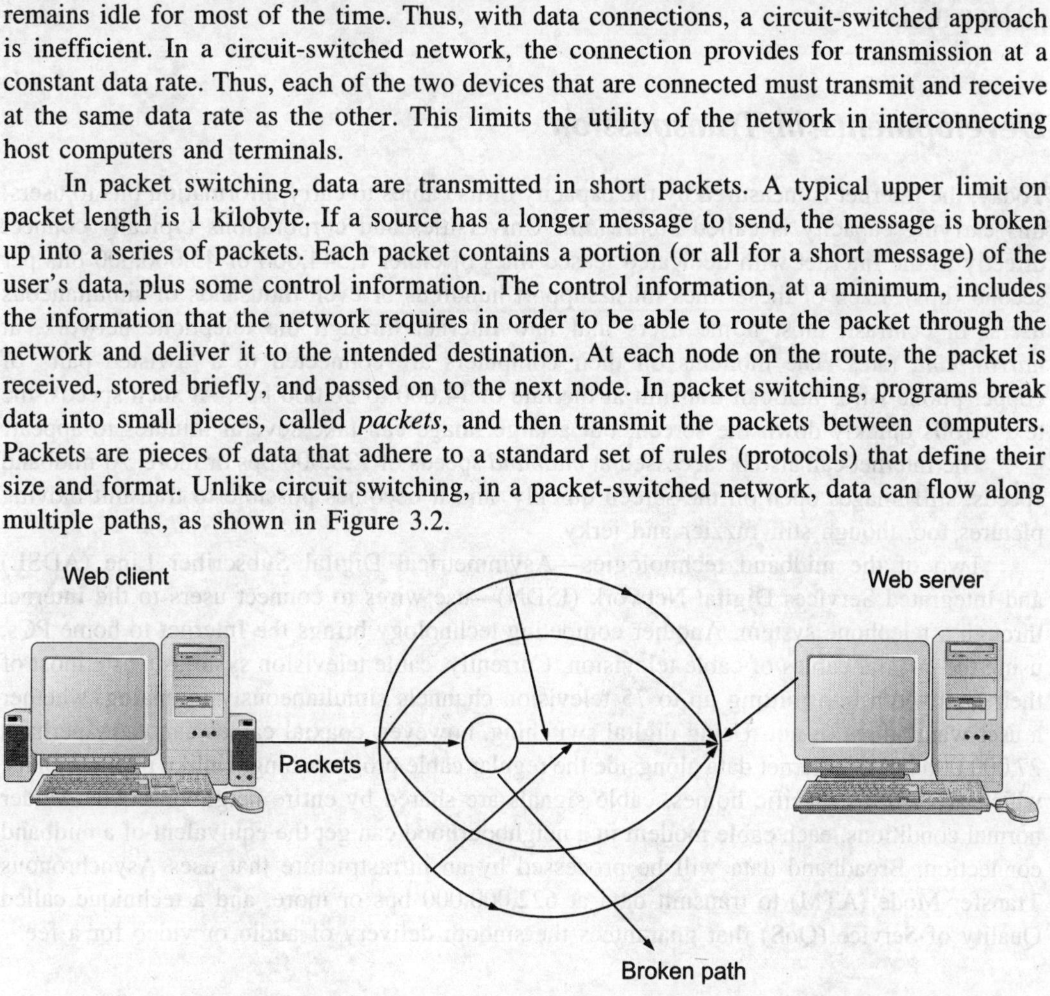

Figure 3.2 A packet switching network with a broken path.

In packet-switched networks, breaking one path does not prevent the data from reaching its destination. The packet will simply find a different path. Each packet must contain its destination address. As the packet travels from one computer to another, each computer examines the packet's address and routes the packet to its next intermediate hop or directly to the destination. The Internet is a packet-switched network. Think of a packet in a packet-switched network as a traveller flying from New Delhi to Mumbai. Depending on the available flights, the traveller may be able to fly non-stop (if the packet is lucky enough to get a direct connection). In most cases, however, the traveller must stop at airports along the way (possibly in Ahmedabad or Jaipur). In a similar way, a packet may visit several computers as it travels across the Internet. As signals travel through network media (cables and wires), they become weak. Engineers refer to this weakening of signals as attenuation. To overcome this, the network designers use special networking devices called *repeaters* which amplify network data.

Developments in Transmission

Today, the Internet is measured by the capacity of its cables to carry information bits to users; this carrying capacity is called *bandwidth*. Universities and corporations typically connect directly to the Internet with dedicated leased lines of either 1,544,000 or 45,000,000 bits per second (bps). Each of these lines must support hundreds or even thousands of simultaneous users. In contrast, most home users dial into Internet through the telephone network, at *narrowband* rates. The modems on their computers are connected to a "twisted pair" of copper phone wires that can transmit at the rate of 14,000 to 56,000 bps. At such speeds, the text scrolls quickly down the screen, but a large image can take several minutes to appear.

The Internet can also be accessed at *midband* speeds of 128,000 bps or more. At midband speeds, still images open on the screen quickly, and it becomes possible to transmit moving pictures too, though still fuzzier and jerky.

Two of the midband technologies—Asymmetrical Digital Subscriber Line (ADSL) and Integrated Services Digital Network (ISDN)—use wires to connect users to the Internet through a telephone system. Another competing technology brings the Internet to home PCs, using the coaxial cables of cable television. Currently, cable television systems waste most of their bandwidth transmitting up to 75 television channels simultaneously in analog, whether a user wants them or not. Using digital switching, however, coaxial cables can carry perhaps 27,000,000 bps of Internet data alongside the regular cable programming. Unlike phone signals, which are sent to specific homes, cable signals are shared by entire neighbourhoods. Under normal conditions, each cable modem in a neighbourhood can get the equivalent of a midband connection. Broadband data will be processed by an infrastructure that uses Asynchronous Transfer Mode (ATM) to transmit data at 622,000,000 bps or more, and a technique called Quality of Service (QoS) that guarantees the smooth delivery of audio or video for a fee.

Network Routers

Network designers use routers to transfer or route data between networks that use different network technologies. Since the Internet is comprised of various networks that use many different network technologies, routers are an integral part of the Internet. A router has an address on the network. Using the addressing capability of routers, the nodes on a network can send packets destined for another network to a router. The router, in turn, will transfer the packet to the other network. To manage network traffic, network designers also use routers to segment large sections of a Local Area Network (LAN) to smaller segments, called *subnets*. To route data, routers commonly use routing tables, which are similar to a lookup database. Using a routing table, routers can look up the correct path (or the best route) from the packet's current location to any destination on the network. Depending on the network's requirements, a designer can implement routing tables as static or dynamic. With a static routing table, the network administrator must manually update the table. Network software automatically updates the dynamic routing tables. The advantage of dynamic routing tables is that, should a part of the network get bogged down with a lot of traffic, the network software can update the routing tables to route packets around the current bottleneck.

Network Switches

A network switch is a small hardware device that joins multiple computers together within one local area network (LAN). Technically, network switches operate Data Link Layer. Network switches appear nearly identical to network hubs, but a switch generally contains more intelligence (and a slightly higher price tag) than a hub. Unlike hubs, network switches are capable of inspecting data packets as they are received, determining the source and destination device of each packet, and forwarding them appropriately. By delivering messages only to the connected device intended, a network switch conserves network and offers generally better performance than a hub. Mainstream Ethernet network switches support either 10/100 Mbps Fast Ethernet or Gigabit Ethernet (10/100/1000) standards. Different models of network switches support differing numbers of connected devices. Most consumer-grade network switches provide either four or eight connections for Ethernet devices. Switches can be connected to each other, a so-called *daisy chaining* method to add progressively larger number of devices to a LAN.

Connectionless versus Connection-oriented Protocols

Connectionless protocols differ from connection-oriented protocols in the way requests and responses to requests are handled. With a connectionless protocol, clients connect to the server, make a request, get a response, and then disconnect. With a connection-oriented protocol, clients connect to the server, make a request, get a response, and then maintain the connection to service future requests.

An example of a connection-oriented protocol is FTP. When you connect to an FTP server, the connection remains open after you download a file. The maintenance of this connection requires system resources. A server with too many open connections quickly gets bogged down. Consequently, many FTP servers are configured to allow only 250 open connections at one time, that is, only 250 users can access the FTP server at once. Additionally, processes that are not disconnected cleanly can cause problems on the server. The worst of these processes is running out of control, using system resources, and eventually crashing the server. The best of these processes simply eat up system resources. In contrast, HTTP is a connectionless protocol. When clients connect to the server, they make a request, get a response, and then disconnect. Since the connection is not maintained, no system resource is used after the transaction is completed. Consequently, HTTP servers are only limited to active connections and can generally do thousands of transactions with low system overhead. The drawback to connectionless protocols is that when the same client requests additional data, the connection must be re-established. To the Web users, this means a waste of time and energy.

Signal Bandwidth

The primary limit on any communications channel is its bandwidth. Bandwidth merely specifies a range of frequencies, from the lowest to the highest, that a channel can carry or that are present in the signal. Bandwidth is expressed in a different way for analog and digital circuits. In analog technology, the bandwidth of a circuit is the difference between the lowest and the highest frequencies that can pass through the channel. Engineers measure analog bandwidth in kilohertz or megahertz. In a digital circuit, the bandwidth is the amount of information that can pass through a channel. Engineers measure digital bandwidth in bits, kilobits, or megabits per second.

Channel Bandwidth

The bandwidth of a communications channel defines the frequency limits of the signals that they carry. This channel bandwidth may be physically limited to the medium used by the channel or artificially limited by communications standards. The bandwidths of radio transmissions, for example, are artificially limited, by law to allow more different modulated carriers to share the air waves at the same time while preventing interference between them.

In wire-based communications channels, bandwidth is often limited by the wires. Certain physical characteristics of wires cause degradations in their high frequency transmission capabilities. The capacitance between conductors in a cable pair, for instance, increasingly degrades signals as their frequencies rise, until it reaches a point at which a high frequency signal might not be able to traverse more than a few centimetres of wire. Amplifiers or repeaters, which boost signals so that they can travel longer distances, often cannot handle very low or very high frequencies.

Most of the telephone channels also have an artificial bandwidth limitation imposed by the telephone company. To get the greatest financial potential from the capacity of their transmission cables, microwave systems, and satellites, telephone carriers normally limit the bandwidth of telephone signals. One reason why bandwidth is limited is that many separate telephone conversations can be stacked atop one another through multiplexing techniques, which allow a single pair of wires to carry hundreds of simultaneous conversations.

Routing Packets

As an individual packet travels from one network to another, the computers through which the packet travels determine the most efficient route for getting the packet to its destination.

The most efficient route changes from second to second, depending on how much traffic each computer on the Internet is handling at each moment. The computers that decide how best to forward each packet are called ***routing computers, router computers, routers, gateway computers*** (because they act as the gateway from a LAN or WAN to the Internet), or ***border routers*** (because they are located at the border between the organization and the Internet). The programs on router computers that determine the best path on which to send each packet contain rules called ***routing algorithms***. The programs apply their routing algorithms to information they have stored in routing tables or configuration tables. This information includes lists of connections that lead to particular groups of other routers, rules that specify which connections to use first, and rules for handling instances of heavy packet traffic and network congestion.

Individual LANs and WANs can use a variety of different rules and standards for creating packets within their networks. The network devices that move packets from one part of a network to another are called *hubs*, *switches*, and *bridges*. Routers are used to connect networks to other networks. You can take a data communications and networking class to learn more about these network devices and how they work. When packets leave a network to travel on the Internet, they must be translated into a standard format. Routers usually perform this translation function. As you can see, routers are an important part of the infrastructure of the Internet. When a company or organization becomes part of the Internet, it must connect at least one router to the other routers (owned by other companies or organizations) that make up the Internet. Figure 3.3 is a diagram of a small portion of the Internet that shows its router-based architecture. The figure shows only the routers that connect each organization's WANs and LANs to the Internet, not the other routers that are inside the WANs and LANs or that connect them to each other within the organization. The Internet also has routers that handle packet traffic along the Internet's main connecting points. These routers and the telecommunications lines connecting them are collectively referred as the ***Internet backbone***. These routers, sometimes called ***backbone routers***, are very large computers that can each handle more than 3 billion packets per second! You can see in Figure 3.3 that a router connected to the Internet always has more than one path to which it can direct a packet. By building in multiple packet paths, the designers of the Internet created a degree of redundancy in the system that allows it to keep moving packets, even if one or more of the routers connecting lines fails.

The Internet Protocol Suite

The problem of Internetworking is how to build a set of protocols that can handle communications between two or more computers, using any type of operating system, and connected using any kind of physical medium. To complicate matters, we assume that no connected system has any knowledge about the other systems. There is no way of knowing where the remote systems is, what kind of software it uses, or what kind of hardware platform it runs on.

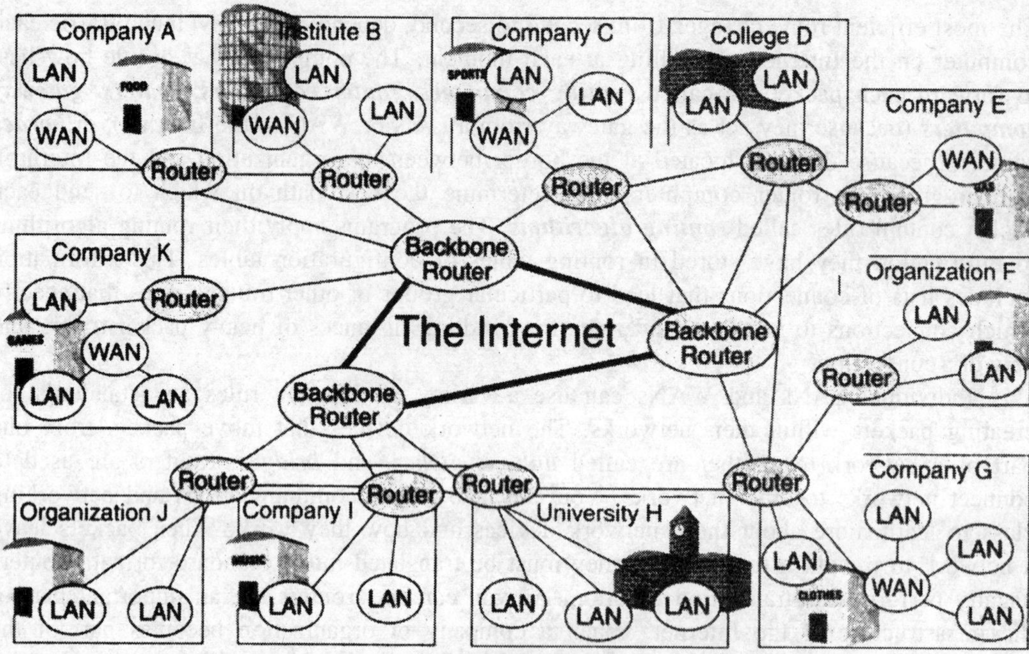

Figure 3.3 Router-based architecture of the Internet.

A Protocol is defined as a set of rules governing the exchange of data between two entities. The key elements of a protocol are:

1. Syntax, which includes such things as data format and signal levels.
2. Semantics, which includes control information for coordination and error handling.
3. Timing, which includes speed matching and sequencing.

TCP/IP is the networking protocol of the Internet, and an extension of intranets. For TCP/IP to work, your network interfaces need to be assigned IP addresses. Addresses are assigned to interfaces and not to computers. So, one computer can have more than one IP address. For example, if you have two network cards on your computer, then each of them will have a different IP address—either static or dynamic. Similarly, if you have a proxy server running, then the computer to which it is installed should have a static IP address. Now, the same machine has to establish a dial-up link to the Internet through, say VSNL. Then the dial-up adapter would be assigned a different dynamic address.

The Internet was designed to embody a series of design principles, which are as follows:

1. ***Interoperable.*** Here, the system supports computers and software from different vendors.
2. ***Layered.*** In this, the collection of Internet protocols works in layers, with each layer building on the layers at lower levels.
3. ***Simple.*** This principle states that each of the layers in the architecture provides only a few functions or operations. This means that application programmers are hidden from the complexities of the underlying hardware.

4. ***End-to-end.*** Here, the Internet is based on 'end-to-end' protocols. This means that interpretation of data happens at the application layer and not at the network layer.

IP Address System

Figure 3.4 shows the structure of IP version 4 and it can be summarized as follows:

A standard IP header is around 20 bytes. There are options to add more bytes.

Ver stands for version, which is IP version 4.

IHL stands for Internet Header Length. Typically it is 5 bits. However, it has two bytes available and therefore the longest header is 60 bits.

TTL is time to live. Maximum is 255 seconds.

Total length for the packet is 16 bits. So, the maximum packet size is 64K.

The header checksum must be recomputed on a hop-by-hop basis since each router hop decrements TTL by one.

The source and destination address is 4 bytes long each.

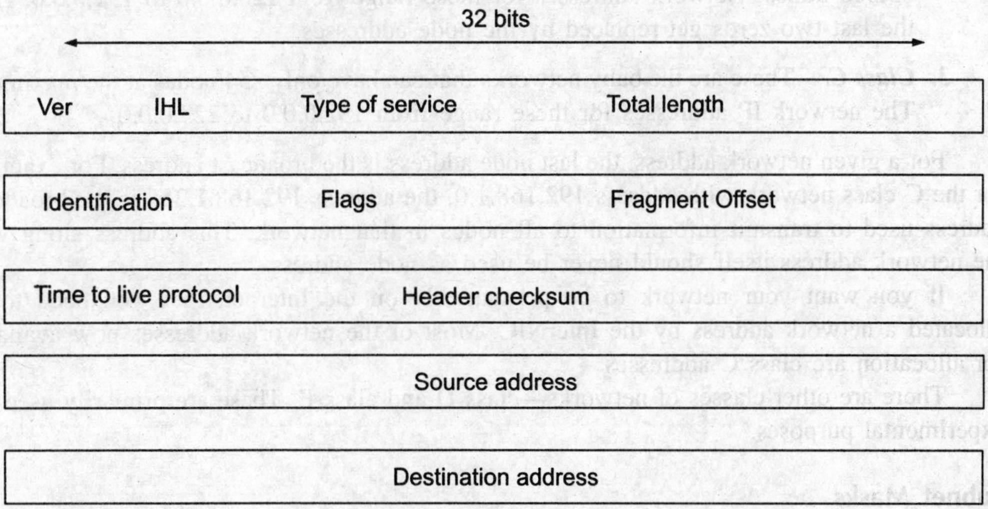

Figure 3.4 IPv4 structure.

An IP address is a number that represents a device uniquely on the Internet or on your company's intranet. This number is actually a binary one, but for convenience sake it is normally written as four decimal numbers. For instance, a typical IP address would be something like 192.168.1.1. The four constituent numbers together represent the network that the computer is on, and the computer (interface) itself. Let us first look at the network address part. The IP addresses for networks on the Internet are allocated by the InterNIC. If you have an Internet connection, then you would be allocated a network address by the agency that registered you, like the InterNIC. Let us assume this as 192.6.132.0, a class C network. Then all the machines on this network will have the same network address. And the last 0 will be replaced by a number from 1 to 254 for the node address. So, nodes will have addresses 192.6.132.1, 192.6.132.2, and so on, up to 192.6.132.254 (see Table 3.2).

TABLE 3.2 Classes of Networks

Type	*Example*	*Explanation*
Class A	[125.] 100.100.100	The part within the box is the network part of the IP address, and the rest identifies a unique node or interface on that network.
Class B	[190.100.] 100.100	You can identify the class of the network from the first of the four numbers that form the IP address.
Class C	[220.100.] [100.] 100	

Depending on the size of the network, the IP-based networks are divided into three classes.

1. ***Class A.*** These networks have their network addresses from 1.0.0.0 to 126.0.0.0, with the zeros being replaced by node addresses. Class A networks are mega monster networks, with up to 16 million plus connections.
2. ***Class B.*** These are smaller networks in comparison, i.e. they can have only about 65,000 nodes! Network addresses for these range from 128.0.0.0 to 191.0.0.0. Here the last two zeros get replaced by the node addresses.
3. ***Class C.*** These are the baby networks that can have only 254 nodes at the maximum. The network IP addresses for these range from 192.0.0.0 to 223.0.0.0.

For a given network address, the last node address is the broadcast address. For example, for the C class network with address 192.168.1.0, the address 192.168.1.255 is the broadcast address used to transmit information to all nodes in that network. This address along with the network address itself should never be used as node address.

If you want your network to be permanently on the Internet, then you need to be allocated a network address by the InterNIC. Most of the network addresses now available for allocation are class C addresses.

There are other classes of networks—class D and class E. These are primarily used for experimental purposes.

Subnet Masks

In an IP network, every machine on the same physical network sees all the data packets sent out on that network. As the number of computers on a network grows, network traffic will grow manifold, bringing down performance drastically. In such a situation, you would divide your network into different subnetworks and minimize the traffic across the different subnetworks. Interconnectivity between the different subnets would be provided by routers, which will only transmit data meant for another subnet across. To divide a given network address into two or more subnets, you use subnet masks. The default subnet mask for class A networks is 255.0.0.0, for class B it is 255.255.0.0, and for class C 255.255.255.0, which signify a network without subnets.

The InterNIC has (RFC 1597-Address Allocation for Private Internets) allocated particular blocks of network addresses for use in intranets. These IP addresses do not conflict with those of existing Internet hosts and will not be handed out for use on the Internet.

The address blocks are:

Class A: 10.0.0.0
Class B: From 172.16.0.0 to 172.31.0.0
Class C: From 192.168.0.0 to 192.168.255.0

Computers on networks using the above given IP addresses will be treated as private ones and they can communicate only within the company intranet. However, they can still access the outside world using proxy servers. This adds to the security of their intranet. Therefore, their intranet should always use addresses from these reserved groups only.

Now, which IP address class should you use for your intranet? The answer depends on the number of hosts that are going to be connected to the intranet. Any machine connected to the network, whether server or client, is called a *host*.

Without subnetting, you can have the configurations shown in Table 3.3.

TABLE 3.3 Number of Machines on each Subnet

Number of machines to be connected	*Class of network*	*Network addresses*
254 or less	C	192.168.0.0 to 192.1678.255.0
255 to 65.534	B	172.16.0.0 to 172.31.0.0
65.535 to 16.777.214	A	10.0.0.0

Thus, if you have a class C network that is not permanently connected to the Internet, your network address can be any one from 192.168.1.0 to 192.168.255.0. If you have selected 192.168.1.0 as your network address, you can have 254 hosts having addresses from 192.168.1.1 to 192.168.1.254 without subnetting. 192.168.1.255 is the broadcast address and 192.168.1.0 is the network address for this network.

Translating IP Numbers to User-friendly Domain Names

Computers in your network (and on the intranet) know each other by their IP addresses. But remembering numbers is not an easy task. Remembering names is much more easier—you remember all your friends and relatives by their names, rather than by their phone numbers. A way was thus devised to associate IP addresses with names that can be easily remembered. Type a name like *xlri.ac.in* into a browser, and a "name lookup" occurs behind the scenes to find the associated IP address—just as you would do a "name lookup" in a phone directory to find a phone number for a name you know. This was once done by using a "hosts" file on every node. The hosts file is simply a list of IP addresses and corresponding names, like a phone directory. Any name lookup, i.e. the process of identifying the IP address associated with a name, will first check the hosts file (if there is one) on the machine making the query, to see whether the name exists.

In the early days of the Internet, hosts files were used to associate machines with names. But soon that became impossible, with millions of hosts already connected and that figure growing by 10 per cent every month. The way out was the DNS: the Domain Name Server. The DNS is a distributed, scalable database of IP addresses and their associated names. It is distributed in the sense that unlike the hosts files, no single computer contains all the DNS information in the world. The DNS data is distributed across many name servers. It is scalable in the sense that you can increase the volume of total DNS data and requests from machines for the same data, without significantly increasing the querying time. Otherwise, the World Wide Web would really have become the world wide wait.

The Internet Naming Conventions

Computers on the Internet identify each other by their IP addresses such as 209.194.84.59, and so on. But remembering numbers is a gift only few of us possess. Names like *yahoo.com* are preferred in such a situation. The Internet is divided into a number of registries or top level domains (TLDs) as shown in Table 3.4.

TABLE 3.4 Top-Level Domain Names

Domain name	*Actual name*
com	Commercial
net	Networks
edu	Educational
jp	Japan
us	United States
de	US Military
org	Organizations
gov	Government
ru	Russian Federation
cn	China
in	India

The Internet naming conventions call for the type of website to be identified by the registry—the portion after the dot in any Web address. For example, the sites that come under the *.com* registry are commercial sites or sites belonging to commercial organizations. Similarly, *.gov* indicates government bodies, and *.org* represents non-profit organizations and societies. But unfortunately, that is not always the case. The *.com* registry has been by far the most popular, and everybody seems to opt for *.com*.

Uniform or Universal Resource Locators (URLs)

The URLs provide a uniform way of identifying resources that are available using Internet protocols (IP). To understand the concept of URLs, you need to know about URL schemes and formats, how URLs are defined, and how to use escape codes in URLs. The basic mechanism that makes URLs so versatile is the standard naming scheme. The URL schemes name the protocol that the client will use to access and transfer the file. Web clients use the name of the protocol to determine the format for the information that follows the protocol name. The protocol name is generally followed by a colon and two forward slashes. The colon is a separator. The double slash marks indicate that the protocol uses the format defined by the Common Internet Scheme Syntax (CISS). The CISS is a common syntax for URL schemes that involve the direct use of IP-based protocols. These protocols specify a particular host on the Internet by a unique numeric identifier called an IP address or by a unique name that can be resolved into the IP address. The information after the double slashes follows a format that is dependent on the protocol type referenced in the URL. Here are two general formats:

1. *protocol://hostname:port/path_to_resource*
2. *protocol://username:password@hostname:port/path_to_resource*

If you use a DOS/Windows-based system, you normally type a backslash to change directories and manoeuvre around the system. Consequently, you might have to remind yourself that the Web follows the UNIX syntax for slashes, and the slashes you type for URLs should be forward slashes.

Hostname information used in URLs identifies the address of a host and is broken down into two or more parts separated by periods. The periods are used to separate domain information from the hostname. The common domain names for Web servers begin with www, such as *www.xlri.com,* which identifies the Web server called *xlri* in the commercial domain. Domains you can specify in your URLs include:

com — Commercial sites
edu — Educational sites
gov — Nonmilitary government sites
mil — Military sites
net — Network sites (developers, Internet Service Providers, and so on)
org — Organizational sites

Defining Port Information in URLs

Ports are rather like telephone jacks on the Web server. The server has certain ports allocated for certain things, for instance, port 80 is for incoming requests for hypertext documents. The server listens to a particular port. When it hears something, in essence, it picks up the phone and connects the particular port. Port information used in URLs identifies the port number to be used for the connection. If you do not specify a port number, a default value is assumed as necessary. Generally, you do not have to specify port numbers in your URLs unless the connection is to be made to a port other than the default. The default values for ports are defined in Table 3.5.

Defining Protocol Schemes

Most protocol schemes follow the two general forms of URLs discussed earlier. Protocol schemes conforming to the CISS standard use the double slashes. The CISS compliant

TABLE 3.5 Ports for Protocols

Protocol	*Port*
File Transfer Protocol (FTP)	Port 21
Gopher	Port 70
HTTP	Port 80
Network News Transfer Protocol (NNTP)	Port 119
Telnet	Port 23
Wide Area Information Server (WAIS)	Port 210

protocols are FTP, Gopher, HTTP, NNTP, WAIS, and File. Protocols that do not conform to the CISS standard omit the double slashes. Non-compliant protocols include Mailto and News. Table 3.6 shows the URL scheme associated with each protocol.

TABLE 3.6 URL Schemes Associated with each Protocol

Protocol acronym	*Full protocol name*	*Example*
FTP	File Transfer Protocol	*ftp://username:password@hostname:port/*
Gopher	Gopher protocol	*gopher://hostname:port/path_to_resource*
HTTP	HyperText Transfer Protocol	*http://hostname:port/path_to_resource*
Mailto	Electronic mail address	*mailto:username@host*
Usenet news	News	*news:newsgroup-name news:message-number*
NNTP	Usenet news accessed with Network News Transfer Protocol	*nntp://hostname/newsgroup-name*
WAIS	Wide Area Information Servers	*wais://hostname:port/database*
telnet	Remote login sessions	*telnet://username:password@hostname: port*
File	Files on local host	*file://hostname/path_to_resource*

Defining URLs

The URLs consist of characters defined by the ASCII character set. The URL specification allows the use of uppercase and lowercase letters. Because URLs typed in uppercase are generally treated the same as URLs typed in lowercase, most Web publishers use only the lowercase letters in their URLs. A result of this is that most Web documents and object files are named in lowercase letters as well. If you are on a system that has case-sensitive file naming, such as UNIX, you will find that naming your files in lowercase is extremely useful in avoiding possible conflicts. Although URLs consist of characters defined by the ASCII character set, you cannot use all ASCII characters in your URLs. You can use the letters a–z, the numerals 0–9, and a few special characters as given in Table 3.7.

TABLE 3.7 Special Characters used in URLs

Character	*Symbol*
Asterisk	*
Dollar sign	$
Exclamation point	!
Hyphen	-
Parentheses (left and right)	( )
Period	•
Plus sign	+
Single quotation mark	' '
Underscore	_

You are limited to these characters because other characters used in URLs have specific meanings, as in the following:

1. ***Colon* (:).** The colon is a separator. It separates the protocol from the rest of the URL scheme, e.g. *http://xlri.com/xlrifound.html*. It separates the host name from the port number as in *http://www.xlri.com:80/*. Also, it separates the user name from the userid, as you can find in *ftp://anonymous:joseph@xlri.com/*.

2. ***Double slash* (//).** They indicate that the protocol uses the format defined by the CISS. They separate the protocol from the URL scheme.

3. ***Single slash* (/).** This is used to separate the path from host name and port. The slash is also used to denote the directory path to the resource named in the URL, e.g. *http://xlri.com/xlrihp.html.*

4. ***Tilde* (~).** This is generally used at the beginning of the path to indicate that the resource is in the specified user's public html directory, e.g. *http://www.aloha.com/~joseph*

5. ***Percentage* (%).** This identifies an escape code. Escape codes Book%20Table%20 of%20 Contents are used to specify special characters in URLs which otherwise have a special meaning, or are not allowed for access.

6. ***At* (@) *symbol.*** This is used in mail accounts to identify the site to which the mailer belongs, as in mailto:joseph@xlri.com. It separates the user name and/or password information from the host name in the URL.

7. ***Question* (?) *mark.*** This is used in the URL path to specify the beginning of a query string. Query strings are passed to CGI scripts. All the information following the question mark is the data that the user has submitted and so are not interpreted as part of the file path. e.g. /usr/cgi-bin/useit.pl?keyword.

8. ***Plus* (+) *sign.*** This is used in query strings as a place-holder between words, e.g. useit.pl?word1+word2+word3. Instead of using spaces to separate words that the user has entered in the query, the browser uses the plus sign.

9. ***Equal* (=) *sign.*** This is used in query strings to separate the key assigned by the publisher from the value entered by the user, e.g. useit.pl?username=joseph. Here, the user name is the key assigned by the publisher and the value entered by the user is Joseph.

10. ***Ampersand* (&) *sign.*** This is used in query strings to separate sets of keys and values, e.g. pl?name-Joseph&question. In this sample URL, name is the first key assigned by the publisher and the value entered by the user is Joseph. The second key assigned by the publisher is a question, and the value entered by the user is "why not".

Dynamic IP Addressing vs Static IP Addressing

In assigning IP addresses to machines, you have two choices. You can either go around typing in the individual address on each machine or you can set up one machine to assign IP addresses to the others. The second one, called dynamic addressing, is preferred for three reasons. First, it makes the job of administering the network, such as adding new clients, avoiding IP clashes, and so on, a lot easier. And second, since only those machines that are switched on will need an IP address, you could potentially have more machines on your network with dynamic addressing, than you could with static addressing. You do dynamic addressing with Dynamic Host Configuration Protocol (DHCP). To make DHCP work on your network, you have to set up a DHCP server.

Next Generation IP

The current version of IP is version 4 (IPv4). Under this version, the Internet addresses are 32 bits long and written as four sets of numbers separated by periods, e.g. 130.211.100.5. This format is also called dotted quad addressing. You may be familiar with addresses like *www.yahoo.com.* Behind each one of these character addresses is a 32-bit numerical address.

With IPv4, the maximum number of available addresses is slightly over 4 billion (2^{32}). This is a large number but because of the block assignments of IP numbers to individual organizations, these numbers may run out over the next few years. For this reason, the various Internet Society boards began to craft in the early 1990s the Next Generation Internet Protocol (Ipng). This protocol which was renamed IP version 6 (IPv6) has just begun to be adopted and it utilizes 128-bit addresses.

IPv6

On June 8, 2011 the Internet Society together with several other big companies and organizations held World IPv6 Day, a global 24 hour test of IPv6.

One critical problem is the lack of address space. Ipv4 which uses 32 bit addressing, theoretically has more than 4 billion addresses. But because of IP class implementation, it is not possible to use all of them. The solution is Ipv6 which has 128- bit addressing space. The address size for Ipv6 has been increased to 128 bits. This solves the problem of the limited address space of Ipv4 and offers a deeper addressing hierarchy and simpler configuration. There will come a day when you will hardly remember how it felt to have only 32 bits in an IP address. Network administrators will love the autoconfiguration mechanisms built into the protocol. Multicast routing has been improved, with the multicast address being extended by a scope field. And a new address type has been introduced, called Anycast address, which can send a message to the nearest single member of a group.

The Ipv6 header has a fixed length of 40 bytes. This actually accommodates only an 8 byte header plus two 16 byte IP addresses (source and destination address) [see Figure 3.5]. Some fields of the Ipv4 header have been removed or have become optional. This way, packets can be handled faster with lower processing costs.

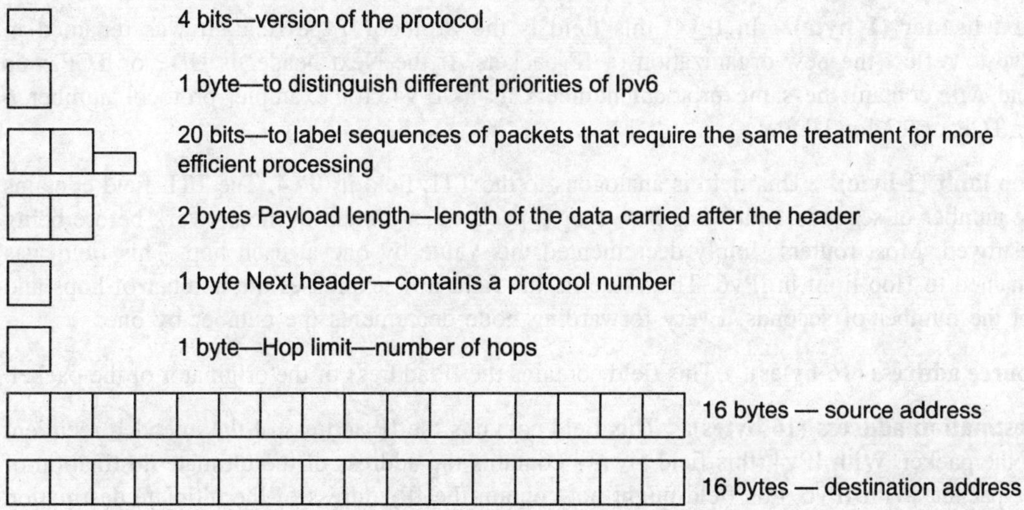

Figure 3.5 General header structure of IPv6.

In IPv6, five fields from the IPv4 header have been removed:

- Header Length
- Identification
- Flags
- Fragment Offset
- Header Checksum

Version (4 bits). This is a 4 bit field and contains the version of the protocol. In the case of IPv6, the number 5 could not be used because it had already been assigned an experimental stream protocol.

Traffic class (1 byte). This field replaces the Type of Service field in IPv4. This field facilitates the handling of real-time data and any other data that requires special handling. This field can be used by sending nodes and forwarding routers to identify and distinguish between classes or priorities of IPv6 packets.

Flow label (20 bits). This field distinguishes packets that require the same treatment, in order to facilitate the handling of real-time traffic. A sending host can label sequences of packets with a set of options, routers keep track of flows and can process packets belonging to the same flow more efficiently because they do not have to reprocess each packet's header. A flow is uniquely identified by the flow label and the address of the source node.

Payload length (2 bytes). This field specifies the payload, i.e. the length of data carried after the IP header. The calculation in IPv6 is different from the one in IPv4. The Length Field in IPv4 includes the length of the IPv4 header, whereas the Payload Length field in IPv6 contains only the data following the IPv6 header. Extension headers are considered part of the payload and are therefore included in the calculation.

Next header (1 byte). In IPv4, this field is the Protocol Type field. It was renamed in IPv6 to reflect the new organization of IP packets. If the Next header is UDP or TCP, this field will contain the same protocol numbers as in IPv4, for example, protocol number 6 for TCP or 17 for UDP.

Hop limit (1 byte). This field is analogous to the TTL field in IPv4. The TTL field contains the number of seconds, indicating how long a packet can remain in the network before being destroyed. Most routers simply decremented this value by one at each hop. This field was renamed to Hop limit in IPv6. The value in this field now expresses the number of hops and not the number of seconds. Every forwarding node decrements the number by one.

Source address (16 bytes). This field contains the IP address of the originator of the packet.

Destination address (16 bytes). This field contains the IP address of the intended recipient of the packet. With IPv4, this field always contains the address of the ultimate destination of the packet. With IPv6, this field might not contain the IP address of the ultimate destination if a Routing header is present.

Extension Headers

The IPv4 header can be extended from a minimum of 20 bytes to 60 bytes in order to specify options such as Security Options, Source Routing, or Timestamping. This capacity has rarely been used because it causes a performance hit.

The simpler a packet header, the faster the processing. IPv6 has a new way to deal with options, that has substantially improved processing. It handles options in additional headers called Extension headers.

The current IPv6 specification defines six Extension headers:

- Hop-by-Hop Options header
- Routing header
- Fragment header
- Destination Options header
- Authentication header
- Encrypted Security Payload header

Transmission Control Protocol (TCP)

The Internet uses packet switching hardware that can become overrun with datagrams. Since this necessitates an additional communication software, the TCP has been invented. All computers that connect to the Internet, run TCP/IP software.

TCP solves several problems that can occur in a packet switching system. If a router becomes overrun with datagrams, it must discard them. As a result, a datagram can be lost in its trip through the Internet. TCP automatically checks for lost datagrams and handles the problem. The Internet has a complex structure with multiple paths that datagrams can travel. When the hardware in a router fails or a network fails, the other routers start sending datagrams along a new path, analogous to the way cars detour around a barricade on a road. As a result of the change in routes, some datagrams can arrive at the destination in a different order than they were actually sent in. TCP automatically checks the incoming datagrams and puts the data back in order. Network hardware failures sometimes result in duplication of datagrams. TCP automatically checks for duplicate datagrams and accepts only the first copy of data that arrives. TCP software makes it possible for two computer programs to communicate across the Internet in a manner similar to the way humans use a telephone. Once the programs establish a connection, they can exchange arbitrary amounts of data and then terminate communication.

Although TCP and IP can be used separately, they were designed at the same time to work as part of a unified system, and were engineered to cooperate and to complement each other. TCP provides a connection-oriented, reliable, byte stream service. The term connection-oriented means that the two applications using TCP (normally considered a client and a server) must establish a TCP connection with each other before they can exchange data. There are exactly two end points communicating with each other on a TCP connection. TCP provides reliability by doing the following:

1. The application data is broken into what TCP considers the best sized chunks to send. The unit of information thus passed by TCP to IP is called a *segment*.
2. When TCP sends a segment it maintains a timer, waiting for the other end to acknowledge the reception of the segment. If an acknowledgment is not received in time, the segment is retransmitted.
3. When TCP receives data from the other end of the connection, it sends an acknowledgement.
4. TCP maintains a checksum on its header and data. This is an end-to-end checksum whose purpose is to detect any modification of the data in transit. If a segment arrives with an invalid checksum, TCP discards it and does not acknowledge receiving it.
5. Since TCP segments are transmitted as IP datagrams, and since IP datagrams can arrive out of order, TCP segments can arrive out of order. A receiving TCP resequences the data if necessary, passing the received data in the correct order to the application.
6. Since IP datagrams can get duplicated, a receiving TCP must discard duplicate data.
7. TCP also provides flow control. Each end of a TCP connection has a finite amount of buffer space. A receiving TCP only allows the other end to send as much data as the receiver has buffers for. This prevents a fast host from taking all the buffers on a slower host.

IP Datagrams

IP is the workhorse protocol of the TCP/IP protocol suite. All TCP data gets transmitted as IP datagrams. IP provides an unreliable, connectionless datagram delivery service. By unreliable, it is meant that there are no guarantees that an IP datagram successfully reaches its destination. The term connectionless means that IP does not maintain any state information about successive datagrams. Each datagram is handled independently from all other datagrams. This also means that IP datagrams can get delivered out of order. If a source sends two consecutive datagrams (first A, then B) to the same destination, each is routed independently and can take different routes, with B arriving before A.

TCP/IP Protocol Suite Architecture

A protocol suite, such as TCP/IP, is the combination of different protocols at various layers. TCP/IP is normally considered to be a four layer system as shown in Figure 3.6.

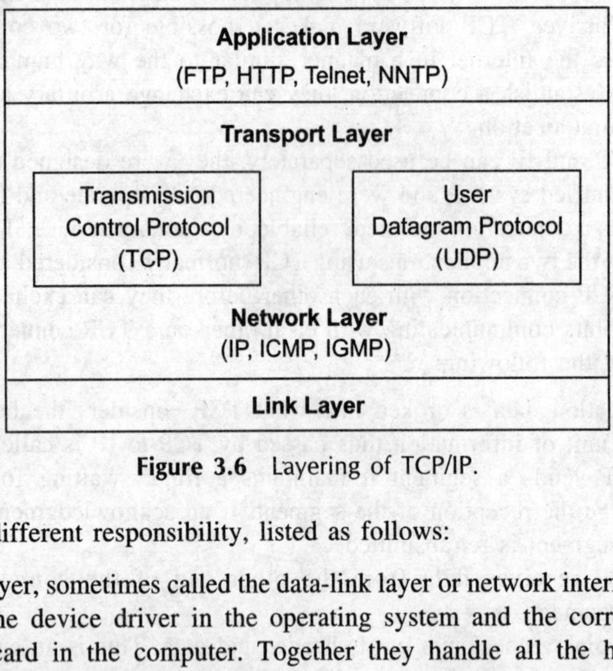

Figure 3.6 Layering of TCP/IP.

Each layer has a different responsibility, listed as follows:

1. The link layer, sometimes called the data-link layer or network interface layer, normally includes the device driver in the operating system and the corresponding network interface card in the computer. Together they handle all the hardware details of physically interfacing with the cable.
2. The network layer (also called the Internet layer) handles the movement of packets around the network. Routing of packets, for example, takes place here. Internet Protocol provides the network layer in the TCP/IP protocol suite.
3. The transport layer provides a flow of data between two hosts, for the application layer above. In the TCP/IP protocol suite, there are two vastly different protocols: TCP and User Datagram Protocol (UDP).

The application layer handles the details of the particular application. One application box is labelled the FTP client and the other, the FTP server. Each layer has one or more protocols for communicating with its peer at the same layer. One protocol, for example, allows the two TCP layers to communicate, and another protocol lets the two IP layers communicate. The application layer is a user process, while the lower three layers are usually implemented in the kernel (the operating system). There is another critical difference between the top layer and the lower three layers. The application layer is concerned with the details of the application and not with the movement of data across the network. The lower three layers know nothing about the application but handle all the communication details.

The purpose of the network interface layer and the application layer are obvious: the former handles the details of the communication media while the latter handles the one specific user application. To understand the difference between the network layer and the transport layer, we connect two or more networks with a router. Figure 3.7 shows two networks connected with a router—an Ethernet and a token ring. The application layer and the transport layer use end-to-end protocols. The network layer, however, provides a hop-by-hop protocol and is used on the two end systems and an every intermediate system. A router, by definition, has two or more network interface layers (since it connects two or more networks). A system with multiple interfaces is called *multihomed.*

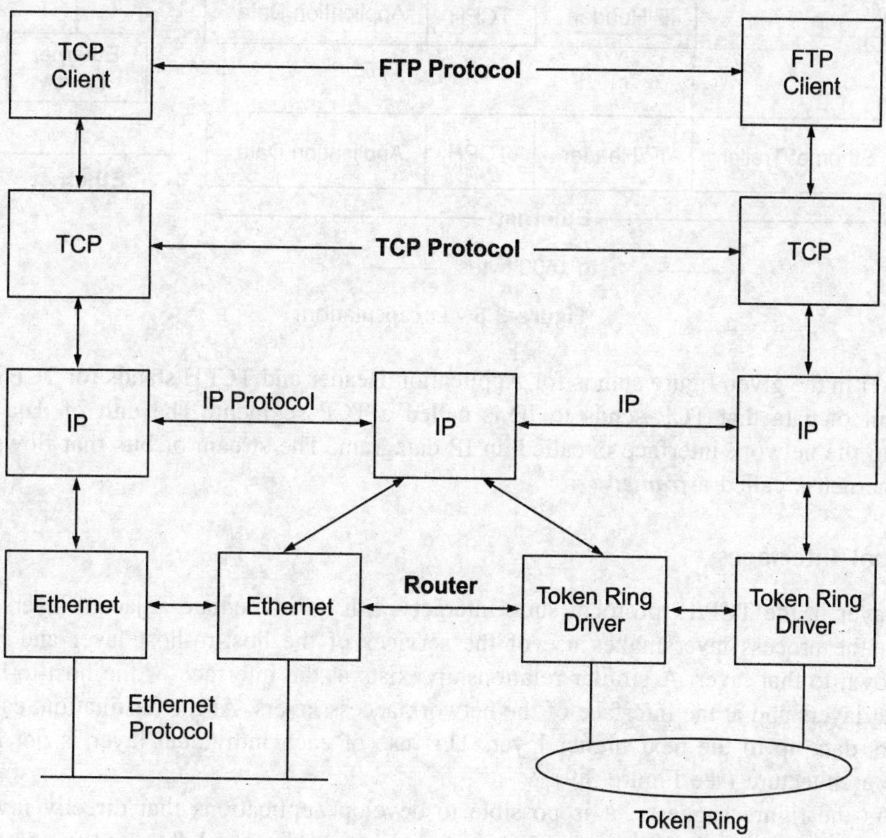

Figure 3.7 Two networks connected with a router.

Encapsulation

Encapsulation is the packaging of attributes and functionality to create an object, essentially the one whose internal structure remains private, though accessible by other objects through a clearly defined interface. Encapsulation ensures security (see Figure 3.8).

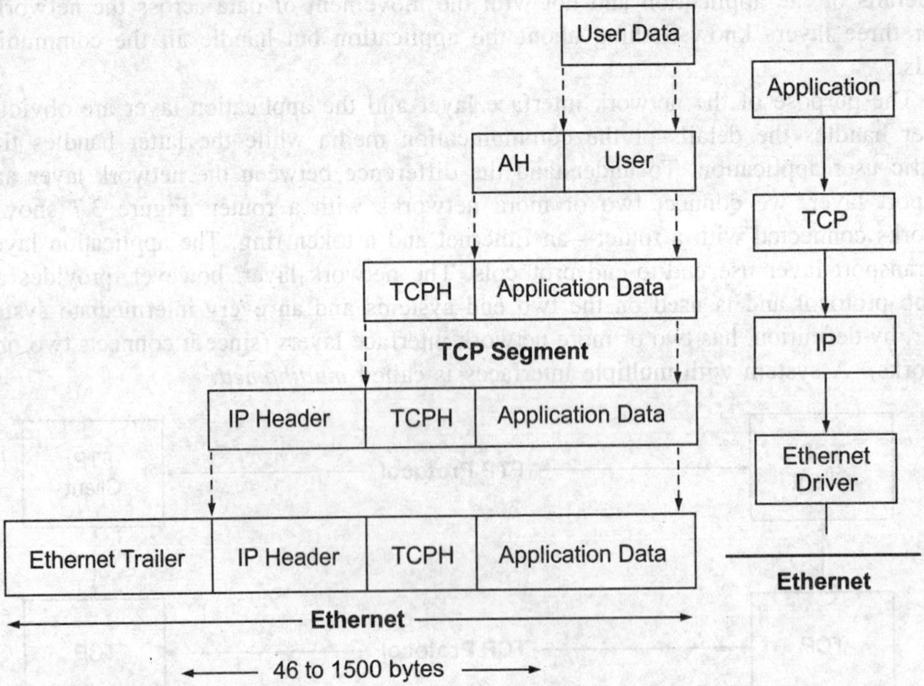

Figure 3.8 Encapsulation.

AH in the given figure stands for Application Header and TCPH stands for TCP Header. The unit of data that TCP sends to IP is called a TCP segment. The unit of data that IP sends to the network interface is called an IP datagram. The stream of bits that flows across the Ethernet is called a *frame*.

Protocol Interfaces

Each layer in the TCP/IP protocol suite interacts with its immediate adjacent layers. At the source, the process layer makes use of the services of the host-to-host layer and provides data down to that layer. A similar relationship exists at the interface of the host-to-host and Internet layers and at the interface of the network access layers. At the destination, each layer delivers data up to the next higher layer. This use of each individual layer is not required by the architecture (see Figure 3.9).

As the figure suggests, it is possible to develop applications that directly invoke the services of any one of the layers. Most applications require a reliable end-to-end protocol and thus make use of TCP. Some special-purpose applications, such as the simple network

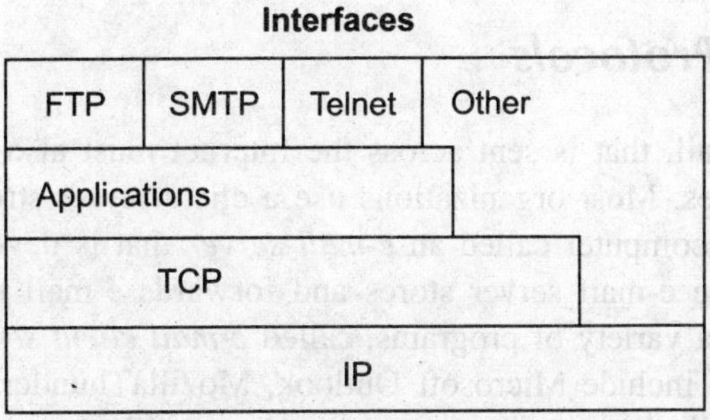

Figure 3.9 TCP/IP protocol suite.

management protocol (SNMP), use an alternative host-to-host protocol known as the user datagram protocol (UDP); others may make use of IP directly. Applications that do not involve internetworking and that do not need TCP, have been developed to invoke the network access layer directly.

Web Page Request and Delivery Protocols

The Web is software that runs on computers that are connected to each other through the Internet, Web client computers run software called *Web client software* or *Web browser software*. Examples: popular Web browser software include Google Chrome, Microsoft Internet Explorer, and Mozilla Firefox. Web browser software sends requests for Web page files to other computers, which are called *Web servers*. A Web server computer runs software called *Web server software*. Web server software receives requests from many different Web clients and responds by sending files back to those Web client computers. Each Web client computer's Web client software renders those files into a Web page. Thus, the purpose of a Web server is to respond to requests for Web pages from Web clients. This combination of client computers running Web client software and server computers running Web server software is an example of a client/server architecture.

The set of rules for delivering Web page files over the Internet is in a protocol called the *Hypertext Transfer Protocol* (HTTP), which was developed by Tim Berners-Lee in 1991. When a user types a domain name (for example, www.yahoo.com) into a Web browser's address bar, the browser sends an HTTP-formatted message to a Web server computer at Yahoo! that stores Web page files. The Web server computer at Yahoo! then responds by sending a set of files (one for the Web page and one for each graphic object, sound, or video clip included on the page) back to the client computer. These files are sent within a message that is HTTP formatted.

To initiate a Web page request using a Web browser, the user types the name of the protocol, followed by the characters before the domain name. Thus, a user would type http://www.yahoo.com to go to the Yahoo! Web site. Most Web browsers today automatically insert the http:// if the user does not include it. The combination of the protocol name and the domain name is called *Uniform Resource Locator* (URL) because it lets the user locate a resource (the Web page) on another computer (the Web server).

Electronic Mail Protocols

Electronic mail, or e-mail, that is sent across the Internet must also be formatted according to a common set of rules. Most organizations use a client/server structure to handle e-mail. The organization has a computer called an *e-mail server* that is devoted to handling e-mail. Software running on the e-mail server stores and forwards e-mail messages. People in the organization might use a variety of programs, called *e-mail client software*, to read and send e-mail. These programs include Microsoft Outlook, MozillaThunderbird, Pegasus Mail, and many others. The e-mail client software communicates with the e-mail server software on the e-mail server computer to send and receive e-mail messages.

Many people also use e-mail on their computers at home. In most cases, the e-mail servers that handle their messages are operated by the companies that provide their connections to the Internet. An increasing number of people use e-mail services that are offered by Web sites such as Yahoo! Mail, Microsoft's Hotmail, or Google's Gmail. In these cases, the e-mail servers and the e-mail clients are operated by the owners of the Web sites. The individual users only see the e-mail client software (and not the e-mail server software) in their Web browsers when they log on to the Web mail service.

With so many different e-mail client and server software choices, standardization and rules are very important. If e-mail messages did not follow standard rules, an e-mail message created by a person using one e-mail client program could not be read by a person using a different e-mail client program. As you have already learned in this chapter, rules for computer data transmission are called protocols. SMTP and POP are two common protocols used for sending and retrieving e-mail. **Simple Mail Transfer Protocol (SMTP)** specifies the format of a mail message and describes how mail is to be administered on the e-mail server and transmitted on the Internet. An e-mail client program running on a user's computer can request mail from the organization's e-mail server using the **Post Office Protocol (POP)**. A POP message can tell the e-mail server to send mail to the user's computer and delete it from the e-mail server; send mail to the user's computer and not delete it; or simply ask whether new mail has arrived. The POP provides support for **Multipurpose Internet Mail Extensions (MIME)**, which is a set of rules for handling binary files, such as word-processing documents, spreadsheets, photos, or sound clips that are attached to e-mail messages.

The **Interactive Mail Access Protocol (IMAP)** is a newer e-mail protocol that performs the same basic functions as POP, but includes additional features. For example, IMAP can instruct the e-mail server to send only selected e-mail messages to the client instead of all messages. IMAP also allows the user to view only the header and the e-mail sender's name before deciding to download the entire message. POP requires users to download e-mail messages to their computers before they can search, read, forward, delete, or reply to those messages. IMAP lets users create and manipulate e-mail folders (also called *mailboxes*) and individual e-mail messages while the messages are still on the e-mail server; that is, the user does not need to download e-mail before working with it.

The tools that IMAP provides are important to the large number of people who access their e-mail from different computers at different times. IMAP lets users manipulate and store their e-mail on the e-mail server and access it from any computer. The main drawback to IMAP is that users' e-mail messages are stored on the e-mail server. As the number of users' increases, the size of the e-mail server's disk drives must also increase. In general, server computers use faster (and thus, more expensive) disk drives than desktop computers. Therefore, it is more expensive to provide disk storage space for large quantities of e-mail on a server computer than to provide that same disk space on users' desktop computers. As the price of all disk storage continues to decrease, these cost concerns become less important. You can learn more about IMAP at the diversity of Washington's IMAP Connection Web site.

Unsolicited Commercial E-mail (UCE, Spam)

Spam, also known as **unsolicited commercial e-mail** (UCE) or **bulk mail**, is electronic junk mail and can include solicitations, advertisements, or e-mail chain letters. The origin of the term *spam* is generally believed to have come from a song performed by the British comedy troupe, Monty Python, about Hormel's canned meat product, SPAM. In the song, an increasing number of people join in repeating the song's chorus: "Spam spam spam spam, spam spam spam spam, lovely spam, wonderful spam. ..." Just as in the song, e-mail spam is a tiresome repetition of meaningless text that eventually drowns out any other attempt at communication.

Besides wasting people's time and their computer disk space, spam can consume large amounts of Internet capacity. If one person sends a useless e-mail to a million people, that unsolicited mail consumes Internet resources for a few moments that would otherwise be available to other users. Once merely an annoyance, spam has become a major problem for companies. In addition to consuming bandwidth on company networks and space on e-mail servers, spam distracts employees who are trying to do their jobs and requires them to spend time deleting the unwanted messages. A considerable number of spam messages include content that can be offensive to recipients. Some employer's worry that their employees might sue them, arguing that the offensive spam they receive while working contributes to a hostile work environment, which can be grounds for harassment allegations. Spam costs businesses more than $40 billion per year in lost productivity and the expenses of dealing with it.

Search Engines

The Internet today contains billions of websites, which is analogous to a library having billions of books. This list of websites is getting longer every second. In such a situation, if one has to search for a particular topic, it becomes almost impossible to find it, as one is aware of possibly a few hundred sites. It is at this point that the search engines come to our rescue.

The first of all search engines was Archie, created in 1990 by Alan Emtage, a student at McGill University in Montreal. The author originally wanted to call the program "archives", but had to shorten it to comply with the Unix world standard of assigning programs and files short, cryptic names.

In 1990, there was no World Wide Web. Nonetheless, there was still an Internet, and many files were scattered all over the vast network. The primary method of storing and retrieving files was via FTP. Archie changed all that. It combined a script-based data gatherer, which fetched site listings of anonymous FTP files, with a regular expression matcher for retrieving file names matching a user query.

One of the first "full text" crawler-based search engines was WebCrawler, which came out in 1994. Unlike its predecessors, it let users search for any word in any webpage, which has become the standard for all major search engines since. It was also the first one to be widely known by the public. Also in 1994, Lycos (which started at Carnegie Mellon University) was launched and became a major commercial endeavour.

Soon after, many search engines appeared and vied for popularity. These included Magellan (search engine), Excite, Infoseek, Inktomi, Northern Light, and AltaVista. Yahoo! was among the most popular ways for people to find web pages of interest, but its search function operated on its web directory, rather than full-text copies of web pages. Information seekers could also browse the directory instead of doing a keyword-based search.

Around 2000, Google's search engine rose to prominence. The company achieved better results for many searches with an innovation called PageRank. This iterative algorithm ranks web pages based on the number and PageRank of other web sites and pages that link there, on the premise that good or desirable pages are linked to more than others. Google also maintained a minimalist interface to its search engine. In contrast, many of its competitors embedded a search engine in a web portal.

Microsoft first launched MSN Search in the fall of 1998 using search results from Inktomi. Microsoft's rebranded search engine, Bing, was launched on June 1, 2009. On July 29, 2009, Yahoo! and Microsoft finalized a deal in which Yahoo! Search would be powered by Microsoft Bing technology.

How Do the Search Engines Work

All search engines have what are called 'robots' or 'spiders', which spend their time going from link to link across the Internet. When they find a new site or an updated site, they will copy some information about the site back to their home database. It is this database, which is interrogated when you run a search. People can register their Web pages with search engines, which means that they usually get listed much more quickly than waiting for the spiders to come across them. They may have the ability to search by some or all of the following search methods:

- Keyword searching
- Concept-based searching
- Refining the search
- Relevancy ranking
- Meta tags

Keyword Searching

This is the most common form of text search on the Web. Most search engines do their text query and retrieval using keywords. Essentially, this means that the search engine pull out the pages containing the words it finds matching the query, and are significant. Words that are mentioned on the top of a document and words that are repeated several times throughout the document are more likely to be deemed important.

Concept-based Searching

Unlike keyword search systems, the concept-based search systems try to determine what you mean, not just what you say. In the best circumstances, a concept-based search returns hits on documents that are about the subject/theme you are exploring, even if the words in the document do not precisely match the words you enter into the query.

Excite is currently the best-known general-purpose search engine site on the Web that relies on concept-based searching. This is also known as clustering—which essentially means that words are examined in relation to other words found nearby.

For example, the word 'heart', when used in the medical/health context, is likely to appear with such words as coronary, artery, lung, stroke, cholesterol, pump, blood, attack, and arteriosclerosis. If the word 'heart' appears in a document with other words such as flowers, candy, love, passion, and valentine, a very different context is established, and the search engine returns links for the pages on the subject of romance.

Refining the Search

Most sites offer two different types of searches—"basic" and "advanced". In a "basic" search, you just enter a keyword without sifting through any pull-down menus of additional options. Depending on the engine though, "basic" searches can be quite complex.

Advanced search refining options differ from one search engine to another, but some of the possibilities include the ability to search on more than one word, to give more weight to one search term than you give to another, and to exclude words that may give wrong results. You may also be able to search on proper names, on phrases, and on words that are in close proximity to other search terms.

Many, but not all search engines allow you to use Boolean operators to refine your search. These are the logical terms AND, OR, NOT, and the so-called proximal locators, NEAR and FOLLOWED BY.

Boolean AND. This means that all the terms you specify must appear in the documents, i.e. "heart" AND "attack". You can use AND if you want to avoid other common irrelevant search results for your query.

Boolean OR. This means that at least one of the terms you specify must appear in the documents, i.e. bronchitis, "acute" OR "chronic". You can use OR if you do not want to miss any relevant search result.

Boolean NOT. This means that at least one of the terms you specify must not appear in the documents. You can use NOT if you anticipate results that would be totally off-base, i.e. nirvana AND Buddhism, NOT Cobain.

Capitalization. This is essential for searching on proper names of people, companies or products. Unfortunately, many words in English are used both as proper and common nouns—Bill, bill, Gates, gates, Oracle, oracle, Lotus, lotus, Digital, digital—the list is endless.

Search Engine Optimization (SEO)

SEO is the practice of increasing both the quality and quantity of website traffic, as well as getting better, exposure to your website or brand, through non-paid search engine results. It is about understanding what people are searching for online, the answers they are seeking, the words they are using, and the type of content they wish to consume. A lot of people search for things. That traffic can be extremely powerful for a business not only because there is a lot of traffic but also because there is a lot of very specific, high-intent traffic. The aim of SEO optimization is to get your website's name or page in the Search Engine Results Pages (SERPs). However, a lot of advertising happens in SERPs.

The world of search engine optimization is complex and ever-changing, but you can easily understand the basics, and even a small amount of knowledge can make a big difference. Search engines are answer machines. They search billions of pieces of content and evaluate thousands of factors to determine which content is most likely to answer your query. Search engines do all of this by discovering and cataloguing all available content on the Internet such as Web pages, PDFs, images, videos, etc. through a process known as *crawling and indexing*, and then ordering it by how well it matches the query in a process we refer to as *ranking*.

Google is responsible for most of the search engine traffic in the world. How does Google determine which pages to return in response to what people search for? How do you get all of this valuable traffic to your site?

Criteria for SEO[3]

Search engines process and store information they find in an index, a huge database of all the content they have discovered and deemed good enough to serve up to searchers.

When someone performs a search, search engines scour their index for highly relevant content and then orders that content in the hope of solving the searcher's query. This ordering of search results by relevance is known as *ranking*. In general, you can assume that the higher a website is ranked, the more relevant the search engine believes that site is to the query.

The criteria for SEO involve the following steps:

1. ***Crawl accessibility.*** Crawl accessibility is needed so that search engines can reach your site and index all the pages. Making sure your site gets crawled and indexed is a prerequisite to showing up in the SERPs. If you already have a website, it might be a good idea to start off by seeing how many of your pages are in the index. This will yield some great insights into whether Google is crawling and finding all the pages you want it to. Google is looking for pages that contain high-quality, relevant information about the searcher's query. They determine relevance by 'crawling' (or reading) your website's content and evaluating (algorithmically) whether that content is relevant to what the searcher is looking for, mostly based on the keywords it contains.

3. https://moz.com/beginners-guide-to-seo

They determine 'quality' by a number of means, but prominent among those is still the number and quality of other websites that link to your page and your site as a whole. Increasingly, additional elements are being weighed by Google's algorithm to determine where your site will rank, such as:

- How people engage with your website
- Your site's loading speed and 'mobile-friendliness'
- How much unique content you have

There are hundreds of ranking factors Google's algorithm considers in response to searches, and they are constantly updating and refining their process.

2. ***Compelling content on the website.*** The content should answer the searcher's query. Content is more than just words; it is anything meant to be consumed by searchers—there is video content, image content, and of course, text. If search engines are answer machines, content is the means by which the engines deliver those answers. Any time someone performs a search, there are thousands of possible results, so how do search engines decide which pages the searcher is going to find valuable? A big part of determining where your page will rank for a given query is how well the content on your page matches the query's intent. In other words, does this page match the words that were searched and help fulfill the task the searcher was trying to accomplish?

   Because of this focus on user satisfaction and task accomplishment, there is no strict benchmarks on how long your content should be, how many times it should contain a keyword, or what you put in your header tags. All those can play a role in how well a page performs in search, but the focus should be on the users who will be reading the content.

3. ***Keyword optimization.*** Keyword optimization is for attracting searchers and search engines. The first step in search engine optimization is really to determine what it is you are actually optimizing for. This means identifying the terms people are searching for (also known as 'keywords') based on which you want your website to get a rank in search engines like Google.

   The first factor to consider is how many people are actually searching for a given keyword. The more people there are searching for a keyword, the bigger the audience you stand to reach. Conversely, if no one is searching for a keyword, there is no audience available to find your content through search. The second factor is relevance. If a term is frequently searched for, that is considered to be relevant. The third factor is competition. This means understanding the relative competition (and likelihood to rank) for specific terms. A person wanting to optimize his website should consider the following aspects about his prospective customers:

   - What types of things are they interested in?
   - What problems do they have?
   - What type of language do they use to describe the things that they do, the tools that they use, etc.?
   - Who else are they buying things from?

Once you have answered these questions, you will have an initial 'seed list' of possible keywords and domains to help you get additional keyword ideas and to put some search volume and competition metrics around. Once you have taken the time to understand how your prospects talk and what they search for, have looked at the keywords driving traffic to your competitors and related sites, and have also looked at the terms driving traffic to your own site, you need to work to understand which terms you can conceivably rank for and where the best opportunities actually lie.

Once you have your keyword list, the next step is actually implementing your targeted keywords into your site's content. Each page on your site should be targeting a core term, and a 'basket' of related terms.

4. ***Great user experience.*** Information architecture refers to how you organize the pages on your website. The way that you organize your website and interlink between your pages can impact how various content on your site ranks in response to searches. The page should load fast.

   Being that well over half of all Web traffic today comes from mobile, it is safe to say that your website should be accessible and easy to navigate for mobile visitors. Responsive websites are designed to fit the screen of whatever type of device your visitors are using.

5. ***Share-worthy content.*** The more popular and important a site is, the more weight the links from that site carry. A site like Wikipedia, for example, has thousands of diverse sites linking to it. This indicates it provides lots of expertise, has cultivated authority, and is trusted among those other sites.

   Creating unique, high-quality resources is no easy task, but it is well worth the effort. High-quality content that is promoted in the right ways can be widely shared. It can help to create pieces that have the following traits:

   - Elicits strong emotions (joy, sadness, etc.)
   - Something new, or at least communicated in a new way
   - Visually appealing
   - Addresses a timely need or interest

Creating a resource like this is a great way to attract a lot of links to one page. You could also create a highly-specific resource that targeted a handful of websites. You might see a higher rate of success, but that approach is not so scalable.

Users who see this kind of unique content often want to share it with friends, and bloggers/tech-savvy Webmasters who see it will often do so through links. These high-quality, editorially earned votes are invaluable to building trust, authority, and rankings potential.

Since Google's algorithm is still largely based on links, having a number of high-quality links to your site is obviously incredibly important in driving search traffic—you can do all the work you want on on-page and technical SEO. If you do not have links to your site, you will not show up in search results listings.

The process of creating and promoting content that will get you links and social shares is a labor-intensive one. Once again, you will find more detailed step-by-step guides to the various aspects of content marketing below, and there are a lot of different ways to effectively create content, help it to get discovered, and rank well in search results.

Software Agents

E-commerce is changing the way business is being done in the Information Age. To gain a competitive edge, businesses are in need of new computational models and infrastructure. To address this need, businesses are developing a model of inter-organizational e-commerce. According to this model, different users are represented by autonomous software agents interconnected via the Internet. The agents act on behalf of their human users/organizations to perform information gathering tasks, such as locating and accessing information from various sources, filtering unwanted information, and providing decision support.

Information Overload

The information overload can be illustrated with the example of Sun Microsystems which reports that employees receive on an average over 100 e-mail messages a day. For Sun, that is a million and a quarter messages a day. The content of the Web grows by an estimated 170,000 pages daily. Also, surveys of data warehouse projects reveal that a number of the larger retail and telecommunications companies have multiple terabyte databases.

The Web has provided end users with 'point-and-click' applications that enable them to browse and navigate through gigabytes and terabytes of data to their heart's content. Unfortunately, end users are often overwhelmed. They spend most of their time navigating and sorting through the data, spending little time interpreting and even less time actually doing something about what they find. The end result is that much of the data we gather goes unused.

Value of Software Agents in a Networked World

An agent can be defined as one that acts or exerts power. It can be an autonomous, (preferably) intelligent, collaborative, adaptive, computational entity. Here, intelligence is the ability to infer and execute needed actions, and seek and incorporate relevant information, given certain goals.

Intelligent Agent (IA) is an agent, which has the capability to deal with new and trying situations. IA must have autonomous and rational properties. Intelligent Agent is a software program that uses agent communication protocols to exchange information for automatic problem solving. IA might have services capabilities, ability for autonomous decision, and commitments features. Some other criteria such as cooperation, negotiation, and conflict resolution make IA more personalized.

The range of firms and universities actively pursuing agent technology is quite broad, and the list is ever-growing. It includes small non-household names (e.g. Icon, Edify and Verity), medium-size organizations (e.g. Carnegie Mellon University (CMU), General Magic,

Massachusetts Institute of Technology (MIT), the University of London), and the real big multinationals (e.g. Alcatel, Apple, AT&T, BT, Daimler-Benz, HP, IBM, Microsoft, Oracle, Sharp). Clearly, these companies are by no means completely homogeneous, especially if others such as Reuters and Dow Jones are appended to this list.

Software agents have synonyms including knowbots (i.e. knowledge-based robots), softbots (software robots), taskbots (task-based robots), userbots, robots, personal agents, autonomous agents, and personal assistants. There are some good reasons for having such synonyms. Firstly, the agents come in many physical guises: for example, those that inhabit the physical world, for example, a factory, are called robots; those that inhabit vast computer networks are sometimes referred to as softbots; those that perform specific tasks are sometimes called taskbots; and autonomous agents refer typically to mobile agents or robots which operate in dynamic and uncertain environments. Secondly, agents can play many roles, say, personal assistants or knowbots, which have expert knowledge in some specific domain. Furthermore, due to the multiplicity of roles that agents can play, there is now a plethora of adjectives which precede the word agent: search agents, report agents, presentation agents, navigation agents, role-playing agents, management agents, search and retrieval agents, domain-specific agents, development agents, analysis and design agents, testing agents, packaging agents, and help agents.

A major advantage of employing software agents with intranet, the Internet, and extranet applications is that they are able to assist in locating and filtering all the data. They save time by making decisions about what is relevant to the user. They are able to sort through the network and the various databases effortlessly and with unswerving attention to detail to extract the best data. They are not limited to hard (quantitative) data, but can also be useful in obtaining soft data about new trends that may cause unanticipated changes and opportunities in local or even global markets. With an agent at work, the competent user's decision-making ability is enhanced with information rather than paralyzed by too much input. Agents are Artificial Intelligence's answer to a need created by internetworked computers.

Information access and navigation are today's major applications of software agents in the intranet, the Internet, and the extranet worlds, but there are other reasons why this technology is expected to grow rapidly.

1. ***Mundane personal activity.*** In a fast-paced society, time-strapped people need new ways to minimize the time spent on routine personal tasks such as shopping for groceries or travel planning, so that they can devote more time to professional activities.
2. ***Search and retrieval.*** It is not possible to directly manipulate a distributed database system in an e-commerce setting with millions of data objects. Users will have to relegate the task of searching and cost comparison to agents. These agents will perform the cumbersome, time-consuming tasks of searching databases, retrieving and filtering information, and delivering it back to the user.
3. ***Repetitive office activity.*** There is a pressing need to automate tasks performed by administrative and clerical personnel in functions such as sales or customer support, to reduce labour costs and increase office productivity. Today, labour costs are estimated to be as much as 60 per cent of the total cost of information delivery.

4. ***Decision support.*** There is a need for increased support for tasks performed by knowledge workers, especially in the decision-making area. Timely and knowledgeable decisions made by these professionals, greatly increase their effectiveness and the success of their business in the marketplace.

5. ***Domain experts.*** It is advisable to model costly expertise and make it widely available. Examples of expert software agents could be models of real-world agents such as translators, lawyers, diplomats, union negotiators, and stockbrokers.

To date, the list of tasks to which commercially available agents and research prototypes have been applied includes advising, alerting, broadcasting, browsing, critiquing, distributing, enlisting, empowering, explaining, filtering, guiding, identifying, matching, monitoring, navigating, negotiating, organizing, presenting, querying, reminding, reporting, retrieving, scheduling, searching, securing, soliciting, sorting, storing, suggesting, summarizing, teaching, translating, and watching.

On the whole, the software agents make the networked world less forbidding, save time by reducing the effort required to locate and retrieve data, and improve productivity by off-loading a variety of mundane, tedious and mindless tasks.

A Typology of Agents[4]

Firstly, the agents may be classified by their mobility, i.e. by their ability to move around some networks. They can thus be called *static* or *mobile* agents.

Secondly, they may be classed as either *deliberative* or *reactive*. Deliberative agents derive from the deliberative thinking paradigm: the agents possess an internal, symbolic, reasoning model and they engage in planning and negotiation in order to achieve coordination with other agents.

Thirdly. agents may be classified along several ideal and primary attributes which they need to exhibit. Some of them are: autonomy, learning and cooperation. We appreciate that any such list would be contentious. Hence, we are not claiming that this is a necessary or a sufficient set. *Autonomy* refers to the principle that agents can operate on their own without any need for human guidance, even though this would sometimes be invaluable. Hence, agents have individual internal states and goals, and they act in such a manner as to meet its goals on behalf of its user. A key element of their autonomy is their proactiveness, i.e. their ability to take the initiative rather than act simply in response to their environment. Cooperation with other agents is of great importance because it is the reason for having multiple agents in the first place in contrast to having just one. In order to cooperate, agents need to possess a social ability, i.e. the ability to interact with other agents and possibly humans via some communication language. Having said this, it is not possible for agents to coordinate their actions without cooperation. Lastly, for agent systems to be truly smart, they would have to *learn* as they react and/or interact with their external environment. In our view, agents are (or should be) disembodied bits of intelligence. Though we will not attempt to define what intelligence is, we maintain that a key attribute of any intelligent being is its ability to

4. www.sce.carletan.ca/netmessage/docs/agentsoverview/ao.html.

learn. Learning may also take the form of increased performance over time. We use these three minimal characteristics in Figure 3.10 to derive four types of agents to include in our typology: *collaborative agents, collaborative learning agents, interface agents* and *truly smart agents*.

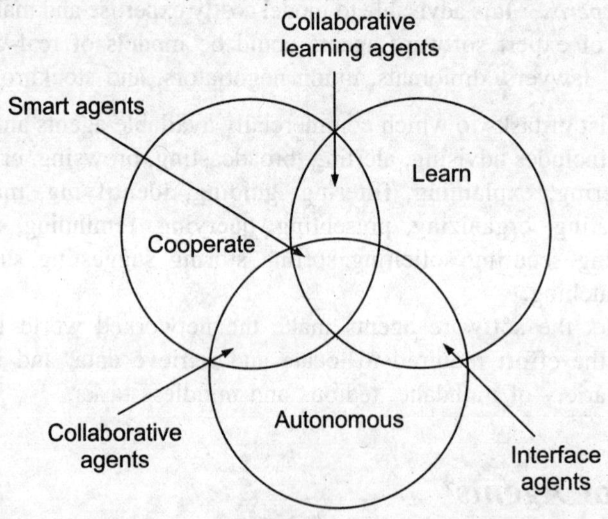

Figure 3.10 A partial view of agent typology.

A Panoramic Overview of the Different Agent Types

Let us now have an overview of the different agent types in Figure 3.11.

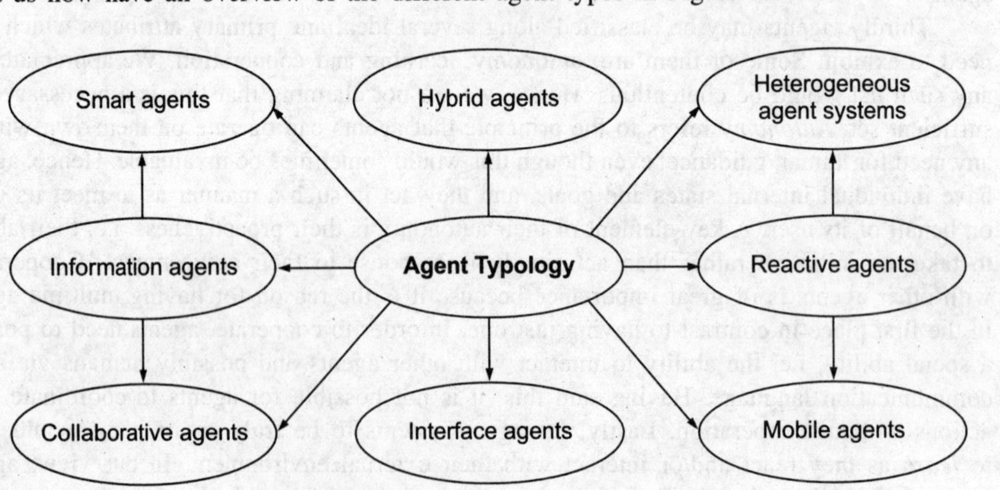

Figure 3.11 Classification of software agents.

Collaborative Agents

Collaborative agents emphasize autonomy and cooperation (with other agents) in order to perform tasks for their owners. They may learn, but this aspect is not typically a major emphasis of their operation. In order to have a coordinated set-up of collaborative agents, they may have to negotiate and reach mutually acceptable agreements on some matters.

In brief, the general characteristics of these agents include autonomy, social ability, responsiveness and proactiveness. Hence, they are able to act rationally and autonomously in an open and time-constrained multi-agent environment. They tend to be static, large, coarse-grained agents. They may be benevolent, rational, truthful, or some combination of these, or none. Typically, most recently implemented collaborative agents do not perform any complex learning, though they may or may not perform limited parametric or rote learning.

The motivation for having collaborative agent systems may include one or several of the following:

1. To solve problems that are too large for a centralized single agent to do due to resource limitations or the sheer risk of having one centralized system.
2. To allow interconnecting and interoperation of multiple existing legacy systems, e.g. expert systems, decision support systems, and so forth.
3. To provide solutions to inherently distributed problems, e.g. distributed sensor networks or air-traffic control.
4. To provide solutions in the form of distributed information sources, e.g. for distributed online information sources, it is natural to adopt a distributed and collaborative agent approach.
5. To provide solutions where the expertise is distributed, e.g. in healthcare provisioning.
6. To enhance modularity (which reduces complexity), speed (due to parallelism), reliability (due to redundancy), flexibility (i.e. new tasks are composed more easily due to the more modular organization) and reusability at the knowledge level (hence shareability of resources).
7. To research into other issues, e.g. understanding interactions among human societies.

Interface Agents

Interface agents emphasize autonomy and learning in order to perform tasks for their owners. The key metaphor underlying interface agents is that of a personal assistant who is collaborating with the user in the same work environment. Note the subtle emphasis and distinction between collaborating with the user and collaborating with other agents as is the case with collaborative agents. Collaborating with a user may not require an explicit agent communication language as is required when collaborating with other agents.

The user's agent acts as an autonomous personal assistant which cooperates with the user in accomplishing some task in the application. As for learning, an interface agent learns typically to assist its user better in four ways: by observing and imitating the user (i.e. learning from the user); receiving positive and negative feedback from the user (learning from the user); receiving explicit instructions from the user (learning from the user); and asking other agents for advice (i.e. learning from peers).

Mobile Agents

Mobile agents are computational software processes capable of roaming Wide Area Networks (WANs) such as the WWW, interacting with foreign hosts, gathering information on behalf of their owners, and coming back home, having performed the duties set by their users. These duties may range from flight reservation to managing a telecommunications network. However, mobility is neither a necessary nor a sufficient condition for agenthood. Mobile agents are autonomous and cooperate, albeit differently from collaborative agents. For example, they may cooperate or communicate with one agent making the location of some of its internal objects and methods known to other agents. By doing this, an agent exchanges data or information with other agents without necessarily giving all its information away.

The need for mobile agents includes the following anticipated benefits:

1. ***Reduced communication costs.*** There may be a lot of raw information that needs to be examined to determine its relevance. Transferring this raw information can be very time-consuming and may even clog the networks. Imagine having to transfer many images just to pick out one. It is much more natural to get your agents to "go" to that location, do a local search/pruning and transfer only the chosen compressed image back across the network. It obviates the need for costly network connections between remote computers as required in Remote Procedure Calls (RPC). It provides a much cheaper alternative as we pay increasingly for network bandwidth and time, such as CompuServe users already do. In the future, we would almost certainly be charged by bytes for bandwidth, though others maintain that the bandwidth would be free.

2. ***Limited local resources.*** The processing power and storage on the local machine may be very limited (perhaps only for processing and storing the results of a search), thereby necessitating the use of mobile agents.

3. ***Easier coordination.*** It may be simpler to coordinate a number of remote and independent requests and just locally collate all the results.

4. ***Asynchronous computing.*** You can set off your mobile agents and do something else and the results will be back in your mailbox, say, at some later time. They may operate when you are not even connected.

5. ***Natural development environment.*** It provides a natural development environment for implementing free market trading services. New services can come and go dynamically and much more flexible services may co-exist with inferior ones, providing more choices for consumers.

6. ***A flexible distributed computing architecture.*** Mobile agents provide a unique distributed computing architecture which functions differently from the static set-ups. It provides for an innovative way of doing distributed computation.

7. ***Rethinking on design process.*** Mobile agents represent an opportunity for a radical and an attractive rethinking of the design process in general. Following on from the latter, it turns the conventional design process on its head, and some truly innovative products should/would emerge out of mobile agent technology.

Information/Internet Agents

Information agents have come about because of the sheer demand for tools to help us manage the explosive growth of information we are currently experiencing, and which we will continue to experience henceforth. Information agents perform the role of managing, manipulating or collating information from many distributed sources.

Interface or collaborative agents started out quite distinct, but with the explosion of the WWW and their applicability to this vast WAN, there is now a significant degree of overlapping. This is inevitable, especially since information or Internet agents are defined using different criteria. They are defined by what 'they do', in contrast to collaborative or interface agents which are defined by what 'they are'. Many of the interface agents built at the MIT Media Labs, for example, are autonomous and learned, but they have been employed in WWW-based roles; hence, they are in a sense, information agents.

Similarly, it is also true that we are drowning in data, being at the same time, starved of information. The underlying hypothesis of information agents is that, somehow they can ameliorate, but certainly not eliminate, this specific problem of information overload and the general issue of information management in this information era.

The motivation for developing information/Internet agents is at least twofold. First, there is simply a yearning need/demand for tools to manage such information explosion. Everyone on the WWW would benefit from them in just the same way as they benefit from search engines such as Google, Spiders, Lycos, or Webcrawlers.

Second, there are vast financial benefits to be gained. Recall that Netscape Corporation grew from relative obscurity to a billion dollar company almost overnight—and a Netscape or Internet Explorer client generally offers browsing capabilities, albeit with a few add-ons.

Information agents have varying characteristics: they may be static or mobile; they may be non-cooperative or social; and they may or may not learn. Hence, there is no standard mode to their operation. Internet agents could be mobile, i.e. they may be able to traverse the WWW, gather information and report what they retrieve to a home location. However, this is not the norm as yet. Information agents may be associated with some particular indexer(s), e.g. a Spider. A Spider is an indexer, able to search in depth, the WWW, and store the topology of the WWW in a database management system (DBMS) and the full index of URLs in the WAIS. Other search/indexing engines or spiders such as Lycos or Webcrawler can be used similarly to build up the index. Indeed, there are currently more than twenty spiders on the WWW.

The user information agent, which has been requested to collate information on some subject, issues various search requests to one or several URL search engines to meet the request. Some of this search may even be done locally if it has a local cache. The information is collated and sent back to the user.

Reactive Software Agents

Reactive agents represent a special category of agents which do not possess internal, symbolic models of their environments; instead they act/respond in a stimulus-response manner to the present state of the environment in which they are embedded. However, the most important points to be noted about the reactive agents are not these (i.e. languages, theories or architectures), but the fact that the agents are relatively simple and they interact with other agents in basic ways. Nevertheless, complex patterns of behaviour emerge from these interactions when the ensemble of agents is viewed globally.

Traditional Artificial Intelligence (AI) has staked most of its bets on the latter, which holds that the necessary and sufficient condition for a physical system to demonstrate intelligent action is that it is a physical symbol system. On the contrary, the physical grounding hypothesis challenges this long-held view, arguing that it is flawed fundamentally, and that it imposes severe limitations on symbolic AI-based systems. This new hypothesis states that in order to build a system that is intelligent, it is necessary to have representations grounded in the physical world.

The key benefit which motivates the reactive agents is the hope that they would be more robust and fault tolerant than other agent-based systems, e.g. an agent may be lost but without any catastrophic effects. Other benefits include flexibility and adaptability, in contrast to the inflexibility, slow response times and brittleness of classical AI systems. Another benefit, it is hoped, is that this type of work would address the frame problem which has so far proved intractable with traditional AI techniques such as non-monotonic reasoning.

Other challenges include the following:

1. Expanding the range and number of applications based on reactive agents.
2. Yearning need for a clearer methodology to facilitate the development of reactive software agent applications. This may or may not require the development of more associated theories, architectures and languages. Much of the current approaches are on the basis of trial and error.
3. Issues such as scalability and performance need to be addressed, though these are unlikely to be important until clearer methodologies are developed and evaluated.

Hybrid Agents

So far, we have reviewed five types of agents: collaborative, interface, mobile, Internet and reactive agents. The debates as to which of them is better are rather academic, and frankly, sterile, rather too early to get into. Since each type has (or promises) its own strengths and deficiencies, the trick (as always) is to maximize the strengths and minimize the deficiencies of the most relevant technique for your particular purpose. Frequently, one way of doing this is to adopt a hybrid approach which brings together the strengths of both the deliberative and reactive paradigms. Hence, hybrid agents refer to those whose constitution is a combination of two or more agent philosophies within a singular agent. These philosophies include a mobile philosophy, an interface agent philosophy and collaborative agent philosophy.

Hybrid agent architectures are still relatively few in number but the cause for having them is overwhelming. There are usually three typical criticisms of hybrid architectures in general. Firstly, hybridism usually translates to ad hoc or unprincipled designs with all its related problems. Secondly, many hybrid architectures tend to be very application-specific. Thirdly, the theory which undermines the hybrid systems is not usually specified. Therefore, we see the challenges for hybrid agents research quite similar to those identified for reactive agents. In addition to these, we would also expect to see the hybrids of philosophies other than those of reactive/deliberative ones. For example, there is scope for more hybrids within a singular agent: combining the interface agent and mobile agent philosophies, which would enable mobile agents to be able to harness features of typical interface agents; or some other combination.

Heterogeneous Agent Systems

Heterogeneous agent systems, unlike hybrid systems described in the preceding section, refer to an integrated set-up of at least two or more agents which belong to two or more different agent classes. A heterogeneous agent system may also contain one or more hybrid agents.

The essential argument is that the world abounds with a rich diversity of software products, providing a wide range of services for a similarly wide range of domains. Though these programs work in isolation, there is an increasing demand to have them interoperate—hopefully, in such a manner that they provide added value as an ensemble than they do individually. The hypothesis is that this is plausible. Indeed, a new domain called agent-based software engineering has been invented in order to facilitate the interoperation of miscellaneous software agents. A key requirement for interoperation amongst heterogeneous agents is having an Agent Communication Language (ACL) through which the different software agents can communicate with each other. The potential benefits for having the heterogeneous agent technology are as follows:

1. Standalone applications can be made to provide value-added services in order to participate and interoperate in cooperative heterogeneous set-ups.
2. The software legacy problem may be ameliorated since it could obviate the need for costly software rewrites, as they are given new leases of life by their interoperation with other systems. At the very least, the heterogeneous agent technology may lessen the blow or effect of routine software maintenance, upgrades or rewrites.
3. Agent-based software engineering provides a radical new approach to software design, implementation and maintenance in general, and software interoperability in particular. Its ramifications (e.g. moving from passive modules in traditional software engineering to proactive agent-controlled ones) would only be clear as this methodology and its tools become clearer.

Smart Agents

Smart agents are those agents which can learn, cooperate, and are autonomous. In a way, all agents are smart. But for our understanding, when these three qualities are combined in an agent, we call it smart.

Software Agents at Work

Auction watchers, comparison shoppers, personal web spiders, newshounds, site recommenders, and portfolio assistants are some of the agents operating in today's e-commerce world. It does not stop with these. The pace at which existing and experimental agent technologies are being applied to the virtual world has quickened. This is evident from the papers presented in conferences[5] on software agents. A good place to monitor new applications of software agents and to keep an eye on both their immediate and long-term future is the Bot Spot website (*www.botspot.com*).

The use of the Internet has accelerated at an unprecedented pace. However, its effective use by humans or decision support machine systems has been hampered by some dominant characteristics of the Infosphere. First, information available from the Internet is unorganized, multi-modal, and distributed on server sites all over the world. Second, the number and variety of data sources and services is dramatically increasing every day. Furthermore, the availability, type and reliability of information services are constantly changing. Third, the same piece of information can be accessed from a variety of different information sources. Fourth, information is ambiguous and possibly erroneous due to the dynamic nature of the information sources and potential information updating and maintenance problems. Therefore, information is becoming increasingly more difficult for a person or machine system to collect, filter, evaluate, and use in problem solving. As a result, the problem of locating information sources, accessing, filtering, and integrating information in support of decision making, as well as coordinating information retrieval and problem solving efforts of information sources and decision-making systems has become a very critical task. Intelligent Software Agents are being used to address these challenges.

Most of the current agent-oriented approaches have focused on what we call *interface agents*, which is a single agent with simple knowledge and problem solving capabilities, whose main task is information filtering to alleviate the user's cognitive overload. Another type of agent is the *SoftBot,* a single agent with general knowledge that performs a wide range of user-delegated information-finding tasks. Unless the agent has beyond the state-of-the-art learning capabilities, it would need considerable reprogramming to deal with the appearance of new agents and information sources in the environment. Because of the complexity of the information finding and filtering task, and the large amount of information, the required processing would overwhelm a single agent. So a proposed solution is to use multi-agent computer systems to access, filter, evaluate, and integrate this information. Such multi-agent systems can compartmentalize specialized task knowledge, organize themselves to avoid processing bottlenecks, and can be built expressly to deal with dynamic changes in the agent and information-source landscape. In addition, Multiple Intelligent Coordinating Agents are ideally suited to the predominant characteristics of the Infosphere, such as the heterogeneity of the information sources, and the presence of multiple users with related information needs.

Internet Standards and Specifications

Many standards are in place on the Web to enable information to be transferred the way it is. The Internet is not a single, unified network, and so it is not surprising that it is not controlled by a single body. Although there are standards, there is no authority to enforce them. If any organization deviates from the collective standards, it loses the benefits of global connectivity. Groups such as the InterNIC do exist to carry out central management

5. http://agents.media.mit-edu/publications/

functions for the Internet. The ultimate authority for the technical direction of the Internet rests with the Internet Society (ISOC). This professional society is concerned with the growth and evolution of the worldwide Internet, with the way in which the Internet is and can be used, and with the social, political and technical issues. It is a voluntary organization whose goal is to promote global information exchange. The structure of the Internet governance hierarchy is shown in Figure 3.12.

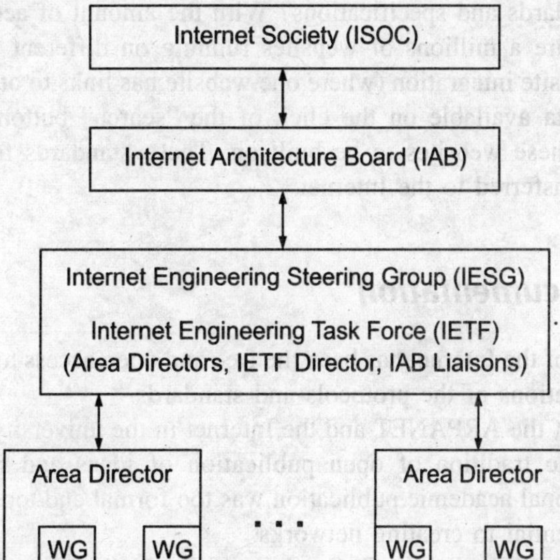

Figure 3.12 Internet administrative structure.

The four groups in the structure are the ISOC and its board of trustees, the IAB, the IESG, and the IETF. The area directors work with their working groups (WGs).

ISOC appoints a council, the IAB that has responsibility for the technical management and direction of the Internet. The IAB is responsible for overall architectural considerations in the Internet. It also serves to adjudicate disputes in the standards process and is responsible for setting the technical direction, establishing standards, and resolving problems in the Internet. The IAB also keeps track of various network addresses.

The IAB is supported by the IETF, the protocol engineering and development arm of the Internet. It is a large, open, international community of network designers, operators, vendors and researchers concerned with the evolution of the Internet architecture and the smooth operation of the Internet.

The IETF is divided into eight functional areas such as:

1. Applications
2. Network management
3. Operational requirement
4. Routing
5. Security

6. Transport
7. User services
8. Internet

The Evolution of Standards and Specifications

Why do we need standards and specifications? With the amount of activity going on in the Internet, where there are a millions of websites running on different platforms, with cross platform and cross website integration (where one website has links to other websites) forming the crux of all the data available on the click of the "search" button, there is a need for certain standards for these websites to be built on. These standards form the basis for the information that is transferred to the Internet.

The Role of Documentation[6]

A key to rapid growth of the Internet has been the free and open access to the basic documents, especially the specifications of the protocols and standards.

The beginnings of the ARPANET and the Internet in the university research community promoted the academic tradition of open publication of ideas and results. However, the normal cycle of traditional academic publication was too formal and too slow for the dynamic exchange of ideas essential to creating networks.

In 1969, a key step was taken by S. Crocker (then at UCLA) in establishing the Request for Comments (RFC) series of notes. These memos were intended to be an informal, fast distribution way to share ideas with other network researchers. At first, the RFCs were printed on paper and distributed via snail mail. As the FTP came into use, the RFCs were prepared as online files and accessed via FTP. Now of course, the RFCs are easily accessible via the World Wide Web at dozens of sites around the world.

The task of the RFCs was to create a positive feedback loop, with ideas or proposals presented in one RFC triggering another with additional ideas, and so on. When some consensus (or at least a consistent set of ideas) comes together, a specification document is prepared. Such a specification is then used as the base for implementation by various research teams.

Internet Service Provider (ISP)

The US Government's 1991 decision to end subsidizing the NSFNET backbone beginning in 1995, sparked a massive restructuring aimed at shaping the Internet into a faster and a more productive tool for the business. The InterNIC compilation of public access dial-up providers listed 80 vendors in December 1993. A year later, the list cited more than 1500 providers. Figure 3.13 illustrates how the providers work.

---

6. http://www.isoc.org/internet/history/brief.html

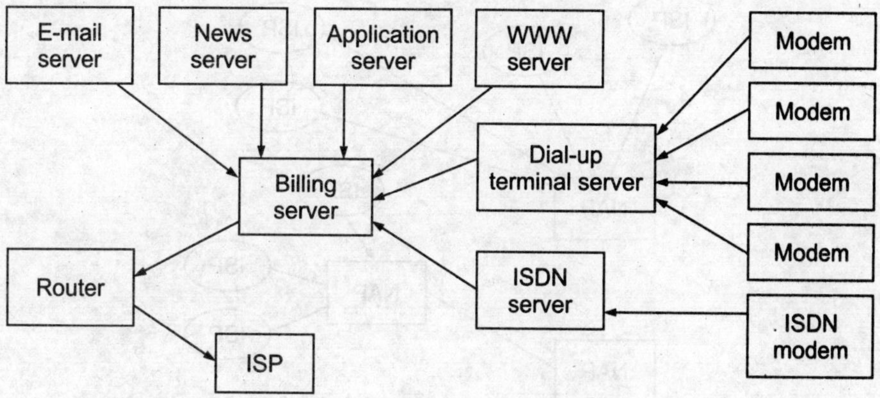

Figure 3.13 Architecture of public access providers.

Commercialization of the Internet has taken place in two spheres: commercialization of users and commercialization of ISPs. At first, companies that accessed the Internet through the existing non-profit mid-level networks were offered a lower level of membership than the academic members. As restrictions were dismantled, commercial use of the Internet became more common. As soon as the commercialization was announced, ISPs came into existence to provide paid access to the various Internet applications and resources for both companies and individuals. Established telecommunications, cable and commercial online companies began to offer this service. Soon, others followed.

From a physical standpoint, the Internet is a network of thousands of interconnected networks. Included among the interconnected networks are:

1. The interconnected backbones that have international reach
2. A multitude of access/delivery sub-networks
3. Thousands of private and institutional networks connecting various organizational servers and containing much of the information of interest. The backbones are run by Network Service Providers (NSPs). The delivery subnetworks are provided by the local and regional ISPs (see Figure 3.14). The ISPs exchange data with the NSPs at the Network Access Points (NAPs).

When a user issues a request on the Internet from a computer, the request traverses an ISP network, moves over one or more of the backbones and across another ISP network, to the computer containing the information of interest. The response to the request follows a similar path. For any given request and associated response, there is no preset route. In fact, the request and response are each broken into packets, and the packets can follow different paths. The paths traversed by the packets are determined by special computers called *routers*. The routers have updateable maps of the networks on the Internet, that enable them to determine the paths for the packets.

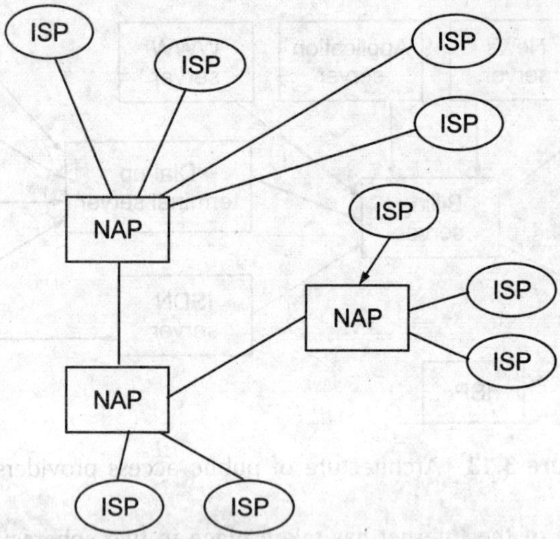

Figure 3.14 NAPs and ISPs.

Markup Languages and the Web

Web pages can include many elements, such as graphics, photographs, sound clips, and even small programs that run in the Web browser. Each of these elements is stored on the Web server as a separate file. The most important parts of a Web page, however, are the structure of the page and the text that makes up the main part of the page. The page structure and text are stored in a text file that is formatted, or marked up, using a text markup language. **A text markup language** specifies a set of tags that are inserted into the text. These **markup tags**, also called **tags**, provide formatting instructions that Web client software can understand. The Web client software uses those instructions as it renders the text and page elements contained in the other files into the Web page that appears on the screen of the client computer.

The markup language most commonly used on the Web is HTML, which is a subset of a much older and far more complex text markup language called **Standard Generalized Markup Language (SGML)**. Figure 3.15 shows how HTML, XML, and XHTML have descended from the original SGML specification. SGML was used for many years by the publishing industry to create documents that needed to be printed in various formats and that were revised frequently. In addition to its role as a markup language, SGML is a **meta language**, which is a language that can be used to define other languages. Another markup language that was derived from SGML for use on the Web is **Extensible Markup Language (XML)**, which is increasingly used to mark up information that companies share with each other over the Internet. The X in XML comes from the word extensible; you might see the word extensible shown as extensible. XML is also a meta language because users can create their own markup elements that extend the usefulness of XML (which is why it is called an "extensible" language).

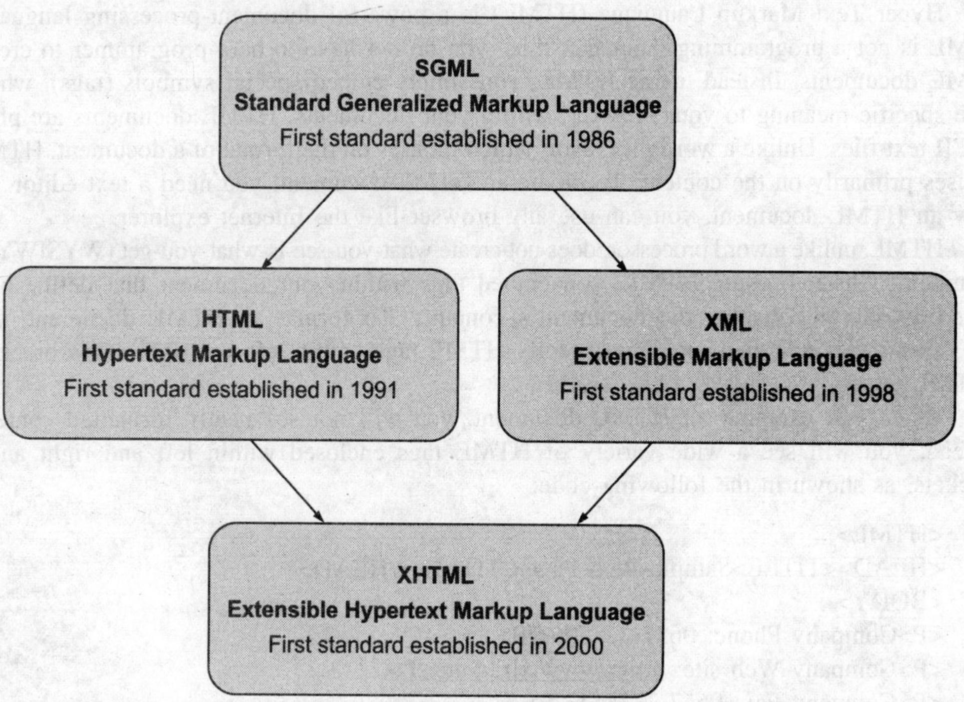

Figure 3.15 Development of markup languages.

The World Wide Web Consortium (W3C), a not-for-profit group that maintains standards for the Web has presented its first draft form of XML in 1996; the W3C issued its first formal version recommendation in 1998. Thus, it is a much newer markup language than HTML. In 2000, the W3C released the first version of a recommendation for a new markup language called *Extensible Hypertext Markup Language* (XHTML), which is a reformulation of HTML version 4.0 as an XML application. The Online Companion includes a link to the W3C XHTML Version 1.0 Specification.

Hypertext allows the visual blurring of boundaries, renaming whole nodes and links to bring all the texts you receive into an indistinguishable aggregate of nodes and links. There would be no one central individual text with the others relegated to comments on, yet the whole could also be read as an integrated, communal discourse not co-authored in the traditional way, but conjoined by the editor's activities. The natural mode of hypertext is compilation rather than linear creation. Hypertext documents are chiefly made up of links to other documents, or other lists of links.[7] Every file, site, movie or sound file, or anything on the Web has a unique URL to identify in which computer it is located, where it is within that computer, and its specific file name. Every Hypertext link on every Web page in the world contains one of the URLs. When a link on a Web page is clicked, a request is sent to retrieve the unique document on some computer in the world that is uniquely identified by that URL. A whole cluster of internationally accepted standards (such as TCP/IP and HTML) make possible this global information retrieval phenomenon that transcends all political and language boundaries.

7. http://www.hanover.edu/philos/ejournal/archive/v6n3/brent/edintro.html#taylor.

Hyper Text Markup Language (HTML) is a powerful document-processing language. HTML is not a programming language; thus, you do not have to be a programmer to create HTML documents. Instead, using HTML, you simply embed special symbols (tags), which have specific meaning to your browser, within your documents. HTML documents are plain ASCII text files. Unlike a word processor, which focuses on the format of a document, HTML focuses primarily on the content. To create an HTML document, you need a text editor. To view an HTML document, you can use any browser like the Internet explorer.

HTML, unlike a word processor, does not create what-you-see-is-what-you-get (WYSIWYG) documents. Instead, using HTML, you embed tags within your document that define how your browser will display the document's contents. To format an HTML document, you use various tags and elements. You specify HTML tags within left and right angle brackets <HTML tag>.

When you examine an HTML document, you will not see neatly formatted content. Instead, you will see a wide variety of HTML tags enclosed within left and right angle brackets, as shown in the following code:

```
<HTML>
<HEAD><TITLE>Sample Web Page</TITLE></HEAD>
<BODY>
<P>Company Phone: 0657-225506</P>
<P>Company Web site: http://www.xlri.com</P>
<P>Company Fax: 0657-227814</P>
<P>Human Relations: HR@xlri.com</P>
</BODY>
</HTML>
```

If you view the above file in a browser, the screenshot shown in Figure 3.16 will appear.

JavaScript

JavaScript is an object-based scripting language designed primarily for the authors constructing HTML documents for viewing under Netscape Navigator, Internet Explorer and other such browsers. It runs both on the server and the client side. On the client side, it can be used to write programs that are executed by a Web browser within the context of a Web page. On the server side, it can be used to write Web server programs that can process information submitted by a Web browser and then used to update the browser's display accordingly.

It is a cross-platform scripting language developed by Netscape. Client-side JavaScript is typically executed in a browser that supports the language. It is an interpreted object-oriented language that can be included in HTML pages. You can access a number of elements in your HTML page and manipulate them using JavaScript. This helps in the creation of dynamic HTML pages capable of responding to user events like mouse clicks, key presses, selection of elements in a form, and so on.

Different components of an HTML page (including elements belonging to a form) are represented as objects that can be accessed by JavaScript. These objects are organized in a hierarchy that begins at the top with the window object. A window represents a browser window or frame. Objects have properties and methods associated with them, and the properties may actually be references to other objects contained in an object. A window thus has several properties such as frames and a history property. Other properties contain information about the window itself, for example, its height and width.

Objects may also have methods associated with them. For instance, a window object has an **alert** method that can be used for throwing an Alert dialog box, a **moveTo()** method that allows you to move the window, a **resizeTo()** method that allows you to change the size of the window, and so on.

Objects can also have events with associated event handlers. In the case of a window, therefore, when the window is loaded, a load event occurs, which can be handled by a user-defined function. The "onLoad" **event** handler is used to specify the function that will handle this. Similarly you can provide your own functions to handle events like unload, window move, window resize, etc.

Using JavaScript you can, for example:

- Create a form that lets the user click on a displayed map of India to obtain the current average housing cost vis-á-vis the per capita income for each state.
- Design a Web page that automatically displays a different thought-provoking quotation at the top of the page every time a page is accessed.
- Add a random number wheel to your Web page that spins at the push of a button, and then, based on the number it stops on, teleports the viewer to a particular website from an extensive list of your favorite sites.
- Construct an online form that lets users determine the closest city where certain required merchandise is available.
- Build the front-end of a multimedia playback device that uses Java applets to playback different types of files, including shockwave animation files, and real audio sound files.
- Create a fortune-telling page that collects some information about the viewer and then displays a personalized set of predictions about that person's life and prospects.
- Design an online tutorial that shows other people how to write scripts using tools like JavaScript.

JavaScript supports a number of constructs found in languages like C. Here are some commonly used JavaScript statements: break, continue, do ... while, for, function, if ... else, return, var, etc.

EXAMPLE

```
<HTML><HEAD></HEAD>
<BODY>

This is static text<P>
        <SCRIPT LANGUAGE="Javascript">
            document.write('Random number:' + Math.random());
        </SCRIPT>
    </BODY>
    </HTML>
```

This is a very simple example containing some JavaScript code inside the BODY tag of the HTML file. JavaScript code is enclosed by <SCRIPT LANGUAGE=" "JavaScript"> and </SCRIPT> tags.

When this page is displayed, there are two lines in it. The first is "This is static text"; the second displays a random number. The difference is that while the first line is a regular static HTML element, the second line is generated as a result of execution of the JavaScript code. When the browser encounters the <SCRIPT> tag, it interprets and executes the code. In this case, we are using the "write" method of document. The **write()** function can be used to write data to this document. We are also using the **random** function in math for generating a random number.

This small script has in essence made the HTML page dynamic. If you reload it, you will see a different random number. The reason for this is that the code has executed again, resulting in the display of a new random number.

Running Scripts

To run, scripts built with javaScript must either be embedded in an HTML document or be referenced as an external file which is loaded with the HTML document and then evaluated. Navigator interprets the inline code directly.

A Web browser displays a Web page as a result of the browser acting on the instructions contained in an HTML file. The browser reads the HTML file and displays the elements of the file as they are encountered. The file may contain the embedded JavaScript code. The process of reading an HTML field and identifying the elements contained in the file is referred to as *parsing*. When a script is encountered during parsing, the browser executes the script before continuing with further parsing.

Some scripts may define functions for handling events that are generated by user actions. For example, you might write a script to define a function for handling the event 'filling a form' or 'clicking a link'. The event handlers can then perform actions such as validating the form's data, generating a custom URL for the link, or loading a new Web page.

The GET method is used to retrieve the information contained at the specified URL. This method may also be used to submit data collected in an HTML form or to invoke a CGI program. When the server processes a GET request, it delivers the requested information (if it can find), but appends at the front of the information an HTTP header that provides data about the server, identifies any errors that occurred in processing the request, and describes the type of information being returned as a result.

The HEAD method is similar to the GET method except that when a Web server processes a HEAD request, it only returns the HTTP header data and not the information that was the object of the request. The HEAD method is used to retrieve information about a URL, without actually obtaining the information addressed by the URL.

The POST method is used to inform the server that the information appended to the request is to be sent to the specified URL. The POST method is typically used to send form data and other information to CGI programs. The Web server responds to a POST request by sending back header data followed by any information generated by the CGI program as the result of processing the request.

The Java programs that can be executed by the Web browser are called *applets* rather than applications, because they cannot be run outside of the browser's own window. Programmers create java applets using the built-in programming features of the Java Developer's Kit. Web pages written in HTML reference java applets using the <APPLET> tag. When a Web page that references a Java applet is loaded by a browser, the browser requests the applet code from the Web server. When the browser receives the applet code, it executes the code and allocates a fixed area of the browser window. This area is identified by attributes specified with the applet tag. The applet is not allowed to update the browser display or handle events outside of its allocated window area. By way of comparison, JavaScript provides access to the entire Web page, but does not support many of the more advanced object-oriented programming features of Java.

JavaScript statements can be included in HTML documents by enclosing the statements between an opening <script> tag and a closing </script tag>. Within the opening tag, the LANGUAGE attribute is set to "JavaScript" to identify the script as being JavaScript as opposed to some other scripting language, such as VisualBasic.

XML

Although computers are now able to handle electronic documents that contain images, music and video, many documents are still bound within a text framework. For text and other media to be combined, exchanged and published, it must be organized within some kind of infrastructure. The XML standard provides such a platform. The name 'XML' is an acronym for 'Extensible Markup Language' (with 'X' replacing 'E' for aesthetic impact). This language is not owned or dominated by any single commercial interest. It was developed by the W3C (the World Wide Web Consortium), and has been shaped by experience of previous markup languages.

XML is an ideal data format for storing structured and semi-structured text intended for dissemination and ultimate publication on a variety of media. Indeed, XML has its roots in this domain. An XML document contains special instructions, called tags, which enclose identifiable parts of the document.

Beyond the world of publishing, information passed between programs and computer systems is becoming richer and more complex as new network-based applications are devised. Such information needs to be **self-describing,** so that the client software can interpret and perform user-driven actions on the data without needing to reconnect to the server. Despite its historical roots in publishing, XML is also suited to the task of unambiguously identifying complex data structures that may never be viewed or printed:

```
<transaction>
<time date='19980509"/>
<amount>123</amount>
<currency type='Rupees"/>
```

```
<from id="X98765>Ravi</from>
<to id="X56565>Bimal</to>
</transaction>
```

An example of a standard that utilizes XML in this way is SMIL (the Synchronized Multimedia Integration Language), which employs XML markup to identify and manage the presentation of files containing text, images, sound and video fragments to create a multimedia presentation.

An XML document has both a logical and a physical structure. The logical structure allows a document to be divided into named units and sub-units, called **elements.** The physical structure allows components of the document, called **entities,** to be named and stored separately, sometimes in other data files so that information can be reused and non-XML data (such as image data) can be included by reference. For example, each chapter in a book may be represented by an element, containing further elements that describe each paragraph, table and image, but image data and paragraphs that are reused (perhaps in other documents) are stored in separate entity files.

The logical structure involves a number of constraints that must be obeyed in all valid XML documents. A document can be checked for conformance using a **parser,** which reports any errors it finds. Documents composed of a number of entities must first be assembled using an **entity manager.** The standard describes software that can perform both these functions as an **XML processor**, though the term 'parser' is commonly promoted to mean the same thing.

XML is actually a **meta-language**, meaning that it is a language that describes other languages. There is no predefined list of elements. XML provides complete freedom to employ elements with names that are meaningful to the application. However, it is possible to prevent tag-naming anarchy with an optional mechanism for predefining the elements allowed in a specific class of documents. A DTD (Document Type Definition) defines the elements allowed, and a **validating parser** compares the DTD rules against a given document to determine the validity of the document. This feature allows software translation filters to be developed with the confidence that the markup used during document preparation conformed to a known specification, and was applied consistently. A number of industry standards for data exchange and publication may be defined in terms of a suitable DTD (there is a DTD for the SMIL format mentioned above).

XML documents can be created and edited using existing text editors and word processors, but special XML-sensitive editors also exist. These editors use the DTD to guide authors, preventing both XML syntax errors and logical document structure errors from occurring. Typically, the tags are replaced by icons selected from a menu of suitable options within the current context. XML encourages the use of elements with names that describe the nature of an object, as opposed to describing how it should be displayed or printed, and this general markup approach has one fundamental advantage over the traditional style-based instructions. The information is self-describing, so it can be located, extracted and manipulated as desired. However, this move away from style-specific formatting means that an appropriate presentation of the document cannot be produced automatically. It is not obvious (at least to a computer program) how the content of an element called Paragraph or Emphasis should be presented, let alone one named Company or Pricecode. A **style sheet** is therefore needed to specify an output format for each element. The great advantage of this approach is that alternative style sheets can be applied at any time, changing the format to suit the intended audience or the capabilities of the publishing medium. An advanced style sheet language should be able to generate standard text, such as a prefix, and also rearrange components of the document, as well as perform the more basic task of selecting appropriate fonts and styles.

XML may be used as an exchange format for **relational database** systems. In this scenario, the XML tags are being used as a convenient data wrapper during transfer of records, fields and relationships between systems. When the data is derived from multiple tables, connected by **one-to-many** relationships, the structured yet repeatable nature of XML elements is ideal for storing any number of related data fields.

Traditional Web technology has been described as 'pull technology', because the Web browser 'pulls' the HTML encoded documents from the Web server, which simply waits for requests for a Web page or other data file. The Web client is active, and the server is passive. The concept behind push technology is that the Web server pushes or sends data to each client, without waiting for a request. The client browser is updated dynamically as the base information changes. One obvious application for this is a news update service.

Increasing interest in client-sided scripting technology is a reaction to the realization that complex services, requiring a high degree of processing power, are best provided by the client computer. The server can then concentrate on its prime purpose, which is to deliver the software and data to each client. For example, a Java program can read and make sense of XML data, and can respond sensibly to operations requested by the applet. Optional data may be hidden or revealed, a table of contents may be created, expanded or retracted, or information may be rearranged or styled in different ways, without further interaction with the Web server.

XML can be used to mark up semi-structured documents, such as reference works, training guides, technical manuals, catalogues, academic journals and reports. Among many other niche applications, XML can also be used to mark up patents, examination papers, financial statements and research papers. New and more specialized uses include support for the presentation of data in the next generation of mobile telephone.

All the features of a typical document can be represented by XML tags. Taking the example of a reference book, objects such as chapters, titles, notes, paragraphs, lists and tables can all be explicitly identified by name:

```
<chapter>
<title>An example XML fragment</title>
<note>
<para>This note contains two paragraphs.</para>
<para>The second paragraph.</para>
</note>
</chapter>
```

XML also facilitates the generation and management of **metadata**, which is data about other data. Taking the reference book example, typical metadata would include the contents, the index, and the date the book was published. None of these items are part of the text of the book, but are simply the background information or an aid to searches or classification.

Intranets and Extranets

Not all TCP/IP networks connect to the Internet. Many companies build internets (small "i"), or interconnected networks, that do not extend beyond their organizational boundaries. An intranet is an interconnected network (or internet), usually one that uses the TCP/IP protocol set, and does not extend beyond the organization that created it. An extranet is an intranet that has been extended to include specific entities outside the boundaries of the organization, such as business partner's customers, or suppliers. Although fax, telephone, e-mail, and overnight express carriers have been the main communications tools for business for many years, extranets can replace many of them at a lower cost.

Public and Private Networks

A public network is any computer network or telecommunications network that is available to the public. The Internet is one example of a public network. Although, a company can operate its extranet using a public network, very few do because of the high level of security risks. The internet, as you will learn in later chapters, does not provide a high degree of security in its basic structure.

A private network is a private, leased-line connection between two companies that physically connects their intranets to one another. A leased line is a permanent telephone connection between two points. Unlike the normal telephone connection you create when you dial a telephone number, a leased line is always active. The advantage of a leased line is security. Only the two parties that lease the line to create the private network have access to the connection. The largest drawback to a private network is cost. Leased lines are expensive. Every pair of companies wanting a private network between them requires a separate line connecting them. For instance, if a company wants to set up an extranet connection over a private network with seven other companies, the company must pay the cost of seven leased lines, one for each company. If the extranet expands to 20 other companies, the extranet-sponsoring company must rent another 13 leased lines. As each new company is added, costs increase by the same amount and soon become prohibitive.

Vendors refer to this as a scaling problem; that is, increasing the number of leased lines in private networks is difficult, costly, and time consuming. As the number of companies that need to join the extranet increases, other networking options become appealing.

Virtual Private Network (VPN)

A Virtual Private Network (VPN) is an extranet that uses public networks and their protocols to send sensitive data to partners, customers, suppliers, and employees using a system called *IP tunneling* or *encapsulation.* IP tunneling effectively creates a private passageway through the Public Internet that provides secure transmission from one computer to another. The virtual passageway is created by VPN software that encrypts the packet content and then places the encrypted packets inside another packet in a process called *encapsulation.* The outer packet is called an *IP wrapper*. The Web server sends the encapsulated packets to their destinations over the Internet. The computer that receives the packet unwraps it and decrypts the message using VPN software that is the same as, or compatible with, the VPN software used to encrypt and encapsulate the packet at the sending end. The "virtual" part of VPN means that the connection seems to be a permanent, internal network connection, but the connection is actually temporary.

Each transaction between two intranets using a VPN is created, carries out its work over the Internet, and is then terminated. VPN software must be installed on the computers at both ends of the transmission. A VPN provides security shells, with the most sensitive data under the tightest control. The VPN is like a separate, covered commuter lane on a highway (the Internet) in which the passengers are protected from being seen by the vehicles travelling in the other lanes. Company employees in remote locations can send sensitive information to company computers using the VPN private tunnels established on the Internet.

Unlike private networks using leased lines, VPNs establish short-term logical connections in real time that are broken once the communication session ends. Establishing VPNs does not require leased lines. The only infrastructure required outside each company's intranet is the Internet.

Cloud Computing

Simply put, cloud computing is the delivery of computing services—servers, storage, databases, networking, software, analytics, intelligence and more—over the Internet ('the cloud') to offer faster innovation, flexible resources and economies of scale. You typically pay only for cloud services you use, helping lower your operating costs, run your infrastructure more efficiently and scale as your business needs change.

With increase in computer and mobile users, data storage has become a priority in all fields. Large- and small-scale businesses today thrive on their data and they spent a huge amount of money to maintain this data. It requires a strong IT support and a storage hub. Not all businesses can afford high cost of in-house IT infrastructure and back up support services. For them, cloud computing is a cheaper solution. Perhaps, its efficiency in storing data, computation and less maintenance cost has succeeded to attract even bigger businesses as well.

Cloud computing decreases the hardware and software demand from the user's side. The only thing that user must be able to run is the cloud computing systems interface software, which can be as simple as Web browser, and the cloud network takes care of the rest. We all have experienced cloud computing at some instant of time; some of the popular cloud services we have used or we are still using are mail services like gmail, hotmail or yahoo, etc.

In an in-house IT server, you have to pay a lot of attention and ensure that there are no flaws into the system so that it runs smoothly. And in case of any technical glitch, you are completely responsible; it will seek a lot of attention, time and money for repair. Whereas, in cloud computing, the service provider takes the complete responsibility of the complication and the technical faults.

Unlike traditional computing where data is stored on your PC's local hard drive, the data in the cloud is stored on many physical and/or virtual servers that are hosted by a third-party service provider. An example of a cloud computing file storage provider is Dropbox. Dropbox files can be accessed from any device via the Internet.

Some common services that are hosted in the cloud are hosted desktop, provided by companies like AT&T; hosted email like Gmail, provided by companies like Google; cloud storage, provided by companies like Dropbox; and streaming music, provided by companies like Spotify. These services, applications and files are stored in the cloud and can be accessed by users via any device.

Advantages

1. ***Worldwide access.*** Cloud computing increases mobility, as you can access your documents from any device in any part of the world. For businesses, this means that employees can work from home or on business trips, without having to carry around documents. This increases productivity and allows faster exchange of information. Employees can also work on the same document without having to be in the same place.

2. ***Security.*** Many cloud providers offer a broad set of policies, technologies and controls that strengthen your security posture overall, helping protect your data, apps and infrastructure from potential threats.

3. ***More storage.*** In the past, memory was limited by the particular device in question. Cloud computing provides increased storage, so you will not have to worry about running out of space on your hard drive.

4. ***Automatic updates.*** The cloud computing provider is responsible for making sure that updates are available—you just have to download them. This saves you time, and furthermore, you do not need to be an expert to update your device; the cloud computing provider will automatically notify you and provide you with instructions.

5. ***Reduced cost.*** Cloud computing eliminates the capital expense of buying hardware and software and setting up and running on-site datacenters—the racks of servers, the round-the-clock electricity for power and cooling, and the IT experts for managing the infrastructure. It adds up fast.

6. ***Speed.*** Most cloud computing services are provided as self-service and on demand, so even vast amounts of computing resources can be provisioned in minutes, typically with just a few mouse clicks, giving businesses a lot of flexibility and taking the pressure off capacity planning.

Types of Cloud Services

Most cloud computing services fall into four broad categories—infrastructure as a service (IaaS), platform as a service (PaaS), serverless and software as a service (SaaS). These are sometimes called the *cloud computing stack* because they build on top of one another. Knowing what they are and how they are different makes it easier to accomplish your business goals.

1. ***Infrastructure as a service (IaaS).*** Infrastructure as a service provides companies with computing resources—servers, networking, storage and datacenter space—on a pay-per-use basis.

   The benefits of IaaS are as follows:
   - No need to invest in your own hardware
   - Infrastructure scales on demand to support dynamic workloads
   - Flexible, innovative services available on demand

2. ***Platform as a service (PaaS).*** Platform as a service refers to cloud computing services that supply an on-demand environment for developing, testing, delivering and managing software applications. PaaS is designed to make it easier for developers to quickly create Web or mobile apps, without worrying about setting up or managing the underlying infrastructure of servers, storage, network and databases needed for development.

   The benefits of PaaS are given below:
   - Develop application and get to market faster
   - Deploy new Web applications to the cloud in minutes
   - Reduce complexity

3. ***Software as a service (SaaS).*** Software as a service is a method for delivering software applications over the Internet, on demand and typically on a subscription basis. With SaaS, cloud providers host and manage the software application and underlying infrastructure and handle any maintenance like software upgrades and security patching. Users connect to the application over the Internet, usually with a Web browser on their phone, tablet or PC.

   The benefits of SaaS are as follows:
   - Sign up and rapidly start using innovative business apps
   - Accessibility apps and data from any connected computer
   - No loss data of if your computer breaks because the data is in the cloud
   - The service is able to dynamically update the software.

Popular Cloud Computing Services

- ***iCloud.*** Apple's iCloud allows you to store music, documents, photos, and other files via WiFi. You can then access them from all of your devices.

- ***Google Cloud Connect for Microsoft Office.*** Google Cloud Connect allows various users to interact using Microsoft Office. This includes simultaneous sharing and editing of Microsoft Word, PowerPoint, and Excel documents.

- ***IBM SmartCloud.*** IBM SmartCloud provides numerous services for IT companies, such as developing applications in the cloud or using the cloud as a backup for your company files.

Internet of Things (IoT)

The term IoT encompasses everything connected to the Internet, but it is increasingly being used to define objects that 'talk' to each other. The Internet of Things is made up of devices, from simple sensors to smartphones and wearables, connected together. This includes everything from cellphones, coffee makers, washing machines, headphones, lamps, wearable devices and almost anything else you can think of. This also applies to the components of machines, for example, a jet engine of an airplane or the drill of an oil rig. The analyst firm, Gartner says that by 2020, there will be over 26 billion connected devices.

But, why on the earth would you want so many connected devices talking to each other? There are many examples for what this might look like or what the potential value might be. Say for example, you are on your way to a meeting; your car could have access to your calendar and already know the best route to take. If the traffic is heavy your car might send a text to the other party notifying them that you will be late. What if your alarm clock wakes up you at 6 a.m. and then notifies your coffee maker to start brewing coffee for you? What if your office equipment knew when it was running low on supplies and automatically re-ordered more? What if the wearable device you used in the workplace could tell you when and where you were most active and productive and shared that information with other devices that you used while working?

Devices and objects with built-in sensors are connected to an Internet of Things platform, which integrates data from the different devices and applies analytics to share the most valuable information with applications built to address specific needs. These powerful IoT platforms can pinpoint exactly what information is useful and what can safely be ignored. This information can be used to detect patterns, make recommendations, and detect possible problems before they occur. For example, if I own a car manufacturing business, I might want to know which optional components are the most popular. Using Internet of Things technology, I can use sensors to detect which areas in a showroom are the most popular, and where customers linger longest or drill down into the available sales data to identify which components are selling fastest.

With the insight provided by advanced analytics comes the power to make processes more efficient. Smart objects and systems mean you can automate certain tasks, particularly when these are repetitive, mundane, time-consuming or even dangerous.

EXERCISES

1. Log into *www.time.com* and trace all the paths of the site by clicking the hyperlinks. Develop a tree diagram of all of the hyperlinks allowed from the site.
2. Describe the physical structure of the Internet.
3. What is a protocol and which protocols handle Internet communications?
4. List the client-server protocols of the Internet.

5. How does the Internet survive without a governing body? How is a dispute currently solved?
6. Visit the websites of IETF (*www.ietf.org*) and IANA (*www.iana.org*). Based on the contents of these sites, what role does each play in the governance of the Internet?
7. Several domain name disputes have arisen on the Internet. Search the *Yahoo!*, the site for some of the interesting domain name controversies.
8. Why is IPv6 needed?
9. Find out who have implemented IPv6.
10. What is an intelligent agent?
11. List two characteristics of agent technology that will be useful for the marketplace.
12. Give the history of hypertext and hypermedia.
13. Why is google.com a big success? How do they make profit? What is special about google's search engine?
14. What is the difference between HTML and XML?

CHAPTER

4

e-Marketing

LEARNING OBJECTIVES

After reading this chapter, you should be able to:

- Understand the difference between traditional marketing and web marketing.
- Identify web presence goals.
- Explain the e-marketing value chain and the e-marketing metrics.
- Understand the browsing behaviour model.
- Understand the basics of e-advertising.

Google

It has been estimated that Google runs over one million servers in data centres around the world, and processes over one billion search requests and about twenty-four petabytes of user-generated data every day. Google's rapid growth since its incorporation has triggered a chain of products, acquisitions, and partnerships beyond the company's core web search engine. The company offers online productivity software, such as its Gmail email service, and social networking tools, including Orkut and, more recently, Google Buzz and Google+. Google's products extend to the desktop as well, with applications such as the web browser Google Chrome, the Picasa photo organization and editing software, and the Google Talk instant messaging application. Notably, Google leads the development of the Android mobile operating system, as well as the new Google Chrome OS, but is best known as the main operating system on the Cr-48 and also on commercial Chromebooks since 15 June 2011, among them the Samsung Series 5 and Acer AC700 Alexa lists the main U.S.-focused google.com site as the Internet's most visited website, and numerous international Google sites (google.co.in, google.co.uk etc.) are in the top hundred, as are several other Google-owned sites such as YouTube, Blogger, and Orkut. Google also ranks number two in the BrandZ brand equity database. The dominant market position of Google's services has led to criticism of the company over issues including privacy, copyright, and censorship.

In January 1996, Larry Page and Sergey Brin of the Stanford University had begun collaboration on a search engine called BackRub, named for its unique ability to analyze the "back links" pointing to a given Website. In September 1998, Google Inc. opened its door in Menlo Park, California. Already Google.com, still in beta, was answering 10,000 search queries each day. Google quickly outgrew the confines of its Menlo Park home, and by February 1999 had moved to an office on University Avenue in Palo Alto. At eight employees, Google's staff had nearly tripled, and the service was answering more than 500,000 queries per day. Interest in the company had grown as well. Red Hat signed on as its first commercial search customer drawn in part by Google's commitment to running its servers on the open source operating system Linux.

With the move to the Googleplex, Google's current headquarters in Mountain View, California, the Google kernel continued to grow—attracting staff and clients and drawing attention from users and the press. To extend the power of its keyword-targeted advertising to smaller businesses, Google introduced AdWords, a self-service ad program that could be activated online with a credit card in a matter of minutes. And in the late 2000, to enhance users' power to search from anywhere on the Web, Google introduced the Google Toolbar. This innovative browser plug-in made it possible to use Google search without visiting the Google homepage, either using the toolbar's search box or right-clicking on text within a Web page, as well as enabling the highlighting of keywords in search results. The Google Toolbar would prove enormously popular and has since been downloaded by millions of users.

As 2000 ended, Google was already handling more than 100 million search queries a day. The first half of 2001 saw a series of partnerships and innovations that would bring Google search to a worldwide audience of mobile users. Meanwhile, Google had acquired a cornerstone of Internet culture. In February, Google took on the assets of Deja.com and began the arduous task of integrating the huge volume of data in the Internet's largest Usenet archive into a searchable format. In short order, Google introduced improved posting, post removal, and threading of the 500 million-plus messages exchanged over the years on Usenet discussion boards.

Meanwhile, the Google search engine evolved again and learned to crawl several new kinds of information. File type search added a dozen formats to Google's roster of searchable documents. In December, Google Image Search, first launched during the summer with 250 million images, came out of beta with advanced search added and an expanded image index. Online shopping took a leap forward with the beta launch of Google Catalog Search, which made it possible for Google users to search and browse more than 1,100 mail order catalogues that previously had been available only in print.

Google's success in charting the public Internet had helped make it the Internet search engine of choice. But Googlebot, the robot software that continually crawls the Web to refresh and expand Google's index of online documents, had to turn back at the corporate firewall—which left employees, IT managers and productivity-conscious executives wishing for a way to bring the power of Google search into their workplaces.

Their wish came true in February of 2002, with the introduction of the Google Search Appliance, a plug-and-play search solution in a bright yellow box. Soon it was crawling company intranets, e-commerce sites and university networks, with organizations from Boeing to the University of Florida powering their searches with "Google in a box".

The Company's automated search technology enables people to obtain nearly instant access to relevant information from its online index. Google generates revenue primarily by delivering online advertising. Businesses use its AdWords program to promote their products and services with targeted advertising. In addition, the third-party Websites that comprise the Google Network use the Company's AdSense program to deliver relevant advertisements that generate revenue. In August 2006, the Company acquired Neven Vision, an online photo-search company. On October 10, 2006, the Company acquired the online video company, YouTube. In October 2006, the Company also acquired JotSpot. JotSpot has developed a series of online productivity software programs that offer many of the functions of Microsoft Office programs, such as Microsoft Word or Excel spreadsheets. JotSpot applications are delivered as Web-based services. In March 2007, the Company acquired Adscape Media Inc., a company that makes technology to deliver advertising over the Internet for placement within videogames.

Advertising

Seventy-three per cent of Google's revenue is derived from its advertising programs. In 2022, out of the $282 billion revenues, $209 billion came from advertising. Google has implemented various innovations in the online advertising market that helped make it one of the biggest brokers in the market. Using technology from the company DoubleClick, Google can determine user interests and target advertisements so that they are relevant to their context and the user that is viewing them. Google Analytics allows website owners to track where and how people use their website, for example, by examining click rates for all the links on a page. Google advertisements can be placed on third-party websites in a two-part program. Google's AdWords allows advertisers to display their advertisements in the Google content network, through either a cost-per-click or cost-per-view scheme. The sister service, Google AdSense, allows website owners to display these advertisements on their website, and earn money every time ads are clicked.

Discussion Questions

1. Why google search-engine has become a great success? Compare google search-engine technology with that of askjeeves.
2. Discuss vertical and horizontal integration used by google.
3. How did google manage to break through corporate firewalls?
4. How does google make money through their search-engine?

Nearly 3 billion people around the world are tapping into the Internet. With the Internet growing at an astonishing pace in recent years, marketers around the world are racing to take advantage of its interactive nature, to communicate and foster exchanges and relationships with customers, suppliers, and the public. Also, the amount of transactions on the Internet are increasing exponentially, as shown in Table 4.1.

The accelerating confluence of traditional print and broadcast media with new digital media like the Internet has created dynamic new channels for marketers. At the same time, advertisers have begun demanding greater economic efficiency in reaching target customers. The Internet is changing the design and implementation of marketing strategies. This dynamic technology provides marketers with efficient and powerful methods of designing, promoting, and distributing products, conducting research, and gathering market information.

Table 4.1 Worldwide retail e-commerce sales (in billions of Dollars)[1]

Year	*Worldwide retail e-commerce revenues in billions of US dollars*
2014	1,336
2016	1,845
2018	2,841
2022	5,200

E-marketing can include any Internet-based promotion, including websites, targeted e-mail, Internet bulletin boards, sites where customers can dial-in and download files, and so on. The term does not have a strict meaning though, and many marketing managers use it to describe any computer-based marketing tool.

Traditional Marketing

If marketing is whatever you do to promote the sale of your products or services, then it should include:

1. Market research—from competitive information-gathering to industry awareness to soliciting customer opinions and preferences
2. Publicity from press releases to the positioning of your company and its offerings in the marketplace
3. Advertising that is text-based (classifieds) and graphic-based (display)
4. Sales, including distribution and merchandising
5. Customer service and customer support.

Traditional marketing seems to fall far short of three features. There are certain problems associated with it, which can be listed as follows:

1. Traditional marketing is often expensive. It can cost a lot of money to produce and print brochures, product sheets, and catalogues. It is also expensive to keep support personnel on hand to answer inquiries from customers, and it costs a lot of money in postage and shipping fees to send information to prospective customers.
2. Traditional marketing can be a very time-consuming process. Mistakes have to be corrected; you have to go back to the ad agency or printer to revise, add or delete, and you often have to wait for months for an ad that you have placed to appear in a publication.
3. Traditional marketing often has a "hit and miss" quality. Marketers often send out bulk of mails to customers and yet receive a tiny response. Moreover they feel that they do not cater to the taste of the consumers or rather that they do not come across the right consumer.

---

1. https://www.statista.com/statistics/379046/worldwide-retail-e-commerce-sales/

Businesses have always made their presence felt by establishing shops, factories, warehouses, and office buildings. An organization's presence is the public image it presents to its stakeholders. The stakeholders of a firm include its customers, suppliers, employees, stockholders, neighbours, and the general public. Companies tend not to worry much about the image they project until they make their mark. Initially, they focus only on their survival. On the Web, making one's presence felt is much more important. The only contact that customers and other stakeholders have with a firm on the Web might be its website or its Web pages. Therefore, creating an effective and appealing Web page is essential even for the smallest and the newest firm operating on the Web.

Identifying Web Presence Goals

When a business creates a physical space in which to conduct its activities, its managers focus on very specific objectives. Few of these objectives are image-driven. An ambitious businessman must find a location that will be convenient for customers to access, with sufficient floor space features to allow the selling activity to occur, and they must take into consideration, the room space to store inventory and provide working space for employees. An added feature is the interior decoration which could enhance the business ambience, and at the same time attract customers. The success of a business relies on fulfilling these objectives in a tangible, physical location.

On the Web, businesses and other organizations have the advantage of creating a space of their own choice, design and other embellishments, good enough to make a distinctive presence. A website can have images, and can activate them by animation, thus making the customers feel and enjoy its presence. It can serve as a sales brochure, a product showroom, a financial report, an employment ad, or a customer contact point. Each entity that establishes a Web presence should decide which tasks the website must accomplish, and which tasks are most important and need to be included for promoting their business.

Different firms, even those in similar business, may establish different Web presence goals. For example, Coca-Cola and Pepsi are two companies that have established very strong brand images and are in the same business, but have developed very different Web presences.

Refer to their websites and identify the differeces.

Achieving Web Presence Goals

An effective site is the one that creates an attractive presence that meets the objectives of the business or the organization. These objectives include:

1. Attracting visitors to the website
2. Making the site interesting enough so that visitors stay and explore
3. Convincing visitors to follow the site's links to obtain information
4. Creating an impression consistent with the organization's desired image

5. Building a trusting relationship with visitors
6. Reinforcing positive images that the visitor might already have about the organization
7. Encouraging visitors to return to the site.

The Uniqueness of the Web

When firms first started creating websites in the mid 1990s, they often built simple sites that conveyed basic information about their businesses. Few firms conducted any market research to see what kinds of things potential visitors might want to obtain from these websites, and even fewer considered what business infrastructure improvement would be needed to keep the site alive. For example, few firms had e-mail address links on their sites. Those firms that did include an e-mail link, often understaffed the department responsible for answering visitors' e-mail messages. Thus, many of the visitors' e-mails remained unanswered. The failure to understand how the Web is different from other presence-building media is one reason why so many businesses fail to achieve their Web objectives. The scenario has changed for the better in the recent times with the prominence of Internet technologies over others.

Now, most of the websites that are designed to create an organization's presence in the web medium include links to a fairly standard information set. The sites give visitors easy access to its history, statements about its objectives or mission, information about products or services offered, financial information, and means of communication with the organization. Such sites achieve varying levels of success, depending largely on how they convey these information. Presentation is important, so also is realizing the fact that the Web is an interactive medium.

Meeting the Needs of Website Visitors

Businesses that are successful on the Web realize that every visitor to their website is a potential customer. Thus, an important concern for businesses crafting a Web presence is the variation in the visitors' characteristics. People who visit a website seldom arrive at it by accident; they are at it for a specific reason. The Web designer who makes a site useful for everyone, needs to keep in mind some of the possible reasons listed as follows:

- Learning about products or services that the company offers.
- Buying the products or services that the company offers.
- Obtaining information about warranties or service and repair policies for products they have purchased.
- Obtaining general information about the company or organization.
- Obtaining financial information for making an investment or credit-granting decision.
- Identifying the people who manage the company or organization.
- Obtaining contact information of a person or a department in the organization.

E-marketing Value Chain

As such, e-marketing thrives with the maintenance of strong relationship between the company and the customer. It is like a chain—the company acquires customers, fulfills their needs and offers support (before and after purchase), and gains their confidence so that they return to it again. Thus the customer value is upheld. This is illustrated in Figure 4.1.

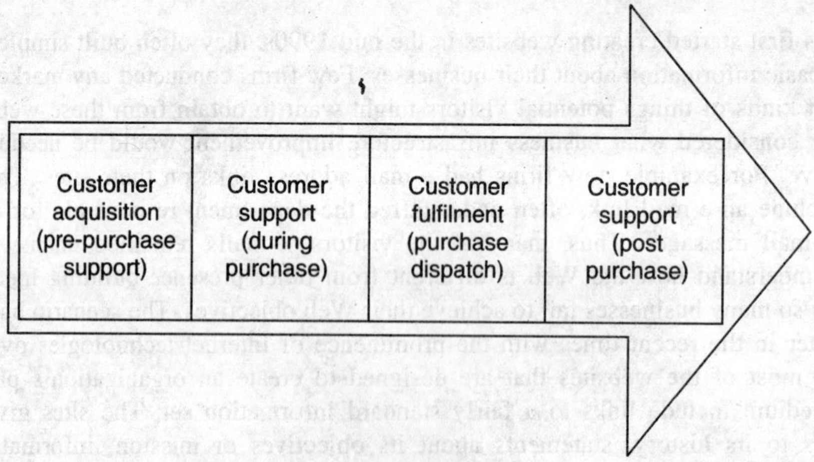

Figure 4.1 E-marketing value chain.

Site Adhesion: Content, Format, and Access

Content

A customer accesses a website for the content of that site. Initially a customer will want to navigate quickly to gain a clear understanding of the site's progression to more detailed information. The key to this is to match a user's psychological and technological sophistication profile with that of the site's initial and subsequent impact.

Format

The format of an organization's site is important with respect to the customer's technical sophistication. Vendors need to create a balance between information provision and information delivery speed. The selection of data format is crucial, as initially the goal is to create viewer interest and engage the viewer in a prolonged interaction.

Access

Online data access depends on the bandwidth requirement. The clear rule in the initial interaction phase is to use as minimal a bandwidth as is feasible to facilitate as wide an audience as possible.

Maintaining a Website

Creating a website that meets the needs of visitors with such a wide range of motivations can be challenging. Not only do website visitors arrive with different needs, but also they arrive with different experience and expectation levels. In addition to the problems posed by the diversity of visitor characteristics, technology issues can also arise. These website visitors will be connected to the Internet through a variety of communication channels that provide different bandwidths and data transmission speeds. They also will be using several different Web browsers. Even those who are using the same browser can have a variety of configurations. The wide array of browser add-in and plug-in software adds yet another dimension to visitor variability. Considering and addressing the implications of these many visitor characteristics when building a website can help convert those visitors into customers.

One of the best ways to accommodate a broad range of visitor needs is to build flexibility into the website's interface. Many sites offer separate versions with and without frames and give visitors the option of choosing either one. Some sites offer a text-only version. As researchers at the Trace Center (*http://trace.wisc.edu/*) note, this can be an especially important feature for visually impaired visitors who use special browser software, such as the **IBM Home Page Reader**, to access website content. The **W3C Web Accessibility Initiative** site includes a number of useful links to information regarding these issues.

If the site design uses graphics, the site can give the visitor the option to select smaller versions of the images so that the page will load on a low-bandwidth connection in a reasonable amount of time. If the site includes streaming audio or video clips, it can give the visitor the option to specify a connection type so that the streaming media adjusts itself to the bandwidth of that connection.

A good site design lets visitors choose among information attributes such as level of detail, forms of aggregation, viewing format and downloading format. Many e-commerce websites give visitors a selectable level of detail, presenting products information by product line. The site presents one page for each line of products. A product line page contains pictures of each item in that product line, accompanied by a brief description. Using hyperlinked graphics for the product pictures, the site offers visitors the option of clicking the product picture to get the page containing a detailed description of that product.

Websites can also offer visitors, multiple information formats by including links to files in those formats. For example, the page offering financial information could include links to an HTML file, an Adobe PDF file, and an Excel spreadsheet file. Each of these files could contain the same financial information, though in different formats, allowing visitors to choose the format that best suits their immediate needs. Visitors looking for a specific financial fact might choose the HTML file so that the information would appear in their Web browsers. Other visitors who want a copy of the entire annual report as it was printed would select the PDF file and either view it in their browsers or download and print the file. Visitors who want to conduct analyses on the financial data would download the spreadsheet file and perform calculations using the data in their own spreadsheet software.

To be successful in conveying an integrated image and offering information to potential customers, businesses should try to meet the following goals when constructing their websites:

- Convey an integrated image of the organization.
- Offer easily accessible facts about the organization.
- Allow visitors to experience the site in different ways and at different levels.
- Provide visitors with a meaningful, two-way (interactive) communication link with the organization.
- Sustain visitor attention and encourage return visits.
- Offer easily accessible information about products and services and how to use them.

Metrics Defining Internet Units of Measurement

The e-commerce world has, since inception been attempting to measure parameters associated with the Web and websites in order to assess two things:

1. Advertising—how many people saw our banner ad?
2. Visitation—how many people came to our site?

For advertising, the metrics measured and their interpretation depend on the position of the measurer. The advertising perspective is that metrics can give the advertiser the most accurate interpretation of the customer-to-site usage ratio, but this has come under increasing scrutiny as the technology and systems associated with Web interfaces and networks become well understood by the advertisers. There is a problem with using hits as a measuring tool. What advertisers want to measure includes the number of unique visitations to a site, as well as multiple other parameters, such as the duration of each visit. The number of hits (visits) is calculated based on a frame of text or image file. Sometimes, a single page may be made up of many of these. Thus, it distorts the hit count. An alternative is to use a metric calculation which uses the whole page as a metric. The problem with this is that a page is cached into the memory of a 'reader' or a Web browser. One visit to the page counts as one hit. But if the user then swaps between tasks and pages, this page may actually be read many times, which should be counted as multiple hits. Another problem is the user who utilizes a 'bot' or a self-propelled search engine to find some information. This search agent will visit sites on the owner's behalf, but will not actually report anything about the sites visited back to the owner, thus throwing off the hit count.

In software metrics theory, one problem is the separation of direct and indirect metrics or measurement. Direct measurement of an attribute is the measurement that does not depend on the measurement of any other attribute. Indirect measurement of an attribute is the measurement that involves the measurement of one or more other attributes. Examples of direct metrics are shown in Table 4.2.

TABLE 4.2 Examples of Direct Metrics

Number of individual, authenticated user sessions
Authenticated user sessions by location
Authenticated user profiles by region
Top 'entry' and 'exit' pages by authenticated users
Most-downloaded files
Advertising 'captures'
Most-active, authenticated organizations accessing the site
Most-active countries, states, cities, and regions by authenticated users
Organizational breakdown of site access by authenticated users
Maximal, minimal, average number of authenticated users per period
Most-used browsers
Spiders or bot activity
Most-used platforms
Successful form submissions
Failed form submissions
Server error log (404 errors and the like)
Top referencing sites

Examples of indirect metrics can be seen in Table 4.3.

TABLE 4.3 Examples of Indirect Metrics

Number of hits per page
Number of successful hits per page
Number of hits for total site
Number of hits per page, per session, per individual user
Average user session time in seconds
Most-accessed segments
Top paths through site
Views of banners
Hits by user groups
Total hits
Cached hits
Successful hits
Failed hits

Many organizations are using the indirect metrics, as advertised by the vendors of packages and software tools, and this will significantly hinder the ability of the executives of these firms to track directly the impact of their dollars being spent on their websites. However, having some of these metrics even as partial views of the activities occurring in a site, is better than having nothing. Organizations in the online customer acquisition phase have attempted to refine some of the indirect metrics to their needs, by understanding their limitations. These include the following:

1. ***Click-through captures.*** How many users click through to the next stage in the customer acquisition process?
2. ***Time spent.*** How long did the viewer stay at the site and which items, pages or routes did the viewer select to navigate through the site?
3. ***Time spent searching.*** Did the viewer use the 'site map' or 'search' feature, and if so for what and for how long?
4. ***Time spent before click-through.*** How long did a viewer linger in the opening stages of the interaction and where?
5. ***E-mails and telephone calls.*** How many e-mails or calls did this section generate and on what issues?
6. ***Registered users.*** If the site has a registration facility, what is the rate?

By assessing these metrics in conjunction with data from other sources such as the direct sales and marketing channels, an organization can estimate the content, format, and accessibility of the online site. Though not perfect, it does provide a useful set of parameters from which to judge the site's effectiveness to retain eyeballs and potential future customers.

The Browsing Behaviour Model

Customers of an e-commerce site interact with it through a series of consecutive and related requests made during a single visit called *session*. Within a session, customers can issue requests of different types, such as Login, Browse, Search, Add to Shopping Cart, or Pay. Different customers may exhibit different patterns of navigation through an e-commerce site and therefore may invoke the different functions provided by the site in different ways and in different frequencies. Some customers may be heavy buyers while others may be occasional buyers who do extensive searching and browsing, but very rarely buy from the site. The customer's behaviour while interacting with an e-commerce site has impacts on the IT resources of the site and on the revenue of the e-store. Thus, it is important to be able to characterize the behaviour of customers or groups of customers of an e-commerce site.

The customer model captures elements of user behaviour in terms of navigational patterns, e-commerce functions used, frequency of access to the various e-commerce functions, and times between access to the various services offered by the site. A customer model can be used for navigational and workload prediction, so that better websites can be modelled.

Browsing Behaviour Model of an Online Video Store

Let us use an example of an online video store to give an informal introduction to the user behaviour model of an e-commerce site. Consider an online video store in which customers can perform the following functions:

1. Connect to the home page and browse the site by following links to bestseller videos and promotions of the week per video category.

2. Search for titles according to various criteria including keywords and title.
3. Select one of the videos that results from a search and view additional information such as a brief description of the product/products, price, shipping time, ranking, and reviews.
4. Register as a new customer of the virtual video store. This allows the user to provide a username and a password, payment information (e.g. credit card number), mailing address, and e-mail address for notification of order status and videos of interest.
5. Login with a username and password.
6. Add items to the shopping cart.
7. Pay for the items added to the shopping cart.

Thus, during a visit to the online video store, a customer issues requests that will cause these functions to be executed. For example, a customer may cause a search to be executed by submitting a URL that specifies the name of an application to be run at the server through a server Application Programming Interface (API) and the keywords to be used in the search. The application will then execute a search in the site database and return an HTML page with all the videos that match the search criteria. Remember that the sequence of consecutive requests issued by the same customer during a single visit to an e-commerce site is called a *session*.

A customer may be classified as being in different states, according to the type of function (i.e. request) requested during a session. For example, the customer may be browsing, searching, registering as a new customer, logging in, adding videos to the shopping cart, selecting the result of a search, or paying for the order. The possible transitions between states depend on the layout of the site. For example, one customer may go from the home page to search, from search to select, from select to add to cart, and from there to the payment area. Another customer may go from the home page to the browse state before doing a search and leaving the online video store without buying anything. To capture the possible transitions between the states in which a customer may be found, we need a model that reflects the navigational pattern of a user during a visit to an e-commerce site (Figure 4.2).

The given model is in the form of a graph and is called the Browser Behaviour Model Graph (BBMG).[2] The nodes of the BBMG, represented by rectangles, depict the states a customer is in during a visit to the e-commerce site. Arrows connecting the states indicate possible transitions between them.

Entry

This is a special state that immediately precedes a customer's entry to the online store. This state is part of the BBMG as a modelling convenience and does not correspond to any action initiated by the customer.

Home

This is the state a customer is in, after selecting the URL for the site's home page.

2. Menasce D.A., Almeida V.A.F., *Scaling for E-business*, Prentice-Hall PTR, NJ, USA, 2000, p. 45.

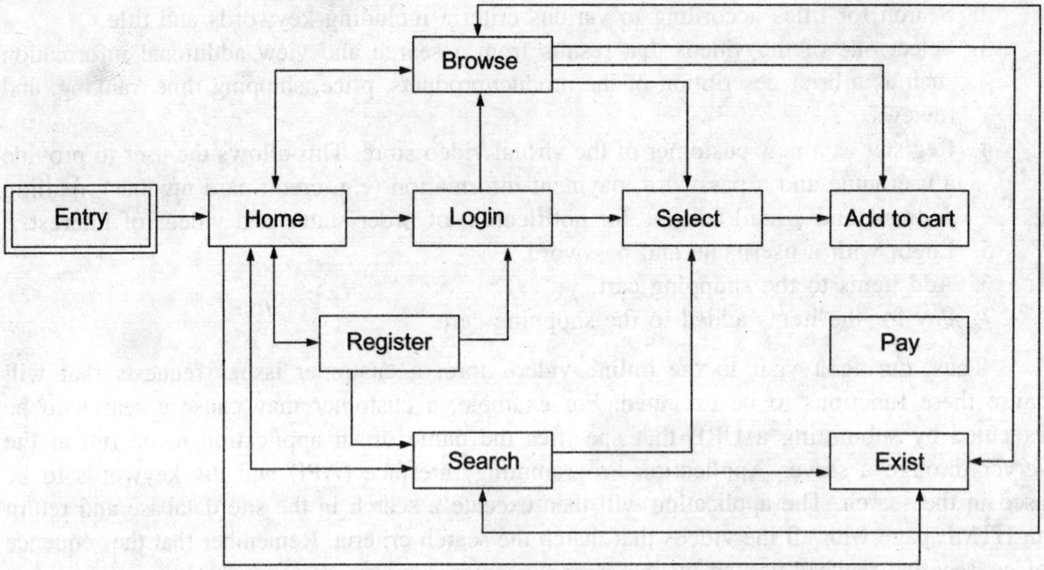

Figure 4.2 States and transitions of the BBMG for the virtual videostore.

Login

A customer moves to this state after requesting a login to the site. Sometimes, even a home page may ask him to login.

Register

To have an account created by registering with the online videostore, the customer selects the proper link for the registration page, thus making a transition to the Register state.

Search

A customer goes to this section after issuing a search request.

Browse

This is the state reached after a customer selects one of the links available at the site to view any of the pages of the site. These links include the list of bestsellers and weekly promotions.

Select

A search returns a list of zero or more links to videos. By selecting one of these links, a customer moves to this state.

Add to Cart

A customer moves to this state upon selecting the button that adds a selected video to the shopping cart.

Pay (Billing)

When ready to pay for the items in the shopping cart, the customer moves to the Billing section.

Exit

Customers may leave the site from any state. Thus, there is a transition from all states, except the entry state, to the exit state.

In the case of Figure 4.2, customers can enter the virtual videostore at only three states: Home, Browse, and Search. From the Home state, they can visit the Register, Login, Browse, and Search states, as well as exit from the site. This figure reflects all possible transitions between states. However, during a single visit to the e-store, a customer may not visit all states, or there may be different visits by the same customer to the site, or there may be visits from different customers in terms of the frequency by which these states are visited. Thus, to characterize the user behaviour during a visit to the site, one must also capture the frequency with which transitions occur. Consider that during a visit to the e-commerce site, a customer visits the Select state forty times. Out of these, the customer moves to the Search state sixteen times, to the Browse state fifteen times, to the Add to Cart state eight times, and once to the Exit state. We can then say that the transition frequencies out of the Select state are: 0.40 (=16/40) to Search state, 0.375 (=15/40) to Browse state, 0.2 (=8/40) to Add state, and 0.025 (=1/40) to Exit state.

In general, we label each transition in the BBMG with the frequency with which a customer follows the path between two states. Since we use BBMGs to characterize the behaviour of many similar visits to the site, we refer to the transition frequencies as transition probabilities.

For example, according to the BBMG of Figure 4.2, customers have a 10 per cent probability of leaving the site after performing a search. This is indicated by a transition from the Search state to the Exit state. From the Search state, customers have a 20 per cent probability of going to the Home state, a 25 per cent probability of doing another search, a 20 per cent probability of selecting one of the videos that resulted from the search, and a 25 per cent probability of going to the Browse state.

Different types of users may be characterized by different BBMGs in terms of the transition probabilities. As an example, consider two customer profiles—occasional and frequent buyers. The first category is composed of customers who use the Web store to find out about existing products, such as new books or best fares and itineraries for travel, but exit most of the time without buying or selecting. The second category is composed of customers who have a higher probability of buying if they see a product that interests them and is affordable. Thus, workload characterization for e-commerce entails in determining the set of BBMGs that best characterize customer behaviour. Note that it is possible for the same customer to exhibit different types of behaviour during each visit to the site. Thus, a BBMG is in fact associated to a visit to the site and not necessarily to a specific customer.

Aggregate Metrics for E-business Sites

Since the Web became a widely used vehicle to support all sorts of applications, including e-business, the need arose to devise metrics to measure a site's efficiency in attaining its goals. Table 4.4 lists common e-business functions when customers get on to an e-business website.

TABLE 4.4 Aggregate Metrics for E-Business Sites

Category	*Function*	*Description*
Common	Login	Login to the site
	Register	Register as a new user
	Search	Search site database
	Select	View one of the results of a search
	Browse	Follow links within the site
Retail	Add Item	Add item to shopping cart
	Remove Item	Remove item from shopping cart
	See Shopping Cart	Check contents and value of shopping cart
	Create Registry	Create a gift registry
	Add to Registry	Add item to gift registry
	Check Status	Check status of previous order
	Pay	Pay for items in shopping cart
Information	Download	Download software/report/music
	Subscribe	Subscribe to regular downloads
	Listen	Listen to real-time audio (e.g. lecture)
	Watch	Watch real-time movie

Many metrics have been used to assess the success of sites in terms of popularity and/or revenue generated.

Hits/Second

This measures the number of requests for objects served in each second by a website. A page is usually composed of one HTML file and several other embedded image files that are automatically requested from the Web server when a user requests the HTML document. So, hits/second counts not just the HTML pages but all embedded objects in a page as separate requests, which does not give a precise idea of the number of times a specific page, with its advertisement banners, was viewed.

Page Views/Day

This reflects the number of individual pages served per day. A company paying for a banner ad to be posted on a page may be interested in the number of times its ad is being seen. Very popular sites can display a few hundred million page views per day.

Click-throughs

This measures the percentage of users who not only view an online ad but also click on it to get to the Web page behind it. This metric is oriented more towards assessing the impact of online ads. However, this measure can be misleading. If the message in the banner ad is too general, it may draw a larger number of clicks than a more specific message. However, users who respond to the more specific messages are more likely to be interested in the product being advertised than those who react to the more general message.

Unique Visitors

This indicates how many different people visited a website during a certain period of time. Many times it is more important to know how many different people visited your site than the total number of visits received during a certain period.

Revenue Throughput

This is a business-oriented metric that measures the number of dollars/sec derived from sales from an e-commerce site. This measure implicitly represents customer and site behaviour. A customer who is happy with the quality of service (e.g. response time) of an e-business site will shop at the Web store, and the revenue throughput will increase.

Potential Loss Throughput

This is another business-oriented metric that measures the amount of money in customers' shopping carts that is not converted into sales because the customer leaves the site due to poor performance or other reasons.

Online Marketing

Online marketing means using the power of online networks, computer communications and digital interactive media to reach your marketing objectives. Online marketing will not replace traditional forms of marketing anyway. Instead, it will both add to and subtract from today's marketing mix. It will add more interactivity. But it will subtract costs. It will add more customer choices. But it will remove marketing's dependence on paper. It will add "information value" to products and services. But it will take away barriers to starting a business or extending a business into international markets. And most importantly, it will turn upside down some old notions we have held of what marketing is all about.

There are three new market segments which are as follows:

Cyberbuyers

These are professionals who spend a good deal of time online, mainly at their places of business. These professionals often have to make complex purchasing decisions that require reams of data and difficult to locate sources of supply, all within a tight time frame. That is a perfect fit with the capabilities of online technology.

Cyberconsumers

These are the home computer users wired up to commercial online services and the Internet. This group represents the pot of gold, and marketers simply need to find ways to make it more attractive to shop and buy online than to go to the local store.

Cybersurfers

They use online technology to expand their horizons, challenge their abilities, and for fun. This segment is typically younger, and possesses shorter attention spans.

Some of the important aspects of marketing are advertising, sales, security of the transactions and the mode of payment used for payments. And all of these have had to adapt and change themselves according to the demands of the Internet.

How Should Buyers Pay Online?

The marketplace, as usual, is responding quickly to this concern. A few basic models or approaches to net-based sales transactions are beginning to come into focus. They are:

1. The consumer, responding to net-based marketing presentation, sends in a cheque, or calls and verbally transmits a credit card number, over the merchant's telephone. This is a fairly traditional approach, and no financial transaction takes place on the Internet.
2. The consumer (i) sets up an account with a merchant or a third party organization, (ii) leaves his or her credit card number by means other than the Internet, and (iii) gives the merchant the authorisation to bill the account, whenever the consumer chooses to buy something.
3. The consumer leaves his or her credit card number on an unsecure online order form. With this approach, the consumer is put at some risk that the credit card number will be compromised, but the risk is perhaps not much greater than giving it out over the phone.
4. The consumer uses a secure (encrypting) client software program to transfer his or her encrypted credit card number to a secure (decrypting) merchant server.
5. The consumer exchanges traditional currency (cash, cheque, credit card authorization) for some form of digital currency, and then spends units of that currency whenever and wherever he or she likes. This requires some form of "electronic wallet" to hold the currency and an account set up between the currency provider and the participating merchants.

Advantages of Online Marketing

Some of the advantages of online marketing can be listed in the following manner:

1. Online marketing offers bottom-line benefits that tie in directly to the demands placed on the organization trying to make a transition into the new economy.

2. Online marketing can save money and help you stretch your marketing budget. Electronic versions of catalogues, brochures, and specification sheets do not have to be printed, packaged, stored, or shipped. These can be updated online, and hence, you need not have to send them back to the printer for changes. This saves a lot of money.
3. Online marketing can save time and cut steps from the marketing process. Marketers no longer have to wait for one of their sales representatives to give them the desired information. They can get it online on their own. E-mail allows you to exchange information with potential buyers quickly. It helps you get your message out to the market sooner, with online brochures, catalogues and so on.
4. Online marketing gives customers another way to buy, while enabling them to take control of the purchasing process. Today, customers want more. They want more information about the products they buy, more input into the product itself, and support after the sale. Smart marketers can leverage the inherent interactivity of online communications by encouraging the customer to get engaged in making decisions about the product. They can choose the colour, select the shipping method, and place the purchase order themselves. The more you can get the customer involved in the process of customizing the product and the selling process to meet their particular needs, the more likely it is that you will get the sale.
5. Online marketing can be information-rich and interactive. It appeals to information-hungry buyers and analytical buyers. It allows buyers and current customers to search and locate the information they need quickly.
6. Online marketing can offer you instant international reach and indeed, online networks have created an instant global community. Online marketing erases the time and distance barriers that get in the way of conducting business transactions with customers in other countries.
7. Online marketing can lower barriers to entry and offer equal opportunity for access. When you are doing business online, distinctions related to the ethnic background or gender or even the size of business do not seem to matter as much. The online world is a great leveller. And online marketing helps to lower many of the marketplace barriers that have held some would be entrepreneurs from full participation in the free market system.
8. Online marketing can be continuously available. One of the best attributes of an online information server is that it is always on the job, twenty four hours a day, 365 days a year.

Various Businesses that Can Flourish on the Internet

Banking

The advent of Automated Teller Machines has long extended banking into the realm of computer-network-enabled services. Now, online banks are being set up exclusively to serve clients through the Internet, with the full range of banking services—deposits, withdrawals, funds transfer, loans and other forms of transactions. Simultaneously, online financial services are being offered by other companies, bringing investment opportunities to customers. And several companies are offering e-cash services.

Databanks

In the information economy, pure data is emerging as a hot commodity. With the ease and low cost of delivering information over the Internet pushing down prices, data-vendors are building profitable businesses in the marketspace. Convenient mechanisms for searching databases are making information services user-friendly as well. And importantly, businesses are also springing up to enable data-shoppers to hunt for the information they need, in the form of search engines which search millions of documents on the Internet to track down information.

Music

Since it is recorded and stored digitally, music as well as the other audio products are the perfect products for distribution over the Internet. Instead of buying cassettes or CDs, customers can simply download the recordings from the site. The world's top music labels are setting up websites from which Internet shoppers can buy their favourite pieces. They are also creating customer involvement by setting up virtual communities of music aficionados who can access sample, trivia, and other value-added information, such as lyrics and scores, directly through the Internet.

Retailing

Two genres of online shopping malls are being set up by digital entrepreneurs. The first consists of multimedia catalogues which shoppers can download through the Internet without taking physical delivery. The second variety is a supermarket service that offers gateways to the websites of scores of other shops, acting as a single window for virtual shoppers. With electronic payment systems becoming secure, customers will soon complete entire retailing transactions on the Internet.

E-advertising

Advertising is a $500 billion worldwide industry that, until now, has been mainly a one-way street, with consumers passively absorbing advertising messages. Advertisers hoped that potential buyers would remember their slogan or jingle long enough to make a trip to the store and purchase the product.

This has changed with the advent of interactivity. The new concept of 'interactivity' has overpowered the traditional concept of advertising, by putting the buyer in the driver's seat. Interactivity allows consumers to increase their control over the buying process. We are all deluged with an overflow of data. We long for a sense of mastery over the information that washes over us. Given the opportunity, we will be more selective about the kind of information we choose to receive. Interactivity gives us that option. Thus, the audience is not captive any more, and the marketers would have to work harder than before to entice them. The marketing efforts will have to be information-rich and user-friendly.

Web-based advertising has become an important part of a company's media mix. Numerous companies are committing large advertising budgets to the Internet.

Following are the reasons for the growing importance of e-advertisements:

1. People increasingly prefer to surf the Internet rather than watch TV.
2. The target audience goes to the advertisement, rather than the other way around.
3. Development of business search engines by companies such as C2B Technologies, which aim to link buyers with online bargain sites for over a million products for comparison-shopping purposes.
4. Yahoo! has a business unit which offers contests and prizes to online participants, which drive players to the websites of different clients. To play, participants must provide certain data, including their preference of advertisements and tastes, which presents a valuable database as to customer preferences.
5. The growth of e-business. Dell Computers, for example, estimates that by 2005, 85 per cent of its sales will be through the Internet.
6. The Internet is not geographically restricted. *Amazon.com* sells 20 per cent of its books to foreign destinations, whereas a physical book store serves an area of only a few square miles.[3]

Various Means of Advertising

E-mail

The advantages of e-mail are its low cost and its ability to reach a wide variety of targeted audiences. Most companies develop a customer database, to whom they send e-mails. E-mail is emerging as a marketing channel that affords cost-effective implementation and better, quicker response rates than other advertising channels. Marketers should be racing to embrace the medium. Sometimes, it may also happen that when every marketer starts inundating prospects and customers with e-mail, the consumers may react negatively.

Banners

They make up 50 per cent of online ad revenues, but their effectiveness may be waning. When IBM kicked off banner ads in 1994 on tech site Hotwire, 30 per cent of the people who saw the ads clicked on them. Now the overall click-through rate for banner ads has dropped to a measly 0.3 per cent.

But it is the most commonly used form of advertising on the Internet. As you surf your way through the information superhighway, banners are everywhere. The smaller the file size, the quicker it gets loaded. Typically, a banner contains a short text or a graphical message to promote a product. A major advantage of using banners is the ability to customize them to the target audience. One can decide which market segment to focus on.

3. http://www.w3.org/history

Skyscrapers

These are the extra-long skinny ads running down the right or left side of a website.

Banner Swapping

Banner swapping is nothing but a direct exchange of links between websites. To be precise, company A may agree to display a banner (in the form of a link) of company B in exchange for company B displaying company A's banner.

Streaming Video and Audio

Companies and content networks including RealNetworks, NetRadio, and MusicVision, insert ads for marketers into music and video clips, as consumers listen to them. It is much more like the TV that marketing advertisers know and trust. You can get click-through rates of about 3.5 per cent, according to RealNetworks. Its widespread use will depend on high-speed Internet connections.

Effectiveness Tracking

This is an upstart DynamicLogic designed by a pioneering service to help traditional advertisers gauge the impact of their marketing by placing tiny files, called cookies, on viewers' computers. This helps them track where people go after seeing their ads.

Mini-sites, Pop-ups

These ads burst upon the screens, allowing companies such as Volvo and SmithKline Beecham's Oxy acne medicine to dish up games and product information. Mini-sites allow advertisers to market without sending people away from the site they are visiting. This type of advertising also gets higher click rates. Sometimes, these can be intrusive and annoying.

Interstitials

Visit the railway site (www.indianrail.gov.in). When the site uploads, a new window will open in your browser from Citibank, asking you to apply for a loan. These windows are called interstitials, and they demand your attention because you must click on them, even if only to close the window. It is estimated that the click-through rates are as high as 5 per cent.

Sponsorships

Sponsorships can vary from a simple sponsorship of an e-mail list to much more sophisticated site sponsorship deals. For example, the e-retailer 800.com (*www.800.com*) sponsored a list of the top 10 videos which appeared alongside the 800.com logo on the Hollywood stock exchange (*www.hsx.com*). By clicking on one of the video titles, visitors were transported to the 800.com site, where they could purchase the video. The advantage of sponsorships is that they can help to build a sponsor's brand by presenting it within the context of the sponsored site and by creating value for visitors to that site.

Coupons

Companies such as cool savings (*www.coolsavings.com*) offer their members discount coupons which they can print out and then use for both online and offline retailers. Coupons can be an attractive marketing mechanism because they encourage product trial, and they are a way of selectively discounting prices to the most price sensitive customers (those are willing to go to website and print out a coupon).

Pay Per Advertising View

Companies such as Cyber Gold "pay" customers to view advertisements. The approach uses the accountability of the Web to reward consumers for processing the "right" kind of information.

Loyalty Programs

Companies such as click rewards (*www.clickwards.com*) offer their members the chance to earn a currency, such as airline miles, by shopping at their network of partner sites. The economics of customer retention are well known. An existing, loyal customer is much more profitable than a new one, so rewarding existing customers to encourage them to remain loyal can be a good tactic.

Partnerships

While many offline companies arrange partnerships, the use of partnerships is more pervasive in the New Economy. Similar to the manner in which complementary companies often collaborate to push a new technology, Web companies often partner with complementary sites to quickly provide a more value-enhanced service to site visitors. One prevailing strategy is to select a customer niche and provide services that encompass the customer's entire needs in that area.

Innovative Customer Acquisition

As the Internet market becomes more competitive, competitive advantage will be derived from innovative marketing. One form of innovative marketing is to ally with groups (or associations) and provide a complementary service that benefits the group's membership. By creating such an alliance, a new site can launch with a large customer base without incurring expensive and risky marketing fees. In such an arrangement, a site generally pays the group a fee for access to its membership.

Providing Information

The Web allows sites to instantly offer information that is relevant to their customer base. Many sites provide instantly accessible information to their customers as a form of marketing and product differentiation. The e-commerce market for travel (airlines, hotels, etc.) is very competitive, with many well-funded players. Sites try to differentiate themselves by offering vast amounts of information to their customers. Travel information can range from top restaurant and hotel information targeted toward expense account business travellers, to time-sensitive travel information to budget-minded leisure travellers. Customers evaluate the information they receive and establish a relationship with the site that best meets their needs. Sites try to capitalize on this relationship by offering e-commerce opportunities like travel reservation services.

Leverage the Customer Base

A primary goal of e-commerce businesses today is to invest heavily in creating a large customer base and establishing a relationship of trust with their customers. Many firms are trying to establish a reputation that conveys to its customer base that they are a solid company that is good at fulfilling e-commerce orders. Eventually, as a company establishes a large and loyal customer base, the goal is to leverage this relationship by offering an expanded product/service selection to its customers. Amazon has successfully leveraged its customer base. Within four months of offering CDs and six weeks of offering videos, Amazon was the top-selling site for both products.

Personalized Online Communications

Online companies have the opportunity to reduce mass-marketing expenses and increase response rates by developing marketing strategies that centre around each individual customer. The manner in which transactions occur on the Internet provides e-commerce companies with detailed information on their customers. Information derived from customers registering preferences and demographic information, as well as firms analyzing past purchases and Web-surfing habits, provides e-commerce companies the opportunity to create a one-to-one marketing relationship with each of their customers. In addition to this information, many e-commerce companies use their sites to establish a two-way dialogue with their customers. This dialogue provides additional information regarding product desires and better avenues to market them. We categorize personalized marketing into five primary forms: (1) permission marketing, (2) personalized recommendations, (3) personalized advertisements, (4) personalized web pages, and (5) personalized e-commerce stores.

1. ***Permission marketing.*** Seth Godin coined the term permission marketing to describe how successful e-mail campaigns can result from creating relationships with customers. Permission marketing has become the current rage of online marketers and has led to increases in marketing response rates. Permission marketing presumes that successful marketing campaigns can be created by establishing a mutually beneficial and trusting relationship between the firm and its customers. In exchange for some offered benefit, customers volunteer information about themselves and, in essence, ask to be marketing targets. Once customers initiate this relationship, they anticipate e-mail messages because they know that these messages will be on relevant topics. By using the permission marketing philosophy, online firms create a valuable database of customers who have given the firm the permission to market to them and are receptive to marketing messages. Permission marketing e-mails must be relevant to the consumer. Relevance can range from general interest to very specific interest. Response rates and trust can increase by sending permission marketing e-mails that are highly specific to customers' interests. Many online firms ask their permission

marketing customers for detailed personal information when they sign up for e-mails. This information allows them to send more targeted e-mails to specific segments of the firm's customer base. Customers appreciate these targeted e-mails, and this increases their relationship level with the firm. The associated increased trust level may also induce customers to reveal additional information about themselves.

2. ***Personalized recommendations.*** Many e-commerce sites have personalized services that make specific merchandise recommendations for each user based on past purchases, web pages viewed, and survey information that the user has provided.
3. ***Personalized advertisements.*** Websites increasingly are using personalized technology software to determine dynamically, in real time, which Web advertisements should be exposed to viewers. ZDNET uses personalization technology that is based on an analysis of five user profile and impression environment variables. Variables used include the user's past click behaviour, time of day, the page, recency/frequency of visits, and search keywords. Based on these variables, users are given a relevancy score (i.e. indicator of the probability of a click), and ads that are most likely to be of interest to the viewer are displayed.
4. ***Personalized Web pages.*** Many portals and e-commerce sites allow users to create their own personalized Web page. This allows users to create a Web page that caters exactly to their interests. Personalization encourages users to return more often and increases the user's familiarity and trust with the Web page. This leads to users spending more time on the website, thereby increasing advertising exposure time. Since a creator/user of a personalized Web page reveals detailed personal information, the site sponsoring the personalized Web page can deliver more targeted consumers to advertisers. This results in an opportunity to charge increased ad rates to reach specific customer groups. At portal site Excite, users can create a personalized portal page using Excite's 'My Excite' service. Excite found that users who create a 'My Excite' personal page come back five times as often as others, and view twice the number of pages compared to Excite users who do not have a personal page. This has allowed Excite to reap higher advertising revenues. In addition, personalization increases users' switching costs.
5. ***Personalized e-commerce stores.*** One of the goals of online merchants is to use Internet technology and their knowledge about individual consumers to tailor their products and services for each of their customers. Jeff Bezos, Amazon's chairman, has stated that one of his goals is to have his "store redecorated for each and every customer." However, he cautions that it could take up to 10 years to achieve such individual customization. Office Depot offers its small-business customers personalized catalogues, allowing businesses to create real-time unique catalogues for their employees, based on their buying authority. In addition to making their customers' shopping experience more pleasant, personalization is a key tool for increasing switching costs. If a customer is satisfied and becomes dependent on a site that offers personalized services, it will be more costly to switch sites. Even if a competing site offers superior services, there is a certain inertia that often slows users from switching sites.

Conducting Online Market Research

The Internet is a powerful and cost-effective tool for conducting market research regarding consumer behaviour, identifying new markets, and testing consumer interest in new products. Interest in interactive Internet research methods is on the rise. Market research that utilizes the Internet is frequently more efficient, faster, and cheaper, and allows the researcher to access a more geographically diverse audience than those found in offline surveys. Furthermore, the size of a market research sample is a key determinant of research design. The larger the sample size, the larger the accuracy and the predictive capabilities of the results. On the Web, market researchers can conduct a very large study much more cheaply than with other methods.

The Internet-based market research is often done in an interactive manner by allowing personal contacts with customers, and it provides marketing organizations with greater ability to understand the customer, market, and the competition. For example, it can identify early shifts in products and customer trends, enabling marketers to identify products and marketing opportunities and to develop those products that customers really want to buy. It also tells management when a product or a service is no longer popular. To learn more on market research on the Web, see the tutorials at *Webmonkey.com.*

Online market researchers have to address numerous issues. For example, customers may refuse to answer certain questions. Also, the administration of questionnaires can be lengthy and costly. Furthermore, researchers risk losing people who do not complete online questionnaires because they may not have the latest, fastest computers or a fast Internet connection. For example, long download times and slow processing of Web-based questionnaires lead only to frustration on the part of the customers; it can convince them not to return to a site, leading to lost respondents and future sales.

Online Market/Research Process and Results

The steps in conducting online research are shown in Figure 4.3.

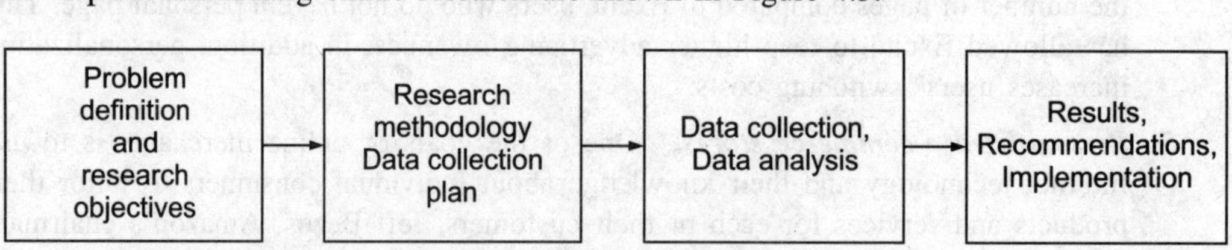

Figure 4.3 Steps needed in online research.

Steps in Collecting Market Research Data

1. Define the research issue and the target market.
2. Identify newsgroups and Internet communities to study.
3. Identify specific topics for discussion.
4. Subscribe to the pertinent groups; register in communities.
5. Search discussion group topic and content lists to find the target market.

6. Search e-mail discussion group lists.
7. Subscribe to filtering services that monitor groups.
8. Enter chat rooms, whenever possible.

Content of the Research Instrument

1. Post strategic queries to groups.
2. Post surveys on your website. Offer rewards for participation.
3. Post strategic queries on your website.
4. Post relevant content to groups with a pointer to your website survey.
5. Post a detailed survey in special e-mail questionnaires.
6. Create a chat room and try to build a community of consumers.

Target Audience of the Study

1. Compare your audience with the target population.
2. Determine your editorial focus.
3. Determine your content.
4. Determine what Web services to create.

Responses can be validated as they are entered, and other elements can be added to the questionnaire, such as graphics, logos, and links to other Web pages. Also, data re-entry errors are eliminated and statistical analyses can he done in minutes. Data from prospective participants can also be collected across international borders. In addition, the participants have the flexibility of responding at any time, at their own convenience. Real-time information and reporting can also be accomplished.

Tracking Customer Movements on the Internet

Through the Internet, it is possible to learn about customers by *observing their behaviour on the Internet* rather than interacting with them and posing questions to them. Many marketers keep track of consumers' Web movements using cookie files attached to a user's browser to help track a Web surfer's movements online, whether or not consumers are aware of it.

Limitations of Online Research

Online research is not suitable for every client or product. Although the Web-user demography is rapidly diversifying, it is still skewed towards certain population groups, such as those with Internet access. If a company manufactures a consumer product such as laundry detergent, Internet research may not be an ideal research tool, because it may not reach enough of the company's target market which in this case may be uneducated women in Indian villages.

Building Customer Relationship Based on One-to-One Marketing

One-to-one marketing is a type of relationship marketing. Relationship marketing is the overt attempt of exchange partners to build a long-term association, characterized by purposeful cooperation and mutual dependence on the development of social as well as structural bonds. It includes the concepts of loyalty and trust.

To be a genuine one-to-one marketer, a company must be able and willing to change its behaviour towards an individual customer based on what they know about that customer. So, one-to-one marketing is really a simple idea—"Treat different customers differently." It is based on the fact that no two customers are alike.

One-to-one marketing involves much more than just sales and marketing, because a firm must be able to change how its products are configured or its services are delivered based on the needs of individual customers. Smart companies have always encouraged the active participation of customers in the development of products, services, and solutions. For the most part, however, being customer oriented has always meant being oriented to the needs of the typical customer in the market—the average customer. But in order to build enduring one-to-one relationships, a company must continuously interact with customers and address their needs individually.

The actual, detailed mechanics of building a one-to-one relationship depends on understanding the various ways in which customers are different and how these differences should affect the firm's behaviour towards particular, individual customers. One reason so many firms are beginning to focus on one-to-one marketing is that this kind of marketing can create high customer loyalty and, as a part of the process, help a firm's profitability.

A company increases loyalty in its own customers—one customer at a time—by establishing a learning relationship with each customer, starting with the most valuable customers. Think of a learning relationship as a relationship that gets better with every new interaction. A customer tells a company of some need (or they learn about it otherwise), and the company customizes its product or service to meet this need. With each interaction and recustomization, the company better fits its product to this particular customer. Thus, the company makes the product more valuable to this customer. Then the customer is more likely to remain loyal to the company.

One of the benefits of doing business over the Internet is that it enables companies to better understand their customers' needs and buying habits, which in turn enables them to improve and frequently customize their future marketing efforts.

Market Segmentation

For years, companies used direct mail to contact customers. However, they did it regardless of whether the products or services were appropriate for the individuals on the company's mailing list. The cost of the direct mailings was about $1 per customer, and only 1 to 3 per cent responded. This meant that the cost per responding customer was between $33 and $100. Obviously, this type of direct marketing was not cost-effective.

In segmentation, the company breaks thousands of customers into smaller demographic segments and tailors its campaigns to each of those segments. Segmentation is done with the aid of tools such as data modeling, warehousing, and mining. Using data mining and Web mining, businesses can look at consumer buying patterns to slice segments even finer. Unfortunately, this is not an easy process, and it requires considerable resources and computer support. Most of the segmentation success stories involve large companies. For example,

Royal Bank of Canada segments its 10 million customers at least once a month to determine credit risk, profitability, and so on. Their segmentation is very successful. The response to Royal Bank of Canada's advertising campaigns has increased from 3 to 30 per cent. Segmentation is less expensive than one-to-one personalization. It is also easier to obtain and maintain the necessary data. Segmentation is important when the Internet goes for localization for advertisement, especially in India with so many different states and languages (See Table 4.5).

TABLE 4.5 Consumer Market Segmentation in India

Segmentation	*Bases/Descriptors*
Geographic	Region and states
	Size of state, city, district, village
	Statistical area
	Population density
	Climate
Demographic	Age
	Occupation
	Sex
	Education
	Family size
	Religion
	Family life cycle
	Caste
	Income
	Linguistic groups
Psychosocial	Social classes
	Lifestyles
	Personality
Cognitive, Affective, Behavioural	Attitudes
	Benefits sought
	Loyalty status
	Readiness stage
	Usage rate
	Perceived risk
	User status
	Innovativeness
	Usage situation
	Involvement

Data Mining and Marketing Research

Customer data accumulates daily in an ever-increasing quantity. Large companies such as retailers, telecommunication companies, PC makers, and car manufacturers build large data warehouses to store such information. To sift through the large amounts of data (e.g., in order to analyze buying habits), marketers use data mining tools.

Data mining derives its name from the similarities between searching for valuable business information in a large database and mining a mountain for a vein of valuable ore. Both processes require either sifting through an immense amount of material or intelligently probing it to find exactly where the value resides. Given databases of sufficient size and quality, data mining technology can generate new business opportunities by providing these capabilities.

- ***Automated prediction of trends and behaviours.*** Data mining automates the process of finding predictive information in large databases. Questions that traditionally required extensive hands-on analysis can now be answered directly and quickly from the data.
- ***Automated discovery of previously unknown patterns.*** Data mining tools identify previously hidden patterns. An example of pattern discovery is the analysis of retail sales data to identify seemingly unrelated products that are often purchased together, such as baby diapers and beer. Other pattern discovery problems include detecting fraudulent credit card transactions and identifying anomalous data that may represent data entry keying errors.

The following are the major characteristics and objectives of data mining:

1. Relevant data are often difficult to locate in very large databases.
2. In some cases, the data are consolidated in data warehouses and data marts; in others, they are kept in databases or in Internet and intranet servers. Data mining tools help remove the information buried in corporate files or archived in public records.
3. "The "miner" is often an end-user empowered by "data drills" and other power query tools to ask ad hoc questions and get answers quickly, with little or no programming skills.
4. "Striking it rich" often involves finding unexpected, valuable results.
5. Data mining tools are easily combined with spreadsheets and other end-user software development tools; therefore, the mined data can he analyzed and processed quickly and easily.
6. Data mining yields five types of information: (a) association, (b) sequences, (c) classifications, (d) clusters, and (e) forecasting.

Data miners can use several tools and techniques. The most well-known tools of data mining are:

- ***Neural computing.*** Neural computing is a machine learning approach by which historical data can be examined for patterns. Users equipped with neural computing tools can go through huge databases and, for example, identify potential customers for a new product or search for companies whose profiles suggest that they are headed for bankruptcy.

- ***Intelligent agents.*** One of the most promising approaches to retrieving information from the Internet or from intranet-based databases is through the use of intelligent agents.
- ***Association analysis.*** This approach uses a specialized set of algorithms that sorts through large data sets and expresses statistical rules among items.

Data mining can also be used to analyze websites. Web mining is the application of data mining techniques to discover actionable and meaningful patterns, profiles, and trends from Web resources. The term Web mining is being used in two different ways. The first, Web content mining, is very similar to text mining. It is the process of information discovery from millions of Web documents. The second, Web usage mining, is the process of analyzing Web access logs (or other information connected to user browsing and access patterns) on one or more Web localities. Table 4.6 shows various industries where data mining can be used.

TABLE 4.6 Data Mining Applications

Industry	*Applications*
Retailing and sales distribution	Predicting sales, determining inventory levels and schedules.
Banking	Forecasting levels of bad loans and fraudulent credit card use, predicting credit card spending by new customers, predicting customer response to offers.
Airlines	Capturing data on where customers are flying and the ultimate destination of passengers who change carriers in mid-flight; thus, airlines can identify popular locations that they do not service and check the feasibility of adding routes to capture lost business.
Broadcasting	Predicting what is best to air during prime time and how to maximize returns by interjecting advertisements.
Marketing	Classifying customer demographics that can be used to predict which customers will respond to a mailing or buy a particular product.

Intelligent Agents in Marketing and Customer-related Applications

As the number of customers, products, vendors, and information increases, it becomes uneconomical, or even impossible, to match customers and products and consider all relevant information. The practical solution to handle the information overload is to use intelligent and software agents.

Agents are used to support many tasks. One of the primary reasons for using such agents is to overcome the tremendous amount of information overload. When going through the purchasing decision process described earlier, for example, a customer must examine large numbers of alternatives, each of which is surrounded by considerable amounts of information.

A search engine is a computer program that can automatically contact other network resources on the Internet, search for specific information or keywords, and report the results. This type of request is repetitive, and answering such requests is costly when done by a human. Search engines deliver answers economically and efficiently by matching questions with FAQ templates, which include standard questions and "canned' answers to them.

Unlike search engines, an intelligent agent can do more than just "search and E-match." For example, it can monitor movement on a website to check whether a customer seems lost or ventures into areas that may not fit his or her profile, and the agent can notify the customer and provide assistance. Depending on their level of intelligence, agents can do many other things, some of which are demonstrated here. Of the many agent applications, we cover only several representative ones (See Figure 4.4).

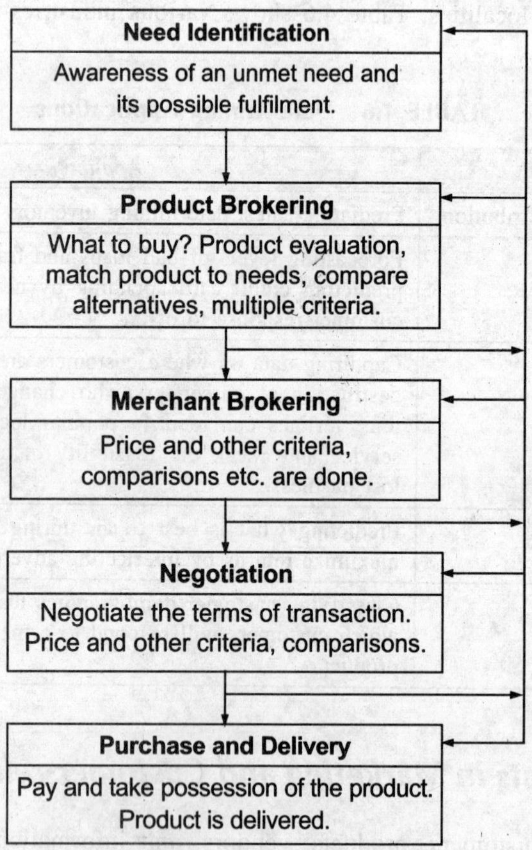

Figure 4.4 Agent-purchasing.

Need Identification

Agents can assist the buyer with need identification by providing product information and stimuli. For example, *amazon.com* provides its customers with an agent that continuously monitors sets of data (such as the arrival of new books) and notifies customers when a book in their area of interest arrives. Similar agents watch for stocks to go below or above a certain level, sending the customer an e-mail when that level is reached. *Expedia.com* notifies customers about low airfares to a customer's desired destination whenever they become available.

Product Brokering

Once a need is established, customers search for a product (or service) that will satisfy this need. Several agents are available to assist customers with this task.

The pioneering agent in this category was firefly. This agent, which was purchased by Microsoft and is no longer available independently, initially helped users find music they were likely to enjoy. Firefly (and similar agents) use a collaborative filtering process to build profiles of people who visit a website. Firefly provided users with a tool that identified them when they visited sites participating in the Firefly program and recommended products/services to them. Based on people's likes (favourite movies, music, interests), Firefly helped marketers predict what customers were likely to want next. This allowed marketers to reach out to consumers with a customized pitch, that was cheaper and more effective than mass advertising. It made product recommendations based on the prioritization of attributes, such as price and delivery time, by users.

Merchant Brokering

Once a customer knows what product he or she wants, the customer needs to find *where* to buy it. Bargain Finder (from Andersen Consulting) was the pioneering agent in this category. The agent, used in online CD shopping, queried the price of a specific CD from a number of online vendors and returned a list of prices. However, this system has encountered problems because vendors who do not want to compete on price only have managed to block out the agent's requests.

Negotiation

The concept of "market" implies negotiation, mostly about prices. In B2B transactions, negotiation is very common. The benefit of dynamically negotiating a price is that the decision is shifted from the seller to the marketplace. In a fixed-price situation, if the seller fixes a price that is too high, sales will suffer. If the price is set too low, profits will be lower. Electronic support of negotiation can be extremely useful.

Kasbah also uses intelligent agents in the negotiation process. Kasbah agents (*kasbah.com*) can negotiate with each other following specific strategies assigned by their creators. However, this agent's usefulness is limited by the fact that price is the only parameter considered.

Agents can negotiate in pairs, or one agent can negotiate for a buyer with several sellers' agents. In such a case, the contact is done with each seller's agent individually, but the buyers agent can conduct comparisons.

Purchase and Delivery

Agents are used extensively during the actual purchase, including arranging payment and delivery with the customer. For example, if a customer makes a mistake when completing an electronic order form, an agent will point it out immediately. When customers buy stocks, for example, the agent will tell the customers when a stock they want to buy on margin is not marginable, or when the customer does not have sufficient funds. Delivery options at *amazon.com,* for example, are posted by agents and the total cost is calculated in real-time.

Measuring the Effectiveness of E-advertising

As more companies rely on their websites to make a favourable impression on potential customers, the issue of measuring website effectiveness has become important. Mass media efforts are measured by estimates of audience size, circulation, or number of addressees. When a company purchases mass-media advertising, it pays a dollar amount for each thousand persons in the estimated audience. This pricing metric is called cost per thousand or cost per metric, and is often abbreviated as CPM in short for cost per thousand impressions.

In reality, measuring Web audiences is more complicated because of the Web's interactivity and also because the value of a visitor to an advertiser depends on how much information the site gathers from the visitor (for example, name, address, e-mail address, telephone number, and other demographic data). Since each visitor voluntarily provides or refuses to provide these bits of information, all visitors are not of equal value. Internet advertisers have developed some web-specific metrics, described in this section, for site activity, but these are not generally accepted and are currently the subject of debate.

When a visitor requests a page from the website, it is counted as one visit. Further page loads from the same site are counted as part of the visit for a specified period of time. This period of time is chosen by the administrators of the site and is dependent on the type of the site. A site that features stock quotes, might use a short time period, because visitors may load the page to check the price of one stock, and reload the page 15 minutes later to check another stock's price. A museum site would expect a visitor to load multiple pages over a longer time period during a visit, and would use a longer visit time window. The first time a particular visitor loads a website page is called a *trial visit*; subsequent page loads are called *repeat visits*. Each page loaded by a visitor counts as a page view. If the page contains an ad, the page load is called an *ad view*. Some Web pages have banner ads that continue to load and reload as long as the page is open in the visitor's Web browser. Each time the banner ad loads is called an *impression*, and if the visitor clicks the banner ad to open the advertiser's page, that action is called a click, or a *click-through*. Banner ads are often sold on a cost per thousand impressions or CPM basis. Rates vary greatly and depend on how much demographic information the website obtains about its visitors, but most are within the range of $1 to $100 CPM.

One of the most difficult things for companies to do as they move on to the Web is to determine the costs and benefits of advertising on the Web. Many companies are experimenting with new metrics they have created that consider the number of desired outcomes that their advertising yields. For example, instead of comparing the number of click-throughs that companies obtain per dollar of advertising, they measure the number of new visitors to their site that buy for the first time after arriving at the site via a click-through. They can then calculate the advertising cost of acquiring one customer on the Web and compare it to the cost of acquiring one customer through traditional channels.

Internet Marketing Trends

Technology-enabled Relationship Management

The nature of the Web, with its two-way communication features and traceable connection technology, allows firms to gather much more information about customers' behaviour and preferences than they can using micro-marketing approaches. Now, companies can measure a large number of things that are happening as customers and potential customers gather information and make purchase decisions. The idea of technology-enabled relationship management has become possible when promoting and selling via the Web. Technology-enabled relationship management occurs when a firm obtains detailed information about a customer's behaviour, preferences, needs, and buying patterns and uses that information to set prices, negotiate terms, tailor promotions, add product features, and otherwise customize its entire relationship with that customer. Although companies can use technology-enabled relationship management concepts to help manage relationships with vendors, employees, and other stakeholders, most companies currently use these concepts to manage customer relationships. Thus, technology-enabled relationship management is often called Customer Relationship Management (CRM) or Electronic-Customer Relationship Management (E-CRM). Table 4.7 compares technology-enabled relationship management with traditional seller-customer interactions in seven dimensions.

Successful, new Web-marketing approaches involve enabling the potential customer to find information easily and to customize the depth and nature of that information, and encourages the customer to buy. Firms should track and examine the behaviours of their website visitors, and then use that information to provide customized, value-added digital products and services in the marketspace. Companies that use these technology-enabled relationship management tools to improve their contact with customers will be more successful on the Web, than firms that adapt advertising and promotion strategies that were successful in the physical world but that are less effective in the virtual world.

The results of a survey of global chief executive officers indicate significant Internet growth and business usage over the next five years, with 92 per cent of executives projecting revenues derived from e-commerce. Although the information technology that supports electronic marketing currently accounts for just 8 per cent of the United States' total economic output, over the last five years, it has fuelled more than one-third of economic growth in the United States. The remarkable growth and impact of the Internet and World Wide Web have spurred almost every business to explore e-marketing strategies to enrich relationships with customers, employees, and suppliers. In fact, the characteristics and availability of the e-commerce infrastructure are driving strategic planning.

TABLE 4.7 E-CRM vs CRM

Dimensions	*Technology-enabled relationship management (E-CRM)*	*Traditional relationships with customers (CRM)*
Advertising	Provide information in response to specific customer inquiries	"Push and sell" a uniform message to all customers
Targeting	Identifying and responding to specific customer behaviours and preferences	Market segmentation
Promotions and discounts offered	Individually tailored to customer	Same for all customers
Distribution channels	Direct or through intermediaries; customer's choice	Through intermediaries chosen by the seller
Pricing of products or services	Negotiated with each customer	Set by the seller for all customers
New product features	Created in response to customer demands	Determined by the seller based on research and development
Measurements used to manage the customer relationship	Customer retention; total value of the individual customer relationship	Market share; profit

Target Markets

Marketing strategy involves identifying and analyzing a target market and creating a marketing atmosphere that satisfies the individuals in that market. Increasingly, marketeers are reaching those individuals through the Internet. Currently, about 110 million Americans access the Internet either at home or at work. Although Internet access outside the US has lagged behind in usage, people around the world are rapidly discovering the Web's potential for communication and e-marketing. Internet use by consumers in other countries—especially Japan (26.9 million users), Germany (19.1 million), the United Kingdom (17.9 million), China (15.8 million), and Canada (13.28 million)—is escalating rapidly.

Although men have long dominated Internet usage statistics, women are increasingly using the Internet for work and to simplify their lives, especially to save time and money. There are 27 million women online in the US, about 46 per cent of American Internet users, but some experts predict that women would have outnumbered men (60 per cent to 40 per cent) on the Internet by 2002. Women are also shopping online—53 per cent of women visitors make online purchase. Internet access by American minority groups is also increasing, with 6.9 million Hispanics, 4.9 million blacks, and 4 million Asians online today. Marketers are also interested in the increasing use of the Internet by teenagers and seniors over the age of 55 years. The 11 million American teenagers using the Internet, spent \$161 million online this year, and experts project that their numbers will reach 15.3 million and \$1.4 billion in 2002. Seniors spent \$3.5 billion online this year and are projected to reach $16.7 billion in online spending by 2002. Such important target markets booming with Internet use, more and more companies are finding market opportunities online.

Product Considerations

The exponential growth of the Internet and the World Wide Web presents significant opportunities for marketing products to both organizations and consumers. Through e-marketing strategies, companies can provide products, including goods, services, and ideas, that offer unique benefits and improve customer satisfaction. Computers and computer peripherals, industrial supplies, and packaged software are the leading organizational purchases online. Consumer products account for a small but growing percentage of Internet transactions, with securities trading, travel/tourism, and books among the hottest consumer purchases. The online marketing of goods such as computer hardware and software, books, videos, CDs, toys, automobiles, and even groceries is accelerating rapidly. Ideas such as marriage counselling, medical advice, tax/legal advice, and even psychic services, are being successfully marketed online as well.

Services may have the greatest potential for online marketing success. Many websites have sprung up to offer or enhance services ranging from home and car-buying-assistance to grocery shopping and travel reservations, and in the travel industry, for example, the ease and relatively low cost of booking travel arrangements online has fuelled online ticket sales, with bookings increasing from $276,000 in 1996 to $1.9 million in 1998. They are projected to reach $8.9 million by 2002.

E-branding

A known and respected brand name can present to potential customers, a powerful statement of quality value and other desirable qualities in one recognizable element. Branded products are easier to advertise and promote, because each product carries the reputation of the brand name. Companies have developed and nurtured their branding programmes in the physical marketplace for many years. Consumer brands such as Ivory soap, Walt Disney entertainment, Maytag appliances, and Ford automobiles have been developed over many years with the expenditure of tremendous amounts of money. However, the value of these and other trusted major brands far exceeds the cost of creating them.

Elements of Branding

The key elements of a brand are differentiation, relevance, and perceived value. Product differentiation is the first condition that must be met with to create a product or a service brand. The company must clearly distinguish its product from all others in the market. This makes branding for products such as salt, nails, or plywood difficult, but not impossible.

If a brand has established that it is different from competing brands and that it is relevant, and inspires a perception of value to potential purchasers, those purchasers will buy the product and become familiar with how it provides value. Brands become established only when they reach this level of purchaser-understanding.

In traditional marketing, "branding" campaigns are designed to embed a company or a product name in your consumer psyche. Firms often use a combination of persuasive, emotional advertising campaigns and public relations to encourage a link between a positive "feeling" and a product. If it works, it can make you want to spend your hard-earned money as fast as possible. Online companies are putting branding to work with remarkable success. Research shows the brand names of seven Internet companies are already recognized by more than 50 million US adults, giving them 'mega-brand' status. According to Opinion Research Corporation International, the following Internet names are top-of-mind with Americans: America Online, Yahoo!, Netscape, *amazon.com*, *Priceline.com*, Infoseek, and Excite. Intelliquest conducted a research and asked 10,000 randomly selected Internet users (unaided by a list of possibilities) to name the sites they associate with certain products. Following is the result:

- Books: *Amazon.com* (56%)
- Music: *CDNow* (24%)
- Computer Software: *Microsoft* (30%)
- Computer Hardware: *Dell* (20%)
- Clothing: *TheGap* (12%)
- Travel: *AOL, Yahoo!, Travelocity* (each 8%)
- Autos: *Yahoo!* (6%)

This clearly shows the effect that e-branding has on the psyche of the consumer. This e-branding criteria is summarized in Table 4.8.

TABLE 4.8 e-branding Criteria

Element	*Meaning to the customer*
Differentiation	In what significant ways is this product or service unlike its competitors?
Relevance	How does this product or service fit into my life?
Perceived value	Is this product or service good?

However, a debate still rages in the business departments of many Internet companies over the importance of branding. How much effort should they spend on e-branding initiatives, that is, building up an online brand? Will those resources be better spent promoting e-commerce efforts which offer tangible returns?

Spiral Branding

The Internet does indeed open new possibilities and new dangers for anyone who ignores the signs. The advent of Internet sites and mailings make possible a new form of marketing called *spiral branding*.

There are two reasons. First, as consumers, it pays to be aware of the tactics marketers are using to influence us. Second, many of us will need to understand and use these techniques ourselves, in our own businesses.

The word "spiral" describes the accelerating benefits of a positive feedback loop. Bill Gates, for instance, often talks about the upward spiral of his Windows business. Since there are more software, customers purchase more Windows machines and since there are more customers, developers build more software which attract more customers. And so goes the cycle.

Savvy marketers use these concepts to create a three-stage branding spiral. First, you use television, print or radio to attract people's attention and send them to the Web. Second, you use the Web to get those customers take interest (via specialized content and interactive services) in your products. You also collect their e-mail addresses. Third, you use e-mail to remind and induce them to return to the Web again. E-mail closes the loop and takes people around the spiral again.

The keys to spiral branding are:

1. Use each media for its best purpose (for instance, don't try to create a television experience on the Web).
2. Do it fast (get something up now and fine-tune as you go along).
3. Iterate constantly (make improvements each time around the spiral).

Branding is about harnessing the free-association game to your advantage; building an e-commerce powerhouse may be a company's stated objective, but it will not get far unless it puts e-branding first.

The Internet is transforming customer buying behaviour, with major consequences for how the new breed of consumer develops familiarity with, and ultimately loyalty to, the brand. Marketers who strive to capitalize on these shifts—as all successful marketers must do—will have to better align their branding investments with new data about how customers shop and buy online. Only by strategically recomposing the marketing mix can marketers drive traffic, build brand equity and capture customer loyalty in the Internet age.

While print, television, radio and related marketing vehicles are hardly superfluous, the data does suggest that "old media" investments will be less effective in building visibility and brand equity over the Web than a range of alternative programs and tools that better align with online customer buying behaviour. Successful marketers will experiment with these emerging strategies to reach out to and connect with their Web-savvy constituents. The following strategies appear particularly promising.

Search Engine Optimization

With nearly half of all Web users citing search engines as their primary portals to new sites, marketers must re-examine their strategies for optimizing their rankings in search results. Appearing among the first few pages of search results on the top search engines is a black-magic science practiced by (usually expensive) outsourcers who specialize in the real-time adjustments that are the key to maximizing visibility on search engines. Today more than 90% searches are done through google (Figure 4.5).

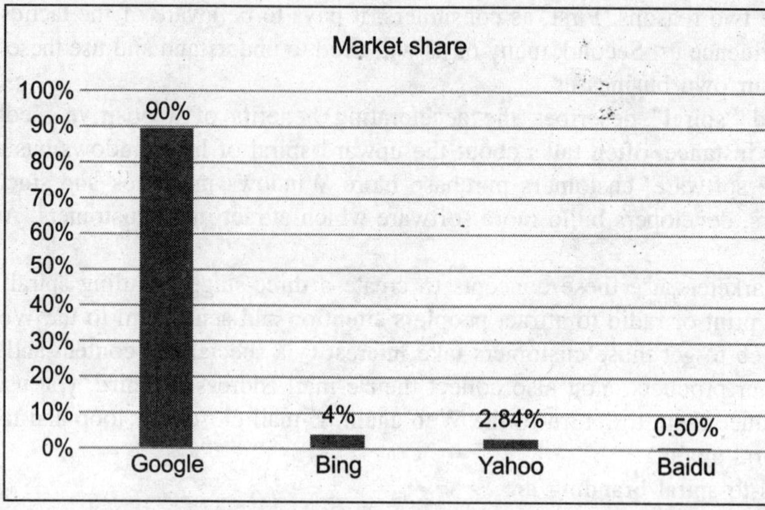

Figure 4.5 Search engine market share[4].

Affiliate Networks

Online marketers need to carefully plan and manage partner programs that give them a broad reach of links on affiliate sites across the Internet. Where 20 per cent of Web users cite "random surfing" as their top means of finding new sites, marketers must have extensive links in place, to maximize their reach to customers throughout the Internet. So-called "affiliate networks"—which typically reward referring to sites with a commission or bounty based on click-throughs, sales leads or completed transactions—are generally much more cost-effective than standard cost-per-thousand banner campaigns.

Advocacy Marketing

Often the most powerful recommendation for a company is that of a satisfied customer to a friend. With 20 per cent of surfers citing word of mouth from friends as their top means of finding new sites, companies need to provide incentives (e.g. discounts, loyalty currencies) and simple mechanisms (e.g. Web-based e-mail forms, pass-along e-mail newsletters) to enlist their customers as marketing advocates to their friends—a strategy often referred to as "viral marketing" by online marketers.

Permission E-mail

When customers explicitly opt into permission marketing relationships, e-mail can be one of the most cost-effective and brand-positive means of acquiring new customers and remarketing to existing customers. Savvy Internet marketeers have realized that "e-mail marketing" does not need to be synonymous with "spam". Instead, a range of strategies such as customer relationship e-mail, corporate e-mail newsletters, reminder services, permission networks,

4. http://marketshare.hitslink.com/search-engine-market-share.aspx?qprid=4??

sponsored independent newsletters, discussion lists, and partner co-marketing can drive online traffic and enhance brand equity.

Personalization and Mass Customization

Marketeers can dramatically enhance customers' online experience by personalizing their Web presence and allowing customers to configure products and services (enabled by mass-customized back-end processes). Sites can improve customer loyalty and build exit barriers with services such as personalized customer interfaces, behaviour-based recommendations and individual product configuration. Personalization is the very essence of experiential branding, whereby customers impact a product or service to reflect a bit of themselves through a one-to-one interaction with the brand.

E-care

A key component of any brand experience is the quality of customer service and support. While companies have long striven for customer service excellence in the offline environment, they are finding that customer expectations for online service present many unfamiliar challenges, such as managing a torrent of customer e-mail inquiries and enabling efficient self-service knowledge bases. With the proper allocation of resources, however, companies can experience brand-positive efficiencies, delivering quality customer service more efficiently online than through traditional channels. Companies that disappoint the user's expectations, however, will damage their online brand equity.

Conventional offline branding is a promise, a relationship built over time, across a wide range of media, gradually giving customers and would-be customers an impression of the organization and an expectation of its products or services. E-branding is immediate. It is not based on the promise; it is based on that dynamic flow of information or the transaction at hand. E-branding is the experience of the words, images, and applications available on your site. Creating the experience is creating what you wish users to feel and think about you, as they operate quite independently from one on the digital frontier. The experience, then, is your brand. While existing brand equity can be brought to the online experience by your customers, it can be destroyed in an instant through a negative interaction with your website, banner ad, or multimedia presentation.

Marketing Strategies

Permission-marketing Strategies

Many businesses would like to send e-mail messages to their customers and potential customers to announce new products, new product features, or sales on existing products. However, print and broadcast journalists have severely criticized some companies for sending e-mail messages to customers or potential customers. Some companies have even faced legal action after sending out mass e-mails. Unsolicited e-mail is often considered to be a spam.

Many businesses are finding that they can maintain an effective dialogue with their customers by using automated e-mail communications. Sending one e-mail message to a customer can cost less than one cent if the company already has the customer's e-mail address. Purchasing the e-mail addresses of persons who have asked to receive specific kinds of e-mail messages will add between a few cents and a dollar to the cost of each message sent. Another factor to consider is the conversion rate. The conversion rate of an advertising method is the percentage of recipients who respond to an ad or promotion. Conversion rates on requested e-mail messages range from 10 per cent to over 30 per cent. These are much higher than the click-through rates on banner ads, which are currently under 1 per cent and decreasing.

The practice of sending e-mail messages to people who have requested information on a particular topic or about a specific product is called opt-in e-mail and is part of a marketing strategy called *permission-marketing*. Thus, a marketing strategy that only sends specific information to persons who have indicated an interest in receiving information about the product or service being promoted should be more successful than a marketing strategy that sends general promotional messages through the mass media. One website that offers opt-in e-mail services is *yesmail.com*.

To induce potential customers to accept or opt in to advertising information sent via e-mail messages, the seller must provide some incentive. This incentive could be entertainment, a chance to win a prize, or even a direct cash payment. For example, *AllAdvantage.com* is a company that pays web users for permission to monitor their web surfing activities. After tracking these users, *AllAdvantage.com* presents targetted ads to them. Advertisers are willing to pay a premium to have access to persons who have demonstrated by their Web surfing habits, that they are interested in the products or services offered by the advertisers.

Brand-leveraging Strategies

Rational branding is not the only way to build brands on the Web. One method that is working for well-established websites is to extend their dominant positions to other products and services. Yahoo! is an excellent example of this strategy. Yahoo! was one of the first directories on the Web. It added a search engine function early in its development and has continued to parlay its leading position by acquiring other Web businesses and expanding its existing offerings. Then, Yahoo! acquired *GeoCities* and *Broadcast.com*, and entered into an extensive cross-promotion partnership with a number of Fox entertainment and media companies. Yahoo! continues to lead its two nearest competitors, Excite and Infoseek, in ad revenue by adding features that Web users find useful and that increase the site's value to advertisers. *Amazon.com's* expansion from its original book business into CDs, videos, and auctions is another example of a website leveraging its dominant position by adding features useful to existing customers.

Affiliate-marketing Strategies

Of course, this leveraging approach only works for firms that already have websites that dominate a particular market. As the Web matures, it will be increasingly difficult for new entrants to identify unserved market segments and attain dominance. A tool that many new, low-budget websites are using to generate revenue is affiliate marketing. In affiliate marketing, one firm's (the affiliate firm's) website includes descriptions, reviews, ratings, or other information about a product that is linked to another firm's site that offers the item for sale. For every visitor who follows a link from the affiliate's site to the seller's site, the affiliate site receives a commission. The affiliate site also obtains the benefit of the selling site's brand in exchange for the referral.

One of the more interesting marketing tactics made possible by the Web is cause marketing, which is an affiliate-marketing program that benefits a charitable organization (and thus, supports a "cause"). In cause marketing, the affiliate site is created to benefit the charitable organization. When visitors click a link on the affiliate's Web page, a donation is made by a sponsoring company. The page that loads after the visitor clicks the donation link carries advertising for the sponsoring companies. Many companies have found that the click-through rates on these ads are much higher than the typical banner ad click-through rates. A leading retail Web florist, *proflowers.com*, has had excellent results advertising on *The Hunger Site* page. When a visitor clicks the button on this page, a group of sponsoring advertisers donates food to a hungry person and a page appears in the visitor's browser with ads for the sponsors.

Viral-marketing Strategies

Traditional marketing strategies have always been developed with an assumption that the company was going to communicate with potential customers directly or through an intermediary that was acting on behalf of the company, such as a distributor, retailer, or independent sales organization. Since the Web expands the types of communication channels available, including customer-to-customer communication, another marketing approach has become popular on the Web. Viral marketing relies on existing customers to tell other persons—the company's prospective customers—about the products or services they have enjoyed using. Much as affiliate marketing uses websites to spread the word about a company, viral marketing approaches individual customers to do the same thing. The number of customers increases much as a virus multiplies, thus the name.

Content Marketing

Content marketing is a marketing technique of creating and distributing relevant and valuable content to attract, acquire, and engage a clearly defined and understood target audience, with the objective of driving profitable customer action.

Content marketing is the art of communicating with your customers and prospects without selling. It is non-interruption marketing. And they do. Content marketing is being used by some of the greatest marketing organizations in the world, including P&G, Microsoft and Cisco Systems.

Social Media Marketing

Social media is becoming one of the most important aspects of digital marketing, which provides incredible benefits that help reach millions of customers worldwide. Social media trends play a vital role in finding ways to engage and interact with customers. Social media transformation is not only a technological shift but also an organizational change which occurs at the intersection of businesses, customers, and technology. Due to this transformation, social media is continuously becoming an important component in the customer decision journey. The first step begins with a complete understanding of the customer journey and its marketing implications. Earlier, there was a linear customer journey where marketers could control a brand's message, but now they are trying to capture the attention of customers on a fragmented journey. According to some surveys, mobile sessions that average a mere 70 seconds long, many times per day are influencing buying decisions. In many ways, these micro-moments have become the footsteps that lead people to purchase products or services. There is no denying that social media marketing has many advantages for startups and established brands. By regular updating the right social media marketing strategy, it will lead to increased traffic, better SEO, improved brand loyalty, healthier customer satisfaction and much more.

TABLE 4.9 Social Networking Sites in India

Social networking sites in India	*Unique visitors (million)*
Facebook	195
Twitter.com	23.3
LinkedIn.com	30
YouTube	60

At the end of 2018, more than 3 billion people in the world are using social media[5] (see Table 4.10).

TABLE 4.10 Users of Social Media in the World

Social media	*Active users*
Facebook	2 billion
Instagram	1 billion
Twitter	330 million
LinkedIn	500 million
Snapchat	300 million

The total ad revenues is estimated to be $74561 million in 2018[6].

5. https://sproutsocial.com/insights/social-media-statistics/
6. https://www.statista.com/outlook/220/100/social-media-advertising/worldwide

Social Media Marketing Strategy

The following steps are involved in the social media marketing strategy (Figure 4.6):

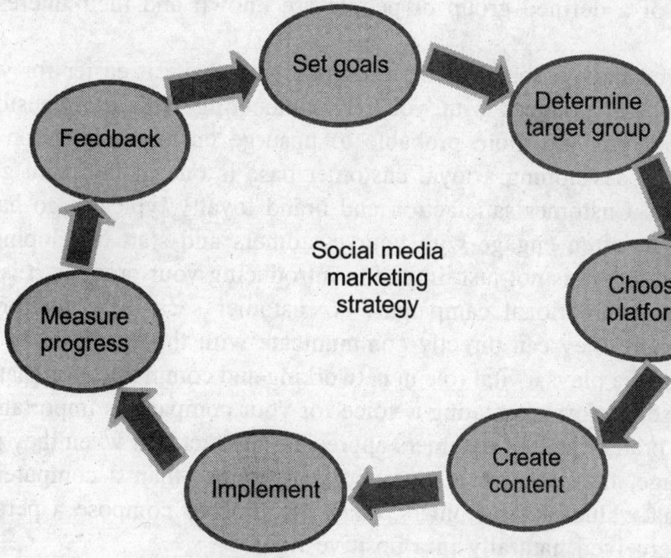

Figure 4.6 Social media marketing strategy.

1. ***Establish social media goals.*** The first step to a successful social media marketing plan is to establish what you want to achieve. Do you have goals to increase brand awareness, generate leads, inform and educate, drive traffic to your site and retain customers? For an advertising strategy, social media marketing is possibly the most cost-effective way.
2. ***Choose your target group.*** Today, thanks to social media, understanding your target audience is not as complicated as it used to be. You have the right tools in hand that help you target varied demographics and connect to your prospective audience. When creating your social media marketing strategy, understanding your audience can make it more precise and result-oriented. Not only do you get to enhance your relationship with your existing customers, but you are also able to find untapped opportunities.
3. ***Choose the right social media platforms.*** Choosing which social media platforms you want to utilize can be overwhelming and a daunting task. You do not have to be present on all platforms. There are many platforms to choose from. If you do not know where to begin, start with the basics—Facebook, Twitter, Instagram, Pinterest, LinkedIn and Google+. A few other social media sites to consider are Houzz, Hometalk, Disqus, Snapchat, Tumblr, Vine, Whatsap, Zillow, and YouTube.
4. ***Create content to improve brand awareness.*** Having a social media marketing strategy will help you not only in growing your presence, but also in maintaining your reputation. To get started, create social media profiles for your business and

start networking with others. Social media is a good way for engaging and interacting customers. The more you communicate with the audience, the more chances you have of conversion. Set up a two-way communication with your target audience so that the wishes of a defined group of people are known and their interests are catered with ease.

When you have a social media presence, you make it easier for your customers to find you and connect with you. By connecting with your customers through social media, you are more probable to upsurge customer retention and customer loyalty. Since developing a loyal customer base is one of the main goals of almost any business. Customer satisfaction and brand loyalty typically go hand in hand. It is essential to often engage with your customers and start developing a bond with them. Social media is not just limited to introducing your product, it is also a leading platform for promotional campaigns. A customer sees these platforms as service channels where they can directly communicate with the business.

Social media plays a vital role in networking and communication platform. With the help of these platforms, creating a voice for your company is important in improving the overall brand image. Customers appreciate the fact that when they post comments on your page, they receive a modified reply rather than a computerized message. A brand that values its customers, takes the time to compose a personal message, which is perceived naturally in a positive light.

One of the other benefits of social media is that it also helps increase your website traffic. By sharing your content on social media, you are giving users a reason to click-through to your website. On your social account, the more quality content you share, the more inbound traffic you will generate while making conversion opportunities.

Social media presence is becoming a vital factor in calculating rankings. These days, to secure a successful ranking, SEO requirements are continuously varying. Therefore, it is no longer enough to simply optimize your website and regularly update your blog. Businesses sharing their content on social media are sending out a brand signal to search engine that speaks to your brand validity, integrity, and constancy.

Marketers need an intelligent approach to design and market micro-moments. Personalized content and call-to-action can add value to the business. Marketers should act seamlessly in real-time and across different channels using a combination of search data and trends.

Customers expect the convenience that allows them to start their buying journey on one channel and end it on another.

5. ***Measure results.*** Track your social media ROI to prove your social campaigns are valuable. If you do not measure the results of your social media marketing campaign, you will not know if your strategy is effective. There are lots of tools out there that will help you measure the effectiveness of your posts. Some social media platforms have analytics already built in so you are able to compare them.

To measure the success of your efforts in social media marketing, you have to link business objectives with social media marketing goals. Then, for each of the social media marketing goals, you have to find the metrics. This is charted in Table 4.11[7].

---

7. https://blog.hootsuite.com/social-media-metrics/

TABLE 4.11 Linking Business Objectives with Social Media Marketing Goal and Metrics

Business objective	*Social media goal*	*Metrics*
Grow the brand	Increase awareness	Followers, shares, etc.
Turn customers into advocates	Engagement	Comments, likes, @mentions, etc.
Drive leads and sales	Conversions	Website clicks, e-mail signups
Improve customer retention	Consumer sentiments	Testimonials, social media sentiments

(i) Metrics for increasing awareness. These include the following:

(a) **Brand awareness** is the attention your brand gets, across all social media, during a *reporting period*. Attention can be expressed through a variety of social media metrics, including @mentions, shares, links, and impressions.

(b) **Audience growth rate** measures the speed at which your brand's following increases on social media. It's *how quickly* you gain followers.

(c) **Post reach** denotes how many people have seen a post since it went live.

(d) **Potential reach** measures the number of people who could, realistically, see a post during a reporting period.

(e) **Social share of voice (SSoV)** measures how many people are mentioning your brand on social media *compared* to your competitors.

(ii) Metrics for engagement analysis. These involve the following:

(a) **Applause rate** is the number of approval actions (e.g., likes, favorites) a post receives relative to your total number of followers.

(b) **Average engagement rate** is the number of engagement actions (e.g., likes, shares, comments) a post receives relative to your total number of followers.

(c) **Amplification rate** is the ratio of shares per post to the number of overall followers.

(d) **Virality rate** is the number of people who shared your post relative to the number of unique views (i.e., impressions) it had during a reporting period.

(iii) Conversion metrics to measure effectiveness of social engagement. These include the following:

(a) **Conversion rate** is the number of visitors who, after clicking on a link in your post, take action on a page (e.g., subscribe to your newsletter; download a gated content asset; register for a webinar) against that page's total visitors.

(b) **Click-through rate (CTR)** is how often people click on the call-to-action link in your post.

(c) **Bounce rate** is the percentage of page visitors who click on a link in your post, only to quickly leave the page they land on without taking an action.

(d) **Cost-per-click (CPC)** is the amount you pay per individual click on your sponsored social media post.

(e) **Cost per thousand impressions (CPM)** is the amount you pay every time a thousand people scroll past your sponsored social media post.

(f) **Social media conversion rate** is the total number of conversions that came from social media, expressed as a percentage.

(g) **Conversation rate** is the ratio of comments per post to the number of overall followers you have.

(iv) Customer metrics for measuring customer sentiments. These include the following:

(a) **Customer testimonials** are any customer review, assessment, comment, endorsement, or interview relating to a brand.

(b) **Customer satisfaction (CSat) score** is a metric that measures how happy people are with your product or service.

(c) **Net promoter score (NPS)** is a metric that measures customer loyalty.

Social Media Analytics to Support Measurements

1. ***Facebook analytics.*** Marketers who run a Facebook business page have access to the comprehensive Facebook analytics dashboard. Developed with insights from Facebook's two billion users, the platform offers recommendations on how to reach the largest audience on social media.

Once you have clicked on the business page you want to monitor, the Insights tab is your go-to place for all things analytics. The overview section offers a summary of the page's performance. Here, you can choose to a time range of one day, one week or the last 28 days. If one of the goals of your campaign is to increase the number of people who follow or like the page, you will find this information in the Follower and Like tabs. Here, you will be able to analyze the page's popularity over time, and see where the new Follows and Likes are happening.

On Facebook, reach measures the number of people who had any posts from your page appeared on their screen. If someone decided to hide posts from your page, you can find that info here, too. Here, you will find where your page traffic is coming from. You can also measure the views for each section page, including About, Photos, Home, etc., which will help you understand what areas are most popular. The posts tab shows you how your page posts are performing, and also offers insights on the best times to post and the types of posts that are most successful.

2. ***Twitter analytics.*** Twitter offers a month-by-month summary of your account's performance. It gives an overview of your follower count, tweet impressions, profile visits and mentions. Highlights from each month include your account's top tweet, top follower and top mention. This is a good place to get a snapshot of your best performing content. In the Tweets tab, track the engagements and impressions on your tweets over a selected period. If you have promoted any tweets, you can track those analytics here, too. Keep tabs on your audience in this section of the analytics dashboard. This is where you can learn about your audience's demographics and thematic interests. You can also add a comparison audience to see how your followers differ from other users.

3. ***Instagram analytics.*** Instagram insights are available for business profiles and accounts with a high number of followers. In addition to analytics on your content, Instagram insights will also provide information about who your followers are, when they are online, and more. Insights and metrics about your account include:
    - **Impressions:** The number of times your posts were on screen
    - **Reach:** The number of unique post views
    - **Website clicks:** The number of clicks on the link included in your profile
    - **Profile visits:** The number of times your username is clicked on
4. ***Snapchat analytics.*** Snapchat has been upping its analytics game of late, especially when it comes to delivering insights on paid content. Snap Ad Reporting lets marketers monitor campaigns in real time, and even tracks whether snaps drove viewers to your store. It finds out exactly how many people are engaging with your snaps. Some marketing campaigns may have the goal of getting snappers to take screenshots. Even if it is not a direct goal, knowing that users felt compelled to take a snapshot of your content is a strong metric.
5. ***Pinterest analytics.*** For businesses on the Pinterest analytics platform, marketers can monitor what pins people like, how much traffic goes to your site, and what people are pinning from your website. Knowing how many times your Pin has shown up across Pinterest is a good metric to measure against closeup and click metrics.
6. ***LinkedIn analytics.*** Company page analytics on Linkedln can be used to monitor traffic to and from your page and learn more about your visitor demographics in this section. If your social media strategy involves posting content on LinkedIn, this section will allow you to track the reach of each post and analyze engagement. You can also track actions on each post, such as how many followers or profile visits you gained. Here, you can monitor follower trends over periods of time, and investigate whether they were acquired organically or through paid content. You will also get demographics about your followers in this section, including industry and seniority data. Marketers can also benchmark audience growth by comparing followers with other companies.

Website Naming Issues

Firms that have a major investment in branding a product or a service must protect that investment. In Chapter 5, you learned about the security issues surrounding website naming. The legal and marketing aspects of website naming can be very much complicated. Although a variety of state and federal laws protect trademarks, the procedure for creating and using website names that are not trademarks can present some challenging issues. Obtaining identifiable names to use for branded products on the Web can be just as important as ensuring legal trademark protection for an existing brand investment.

In 1998, a poster art and framing company named Artuframe opened for business on the Web. With quality products and an appealing site design, the company was doing well, but it was concerned about its URL, which was *www.artuframe.com.* After searching for a more appropriate URL, the company's president found the website of Advanced Rotocraft Technology, an aerospace firm, at the URL *www.art.com.* After finding out that Advanced Rotocraft Technology's site was drawing 150,000 visitors each month who were looking for something art-related, Artuframe offered to buy the URL. The aerospace firm agreed to sell the URL to Artuframe for $450,000. Artuframe immediately changed its URL to *Art.com* and experienced a 30 per cent increase in site traffic, the day after implementing the name change. The newly named site however, did not rely on the name change alone. It has since then entered a joint marketing agreement with Yahoo! that places an ad for *Art.com* on art-related search result pages. *Art.com* has also created an affiliate program with businesses that sell art-related products and other organizations that have websites devoted to art-related topics.

Another company that invested in an appropriate URL was *Cars.com.* The firm paid $100,000 to the speculator who had originally purchased the rights for the URL. *Cars.com* is a themed-portal site that displays ads for new cars, used cars, financing, leasing, and other car-related products and services. The major investors in this firm are newspaper publishers that wanted to retain an interest in automobile-related advertising as it moved online. Classified automobile ads are an important revenue source for many newspapers.

Table 4.12 lists domain names that have been sold for more than $1 million each.

TABLE 4.12 Domain Names that were Sold

Domain name	*Price*
Business.com	$7.5 million
Altavista.com	$3.3 million
Loans.com	$3.0 million
Wine.com	$3.0 million
Autos.com	$2.2 million
Express.com	$2.0 million
WallStreet.com	$1.0 million
iPhone.com	$1.0 million
Invest.com	$1.0 million
Flying.com	$1.1 million
Scores.com	$1.2 million
DataRecovery.com	$1.6 million
CreditCheck.com	$3.0 million

Although most domains that have high value are dot-com sites, the name *engineering.org* sold at an auction to the American Society of Mechanical Engineers, a not-for-profit organization, for just under $200,000.

Several legitimate online businesses, known as URL brokers, are in the business of selling or auctioning domain names that they believe others will find valuable. Companies selling "good" (short and easily remembered) domain names include *Domains.com*, *DomainRace.com*, *GreatDomains.com*, and *HitDomains.com*. *Unclaimed Domains* sells a subscription to lists of recently expired domain names that it publishes periodically, and the Netcraft website has a URL search function to search for words in URLs. The Internet Corporation for Assigned Names and Numbers (ICANN) maintains a list of accredited domain http://www.fka200.com/2009/01/03/a-list-of-some-of-the-top-domain-name-sales-ever-most-expensive-domains/ name registrars, which are companies that have been authorized by ICANN to sell the rights to use specific domain names ending in com, net, and org.

Advertising-supported Model

The advertising-supported business model is the one used by network television in the United States. Broadcasters provide free programming to the audience along with advertising messages. The advertising revenue is sufficient to support the operations of the network and the creation or purchase of the programs.

Many observers of the Web in its early growth period, believed that the potential for Internet advertising was tremendous. However, after a few years of experience trying to develop profitable advertising-supported business models, many of those observers are less optimistic. The success of Web advertising has been hampered by two major problems. First, as discussed earlier, no consensus has emerged on how to measure and charge for site visitor views. Since the Web allows multiple measurements, such as of number of visitors, number of unique visitors, number of click-throughs, and other attributes of visitor behaviour, it has been difficult for web advertisers to develop a standard for advertising charges, such as the CPM measure used for mass-media outlets. In addition to the number of visitors or page views, stickiness is a critical element for creating a presence that will attract advertisers. Recall from Chapter 3 that the stickiness of a website is its ability to keep visitors at the site and to attract repeat visitors. People spend more time at a sticky website and are thus exposed to more advertising.

The second problem is that very few websites have sufficient numbers of visitors to interest large advertisers. Most successful advertising on the Web is targeted to very specific groups. However, it can be difficult to determine whether a given website is attracting a specific market segment or not, unless that site collects demographic information, which the visitors are increasingly reluctant to provide because of privacy concerns.

Only a few general-interest sites have generated sufficient traffic to be profitable based on advertising revenue alone. One of these is Yahoo!, which was one of the first Web directories. Many people use Yahoo! as a starting point for searching the Web, and the number of visitors increase day by day. This has made it possible for Yahoo! to expand its Web directory into one of the first portal sites. Because the Yahoo! portal's search engine presents visitors' search results on separate pages, it can include advertising on each results page that is triggered by the terms in the search. For example, when the Yahoo! search engine detects that a visitor has searched on the term "new car deals", it can place a Ford ad at the top of the search results page. Ford is willing to pay more for this ad because it is directed only at visitors who have expressed interest in new cars. This example demonstrates one attractive option for identifying a target market audience without collecting demographic information from site visitors. Unfortunately, only a few high-traffic sites are able to generate significant advertising revenues this way. Besides Yahoo!, the main portal sites in this market today are Excite, Infoseek, and Lycos. Smaller general-interest sites, such as the Web directory *refdesk.com*, have had much more difficulty than the larger search engine sites in attracting advertisers. This may change in the future as more people use the Web.

Newspaper publishers have experimented with various ways of establishing a profitable presence on the Web. It is unclear whether a newspaper's presence on the Web helps or hurts the newspaper's business as a whole. Although it provides greater exposure for the newspaper's brand and a larger audience for advertising that the paper carries, it can also take away sales from the print edition, a process called *cannibalization*. Newspapers and other publishers worry about cannibalization, because it is very difficult to measure. Some publishers have conducted surveys in to find out whether people have stopped buying their favourite newspaper because the contents they want to see are available online, but the results of such surveys are not very reliable.

Many leading newspapers, including *The Washington Post* and *The Los Angeles Times*, have established online presences in the hope that they will generate enough revenue to cover the cost of creating and maintaining the website. The **Internet Public Library Online Newspapers** page includes links to hundreds of newspaper sites around the world.

Although attempts to create general-interest websites that generate sufficient advertising revenue to be profitable have met with mixed results, sites that target niche markets have been more successful. For newspapers, classified advertising is very profitable. Therefore, it is not a surprise that websites which specialize in providing only classified advertising, have profit potential if they can reach a narrow enough target market.

An implementation of the advertising-supported business model which appears to be successful is web employment advertising. Firms with websites such as *CareerSite.com* and *JOBTRAK* offer international distribution of employment ads. As the number of people using the Web increases, these businesses will be able to move out of their current focus on technology and higher-level jobs and include advertising for all kinds of positions. These sites can use the same approach that search engine sites use to offer advertisers target markets. When a visitor specifies an interest in, for example, engineering jobs in Dallas, the results page can include a targeted banner ad for which an advertiser will pay more, because it is directed at a specific segment of the audience. Employment ad sites can also target specific categories of job seekers by including short articles on topics of interest. This will also ensure that qualified people, who are not necessarily looking for a job, keep coming back to the site; such people are the candidates most highly sought after by employers.

Marketing Strategy on the Web

Finally, it needs to be reiterated that strategy for marketing on the Internet should follow rules such as those given in Table 4.13.

TABLE 4.13 Marketing Strategies for the Web

Strategy	*Rules*
Brands	Your website becomes your most important brand.
Change	Keep in mind that the marketing rules on the Internet are constantly changing.
Conciseness	Keep your pages short, and spread information on several pages.
Content	Content is the king and so make it interesting.
Dynamic sites	Create dynamic sites that use new technologies to adapt information based on user profiles.
Finances	Try new markets with low advertising pricing schemes.
Free giveaways	Create free offerings for your loyal customers.
Global village	Think global, but localize.
Live events	Online events create quick awareness.
Niche markets	The Internet is a series of niche markets and mass markets.
Promotion	Promote your site everywhere.
Syndication	Co-brand your services and products.
Technology	Use Internet technology to maximize your marketing objectives.

The Times of India

Till 2002, *The Times of India* was just another newspaper competing to make its mark and increase its readership. But today, the newspaper has transformed from what was once a plain-looking national newspaper into a global one, which anybody in any part of the world can access with just a click of the mouse.

To put consumers, i.e. the readers, in the center of the flagship media brand, The Times Group had hired a seasoned advertising strategy professional, Rahul Kansal, as Brand Director. The new position of Brand Director was to attempt to address the readers as consumers and a 'brand person' (and not just a content person—Editor) needs to constantly evolve the product offering. When the TOI decided to revamp its brand image, it brought about a lot of changes to its paper as well as its online edition. The Internet hence played a very important role in its remodeling. They changed their page layout, broke the page up into different sections, added pictures to break the monotony, and then went online.

Now, how did going online help them? It integrated the hard copy of the newspaper with the online edition. They made the website a place where people came for more than just news. They introduced the following online features:

- Classified advertisements: There is an option of online search. Since there is no restriction like in the print, more ads can be accommodated. This is also integrated with the printed version.
- Hot links: They provide links to the e-paper that makes the local paper globally available for a subscription, and other favourite links like Bollywood, NRI news, etc.

- News items: Links to the regular sections of the newspaper are also provided, like India, sports, world, weather, entertainment, etc.
- Opinion section: In this section, the views of the various columnists, editor and people on the various current affairs are given.
- Online copies of all supplements.
- Online shopping, games, chats, e-mails.
- Lots of pictures and graphics to make it interesting.
- They also have links to other sites powered by the Times Group, thereby promoting those as well.

Advantages of the Online Edition

- Accessibility—People from Bangalore to Boston, Hyderabad to Houston can all have access to TOI.
- Hourly updates—Any breaking news can be easily found on the website, and people need not wait for the next morning.
- Caters to a wide range of interests and needs—Current affairs, finances, shopping, entertainment, astrology, travel bookings, etc.
- Platform to voice opinions—Opinion polls, letters to the editors, views of columnists and editor.
- Show customers that they too are modern and on par with the changing trends.
- Incorporate features that keep bringing people back to their site—offering the customers more than just news.

All of this and more add up to the Brand—*The Times of India*.

Case Discussion

1. What are the advantages of having an internet version of the newspaper?
2. Visit the site of *The Times of India* and identify the difference between the internet version and the actual newspaper?
3. How does the marketing model fit into the internet version of the newspaper?

EXERCISES

1. Describe the process of Internet shopping. List the major steps involved.
2. What is direct marketing?
3. List the critical success factors of Dell.
4. Why are books such a natural target for e-commerce?
5. List the major methods of Internet advertisement.
6. Compare banner swapping and banner exchange.
7. Compare and contrast 'pulling information' and 'pushing information'.

8. Discuss why banners are important in Internet advertisement.

9. How is the chat room used for advertisement?

10. Why might the use of CPM to charge advertisers be inappropriate as a basis for charting ads?

11. Why do customers like Web-based purchase? What cultural and social factors would affect Indian Web-based purchases?

12. Enter the sites of www.peapod.com and www.Netgrocer.com. Compare the services offered by the two companies and evaluate their chances for success. If you had money to invest, in which of these two companies would you invest?

13. There are many search engines. Try the following ones: www.jango.com and www.compare.com. Try to find a Notebook computer, a vacuum clearner and a plain paper fax machine and compare the prices. Comment on the strong and weak point of each of the search engines.

14. Almost all major car manufacturers allow you to configure your car online. Enter www.toyota.com and www.ford.com and configure a car of your choice. After you decide what you want, examine the payment options.

15. Enter the website www.ipro.com and find what Internet traffic management, Web results and auditing services are provided. What are the benefits of each?

16. Find information about banners in the following sites:
    (a) www.linkexchange.com
    (b) www.coder.com
    (c) www.doubleclick.net/advertisers

17. Investigate the high volume items that are being retailed on the Internet. Some examples are:
    Toys(www.eToys.com)
    Software(www.eggheads.com)
    Movies(www.real.com)
    Find more best selling sites.

18. Study the site traveljini.com and analyse its marketing strategies. A brief history of traveljini is given below:

    The tourism industry in India is fairly developed and there is scope for further development. *Traveljini.com* provides a unique business proposition for the tourism industry by using e-commerce, so as to give tourism in India a greater visibility that is also cost-effective and reliable.

    Traveljini.com Limited was established in June 2000 and is a portal dedicated to the exciting business of travel. It is one of India's premier travel portal backed by strong offline presence across the country.

    Traveljini.com offers a complete solution relating to travel. Some of the services they provide include the best deals on flights, hotels, car rentals, cruises, and leisure holidays, and all these can be booked either online or offline. The site boasts of the most exhaustive travel-related information and has a slew of unique support services to ensure that a tourist's travel experience is unmatched. This guarantees that it is the one site that discerning travellers must check before setting out.

In over two years, Traveljini has established itself as the India's leading Internet travel company in terms of:

- brand recall
- depth of content
- transaction capability

Traveljini aims to set benchmarks in customer service, using the latest technologies in product development and delivery. They use fully-automated, customized software, a brick-and-mortar travel agency and an efficient customer service cell, which allows them to serve their clients to a hitherto unprecedented degree.

"To become the largest Travel Distribution Company in India by the simple expedient of putting the customer first."

TJ Travel Services Limited is another wholly-owned subsidiary of *Traveljini.com*. It is an IATA accredited travel agency, which provides back-end support for corporate business travel as well as handling flight ticketing in both the domestic and international sectors, for conferences, incentive travel and events.

Traveljini.com books domestic flights in India and international flights as well. They have an application called the Smart Fare Finder for special fares to various international destinations on the leading airlines of the world.

They also provide assistance in visa processing. They can also book hotel rooms in India and abroad. To make it easy for the customer, they offer easy access to their global hotel reservation system, so one can check real-time availability of rooms in 30,000 hotels around the world. They have every kind of holiday that a traveller might want, from a cruise to a weekend to a romantic honeymoon.

If someone wants a holiday designed specially for him and his family, he can access Customjini. They allow buying of foreign exchange through their network and which is then delivered to the customer's doorstep. A service called Mapjini can be used to find ways in over 60 Indian cities if the need be. Business travellers can seek their services to organize a conference, a meeting, incentive travel or an exhibition. They also book cars in India for all kinds of travellers.

CHAPTER

5

e-Security

LEARNING OBJECTIVES

After reading this chapter, you should be able to:

- Understand the goals of information security.
- Explain the methods used for defense against attack on computer systems.
- Describe the different kinds of attacks on computer systems.
- Understand the firewalls and why do we need them.
- Understand the enterprise-wide security system.
- Describe the encryption techniques used in secure transactions.
- Understand digital signatures and how they are used.

Security Breach

Karan Bahree, 24, from New Dehli sold a CD containing the confidential details of 1,000 British bank accounts to an undercover reporter from the UK based newspaper Sun. He was an employee of the call centre called **Infinity eSearch**. According to The Sun, the information, which includes addresses, passwords, phone numbers and driving license and passport details, was purchased for £3 per customer. Financial institutions such as Barclays, Lloyds TSB, the Nationwide and HSBC were affected[1]. A call centre is a centralized office used for the purpose of receiving and transmitting a large volume of requests by telephone. Many call centres have been built in developing countries like India because of cheap labour. This means that the companies get cheap land and labour, and can often benefit from grants to encourage them to improve employment in a given area.

1. OUT-LAW News, 27/01/2006.

Case Discussion

1. Discuss the areas where privacy becomes an issue in computer usage.
2. Discuss how information systems can be protected from unauthroized access and usage.
3. What is the importance of privacy with regard to computer information systems?

Cars, fridges, houses, factories, gadgets, etc., are being controlled and monitored remotely using computers. At the same time, more and more people around the globe have access to these new technologies and depend on them in their daily life. But, the mass of interconnected things, referred to as the Internet of Things (or Internet or Everything), and technological innovation come with a risk—they increase the number of potential targets for malicious cyber activity.

Malicious cyber activity is a growing challenge for organizations worldwide. It ranges from straightforward online fraud to sophisticated cyber espionage and calculated cybercrime, used to steal secrets and other information stored digitally on systems and networks. Malicious cyber activities have the potential not just to seriously harm an organization's business and reputation, but also to compromise a nation's security, stability and prosperity. The number of incidents has spiked in recent years, as perpetrators aggressively exploit flaws in digital infrastructure. This has catapulted cyber security to front-of-mind for business leaders, regulators and politicians who are anxious to shore up defences and improve resilience.

Cyber adversaries are constantly devising new ways to exploit vulnerable systems and networks. This is forcing organisations—from banks to energy companies, and from government agencies to charities—to strengthen their cyber defences.

Information System Security

Any business, whether it is a traditional brick-and-mortar business, a brick-and-click e-business, or a pure-play e-business, needs to be concerned about network security. The Internet is a public network consisting of thousands of private computer networks connected together. This means that a private computer network system is exposed to potential threats from anywhere on the public network. Protection against these threats requires businesses to have stringent security measures in place. In the physical world, crimes often leave evidence—finger prints, footprints, witnesses, video on security cameras and so on. Online, a cyber-crime also leaves physical, electronic evidence, but unless good security measures are taken, it may be difficult to trace the source of a cyber-crime.

As seen in Figure 5.1, the goals of security are:

1. Integritiy of the data sent and received.
2. Confidentiality of the data so that it is not accessible to others.
3. The data ought to be available to the people for whom it is meant.

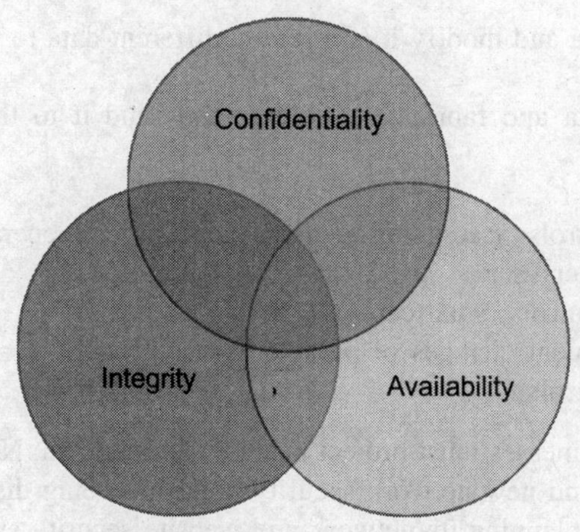

Figure 5.1 Security goals.

As shown in Figure 5.2, the data sent from the source ought to reach in destination without any tampering as shown in Figure 5.2(a). But the above criteria shown in Figure 5.2(a) may be violated by the following:

1. Interrupt the data and cut it off as shown in Figure 5.2(b).
2. Intercept the data with the intent of spying on it as shown in Figure 5.2(c).

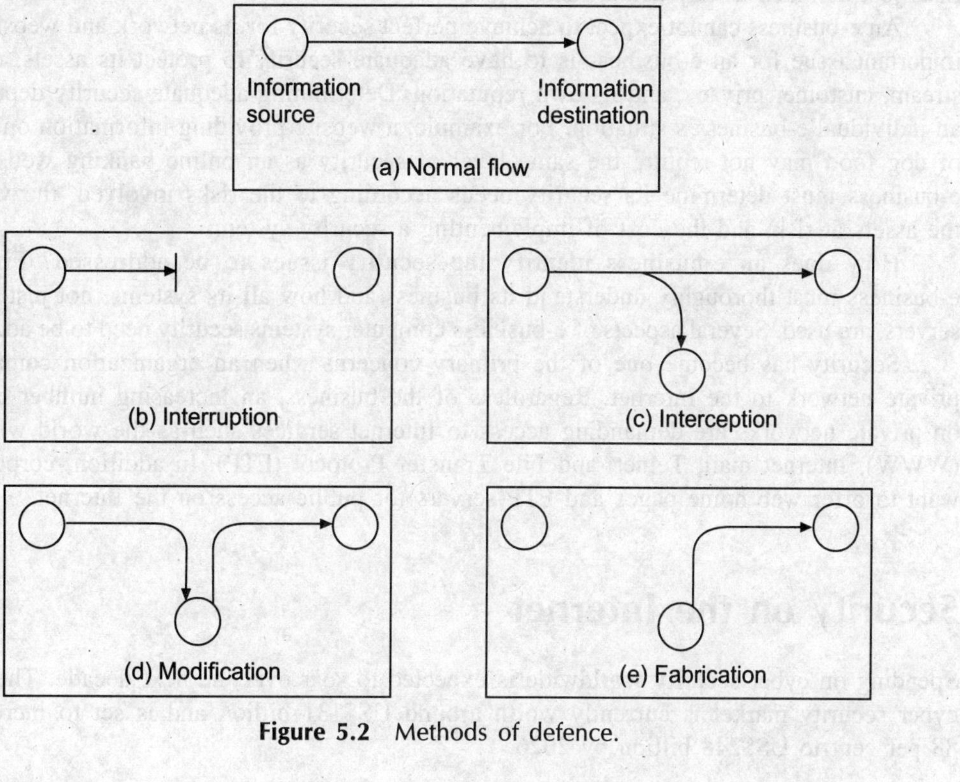

Figure 5.2 Methods of defence.

3. Interrupt the data and modify it and send a different data to the receiver as shown in Figure 5.2(d).
4. Obstruct the data and fabricate new data and send it to the receiver as shown in Figure 5.2(e).
   - Encryption
   - Software Controls (access limitations in a data base, in operating system protect each user from other users)
   - Hardware Controls (smartcard)
   - Policies (frequent changes of passwords)
   - Physical Controls

Additionally, e-businesses must protect against the unknown. New methods of attacking networks and websites and new network security holes are being discovered with disturbing frequency. By carefully planning its network and website security system, an e-business can protect itself against many known and as yet unknown threats. An e-business must always be prepared for network and website attacks, or risk the loss of assets.

Another very important reason to protect an e-business's network and website is to protect the e-business's relationships with its customers. Many Internet users perceive that there is a large risk to their privacy and security when they buy products and services or submit personal information online. Although the perception of risk may be greater than the actual risk, it is still a cause for concern. An e-business must address customers' perceived risks just as much as any actual risks.

An e-business cannot expect to achieve perfect security for its network and website. The important issue for an e-business is to have adequate security to protect its assets, revenue stream, customer privacy, and its own reputation. Determining adequate security depends on an individual e-business's situation. For example, a website providing information on flavors of dog food may not require the same level of security as an online banking website. An e-business must determine its security needs according to the risks involved, the value of the assets at risk, and the cost of implementing a security system.

How does an e-business identify the security issues to be addressed? First, the e-business must thoroughly understand its business and how all its systems, not just its web servers, are used. Several aspects of e-business computer systems security need to be addressed.

Security has become one of the primary concerns when an organization connects its private network to the Internet. Regardless of the business, an increasing number of users on private networks are demanding access to Internet services such as the world wide web (WWW), Internet mail, Telnet, and File Transfer Protocol (FTP). In addition, corporations want to offer web home pages and FTP servers for public access on the Internet.

Security on the Internet

Spending on cyber security worldwide is expected to soar over the next decade. The global cyber security market is currently worth around US$131 billion and is set to increase by 88 per cent to US$248 billion by 2026.

Several trends support the growth outlook for cyber security spending:

- ***Expanding threat of cyber attacks.*** Malicious cyber activity is on the rise, as criminals use ever-more sophisticated strategies to infiltrate systems and networks.
- ***Mounting exposure to cyber risk.*** The rapid expansion of internet-enabled economic activity and the number of connected devices and systems increase the likelihood of widespread malicious cyber activity. People in far corners of the globe are gaining online access, as the world becomes more digitised and interconnected. This is partly due to smartphone penetration, which has risen markedly in many countries. Everyday items such as watches, fridges and cars are now Internet-connected, as are important customer databases, power plants and government payment systems. This increases the volume and quality of information shared electronically, and widens the range of potential targets for perpetrators.
- ***Growing risk awareness.*** Recent high-profile cases of malicious cyber activity and media coverage of data breaches have made companies and other organizations increasingly aware of the risks cyber adversaries pose to their businesses.
- ***Increasing regulation of cyber risk.*** Governments worldwide are increasingly concerned that cyber attacks could hit crucial economic sectors. Many are issuing new laws to ensure organizations bolster their cyber security controls. The expected growth in cyber-related regulation is likely to prompt organizations to increase their security spending.
- ***Cyber security is no longer just firewalls and off-the-shelf virus software.*** In recent years, it has evolved significantly to encompass a sophisticated range of products and services, as well as activities within organizations to build and operate their cyber security system.

Looking at Table 5.1, one can see the amount of money being spent on security of computer systems.

TABLE 5.1 Global Spending on Internet Security Software 1998–2003[2]

Year	*Revenues (in billion $)*
2014	70.84
2015	84
2016	92
2017	99
2018	106

Network administrators have increasing concerns about the security of their networks when they expose their organization's private data and networking infrastructure to Internet crackers. To provide the required level of protection, an organization needs a security policy to prevent unauthorized users from accessing resources on the private network and to protect

2. www.epaynews.com

against the unauthorized export of private information. Even if an organization is not connected to the Internet, it may still want to establish an internal security policy to manage user access to certain portions of the network and protect sensitive or secret information.

The fundamental problem may be that the Internet was not designed to be very secure, i.e. open access for the purposes of research was the prime consideration at the time the Internet was implemented. However, the phenomenal success of the Internet, combined with the introduction of different types of users, including unethical users, has aggravated existing security deficiencies to the extent that wide-open Internet sites risk inevitable break-ins and resultant damages. Other factors include the following:

1. ***Vulnerable TCP/IP services.*** A number of the TCP/IP services are not secure and can be compromised by knowledgeable intruders; services used in the local area networking environment for improving network management are especially vulnerable.
2. ***Ease of spying and spoofing.*** A majority of Internet traffic is unencrypted; e-mail, passwords, and file transfers can be monitored and captured using readily-available software. Intruders can then reuse passwords to break into systems.
3. ***Lack of policy.*** Many sites are configured unintentionally for wide-open Internet access, without regard for the potential for abuse from the Internet; many sites permit more TCP/IP services than they require for their operations, and do not attempt to limit access to information about their computers that could prove valuable to intruders.
4. ***Complexity of configuration.*** Host security access controls are often complex to configure and monitor; controls that are accidentally misconfigured often result in unauthorized access.

Sites that ignore these problems face some significant risk that they will be attacked by intruders and that they may provide intruders with a staging ground for attacks on other networks. Even sites that do observe good security practices, face problems with new vulnerabilities in networking software and the persistence of some intruders.

Some of the problems with Internet security are the result of inherent vulnerabilities in the services (and the protocols that the services implement), while others are a result of host configuration and access controls that are poorly implemented or overly complex to administer. This is further aggravated by the tremendous growth of the Internet and the way it is used. Businesses and agencies now depend on the Internet for communications and research, and thus have much more to lose if their sites are attacked. The following sections describe the problems on the Internet and the factors that contribute to these problems:

1. ***How secure is the server software?*** Security should be in place to prevent any unauthorized remote logon to the system. It should be extremely difficult to make changes to the server software. The servers themselves should be physically located in a secure environment.
2. ***How secure are communications?*** Customer credit card information and other sensitive data that is being transmitted across the Internet must be protected.
3. ***How is the data protected once it is delivered to the e-business?*** Is it stored in unencrypted text files at the website? Is it moved to offline storage?

4. ***How are credit card transactions authenticated and authorized?*** Credit card transactions must be authenticated and authorized, so as to make it more secure for the users.

Besides implementing secure technologies, an e-business should develop security policies and procedures. Everyone working in an e-business should understand his or her responsibilities for keeping the business secure. Also, a plan of action should be ready to deal with any potential security problem.

The biggest potential security problem in an e-business is of human, rather than of electronic origin. The weakest link in any security system is the people using it. The employees of an e-business may not understand the security policy. Sometimes, the security policy is so burdensome that the employees are not able to follow it, or refuse to follow it because it makes it difficult for them to get their work done. For example, employees may get annoyed at having to make frequent changes to logon passwords. At times, they may not understand the importance of security measures. Educating employees about the need for security and their role in the security processes is essential. Table 5.2 summarizes the general security issues that e-businesses must consider.

TABLE 5.2 General Security Issues

Issue	*Comment*
Connection to the Internet	Private computer networks are at risk from potential threats from anywhere on the public Internet network.
Unknown risks	New security holes and methods of attacking networks are being discovered with alarming frequency.
Customer privacy and security of customer information	Not only must steps be taken to protect the privacy of customer information, but also customers must be made aware of those steps and have confidence in them.
Security consciousness	Management and employees must understand the importance of security policies and procedures.

Security risks associated with a network and a website can be addressed in some ways as follows:

Network and Website Security Risks

As part of planning a startup e-business' security, management should become familiar with network and web server security risk terminology. Originally, hacker was a term used to describe gifted software programmers. Today, hacker is a slang term used to refer to someone who deliberately gains unauthorized access to individual computers or computer networks. Ethical hackers use their skills to find weaknesses in computer systems and make them known, without regard for personal gain. Malicious hackers, also called crackers, gain access to steal valuable information such as credit card numbers, attempt to disrupt service, or cause any other damage. Since there is a wide press coverage of computer system security breaches, the terms "hacker" and "cracker" are now generally used interchangeably for those involved in malicious, unauthorized computer system access.

An e-business must protect itself against unauthorized access to its computer network, denial-of-service traffic overloads, and the intrusion of destructive viruses.

Denial-of-Service Attacks

A Denial-of-Service or DoS attack is an attack on a network that is designed to disable the network by flooding it with useless traffic or activity. A distributed denial-of-service, or DDoS, attack uses multiple computers to launch a DoS attack. While a DoS attack does not do any technical damage, it can do substantial financial damage to an e-business, because every second an e-business's network or a website is down, it may result in lost revenues.

The attacker first breaks into hundreds or thousands of random, insecure computers on the Internet and installs an attack program. Then he coordinates them all to attack the target simultaneously. Thereafter, the target is attacked from many places at once; the traditional defences just do not work, and the system crashes.

These attacks are incredibly difficult, if not impossible, to defend against. In a traditional denial-of-service attack, the victim's computer might be able to figure out where the attack is coming from and shut down those connections. But in a distributed attack, there is no single source. The computer should shut down all connections except the ones it knows to be trustworthy, but that does not work for a public Internet site.

So far, these attacks are strictly denial-of-service. They do not affect the data on the websites. These attacks cannot steal credit card numbers or proprietary information. They cannot transfer money out of your bank account to trade stocks in your name. Attackers cannot gain financially from these attacks. Still, they are very serious. For most big corporations, the biggest risk of a security breach is loss of income or loss of reputation, either of which is achieved by a conspicuous denial-of-service attack. The real problem is that there are hundreds of thousands, possibly millions, of innocent, naive computer users who are vulnerable to attack. They are using DSL or cable modems, they're always on the Internet with static IP addresses, and they can be taken over and used as launching pads for these attacks.

Viruses

Viruses are the most common security risk faced by e-businesses today. A virus is a small program that inserts itself into other program files that then become "infected", just as a virus in nature embeds itself in normal human cells. The virus is spread when an infected program is executed, and this further infects other programs. Examples of virus effects include inability to boot, deletion of files or entire hard drives, inability to create or save files, and thousands of other possibilities. A logic bomb is a virus whose attack is triggered by some event such as the date on a computer's system clock. A logic bomb may simply release a virus or it may be a virus itself. Viruses are generally introduced into a computer system via e-mail or by unauthorized network access. Virus examples include Stoned, Michelangelo, and AutoStart 9805.

Trojan horse. This takes its name from a story in Homer's Iliad, and is a special type of virus that emulates a benign application. It appears to do something useful or entertaining but actually does something else as well, such as destroying files or creating a "back door" entry point to give an intruder access to the system. A Trojan horse may be an e-mail in the form of attachment or a downloaded program. Trojan horse examples include BackOrifice, VBS/Freelink, and BackDoor-G.

Worm. This is a special type of virus that does not directly alter program files. Instead, a worm replaces a document or an application with its own code and then uses that code to position itself. Worms are often not noticed until their uncontrolled replication consumes system resources and slows down or stops the system. Worm examples include VBS/Loveletter, a VBS/Godzilla.worm, and Happy99.

A macro is a short program written in an application such as Microsoft Word or Excel to accomplish a series of keystrokes. A macro virus is a virus that infects Microsoft Word or Excel macros. Macro viruses can be introduced into a computer system as part of a Word or an Excel document received as an e-mail attachment, or as a file on disk. Opening the e-mail attachment or file triggers the macro virus.

Some viruses are, however, just hoaxes. Several antivirus software vendors maintain up-to-date information such as the Virus Information Library at *McAfee.com*, the AntiViral Pro Virus Encyclopedia on viruses, worms, Trojan horses, and hoaxes. E-businesses also face other security issues related to doing business on the Web, such as website defacement, information theft, and data spills.

Spyware

Spyware is Internet jargon for Advertising Supported software (Adware). It is a way for shareware authors to make money from a product, other than by selling it to the users. There are several large media companies that offer them to place banner ads in their products in exchange for a portion of the revenue from banner sales. This way, you do not have to pay for the software and the developers are still getting paid. If you find the banners annoying, there is usually an option to remove them, by paying the regular licensing fee. This usually involves the tracking and sending of data and statistics via a server installed on the user's PC and the use of your Internet connection in the background. Spyware examples include CoolWebSearch,Internet Optimizer (also known as DyFuCaZango (formerly 180 Solutions), HuntBar (also know as WinTools).

Adware. Adware is any software application in which advertising banners are displayed while the program is running. The authors of these applications include additional code that delivers the ads, which can be viewed through pop-up windows or through a bar that appears on a computer screen. The justification for adware is that it helps recover programming development cost and helps to hold down the cost for the user.

Adware has been criticized because it usually includes code that tracks a user's personal information and passes it on to third parties, without the user's authorization or knowledge. Adware examples include Bearshare, Bonzi Buddy, Comet Cursor and DivX.

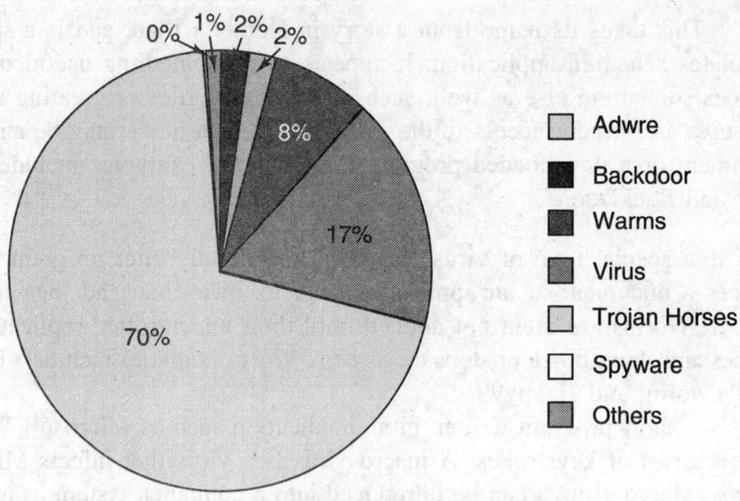

Figure 5.3 Percentage of malware.[3]

How are Sites Hacked?

Distributed systems based on the client/server model have become common. In recent months, we can see an increase in the development and the use of distributed sniffers, scanners, and denial-of-service tools. Attacks using these tools can involve a large number of sites simultaneously and focus to attack one or more victim hosts or networks.

In a typical distributed attack system, the 'intruder' controls a small number of 'masters', which in turn control a large number of 'daemons'. These daemons can be used to launch packet flooding or other attacks against the 'victims' targeted by the intruder.

In the incidents that have occurred so far, daemons were installed on several hundred sites, typically through the exploitation of well-known vulnerabilities that lead to root privileges on the compromised machines. Though some implementations of the daemon program do not require root privileges to launch attacks, in practice most of the daemons are concealed by the installation of 'root kits' designed to hide evidence of intrusion. There are indications that the processes for discovering vulnerable sites, compromising them, stalling daemons, and concealing the intrusion are largely automated, with each step being informed in 'batch' mode against many machines in one session. Daemons have been discovered on a variety of operating systems with varying levels of security and system management.

Once installed and operated, the daemon announces its presence to several (usually three or four) predefined masters and waits for further commands. The master program records that the daemon is ready to receive commands in an internal list, which can be retrieved by the intruder. Masters can cause daemons in the list to launch attacks, shut down gracefully, or even announce themselves to a new master server. Intruders have used cryptographic techniques to conceal the information recorded by the master and daemons.

3. http://en.wikipedia.org/wiki/File:Malware_statics_201

At the command from an intruder, the master can issue attack requests to the daemons in its list. These requests contain information about the requested attack such as the address of the victim, the duration, and other parameters. The master programs frequently operate as ordinary user programs on compromised hosts, where their activity can easily be hidden.

Security Incidents on the Internet

As an evidence of the above, three problems have occurred within a short period of time. In the first, persistent vulnerabilities in the UNIX sendmail program were discovered. Sites which had not corrected their sendmail programs, were forced to scramble to correct the programs before their vulnerabilities were attacked. However, due to the complexity of the sendmail program and networking software in general, three subsequent versions of sendmail were found to still contain significant vulnerabilities. The sendmail program is used widely, and sites without firewalls to limit access to sendmail are forced to react quickly whenever problems are found and vulnerabilities revealed.

In the second, a version of a popular and a free FTP server was found to contain a Trojan horse that permitted privileged access to the server. Sites using this FTP server, but not necessarily the contaminated version, were again forced to react very carefully and quickly to this situation. Many sites rely on the wealth of free software available on the Internet, especially security-related software that adds capability for logging, access control, and integrity checking that vendors often do not provide as part of the operating system. While the software is often of high quality, sites may have little recourse other than to rely on the authors of the software if it is found to have vulnerabilities and other problems.

The third problem has the strongest implications: intruders had broken into potentially thousands of systems throughout the Internet, including gateways between major networks, and installed sniffer programs to monitor network traffic for usernames and static passwords typed in by users to connect to networked systems. The intruders had used various known techniques for breaking into systems, as well as using passwords that had been "sniffed". One of the implications of this incident is that static or reusable passwords are obsolete for protecting access to user accounts. In fact, a user connecting to a remote system across the Internet may be unintentionally placing that system at the risk of attack by intruders who could be monitoring the network traffic to the remote system.

Weak Authentication

Security handling teams estimate that many incidents stem from the use of weak, static passwords. Passwords on the Internet can be "cracked" in a number of different ways. However, the two most common methods are by cracking the encrypted form of the password and by monitoring communications channels for password packets. The UNIX operating system usually stores an encrypted form of passwords in a file that can be read by normal users. The password file can be obtained by simply copying it. It can also be obtained by a number of other intruder methods. Once the file is on hand, an intruder can run readily-available password cracking programs against the passwords. If the passwords are weak, e.g. less than 8 characters, and so on, they could be cracked and used to gain access into the system.

Ease of Spying

It is important to note that when a user connects to her account on a remote host using Telnet or FTP, the user's password travels across the Internet unencrypted or in plain text. Thus, another method for breaking into systems is to monitor connections for IP packets bearing a username and a password, and then using them on the system for normal login. If the captured password is to an administrator's account, then the job of obtaining privileged access is made much easier. As noted previously, hundreds and possibly thousands of systems across the Internet have been penetrated as a result of monitoring for usernames and passwords. E-mail, as well as the contents of Telnet and FTP sessions, can be monitored and used to learn information about a site and its business transactions. Most users do not encrypt e-mail, since they assume that e-mail is secure and thus safe for transmitting sensitive information.

Ease of Spoofing

The IP address of a host is presumed to be valid and is therefore trusted by TCP and UDP services. A problem is that, using IP source routing, an attacker's host can masquerade as a trusted host or a client. Briefly, IP source routing is an option that can be used to specify a direct route to a destination and return path back to the origin. The route can involve the use of other routers or hosts that normally would not be used to forward packets to the destination. An example of how this can be used such that an attacker's system could masquerade as the trusted client of a particular server is as follows:

1. The attacker would change her host's IP address to match that of the trusted client.
2. The attacker would then construct a source route to the server, that specifies the direct path the IP packets should take to the server and should take from the server back to the attacker's host, using the trusted client as the last hop in the route to the server.
3. The attacker sends a client request to the server using the source route.
4. The server accepts the client's request as if it came directly from the trusted client, and returns a reply to the trusted client.
5. The trusted client, using the source route, forwards the packet on to the attacker's host.

Many UNIX hosts accept source routed packets and will pass them on as the source route indicates. Many routers will accept source routed packets as well, whereas some routers can be configured to block source routed packets.

E-mail on the Internet is particularly easy to spoof and, without enhancements such as digital signatures, generally cannot be trusted. As a brief example, consider the exchange that takes place when Internet hosts exchange mail. The exchange takes place using a simple protocol consisting of ASCII-character commands. An intruder could easily enter these commands on Telnet to connect directly to a system's Simple Mail Transfer Protocol (SMTP) port. The receiving host trusts this sending host, and thus the origin of the mail is spoofed easily by entering a sender address that is different from the true address. As a result, any user, without privileges, can falsify or spoof e-mail.

Other services, such as Domain Name Service (DNS), can be spoofed, but with more difficulty than e-mail. These services still represent a threat that needs to be considered when using them.

How Vulnerable are the Internet Sites?

The Internet, while being a useful and a vital network, is at the same time vulnerable to attacks. Sites that are connected to the Internet face significant risk in some form by intruders. The following factors would influence the level of risk:

- Number of systems connected to the site
- Services utilized by the site
- Interconnectivity of the site to the Internet
- Site's profile, or how well-known the site is
- Site's readiness to handle computer security incidents.

The more the number of systems that are connected, obviously the harder it is to control their security. Equally, if a site is connected to the Internet at several points, it is likely to be more vulnerable to attacks than a site with a single gateway. At the same time, though, how well prepared a site is, and the degree to which the site relies on the Internet, can increase or decrease the risk. A site's high profile could attract more potential intruders who wish to do some harm to the site's image. It should be mentioned though, that "quiet", less-frequently used sites are also attractive to intruders since they can more easily hide their activity.

Sites that use recommended procedures and controls for increasing computer security have significantly lower risks of attack. Firewalls, combined with one-time passwords that are immune from monitoring or guessing, can increase greatly a site's overall level of security and make using the Internet quite safe.

Website Defacement

Website vandalism or defacement can be the result of a hacker breaking into a network, accessing the website files, and modifying the HTML to physically change Web pages. Not only do website defacements embarrass an e-business, but some website defacements can have serious financial repercussions. Aastrom Biosciences. Inc., a Michigan based medical products company, experienced a serious defacement created to manipulate its stock price. In February 2000, a bogus news release announcing a merger with a California biopharmaceutical company, Geron Corporation, was posted on Aastrom's website. Stock prices for both companies rose: Aastrom shares rose from $4 to $4.41 and Geron shares rose from $47.19 to $51. After discovering the defacement, Aastrom notified Geron, and representatives of both companies advised officials with the NASDAQ index, where both stocks are traded, that there was no merger.

Electronic Industrial Espionage

It is a major risk and a big dollar issue that most companies are reluctant to discuss openly—electronic industrial espionage. Often, e-businesses that have been hacked and had business secrets stolen are too embarrassed to admit the break-in. However, in late October 2000, one very high-profile company, Microsoft, found itself scrambling to deal with first rumours and then published reports of a serious hacking incident with industrial espionage overtones.

The apparent culprit was a Trojan horse virus named QAZ Trojan that was first identified in mid-July in China. The QAZ Trojan virus infects a computer system when a user opens an e-mail attachment containing the virus. Then the virus replaces the system's Notepad text editor with its own code, searches for other shared hard drives to infect, and sends the IP addresses of infected computers to an outside e-mail address. This creates a "back door" a hacker can use to enter a system, search for passwords, and install software programs to allow remote control of the computer. Although by August 2000, all major antivirus software makers had included the QAZ Trojan information in their downloadable virus updates, somehow the QAZ Trojan virus was used to create a "back door" in Microsoft.

Credit Card Fraud and Theft of Customer Data

Almost all B2C purchase transactions involve credit cards. An e-business that accepts credit cards in payment for goods and services, must secure the credit card information in transit to its website, and it must secure stored credit card information. Also, systems must be in place for credit card transaction authentication (verifying that the person placing the order really is the holder of the credit card used in the transaction), and credit card authorization (verifying that the charge can be made to the card number).

A hacker can break into a database server and steal thousands of credit card numbers and other information in a matter of moments, and an e-business might not even recognize that the hacker was there. For example, one of the largest reported cases of stolen credit card information took place in January 1999 (but was not reported until much later) when information on 485,000 credit cards, including card numbers, expiration dates, names, and addresses, was stolen from an e-business website and stored at a US government agency's website, where the agency's website administrator discovered the data. There was no reported evidence of fraudulent use, and some of the accounts were not active. But this event highlights the risk to a vulnerable e-business of the theft of sensitive information.

Security and E-mail

E-mail users who desire confidentiality and sender authentication use encryption. Encryption is simply intended to keep personal thoughts personal. There are two good programs to encrypt e-mails and they are: Pretty Good Privacy (PGP), and Privacy Enhanced Mail (PEM).

E-mail is typically encrypted for the reason that all network correspondence is open for eavesdropping. Internet e-mail is obviously far less secure than the postal system, where envelopes protect correspondence from casual snooping. In contrast, the header area of any e-mail message will show that it has passed through a number of nodes on its way to you. Each of these nodes presents the opportunity for snooping.

Privacy Enhanced Mail Standard

PEM is the Internet Privacy Enhanced Mail standard, designed, proposed, but not yet officially adopted by the Internet Activities Board, to provide secure electronic mail over the Internet.

Designed to work with current Internet e-mail formats, PEM includes encryption, authentication, and key management, and allows use of both public-key and secret-key crypto-systems. The system supports multiple cryptographic tools: for each mail message, the specific encryption algorithm, digital signature algorithm, hash function and so on, are specified in the header. PEM explicitly supports only a few cryptographic algorithms; others may be added later. It uses the DES algorithm for encryption and the RSA algorithm for sender authentication and key management. PEM also provides support for non-repudiation, which allows the third-party recipient of a forwarded message to verify the identity of the message originator (not just the message forwarder) and to verify whether any of the original text has been altered.

Pretty Good Privacy (PGP)

Pretty Good Privacy (PGP) is the implementation of public-key cryptography based on RSA. It is a free software package developed by Phillip Zimmerman, that encrypts e-mail. Since being published in US as freeware in June 1991, PGP has spread rapidly and has since become the de facto worldwide standard for encryption of e-mail. It is freely available for DOS, Macintosh, UNIX, Amiga, VMS, Atari, and OS/2 systems. PGP provides secure encryption of documents and data files that even advanced supercomputers are hard pressed to "crack". The process is so simple that anyone with a PC can do it with almost no effort. For authentication, PGP employs the RSA public-key encryption scheme and the MD5 (Message Digest version 5) developed by Rivest, a one-way hash function to form a digital signature that assures the receiver that an incoming message is authentic (that it comes from the alleged sender and that it has not been altered).

Network and Website Security

The best way to recognize when a hacker is attempting unauthorized network access is to monitor network performance. Setting up, logging, and monitoring established network reference points, called benchmarks, can alert an e-business to security problems. A skilled system administrator and other well-trained technicians, who use these benchmarks to monitor and manage the network and servers, are critical. Other tools such as passwords, firewalls, intrusion detection systems, and virus scanning software should be used to protect an e-business' network and website.

A password is a code, or more often a common word, used to gain access to a computer network. Passwords are only effective when used properly. Often a computer user chooses a bad password, such as a short, common word—a name, or birthday—so that the user can remember the password easily. One way hackers penetrate network security is by using software that "guesses" a password by trying millions of common words until one of the words is accepted. Passwords that require a minimum length of six characters in a mix of letters and numbers increase the number of potential passwords into billions and make it more difficult for a hacker to guess them. A computer user should also change passwords regularly. If a user has access to multiple systems, it is a good idea to have different passwords on each system.

A firewall is a software or a hardware used to isolate and protect a private system or a network from the public network. A firewall provides an easy-to-manage entry point to multiple systems behind it. Firewalls can control the type of information that is allowed to pass from the public network to the private network, as well as what services inside the firewall are accessible from the outside. Firewalls can also log activity, to provide an audit trail in case the network is penetrated.

Intrusion detection is the ability to analyze real-time data to detect, log, and stop unauthorized network access as it happens. Businesses can install intrusion detection systems that monitor the network for real-time intrusions and respond to intrusions in a variety of user-detected ways. An intrusion detection system can defend a website against DoS attacks by adding more servers to increase the traffic the website can handle, by using filters and routers to manage traffic, and by having a backup plan to reroute legitimate traffic during an attack. Cisco's Secure Intrusion Detection System, and Network ICE's ICEpac Security Suite are two examples of intrusion detection systems.

Virus scanning software, including e-mail virus scanning, should be installed on all network computers. Antivirus software should be kept updated. Communication ports should be used to allow data to enter and exit the network. The system administrator should close all unused communication ports. Up-to-date security patches for operating systems should be installed as soon as the patches are available, to prevent hackers from exploiting built-in system weaknesses.

Transaction Security and Data Protection

Transaction security, especially for credit card transactions, and the protection of customer data are as important as website and network security. Tools to protect transaction data and customer data include:

- Using a predefined key to encrypt and decrypt the data during transmission;
- Using the Secure Sockets Layer (SSL) protocol to protect data transmitted over the Internet. SSL provides encryption of data between the browser on the customer's computer and the software on the Web server, allowing data such as credit card information to be transmitted securely. SSL uses digital certificates so that a Web browser can authenticate the server it is connected to, making sure that credit card data is going to the appropriate server;
- Moving sensitive customer information such as credit card numbers offline, or encrypting the information if it is to be stored online;
- Removing all files and data from storage devices, including disk drives and tapes, before getting rid of the devices; and
- Shredding all hard-copy documents containing sensitive information before trashing them.

Of course, an e-business's security solutions are only as strong as its weakest link—often its employees. An e-business must maintain a security-oriented culture, starting at the top, in order for employees to take security seriously. An e-business should also consider having its security systems tested or audited.

Security Audits and Penetration Testing

Security audits can provide an overall assessment of an e-business' systems and security issues by checking for vulnerabilities in those systems and providing recommendations for fixing those vulnerabilities. Security consultants such as DefendNet Solutions Inc., Internet Security Systems, and Pinkerton Systems Integration offer security auditing services.

Accounting firms, such as Ernest & Young, also offer security auditing services. Some of the Big Five international accounting firms use the American Institute of Certified Public Accountants (AICPA) WebTrust seal and audit criteria. The WebTrust seal indicates to customers that the website is verified as being safe and secure by the AICPA. The AICPA audit criteria cover best business practices, site security, and customer information privacy. Some accounting firms use their own audit seal instead of, or in addition to, the AICPA WebTrust seal.

When evaluating security consultants who will perform the penetration testing, there are several factors to consider. They can be listed as follows:

1. Get evidence that the security consultants have insurance to protect against accidental system damage or down time.
2. Have everyone on the consultant's penetration team sign a non-disclosure agreement.
3. Consider requiring a third-party background check on each member of the consultant's penetration team.
4. Decide whether it makes sense to use a security consultant who employs former hackers.
5. Determine if the consultant's team is going to use packaged security scanning software that could be employed by the in-house staff, or if they are using custom tools.
6. Develop a clear scope for the penetration test and a workable time frame.
7. Determine whether to have a DoS attack done, and if so, when to schedule it to least disrupt customer access.
8. Make sure the final report from the consultant includes an accounting of all attacks attempted and whether or not they were successful, a return of all the paper or electronic information gathered by the consultant, and recommendations on how to fix up any problems discovered during the tests.

Individual PC Security Risks

Often managers in an e-business use stand-alone personal computer during the start up phase, until funds are available to build and operate a network or until the e-business can outsource its IT operations. Additionally, some e-businesses offer their employees the opportunity to telecommute—allowing an employee to use his or her home computer, or installing a business-owned personal computer in the employee's home. Certainly, business employees often work on business files at home. Due to these factors, it is important for an e-business to understand that individual PCs are also at risk from hackers.

E-business Risk Management Issues

An e-business should manage its e-business risks as a business issue, not just as a technology issue. An e-business must consider the direct financial impact of immediate loss of revenue, compensatory payments, and future revenue loss from e-business risks such as:

1. Business interruptions caused by website defacement or denial-of-service attacks;
2. Litigation and settlement costs over employees' inappropriate use of e-mail and the Internet;
3. Product or service claims against items advertised and sold via a website;
4. Web-related copyright, trademark, and patent infringement lawsuits; and
5. Natural or weather-related disasters.

An e-business should put in place an effective risk management program that includes the following:

- Network and website security and intruder detection programs
- Antivirus protection
- Firewalls
- Sound security policies and procedures
- Employee education.

Another important component of a risk management program is the transfer of risk via insurance. Table 5.3 illustrates some of the different kinds of insurance coverage an e-business should consider when developing an effective risk management program. It is a good idea for an e-business's management to consult with a commercial insurance broker that offers e-risk management services, to help develop a risk management plan including insurance coverage.

TABLE 5.3 E-risk Insurance

E-risk insurance	*Coverage*
Computer Virus Transmission	Protects against losses that occur when employees open infected e-mail attachments or download virus-laden software.
Extortion and Reward	Responds to Internet extortion demands and/or pays rewards to help capture saboteurs.
Unauthorized Access/ Unauthorized Use	Covers failure to protect against third-party access to data and transactions.
Specialized Network Security	Responds to breach of network security and resulting losses.
Media Liability	Protects against intellectual property infringement losses.
Patent Infringement	Covers defensive and offensive costs when battling over patent infringement issues.
Computer Server and Services Errors & Omissions	Protects e-businesses against liability for errors and omissions when their professional advice causes a client's financial loss.

The Firewall Concept

An Internet firewall is a system or group of systems that enforces a security policy between an organization's network and the Internet. The firewall determines which inside services may be accessed from the outside, which outsiders are permitted access to the permitted inside services, and which outside services may be accessed by insiders. For a firewall to be effective, all traffic to and from the Internet must pass through the firewall, where it can be inspected. The firewall must permit only authorized traffic to pass, and the firewall itself must be immune to penetration. Unfortunately, a firewall system cannot offer any protection once an attacker has got through or around the firewall.

It is important to note that an Internet firewall is not just a router, a bastion host, or a combination of devices that provides security for a network. The firewall is part of an overall security policy that creates a perimeter defence designed to protect the information resources of the organization. This security policy must include published security guidelines to inform users of their responsibilities; corporate policies defining network access, service access, local and remote user authentication, dial-in and dial-out, disk and data encryption, and virus protection measures and employee training. All potential points of network attack must be protected with the same level of network security. Setting up an Internet firewall without a comprehensive security policy is like placing a steel door on a tent.

A firewall is an approach to security. It helps implement a larger security policy that defines the services and access to be permitted, and it is an implementation of that policy in terms of a network configuration, one or more host systems and routers, and other security measures such as advanced authentication in place of static passwords. The main purpose of a firewall system is to control access to or from a protected network, i.e. a site. It implements a network access policy by forcing connections to pass through the firewall, where they can be examined and evaluated.

A firewall system can be a router, a personal computer, a host, or a collection of hosts, set up specifically to shield a site or a subnet from protocols and services that can be abused from hosts outside the subnet. A firewall system is usually located at a higher-level gateway, such as a site's connection to the Internet. However, firewall systems can be located at lower-level gateways to provide protection for some smaller collection of hosts or subnets.

Why Firewalls?

The general reasoning behind firewall usage is that without a firewall, a subnet's systems expose themselves to inherently insecure services, and to probes and attacks from hosts elsewhere on the network. In a firewall-less environment, network security relies totally on host security and all hosts must, in a sense, cooperate to achieve a uniformly higher level of security. The larger the subnet, the less manageable it is to maintain all hosts at the same level of security. As mistakes and lapses in security become more common, break-ins occur not as the result of complex attacks, but because of simple errors in configuration and inadequate passwords.

A firewall approach provides numerous advantages to sites by helping to increase overall host security. The following sections summarize the primary benefits of using a firewall.

Protection of Vulnerable Services

A firewall can greatly improve network security and reduce risks to hosts on the subnet by filtering inherently insecure services. As a result, the subnet network environment is exposed to fewer risks, since only selected protocols will be able to pass through the firewall.

For example, a firewall could prohibit certain vulnerable services such as Network File System (NFS) from entering or leaving a protected subnet. This provides the benefit of preventing the services from being exploited by outside attackers, but at the same time permits the use of these services with greatly reduced risk of exploitation.

Firewalls can also provide protection from routing-based attacks, such as source routing, and attempts to redirect routing paths to compromised sites via Internet Control Message Protocol or ICMP redirects. A firewall could reject all source-routed packets and ICMP redirects and then inform administrators of the incidents.

Controlled Access to Site Systems

A firewall also provides the ability to control access to site systems. For example, some hosts can be made reachable from outside networks, whereas others can be effectively sealed off from unwanted access. A site could prevent outside access to its hosts except for special cases such as mail servers or information servers.

This brings to the fore an access policy that firewalls are particularly adept at enforcing: do not provide access to hosts or services that do not require access. If, for example, a user requires little or no network access to her desktop workstation, then a firewall can enforce this policy.

Concentrated Security

A firewall can actually be less expensive for an organization in that all or most modified software and additional security software could be located on the firewall systems as opposed to being distributed on many hosts. In particular, one-time password systems and other add-on authentication software could be located at the firewall as opposed to each system that needed to be accessed from the Internet.

Enhanced Privacy

Privacy is of great concern to certain sites, since what would normally be considered innocuous information, might actually contain clues that would be useful to an attacker. Using a firewall, some sites wish to block services such as finger and Domain Name Service. Finger displays information about users, such as their last login time, whether they have read mail, and other items. But, finger could leak information to attackers about how often a system is used, whether the system has active users connected, and whether the system could be attacked without drawing attention.

Firewalls can also be used to block DNS information about site systems; thus, the names and IP addresses of site systems would not be available to Internet hosts. Some sites feel that by blocking this information, they are hiding information that would otherwise be useful to attackers.

Need for Usage Statistics on Network

If all access to and from the Internet passes through a firewall, the firewall can log accesses and provide valuable statistics about network usage. A firewall, with appropriate alarms that sound when suspicious activity occurs, can also provide details on whether the firewall and network are being probed or attacked.

It is important to collect statistics about network usage and evidence of probing for a number of reasons. Of primary importance is, knowing whether the firewall is withstanding probes and attacks, and determining whether the controls on the firewall are adequate. Network usage statistics are also important as input into network requirements studies and risk analysis activities.

Policy Enforcement

Lastly, but perhaps most importantly, a firewall provides the means for implementing and enforcing a network access policy. In effect, a firewall provides access control to users and services. Thus, a network access policy can be enforced by a firewall, whereas without a firewall, such a policy depends entirely on the cooperation of the users. A site may be able to depend on its own users for their cooperation. However, it cannot or it should not depend on the Internet users in general.

Firewall Components

The primary components (or aspects) of a firewall are:

1. Network policy
2. Advanced authentication mechanisms
3. Packet filtering
4. Application gateways.

The following sections describe each of these components in detail.

Network Policy

There are two levels of network policy that directly influence the design, installation and use of a firewall system. The higher-level policy is an issue-specific network access policy that defines those services which will be allowed or explicitly denied from the restricted network, how these services will be used, and the conditions for exceptions to this policy. The lower-level policy describes how the firewall will actually go about restricting the access and filtering the services that were defined in the higher level policy. The following sections describe these policies in brief.

Service access policy. The service access policy should focus on Internet-specific use issues as defined above, and perhaps all outside network access (i.e., dial-in policy, and SLIP and PPP connections) as well. This policy should be an extension of an overall organizational policy regarding the protection of information resources in the organization. For a firewall to be successful, the service access policy must be realistic and sound, and should be drafted before implementing a firewall. A realistic policy is one that provides a balance between protecting the network from known risks, while still providing users access to network resources. If a firewall system denies or restricts services, it usually requires the strength of the service access policy to prevent the firewall's access controls from being modified on an ad hoc basis. Only a management-backed sound policy can provide this.

A firewall can implement a number of service access policies. However, a typical policy may be to allow no access to a site from the Internet, but allow access from the site to the Internet. Another typical policy would be to allow some access from the Internet, but perhaps only to selected systems such as information servers and e-mail servers. Firewalls often implement service access policies that allow some user access from the Internet to selected internal hosts, but this access would be granted only if necessary and only if it could be combined with advanced authentication.

Firewall design policy. The firewall design policy is specific to the firewall. It defines the rules used to implement the service access policy. One cannot design this policy in a vacuum isolated from understanding issues such as firewall capabilities and limitations, and threats and vulnerabilities associated with TCP/IP. Firewalls generally implement one of the following two basic design policies:

1. Permit any service unless it is expressly denied
2. Deny any service unless it is expressly permitted.

A firewall that implements the first policy allows all services to pass into the site by default, with the exception of those services that the service access policy has identified as disallowed. A firewall that implements the second policy denies all services by default, but passes those services that have been identified as allowed. This second policy follows the classic access model used in all areas of information security.

The first policy is less desirable, since it offers more avenues for getting around the firewall, i.e. users could access new services currently not denied by the policy (or even addressed by the policy) or run denied services at non-standard TCP/UDP ports that are not denied by the policy. Certain services such as X Windows, FTP, Archie, and RPC cannot be filtered easily and are better accommodated by a firewall that implements the first policy. The second policy is stronger and safer, but is more difficult to implement and may impact users in that certain services such as those just mentioned may have to be blocked or restricted.

The relationship between the high-level service access policy and its lower level counterpart is reflected in the discussion above. This relationship exists because the implementation of the service access policy is heavily dependent upon the capabilities and limitations of the firewall system, as well as upon the inherent security problems associated with the wanted Internet services. For example, wanted services defined in the service access policy may have to be denied if the inherent security problems in these services cannot be effectively controlled by the lower level policy and if the security of the network takes precedence over other factors. On the other hand, an organization that is heavily dependent on these services to meet its mission may have to accept higher risk and allow access to these services. This relationship between the service access policy and its lower-level counterpart allows for an iterative process in defining both, thus producing the realistic and sound policy initially described.

The service access policy is the most significant component of the four described here. The other three components are used to implement and enforce the policy. (And as noted above, the service access policy should be a reflection of a strong overall organization security policy.) The effectiveness of the firewall system in protecting the network depends on the type of firewall implementation used, the use of proper firewall procedures, and the service access policy.

Advanced Authentication

Security lapses on the identity of Internet users have occurred in part due to the weaknesses associated with traditional passwords. For years, users have been advised to choose passwords that would be difficult to guess, or not to reveal their passwords. However, even if users follow this advice (and many do not), the fact that intruders can and do monitor the Internet for passwords that are transmitted in the clear has rendered traditional passwords obsolete.

Advanced authentication measures such as smartcards, authentication tokens, biometrics, and software-based mechanisms are designed to counter the weaknesses of traditional passwords. While the authentication techniques vary, they are indeed similar in one aspect. The passwords generated by advanced authentication devices cannot be reused by an attacker who has monitored a connection. Given the inherent problems with passwords on the Internet, an Internet-accessible firewall that does not use or does not contain the hooks to use advanced authentication makes little sense.

Some of the more popular advanced authentication devices in use today are called one-time password systems. A smartcard or authentication token, for example, generates a response that the host system can use in place of a traditional password. The token or card works in conjunction with software or hardware on the host, and therefore, the generated response is unique for every login. The result is a one-time password which, if monitored, cannot be reused by an intruder to gain access to an account.

Since firewalls can centralize and control site access, the firewall is the logical place for the advanced authentication software or hardware to be located. Although advanced authentication measures could be used at each host, it is more practical and manageable to centralize the measures at the firewall. Figure 5.4 illustrates that a site without a firewall using advanced authentication permits unauthenticated application traffic, such as Telnet or FTP, directly to site systems. If the hosts do not use advanced authentication, then intruders could attempt to crack passwords or could monitor the network for login sessions that would include the passwords. The figure also shows a site with a firewall using advanced authentication, such that Telnet or FTP sessions originating from the Internet to site systems must pass the advanced authentication before being permitted to the site systems. The site systems may still require static passwords before permitting access. However, these passwords would be protected against exploitation, even if the passwords are monitored, as long as the advanced authentication measures and other firewall components prevent intruders from penetrating or bypassing the firewall.

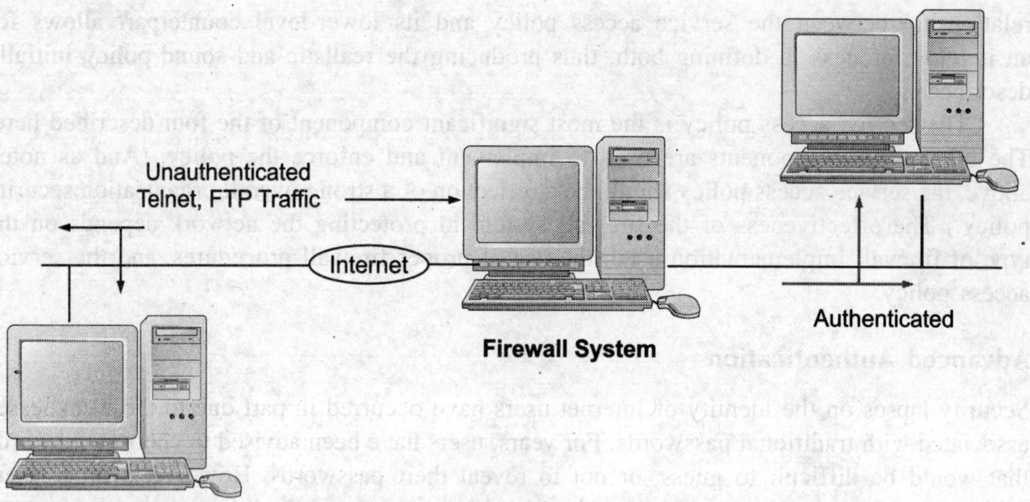

Figure 5.4 Advanced authentication on a firewall to pre-authenticate Telnet, FTP traffic.

Packet Filtering

IP packet filtering is done, usually, using a packet filtering router designed for filtering packets, as they pass between the router's interfaces. A packet filtering router usually can filter IP packets based on some or all of the following fields:

1. Source IP address
2. Destination IP address
3. TCP/UDP source port
4. TCP/UDP destination port.

Not all packet filtering routers currently filter the source TCP/UDP port, though vendors have now started incorporating this capability. Some routers examine the router's network interfaces in which a packet arrives, and then use this as an additional filtering criterion. Some UNIX hosts provide packet filtering capability, although most do not.

Filtering can be used in a variety of ways to block connections from or to specific hosts or networks, and to block connections to specific ports. A site might wish to block connections from certain addresses, such as from hosts or sites that it considers to be hostile or untrustworthy. Alternatively, a site may wish to block connections from all addresses external to the site (with certain exceptions, such as SMTP for receiving e-mail) (see Figure 5.5).

As an example of packet filtering, consider a policy to allow only certain connections to a network of address 123.4.*.*. Telnet connections will be allowed to only one host, 123.4.5.6, which may be the site's Telnet application gateway, and SMTP connections will be allowed to two hosts, 123.4.5.7 and 123.4.5.8, which may be the site's two electronic mail gateways. NNTP (Network News Transfer Protocol) is allowed only from the site's NNTP feed system, 129.6.48.254, and only to the site's NNTP server, 123.4.5.9, and NTP (Network Time Protocol) is allowed to all hosts. All other services and packets are to be blocked. An example of the rule-set is in Table 5.4.

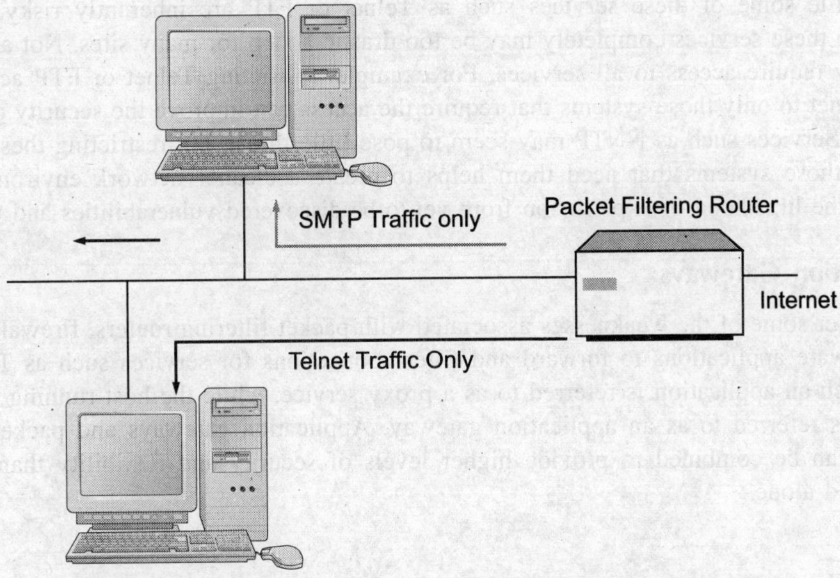

Figure 5.5 Representation of packet filtering on Telnet and SMTP.

TABLE 5.4 Packet Filtering Table

Type	*Source address*	*Destination address*	*Source port*	*Destination port*	*Action*
TCP	*	123.4.5.6	>1023	23	permit
TCP	*	123.4.5.6	>1023	25	permit
TCP	*	123.4.5.6	>1023	2	permit
TCP	129.6.58.254	123.4.5.6	>1023	119	permit
UDP	*	123.4.*.*	>1023	123	permit
*	*	*	*	*	deny

The first rule allows TCP packets from any source address and port greater than 1023 on the Internet to the destination address of 123.4.5.6 and port of 23 at the site. Port 23 is the port associated with the Telnet server, and all Telnet clients should have unprivileged source ports of 1024 or higher. The second and third rules work in a similar fashion, except packets to destination addresses 123.4.5.7 and 123.4.5.8, and port 25 for SMTP, are permitted.

The fourth rule permits packets to the site's NNTP server, but only from source address 129.6.48.254 to destination address 123.4.5.9 and port 119 (129.6.48.254 is the only NNTP server that the site should receive news from, thus access to the site for NNTP is restricted to only that system). The fifth rule permits NTP traffic, which uses UDP as opposed to TCP, from any source to any destination address at the site. Finally, the sixth rule denies all other packets—if this rule is not present, the router may or may not deny all subsequent packets. This is a very basic example of packet filtering. Actual rules permit more complex filtering and greater flexibility.

While some of these services such as Telnet or FTP are inherently risky, blocking access to these services completely may be too drastic a step for many sites. Not all systems generally require access to all services. For example, restricting Telnet or FTP access from the Internet to only those systems that require the access can improve the security of users at no cost. Services such as NNTP may seem to pose little threat, but restricting these services to only those systems that need them helps to create a cleaner network environment and reduces the likelihood of exploitation from yet-to-be-discovered vulnerabilities and threats.

Application Gateways

To counter some of the weaknesses associated with packet filtering routers, firewalls need to use software applications to forward and filter connections for services such as Telnet and FTP. Such an application is referred to as a proxy service, while the host running the proxy service is referred to as an application gateway. Application gateways and packet filtering routers can be combined to provide higher levels of security and flexibility than if either were used alone.

What Should a Firewall Contain?

Once the decision is made to use firewall technology to implement an organization's security policy, the next step is to procure a firewall that provides the appropriate level of protection and is cost-effective. However, what features should a firewall have, at a minimum, to provide effective protection? One cannot answer this question entirely with specifics, but it is possible to recommend that, in general, a firewall should have the following significant features or attributes.

1. Be able to support a "deny all services except those specifically permitted" design policy, even if that is not the policy used;
2. Support your security policy, not impose one;
3. Be flexible and able to accommodate new services and needs if the security policy of the organization changes;
4. Contain advanced authentication measures, or should contain the hooks for installing advanced authentication measures;
5. Employ filtering techniques to permit or deny services to specified host systems, as needed;
6. Use proxy services for services such as FTP and Telnet, so that advanced authentication measures can be employed and centralized at the firewall. If services such as NNTP, http, or gopher are required, the firewall should contain the corresponding proxy services;
7. Contain the ability to centralize SMTP access, to reduce direct SMTP connections between site and remote systems. This results in centralized handling of site e-mail;
8. Accommodate public access to the site, such that public information servers can be protected by the firewall but can be segregated from site systems that do not require the public access;

9. Contain the ability to concentrate and filter dial-in access;
10. Contain mechanisms for logging traffic and suspicious activity, and also mechanisms for log reduction so that logs are readable and understandable;
11. Be developed in a manner that its strength and correctness is verifiable. It should be simple in design so that it can be understood and maintained;
12. Be updated with patches and other bug fixes, at regular time intervals.

If the firewall requires an operating system such as UNIX, a secured version of the operating system should be a part of the firewall, with other security tools as necessary to ensure firewall host integrity. The operating system should have all patches installed.

The IP filtering language should be flexible, user-friendly to program, and should filter on as many attributes as possible, including source and destination IP address, protocol type, source and destination TCP/UDP port, and inbound and outbound interface.

There are undoubtably more issues and requirements, however many of them will be specific to each site's own needs. A thorough requirements definition and high-level risk assessment will identify most issues and requirements; however it should be emphasized that the Internet is a constantly changing network. New vulnerabilities can arise, and new services and enhancements to other services may represent potential difficulties for any firewall installation. Therefore, flexibility to adapt to changing needs is an important consideration.

Benefits of an Internet Firewall

Internet firewalls manage access between the Internet and an organization's private network. Without a firewall, each host system on the private network is exposed to attacks from other hosts on the Internet. This means that the security of the private network would depend on the "hardness" of each host's security features and would be only as secure as the weakest system.

Internet firewalls allow the network administrator to define a centralized "choke point" that keeps unauthorized users such as hackers, crackers, vandals, and spies, out of the protected network, prohibits potentially vulnerable services from entering or leaving the protected network, and provides protection from various types of routing attacks. An Internet firewall simplifies security management, since network security is consolidated on the firewall systems rather than being distributed to every host in the entire private network.

Firewalls offer a convenient point where Internet security can be monitored and alarms generated. It should be noted that for organizations that have connections to the Internet, the question is not whether attacks will occur but, when do they occur? Network administrators must audit and log all significant traffic through the firewall. If the network administrator does not take the time to respond to each alarm and examine logs on a regular basis, there is no need for the firewall, since the network administrator will never know if the firewall has been successfully attacked!

For the past few years, the Internet has been experiencing an address space crisis that has made registered IP addresses a scarce resource. This means that organizations wanting to connect to the Internet may not be able to obtain enough registered IP addresses to meet the demands of their user population. An Internet firewall is a logical place to deploy a Network Address Translator (NAT) that can help alleviate the address space shortage and eliminate the need to renumber when an organization changes its ISPs.

An Internet firewall is the perfect point to audit or log Internet usage. This permits the network administrator to justify the expense of the Internet connection to management, pinpoint potential bandwidth bottlenecks, and provide a method for departmental charge-backs if this fits the organization's financial model.

An Internet firewall can also offer a central point of contact for information delivery service to customers. The Internet firewall is the ideal location for deploying World Wide Web and FTP servers. The firewall can be configured to allow Internet access to these services, while prohibiting external access to other systems on the protected network.

Finally, some might argue that the deployment of an Internet firewall creates a single point of failure. It should be emphasized that if the connection to the Internet fails, the organization's private network will still continue to operate though the Internet access is lost. If there are multiple points of access, each one becomes a potential point of attack that the network administrator must firewall and monitor regularly.

By adequately securing little corners of cyberspace, you can instil and maintain the right levels of trustworthiness that your customers both demand and deserve. We have seen that e-security requires a holistic approach. It is as much a set of behaviours as it is a bundle of software tools and network sniffers which, by themselves, might leave us with a false sense of security. Analogies abound in our everyday lives. We buy expensive alarm systems for our homes, move around elite communities, opt for a German Shepherd or a Doberman Pinscher, and yet we know that these are only partial solutions.

True security requires that you educate your staff, develop manageable security policies and procedures, and create a secure organization (whether it be one or many employees) that enforces those policies. It requires that you properly configure your network for your organization, without assuming that off-the-shelf configurations are right for you. It also means investing in the tools and expertise that you deem necessary to evaluate and monitor your network in order to detect intrusions before they actually happen, as well as develop a clear strategy for dealing with an intrusion when it inevitably happens. Finally, a secure network calls for constant vigilance. This means keeping up with the technological changes around you by reading trade journals and periodicals, joining user groups that discuss security issues and disseminate the latest security information, and attending conferences, seminars, and any relevant training that will keep you abreast of evolving security needs.

Defining an Enterprise-wide Security Framework

Traditionally, organizations have relied on policies to communicate high-level directives from the management. These documents, once issued, provide a top-down influence for everyone in the company—from business units to departments to individual employees. Furthermore, these policies typically were developed at one time in the organization's evolution to capture the current environment. One of the major challenges for an organization in this area is the continued growth and adaptation of the policies to mirror the transformation within the organization. The fastest area of growth and change within an organization is Information Systems. With the rapid development and push towards new technologies, organizations find themselves striving to maintain current technical environments with outdated policies. Secondly, with the emergence of new technology strategies such as Intranets and Extranets, security and protection of informational assets has become paramount.

The first step is an enterprise-wide Information Systems security policy that is consistently enforced even as business needs change. Unfortunately, most companies have only bits and pieces of security scattered throughout the organization. These may make some departments or individuals feel safe, but they do little to protect the enterprise as a whole. A security policy should include People, Policy, and Technology. The security process is a mixture of these three elements. Each element depends in some manner on the other elements. Also, issues receive greater coverage when the elements are combined. The controls environment is greatly enhanced when these three elements work in concert. A simple diagram will suffice to illustrate this (see Figure 5.6). This diagram shows the basic elements and also the coverage areas.

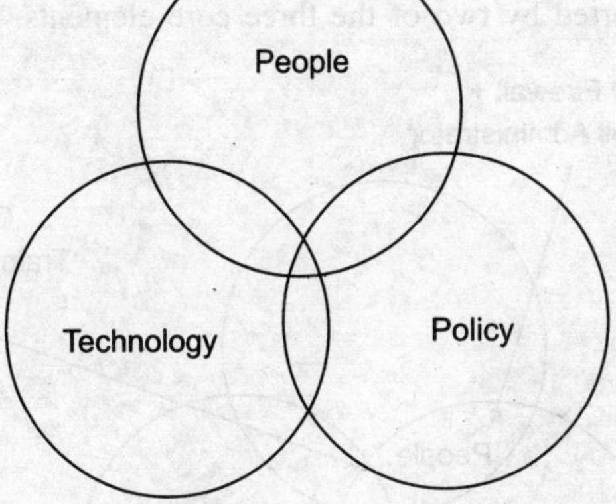

Figure 5.6 People, policy and technology model.

As you move towards the union of these elements, the controls environment increases—there is greater coverage. Let us understand these three elements individually.

People. This core element is the most important. The people element comprises the people and various roles and responsibilities within the organization. These are the people that are put in place to execute and support the process. A few key roles include senior management, security administrators, system and IT administrators, end users, and auditors.

Policy. This element comprises the security vision statement, security policy and standards, and the control documentation. This is basically the written security environment—the bible that the security process will refer to for direction and guidance.

Technology. This element includes tools, methods, and mechanisms in place to support the process. These are core technologies—the operating systems, the databases, the applications, the security tools—embraced by the organization. The technology then is the enforcement, monitoring, and operational tools that will facilitate the process.

The concept is that each core element could be measured for effectiveness and coverage. Also, issues can be measured against the model to determine what controls coverage for that issue. The objective then is to move issues into the intersecting areas of the elements—with the final objective of moving the issue into the middle area of greatest coverage. As risk issues are identified, each step to manage the risk will fall into one of the core elements of people, policy, or technology. If the issue is resolved with one of the elements, addressing one of the other elements can enhance this resolution. As the core elements are added to the controls environment and utilized in concert, the issue is then resolved on several fronts—the controls coverage is greater.

The People, Policy, Technology (PPT) Model

The PPT model can be illustrated with a few simple examples. Figure 5.7 shows the PPT model with regards to Internet usage and misuse. Users are educated on the proper usage of the Internet. The controls environment relies solely on the user. An Internet usage policy is written to document proper use of the Internet and the consequences of misuse. The controls environment now is supported by two of the three core elements.

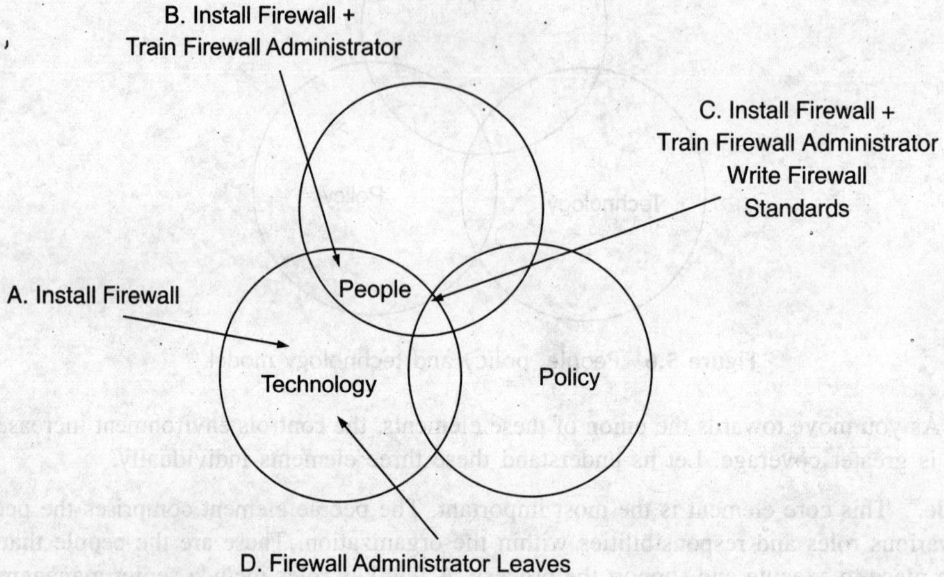

Figure 5.7 Internet connection: Coverage by three elements.

The PPT model is simply the analysis of a risk issue. If the issue is broken down into the three core elements, action items can be determined for each core element. In this manner, control coverage can be moved from one element to two, and ultimately to coverage by all of the elements.

Understanding the Security Framework

Key elements, also referred to as the "Four Pillars" to Information Security, include:

- Solid Senior Management Commitment
- An overall Security Vision and Strategy
- A comprehensive Training and Awareness Program
- A solid Information Security Management Structure including key skill sets and documented responsibilities as depicted in Figure 5.8.

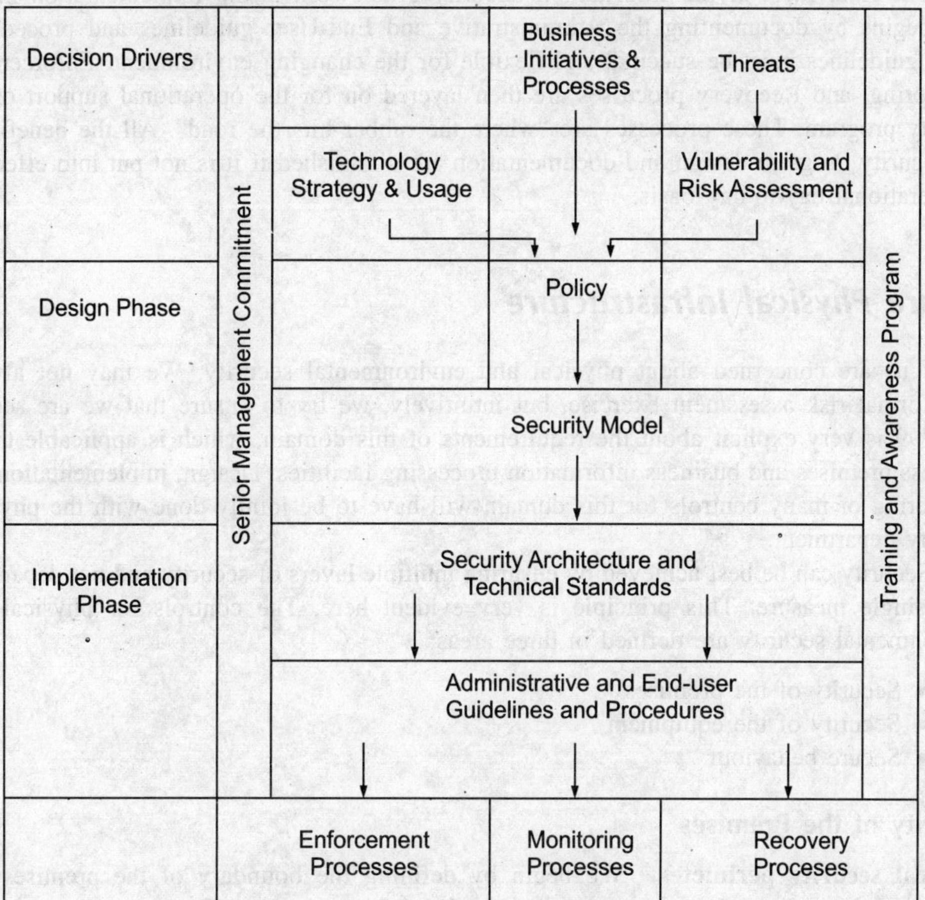

Figure 5.8 Information security management structure.

Within the four "pillars" of the program, several phases are included.

The first is the Decision Driver Phase, which contains factors determining the business drivers of security. These include Technology Strategy and Usage, Business Initiatives and Processes, and Threats, Vulnerabilities and Risk. All these combine to form a unique "Security Profile" of the organization. The "profile" needs to be reflected in the Security Policies and Technical Controls.

The next facet of the Information Security Framework includes the design of the security environment, also called the Design Phase. This is the stage where the organization documents its security policy, the control environment and deals with controls on the technology level. A key element in this process is not only the clear definition of security policy and technical control information, but also the "Security Model" of the enterprise. Information Classifications and Risk Assessment methods fall under this component. These processes allow the organization to manage risk appropriately and identify the risks and value of information assets.

The final facet of the Information Security Framework is the Implementation Phase. This begins by documenting the Administrative and End-User guidelines and procedures. These guidelines must be succinct and flexible for the changing environment. Enforcement, Monitoring, and Recovery processes are then layered on for the operational support of the security program. These processes are "where the rubber hits the road". All the benefits of the Security Program design and documentation are diminished if it is not put into effect on an operational day-to-day basis.

Secure Physical Infrastructure

All of us are concerned about physical and environmental security. We may not always do a formal risk assessment exercise, but intuitively, we try to ensure that we are secure. BS 7799 is very explicit about the requirements of this domain, which is applicable to the business premises and business information processing facilities. Design, implementation and monitoring of many controls for this domain will have to be jointly done with the physical security department.

Security can be best achieved by ensuring multiple layers of security and not depending on a single measure. This principle is very evident here. The controls for physical and environmental security are defined in three areas:

- Security of the premises
- Security of the equipment
- Secure behaviour

Security of the Premises

Physical security perimeter. We begin by defining the boundary of the premises and examining the security requirement, based on the risk assessment. The best way to do this will be to walk around the premises and 'case the joint.' Evaluate all the entry points through which an intruder could come in. Take help of a security agency to do this. Do not depend on your skills as an armchair detective. The classical approach to securing the premises is to create multiple barriers.

Start with the outermost perimeter. How much resistance this perimeter is expected to provide? Based on risk assessment, you need to decide all the physical specifications like height, width for the protective wall. Next, consider all the entry points. Are the doors strong enough? Are the door frames strong enough? Are the windows, ventilators, air-conditioning firmly secured with grills? Do the physical barriers extend from real floor to real ceiling, or is there a gap between false ceiling and real ceiling through which somebody could crawl in? We need to detect the weakest link while assessing the perimeter defence. How are the access points guarded? Are they controlled through card-controlled entry gates? Are watchmen, guards or receptionist monitoring the entry points?

Physical entry controls. Only the authorized persons should be allowed access to the secure areas. This objective could be achieved by having a clear access control policy defining the access rights. Based on this policy, appropriate measures should be in place. These measures may take the form of access control devices like swipe card controlled doors, logging information about visitors and visible identification badges.

Securing offices, rooms and facilities. Location of the secure office within the physically secure perimeter should be chosen with care. All the risks pertaining to fire, flood, explosion, civil unrest and other forms of natural or man-made disaster should be considered. There could also be threat from neighbouring premises, caused by leakage of water, spreading of fire, or storage of toxic/inflammable/explosive material. Even bulk supplies like stationery should not be stored within the secure premises.

The secure location should not be publicized in any manner. No display board, banners, signs to indicate the presence of any important information processing activity. Even the internal telephone directories should not be readily accessible to outsiders.

Support facilities like photocopier, fax machines, which are constantly accessed by everyone, should be located away from the secure area. Suitable intrusion detection systems like CCTV, motion sensors etc. should be installed and regularly tested.

Working in secure areas. Security equipment like CCTV and swipe-card controlled gates are of no use if the persons working in these locations are not trustworthy, or are incompetent, or simply lack awareness of their responsibility. They should be hand-picked and trained for these operations. They should not brag about their nature of work or location. Also, information should be provided on need-to-know basis. Segregation of duties should be scrupulously followed with strict supervision. Third-party personnel should be granted restricted access. No photographic, video, audio or other recording equipment must be allowed inside the premises, unless authorized.

Isolated delivery and loading areas. We have taken care of every aspect of physical security in the above paragraphs, but do we know how canteen facilities get into secured premises? How the trash is taken out? How the courier delivers the parcels? In industrial premises, there could be constant movement of incoming and outgoing material. All this traffic needs to be isolated from the secure office area, so that it does not pose a threat.

Security of the Equipment

Equipment setting and protection. Our next concern is the appropriate security of the equipment. Information processing equipment needs to be handled carefully. The first level of equipment protection depends on physical location. The location should minimize the need for unnecessary access, as well as prevent snooping. It should be such as to minimize the risk of theft as well as the risk from natural disasters like fire, flood, chemicals etc. Also, consider risks like electrical and electromagnetic interference, humidity etc.

Power supplies. Information processing will come to halt in the absence of a suitable power supply. This could be the worst type of a denial-of-service attack. A thorough business risks assessment is necessary to understand the impact on non-availability of power for certain durations. Based on the evaluation, appropriate measures need to be taken.

These could be:

1. Taking power from multiple feeds of electric supply.
2. In case all the electric supplies fail simultaneously, you need to have an uninterruptible power supply (UPS) with adequate battery capacity capable of sustaining the initial load.
3. The UPS could in-turn be supported by backup generator sets.
4. The backup generator would require adequate supply of fuel, which also needs to be stored with replenishment, assured by the suppliers.
5. Proper installation of emergency lights should also be planned; lightning protection should be provided to the power installation and the communication lines.

Cabling security. We really need to remember every detail, including the proverbial last nail. Do we know the physical layout of power cables and communication cables in our premises? The first step will be to obtain wiring diagrams and update them. Then, do a physical inspection and assess the protection needs against damage, interference or interception. Establish the best practices for laying the network cables as well as power cables, and ensure that these are actually implemented. The next step is to decide on additional security protection required for the network. This could be expensive for an old installation. Safety measures like use of armoured conduit cables, underground ducts, or fibre optic cabling will require huge investment and need to be justified based on risk assessment. But simple measures like providing locks to the communication cable patch board, which are often over-looked, should be immediately implemented.

Equipment maintenance. It is normally expected that due care is taken for equipment maintenance, and proper records are maintained. From a security angle, two more measures are required. One is to maintain record of faults that were noticed, and the second step is to maintain records of all equipment sent off the premises for maintenance.

Security of equipment off premises. Shrinking size of computers and expanding wide area networks have made the computer equipment extremely mobile. Processing as well as storage capacity of mobile devices has been following Moore's law of doubling every 18 months. Securing these devices is as important as securing the data centre. Various controls that should be considered are: administrative controls like permissions and corporate policy on use of mobile computers in places like airplanes, physical controls like securing the devices with security chains, alarms, and storing them at non-obvious places, using access control devices like USB tokens, and finally taking adequate insurance cover.

Secure disposal or reuse of equipment. Storage devices have long memory, unless specifically destroyed. Mere deletion is not enough. This becomes important when an old computer equipment is disposed off or transferred to another location. Equipment sent for repair are equally susceptible to reading of data from the 'deleted' storage devices. Every such device should be subjected to a thorough erasing and overwriting to destroy the data. Since some reports claim that the data could be recovered even after multiple overwriting and formatting, it may be desirable to physically destroy the media containing top secret information.

Secure Behaviour

Clear desk and clear screen policy. Our concern for information security should not stop at securing the premises and equipment. Sensitive information could be accessible in many forms, and it is necessary to identify and protect the information in all its incarnations. Classification of information will help to identify the sensitivity, but having an organizational "clear desk and clear screen policy" could ensure actual protection. In brief, it means keep everything under lock and key and do not allow anybody to snoop. The following guidelines should be issued:

- Lock up all documents and media when not being used.
- Protect the computers and terminals through use of key locks, passwords, and screen savers.
- Fax and telex machines used for confidential information should not be left unattended.
- Access to photocopiers and scanners is restricted after office hours.
- Printing of classified information should be supervised and all printouts must be removed immediately.

Removal of property. Any movement of equipment, information or software should be only with proper authorization. All these movements should be logged and records maintained for all outgoing and incoming items. In these days of storage media capable of containing gigabytes of information, this procedure becomes very important. Employees should be made aware that spot checks would be carried out to ensure full compliance.

Security is being paranoid about threats. Physical security is very demonstrative about this paranoia. But, it also sets the tone about the organization's concern about information security.

Information Security Environment in India[4]

Most Indian companies that are aiming to go global will require certifying their ability to maintain proper security levels when scouting for international clients. Information security is no more a mere legal requirement but it is fast becoming a factor for companies to compete on and grow businesses. A "secure and reliable" environment—defined by strong copyright, IT and cyber laws—is an imperative for the growth and future success of the ITES–BPO industries.

NASSCOM has been proactive in pushing this cause and ensuring that the Indian Information Security environment benchmarks with the best across the globe. Indian ITES–

4. www.nasscom.in

BPO companies today adhere to international best practices—they are regularly audited by independent certified auditors, comply with international standards at the highest levels, update procedures and practices regularly and meet, if not exceed the worldwide information security standards to ensure that data and personal information of international customers is adequately protected.

Security Environment in India

Indian companies are known for their quality deliverables. International certifications like ISO 9000 went a long way in establishing this reputation. Likewise following international standards in information security is also helping Indian companies build credibility among customers. While most Indian BPO firms are recognized for high quality processes and services, information security practices need to be constantly reviewed and updated according to the rapidly changing environment. Customer data demands special focus.

Indian companies have robust security practices comparable to those followed by western companies. Indian companies primarily comply with BS 7799—a global standard that covers all domains of security. Companies sign Service Level Agreements (SLA), which have very strict confidentiality and security clauses built into them at the network and data level. Such SLAs also cover all relevant laws that the companies want its offshore providers to comply with and actions that can be taken in case of breaches.

Laws such as the IT Act, 2000, Indian Copyright Act, Indian Penal Code Act and the Indian Contract Act, 1972 provide adequate safeguards to companies offshoring work to US and UK. Most of the BPO companies providing services to UK clients ensure compliance with UK Data Protection Act, 1998 (DPA) through contractual agreements.

Companies dealing with US clients require compliance depending upon the industry served, e.g. Healthcare requires compliance with HIPAA, Financial services require compliance with GLBA. To ensure compliance with such laws, Indian vendors follow security practices as specified by clients such as security awareness, protection of information, non-disclosure agreements, screening of employees, etc. Further, clients conduct periodic audits to ensure compliance. Many companies in India are undergoing/have undergone SAS-70 Audit. SAS-70 assignments helps service companies operating from India to implement and improve internal controls, ensure minimal disruptions to business from clients' auditors, and is potent marketing tool in the face of increasing competition.

EXERCISES

1. Describe how online website operations can be protected from hackers.
2. What is the role of a firewall?
3. Outside firewalls, what are the major technologies used to ensure Internet security?
4. What is the use of a proxy server?

5. What is a denial-of-service attack and how does it affect a business organization?
6. Which is easier to maintain—default deny or default permit?
7. Why should a firm care about IP spoofing attacks that originate from its site but do not pose a threat to its own computer security?
8. What are the necessary components for an organization's security policy?
9. Why should a firewall be able to support a 'deny all services, except those specifically permitted', if this is not the policy expected to be used?
10. Discuss the relative merits of developing firewalls in-house or buying commercial firewall software.
11. What are some of the potentially dangerous internet services, and why?

CHAPTER

6

e-Payment Systems

LEARNING OBJECTIVES

After reading this chapter, you should be able to:

- Know about various kinds of e-payment systems.
- Describe various requirements of digital payment systems.
- Understand the use of credit card payment systems.
- Describe the encryption mechanisms needed for credit cards.
- Understand micropayment systems.
- Know how digital signature works.
- Know about online financial services in India.

American Express Credit Card Authorization

Credit cards are a fact of life. Credit cards provide certain benefits and disadvantages to both card holders and the issuing financial institution. Credit card authorization is the process by which card issuers either approve, refer (i.e. directs the agency to contact Global for further instructions) or deny requests to accept transactions. Approval is based on a validation of the account number and expiration date to verify that a cardholder's account is open and that the transaction will not place the account above any credit limit. Since most authorization requests are approved, the term "authorized transaction" refers to an approved authorization request.

Figure 6.1 depicts the typical flow of an online authorization through a non-Internet payment device such as a point-of-sale terminal or a PC utilizing card processing software.

1. Card information is captured from the magnetic strip by swiping the card through a point-of-sale terminal, or by data entering the card and payment information into

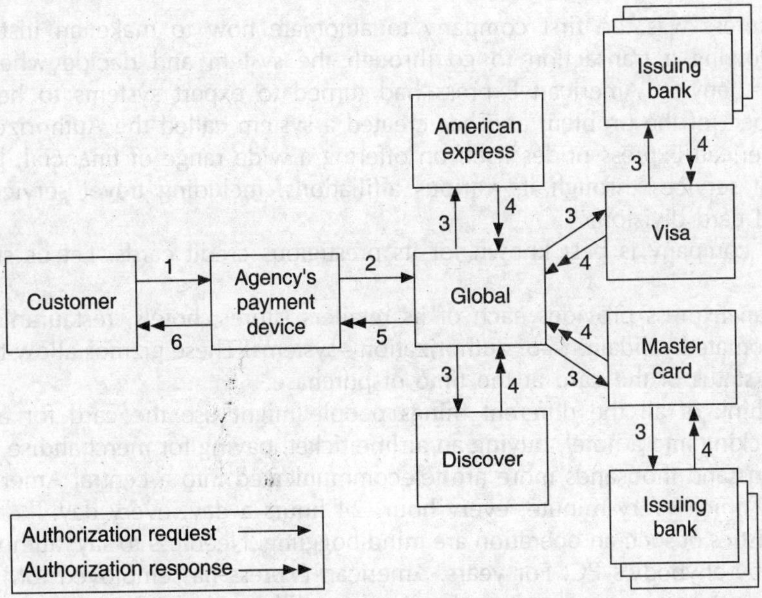

Figure 6.1 Credit card authorization process.

the agency's payment device (e.g. PC-based software). Information from the card (e.g. card type, account number, expiration date) is combined with information about the transaction (e.g. dollar amount) to create the authorization request.

2. The agency's payment device connects to Global's system and transmits the authorization request via one of the five communications methods (i.e. dial-up, leased line, host-to-host, ISDN or wireless).
3. Global's system recognizes the authorization request as being for a Visa, MasterCard, American Express or DiscoverCard. In the case of Visa or MasterCard, the request is transmitted to the appropriate association, which, in turn, routes the request to the member bank which issued the card. If the authorization request is for an American Express or DiscoverCard, Global transmits the request to American Express or Discover, respectively.
4. The card issuer (a Visa or MasterCard issuing bank or American Express or Discover) verifies that the cardholder's account is valid and that the amount of the transaction is less than their remaining credit limit (if such a credit limit exists). The approval (with authorization number), referral or declination is transmitted directly back to Global for American Express and Discover transactions and indirectly back to Global through an association for Visa and MasterCard transactions.
5. Global transmits the response to the agency's payment device.
6. The cardholder is made aware if the transaction is approved or denied. If approved, a confirmation number (which can be the authorization number) is typically provided to the cardholder. Since most authorization requests are approved, the term "authorized" denotes an approved authorization request.

From the cardholder/agency perspective, this process is seamless, taking only seconds for completion. This system is well established today. But 20 years ago, it was not so.

American Express was the first company to automate how to make an instant decision regarding allowing a transaction to go through the system and decide whether to give the credit or deny it. American Express had turned to expert systems to help with this particular aspect of the problem and has created a system called the Authorizer's Assistant in 1987. American Express prides itself on offering a wide range of financial, business and entertainment services through its various affiliations, including travel service, insurance coverage and card division.

But the company is best known for its prestigious credit cards. Let us start with the basics.

American Express provides each of its retailers (stores, hotels, restaurants, bars) with one of its automated validation—or authorization—systems. These gizmos allow the merchant to check the status of the card at the time of purchase.

Now, think of all the different things people might use the card for at any given moment: checking into a hotel, buying an airline ticket, paying for merchandise, etc. Each of these scenarios and thousands more are telecommunicated into a central American Express authorization office every minute, every hour, 24 hours a day, every day.

The logistics of such an operation are mind boggling. Needless to say, authorizations are not handled by anybody's PC. For years, American Express has employed IBM mainframes for the basic authorization procedures involved in each card check.

Think of 100 queries on the same topic with different variables bombarding the mainframe simultaneously in a relatively constant stream. Think about the fact that the mainframe is designed to handle relatively common queries. Then think about how many calls have to be turned over to human experts for actual verification or decision making.

The company's history of involvement with expert systems led it to consider creating an automated authorization system: not just a prototype of a semi-useful, occasionally employed expert system, but one that would work in real time and could be connected to the installed mainframe for access to the existing database.

The criteria for the system, in addition to the technical requirements just mentioned, were fairly straightforward:

1. Minimize fraud and credit losses from improper or incorrect authorizations.
2. Assist in making more accurate authorization, more quickly and frequently.
3. Reduce training time and associated costs for authorizers.
4. Stabilize authorization staffing levels by transferring certain responsibilities to the computer system.

The system also had to be able to show its chain of reasoning at given points in the operation. It also had to be fairly easy to maintain, with the ability to incorporate new company policies in a minimal amount of time; obviously, that eliminated compiler-based systems.

American Express looked for the appropriate product and vendor and eventually settled on Inference Corp. to help with its large-scale development plan. This Los Angeles, California-based company is the vendor of the Automated Reasoning Tool, a Lisp development tool usually referred to by its acronym, ART.

Inference agreed to develop the Authorizer's Assistant to conform to all American Express's criteria. Eventually the system had to be fully deployable to American Express for internal use. Two important points about ART are worth mentioning. First, the program allows for incremental rule compilation during development, which means new rules can be inserted without having to go through entire recompilation of an application. This was appealing because of American Express's need for revisions based on corporate policy changes.

Second, ART is capable of synchronous processing. It was important to American Express to be able to exchange data with IBM 3090 to utilize shared information between the two environments.

Started in early 1986, the system began with prototypes. American Express is different from other credit companies in that it has no predefined credit limit. The company imposes spending ceilings for individual cardholders based on their ability to pay their monthly statements, which are always due in full. So often, users of the card may not know how much they are allowed to spend in a given time period until the company determines that may be the cardholder is in over his or her head.

Thus, a dilemma arises if an individual who customarily runs up a maximum of $200 per month suddenly makes a purchase of $15,000. This would require human authorization because of the mitigating factors involved.

Primary concerns are: "Is the card being used by someone other than the original Cardholder? Could it be stolen or a fake? Could the cardholder have gone berserk and embarked upon a murderous shopping spree?" Although the last question is not an official American Express designation, I'm sure it gives you an idea of the possibilities.

Other factors also come into play. If Monday's authorization for a card came in from New York, Tuesday's authorization for the same card came from Manila, Philippines, Wednesday's from Stockholm, Sweden, Thursday's from Mumbai, India, and Friday's from Anchorage, Alaska, something fishy is probably going on.

The system has to be able to track strange travel patterns given the location of previous authorization sites. Not that any of these are strange places to use the card; it is just strange if the user appears to only have stopped in each place for the sole purpose of using the credit card.

As if this was not enough, the system also has to address the problem of discrepancies. When discrepancies do occur, how will the customer be queried? It was decided that the program would help by supplying a set of courteous questions to the merchant on the other end in case a problem arose.

Back to the mechanics. The first prototype took almost six months to complete and consisted of 520 rules configured for forward chaining. Currently, by the time, it was deployed in 1987, it had about 1,500 rules.

Case Discussion

1. Discuss how fraud takes place in credit card companies.
2. What steps are being taken by credit card companies to limit fraud?
3. Credit cards are not a big success in India yet. Can you identify reasons for it?

Main Concerns of Online Payments

In a survey conducted by the Online Banking Association, member institutions rated security as the most important issue of online banking. There is a dual requirement to protect customers' privacy and protect against fraud. Banking Securely: Online Banking via the World Wide Web provides an overview of Internet commerce and how one company handles secure banking for its financial institution clients and their customers. Some basic information on the transmission of confidential data is presented in Security and Encryption on the Web. A multi-layered security architecture comprising firewalls, filtering routers, encryption and digital certification ensures that your account information is protected from unauthorized access:

- Firewalls and filtering routers ensure that only the legitimate Internet users are allowed to access the system.
- Encryption techniques used by the bank (including the sophisticated public key encryption) would ensure that privacy of data flowing between the browser and the Infinity system is protected.
- Digital certification procedures provide the assurance that the data you receive is from the Infinity system.

The growth of e-commerce is dependent, among other factors, on the existence of secure, user-friendly and cost-effective payment systems. Handling payments is a costly process that has been a central part of bank business for the past century. However, it is now being transformed by technological developments, and in particular, the Internet. The importance of the payment function lies in the fact that it could encourage convergence between sectors with disparate objectives, since payment systems are the common denominator of all e-commerce transactions. Conceptually, the alternative means of payment available for e-commerce may be classified as either electronic money (e-money), or electronic access products. The difference between them is that whereas electronic access products basically provide Internet access to traditional products (credit card payments, bank transfers, and the like), e-money is a new concept, and in particular is considered to be "private money not depending on central bank reserves."

Consolidated methods of payment used for distance selling mostly at national level, such as cheque, cash-on-delivery and credit-transfer mechanisms, have proven easy to adapt to electronic transactions. The credit card system has to date been the usual payments instrument for goods ordered over the Internet. This is despite security concerns and relatively higher transaction cost. Nevertheless, the lack of a widely accepted e-payment system is not considered to be a major barrier for the gearing up of e-commerce. The most important factors are undoubtedly user trust and user confidence.

E-payment systems are becoming central to e-commerce as companies look for ways to serve customers faster and at lower cost. Emerging innovations in the payment for goods and services in electronic commerce promise to offer a wide range of new business opportunities. The current state of online electronic payments is in many ways reminiscent of the medieval ages. The merchants of Asia and Europe faced a similar problem while trying to unlock the commercial potential of the expanding marketplace. Those ancient traders faced a number of obstacles, such as conflicting local laws and customs regarding commercial practices, and incompatible and nonconvertible currencies that restricted trade. To circumvent some of these problems, traders invented various forms of payment instruments, such as promissory notes, bills of exchange, gold coins, and barter. The merchants also developed commercial law surrounding the use of these instruments, that proved to be one of the turning points in the history of trade and commerce. We are on the verge of a similar sort of development today with regard to e-payment systems.

Everyone agrees that the payment and settlement process is a potential bottleneck in the fast-moving electronic commerce environment, if we rely on conventional payment methods such as cash, cheques, bank drafts, or bills of exchange. Electronic replicas of these conventional instruments are not well-suited for the speed required in e-commerce purchase processing. For instance, payments of small denominations (micropayments) for bits and pieces of information must be accepted by vendors in real time. Conventional instruments are too slow for micropayments, and the high transaction costs involved in processing them add greatly to the overhead. Therefore, new methods of payment are needed to meet the emerging demands of e-commerce. These new payment instruments must be secure, have a low processing cost, and be accepted widely as global currency tender.

History's Lesson about Payments: People Drive Change

The development of money is not dependent solely on objective characteristics. Subjective valuations play a critical role. Ultimately consumers determine what form of money is most desirable—people simply substitute cheaper and more convenient forms of money for expensive and inconvenient forms. It is ultimately through this substitution in use that new money forms embed themselves in the marketplace.

Up until that time, it was assumed that money and payment systems had been invented and imposed by the state. Money is a social phenomenon, with its roots in the barter economy; payment systems evolved out of the barter economy—and empowered buyers and sellers—with the development of money as a medium of exchange. Buyers and sellers recognized that doing business became much more efficient if everyone used a commonly accepted form of payment.

The notion of money continues to evolve, driven by overwhelming marketplace preference for increased convenience and efficiency, and decreasing risk and costs. The modern payment card system is an excellent example of this organic, socially-driven growth—the creation of new forms of exchange that continue to make life easier and more efficient. So long as the human condition continues to change, payment systems will continue to evolve, driven by those powerful market forces.

Digital Payment Requirements

For any digital payment system to succeed, the criteria given in Table 6.1 ought to be satisfied.

TABLE 6.1 Digital Payment Requirements

Criteria	*Need for the criteria*
Acceptability	Payment infrastructure needs to be widely accepted.
Anonymity	Identity of the customers should be protected.
Convertibility	Digital money should be convertible to any type of fund.
Efficiency	Cost per transaction should be near zero.
Integration	Interfaces should be created to support the existing system.
Scalability	Infrastructure should not breakdown if new customers and merchants join.
Security	Should allow financial transactions over open networks.
Reliability	Should avoid single points of failure.
Usability	Payment should be as easy as in the real world.

Online Payment Categories

Online payments can be broadly divided into three categories as shown in Table 6.2.

TABLE 6.2 Online Payment Categories

Category	*Description*
Micropayment	Transaction value less than 5 euros or dollars. Transaction costs are nearly zero.
Consumer payments	Transaction value between 5 and 500 euros or dollars. Payments are executed by credit card transactions.
Business payments	Transaction value more than 500 euros or dollars. Debit cards or invoices are appropriate solutions in this system.

E-payment systems are proliferating in banking, retail, healthcare, online markets, and even in government—in fact, anywhere money needs to change hands. Organizations are motivated by the need to deliver products and services more cost-effectively and to provide a higher quality of service to customers. Research into e-payment systems for consumers can be traced back to the 1940s, and the first applications, the credit cards, appeared soon after. In the early 1970s, the emerging electronic payment technology was labelled electronic funds transfer (EFT). EFT is defined as:

> *any transfer of funds initiated through an electronic terminal, telephonic instrument, or computer or magnetic tape so as to order, instruct, or authorize a fine new institution to debit or credit an account.*[1]

EFT utilizes computer and telecommunication components, both to supply and to transfer money or financial assets. Transfer is information-based and intangible. Thus EFT stands in marked contrast to conventional money and payment modes that rely on physical delivery of cash or cheques (or other paper orders to pay) by truck, train, or airplane.

1. www.itspace.com

Since 1947, significant changes have taken place in funds transfer. You can find them listed here, in Table 6.3.

TABLE 6.3 Significant Innovations in Modern Payment Systems[2]

Year	*Innovations*
1947	Flatbush National Bank issues first general-purpose credit card, for use in select New York shops.
1950	Diners Club Charge Card introduced.
mid-1950s	The development of magnetic ink character recognition (MICR) facilitated more timely processing of cheques, sealed the cheque's standing as the preferred non-cash payment option.
1958	BankAmerica, in Fresno, California, executes the first mass mailing of credit cards.
1967	Westminster Bank installs the first automated teller machine at Victoria, London branch.
1970	The New York Clearing House launches CHIPS—the Clearing House Interbank Payments System which provides US dollar funds transfer and transaction settlements online and in real time.
late 1970s	Chemical Bank launches its Pronto system providing 3000 computer terminals to customers' homes linked to its central computers by telephone. It offers a range of facilities: balance inquiries, money transfers between Chemical Bank accounts, and bill payments to selected local stores. The stumbling block for first-generation home-banking systems in general was, who is to pay for the terminals at home?
1985	Electronic Data Interchange (EDI) extensively used in bank-to-bank payment systems.
1994	Digital cash trials by DigiCash of Holland conducted online.
1995	Mondex electronic currency trials begin in Swedon, England.

Digital Token-based e-Payment Systems

The introduction of charge cards in the early 1900s, beginning with western union in 1914, represented a breakthrough in payments. But while these cards enhanced customer loyalty and stimulated repeat behaviour, they were generally limited to the local market, or in store use. In 1958, Bank of America took a major step forward, introducing what eventually became the modern credit card. Based on extensive test marketing in Fresno, California, it became clear there was a large market for a general purpose bank card featuring a revolving credit facility and wide acceptance. With the launch of Bank of America's card, the consumer was not tied to one merchant or product, but was now free to make credit purchases at a wide range of outlets. As the adoption of the bank card grew, the potential size of the market for transactions expanded geometrically. It was a profound turning point in the history of money.

The development of the modern electronic payment network took an important step forward in the mid-1970s, with the creation of a global joint venture that would eventually be known as visa. Through shared investments, the visa association created a global system

2. Kalakota R. and Whinston A., *Frontiers of Electronic Commerce*, Addison-Wesley, Massachusetts, 1996, p. 296.

to authorize transactions, clear and settle electronic payments, codify operating regulations to protect consumers and merchants alike, and set interoperability standards to ensure that, unlike cash and cheques, a visa card could be used anywhere in the world.

Two developments in the 1990s further broadened the utility of electronic payments.

Debit cards, a popular "pay now" product, allowed consumers to access funds in a demand deposit account to conduct transaction at the point of sale; and e-commerce emerged as mainstream business channel, both relying on and stimulating electronic payments.

The rapid adoption of these relatively recent developments demonstrate the speed at which the payments landscape is changing. Looking forward, there is broad experimentation in ways to migrate electronic payment functions into consumer devices such as mobile phones, PDAs, and other popular electronic products. This process is well underway in some European and Asian markets where mobile phones are nearly as ubiquitous as payment cards. Visa describes this new range of payment choices as "u-commerce," or universal commerce—the ability to conduct commerce anywhere, anytime, or any way.

This shift in consumer preference is driving major changes in personal consumer expenditures (PCE). The growth in card usage as a share of PCE continues to expand relative to cash and cheques.

Also, in most markets around the world, the use of cash and cheques is declining—a trend that is likely to continue. The trend away from cash and cheques is driven by well established benefits of electronic payments to all parties.

Benefits to Buyers

- Convenience of global acceptance, a wide range of payment options, and enhanced financial management tools.
- Enhanced security and reduced liability for stolen or misused cards.
- Consumer protection through an established system of dispute resolution.
- Convenient and immediate access to funds on deposit via debit cards.
- Accessibility to immediate credit. Intuitively, the comparative cost of arranging for a consumer loan relative to the ability to obtain credit at the point of sale is substantial in considering both the direct processing costs as well as the implicit opportunity costs to borrower and lender.

Benefits to Sellers

- Speed and security of the transaction processing chain from verification and authorization to clearing and settlement.
- Freedom from more costly labour, materials and accounting services that are required in paper-based processing.
- Better management of cash flow, inventory and financial planning due to swift bank payment.

- Incremental purchasing power on the part of the consumer.
- Cost and risk savings by eliminating the need to run an in-house credit facility.

A dramatic example of the efficiencies created by electronic payments can be seen in the public sector, where governments have used innovations such as purchasing card to reduce paperwork, enhance financial controls, and create more robust accounting and financial data.

Convenience

Anyone who has searched through pockets for exact change for parking, fumbled with foreign currency, paid exorbitant foreign exchange commissions, tried to cash a cheque in another country or been concerned about carrying a large roll of banknotes can appreciate the convenience of payment cards.

Fundamental to this convenience is the virtually ubiquitous acceptance and utility, whether it is an apparel store in Paris or a crafts shop in Nepal. Payment cards work in brick and mortar environments, over the phone, on the Internet, and through the post. Applications are underway that support new uses such as recurring payments, insurance and payroll disbursements, rent and utility bills, and small ticket transactions such as vending machines and car parks. Consumers place an enormous value on convenience, although this paper has not attempted to measure it. The sheer convenience of being able to access cash at an ATM or conduct a transaction directly at the point of sale with a credit or debit card clearly has had an impact on economic growth.

None of the banking or retailing payment methods in their present form are completely adequate for the consumer-oriented e-commerce environment. Their deficiency is their assumption that the parties will, at some time or other, be in each other's physical presence or that there will be a sufficient delay in the payment process for frauds, overdrafts, and other undesirables to be identified and corrected. These assumptions may not hold good for e-commerce and so, many of these payment mechanisms are being modified and adapted for the conduct of business over networks.

Entirely new forms of financial instruments are also being developed. One such new financial instrument is *electronic tokens,* which are available in the form of electronic cash/ money or cheques. Electronic tokens are designed as electronic analogues of various forms of payment backed by a bank or a financial institution. Simply stated, electronic tokens are equivalent to cash that is backed by a bank.

Transition to Digital Payments in India

Cash is the de-facto mode of payment across the globe. More than 95 per cent of the transactions in India are still cash-based. While demonetization of 2016 wiped out 86 per cent of the currency from the Indian market, the 'currency in circulation' has increased since January 2017 to 19.5 lakh crore rupees (as per the RBI). Other modes of payment, especially digital payments, have grown steadily for the past many years. While credit and debit cards are the most popular cashless modes of payment introduced more than three decades ago in India, the adoption is still slow and steady. There are challenges in adoption due to lack of infrastructure, connectivity and Point-of-Sale (PoS) machines. The penetration is low amongst small ticket merchants as well as tier-2, tier-3 cities since banks lack the will to promote PoS adoption for small businesses.

Demonetization disrupted the cash economy for a while with a rise in digital payments. The growth of digital payments has been accelerated by four years due to demonetization. Since then, the cash is back, but mobile payments are being used twice as much. Currently, less than 5 per cent of the transactions are cashless and there has been a strong push by the government for digital payments. There are plenty of cashless payment options that have grown in the last three years such as UPI, Net Banking, Open banking apps, USSD, AEPS, etc.

Digital payment is a way of payment which is made through digital modes. In digital payments, payer and payee both use digital modes to send and receive money. It is also called *electronic payment.* No hard cash is involved in digital payments. All the transactions in digital payments are completed online. It is an instant and convenient way to make payments.

Digital revolution has provided an easy way to go for digital payments. India has more than 100 crore active mobile connections and more than 22 crore smartphone users. This number is going to increase further with a faster Internet speed. The reach of mobile network, Internet and electricity is also expanding digital payments to remote areas. This will surely increase the number of digital payments.

To talk about cash payments, you have to first withdraw cash from your account. Then, you use this cash to pay at shops. Shopkeeper goes to the bank to deposit the cash which he got from you. This process is time-consuming for you and also for the shopkeeper. But, in digital payments, the money transfers from your account to the shopkeeper's account immediately. This process is automatic and neither you nor the shopkeeper is required to visit the bank.

It is because of this reason that Mobile wallets like Mobikwik, Paytm, Oxigen, Amazon Pay, Google Pay have become the forerunners of the digital payment industry. While these wallets are penetrating into very small businesses and non-tier-1 cities initially with their cash-backs, they have innovated and provided easy user experience that needs minimum learning by a user. For example, payment via scanning a QR Code or simply entering merchant's mobile number is easy. Sending money to a friend to clear debts is just a click-or-two away. To add on to this, apart from simplifying payments, the value added services like bill payments, ticket booking provided by these wallets have made them the preferred payment option of the savvy Indian consumer.

The future of digital payments lies in providing further simplified and secure user experience, while increasing its adoption by leading socio-economic changes at the grass root level. Mobile wallets are good, but still need taking out the smartphone followed by some action by the user, which is no better than taking out the credit card for payment. Next simplification lies in secure identification and payments (by face detection, voice, sound), which can further disrupt and exponentially grow the digital payments wave.

Technological advancements in the digital payment ecosystem are changing our lives significantly and providing the end-consumers with speed, convenience, choice and savings. India, with a large share of 48 per cent of the world's unbanked and financially underserved, is clearly a critical frontier for digital payments. Over the last few years, the digital payment space has grown quite well in India with 400+ organizations working on creating and capturing value in online commerce. India's digital payment industry, which is currently worth around USD 200 billion, is expected to grow five-fold to reach USD 1 trillion by 2023, as per a report by Swiss financial services holding company, Credit Suisse. Digital payments present a huge opportunity for various digitization initiatives in the country.

The digital India mission envisioned by the Government of India is aimed at transforming the country into a digital economy. One major part of this larger program is a special focus on digital payments. The program on digital payments is envisioned with elements such as extending banking facilities to underbanked, banking from anywhere, expanding the base of financial inclusion, creating digital space flywheel opportunities with national identity program and establishing enhanced transparency into the systems. Digital payments are becoming a key part of our daily lives and impacting society, business and the economy at large. Innovative use of technology has enabled digital payment infrastructure and the creation of innovative products such as mobile wallets, i.e., prepaid payment instruments. The private sector in India has taken a giant leap to drive digital payments adoption. At the same time, National Payment Corporation of India (NPCI) developed and introduced Unified Payment Interface (UPI), which provides 24×7×365 mobile payment platform for users to send and receive payments with a simple virtual payment address. This technology innovation was further augmented with the introduction of Bharat Interface for Money (BHIM), which has enabled high-volume cashless payments through mobile phones. The Indian Government's thrust on digital payments is making this space affordable and interoperable, which is benefitting end-consumers, businesses and digital payment sector at large.

Innovations such as, but not limited to, tokenization of card, NFC (Near Field Communication) readers at merchant stores, biometric-enabled transactions and interoperability of wallets are paving ways for the next generation financial world. The rise of non-traditional players such as Apple, Google, Samsung, Starbucks, Vodafone, etc., clearly reflects that this space is no longer a monopoly of the traditional financial institutions. The future customer may transact via smart watches, smart cars and even smart apparel. The expectations from future digital payment modes include:

1. Simpler payment methods
2. Omnipresent merchant networks
3. Frictionless on demand payment options
4. Customer-friendly easy on-boarding and off-boarding provisions
5. Significant reduction in costs in performing digital transactions
6. Cyber security preparedness for the digital payment space warrants a concerted effort globally.

Different Types of Digital Payments

Banking Cards (debit/credit/cash/travel/others)

Cards are provided by banks to their account holders. These have been the most used digital payment modes till now. Many of us use cards for transferring funds and making digital payments. Credit cards, debit cards and prepaid cards are the main types of cards. Banking cards offer consumers more security, convenience, and control than any other payment method. The wide variety of cards available, including credit, debit and prepaid, offers enormous flexibility as well. These cards provide two-factor authentication for secure payments, e.g. secure PIN and OTP. RuPay, Visa, MasterCard are some of the examples of card payment systems. Payment cards give people the power to purchase items in stores, on the Internet, through mail-order catalogues and over the telephone. They save time and money of both customers and merchants, and thus, enable them for ease of transaction.

Without any doubt, the basic means of payment used and initiated via the Internet for consumer transactions till date is the credit card. Credit cards have proved popular for a number of reasons which are as follows:

- The system is familiar to users and was widely used before the advent of e-commerce, thus bolstering the users' confidence.
- Transaction costs are hidden from users (i.e., basically met by sellers, and passed on to all customers, not just credit card users).
- Payment is simple anywhere and in any currency, thus matching the global reach of the Internet.
- The credit-issuing company shares the transaction risk; helping overcome consumers' fear and reluctance to buy goods they have not actually seen, from sellers they do not know (in the physical world, this function was important because it enabled sellers to take payment from buyers they do not know; this trust relationship is needed in both directions for online transactions).

Debit cards are issued by the bank where you have your account. You can use these cards for the money in your account. The payments you make with these cards debit from your account and credit immediately to the payee's account. You can use these cards to make payments to one bank account to another.

Nowadays, as the online banking system continues to gain acceptance and much improvement, many consumers are taking advantage of the system and are shifting from the use of cash and cheques to debit cards. Basically, a debit card is a plastic card issued to the customers by banks and debit card companies. It allows a cardholder to purchase products or services directly from their savings accounts that come from checking machines. Funds used are prepaid and exist in the bank account prior to any transaction made using the card. Debit cards, which are also known as bank card or check card, are significant when making purchases or while travelling. Having debit cards in hand means that buyers do not have to bring huge amounts of cash in their pockets since numerous establishments accept these cards as mode of payment. Almost all stores like shopping centres, restaurants, hotels, airlines, and malls have made their point-of-sale terminals capable of receiving payment from prepaid cards. For a customer, it is easier to swipe than to count cash and coins. Also, Internet shoppers, who buy goods online, use debit cards too. Usually, businesses, which sell through the Internet and deliver by mail, only accept debit or credit cards for fees.

Further, for people who pay their bills through an automated teller machine (ATM), a debit card is vital. By just inserting the card in the machine and pressing the amount to be paid, the payee saves time and effort compared to falling in line to pay to the teller. The remaining amount of money can be checked online or through mobile phone. Another importance of debit cards is that they are used to withdraw cash from ATMs. Consumers who use debits cards can easily track their expenses since these are listed in their bank statements. The number of debit cards issued by banks grew from 182 million in 2010 to 980 million in 2018[3].

Disadvantages of debit cards: Debit cards offer lower levels of security protection than credit cards. Theft of the users' PIN using skimming devices can be accomplished much easily with a PIN input than with a signature-based credit transaction. Unlike a credit card, debit card transactions give you no grace period. They are a quick, pay-now deal.

They can make balancing your account tricky if you are not fastidious about keeping receipts and recording transactions in a timely fashion. It is easy to forget, for example, when you pay at the petrol pump with a debit card and drive off without your receipt.

Some ATM machines charge a fee for their use and then your bank adds another foreign ATM charge (if the machine is not from your bank). Know ahead of time what the fees are and where you can access your money for free, if possible.

Prepaid cards are another type of cards which you use to pay digitally. You must have to recharge these cards before using just like prepaid SIM cards.

Cards are one of the best modes when you pay at portals or e-commerce sites.

Unstructured Supplementary Service Data (USSD)

Unstructured Supplementary Service Data (USSD) is a session-based transmission protocol used by cellular telephones to communicate with the Telecom Service Providers (TSP). The USSD is a capability built into mobile phones, much like the Short Message Service (SMS).

The innovative payment service *99# works on the USSD channel. This service allows mobile banking transactions using basic feature mobile phone; there is no need to have mobile Internet data facility for using USSD-based mobile banking. It is envisioned to provide financial deepening and inclusion of underbanked society in the mainstream banking services. *99# service has been launched to take the banking services to every common man across the country. Banking customers can avail this service by dialling *99#, a Common number across all Telecom Service Providers (TSPs), on their mobile phone and transact through an interactive menu displayed on the mobile screen. Key services offered under *99# service include interbank account to account fund transfer, balance enquiry, mini statement, besides host of other services. *99# service is currently offered by 51 leading banks and all GSM service providers and can be accessed in 12 different languages, including Hindi and English as on 30 November 2016. It is a unique interoperable direct to consumer service that brings together the diverse ecosystem partners such as banks and TSPs. The USSD banking has a transaction limit of ₹5000 per day per customer. The RBI has also set a maximum charge of ₹2.5 per operation.

Aadhaar Enabled Payment System (AEPS)

The term 'AEPS', which stands for Aadhaar Enabled Payment Service, is an Aadhaar-based digital payment mode. A customer needs only his or her Aadhaar number to pay to any

3. http://www.rbi.org.in/scripts/ATMView.aspx.

merchant. The AEPS allows bank to bank transactions. It means the money you pay will be deducted from your account and credited to the payee's account directly.

You need to link your Aadhaar number to your bank account to use this service. Unlike Debit cards and the USSD, the AEPS does not have any charges on transactions. You can use it with the help of PoS machines. You can withdraw or deposit cash, send money to another Aadhaar-linked account with it. The good thing about AEPS is that it does not need your signature, bank account details or any password. It uses your fingerprint as a password. No one can forge your fingerprints, thus it is the most secure digital payment mode.

Unified Payments Interface (UPI)

Unified Payment Interface (UPI) is a payment mode, which is used to make fund transfers through the mobile app. You can transfer funds between two accounts using UPI apps. You will have to register for mobile banking to use UPI apps. Currently, this service is only available for android phone users.

You need to download a UPI app and create a Virtual Payment Address (VPA) or UPI ID. There are too many good UPI apps available such as BHIM, SBI UPI, HDFC UPI, iMobile, PhonePe, etc. It is not mandatory to use the UPI app from your bank to enjoy UPI service. You can download and use any UPI app.

Unified Payments Interface (UPI) is a system that powers multiple bank accounts into a single mobile application (of any participating bank), merging several banking features, seamless fund routing and merchant payments into one hood. It also caters to the 'peer-to-peer' collect request, which can be scheduled and paid as per the requirement and convenience. Each bank provides its own UPI app for Android, Windows and iOS mobile platform(s).

Mobile Wallets

A mobile wallet is a virtual wallet that allows the users to carry their credit card or debit card information electronically on their mobile devices. A smartphone or browser can be used to make purchases of goods or even make merchant payments. A mobile wallet is a way to carry cash in digital format. You can feed your credit card or debit card information in mobile wallet application or you can transfer money online to mobile wallet. Instead of using your physical plastic card to make purchases, you can pay with your smartphone, tablet, or smart watch. An individual's account is required to be linked to the digital wallet to load money in it. Some private companies and most banks have their e-wallets, e.g. Paytm, Freecharge, Mobikwik, Oxigen, mRupee, Airtel Money, Jio Money, SBI Buddy, Itz Cash, Citrus Pay, Vodafone M-Pesa, Axis Bank Lime, ICICI Pockets, SpeedPay, etc.

E-Wallets

E-wallet or mobile wallet is the digital version of your physical wallet with more functionality. You can keep your money in an e-wallet and use it when needed. Use the e-wallets to recharge your phone, pay at various places and send money to your friends. If you have a smartphone and a stable Internet connection, you can use e-wallets to make payments. These e-wallets also give additional cashback offers.

Some of the most used e-wallets are SBI buddy, ICICI Pockets, Freecharge, Paytm, etc.

Point-of-Sale (PoS)

A Point-of-Sale (PoS) is the place where sales are made. On a macro level, a PoS may be a mall, a market or a city. On a micro level, retailers consider a PoS to be the area where a customer completes a transaction such as a checkout counter. It is also known as a point of purchase.

Internet Banking

Internet banking, also known as online banking, e-banking or virtual banking, is an electronic payment system that enables customers of a bank or other financial institution to conduct a range of financial transactions through the financial institution's website.

Micro ATM

A micro ATM is a device that is used by a million Business Correspondents (BC) to deliver basic banking services. The platform enables business correspondents such as a local kirana shop owner to conduct instant transactions.

The micro platform will enable function through low-cost devices (micro ATMs) that are connected to banks across the country. This would enable a person to instantly deposit or withdraw funds regardless of the bank associated with a particular BC. This device is based on a mobile phone connection and is made available at every BC. Customers have to just get their identity authenticated and withdraw or put money into their bank accounts. This money comes from the cash drawer of the BC. Essentially, BCs act as bank for the customers and all they need to do is verify the authenticity of customer using customers' UID. The basic transaction types, to be supported by micro ATM, are deposit, withdrawal, fund transfer and balance enquiry.

Different Types of Online Financial Transactions

National Electronic Fund Transfer (NEFT)

NEFT is a nation-wide payment system facilitating one-to-one funds transfer. Under this scheme, individuals, firms and corporates can electronically transfer funds from any bank branch to any individual, firm or corporate having an account with any other bank branch in the country participating in the scheme. Individuals, firms or corporates maintaining accounts with a bank branch can transfer funds using NEFT. Even such individuals who do not have a bank account (walk-in customers) can also deposit cash at the NEFT-enabled branches with instructions to transfer funds using NEFT. However, such cash remittances is restricted to a maximum of ` 50,000 per transaction. NEFT, thus, facilitates originators or remitters to initiate funds transfer transactions even without having a bank account. Presently, NEFT operates in hourly batches—there are 12 settlements from 8 am to 7 pm on week days (Monday through Friday) and six settlements from 8 am to 1 pm on Saturdays.

Real Time Gross Settlement (RTGS)

The RTGS is defined as the continuous (real time) settlement of funds transfer individually on an order-by-order basis. 'Real time' means the processing of instructions at the time they are received rather than at some time later; 'gross settlement' means the settlement of funds transfer instructions occurs individually. Considering that the funds settlement takes place in the books of the Reserve Bank of India, the payments are final and irrevocable. The RTGS system is primarily meant for large value transactions. The minimum amount to be remitted through RTGS is ₹2 lakh. There is no upper ceiling for RTGS transactions. The RTGS service for customers' transactions is available to banks from 9.00 hours to 16.30 hours on week days and from 9.00 hours to 14:00 hours on Saturdays for settlement at the RBI end. However, the timings that the banks follow may vary depending on the customer timings of the bank branches.

Electronic Clearing System (ECS)

The ECS is an alternative method for effecting payment transactions in respect of the utility bill payments such as telephone bills, electricity bills, insurance premium, card payments and loan repayments, etc., which would obviate the need for issuing and handling paper instruments, and thereby, facilitate improved customer service by banks/companies/corporations/ government departments, etc., collecting or receiving the payments.

Immediate Payment Service (IMPS)

The IMPS offers an instant, 24×7, interbank electronic fund transfer service through mobile phones. It is an emphatic tool to transfer money instantly within banks across India through mobile, Internet and ATM, which is not only safe but also economical both in financial and non-financial perspectives. Through the IMPS, making payment is simple just using the mobile number of the beneficiary.

Advantages of Digital Payments

The advantages of digital payments are discussed below:

1. ***Easy and convenient.*** Digital payments are easy and convenient. You do not need to take loads of cash with you. All you need is your mobile phone or Aadhaar number or a card to pay. UPI apps and e-wallets have made digital payments easier.
2. ***Pay or send money from anywhere.*** With digital payment modes, you can pay from anywhere anytime.
3. ***Discounts from taxes.*** Government has announced many discounts to encourage digital payments.
4. ***Written record.*** You often forget to note down your cash spendings. Or even if you note, it takes a lot of time. But, you do not need to note your spendings every time

with digital payments. These are automatically recorded in your passbook or inside your e-wallet app. This helps in maintaining your record, tracking your spendings and budget planning.

Drawbacks of Digital Payments

Every coin has two sides so as the digital payments. Despite many advantages, digital payments have a few drawbacks also, which are given below:

1. ***Difficult for a non-technical person.*** Most of the digital payment modes are based on mobile phone, Internet and cards. These modes are somewhat difficult for non-technical persons or illiterate persons such as farmworkers, etc.
2. ***Risk of data theft.*** There is a big risk of data theft associated with the digital payment. Hackers can hack the servers of the bank or the e-wallet you are using and easily get your personal information. They can use this information to steal money from your account.
3. ***Overspending.*** You keep limited cash in your physical wallet. Hence, you think twice before buying anything. But, if you use digital payment modes, you have all your money with you always. This can result in overspending.

Credit Cards as e-Payment Systems

Without doubt, the basic means of payment used and initiated via the Internet for consumer transactions till date is the credit card. Credit cards have proved popular for a number of reasons as the following:

1. The system is familiar to users and was widely used before the advent of e-commerce, thus bolstering the users' confidence.
2. Transaction costs are hidden from users (i.e. basically met by sellers, and passed on to all customers, not just credit card users).
3. Payment is simple anywhere and in any currency, thus matching the global reach of the Internet.
4. The credit-issuing company shares the transaction risk; helping overcome consumers' fear and reluctance to buy goods they have not actually seen, from sellers they do not know (in the physical world this function was important because it enabled sellers to take payment from buyers they do not know; online this trust relationship is needed in both directions).

As of December 2018, various banks in India have issued around 41 million credit cards.

The disadvantages of credit cards for e-commerce include the fact that they cannot be used directly for small value payments or peer-to-peer transactions.

Disadvantages of Credit Cards

Credit cards have their own disadvantages. First, the relatively high transaction cost makes them impractical for small-value payments. Second, they cannot be used directly by individuals to make payments to other individuals (peer-to-peer transactions). Third, protecting the security of transactions is vital, especially in the virtual world where there is no payment guarantee to the merchant by a bank. Users' fears about security issues seem to be a consequence of the newness and relative unfamiliarity of the medium, rather than the real risks involved in the system.

Debit Cards as e-Payment Systems

Nowadays, as the online banking system continues to gain acceptance and much improvement, many consumers are taking advantage of the system and are shifting from the use of cash and cheques to debit cards. Basically, a debit card is a plastic card issued to customers by banks and debit card companies. It allows the cardholder to purchase products or services directly from their savings account that come from checking machines. Funds used are prepaid and exists in the bank account prior to any transaction made using the card. Debit cards, which are also known as bank card or check card, are significant when making purchases or while travelling. Having debit cards on hand means that buyers do not have to bring huge amounts of cash in their pockets since numerous establishments accept these cards as mode of payment. Almost all stores like shopping centres, restaurants, hotels, airlines, and malls have made their Point-of-Sale terminals capable of receiving payment from prepaid cards. For a customer, it is easier to swipe than to count cash and coins. Also, internet shoppers who buy goods online use debit cards too. Usually, businesses who sell through the internet and deliver by mail only accept debit or credit cards for fees.

Further, for people who pay their bills through an automated teller machine (ATM), a debit card is vital. By just inserting the card in the machine and pressing the amount to be paid, the payee saves time and effort compared to falling in line to pay to the teller. The remaining amount of money can be checked online or mobile phone. Another importance of debit cards is that they are used to withdraw cash from ATMs. Consumers who use debits cards can easily track their expenses since these are listed in their bank statements. The number of debit cards issued by banks grew from 182 million in 2010 to 500 million in 2014[4].

Disadvantages of Debit Cards

- Debit cards offer lower levels of security protection than credit cards. Theft of the users' PIN using skimming devices can be accomplished much easily with a PIN input than with a signature-based credit transaction. Unlike a credit card, debit card transactions give you no grace period. They are a quick, pay-now deal.

4. http://www.rbi.org.in/scripts/ATMView.aspx.

- They can make balancing your account tricky if you are not fastidious about keeping receipts and recording transactions in a timely fashion. It is easy to forget, for example, when you pay at the gas pump with a debit card and drive off without your receipt.
- Some ATM machines charge a fee for their use and then your bank adds another foreign ATM charge (if the machine is not from your bank). Know ahead of time what the fees are and where you can access your money for free if possible.

Encryption and Credit Cards

Encryption is instantiated when credit card information is entered into a browser or other e-commerce device and sent securely over the network from a buyer to a seller as an encrypted message. This practice however, does not meet the important requirements of an adequate financial system, such as non-refutability, speed, safety, privacy, and security. To make a credit card transaction truly secure and non-refutable, the following sequence of steps must occur before actual goods, services, or funds flow:

1. A customer presents his or her credit card information (along with an authenticity signature, or other information such as mother's maiden name) securely to the merchant.
2. The merchant validates the customer's identity as the owner of the card account.
3. The merchant relays the credit card charge information and signature to its bank or online credit card processors.
4. The bank or processing party relays the information to the customer's bank for authorization approval.
5. The customer's bank returns the credit card data, charge authentication, and authorization to the merchant.

In this scheme, each consumer and each vendor generates a public key and a secret key. The public key is sent to the credit card company and put on its public key server. The secret key is re-encrypted with a password, and the unencrypted version is erased. To steal a credit card number, a thief would have to get access to both a consumer's encrypted secret key and password. The credit card company sends the consumer a credit card number and a credit limit. To buy something from vendor X, the consumer sends vendor X the message, "It is now time T. I am paying Y dollars to X for item Z." Then the consumer uses his or her password to sign the message with the public key. The vendor will then sign the message with its own secret key and send it to the credit card company, which will bill the consumer for Y dollars and give the same amount (less the fee) to X.

Nobody can cheat in this system. The consumer cannot claim that he did not agree to the transaction, because he has signed on it (as in everyday life). The vendor cannot levy fake charges, because he does not have access to the consumer's key. He cannot impose the same charge twice, because the consumer has included the precise time in the message. To become more useful, credit card systems will have to develop distributed key servers and card checkers. Otherwise, a concentrated attack on these sites could bring the system to a halt.

Support for Privacy Enhanced Mail (PEM) and Pretty Good Privacy (PGP) encryption has been built into several browsers. Both of these schemes can be substantially bolstered with the addition of encryption to defeat snooping attacks.

Unfortunately, whether existing credit card companies will accept digital signatures as replacements for real signature is not clear. And so, vendors will have a difficult time when customers dispute the charges made using encrypted credit card numbers over the Internet. When credit card companies do decide to accept digital signatures, they also need to maintain a public server with all the public keys. This method assumes that the credit card company will keep the vendor honest, as is the case with traditional credit card transactions. E-payment processing is not an inexpensive proposition, however. But neither is it fradulent. If e-commerce takes off and small transactions increase without a fully encrypted system in place, fraud will become expensive all the more.

Business Pros and Cons of Credit Card-based Payment

Third-party processing for credit cards entails a number of pros and cons. These companies are chartered to give credit accounts to individuals and act as bill collecting agencies for businesses. Consumers use credit by presenting them for payment and then paying an aggregate bill every month. Consumers pay either by flat fee or individual transaction charge service. Merchants get paid for the credit card drafts that they submit to the credit card company. Businesses get charged a transaction charge ranging between 1 per cent and 3 per cent for each draft submitted.

Credit cards have advantages over cheques in that, the credit card company assumes a larger share of financial risk on both the buyer and the seller in a transaction. Buyers can sometimes dispute a charge retroactively and have the credit card company act on their behalf. Sellers are ensured that they will be paid for all their sales and they need not worry about the fraud. This becomes a convenience for the buyer in that, the credit card transactions are usually quicker and easier than cheque (and sometimes even cash) transactions. One disadvantage to credit cards is that their transactions are not anonymous, and credit card companies do in fact compile valuable data about spending habits.

Record keeping with credit cards is one of the features consumers value most, because of disputes and mistakes in billing. Disputes may arise because different services may have different policies. For example, an information provider might charge for partial delivery of a file (the user may have abandoned the session after reading a part of the file), and a movie distributor might charge depending on how much of the video had been downloaded. The cause of interrupted delivery needs to be considered while resolving disputes. In general, implementing payment policies will be simpler when payment is made by credit card rather than by cash.

The complexity of credit card processing takes place in the verification phase, a potential bottleneck. If there is a lapse in time between the charging and the delivery of goods or services (for example, when an airline ticket is purchased well in advance of the date of travel), the customer verification process is simple because it does not have to be done in real time. In fact, all the relaying and authorizations occur after the customer-merchant transaction is completed, unless the authorization request is denied. However, if the customer wants a report (or even a digital airline ticket) to be downloaded into a PC or other information appliance immediately at the time of purchase, many message relays and authorizations take place in real time, while the customer waits. Such exchanges may require many sequence-specific operations, such as staged encryption and decryption and exchanges of cryptographic keys.

Encryption and transaction speed must be balanced however, as research has shown that online users get impatient and typically wait for 20 seconds before pursuing other actions. Hence, online credit card users must find the process to be accessible, simple, and fast. Speed will have design and cost implications, as it is a function of network capabilities, computing power available at every server, and the specific form of the transaction. The infrastructure supporting the exchange must be reliable. The user must feel confident that the supporting payment infrastructure will be available on demand and that the system will operate reasonably well, regardless of component failures or system load conditions. The builders and providers of this infrastructure are aware of customer requirements and are in fierce competition to fill those needs.

Bitcoin—As a Crypotocurrency

Bitcoin is a form of money that uses cryptography to control its creation and management. Bitcoins are used for electronic purchases and transfers. It is a new form of currency that was created by an unknown person using the alias Satoshi Nakamoto. Transactions are made with no middle men—meaning, no banks! There are no transaction fees and no need to give your real name. More merchants are beginning to accept them. In January 2009, the first block, nicknamed 'Genesis' is launched allowing the initial 'mining' of Bitcoins to take place. Later that month, the first transaction took place between Satoshi and Hal Finney, a developer and cryptographic activist. Bitcoin is not an institution, organisation, or any sort of centralised entity. The special characteristic of Bitcoin is that there is no central authority. It is literally a network of users—known as *peers*—who simply decide to buy and sell goods and services through a mode of virtual currency. Bitcoins are not printed. It is decentralized. They are 'mined' using computing power in a distributed network. According to protocol, only 21 million Bitcoins can be created by miners. So, the main characteristics of Bitcoins are:

1. It is a decentralised currency.
2. It is easy to set up.
3. It is anonymous.
4. It is completely transparent.
5. There is no transaction fee when you buy goods or services using Bitcoin.
6. It is fast.
7. It is non-repudiable.

Every single purchase of Bitcoin is immediately logged digitally on a transaction log that tracks the time of purchase and who owns how many bitcoins. This digital transaction log is called blockchain. The blockchain, records every single transaction and the ownership of every single bitcoin in circulation. Each time a bitcoin changes ownership from seller to buyer, the two parties need to agree on its price. There is no 'fixed' price. Usually, it's the seller's responsibility to give a fair price to the buyer based on what rate bitcoins are being traded in elsewhere. The difference between bitcoins and other currencies is that there is no centralised bank that prints the currency and sets relative values. Through transactions, the value of bitcoin fluctuates through supply and demand. Several marketplaces called *bitcoin exchanges* allow people to buy or sell bitcoins using different currencies. Mt. Gox is the largest bitcoin exchange. More than $1.5 billion worth of bitcoins are currently in circulation around the world.

In October 2009, Bitcoin received an equivalent value in traditional currencies. The New Liberty Standard established the value of a Bitcoin at $1 = 1,309 BTC. The equation was derived so as to include the cost of electricity to run the computer that created the Bitcoins in the first place.

In February 2011, Bitcoin took parity with US dollar. In December 2012, one Bitcoin was equivalent to 13 US Dollars. In March 2019, it was selling in the price range of 5000–5500 US Dollars[5].

Data Protection

Although the number of businesses on the Internet has grown, many of these organizations are simply maintaining a 'Web presence' by providing information about themselves and their products, and have not yet undertaken Internet-based transactions. This inertia is probably due to concern about the security of transactions and user authorization. Technologies concerned with authorization include firewalls, password access, smart cards, and biometrics fingerprinting. However, in order to provide secure electronic transactions (SET), encryption technologies are used. Encryption technologies, which are supported by the appropriate legal mechanisms, have the potential to allow global electronic commerce to develop.

One essential challenge of e-commerce is risk management. Operation of e-payment systems incurs three major risks: fraud or mistake, privacy issues, and credit risk. Preventing mistakes might require improvements in the legal framework. Dealing with privacy and fraud issues requires improvements in the security framework. Curtailing credit risk requires devising procedures to constrict or moderate credit and reduce float in the market.

Risks from Mistake and Disputes: Consumer Protection

Virtually, all e-payment systems need some ability to keep automatic records, for obvious reasons. From a technical standpoint, this is not a problem for electronic systems. Credit and debit cards have them, and even the paper-based cheque creates an automatic record. Once information has been captured electronically, it is easy and inexpensive to keep (it might even cost more to throw it away than to keep it). For example, in many transaction processing systems, old or blocked accounts are never purged and old transaction histories can be kept forever on magnetic tape.

5. http://historyofbitcoin.org/

Given the intangible nature of electronic transactions and dispute resolution relying solely on records, a general law of payment dynamics and banking technology might be that no data need ever be discarded. The record feature is an after-the-fact transcription of what happened, created without any explicit effort by the transaction parties. Features of these automatic records include: (i) permanent storage, (ii) accessibility and traceability, (iii) a payment system database, and (iv) data transfer to payment maker, bank, or monetary authorities.

The need for record keeping for purposes of risk management conflicts with the transaction anonymity of cash. One can say that anonymity exists today only because cash is a very old concept, invented long before the computer and networks gave us the ability to track everything. Although a segment of the payment-making public always desire transaction anonymity, many believe that anonymity runs counter to the public welfare because too many tax, smuggling, and/or money laundering possibilities exist. The anonymity issue raises the question: can e-payments be done without an automatic record feature?

Many recent payment systems seem to be ambivalent on this point. For instance, the Mondex electronic purse touts equivalence with cash, but its electronic wallets are designed to hold automatic records of the card's last twenty transactions with a built-in statement. Obviously, the card-reading terminals, machines, or telephones could maintain records of all transactions. With these records, the balance on any smart card could be reconstructed after the fact, thus allowing additional protection against loss or theft. This would certainly add some value versus cash.

Managing Information Privacy

The e-payment system must ensure and maintain privacy. Every time one purchases goods using a credit card, subscribes to a magazine, or accesses a server, that information goes into the database. Furthermore, all these records can be linked so that they constitute in effect, a single dossier. This dossier would reflect what items were bought, and where and when. This violates the unspoken law of doing business, that privacy of customers should be protected as much as possible.

Managing Credit Risk

Credit or systemic risk is a major concern in net settlement systems, because a bank's failure to settle its net position could lead to a chain reaction of bank failures. The digital central bank must develop policies to deal with this possibility. Various alternatives exist, each with advantages and disadvantages. A digital central bank guarantee on settlement removes the insolvency test from the system because banks will more readily assume credit risks from other banks.

Without such guarantees, the development of clearing and settlement systems and money markets may be impeded. A middle road is also possible; for example, setting controls on bank exposures (bilateral or multilateral) and requiring collateral. If the central bank does not guarantee settlement, it must define, at least internally, the conditions and terms for extending liquidity to banks in connection with settlement.

Designing e-Payment Systems

Despite cost and efficiency gains, many hurdles need to be overcome for the spread of e-payment systems. These include several factors, mostly non-technical in nature, that must be addressed before any new payment method is made successful. They are as follows:

1. ***Privacy.*** A user expects trustworthiness of a secure system; just as the telephone is a safe and a private medium, free of wiretaps and hackers, electronic communication must merit equal trust.
2. ***Security.*** A secure system verifies the identity of two-party transactions through "user authentication", and reserves flexibility to restrict information/services through access control. Tomorrow's bank robbers will need no getaway cars—just a computer terminal, the price of a telephone call, and a little ingenuity. Millions of dollars have been embezzled by computer fraud. No systems are yet foolproof, although designers are concentrating closely on security.
3. ***Intuitive interfaces.*** The payment interface must be as easy to use as a telephone. Generally speaking, users value convenience more than anything.
4. ***Database integration.*** With home banking, for example, a customer wants to play with all his accounts. Separate accounts are stored on separate databases. The challenge before banks is to tie these databases together and allow customers access to any of them while keeping the data up-to-date and error-free.
5. ***Brokers.*** A "network banker"—someone to broker goods and services, settle conflicts, and facilitate financial transactions electronically—must be in place.
6. ***Pricing.*** One fundamental issue is how to price payment system services. For example, should subsidies be used to encourage users to shift from one form of payment to another—from cash to bank payments, from papers based to e-cash? The problem with subsidies is the potential waste of resources, as money may be invested in systems that will not be used. Thus, investment in systems not only might not be recovered, but also substantial ongoing operational subsidies will be necessary. On the other hand, it must be recorded that, without subsidies, it is difficult to fix up an affordable price to all services.
7. ***Standards.*** Without standards, the welding of different payment users into different networks and different systems is impossible. Standards enable interoperability, giving users the ability to buy and receive information, regardless of which bank is managing their money.

None of the above hurdles are insurmountable. Most of these will be overcome within the next few years. These technical problems, experts hope, will be solved as technology is improved and experience is gained. The biggest question concerns how customers will take to a paperless and (if not cashless) a less-cash world.

The Key to Security: Cryptography

Cryptography relies on two basic components: an algorithm (or cryptographic methodology), and a key. Algorithm is the method used to encrypt the message, and key is the object used to decrypt the message. For instance, in a system where letters are substituted for other letters, the "key" is the chart of paired letters and algorithm is the substitution. In modern cryptographic systems, the algorithms are complex mathematical formulae, and keys are strings of bits. If two parties want to communicate, they must use the same algorithm. In some cases, they must also use the same key. Many cryptographic keys must be kept secret. Sometimes algorithms are also kept secret, as the method of encryption may hold the very method used to decrypt the message.

Cryptosystems are being increasingly used in encryption, authentication, integrity, non-repudiation, and management of other crypto systems like key management. A crypto system is a mathematical function for processing data, and there is nothing secret about the function except the key.

Examples of Encryption Techniques

Caesar's Method

This is one of the oldest known techniques of encryption. It traces its history back to Roman times. It is a really simple method of encrypting a message. It involves shifting each letter of the message to a letter that appears *k* letters after it. In the method that was first devised by the Romans, *k* was equal to 3. What this meant was that each letter was shifted 3 places to the right. For example, 'A' would be transformed to 'D', 'B' to 'E', 'C' to 'F', and so on.

So, starting with ABCDEFGHIJKLMNOPQRSTUVWXYZ and sliding everything up by 3, you get DEFGHIJKLMNOPQRSTUVWXYZABC where, D = A, E = B, F = C, and so on. Using this scheme, the plain text "SECRET" encrypts as "VHFUHW". To enable someone else to read the cipher text, you tell him or her that the key is 3. This is clearly a secret key system, the secret key being the value of *k*. Clearly, this is not a very safe system of encryption, as trying all possible values of *k*, namely 1 through 26, can easily crack it.

Letter Pairing

This method is similar to Caesar's method. Here, instead of shifting each letter to some places to its right, letters are paired off with each other in a random manner. For example, consider the pairing A × Z, B × Y, C × X, and so on.

The method overcomes the limitation of Caesar's method and cannot be encrypted even by using various values of *k*. Yet, this is not a safe method at all, and can easily be decrypted by using techniques such as frequency analysis. If a large enough message is intercepted, then by counting the number of times a letter appears, the third party can judge which letter stands for which by comparing the data with the average frequencies of usage of letters of the language. For example, we know that 'E' is the most often used letter, and hence the most repeated letter would probably stand for 'E'.

The two examples given above are simple yet interesting encryption techniques. In the following few pages, we will discuss some of the latest and most widely used encryption techniques.

RSA

RSA stands for Rivest, Shamir and Adleman—the three cryptographers who invented the first practical commercial public key cryptosystem. Today it is used in Web browsers, e-mail programs, mobile phones, virtual private networks, secure shells, and many other places. With sufficiently large keys, you can be confident of foiling the vast majority of attackers. Until recently, the use of RSA was very much restricted by patent and export laws. However, the patent has now expired and US export laws have been relaxed. RSA encryption uses large prime numbers for its purposes.

It works on the basic fact that large numbers are extremely difficult to factorize. If we take the product of two arbitrarily large (but secret) prime numbers of say, 50 digits each and multiply them, then using the most current supercomputing technology it would take more than a thousand years to factorize them. This method has brought to the fore a branch of mathematics called 'number theory' that is till now considered to have no practical applications.

RSA uses two large prime numbers. Numbers must be quite large in length, 100 to 300 bits, and must have a prime value. Only the person who wants to decrypt the message should know these. Using these, a mathematical algorithm is developed which produces a public key. Anyone who wants to encrypt a message uses this algorithm. The key is based on the two large primes used, and is known only to the person who has developed the particular algorithm.

RSA seems to be a reliable and a fast algorithm, but the serious persisting flaws consist of the hiding of two initial numbers chosen from the IP table. Once discovered, intruders can use these numbers to reconstruct the message and the keys.

DES

This is an example of a widely used secret key encryption system. In 1972, the National Institute of Standards and Technology (NIST) decided that a strong cryptographic algorithm was needed to protect non-classified information. The algorithm was required to be cheap, widely available, and very secure. NIST envisioned something that would be available to the general public and could be used in a wide variety of applications. So they asked for public proposals for such an algorithm. In 1974, IBM submitted the Lucifer algorithm, which appeared to meet most of NIST's design requirements.

The modified Lucifer algorithm was adopted by NIST as a federal standard on November 23, 1976. Later its name was changed to Data Encryption Standard (DES). The algorithm specification was published in January 1977, and with the official backing of the government it became a very widely employed algorithm in a short time.

DES encrypts and decrypts data in 64-bit blocks, using a 64-bit key (although the effective key strength is only 56 bits, as explained below). It takes a 64-bit block of plain text as input, and outputs a 64-bit block of cipher text. It always operates on blocks of equal size, and it uses both permutations and substitutions in the algorithm.

Unfortunately, over time, various short cut attacks were found that could significantly reduce the time needed to find a DES key by brute force. And as computers became progressively faster and more powerful, it was recognized that a 56-bit key was simply not large enough for high security applications. As a result of these serious flaws, NIST abandoned their official endorsement of DES in 1997 and began work on a replacement, to be called the Advanced Encryption Standard (AES). Despite the growing concerns about its vulnerability, DES is still widely used by financial services and other industries worldwide to protect sensitive online applications.

Attacks on Crypto Systems

One of the most important perspectives of key management is to prevent attacks or to make attacks practically infeasible. Theoretically, all crypto systems are susceptible to direct key search attacks and, from a theoretical perspective, all keys are breakable. But from a practical point of view, this is not always the case for most of the widely used crypto systems around.

There are basically two types of crypto systems:

Symmetric Key Crypto Systems

This is historically known as the *secret key system*. In this crypto system, the key for the underlying mathematical function can be used to reverse this mathematical function (hence 'symmetric'). There are two types of symmetric key crypto systems: 'stream' ciphers are used in mobile communication, and 'block' ciphers are used for encryption/authentication. Examples of some block ciphers are Data Encryption Standard (DES), International Data Encryption Algorithm (IDEA), and SAFER. Symmetric systems are built by repeatedly using simple mathematical operation involving the key. Thus, they can be executed at a high speed. These crypto systems find their use in systems where a large amount of data is processed.

Asymmetric Key Crypto Systems

This is also known as *public key system*. The key for the underlying mathematical function cannot be easily used to reverse the mathematical function. A separate key is required to do this (hence the name 'asymmetric'). Participants in such a system will have a key pair—public and private key.

This system is based on a one-way mathematical function—easy in one direction but very difficult to reverse, as for example, multiplying two large numbers is easy but factorizing this product can be very difficult. Diffie-Hellman, RSA, El Gamal are based on this theory. Asymmetric key crypto systems are flexible to implement as compared to secret key systems, but are much slower to execute. This system is widely used in digital signature, key management, and entity authentication.

A Matter of Keys

The key for any crypto system is a string of binary digits (bits) that holds information. For a symmetric system, a key is usually a given length of binary string, and any binary string of this length can be a valid key. For example, DES has a 56-bit key (in fact 64, of which 8 are parity check bits). So, any bit string of length 56 can be a DES key.

For asymmetric systems also, the key is a string of binary digits but all such strings are not valid keys. Some RSA versions use 512-bit keys, but every possible 512-bit key is not a valid key. For example, even numbers are not valid. Key lengths of symmetric and asymmetric keys are not directly comparable, and techniques for finding out unknown keys are different for the two systems.

In symmetric system, the technique for finding unknown key for block and stream ciphers is the same. For block ciphers, key can usually be of any binary string of given size. For example, DES has a 56-bit key, Triple DES has a 112-bit key, and it is 128-bit for IDEA and SAFER. So DES has 256 possible keys, triple DES has 2,112 possible keys, and IDEA and SAFER have 2,128 possible keys.

For some data processed by block ciphers, one has to try all possible keys until one finds out a small collection of keys that work. One of these keys would be the unknown key. This form of attack is known as a brute force attack/exhaustive key search and requires a minimum of information to perform such an attack.

The objective for strong block cipher design is to ensure that exhaustive key search takes far longer time and is far more expensive than it is feasible, and that there is no other way of getting the unknown key more quickly and more cheaply than exhaustive search. The complexity of such an attack is quantified by comparing the number of applications of the block cipher in the attack with an exhaustive key search.

Even in cases where the attack compares favourably, there are other points to be considered, such as the amount of data that needs to be processed by the block cipher with the unknown key. While such attacks are specific to the block ciphers, there are two types of attack that have wide applicability: differential cryptanalysis, and linear cryptanalysis. Some carefully chosen data are processed by the block cipher to be analyzed to find the unknown key in differential cryptanalysis. In linear cryptanalysis, the underlying algebraic structure is used to analyze data processed by the block cipher. For the widely used block ciphers such as DES, these attacks are currently impractical, as they require the generation of vast amount of data with the unknown key. For example, differential attack on DES requires the processing of 250 bytes of data and a linear attack requires processing of 246 bytes of data.

Exhaustive Search

An exhaustive attack on a block cipher is very complex. This is because one has to look for all the keys for an exhaustive search, and the larger the number of keys, the harder this is. As an illustration, consider an exhaustive key search for a 56-bit DES key. An exhaustive key search for a DES key will require 256 tests, which is equal to 7.2 × 1016 tests. Assuming

106 testing devices are employed, each capable of performing 106 tests per second, the complete test cycle will require 7.2 × 104 seconds, which is equivalent to 20 hours. In such a scenario, the key might be expected in 10 hours. Obviously, computation of such magnitude is beyond the limit of average desktops. Approximate figures for other block ciphers with different key sizes can be derived by multiplying by an appropriate factor.

Clearly, the feasibility of an attack depends on the computing resources of the attacker. In March 1997, RSA Data Security Inc. issued test challenge DES-I to find a 56-bit DES key (with a $10,000 prize). There were 256 or 72 quadrillion possible DES keys. The key was found 140 days later by an effort distributed over the Internet. It involved 70,000 Internet addresses, each searching through different keys until the correct one was found. At the peak rate, 7 billion keys were being tested per second. At this rate, it would have taken a minimum of 32 days to find the key.

In 1998, RSA DES Challenge II was solved in 56 hours. This time again the effort involved massive computing resource. Electronic Frontier Foundation (EFF) designed DES Breaker at an estimated cost of $80,000. The manufacturing cost of the machine was $130,000. The complete key search took 220 hours. The peak search rate this time was a massive 90 billion keys per second. The latest DES challenge, DES Challenge III was solved in January last year in 22 hours and 15 minutes. It involved the combined efforts of EFF'S Deep Crack and *distributed.net* to find the key.

Private Key and Public Key

In Figure 6.2, the message is encrypted with a public key and sent to the recipient. The recipient opens it with his public key.

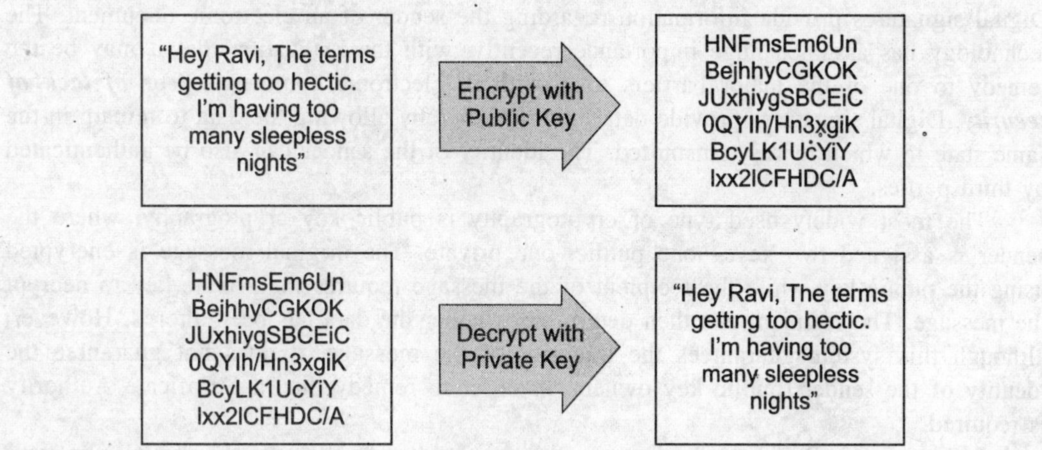

Figure 6.2 Role of public and private key.

For asymmetric key crypto systems, the situation is different. It is generally believed that the difficulty of finding an unknown private key depends upon the difficulty of some well-known mathematical problems. The problem of finding an RSA private key is believed to be equivalent to factorizing a large number that is the product of two large primes. From the invention of asymmetric cryptography (mid-1970s) until recently, there were a number of algorithms that could factor such numbers and they all took roughly the same time. In the last few years, a new algorithm—the General Number Field Sieve (GNFS)—has been invented that can factor a number more quickly than the previous algorithms. The discrete algorithm problem used for El Gamal and DSS has a similar complexity. As with DES, a RSA Data Security challenge number (RSA-130) with 430 bits was issued. This number has been factorized (April 1996), again using an effort distributed over the Net. The total effort used in factorizing RSA-130 is believed to be 500 Mips years (equivalent to a computer running 500 million instructions per second for a year). Such figures make it just about conceivable that with concentrated effort distributed over the Net, it is just possible to factorize a 512-bit number as the product of two primes. This means RSA system with 512-bit private keys are potentially vulnerable to such attacks.

In future, increase in computing speed will make it possible to factorize larger-sized numbers. However, it is entirely possible that overnight someone will invent a new algorithm and all the figures will have to be revised.

Although popular media has floated the perception that DES keyspace is so small that it is possible for anyone with a PC to break any DES-based crypto system, it is far from the truth. Well, it is true that 56-bit key is too small, but not for the computing power of a PC. DES is vulnerable when attacked with an immense computing power. Even after AES becomes the new standard, we will see DES in use for some time to come.

Digital Signature

Digital signatures provide information regarding the sender of an electronic document. The technology has assumed huge importance recently, with the realization that it may be the remedy to one of the major barriers to growth of electronic commerce: ***fear of lack of security***. Digital signatures provide data integrity, thereby allowing the data to remain in the same state in which it was transmitted. The identity of the sender can also be authenticated by third parties.

The most widely used type of cryptography is public key cryptography, where the sender is assigned two keys—one public, one private. The original message is encrypted using the public key while the recipient of the message requires the private key to decrypt the message. The recipient can then determine whether the data has been altered. However, although this system guarantees the integrity of the message, it does not guarantee the identity of the sender (public key owner). In order to remedy this, a Certificate Authority is required.

In Figure 6.3, Ravi (the sender) uses his private key to compute the digital signature. In order to compute the digital signature, a one-way hashing algorithm may be used to first calculate a message digest, as is done by RSA. The message digest is an efficient way to represent the message, as well as being a unique number that can only be calculated from the contents of the message. The sender's private key is used at this point to encrypt the message digest. The encrypted message digest is what is commonly called a digital signature.

A certification authority (CA) performs the task of managing key pairs, while the verification of the person or entity bound to that key pair is initially ascertained at the time of application by the registration authority. A certificate is issued by a CA and links an individual or entity to its public key, and in some cases to its private key. Certification authorities can offer different grades of certificates, depending upon the type of initial identification provided by the individual.

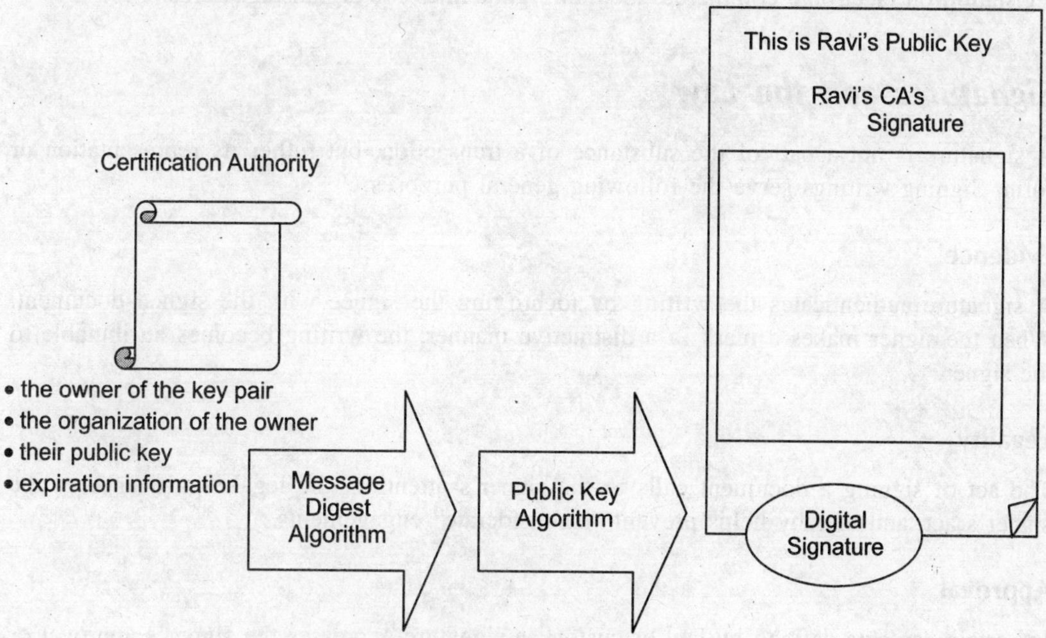

Figure 6.3 Digital signature process.

From an information security viewpoint, these simple "electronic signatures" are distinct from the "digital signatures" and in the technical literature, although "digital signature" is sometimes used to mean any form of computer-based signature. These guidelines use "digital signature" only as it is used in information security terminology, as to mean the result of applying the technical processes.

Legal Position of Digital Signatures

Although the digital signature technology has been available for some time, it has only recently become feasible to use digital signatures to authenticate a document. This breakthrough has made digital signatures one of the most important areas of development within electronic commerce. It is important because the technology and the law governing it must develop in a way that promotes—or at the very least does not inhibit—the growth of electronic commerce.

A substantial amount of legislation regulating the use of digital signatures and their legal status has been enacted. So far, this has been enacted on a state by state basis, resulting in those countries taking contrasting legal positions. International law on digital signatures has yet to be formulated.

Developments are also taking place at a global level. Bodies such as the Internet Engineering Task Force (IETF), the International Organization for Standardization (ISO), and W3C are currently working on standardization of digital signatures. The OECD has issued 'Guidelines for Cryptology Policy', which includes a guide for states on the creation of legislation governing the use of digital signatures. UNCITRAL has also released draft legislation on electronic commerce, including guidelines for digital signatures.

Signatures and the Law

A signature is not a part of the substance of a transaction, but rather its representation or form. Signing writings serve the following general purposes:

Evidence

A signature authenticates the writing by identifying the signee with the signed document. When the signer makes a mark in a distinctive manner, the writing becomes attributable to the signer.

Legality

The act of signing a document calls to the signer's attention, the legal significance of the signer's act, and thereby helps prevent "inconsiderate" engagements.

Approval

In certain contexts defined by law or custom, a signature expresses the signer's approval or authorization of the writing, or the signer's claim that it has legal validity.

Efficiency and Logistics

A signature on a written document often imparts a sense of clarity and finality to the transaction, and may lessen the subsequent need to inquire beyond the face of a document. Negotiable instruments, for example, rely upon formal requirements, including a signature, for their ability to change hands with ease, rapidity, and minimal interruption.

Authenticity

The formal requirements for legal transactions, including the need for signatures, vary in different legal systems, and also vary with the passage of time. There is also variance in the legal consequences of failure to cast the transaction in a required form. The statute of frauds of the common law tradition, for example, does not render a transaction invalid for lack of a "writing signed by the party to be charged", but rather makes it unenforceable in the court, a distinction which has caused the practical application of the statute to be greatly limited in case law.

During this century, most legal systems have reduced the formal requirements, or at least have minimized the consequences of failure to satisfy formal requirements. Nevertheless, sound practice still calls for transactions to be formalized in a manner which assures the parties of their validity and enforceability. In current practice, formalization usually involves documenting the transaction on paper and signing or authenticating the paper. Traditional methods however, are undergoing fundamental change. Documents continue to be written on paper, but sometimes merely to satisfy the need for a legally recognized form. In many instances, the information exchanged to effect a transaction never takes paper form. Computer-based information can also be utilized differently than its paper counterpart. For example, computers can "read" digital information, and transform the information or take programmable actions based on the information. Information stored as bits rather than as atoms of ink and paper can travel near the speed of light, may be duplicated without limit and with insignificant cost.

Although the basic nature of transactions has not changed, the law has only begun to adapt to advances in technology. The legal and business communities must develop rules and practices which use new technology, to achieve and surpass the effects traditionally achieved from paper forms.

To achieve the basic purposes of signatures outlined thus, a signature must have the following attributes:

Signer authentication. A signature should indicate who signed a document, a message or a record, and should be difficult for another person to produce without authorization.

Document authentication. A signature should identify what is signed, making it impracticable to falsify or alter either the signed matter or the signature without detection.

Signer authentication and document authentication are tools used to exclude impersonators and forgers, and are essential ingredients of what is often called a "non-repudiation service" in the terminology of information security profession. A non-repudiation service provides assurance of the origin or delivery of data in order to protect the sender against false denial by the recipient that the data has been received, or to protect the recipient against false denial by the sender that the data has been sent. Thus, a non-repudiation service provides evidence to prevent a person from unilaterally modifying or terminating legal obligations arising out of a transaction effected by computer-based means.

Optimally, a signature and its creation, and its verification processes should provide the greatest possible assurance to both the signer's as well as the document's authenticity with least possible expenditure.

Affirmation

The affixing of the signature should be an affirmative act, which serves the ceremonial and approval functions of a signature and establishes the sense of having legally consummated a transaction.

Digital signature technology generally surpasses paper technology in all these attributes. To understand why, one must first understand how digital signature technology works.

How Digital Signature Technology Works

Digital signatures are created and verified by cryptography. Digital signatures use public key cryptography, which employs an algorithm using two different but mathematically related "keys": one for creating a digital signature or transforming data into a seemingly unintelligible form, and another key for verifying a digital signature or returning the message to its original form. Computer equipment and software utilizing two such keys are often collectively termed an "asymmetric crypto system".

The complementary keys of an asymmetric crypto system for digital signatures are arbitrarily termed private key, which is known only to the signer and used to create the digital signature, and the public key, which is ordinarily more widely known and is used by a relying party to verify the digital signature. If many people need to verify the signer's digital signatures, the public key must be available or distributed to all of them, perhaps by publication in an online repository or directory, where it is easily accessible. Although the keys of the pair are mathematically related, if the asymmetric crypto system has been designed and implemented securely it is "computationally infeasible" to derive the private key from the knowledge of the public key. Thus, although many people may know the public key of a given signer and use it to verify that signer's signatures, they cannot discover that signer's private key and use it to forge digital signatures. This is sometimes referred to as the principle of "irreversibility".

Another fundamental process, termed *hash function*, is used in both creating and verifying a digital signature. A hash function is an algorithm which creates a digital representation or "fingerprint" in the form of a "hash value" or "hash result" of a standard length which is usually much smaller than the message but nevertheless substantially unique to it. Any change to the message invariably produces a different hash result when the same hash function is used. In the case of a secure hash function, sometimes termed as a "one-way hash function", it is computationally infeasible to derive the original message from the knowledge of its hash value. Hash functions therefore enable the software to create digital signatures to operate on smaller and predictable amounts of data, while still providing robust evidentiary correlation to the original message content, thereby efficiently providing assurance that there has been no modification of the message since it was digitally signed.

Thus, the use of digital signatures usually involves two processes—one performed by the signer, and the other by the receiver of the digital signature. They can be discussed as follows:

Digital Signature Creation

This uses a hash result derived from and unique to both the signed message and a given private key. For the hash result to be secure, there must be only a negligible possibility that the same digital signature could be created by a combination of any other message and a private key.

Digital Signature Verification

This is the process of checking the digital signature by reference to the original message and the given public key, thereby determining whether the digital signature was created for that same message using the private key corresponding to the referenced public key.

To sign a document or any other item of information, the signer first delimits precisely the borders of what is to be signed. The delimited information to be signed is termed "message" in these guidelines. Then a hash function in the signer's software computes a hash result unique (for all practical purposes) to the message. The signer's software then transforms the hash result into a digital signature using the signer's private key. The resulting digital signature is thus unique to both the message and the private key used to create it.

Typically, a digital signature (a digitally signed hash result of the message) is attached to its message and stored or transmitted with its message. However, it may also be sent or stored as a separate data element, so long as it maintains a reliable association with its message. Since a digital signature is unique to its message, it is useless if it is wholly disassociated from its message.

Verification of a digital signature is accomplished by computing a new hash result of the original message by means of the same hash function used to create the digital signature. Then, using the public key and the new hash result, the verifier checks: (i) whether the digital signature was created using the corresponding private key, and (ii) whether the newly computed hash result matches the original hash result which was transformed into the digital signature during the signing process. The verification software will confirm the digital signature as "verified" if: (i) the signer's private key was used to digitally sign the message, which is known to be the case if the signer's public key was used to verify the signature because the signer's public key will verify only a digital signature created with the signer's private key, and (ii) the message was unaltered, which is known to be the case if the hash result computed by the verifier is identical to the hash result extracted from the digital signature during the verification process.

Various asymmetric cryptosystems create and verify digital signatures using different algorithms and procedures, but share this overall operational pattern.

The processes of creating a digital signature and verifying it, accomplish the essential effects desired of a signature for many legal purposes:

Signer Authentication

If a public and a private key pair is associated with an identified signer, the digital signature attributes the message to the signer. The digital signature cannot be forged, unless the signer loses control of the private key (a "compromise" of the private key), such as by divulging it or losing the media or device in which it is contained.

Message Authentication

The digital signature also identifies the signed message, typically with far greater certainty and precision than paper signatures. Verification reveals any tampering, since the comparison of the hash results (one made at signing and the other made at verifying) shows whether the message is the same as when signed.

Affirmative Act

Creating a digital signature requires the signer to use the signer's private key. This act can perform the "ceremonial" function of alerting the signer to the fact that the signer is consummating a transaction with legal consequences.

Assurance

The processes of creating and verifying a digital signature provide a high level of assurance that the digital signature is genuinely the signer's. As with the case of modern Electronic Data Interchange (EDI), the creation and verification processes are capable of complete automation (sometimes referred to as machinable), with human interaction required only in exceptional cases. Compared to paper methods such as checking specimen signature cards—methods so tedious and labourious that they are rarely used in practice—digital signatures yield a high degree of assurance without adding greatly to the resources required for processing.

The processes used for digital signatures have undergone thorough technological peer review for over a decade. Digital signatures have been accepted in several national and international standards developed in cooperation with, and accepted by many corporations, banks, and government agencies. The likelihood of a malfunction or a security problem in a digital signature cryptosystem designed and implemented as prescribed by the industry standards is extremely remote and is far less than the risk of undetected forgery or alteration on paper or of using other less secure electronic signature techniques.

Digital Signature and Indian Websites

Some of the websites which use digital signatures are given in Table 6.4.

TABLE 6.4 Indian Websites that use Digital Signature

Shopping and Auctions sites	SifyMall
	Bazee
	Fabmall
	Rediff
Bookings and Reservations	All major airlines
	Indian Railways
Service Companies e-payments	Cellular Providers
	ISPs
Net Banking	ICICI
	HDFC

Following is the list of certifying authorities in India

- SafeScrypt (A Sify-Verisign venture) was the first CA in India.
- National Informatics Centre.
- Tata Consultancy Services.
- Institute of Development and Research in Banking Technology, Hyderabad (IDRBT), the technology arm of the Reserve Bank of India.
- Mahanagar Telephone Nigam Ltd (MTNL).
- ICICI Infotech, which has the contract for the supply and installation of the National Root Certification Authority, with an aim to bring uniformity amongst the different certifying authorities in India.

Public Key Certificates

To verify a digital signature, the verifier must have access to the signer's public key and have assurance that it corresponds to the signer's private key. However, a public and a private key pair has no intrinsic association with any person; it is simply a pair of numbers. Some convincing strategy is necessary to reliably associate a particular person or entity to the key pair.

In a transaction involving only two parties, each party can simply communicate (by a relatively secure "out-of-band" channel, such as a courier or a secure voice telephone) the public key of the key pair each party will use. Such an identification strategy is no small task, especially when the parties are geographically far away from each other, conduct communication over a convenient but insecure channel such as the Internet, are not individuals but rather corporations or similar artificial entities, and act through agents whose authority need to be ascertained. As electronic commerce increasingly moves from a bilateral setting to the many-on-many architecture of the World Wide Web on the Internet, where significant transactions will occur among strangers who have no prior contractual relationship and will never deal with each other again, the problem of authentication/nonrepudiation becomes not merely one of efficiency, but also of reliability. An open system of communication, such as the Internet, needs a system of identity authentication to handle this scenario.

To that end, a prospective signer might issue a public statement, like: "Signatures verifiable by the following public key are mine." However, others doing business with the signer may for good reason be unwilling to accept the statement, especially where there is no prior contract establishing the legal effect of that published statement with certainty. A party relying upon such an unsupported published statement in an open system would run a great risk of trusting a phantom or an imposter, or of attempting to disprove a false denial of a digital signature (non-repudiation), if a transaction should turn out to prove disadvantageous for the purported signee.

The solution to these problems is the use of one or more trusted third parties to associate an identified signer with a specific public key. That trusted third party is referred to as a *certification authority* in most technical standards and in these guidelines.

To associate a key pair with a prospective signer, a certification authority issues a certificate, an electronic record which lists a public key as the "subject" of the certificate, and confirms that the prospective signee identified in the certificate holds the corresponding private key. The prospective signee is called the *subscriber*. The certificate's principal function is to bind a key pair with a particular subscriber. A *recipient* of the certificate desiring to rely upon a digital signature created by the subscriber named in the certificate (whereupon the recipient becomes a *relying party*) can use the public key listed therein to verify if the digital signature was created in corresponding to the private key. If such verification is successful, this chain of reasoning provides assurance that the corresponding private key is held by the subscriber named in the certificate, and that the digital signature was created by that particular subscriber.

To assure both message and identity authenticity of the certificate, the certification authority digitally signs it. This can be verified by using the public key of the certification authority listed in another certificate by another certification authority (which need not be on a higher level in a hierarchy), and that certification can in turn be authenticated by the public key listed in yet another certificate and so on, until the person relying on the digital signature is adequately assured of its genuineness. In each case, the issuing certification authority must digitally sign its own certificate during the operational period of the other certificate used to verify the certification authority's digital signature.

A digital signature, whether created by a subscriber to authenticate a message or by a certification authority to authenticate its certificate (in effect a specialized message), should be reliably time-stamped to allow the verifier to determine whether the digital signature was created during the operational period stated in the certificate, which is a condition upon the verifiability of a digital signature under these guidelines.

To make a public key and its identification with a specific subscriber readily available for use in verification, the certificate may be published in a repository or made available by other means. Repositories are online databases of certificates and other information available for retrieval and use in verifying digital signatures. Retrieval can be accomplished automatically by having the verification program directly inquire the repository to obtain certificates as needed.

Once issued, a certificate may prove to be unreliable, such as in situations where the subscriber misrepresents his identity to the certification authority. In other situations, a certificate may be reliable enough when issued but come to be unreliable sometime thereafter. If the subscriber loses control of the private key ("compromise" of the private key), the certificate becomes unreliable, and the certification authority (either with or without the subscriber's request depending on the circumstances) may suspend (temporarily invalidate) or revoke (permanently invalidate) the certificate. Immediately upon suspending or revoking a certificate, the certification authority must publish notice of the revocation or suspension or notify persons who inquire or who are known to have received a digital signature verifiable by reference to the unreliable certificate.

The Secure e-Payment Process Method

Secured payment transaction system is critical to e-commerce. Without a secured payment transaction system, e-commerce will be a castle built on sand.

There are two common standards used for secure e-payments—SSL and SET. Secure Socket Layer (SSL) and Secure Electronic Transactions (SET) are two major players in the secured payment transaction market. Both use RSA public-key cryptography for encryption and authentication, but SSL and SET are very different protocols to approach payment transaction security.

SSL

SSL is a secured socket layer between HTTP and TCP on a Web server. It is a transport layer security protocol. SSL provides a simple encrypted connection between the client's computer and merchant's server over Internet. It also provides authentication for the merchant's server with its digital certificate from a certificate authority.

This is a secured connection for cyber shoppers to send payment information to e-tailor's Web shop. It can be used as a simple order form including payment information on the Web. But it does not include the payment process protocol with credit card company and issuing banks.

Currently, the fast growing Internet consumer commerce is mainly based on accepting credit card over SSL. One of the reasons for the growth in this direction is that SSL provides secured connection with encryption and authentication between two computers over the Internet. SSL provides a security handshake in which the client and server computers exchange a brief burst of messages. In these messages, they agree upon the level of security they will use to exchange digital certificates and perform other tasks. Each computer unfailingly identifies the other. It is not a problem if the client does not have a certificate, because the client is the one who is sending sensitive information. On the other hand, the server with whom the client is doing business ought to have a valid certificate. Otherwise, you (the client) cannot be certain that the commerce site actually belongs to the one whom it refers to. After identification, the SSL encrypts and decrypts information flowing between the two computers. This means that information in both the HTTP request and the HTTP responses are encrypted. Encrypted information includes the URL the client is requesting, any form containing information the user has completed (which might include a credit card number), and HTTP access authorization data such as user names and passwords. In short, all communication between SSL-enabled clients and servers is encoded. When SSL encodes everything flowing between the client and the server, an eavesdropper will receive only the unintelligible information.

Is SSL really secure? Yes, SSL indeed provides the secured connection for payment transaction between customers and merchants. It is more secure than phone and postal mail delivery. But the security ends at the merchant's site. It does not keep the credit card numbers after the transaction is completed.

SET

SET is a messaging protocol designed by VISA and MasterCard for securing credit card transactions over open networks, such as the Internet.

In the SET protocol, a transaction has three players—the customer, the merchant, and the merchant's bank. SET protocol has three principal features as listed in the following:

- All sensitive information sent within the three parties are encrypted.
- All three parties are required to authenticate themselves with certificates from the SET certificate authority.
- The merchant never sees the customer's card number in plain text.

The third feature actually makes Internet commerce more secure than traditional credit card transactions, such as pay by credit card in store, over phone, or through mail order form. It is also more secure than SSL.

To implement SET in e-commerce on Internet, it requires the SET point-of-sale client software such as SET "electronic wallet" implemented widely in the client's Web browser. It is a big challenge to make such a point-of-sale software widely available to the Internet community.

Online Financial Services in India

Web-based banks figured their pitch was irresistible—by eliminating physical branches, tellers, and bankers' hours, they could slash costs and offer customers higher interest rates and more convenience. But in reality, customers want human contact, or at least an ATM. The multichannel strategy is what is important to people. They want to be able to use the Web. Online banks have also learned that convenience means more than just twenty-four-hour banking. In fact, some aspects of the virtual banking model are flat-out inconvenient. For example, online banks require that deposits be made by cheque or money order, eliminating the cash option available at traditional banks. Adding physical infrastructure, though, adds to an on line bank's operating costs and may force it to lower interest rates paid on savings. Online banks maintain that they still run more efficiently than traditional banks because of practices such as online account managers, loan officers, and so on. That allows them to manage a branch with a smaller staff than a traditional bank. Although a multichannel approach may appeal to customers, the strategy undermines the very premise of online—only institutions, and makes them less distinguishable from traditional banks that also offer Web-banking services. It is a lot easier and cheaper for an existing bank to roll out Internet services than it is for an Internet bank to buy enough ATMs or branches to compete on a national level.

Online banking is also known as cyber banking, home banking, virtual banking, and includes various banking activities that can be conducted from anywhere instead of at a physical bank location. Consumers can use e-banking to pay bills online or to secure a loan electronically. Electronic banking saves a lot of time and money for users. For banks, it offers an inexpensive alternative to branch banking and a chance to enlist remote users. Many physical banks offer home banking services, and EC is used as a major competitive strategy. Online banking is growing in India.

Features of e-Banking in India

1. Can access current account balances at any time.
2. Can obtain charge and credit card statements.

3. Can pay bills online.
4. Can download account transactions.
5. Can transfer money between accounts.
6. Can keep a track of accounts online.
7. Can send e-mails to the bank.
8. Customers have a flexible schedule.
9. Can also use additional services like free phone banking, ATM withdrawals, bill paying.

International banking and the ability to handle trades in multiple currencies are critical for international trade. Although some international retail purchasing can be done with a credit card number, other transactions require international banking support. Many banks offer such services online.

Personal Finance Online

Often electronic banking and portfolio management are combined with personal finance. However, specialized personal finance vendors offer more diversified services, with features like:

1. Bill tracking
2. Tracking of bank accounts, expenditures, and credit cards
3. Portfolio management, including reports and capital gain (losses) computations
4. Investment tracking and monitoring of securities
5. Stock quotes
6. Personal budget organization
7. Record keeping of cash flow, and profit and loss computations
8. Tax computations and preparations
9. Retirement goals, planning, and budgeting.

Online Billing and Bill Paying

People prefer to pay monthly bills like telephone, utility, electricity etc., online. More so, the recipients of such payments are even more eager to receive money online, as the processing costs are lower! In India, banks like ICICI and SBI make it easier with a facility of paying bills from online accounts.

ICICI provides this feature absolutely free of cost and offers customer to view the bill, status checks, and queries. For certain billers, one can see the bill online and pay immediately or schedule the payment of bills. Now there is no more hunting around for the right amount to be paid. Paying these Bills online will ensure that one does not miss any due dates. It acts as a reminder.

SBI on the other hand also provides a feature called Autopay. One can set up AutoPay instructions with an upper limit to ensure that bills are paid automatically whenever they are due. The upper limit ensures that only bills within the specified limit are paid automatically, thereby providing the customer complete control over these payments.

Auxiliary Services

ICICI offers a few auxiliary services online as part of their online services, apart from bill payment and e-banking.

Online shopping: using the Internet banking ID and transaction password, one can visit affiliated shopping sites online and make online transactions.

Online Trading[6]: one of the most popular features of ICICI is their online trading feature. Their products and services offer the following features:

1. Trading in shares
2. Trade in derivatives
3. Investing in mutual funds
4. IPOs and bonds online
5. Personal finance and portfolio, risk management
6. Customer servicing

Some banks like SBI also offer other features like telephone and SMS alerts.

Mutual Funds Online

Mutual funds online are very useful in providing financial assistance and predictions, offering services like[7]

1. Funds fact sheet
2. New launches of Public Offerings
3. Portfolio Trackers and Fund Monitors

These services are available online and provide useful advice on fund management and investments.

While online services are useful and easy to handle, they are definitely not risk free. There are repeated cases of fraud, carding cash, and liquidity risks, etc. which probably deter many. Again, while these are few online financial services available in India, they are definitely not exhaustive as many are still in the pipeline and yet to hit the market, but the day is not far away!

Online Stock Trading: The High Speed Alternative

One can now buy and sell shares online with speeds comparable and at times better than NSE's NEAT Terminal. This speed and reliability comes only with perseverance of a pioneer backed by huge investment in technology! Intra-day price alerts that you can set, customize market watch screen, intra-day tick-by-tick time and price data with chart, for any number of scripts. Technical experts make live calls, the news desk supplying you with the fastest information updates. Even if you load CNX 500 with 500 scripts, it will appear with all live prices in a fraction of a second.[8]

6. www.icicidirect.com
7. www.mutualfundsindia.com
8. www.5paisa.com

No More Paper Hassles

Mutilated certificates, lost certificates, postal delays, and counterfeit shares are a thing of the past. Enter a world of safe, secure and convenient buying, selling and transacting without suffering endless paperwork and delays. Convert your securities to electronic format with the demat account. It is as easy as opening a bank account[9].

e-Banking for Funds Transfer

Buying and selling of shares online can now be done with the help of Internet Banking[10]. E-banking in India is guided by the Information Technology Act, 2000.

The Act provides legal recognition to electronic records, electronic contracts and digital signature. Specifically the Act says "Subject to the provisions of this section, any subscriber may authenticate an electronic record by affixing his digital signature."

Features Offered While Trading in Stocks Online[11]

Several features offered while trading in stocks are enumerated below:

1. ***View positions online.*** The customer can view the status of all his orders online. Every information—as to whether the order has been executed or are waiting in the queue to be executed—can be viewed for their status.
2. ***View transaction history online.*** Transactions details for all the trades done are available online. The customer can also check his Account statements online. This account would be updated regularly on a quarterly basis.
3. ***Online quotes, streaming quotes and ticker.*** The customer gets free online quotes for all his favourite stocks. Quotes are real-time to make sure he receives the best quote for his trades. He can also access the Streaming Quotes, which would give him a feel of the online update of stock prices of his choice. A real-time ticker would run on the screen for him to keep a watch on the stocks of his choice.
4. ***Online news analysis.*** This gets the latest news affecting the markets. ICICI direct research team will analyze the news and explain its impact on the market and stocks.
5. ***Follow the market.*** This gets the latest stock trends by accessing its market centre. Its research team will ensure that you are kept abreast of the latest market happenings. All news and events affecting markets and companies are analyzed and presented in a form which you can understand easily. It gets the complete picture behind the movement of the stocks.

---

9. www.hdfcbank.com
10. *Business India*, Sep. 2001
11. www.icicidirect.com

6. ***IPO centre.*** It tells about all the latest IPOs (Initial Public Offerings) which are about to hit the market and our analysis on these. IPO Calendars, recent IPO listings, Prospectus/Offer Documents, and IPO analysis are few of the features which help the customer keep on top of the IPO markets.

The major online brokers have been getting better and better with improved services and programs. Most online brokers charge the average client, but most will give services and access free to traders who trade actively and maintain above minimum account balances. There are non-brokerage services that can be purchased or accessed for free on the Internet. Many provide information or tools that you cannot get from your broker.[12]

Some of the **major Indian players** in the Online Stock Trading business are:

- ICICIDirect.com
- IndiaInfoline.com
- Fivepaisa.com
- HDFCBank.com
- MyIris.com
- Sharekhan.com
- Indiabulls.com

A Unique e-Broking Service

Stock market investors in India have never had it so good—low brokerage rates and some of the best research, thanks to Internet technology and E-broking. This is a unique model, which combines the rates of a discount brokerage and the service of a boutique house. They ensure independence and integrity as they do not trade on their account, and all employees have to adhere to strict compliance guidelines. Besides high quality investment advice from an experienced research team, the site offers real-time stock quotes, market news, and multiple tools for technical analysis. They have implemented world class security systems to prevent any possibility of misuse, fraud, or data pilferage. They have successfully emerged as one of the leading providers of E-broking services in India.[13]

How Does Online Stock Trading Occur?

Selling of shares is just a click away. Its powerful 3-in-1 concept enables its customer to tie in his saving bank account and his demat account to his brokerage account electronically. This integration ensures that money is transferred to/from the bank account and the shares are transferred from/to the ***DEMAT*** account automatically without any paperwork.[14]

---

12. www.arbtrading.com
13. www.indiainfoline.com
14. www.icicidirect.com

The Advantages

The advantages of opening a Demat Account are many, and a few of them are as follows:

- Shorter settlements, thereby enhancing liquidity.
- No stamp duties on transfer of securities held in Demat form.
- No concept of Market Lots.

How to Transact

Some of the transactions which take place in a Demat account are: **Credit transactions**, **Debit transactions**, and **Pledging of dematerialized securities**.

Credit transactions can take place in your demat account by way of:

- Transfer of securities from the account of a clearing member (market transactions).
- Transfer of securities from the account of another beneficiary (off-market transactions).
- Allotment on public issues directly in your demat account.
- Credit of non-cash benefits like bonus, rights etc., directly in your demat account.

Debit transactions can take place in your demat account by:

- Transfer of securities to the account of a clearing member (market transactions)
- Transfer of securities to the account of another beneficiary (off-market transactions)

In these transactions, securities are transferred from your account to the demat account of the receiver as per instructions on the personalized instruction slip.

These instructions need to be signed by all the account holders and need to be submitted everytime you want to transfer securities from your account, unless you opt for opening an e-broking account with a broker who is registered for providing the e-broking facility.

Pledging of Dematerialized Securities

- Pledgor is the entity who wants to mark a lien on securities owned by him.
- Pledgee is the entity in whose favour the lien is marked.

The process for marking pledges works briefly as follows:

1. Pledgor and the pledgee must have depository accounts.
2. Pledgor must initiate the pledge by submitting to us the details of the securities to be pledged in standard format.
3. The pledgee should confirm this request through his DP.
4. On completion of above processes, a pledge is created on securities.

Share Price Chart

Perhaps in the current business environment, the most important parameter of business is the stocks and shares. *Indiainfoline* is one of the numerous dedicated sites in this field and provides the necessary information about them. Some of the information provided absolutely free on the site is:

- ***Stock:*** Buy/sell recommendations.
- ***Real time:*** News/stories, prices, Commentary, Gainer/losers, New IPO prices, Arbitrage.

- ***Stock statistics:*** Winners/Losers, Circuit hitters, 52 week high/lows, Most active advance/declines, Momentum line, FII investment, MF investment, Long/short position, The arbitrageur, Badla statistics, All India turnover, BSE turnover, Settlement program, Sectoral indices, Sectoral returns, Pivotal performance, Top 200 performance, Book closure, Board meetings, Debt instruments.

There is also a facility to download prices as in BSE, NSE, GDR, and Odd lot.

Stock Ideas

- Daily round-up
- Investment ideas
- Punter's diary
- Bargain hunter
- Wake-up call
- Runaway stocks
- Irate investor
- IPO line
- Grape line

Statistics

This is one of the premier sections, providing GDR/ADR Prices, NSE Prices, Gainers/Losers, Most active, 52 week high/lows, Advance/declines, All India turnover, BSE turnover, FII investments, MF investments, Sectoral returns, Momentum line, Pivotal performance, Top200 performance, Book closure, Record date, Debt instruments, Wealth Builder, Analyze the investment needs.

EXERCISES

1. List four security requirements for safe e-payments.
2. Describe the pros and cons of secret key encryption and public key encryption, and their complementary use.
3. Define digital signature and digital envelope.
4. Describe the security schemes adopted in SSL and SET.
5. Define the concept of micropayments, and provide examples of its use.
6. Define e-cash, and list the different types of e-cash.
7. Explain why the traditional payment systems are inadequate for e-commerce.
8. Why are micropayments so important for the future of e-commerce?
9. Discuss some of the issues involved in international and cross-border financial transactions.
10. Surf the site of ICICI bank and find out the financial services that they offer.
11. What is a digital certificate?

12. Who are the agencies that provide digital certificates in India?
13. What is a key?
14. Explain the symmetric key system.
15. What e-payment security mechanisms are used by various banks in India?
16. What is the RSA algorithm?

CHAPTER

7

e-Customer Relationship Management

LEARNING OBJECTIVES

After reading this chapter, you should be able to:

- Understand the importance of customer relationship management.
- Learn about the need for e-customer relationship tools.
- Describe the E-CRM toolkit.
- Manage customer value orientation.
- Understand the CRM capabilities in the customer life cycle.
- Know CRM and workflow automation.

FedEx

FedEx grew to be a multibillion-dollar company by providing reliable overnight delivery of high-priority, time-sensitive packages and documents. After the parcels are picked up at the customer's site or dropped off at a FedEx location, they are rushed to the local airport and flown to a FedEx hub where they are sorted by destination, loaded on planes and shipped to the destination airport. Packages designated for overnight delivery are delivered to their destination within 24 hours. It operates in four segments: FedEx Express, FedEx Ground, FedEx Freight and FedEx Kinko's. The FedEx Express segment offers various shipping and transportation services for delivery of packages and freight. The FedEx Ground segment provides business and residential money-back-guaranteed ground package delivery services. The FedEx Freight segment offers regional next-day and second-day, and less-than-truckload freight services. The FedEx Kinko's segment provides document solutions and business services. This segment's global network of digitally connected locations offer access to technology for black and white, and colour copying/printing, finishing and presentation services, signs and graphics, Internet access, videoconferencing, outsourcing, managed services, Web-based printing, document management solutions and various ground shipping services. This segment also offers retail products, such as specialty papers, greeting cards, printer cartridges, stationery and office supplies.

To maintain a high degree of reliability in its shipping process, FedEx tracks each package through each step on its path from the shipper to the recipient. When the driver picks up the package, it is logged immediately using Supertracker, a portable, handheld computer containing a bar code reader for capturing the bar code identification on the package and a keyboard for entering additional information such as the destination's zip code. Upon returning to the truck, the driver inserts the Supertracker into a small computer that transmits the data by radio waves to the local dispatch centre, which has a link to the corporate database. Within five minutes of initial pickup, the FedEx database contains the package's identification, location, destination, and route. The location data is updated automatically (using the package's bar code) as the package moves through each step on its way to the destination. Although package pickup and delivery involve a series of steps in different places, the combination of telecommunications and computing permits FedEx to know the location of every package at any time and to make sure that procedures are followed throughout. Any deviation would become obvious quickly.

Package-tracking information is used in many ways. Information about pickups and deliveries is the basis of customer billing. Detailed tracking information supports customer service by permitting customer service agents to tell customers where their packages are:

Customers can access the FedEx Website to obtain the same information.

As a method for managing their own internal operations, FedEx developed a service quality index based on 12 types of events that disappoint customers, including late delivery, damaged or lost packages and complaints. Even a delivery at 10:31 for a package promised for 10:30 is considered a problem. So that they will learn from past problems and mistakes, people throughout the company receive daily feedback reports identifying problems that occurred the previous day.

As other major package delivery and shipping companies built similar systems, FedEx decided to expand from a package delivery company to a fully integrated corporate partner that picks up, transports, warehouses and delivers all of a company's finished goods from the factory to the customer's receiving dock with status data available every step of the way.

Manufacturing and marketing firms that rely on quick, reliable delivery of consumer products and spare parts should plan to transfer most of these delivery functions to logistics firms such as FedEx and UPS that have built processes and information systems needed for quick, reliable delivery.

Initially, FedEx's service was about delivering packages. Gradually, an international information system supported by a telecommunications network became an important part of the package delivery service because this system kept track of each package at all times. Later, the telecommunications network became an essential part of FedEx's expansion into a corporate logistics business that required a highly distributed but tightly controlled information system.

As FedEx moved in these directions, it had to make many decisions about how to transmit information within its worldwide computer network and from pick-up points and other tracking locations into its computer network. In making these decisions it had to evaluate alternatives related to topics such as:

- Which data transmission methods and technologies should be used? For example, where will it be appropriate to use wire-based versus wireless transmission?
- Should the data move through public communication networks or private FedEx channels?

Case Discussion

1. What makes Federal Express a success?
2. Compare Federal Express with UPS and DHL.

Customer Relationship Management (CRM) is defined as the aligning of business strategy with the corporate culture of the organization, along with customer information and a supporting information technology of the customer interactions that promote a mutually beneficial relationship between the customer and the enterprise. Primarily, customer relationship management is a business strategy, but it is a business strategy enabled by the advances in technology. Widespread implementation of customer information, Enterprise Resource Planning (ERP) systems, sales force automation, and integrated point-of-sale systems have made customer information readily available in large volumes. Reduced costs and higher levels of performance for database management platforms allow us to gain access to this customer information and gain new insights into our customers and their behaviour through a variety of analysis methods. Advances in contact management technology and supporting infrastructure allow us to take advantage of this information in increasingly cost-effective and innovative ways. Perhaps most significantly, the Internet provides a completely new way for an enterprise to interact with its customer—the electronic channel, or the e-channel. With consumers buying everything—from groceries to automobiles—on the Internet and the businesses beginning to shift their purchasing activities to industry-oriented virtual marketplaces, the characteristics of customer interaction are constantly changing. In the business environment, the focus is being shifted to customer retention.

The link between customer satisfaction and the return on investment is the profit for a company, as shown in Figure 7.1.

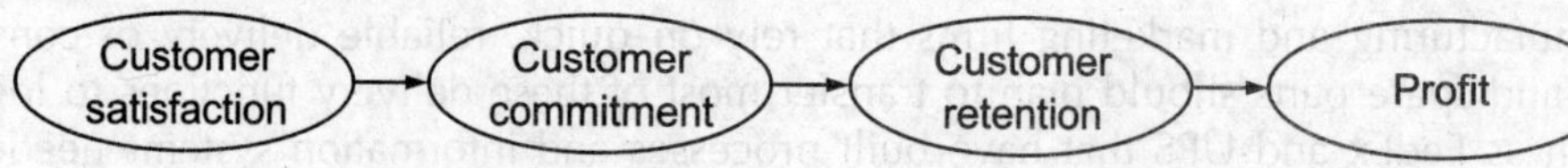

Figure 7.1 Customer satisfaction and profit.

Customer Relationship Management

Beyond the glamour of developing the e-channel, business is investing heavily to deploy customer relationship management in traditional channels. In most cases, these capabilities are developed independently, requiring expensive integration later on to achieve the vision of true customer relationship management on an enterprise-wide scale. Integration of these resources is one of the key challenges of successful deployment of CRM across the enterprise.

This is because it has a direct impact on the consistency of the customer experience with the enterprise. So how does the enterprise integrate systems across functions and channels? It does not happen by accident, but through foresight and planning. All the functions and the channels must come together to develop an enterprise-wide strategy for CRM. Only then can the enabling information technology be fully integrated with maximum efficiency and effectiveness. This technology spreads customer information throughout the enterprise and it must be based on a unified information architecture.

Independently developed CRM capabilities within the various parts of the enterprise usually begin based on function-specific short-term needs. Marketing begins to implement CRM with a variety of products, often combined with integrated suites to plan, execute, and monitor marketing campaigns and perform database marketing. Lead management and sales force automation capabilities are deployed to support the field sales force. Systems that manage the supply chain and product delivery are deployed to support mass customization and to provide up-to-the minute information about the goods in transit, to the customer. Field service representatives and contact centres deploy sophisticated telephony and information systems to provide ongoing customer service and cross-selling.

These separate capabilities do provide a means to support function-specific and channel-specific CRM strategies. Business culture can shift from product-focus to customer-focus. Sales and marketing can focus on retention and increase of share of customers instead of acquisition and market share. Customer service can identify and take advantage of cross-sell and up-sell opportunities. However, customer information does not freely flow across the enterprise. To obtain the vision of customer relationship management, information must move about freely. This requires integration.

Only through the integration of marketing, sales, fulfilment and service across business partnerships, the direct sales force, the telechannel and the e-channel, is the vision of customer relationship management realized. Customer information must flow like water within, around, and through these functions and channels to ensure that the enterprises can build mutually beneficial relationship with the customers, and even amongst their customers. Everyone in the enterprise participating in the conversation with the customer needs access to the latest information on the customer's profile, behaviour, and expressed needs. Marketing provides the latest promotions and offers for individual customers, based on their interactions on the website. Products are customized to meet specific customer needs and customer service is fully done, resulting in increased levels of customer satisfaction and loyalty. With an enterprise-wide view of each customer, the value of each relationship is measurable, and each relationship is managed based on this value. Every customer touch becomes an opportunity to modify customer behaviour in a beneficial way based on the totality of information at the disposal of the enterprise. Achieving this vision results in unprecedented competitive advantage in some industries ... or mere survival in other industries.

E-CRM Solutions

E-Customer Relationship Management or E-CRM solutions are especially valuable to companies that face the following circumstances:

1. Business is driven by mission-critical customer service requirements
2. Current costs for CRM run high
3. Large volumes of information is distributed
4. A complete customer care solution is needed.

E-CRM solutions can be deployed and managed to provide increased revenues and decreased costs for companies while improving customer service. E-CRM goals can be achieved with Internet business strategies, web-based CRM specification development, web systems design and project management, interactive interface design and electronic publishing.

The strategy for e-CRM can be visualized in three stages, as given in Figure 7.2.

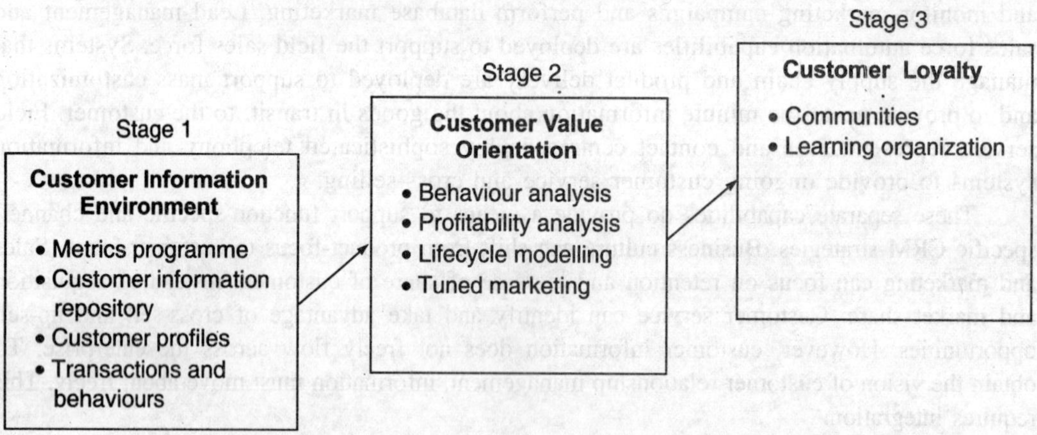

Figure 7.2 Strategies of a customer focussed business.

Customer Information Environment

In the first stage, building up of a customer information environment and acting on it forms the starting point. It consists of Metrics programmes, Customer information repository, and monitoring customer behaviours.

Customer Value Orientation

In the second stage, operational effectiveness is the focus. Customers want value for their money. They believe that they have got value, when the perceived benefits they receive from something exceed the costs of owning it. These components are represented in Figure 7.3.

Customer Loyalty

In the third stage, the focus is on the integration of internal process of the organization with the customer in creating a community.

Moving costly customer services to the Internet is critical to staying competitive. Providing customer services on the Internet means a lot more than just having a website. With the users demanding more services via the Internet, leading companies have realized the importance of their e-services strategies on the Web.

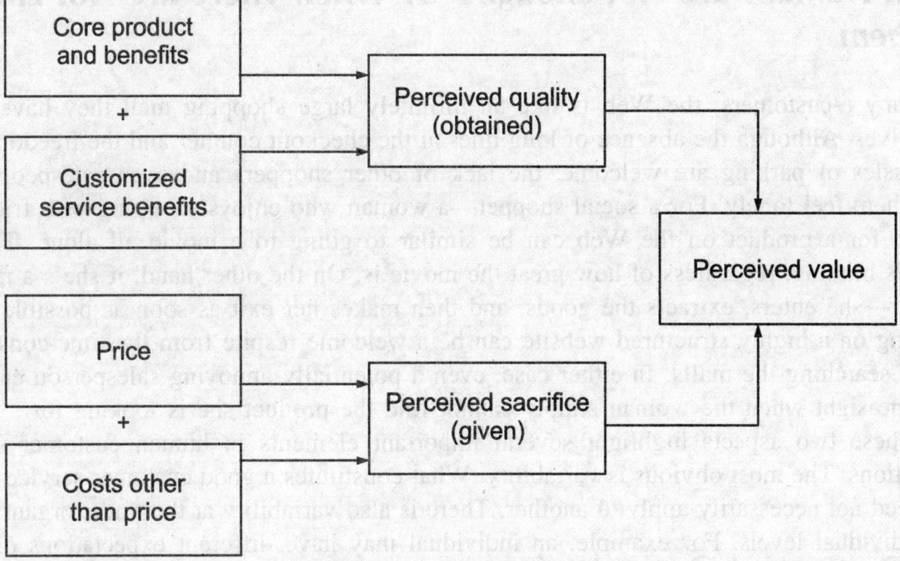

Figure 7.3 Perceived value.

Most companies are focussed on today's most critical business challenge—attracting and retaining customers. These companies require customer-directed e-business solutions and E-CRM to meet those requirements. Companies benefit from huge cost savings and increased revenues. Customers benefit from on-demand access to information, less hassles with better support, and less expensive services.

TABLE 7.1 Valuation of Companies

Company	*Revenues (in billion)*	*Market capitalization (in billion)*
Google	8.57	168.52
Amazon	9.86	89.47
Ebay	2.55	42.13
Yahoo	1.21	21.34
IAC	0.46021	3.18
AOL	0.5514	2.09
Monster	0.26138	1.97

The strategy of the portals is to become global supermarkets providing everything for individuals, families and organizations. Their customer base is what stock market considers to be the most important asset of these companies.

When Humans are Not Enough—Or When There are Not Enough of Them

For many e-customers, the Web is like an infinitely large shopping mall they have all to themselves. Although the absence of long lines at the checkout counter and the freedom from the hassles of parking are welcome, the lack of other shoppers and even salespeople can make them feel lonely. For a social shopper—a woman who enjoys shopping with friends—looking for a product on the Web can be similar to going to a movie all alone. The fun factor is missing, regardless of how great the movie is. On the other hand, if she's a mission shopper—she enters, extracts the goods, and then makes her exit as soon as possible—then shopping on a highly structured website can be a welcome respite from the time-consuming task of searching the malls. In either case, even a potentially annoying salesperson can be a welcome sight when the woman simply cannot find the product she is looking for.

These two aspects highlight several important elements in human customer service interactions. The most obvious is variability. What constitutes a good customer service in one area need not necessarily apply to another. There is also variability at the trade, organization, and individual levels. For example, an individual may have different expectations of what constitutes a good customer service in the airline, hotel, and restaurant industries. He probably has specific expectations about his favourite airline or hotel chain. Furthermore, he no doubt expects different levels of service at each location.

Variability in service can result from a variety of factors. Perhaps the staff in one location has insufficient training to understand their customers' needs. May be, they just do not care. Perhaps they are simply having a bad day. Today, many new products last only for three months in the marketplace, making it virtually impossible for a salesperson to become an expert on a particular product before another replaces it. Clearly, with some products and services, it is simply absurd to expect a salesperson without extensive training to become proficient in interfacing with customers in more than a superficial way.

If someone were to ask the person who manages the customer service division of a business to name his greatest assets and liabilities, he will say it is the people. It is a challenge to attract people and keep them attentive and educate them, but it is usually worth the effort. Good customer service representatives can provide personal, empathetic, quality, reassuring service, especially when they interact with the customer in person. Nothing beats an attentive, knowledgeable sales or support person in terms of bonding customers to a company. Great sales and service representatives create a loyal following that is often independent of the company they represent.

Although there are situations when only a live customer service representative is required, this is not always possible. With today's busy lifestyle, there is simply not enough time to have face-to-face interaction. Increasingly, sales and support interactions occur with the assistance of communications and computer technology, even for costly items. For example, when time is a scarce resource and an unstructured conversation can resolve things in a few seconds, telephone is of great help, especially since it is universally available.

Despite these advantages of personal service sales and service representatives are expensive from a practical perspective, especially in a 24 hours, 7 days support model. In addition, there is the aforementioned variability in service, due to dozens of possible issues, such as a representative's disinterest in a particular product because there are dozens of other products he needs to know about. One of the major limitations of human customer service representatives is that they normally work with customers on a one-on-one basis. Scalability, the ability to work with multiple customers at once, is possible in group presentation situations, but then the personal, one-on-one interaction suffers. There are also errors, of both omission and commission, which can appear in any human-mediated transaction, regardless of the touch point. This is especially true when the transaction involves the manual entry of data.

As the effective interaction distance between customer and support staff increases from personal to phone, to live Web chat, to e-mail interactions, many of the positive qualities of personal interaction normally ascribed to a good customer service representative decrease. The potential for using the touch point in an emotionally intelligent interface diminishes as well. For example, it is much easier to foster an emotional bond with a customer through personal interaction than through e-mail. In addition, human-mediated interactions tend to generate fewer data and less granular data than is available through computer-assisted means. Often, this is simply because someone has to take time to record the data. Furthermore, it may be impossible for some employees to fulfil their data-logging requirements because they may lack the education needed to understand the product or service. For example, a new employee may not be able to differentiate between fabric types, saree styles, or designer labels. Another characteristic of human customer representatives is that they bring with them a variety of security and confidentiality issues, from both an employee and a technology perspective. That is, the equipment the support staff uses must be protected from viruses and break-ins, and employees must be trusted or guarded as well.

How Technology Can Help

Interactive computer and communications technology can assist in the sales and support process in several ways. Telephone, live chat and e-mail can enhance the effectiveness of customer service representatives. Computer-mediated e-mail, chat and animated chat can take over when a human representative is exhausted. They can serve as a filter, answering all but the most difficult questions for the representatives.

Web technology can also help offload the support issue to customers who enjoy helping each other on the Web. For example, Lands' End (*www.LandsEnd.com*) adds to the fun of shopping with its *Shop With a Friend*™ option. Two shoppers can browse together and add items to the same shopping cart. For example, two friends working in different companies can go shopping during their lunch break, just as though they had met and gone shopping in the same brick-and-mortar retail outlet. There is no elaborate data warehousing or cluster analysis involved, just a two-way Web chat connection and a slight modification in their shopping cart model. The customers take care of navigating the Web and helping each other with product selection.

In a similar vein, several vendors, including Cahoots, Hypernix, ICQ, MyESPcom, Third Voice, and WebSideStory, offer live-chat technology to make online shopping less sterile and more emotionally engaging. Their idea is to create a sense of community for a particular website by allowing prospective customers to communicate with each other at any time, even without knowing each other's name.

For example, customers shopping for widgets on a particular website could ask if other customers had a good or bad experience with the widgets purchased there. Anyone visiting that website could respond to the query and discuss the merits and demerits of those widgets. The goal is to improve upon the Web's record of two-thirds cart abandonment. That is, about two-thirds of all shopping carts are abandoned at some point before final checkout. From the perspective of a website owner and the one paying for the live-chat capabilities, the danger is that the discussions may become derogatory and out of control.

Human-mediated personal contact, phone contact, live Web chat, e-mail, and animated Web chat are representatives of the range of possibilities currently available, where animated Web chat represents the greatest level of technological involvement. There are also several technologies on the horizon, such as two-way Web-based video links, but the realities of current bandwidth limitations of the Internet are holding these technologies at bay. Also, the value for each characteristic attributed to a touch point represents a typical case. As with any measurement or estimate, there is variability in the actual value shown.

Reducing Cost Per Contact

One of the effects of adding the appropriate technology to the customer support or sales mix is that there is often a reduction in the cost per contact, i.e. the money spent to connect with each customer. The cost per contact tends to be highest for personal, one-on-one interactions, simply because the representative's full attention is necessarily focussed on a single customer. The customer receives the full benefit of the representative's training during the period of contact, as well as many of the resources that result in direct and indirect costs to the company.

With the addition of phone technology, the support representative is freed somewhat from dealing with one customer to the exclusion of all others. For example, he might be on the phone with one potential customer, while simultaneously composing an e-mail to another potential customer or client, filing papers, cleaning up his desk, or in some way contributing to his own and the company's future success.

Similarly, live, Web-based chat and e-mail have a relatively low cost per contact, in part because the support representative can multitask. For example, in the case of a live chat, the representative can communicate with potential customers on the Web in spurts, and in between sessions, handle other support issues. Furthermore, since e-mail is normally handled in batches, often with canned responses, a customer service representative has time between e-mail runs to perform other functions.

Moving from primarily human to computer-mediated interactions, the cost per contact is potentially even lower. Computer-mediated e-mail, in which e-mail is generated by a bot, can respond to hundreds of e-mails during the time it takes a human to answer one or two. Similarly, computer-mediated chat, where real-time chat bots help customers, can reply to hundreds of queries per second. The same rationale holds for animated chat bots that incorporate emotive, animated graphic characters. The marginal cost of handling an additional customer is an insignificant increase in the server power and Internet bandwidth requirements.

Decreasing Development Time

Customer representatives are expensive to train, to keep motivated, and to retain, especially in this state of the economy. Training a representative for a new product or service may take a few days or up to several weeks, depending on the complexity and the number of products and services the representative is expected to sell or support. Development time is the greatest for representatives who work face-to-face with customers. One reason for this is that it includes recruiting time. Good all-round salespeople and representatives with fascinating manners, speech, dress, and charisma are hard to find. A business may be lucky enough to locate a representative who has excellent live chat skills, but whose squeaky voice may not do in phone support and whose green hair might not present the image the business is looking for in person-to-person sales.

Characteristics of human versus computer-mediated customer service representatives vary over a variety of touch points. This is illustrated in Table 7.2. As you can find, variability in service is the greatest with personal, one-on-one contact and telephone service.

TABLE 7.2 Comparison between Human and Computer Interaction[1]

Characteristic	*Human*				*Computer*		
	Personal	*Phone*	*Live chat*	*E-mail*	*E-mail*	*Chat*	*Anim chat*
Cost per contact	●	◆	■	■	■	■	■
Development time	●	◆	■	■	◆	◆	●
Emotional bond	●	◆	◆	■	■	◆	◆
Emotive	●	◆	◆	■	■	◆	◆
Empathetic	●	◆	◆	■	■	■	◆
Error prone	●	●	●	●	■	■	■
Flexibility	●	●	●	●	◆	◆	◆
Interactivity	●	●	◆	■	■	◆	●
Continuity	■	■	◆	◆	◆	◆	◆
Personal	●	●	●	●	●	●	●
Personality	●	◆	◆	■	■	◆	◆
Quality	●	◆	◆	◆	●	●	●
Reassuring	●	●	◆	■	■	◆	◆
Reliability	◆	◆	◆	◆	●	●	●
Responsive	◆	◆	◆	■	◆	●	●
ROI	■	◆	◆	◆	●	●	●
Scalability	■	■	■	◆	●	●	●
Transference	●	●	■	■	■	■	◆
Variability	●	●	◆	◆	■	■	■

● High; ◆ Medium; ■ Low

1. Bergeron B., *The Eternal E-customer*, McGraw-Hill, New York, 2001, p. 174.

With computer-enabled tools, such as liberty of canned phrases, customer service representatives can be trained to become proficient users of live chat and e-mail even if they are slow typists. As long as the representative can recognise which phrases or responses to use in specific circumstances, even minimal keyboard skills will do. E-mail is one of the most forgiving touch points, since the dialogue does not occur in real time. A customer service representative has time to refer an unintelligible e-mail to a supervisor who can then answer it or route it to the appropriate person to handle.

In comparison to training human customer representatives, computer-mediated e-mail and chat have moderate development times. The likely questions and the corresponding answers have to be gathered and compiled into a knowledge base. The normal software development cycle of testing, modifying, and again testing and re-modifying the code and the knowledge base until everything checks out can take weeks, even with a simple support problem.

Creating Emotional Bonds

Although the golden standard for creating an emotional bond between the customer and a company is to have a dedicated, charismatic salesperson or a representative, technology can be of great help in creating an emotional bond. As illustrated in Table 7.2, personal contact is capable of creating the most profound emotional bond. Live chat is also capable of supporting a meaningful dialogue that can help create an emotional bond, but it is not as powerful as the phone or direct contact. Since e-mail lacks most of the cues we normally associate with a conversation, such as immediacy, it has the lowest likelihood of creating a meaningful emotional bond.

Computer-mediated chat and animated chat, when appropriately implemented, have the best chances of creating an emotional bond with the customer.

Presenting Emotive Content

Human beings are emotional creatures. We react to not only language and voice intonation and the subject, but also to dozens of subtle cues, in the form of physical gestures. For this reason, it can be stated that personal interactions convey the most emotive content. E-mail has the lowest emotive content capacity, in part because of the time factor. Both chat and e-mail can enhance the messages with the use of emotive icons or emotions. Of the computer-mediated options available, animated chat has the greatest potential for conveying emotive messages to a customer.

Displaying Empathy

Great salespeople and customer representatives are empathetic; they can understand the customer's situation or at least give the impression that they do. It is the impression that matters to customers; they want to feel that they have been listened to. This feeling can be communicated best in person, but to some degree over a phone conversation, and to a lesser extent over a live chat conversation. Because it lacks immediacy, e-mail tends to be a poor communications conduit for empathetic thoughts and feelings. Computer-mediated communications, such as e-mail and live chat, do not fare very well when the goal is to communicate feelings that may be difficult for a computer to convey. In this regard, animated chat communications can sometimes convey a sense of understanding, when used as the touch point.

Reducing Human Error

Humans are simply more error-prone than computers when it comes to manipulating symbols and values. Assuming there is an accurate customer data to work with, computer-mediated customer communications can have a much lower error rate than human-mediated communications in tracking orders, verifying charges, and identifying repeat customers.

Increasing Flexibility

While computers might excel in flawlessly following human instructions, good customer service representatives excel in flexibility. Regardless of the touch-point, a good representative, when properly trained, can help rectify errors or retrieve missing data that current computer-mediated systems cannot.

Improving Interactivity

Interactivity, the ability of representatives to respond to a customer's queries in near real-time, is best in person and over the phone. E-mail interactivity suffers from an inherent lag from the time a problem statement is made to the response, but the lag time tends to be smaller when the e-mail is computer-mediated. Chat, whether live or computer-mediated, can support a moderate level of interactivity.

Increasing Continuity

From the customer's perspective, continuity can be extended with computer-mediated chat and e-mail. Continuity is important in forming a bond with customers, especially with personal, and to a lesser extent, phone interactions. Computer-mediated communications can provide infinite continuity. For example, the names used to identify a chat bot can be held constant, and the appearance of animated figures used in animated chat communications can remain constant as well.

Adding a Personal Touch

Even human-mediated communications tend to rely on computer-generated or warehoused customer data to the same extent that computer-mediated communications do. In other words, most touch-points are already leveraging computer technology to provide a personal touch.

Communicating Personality

Computer hardware, programs and websites, all have personalities. However, just as personal interactions tend to have a great potential to exhibit personality, animated chat, where an anthropomorphic figure can communicate with visual cues, text and even voice, has a much greater chance of communicating personalities to customers. The challenge is to create personalities that customers can relate to in a positive way.

Increasing Quality

The quality of customer dialogue tends to be highest when it is controlled by a good salesperson or motivated customer service representative. Phone, live chat, e-mail, and other touch-points can also be of high quality, but are usually not as high as of a good salesperson. Computer technology can help with these other touch-points by minimising variability and otherwise contributing to quality control. Computer-mediated communications can have consistent, high-quality dialogues with customers, because all possible responses can be validated before they are presented to customers.

Providing Reassurance

An important aspect of the sales process is reassuring customers that their purchase decisions are correct, their problems have been solved, and that their products are on the way. Computer technology can be used for something as ordinary as helping reassure customers about the status of their order, or as sophisticated as creating a personal profile of customers and using it to explain why the products they just ordered are in their best interest.

Increasing Reliability

Humans vary in their reliability from person to person and from day to day. Computers are reliable machines as long as human-generated viruses do not attack them. A business can rely on computer-mediated communications with customers as long as it has tightly controlled parameters. In short, computers excel where reliability is an issue.

Improving Responsiveness

Properly trained sales and support staff can do a good job of responding to customer needs in a timely manner. E-mail has the lowest responsiveness of the human-mediated communication, simply because of the inherent delays in e-mail communications. By definition, e-mail carries with it, a perceptible delay that is not noticed or at least is not significant in a live chat, for example. Because of the rapid 24 × 7 response made possible by computers, computer-mediated chat and animated chat are potentially much more responsive than a customer representative or salesperson could be.

Improving Return on Investment (ROI)

Generalizing the Return on Investment (ROI) for a customer representative or computer technology is complicated. There are always specific circumstances, such as the cost of money and the specifications of the people or computer technology involved. However, in today's economy, it is generally understood that the turnover is high. This is especially true in the customer-support area, where temporary and seasonal workers fill a relatively large number of representative jobs. It is because of the variable nature of the labour supply and the low cost per contact for computer-mediated dialogue, that the ROI for computer-mediated support of all types is potentially greater than for human-mediated support.

Increasing Scalability

In general, humans do not scale very well. Most interactions are on a one-on-one basis, such as personal, phone, and live-chat communications. E-mail is scalable because it may be handled in batches, with the same generic answer being applied to hundreds of questions. In contrast, computer-mediated touch points are virtually infinitely scalable, given an adequate infrastructure, including supporting server hardware.

Controlling Transference

Transference is, ascribing the characteristics of one person to another, often at a subconscious level. This may be the result of similarities in appearance, style of speech, or mannerisms and can be a positive or a negative factor in the sales and customer-relations process. For example, a salesman may subconsciously remind a woman of a trusted relative, and she will instinctively believe everything he says. Conversely, the same salesman could remind her of an unscrupulous salesperson she dealt with in the past, and she develops the same negative attitude towards this one. In human-mediated communications, transference occurs primarily with personal contact, but may also occur in phone conversations.

Transference can be an asset in computer-mediated interactions. For example, a business can provide customers with the ability to modify the animation and synthesized speech to suit their preferences. It could present customers with a menu of animated figures including male, female, young and old, from which they could choose. In addition, it could allow customers to specify the speaking style of each figure, from businesslike to casual. Customers do not generally create figures to learn from or deal with what they do not relate to positively.

Decreasing Variability

Variability is a characteristic of human-mediated communications that is virtually absent in properly designed computer-mediated dialogues. This variability may be a nuisance, as for example, if the customer inquires about tax code information. An animated chat bot may not be as engaging as a human, but a business will know, to what information are its customers being exposed.

Where Interactive Web Technology Shines

From the above discussion, it is apparent that of the characteristics listed in Table 7.2, Web-based customer support has the following advantages:

1. Lower cost per contact
2. An emotional bond with the customer
3. An ability to communicate with more emotive content
4. Fewer errors
5. Greater customer interactivity with a website
6. Improved reliability

7. Greater responsiveness
8. Greater return on investment
9. Improved scalability
10. Less variability in the quality and content of communications.

What really matters is how businesses apply these potential benefits of interactive technology to their Web presence. If the goal is to create an Emotionally Intelligent Interface, then a business could use these technologies towards setting the tone of interaction, involving its customers in a mutually beneficial dialogue, and using interactivity to establish a meaningful relationship.

When potential customers visit a website, they should be made to feel comfortable with the company and confident that it can fill their needs efficiently and economically. At a brick-and-mortar store, the sales staff and the layout and decoration of the reception area of the store perform this function. The environment established by the technologies incorporated in the website can dictate customers' responses to the business, and how long their visit to the website lasts. Creating a welcoming environment can entail something as simple as creating a panel of potential customer service representatives and allowing customers to choose which one they would like to interact with, whether the representatives are real or virtual.

E-CRM Toolkit

An E-CRM 'toolkit' covers a wide diversity of channels (see Figure 7.4). In order to bring true customer management across online business, one needs the E-CRM products to fulfil the following criteria:

Content

Is the system delivering the contents a customer wants to see? How is it being managed on the IT platform?

Storefront and Merchandising Services

With large numbers of visitors failing to complete transaction at the checkout, it is needed to ensure that your storefront services propel your customers to the cash point.

E-mail Management

Are e-mail campaigns focussed to provide an offer that customer cannot refuse? How are these tied in with websites so that customers enjoy a seamless experience?

Customer Management

Is the company managing data across all the sales and marketing functions to its best?

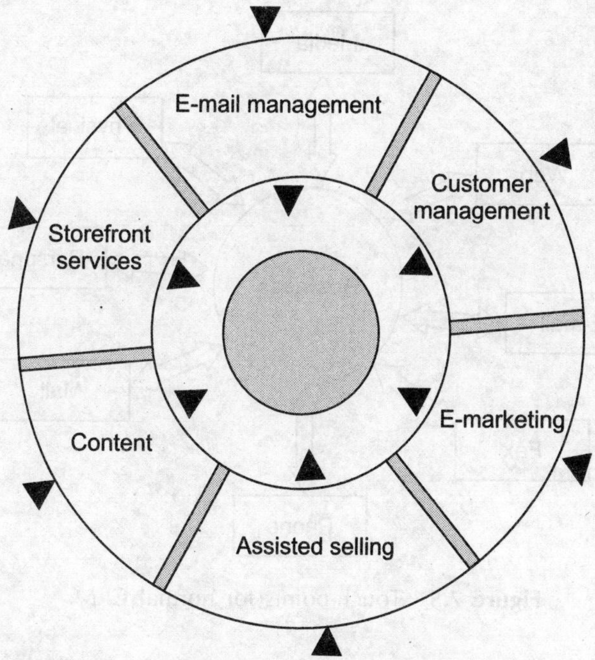

Figure 7.4 E-CRM toolkit.

E-marketing

How well are e-marketing efforts targeted? How well do they combine with online selling operation?

Assisted Selling

One needs only to look at the Dell business model to see how assisted selling can enhance the shopping experience and achieve business success. But what assisted selling approach will work best for any company?

Typical Business Touch-points

Typical business touch-points from a consumer perspective include: Media—TV, radio, newspaper and flyers; Physical—the physical plant, such as a showroom or retail outlet; Personal—direct people contact, including salespeople and customer representatives; Mail—correspondence, bills, and payments through postal service; Phone—telephone communications with sales, marketing, and customer service representatives; Fax–facsimile communications, including quotes and invoices; E-mail—communications via computer regarding orders and services; and Web—information and ordering through the Web. Figure 7.5 illustrates the state where every touch-point is significant. The arrows therein indicate the relative significance of each touch-point.

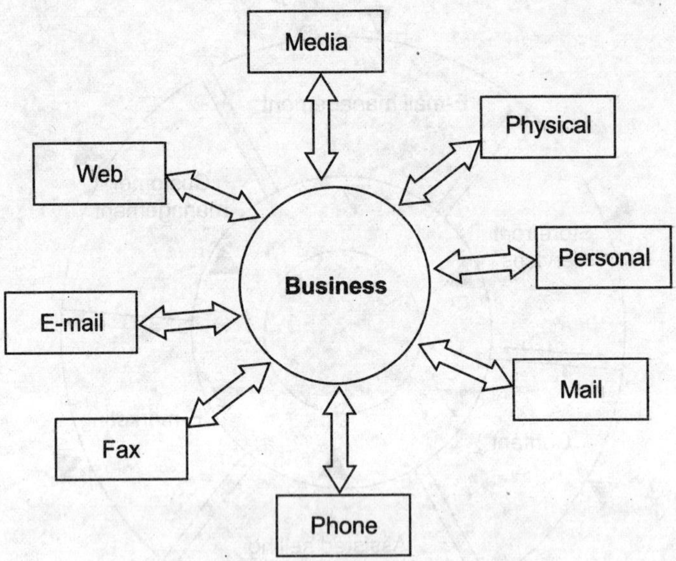

Figure 7.5 Touch-points for normal CRM.

For any company, it simply is not enough to know "who buys what?" in order to build a successful, profitable marketing campaign. It needs to know who its customers are, and how much it should invest on them. This necessitates the maintenance of a consolidated database. The components of the data warehouse can be found in Figure 7.6.

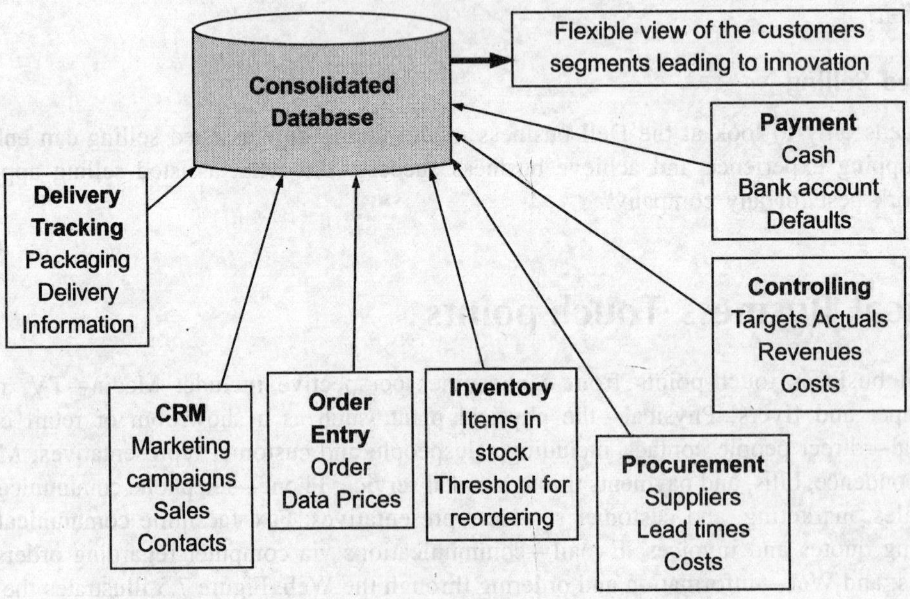

Figure 7.6 Data warehouse architecture.

Converting Clicks to Customers

To leverage technology and thereby realize the greatest benefit from a Web presence, a business must first know what it is after, in terms of a relationship with its customers. Assuming that the goal is to provide a website with an Emotionally Intelligent Interface, management also has to appreciate the possibilities within the business resource and technology constraints. Note that the technologies with the greatest degree of interactivity provide the greatest potential for a sale. A business needs to pull everything together in a way that harmonizes with its customers; the business should use the technology at its disposal so that the odds of creating a loyal customer following are maximized.

Managing Customer Value Orientation and Life Cycle

The CRM industry has matured rapidly over the past few years. Contact managers have evolved into full-function sales force automation systems. CRM front-office suites now support marketing, sales and service. Integration between CRM systems and enterprise resource planning (ERP) systems is becoming more common, if not commonplace.

The E-CRM market is new and rapidly evolving. Implementing CRM for traditional front-office marketing, sales and service operations is becoming the top priority for most companies. That prospect has been challenging enough, being formidable to the new touch-points such as the Web. Integration is still the key. Online or offline, client/server technology is still a major factor. Anyone who has implemented client/server applications between the various contact centres and touch points within an enterprise can afford the complexity and the cost involved in them. In short, CRM is a square peg and e-business is a round hole. However, everything is changing with the introduction of new, Web-based CRM solutions.

To help organize the chaos, E-CRM solutions can be grouped into two categories—Web-based solutions and Web-extended solutions.

The Web-based CRM solutions are designed from the bottom up, exclusively for the Internet. These are very innovative products, initially focussed on the sales (e-commerce) function. More marketing and service capabilities will be soon added.

Web-extended CRM solutions are established (primarily client/server-based) CRM suites, originally designed for enterprise users with extensions, to include web-interface functions. There are three phases of CRM:

1. Acquisition
2. Enhancement
3. Retention.

Each has a different impact on the customer relationship, and each can more closely tie a company with its customer's life.

Acquisition

You acquire new customers by promoting product/service leadership that pushes performance boundaries with respect to convenience and innovation. The value proposition to the customer is the offer of a superior product backed by excellent service.

Enhancement

You enhance the relationship by encouraging excellence in cross-selling and up-selling. This deepens the relationship. The value proposition to the customer is an advantage with greater convenience at low cost (one-stop shopping).

Retention

Retaining profitable customers for life should be the aim. Retention focusses on service adaptability, i.e. it delivers not what the market wants, but what the customers want. The value proposition to the customer enhances a proactive relationship that works well with the best interest of the customers. Today, leading companies focus on retention of existing customers much more than on attracting new customers. The reason behind this strategy is simple: If you want to make money hold on to your good customers. But do not be fooled; it is not as easy as it seems.

All the phases of CRM are interrelated as shown in Figure 7.7. However, performing the tasks well in all the three phases is a difficult proposition, even for the best of companies. Companies often have to choose which one of these dimensions will be their primary focus.

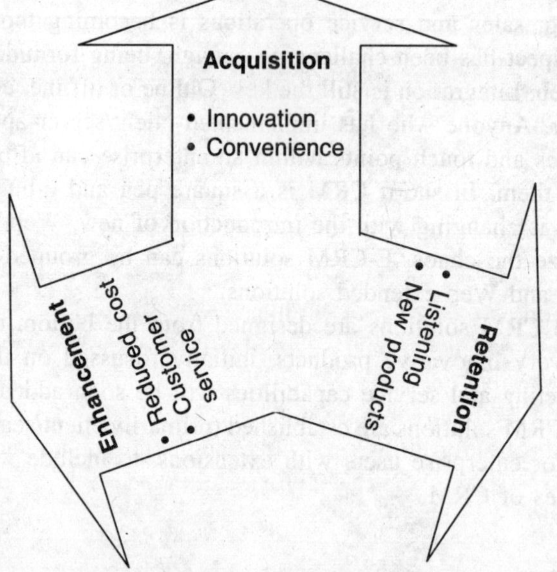

Figure 7.7 The three phases of CRM[2].

The Customer Retention Goal

Attracting and retaining customers has rapidly emerged to be the most mission-critical function of leading businesses. Everything (products, services, pricing, and the like) is a commodity.

2. Kalakota R. and Robinson M., *e-business*, Addison-Wesley, NJ, USA, 1999, p. 114.

Customer retention has replaced cost-effectiveness and cost-competitiveness as the greatest concern of business executives today. It costs five to ten times more to get new customers than to retain the existing ones. It is going to involve more efforts than web interactions to keep the customer brand-loyal.

The Power Shift

Give customers what they want. This can be a challenge, or it can be an opportunity. The same technology that has made it more difficult, can also make it easier. Customers are more important than business people. Companies need to do business with customers in their own way. The key is integration of the various points of customer contact, including Web, contact centres, wireless (field) and others. All customer interactions must be consistent, with clear value delivered to the customer and the company.

E-CRM is not the single answer to attracting and retaining customers, nor are e-customers the only valuable customers. Indeed, Internet is not the only point of contact with the customers, nor are the other digital and online communication tools described in Figure 7.8. Five years and beyond from now, some customers will still prefer the telephone or face-to-face communications.

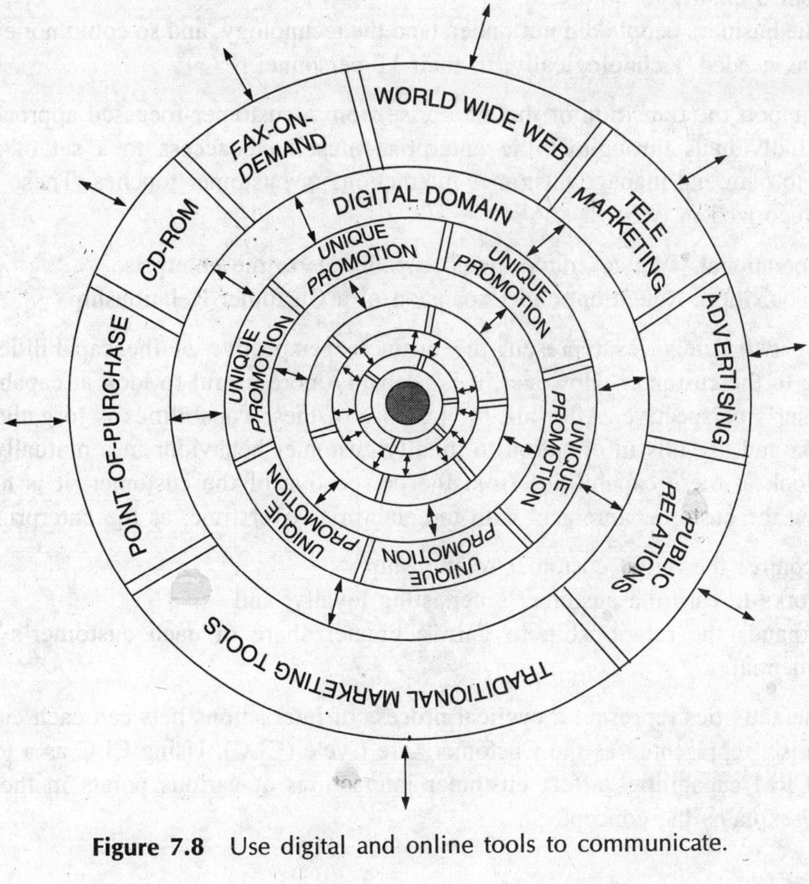

Figure 7.8 Use digital and online tools to communicate.

Customers should not be segmented, based on the assumption that they will predominantly choose one point of contact with business. More likely, customers will have multiple points of contact, including our website, contact centre, sales and field service representatives. They expect a consistent experience from point to point. They expect the company to be easy to do business with.

Very soon, the "e" fancy will subside. Executives in every industry will recognize that the next major phase of the Web phenomenon is actually integration with other points of contact. Blended media is the true killer solution for business.

In the past, if marketers wanted to incorporate technology into their environment, they often looked outside the enterprise for help. Sales frequently outsourced lead management processes, and multiple vendors often managed call centres with information systems completely separated from each other and the enterprise. There were a number of reasons for this, such as the following:

1. Their internal IT department did not understand what was needed.
2. The IT department had other priorities and would take too long to develop the needed technology.
3. The functional areas did not trust their own internal data, believing it to be of too poor a quality to be useful.
4. The business people did not understand the technology, and so could not explain what was needed, technologically, to their IT personnel.

To support the transition of the enterprise from a customer-focussed approach to doing business, individuals throughout the enterprise must have access to a set of capabilities necessary to plan and manage customer interactions or customer touches. These capabilities can be categorized in two ways:

1. Operational, Tactical, or Strategic capabilities to the enterprise
2. Acquisition, Retention, and Expansion of a Customer Relationship

These two categories represent the business perspective of the capabilities and how they relate to the customer. However, it is probably more useful to look at capabilities from the customer's perspective. After all, the purpose of these capabilities is to gather customer information and use this information to modify customer behaviour in a mutually beneficial way. To look at these capabilities from the perspective of the customer, it is necessary to realize how the customer interacts with the enterprise over time, as the enterprise:

1. acquires the initial customer relationship;
2. works to earn the customer's persisting loyalty; and
3. expands the relationship to gain a greater share of each customer's purchasing potential.

These activities represent a cyclical process of interactions between each customer and the enterprise, represented as the Customer Life Cycle (CLC). Using CLC as a tool, we can see how CRM capabilities affect customer interactions at various points in the life cycle. Figure 7.9 explains the concept.

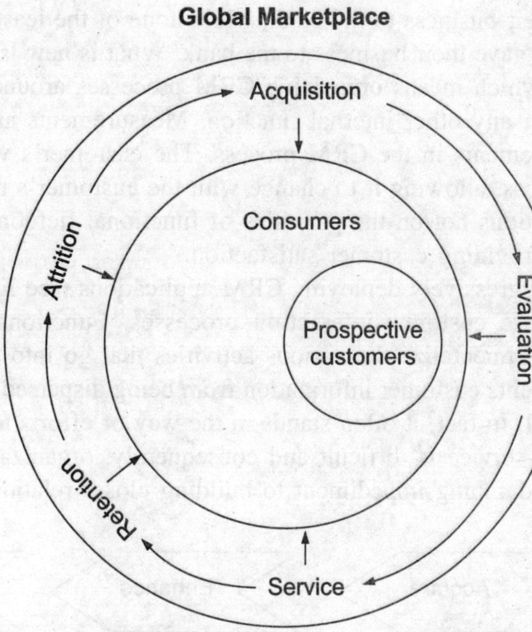

Figure 7.9 Customer life cycle.

CRM Capabilities and the Customer Life Cycle

Customer acquisition consists of the business processes in the CLC leading up to the customer moment, when consumers become customers … or not. This includes *awareness generation, knowledge transfer, consideration, pre-sales, and evaluation*. Capabilities include consumer surveys in business operations, tracking enterprise-wide customer interactions in business management, and market basket analysis in business intelligence. The enterprise clearly requires customer acquisition to maintain and expand revenues and profits. A business without new customer acquisition will shrink and eventually fail. But compared to customer retention and expanding "share of customer", customer acquisition can be expensive.

Expanding the "share of customer" is gaining the largest portion of acquisitions made by each individual customer in the global marketplace. The proportion of a customer's money that goes to a particular enterprise is known as the share of customer. Example capabilities include delivery of new information to a customer through business operations as the customer re-enters the CLC, taking advantage of cross-sell opportunities using business management capabilities, and identifying cross-sell opportunities through business intelligence capabilities. The benefits of expanding "share of customer" are similar to customer retention—additional sales without the cost of acquiring a new customer. However, expanding the share of customer is as valuable as customer retention. Most companies find that their most profitable customers are the ones that spend the largest percentages of their budgets with the enterprise. For example, one bank recently identified that every one of their most profitable customers (the top 20 per cent) gave their business to the bank, while none of the least profitable customers (the bottom 20 per cent) gave their business to the bank. What is new is the customer-centred nature of applications, which means organizing CRM processes around the customer rather than marketing, sales, or any other internal function. Measurements and feedback from the customer enable improvements in the CRM process. The customer's viewpoint becomes an integral part of the process, allowing it to change with the customer's needs. In other words, companies base their actions not on the priorities of functional fiefdoms, but on the overall corporate objective of providing customer satisfaction.

However, before aggressively deploying CRM applications (see Figure 7.10), managers might have to restructure customer-interaction processes. Functional and organizational structures tend to compartmentalize the various activities that go into serving the customer. Such fragmentation prevents customer information from being dispersed far enough within the organization to be useful; in fact, it often stands in the way of efforts to build a relationship. As a result, customized service is difficult and consequently, organizations tend to treat all customers the same—a damning impediment to building closer relationships.

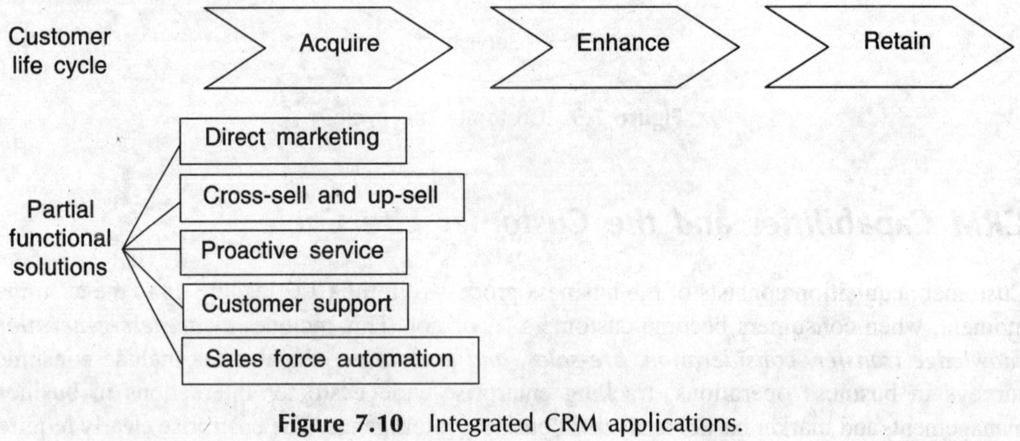

Figure 7.10 Integrated CRM applications.

To counter fragmentation, leading-edge companies strive to take a more customer-centred approach to CRM. There is a growing trend towards managing all the activities that identify, attract, and retain customers in an integrated fashion, that is, managing them as a process that cuts across functional departments. By addressing these activities as a set of CRM processes, organizations can create end-to-end communications and performance accountability for entire sets of activities. In short, a CRM infrastructure is really a portfolio of process competencies.

CRM capabilities supported by Business Operations include:

- Consumer surveys and focus groups
- Delivering information to consumers
- Tracking promotional materials
- Tracking samples
- Managing coupons
- Managing the point of sale

- Billing
- Invoicing
- Fulfilling orders
- Mass customizing products and services

CRM capabilities supported by Business Management include:

- Managing customer touches
- Managing marketing campaigns
- Monitoring marketing campaign performance
- Managing inventory levels
- Driving mass customization
- Managing cross-sell and up-sell opportunities
- Customizing marketing channels, such as the Web
- Personalizing communications
- Driving contact centre scripts
- Capturing key performance metrics

CRM capabilities supported by Business Intelligence include:

- Click stream analysis
- Market basket analysis
- Customer segmentation
- Cross-selling analysis
- Lifetime Customer Value (LTV) analysis
- Recency/Frequency/Monetary (RFM) analysis
- Dimensional "what if" analysis
- Customer profiling
- Cluster analysis
- Factor analysis
- Conjoint analysis
- Discriminant analysis
- Pricing analysis
- Market channel profiling

Each of these capabilities can play a key role in the interaction of the enterprise and the customer. Functions of business operations include some capabilities that are not always associated with CRM, such as billing. But a bill is a regular, predictable customer touch. Why not include a cross-sell offer or product coupon with the bill? Many companies now do this, requiring coordination of billing with CRM capabilities. After all, a consumer who often moves an unsolicited mail directly from the mailbox to the trash can, will nearly always open a bill.

Privacy Issues and CRM

The most sensitive aspect of customer relations is privacy. All of us have boundaries, and don't trust people who become too familiar too soon.

From the business perspective, ubiquitous data and information that flow seamlessly from one touch point to another represents a kind of selflessness, regardless of the business model. The goal of every service-conscious business is to understand not only all customers, but their circumstances as well, and this requires information. In addition to the obvious business opportunities, there are numerous consumer benefits for ready access to personal information, no matter where the location is.

Paradoxically, Internet initially gave the illusion of privacy and anonymity. People could voice their opinions on any subject, view pornography, and read any topic they wanted, without disclosing their identity. However, it was a very short, temporary illusion. In the workplace, e-mails as well as the employees' activities on the Web are often monitored.

There is currently a hot debate over the rights of companies to create dossiers on consumers without their knowledge and then sell the information to third parties. While companies like DoubleClick (*www.DoubleClick.com*) received a lot of media attention for the intentional use of consumer data, other companies such as America Online, which have much more consumer information at their fingertips, have maintained a low profile. America Online, for example, maintains information on 21 million subscribers, including demographics, credit card numbers, and their whereabouts. Although America Online is not currently in the business of selling consumer data, it sells names and addresses to bulk mailers, and buys information about subscribers for targeted advertisements. Some service providers intentionally track subscriber movements with subscribers' knowledge, and sell the information to third parties. Subscribers are given free Internet access and extensive personal profiles.

Tracking consumer-purchasing patterns is not always used with the consumer's best interest in mind. For example, personal tracking data are often used in yield management, a technique designed to maximize revenue and profitability. The idea is that some customers are more profitable than others, especially those placing orders with short lead times. Since suppliers can charge higher prices for orders with short lead times, they reserve capacity for such orders and turn down less profitable, long-range orders. As customers are ranked in terms of profitability and system compatibility, less-profitable customers are deleted from the list and their orders declined. For example, a company may not be able to purchase hotel rooms in bulk for conferences, unless its conferences are to a certain minimum size. This mechanism is great for businesses, but may not be appreciated by some customers.

It is now clear that customer relations are based on a timeless, technology-independent, triad—service, trust, and loyalty. Customers have to trust that a business is working with their best interests in mind. Without trust, which is a major contributor to the emotional bond between a business and its customers, there can be no relationship. Furthermore, even the best intentions are worthless without action. A business must repeatedly provide a valuable, consistent service to prove its customers that the company stands behind its marketing rhetoric. If a business provides its customers with a valuable service and develops a trusting relationship, the business can do all it can to galvanize a loyal customer following.

Data Mining in CRM

Over the past few decades, there has been a constant shift in the way the companies react with their customers. Companies have found that they need to know the customers better, and for that they need to quickly respond to their needs and wants. It is no longer possible to wait until the signs of customer dissatisfaction are obvious, before taking action. To succeed, companies must be proactive and anticipate what a customer desires. This has made the companies to invest heavily into CRM.

To be successful, database marketers must first identify market segments containing customers or prospects with high-profit potential. They then build and execute campaigns that favourably impact the behaviour of these individuals.

The first task, i.e. identifying market segments, requires significant data about prospective customers and their buying behaviours. In practice, massive data stores often impede marketers, who struggle to sift through the minutiae to find the nuggets of valuable information. Data mining applications automate the process of searching the mountains of data to find patterns that are good predictors of purchasing behaviours.

After mining the data, marketers must feed the results into campaign management software that, as the name implies, manages the campaign directed at the defined market segments. In the past, the link between data mining and campaign management software was mostly manual. Successful companies need to react to each and every one of these demands in a timely fashion. The market will not wait for your response, and customers that you have today could vanish tomorrow. Interacting with your customers is also not as simple as it has been in the past. Customers and prospective customers want to interact on their terms, meaning that you need to look at multiple criteria when evaluating how to proceed. You will need to automate the offer, the person, the time and the channel.

The right offer means managing multiple interactions with your customers, prioritizing what the offers will be, while making sure that irrelevant offers are minimized. The right person means that not all customers are cut from the same cloth. Your interactions with them need to move towards highly segmented marketing campaigns that target individual wants and needs. The right time is a result of the fact that interactions with customers now happen on a continuous basis. This is significantly different from the past, when quarterly mailings were cutting-edge marketing. Finally, the right channel means that you can interact with your customers in a variety of ways (direct mail, e-mail, telemarketing, etc.). You need to make sure that you are choosing the most effective medium for a particular interaction.

It is important to realize, though, that data mining is just a part of the overall process but it needs to work with other technologies (for example, data warehousing and marketing automation), as well as with established business practices.

Consider a case where you are a marketing manager for a regional telephone company. You are responsible for managing the relationships with the company's cellular telephone customers. One of your current concerns is customer attention, which has been eating severely into your margins. You understand that the cost of keeping customers around is significantly less than the cost of bringing them back after they leave, so you need to figure out a cost-effective way of doing this.

Instead of providing the customer with something that is proportional to their value to your company (as done traditionally), you should instead be providing the customer with something proportional to your value to them. Give your customers what they need. There are differences between your customers, and you need to understand those differences in order to optimize your relationships. One big spending customer might value the relationship because of your high reliability, and thus would not need a gift in order to continue with it. On the other hand, a customer who takes advantage of all of the latest features and special services might require a new phone or other gift in order to stick around for another year. Or they might simply want a better rate for evening calls because their employer provides the phone and they have to pay for calls outside of business hours. The key is in determining which type of customer you are dealing with.

It is also important to consider timing in this process. You cannot wait until a week before a customer's contract and then pitch them an offer in order to prevent them from churning. By then, they have most likely decided what they are going to do and you are unlikely to affect their decision at such a late date. On the other hand, you do not have to start the process immediately upon signing up a customer. It might be months before they have an understanding of your company's value to them, so any efforts now would also be wasted. The key is finding the correct middle ground, which could very well come from your understanding of your market and the customers in that market. The best way to go about it is to use data mining to automatically find the optimal point.

Clustering and Segmentation Methodology

Customer clustering and segmentation are two of the most important data mining methodologies used in customer-relationship management. They use customer-purchase transaction data to track buying behaviour and create strategic business initiatives. Businesses can use this data to divide customers into segments based on such "shareholder value" variables as current customer profitability, some measure of risk, a measure of the lifetime value of a customer, and retention probability. Creating customer segments based on such variables highlights obvious marketing opportunities.

For example, high-profit, high-value, and low-risk customers are the ones a company wants to keep. This segment typically represents the 10 to 20 per cent of customers who create 50 to 80 per cent of a company's profits. A company would not want to lose these customers, and the strategic initiative for the segment is obviously retention. A low-profit, high-value, and low-risk customer segment is also an attractive one, and the obvious goal here would be to increase profitability for this segment. Cross-selling (selling new products) and up-selling (selling more of what customers currently buy) to this segment are the choices for marketing initiatives.

Within behavioural segments, a business may create demographic subsegments. Customer demographic data does not typically correlate to customer shareholder value, which is why you do not use it together with behavioural data to create segments. However, demographic segmenting can steer marketers into selecting appropriate advertising, marketing channels, and campaigns to satisfy the strategic behavioural segment initiatives.

For example, imagine a bank with a high-profit and a low-profit behavioural customer segment, both of which have a demographic subsegment of young-family, high-income professionals. The marketer would want to ask the following question: Why do these similar demographic segments behave differently, and how do I turn the low-profit group into a high-profit group? It is difficult if not impossible to answer why, but data mining provides an answer to the how. Affinity analysis may reveal that the high-profit group of young, wealthy professionals has a distinct product pattern—mortgages, mutual funds, and credit cards. The low-profit group may have a product pattern that partially fills that of the high-profit group—mutual funds and credit cards. The marketing campaign to increase the profitability of the low-profit segment would thus be to market mortgages to them.

Thus, behavioural clustering and segmentation help derive strategic marketing initiatives by using the variables that determine customer shareholder value. By conducting demographic clustering and segmentation within the behavioural segments, you can define tactical marketing campaigns and select the appropriate marketing channel and advertising for the tactical campaign. It is then possible to target those customers most likely to exhibit the desired behaviour (such as buying a mortgage product, in our bank example) by creating predictive models.

Data mining can be applied to deal with huge customer data. With the results of data mining, one can slice and dice the customer data. Table 7.3 provides the data mining solutions for customer management.

TABLE 7.3 Data Mining Solutions and Customer Management[3]

Data mining task	*Algorithms*	*Business problem*
Classification	Decision trees, Neural network, K-Nearest Neighbour.	Which segments do the customers belong to?
Associations and affinity grouping	Association rule induction.	What-if analysis.
Clustering	Decision trees, K-Nearest Neighbour, Neural networks.	What are some valid ways to segment customers?
Description	Association rule induction, OLAP.	Which variables are important in determining an outcome?

Orbitz

Orbitz, which was founded by a group of big airlines, and its rivals have to make it better still. Some in the industry think that strong competition and negligible buyer loyalty will cause a big shake-out soon. Some of the smaller companies have already been snapped up. Travel makes up the biggest chunk of business-to-consumer e-commerce, accounting for about one-third of online consumer spending. Last year 35 million Americans bought travel online, a 17 per cent increase on 2002, according to the Pho Cus Wright Consumer Travel trends Survey. The survey found that nearly two-thirds of those travellers were happy to buy personal travel either from online agencies or directly from the websites of travel firms, and often used both for different parts of the same trip. The vast majority of customers would consult at least one online travel agency and the website of one supplier before purchasing anything online. Many more people would investigate their travel options online, but then book offline.

3. Morath P., *Success @ e-business*, The McGraw-Hill companies, London, 2000.

Internet travel agents need to entice those browsing to actually book their trips with them, and to get them to buy more of their total travel needs from just one site. One way of doing this is to develop "dynamic packaging". This allows customers to pick all the different elements of their trip from the site, including flights, hotels, hire, local tours, and even tickets to the theatre or sporting events.

In the offline world, such packages have long been put together by tour operators in brochures displayed by travel agents.

What makes a successful travel package comes back to the question of value. It could be the convenience of buying everything in one place, but it could also be the satisfaction of getting a bargain. In packaged deals, the price of the individual components is often opaque. If travellers check the rates of the airlines, hotels and car-hire firms involved, they may sometimes find that, if bought individually, the parts would cost more than the package. This is because packages involve deals between suppliers and travel agents, such as promoting one particular hotel or airline in return for a rate discounted below the lowest advertised price.

Tour operators have been packaging their trips this way for decades. Getting dynamic packaging to work well online for individual consumers is not so straightforward, but the rewards for companies that pull it off could be rich indeed. At present, in America some 20 per cent of travel is bought online. But many in the industry think that travel could become the first big industry with the majority of its sales online, and that the proportion could reach 50 to 70 per cent within a decade. Europe is expected to follow the same pattern, but with a delay of about three years.

If these forecasts prove accurate, they will lead to huge changes in the travel business. Airlines, hotels and car-rental companies were all using computerized reservation systems already, operated by travel agents or telephone-sales reps. Moving these on to the Web did not involve a very big step. After the global slump in travel following the terrorist attacks on September 11, 2001, travel companies were keen to get what business they could from the online agents. Clicking to buy a return flight from Mumbai to London, for instance, is straightforward enough. But a fly-drive holiday from London to India for a family of four, with various hotels, car rental, visit to the Taj Mahal and a return via Kathmandu, may require help from a real person.

Yet the Internet still offers advantages. Having used a website to plan a holiday, a customer is likely to have a fairly good idea of what he wants, by the time he makes that phone call.

Most of the big online travel agents are now also chasing the market for business travel. According to an industry rule of thumb, about 60 per cent of trips are for leisure and 40 per cent for business; but when it comes to expenditure, the ratio is reversed. Many small companies already deal directly with online agents, but for bigger companies booking business travel is a lot more complex than leisure travel.

Business travel is governed by the budgets and rules set by corporate travel departments (such as who gets to fly business class, and in what circumstances), and by discounts negotiated with particular travel suppliers. Nevertheless, with their lower transaction costs, online agents expect to be able to offer cheaper business travel than many offline agents. Some also provide additional services that could be useful for harassed travellers of any kind, business or leisure. For instance, Orbitz employs former air-traffic controllers in its operations centre to keep an eye on potential problems. This means travellers can be alerted to flight delays by e-mail or mobile phone before they set off for the airport.

CRM and Workflow Automation

CRM consists of recording and making available all information pertaining to your customers and using it for effective customer satisfaction. There should be a smooth flow of information from the customer to your organization. This information should be stored in such a way that it is accessible to all concerned people, such as the sales executive, area sales manager, all the way up to the CEO. This makes CRM one of the most critical components of workflow within your organization. It centres around a knowledge base that captures all the customer information.

The information captured contains details on customers at various stages of the customer relationship—suspects, prospects, current and old customers. For each customer, information like the key contacts in the organization, decision makers and their buying cycles, as well as information on each contact is maintained. Basically, all case histories should be easily available.

Figure 7.11 shows how a company's products reach the customers, and the intermediate stages.

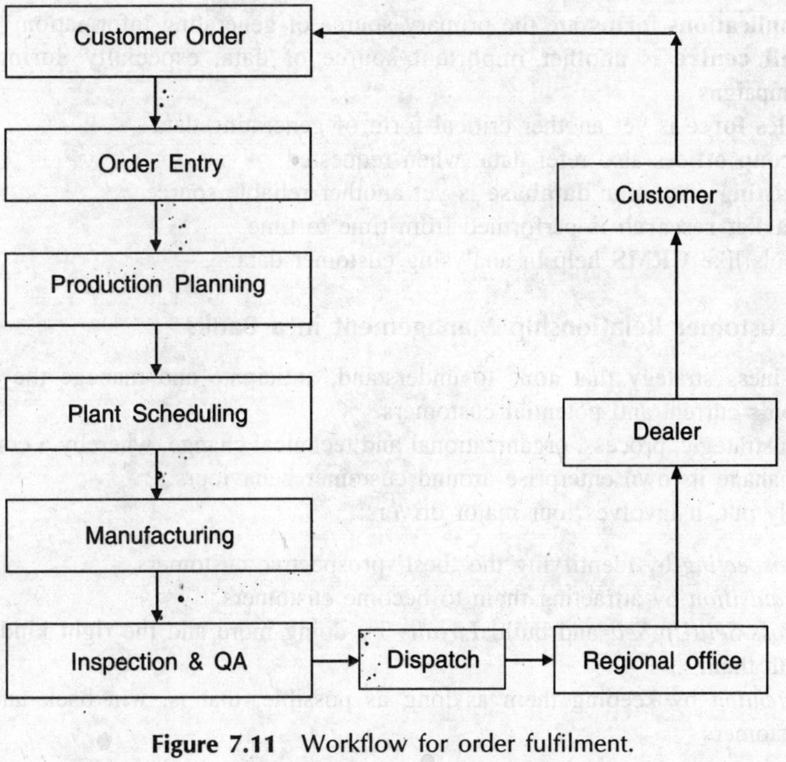

Figure 7.11 Workflow for order fulfilment.

Advanced Planning and Scheduling implies organizing, forecasting and implementing the workflow.

Customer Relationship Management System for a Bank

The scope of Customer Relationship Management System (CRMS) is:

1. Creation of a Web intranet site to manage content and provide a platform for sharing information.
2. Creation of a self-managed cross-functional team.
3. High employee satisfaction.
4. Higher productivity.

CRMS is a tool to help grow the bank's Wealth Management business, better manage the enterprise around customer behaviours and develop products and services to attract, satisfy and retain current and potential customers.

Sources of Data for a CRMS

Almost all facilities are granted to customers based on a detailed understanding of their current circumstances.

- **Applications forms** are the primary source of generating information
- **Call centre** is another important source of data, especially during marketing campaigns
- **Sales force** is yet another critical form of generating data
- **Group offices** also refer data, when requested
- **Existing customer database** is yet another reliable source
- **Market research** is performed from time to time
- Tools like **CRMS** help in analysing customer data.

What is Customer Relationship Management in a Bank?

It is a business strategy that aims to understand, anticipate and manage the needs of an organization's current and potential customers.

It is a strategic, process, organizational and technical change, whereby a company seeks to better manage its own enterprise around customer behaviours.

Simply put, it involves four major drivers:

- *Prospecting* by identifying the 'best' prospective customers
- *Acquisition* by attracting them to become customers
- *Cross-Sell/Up-Sell* and build *Loyalty* by doing more and the right kind of business with them
- *Retention* by keeping them as long as possible, that is, win back and save your customers

Customer Relationship Management is known by different names like 'Total Customer Care', 'Customer Value Management', although globally it is better known by its acronym 'CRM'.

What is Customer Relationship Management System (CRMS)?

The Customer Relationship Management System (CRMS) is a sales support system, developed to further the Bank's personal banking wealth management initiatives. This system is a tool for Customer Service Representatives (CSRs) and Relationship Managers (RMs) aid in the ***sales process***. CRMS drives a more 'customer centric' behaviour, thus helping us deepen relationships with our customers.

CRMS provides:

- Consolidated 'Overview' screen
- Customer 'Demographic' screen
- 'Contact History' screen
- Product 'Cross Sell Opportunities'
- A 'sales referral system' to grow our business with group offices
- Transaction and account details
- Online tracking of sales activity
- Sales/leads reports
- An intranet site (CNS) to view product information
- Update details of customer interactions.

When to Use CRMS?

CRMS is used as a principal tool for servicing customers such as:

- Account-related enquiries
- Transaction history enquiries
- Product campaign enquiries

This in turn can lead to:

- Discussion of customer's needs
- Cross-sell other products and services

The basic objective of CRMS was to manage the sales automation and provide elementary relationship management tools. The system provided functionalities which included an overview of the customer's current relationship, cross-sell opportunities based on a product gap analysis, creating leads and closing sales, scheduling tasks, contact management, notes and sharing of information, referring business to other departments or entities, receiving referrals from the call centre and other businesses.

The problems associated with implementing a CRM are:

- Lack of understanding of CRM—the bank's mission and objectives
- Lack of customer management (customer-centric)
- Variances in application of business processes
- Lack of data integrity and completeness
- Lack of the sales process and how CRMS helps deliver this
- Lack of complete knowledge the functionalities available on the system
- Lack of support infrastructure

The demands of the system to achieve effectiveness are:

- Redesign processes and communicate this efficiently
- Create awareness about CRM practices and its effective usage
- Encourage users to effectively record all contacts and sales
- Provide a recognition platform for the high performers
- Provide clearer communication regarding support
- Address standard questions/problems faced by users

The content information of the CRMS comprises:

- Mission Statement
- Meet the Team (message from senior management)
- What is Customer Relationship Management?
- What is CRMS and how does it fit into the Group's Sales process?
- Business Process Guides
- Roles and Responsibilities Guide for Users
- Problem Reporting Procedures
- CRMS High Fliers
- FAQ
- Glossary

Figure 7.12 shows the workflow in a banking CRM situation.

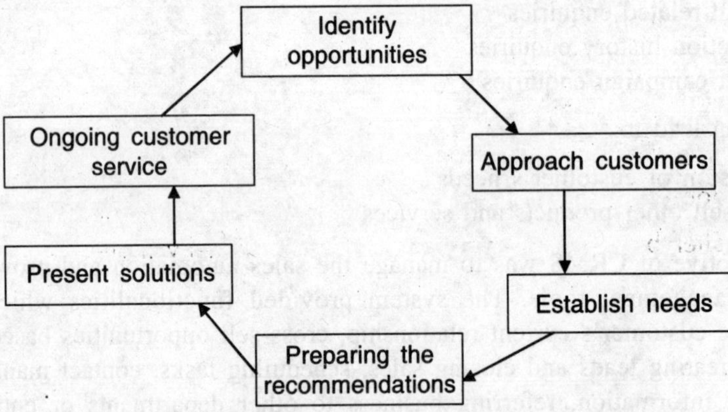

Figure 7.12 Workflow in a banking CRM situation.

Figure 7.13 shows a sales flowchart for a customer enquiry.

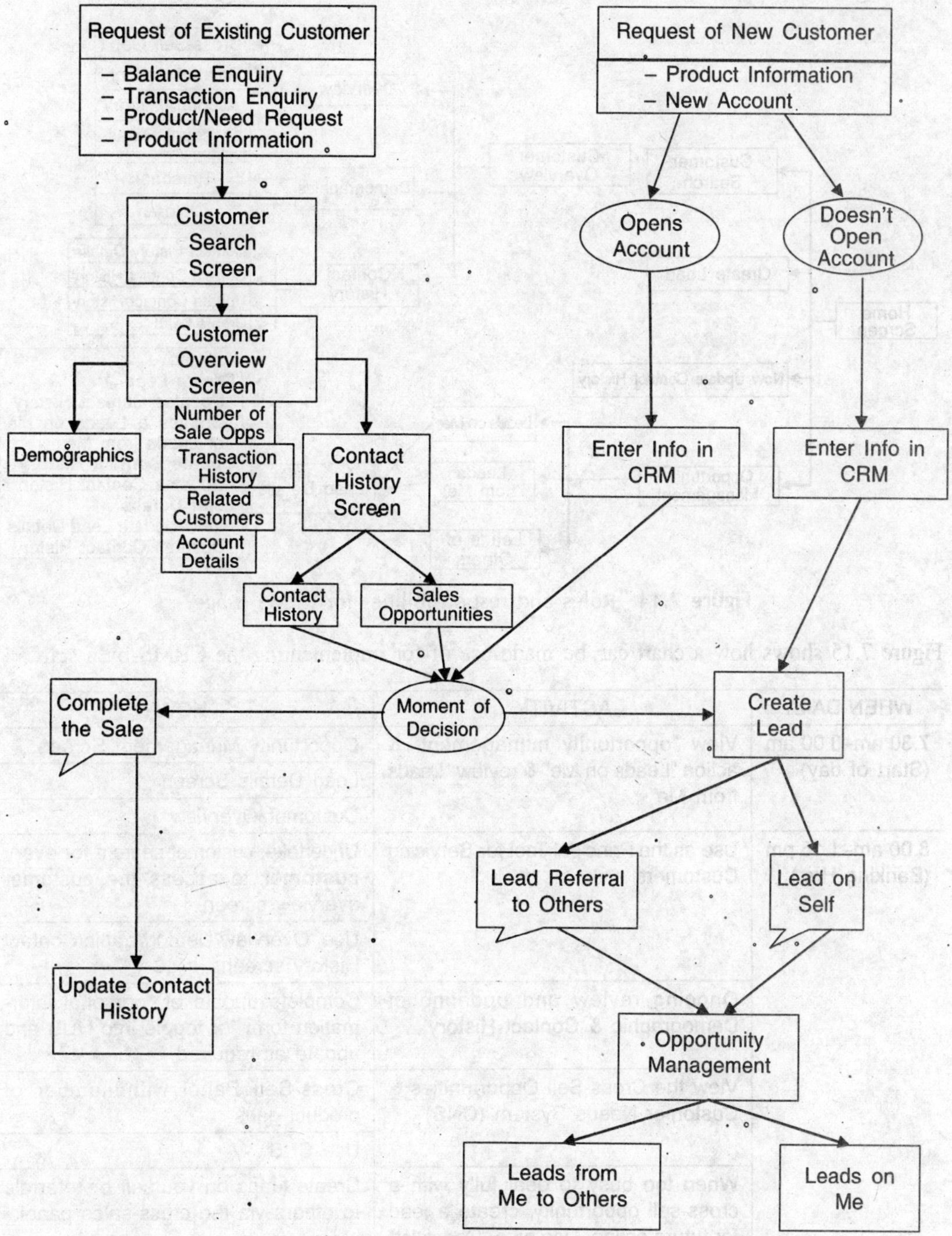

Figure 7.13 CRMS—sales flowchart.

Figure 7.14 shows the roles and responsibilities for CRMS usage.

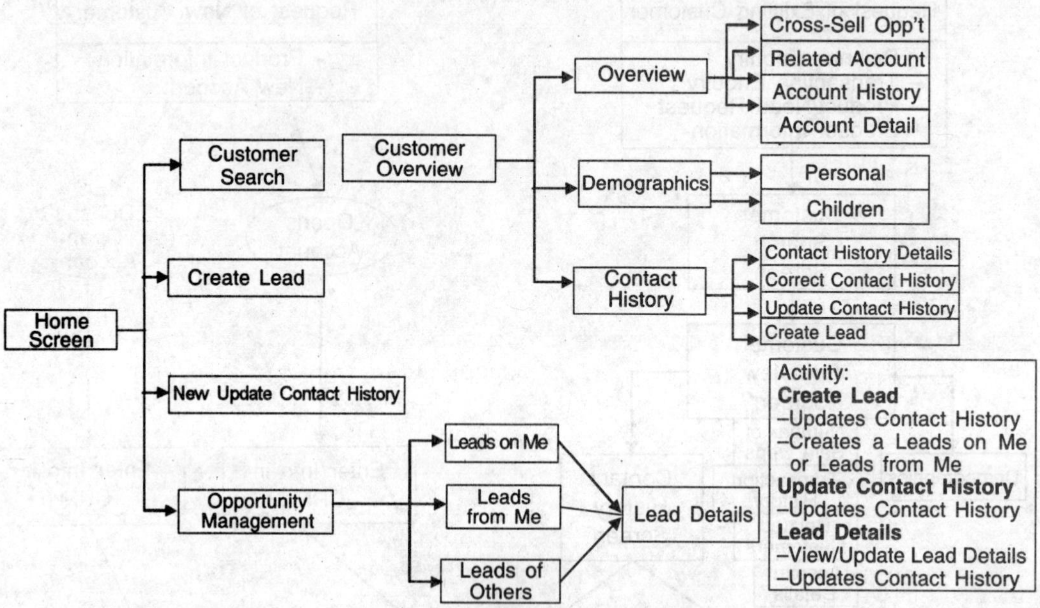

Figure 7.14 Roles and responsibilities for CRMS usage.

Figure 7.15 shows how a chart can be made use of for implementing the CRMS by a staff.

WHEN-DAILY	ACTIVITY	HOW
7.30 am–8.00 am (Start of day)	View "opportunity management" & action "Leads on Me" & review "Leads from Me"	Opportunity Management Screen
		Lead Details Screen
		Customer Overview
8.00 am–1.15 pm (Banking Hrs.)	Use as the Principal Tool for Servicing Customers	Undertake "customer search" **for every customer** to access the customer overview screen
		Use Overview/Demographic/Contact History screens
	Ongoing review and updating of Demographic & Contact History	Complete update of "personal information form" or toggle into HUB and update as required
	View the Cross-Sell Opportunities & Customer Needs System (CNS)	Cross-Sell Panel with number of product gaps
		Use CNS
	When too busy to deal fully with a cross-sell opportunity, create a lead for future action. Use as a "Checklist" for customer product sales by creating appropriate leads **at that time.**	Create leads on yourself or referrals to others via the cross-sales panel

Figure 7.15 Chart to be made use of by a staff member for implementing the CRMS (*Contd.*).

WHEN-DAILY	ACTIVITY	HOW
	Deepen knowledge of the customer by recording relevant information	On the "Overview Screen", record the "Preferred Name, Language and Notes" and use the "Update Contact History" Screen
1.15 pm–3.30 pm	**Review** "checklist" of activities for yourself & others and **update** as required	Open Opportunity Management, action Leads On Me and Leads From Me
	Review leads created during the day to identify any other potential sales opportunities	Review Overview/Demographic/ Contact History
WHEN-WEEKLY	**ACTIVITY**	**HOW**
	Record sales performance	Transfer sales figures from CRMS weekly sales reports onto the individual "Recording Success" worksheet
	Review activity performance against targets	Review Sales Report in preparation for the Weekly Business Development Meetings
WHEN-WEEKLY	**ACTIVITY**	**HOW**
	Review activity and sales performance against target for each product	Review Individual Activity and Sales Performance Spreadsheet in preparation for a one-to-one discussion with your line manager

Figure 7.15 Chart to be made use of by a staff member for implementing the CRMS.

Indianrail.gov.in

This official site of INDIAN RAILWAYS is hosted by the Centre for Railway Information Systems (CRIS), under the Ministry of Railways, Government of India. Launched on January 5, 1999, it has emerged as one of the most accessed websites in India. The site deals with all the information required by the customers—covering the passengers, the suppliers, the contractors, etc.

This site is the direct interface between the Railway Administration and the common citizens of India.

Features Covered in the Site

Although the site is open to all concerned for any relevant information, it can be divided into different sections depending upon the segment of society they cater to specifically. These are as follows:

1. PASSENGER-RELATED FEATURES

Reservation Status This link gives details regarding the following:

• Passenger status	Whether wait-listed or confirmed
• Train schedule	The scheduled departure and arrival timings of the trains

Passenger Info This link gives general information related to journey planning, like:

• Station, Class, Quota, Codes	This is required while booking a ticket for a journey
• International tourists	The location of International Tourist Bureaus in important cities and the special tour plans available to foreign and NRI tourists
• Season tickets	The details including fares for the benefit of students, office-goers and the business community
• Tatkal service	One of the most successful schemes launched to facilitate those who have to move at a very short notice

Passenger Services This link gives guidelines regarding the different types of services available on rail, besides others details like:

• Facilities to passengers on board	Accommodation, luggage, catering, medical, bed-rolls, etc.
• The different types of quotas	The quotas like defence, handicapped, senior citizens, etc.
• Rules for reservation	The general details which are to be kept in mind by the passengers, including some statutory provisions of the Railways Act
• Details regarding special tourist trains	Includes details of special tourist trains like Royal orient trains, Shivalik. Delux Train and the "Toy Trains" connecting the hill stations
• Accident compensation claims	The terms and condition for compensation for passengers involved in any mishap

Time Table This link has features which help the passengers to plan their journey.

- Train/Fare Accommodation
- Trains between important stations
- Fare

Citizens' Charter on Passenger Services This link provides details to the common man regarding the rights of a travelling passenger. It is worth noting that most of the people are not aware of this Charter at all. It also gives detailed information regarding the obligations of the Railways with respect to the different services provided.

FAQs for Passengers This link answers a wide range of queries of an ordinary passenger.

Feedback and Complaints This section obtains feedback and complaints regarding the services by the passengers in specific and the citizens in general.

2. *FEATURES FOR THE COMMON PUBLIC*

About Us There are lots of things about the Railways which the ordinary citizens are not aware of. Detailed information regarding the following topics is given in this link:

- The Indian Railways System
- Planning
- The activities of the different department of the Railways
- Passenger Business
- Freight Operations
- Utilization of Assets
- Safety
- Research and Development
- Statistical Summary
- Organizational Structure

3. *INFORMATION FOR THE INDUSTRY*

Railway Budget It gives details of the Railway Budget for the current financial year. The information and provisions mentioned in it are of immense use to people related to industry, academics, trade and commerce, besides the common citizen.

Status Paper It presents the current status of the Indian Railways in the current economic scenario. It analyses the impact of the current trends after 5 to 10 years, and tries to explore the possibilities to expand and compete with the road transport sector in addition to making substantial profits on its own.

4. *INFORMATION FOR THE RAILWAY SUPPLIERS/CONTRACTORS*

Purchase and Tenders This includes the details of the existing and the pending tenders and contracts for supply of materials to the different units of Railways or for important projects.

5. *INFORMATION FOR THE RAILWAYMEN*

Internal Information for the Employees This link has a limited access and contains the latest guidelines circulars and orders issued by the Railway Board (Ministry of Railways) for the railway employees.

6. *LINKS TO OTHER RAILWAY-RELATED SITES*

There are a number of links of other sites of Indian Railways, like:

- Production Units
- Zonal/Metro Railways
- Public Sector Undertakings (e.g. IRCON, CONCOR, Delhi Metro, Konkan Railway)
- Heritage Sites
- Other sites directly under Ministry of Railways

Case Discussion

1. Log on to the railway site and look at all the customer-service functions that they offer?
2. Though *indianrail.gov.in* is a site that is accessed by many, why are railways not doing any advertising business on the site?
3. Can the railways build a community model on their site?

EXERCISES

1. Describe the typical profile of the Internet users.
2. Describe the purchasing decision-making process on the Web.
3. Explain the concept of customer loyalty and how to increase it using the Web.
4. Enter *amazon.com* and identify all customer services provided for free.
5. Go over a market research website, such as *www.acnielsen.com*, and discuss what might motivate a consumer to provide answers to your queries.
6. Surf *www.e-land.com* and list the types of consumer information you can collect from the site.
7. Enter *www.firefly.net* and share your experiences about how the information you provide might be used by the company for marketing a specific domain.
8. Access the Indian Railways site *indianrail.gov.in* and look at all the customer focus the site has.
9. After navigating the naukri.com site, suggest ways to improve customer service for this site.

CHAPTER

8

e-Supply Chain Management

LEARNING OBJECTIVES

After reading this chapter, you should be able to:

- ➠ Understand the importance of supply chain management.
- ➠ Know how technologoy helps in supply chain management.
- ➠ Understand the benefits of E-SCM.
- ➠ Learn about the major trends in E-SCM.

e-Supply Chain at CISCO

Cisco Systems, Inc. is the worldwide leader in networking for the Internet. Cisco's hardware and software solutions are used to link computers and computer networks so people have easy access to information—regardless of differences in time, place, or type of computer system. Customers benefit from Cisco networking solutions through more efficient exchange of information, which in turn leads to cost savings, process efficiencies, and closer relationships with customers, prospects, business partners, suppliers, and employees. Cisco solutions are the networking foundation for companies, universities, utilities, and government agencies worldwide.

The Company was founded in late 1984 by a small group of computer scientists from Stanford University seeking an easier way to connect different types of computer systems. Cisco Systems shipped its first product in 1986. Since then, Cisco has grown into a multinational corporation with over 47,000 employees in more than 200 offices in 54 countries.

Cisco's products encompass the broadest range of networking solutions available from any single supplier. These solutions include routers, LAN and WAN switches, dial and other access solutions, SNA-LAN integration solutions, Website management tools, Internet appliances, and network management software. The thread that ties these products together is the Cisco IOS™ software platform, which delivers network services and enables networked applications. Cisco's offerings also include industry-leading customer services for network design, implementation, maintenance, and support.

Cisco has been at the heart of many historic changes in technology, and that continues to be true today. Now, at a time when the technology industry is going through a period of dramatic change, Cisco is the market leader in multiple areas, such as routing and switching, unified communications, wireless and security. The company helped catalyze the industry's move toward IP and, now that it is fully underway, the company is at the centre of fundamental changes in the way the world communicates.

The emergence of the network as a platform is changing the entire value chain of technology and placing the network squarely at the centre of innovation: as many as 14 billion devices will be connected to the Internet by 2010. The explosion of devices will be fuelled by more and more services and tasks being handled online, from phone calls to personalized searches to downloading videos, games and other forms of entertainment.

The role of the network is evolving beyond that of infrastructure. It is emerging as a secure platform for delivering the customized and personalized experience that 21st century users expect—whether that means delivering new services as a carrier, boosting productivity for businesses of any size or consumers looking for real-time, personalized entertainment and services.

Cisco is leading the transition to a network-centric technology environment. By combining its core strength (IP) with intelligence, the company is creating a powerful communications platform that will serve as the basis for the convergence of data, voice, video and mobile communications in a secure, integrated architecture.

Below are three examples of how the transition to a network-centric architecture is having profound and dramatic effect on entire industries:

1. ***IP communications and IP video.*** Communications networks are going through a transformation empowered by the Internet and networking technology. When the Internet was at its earliest stages as a business and consumer tool, Cisco had a vision for how IP technology would transform voice and video communications. In 1998, Cisco acquired a small Voice over Internet Protocol (VoIP) company and began developing this technology. Today Cisco is the global leader in IP communications equipment, selling over 7.5 million IP phones worldwide, including to more than 70 per cent of Fortune 500 companies. Now Cisco is building on that leadership to develop IP-based video technologies to transform the way video content is delivered to the home and within companies. We are aggressively moving into a new realm of IP, with the promise of IPTV on the horizon, and pervasive video on the Internet.
2. ***Emergency responder communications.*** Cisco has developed IP-based technology that addresses today's voice communications interoperability requirement, enabling communications across any type of device, whether push-to-talk (radio) systems, cell phones or landline phones. This technology, called IPICS (IP Interoperability and Collaboration System) is now being field tested in several locations in the United States. This is one of the industry's first systems designed to easily integrate disparate push-to-talk radio systems together with widely deployed voice, video and data networks. One of the most promising features of the IPICS technology

is it can enable preexisting communications systems to interoperate, eliminating the need to completely replace deployed systems. Cisco IPICS delivers the "right information to the right person in the right format at the right time."

3. ***Health care information technology.*** Quality health care is one of our most vital national needs. There is a growing consensus that our health care system is outdated, inefficient, and most worrisome, prone to errors. The Bush Administration has worked to modernize the health care system through electronic health records and information sharing that will improve the quality of health care and reduce costs. Cisco has taken a leadership position in driving this change. First, it has developed the technologies that enable the networking of health information. Second, it is helping create regional and national health data networks that will enable information sharing so that critical patient information is available to health care providers in a timely fashion. Finally, Cisco is practicing what it preaches by adopting health care IT within its own health programs and creating incentives for employees' doctors to modernize their systems.

Research and Development

Cisco innovates in many different ways: via technology development and the expansion of technologies after their initial invention, and through adjacent technology and market extension. We also innovate through world-class integration and scaling of acquisitions, by starting new business models, and in the way we partner with other companies.

Linksys Takes Cisco Into the Home

Cisco has extended its networking technology expertise in the enterprise and service provider markets into the high-growth consumer networking market with the addition of its Linksys Division in June 2003.

Linksys has the most extensive product line in home networking, with more than 70 products including wireless routers and access points for simultaneous sharing of broadband Internet connections, wireless network adapters and wireless print servers as well as traditional wired products such as Ethernet routers and cable modems, unmanaged switches and hubs, print servers and network attached storage for easy sharing of digital music, photo and video media files.

With Cisco's networking expertise and Linksys' user-friendly features, consumer and small medium business (SMB) users will be able to build high quality networks designed for the home or small office environment. A home network enables families to better utilize their broadband Internet connections by offering the ability to share Internet access using either wired or wireless connections.

Case Discussion

1. Discuss the innovative features CISCO has adopted to be a market leaders.
2. How are knowledge assets made use of in CISCO?
3. How was e-supply chain management innovated by CISCO?

E-commerce is slowly affecting the distribution channels through which consumers and businesses have traditionally bought and sold goods and services. The online channel provides sellers with the ability to reach a global audience and operate with minimal infrastructure, reduced overheads, and greater economies of scale, while providing consumers with a broad selection and unparalleled convenience. As a result, a growing number of consumers do business transactions on the Web, such as buying products, trading securities, paying bills, and purchasing airline tickets. Essentially, e-commerce is all about the transactional business process of selling and buying via the Internet. **e-Supply Chain** refers in particular to the management of supply chain, using the Internet technologies.

Communication is in real time and data can be integrated with back office systems, reducing paperwork. Using the Web to eliminate paper transactions can generate substantial savings of cost and time. It facilitates the removal of purchase orders, delivery confirmations, bills of material and invoices. The switch away from paper can also speed up response and improve communications with those in different time zones or who work outside normal office hours, such as a customer's night shift supervisor. Another significant potential benefit is a reduction in the errors associated with activities such as re-keying data, receiving orders by telephone calls and handwritten faxes.

The Web permits improvements in both procurement and fulfilment, particularly in terms of stock availability and on-time delivery. Visibility throughout the entire supply must be completely transparent to achieve full customer satisfaction and leverage the full benefits of e-logistics. This is achieved through the movement of information in tandem with goods and services. Customers thus have complete real-time consignment status information over the Web, while suppliers and delivery companies can save on the staff time previously devoted to answering queries on order status. This is an essential difference between 'old economy' and 'new economy' logistics. The challenges posed by greater inventory pipeline visibility are not just technical in nature, they also include issues concerning openness and partnership relations. Collaboration is necessary for more precise forecasting, scheduling and resource planning.

At the warehouse and distribution level, facilities must provide inventory control at the individual shipment or even item level. Distribution and warehouse centres must have the flexibility to meet the diverse requirements of customers. This need for flexibility and adaptability is further driven by new forms of international competition, increasing levels of globalisation that mean ever-changing customer requirements. Again, inventory visibility and information transparency in the e-logistics system are the keys to success. e-logistics also improves the delivery of goods and services at reduced cost through development of methods for supply chain management, including advances in data management, and increasingly sophisticated planning and scheduling systems.

Just in Time (JIT) production has been around for decades but traditionally has mainly been used when supplying a relatively small number of customers. Information Technology now makes it possible to overcome the administrative problems associated with building large numbers of individual orders on a JIT basis. In some sectors, this will facilitate a move towards the system, epitomised by Dell, of building products to order, in a high volume plant, and shipping them direct to the end user. Real value emerges from the combination of the e-logistics system with other information technology-based processes such as MRP or ERP, and market information and customer data systems. In addition, the integration of a company's computerised Management Information Systems with its logistics software and data facilitates the analysis of buying and selling patterns to serve customers better and cut costs.

The amalgamation of supply chain management and customer relationship management can radically improve competitiveness. Cost reductions and customer service enhancements occur in conjunction with each other, rather than being mutually exclusive as assumed in 'old economy' strategic thinking. The objective of the right product in the right place at the right time and cost is accommodated to a greater extent than previously possible.

e-logistics enables organizations to see the big picture by capturing and sifting through data for procurement and fulfilment. Ultimately, management of the entire supply chain is e-enabled, and logistics-generated data can feed back into strategic and tactical decisions made by other parts of the organization. The Internet ultimately provides access to true rather than forecasted supply and demand information. E-logistics also permits a closer integration of a company's internal business systems with collaborative information from partners and Web-based functions and information. In essence, e-logistics represents the foundation for improved business processes, allowing for real-time visibility, seamless channel linkage and collaborative solutions in the supply chain.

e-business communities can target new markets by offering low entry costs, relatively minimal complexity with more flexibility and a convenient way of transacting business. The trend of outsourcing and strategic alliances in most industries provides an added impetus to support the sharing of supplier, customer, and corporate information, that was once proprietary with competitors and other cross-industry players. Businesses today are finding themselves in an environment in which unprecedented information-sharing among all participants is driving fundamental changes in the interactions, business practices, and operations of everyone involved (see Figure 8.1).

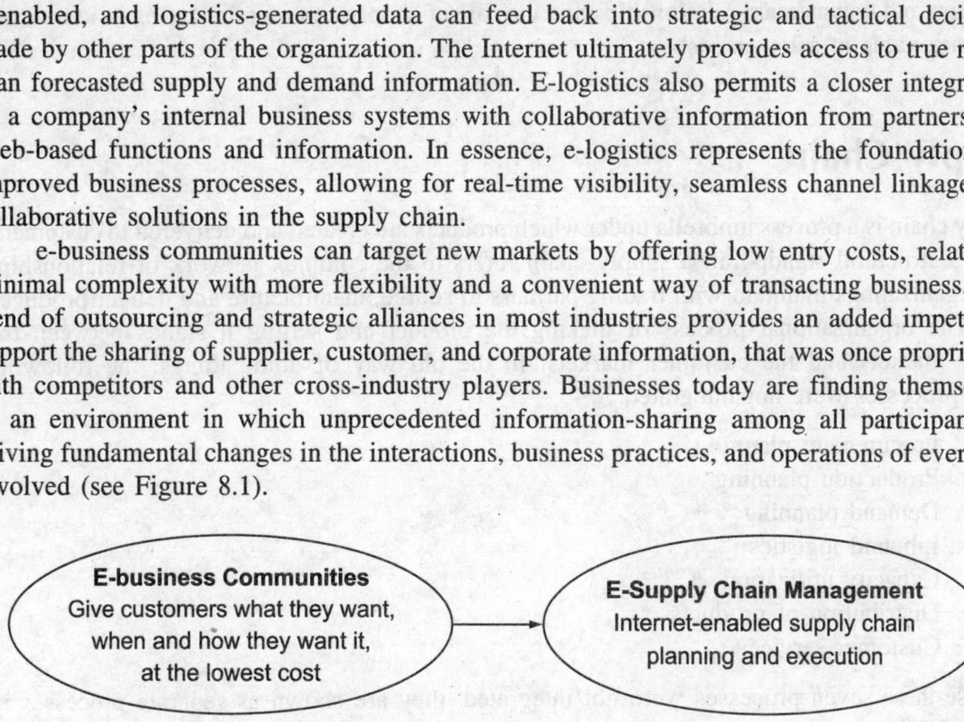

Figure 8.1 e-SCM—value proposition.

One needs only to consider the recent collaboration between the "big three" auto makers in the USA in launching the automotive network exchange (ANX), to further understand the impending effects of electronic business communities. ANX will establish a standard method for parts suppliers to communicate with and obtain order information from the auto manufacturers. The potential result will be a lower cost structure for the entire auto industry, in which all participants will benefit. At the same time, such benefits will greatly modify the competitive strategies and interactions among all participants. It is a Web-based relationship in the supply chain. The growth of Web-based e-commerce has generated a number of approaches for creating a model of how it impacts business.

Business partners and customers connect together through the Internet to participate in commercial trading and participate in communications and interaction. Each of these areas has a set of strategic activities and issues. Opportunities for creating values occur in each of these. Compared to logistics, the discipline it developed from, Supply Chain Management (SCM) is a relatively new term. While overall logistical concepts have been around for many centuries, SCM did not make its appearance in the literature until the last decade. For a long time, logistics was a concept limited to the military sector, and it is only since the middle of the 20th century that logistics has come to be accepted in the business sector. Today, SCM may be described as the integrated management approach for planning and controlling the flow of materials from suppliers, through the distribution channel, to the end user. Compared to the internal focus of traditional logistic approaches, SCM emphasizes the management of upstream and downstream relationships and the role of supply chain optimization in increasing customer value at a lower cost.

Supply Chain

Supply chain is a process umbrella under which products are created and delivered to customers. From a structural standpoint, a supply chain refers to the complex network of relationships that organizations maintain with trading partners to source, manufacture and deliver products.

The organizational process of making the product and selling it stands between the supply markets and the customer markets. In the old way of doing things, the following seven processes were not integrated:

1. Procurement planning
2. Production planning
3. Demand planning
4. Inbound logistics
5. Capacity utilization
6. Distribution of products
7. Customer service

Because these seven processes were not integrated, they are shown as separate processes in Figure 8.2.

The New Way

The flow of materials and information through a business, from the initial purchasing function through the operation and eventually to the customers, is known as the supply chain.

The concept of SCM is a holistic view of coordinating functions that transfer data and material resources from the suppliers to consumers in the finished form to make the process efficient and cost effective. The importance of e-commerce to manufacturing and distribution is undoubtedly a part of SCM. If high speed, low cost, communication and collaboration with customers and suppliers are critical success factors for effective SCM, then the e-chain is the future. Let us visualize the new way of managing the supply chain as in Figure 8.3.

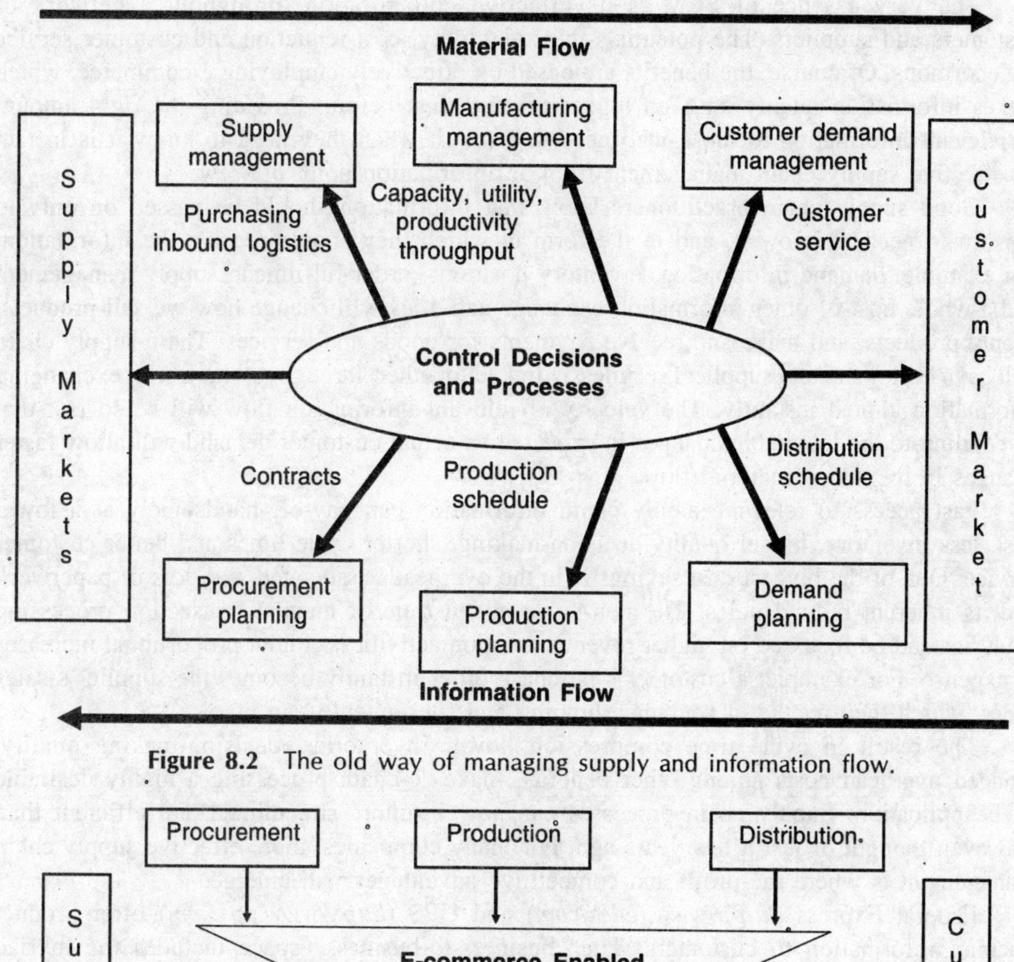

Figure 8.2 The old way of managing supply and information flow.

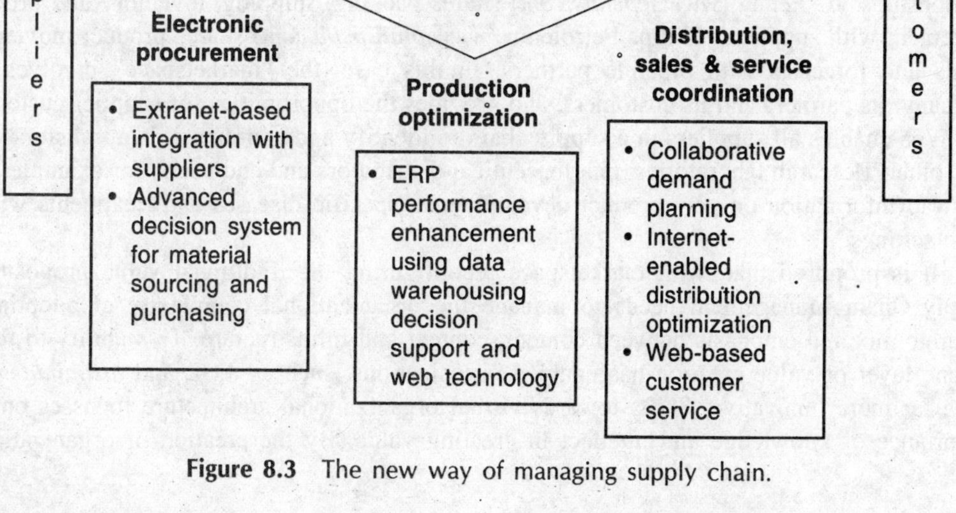

Figure 8.3 The new way of managing supply chain.

The very essence of SCM is its effective collaboration throughout a network of customers and suppliers. The potentials in productivity, cost reduction and customer service are enormous. Of course, the benefits are based on effectively employing e-commerce, which makes information quality an even higher priority than before. Providing the right amount of relevant information to those who need to know it when they need to know it is in fact an effective supply chain management from an information point of view.

Good supply chain practitioners know that information should be passed on only to those who need to know it, and in the form in which they should receive the information. For example, demand information, inventory positions, order-fulfilment, supply management and a whole host of other information exchange activities will change how we sell products, supply products, and make and receive payments for goods and services. The e-supply chain will have customers and suppliers seamlessly linked together, throughout the world, exchanging information almost instantly. The velocity of relevant information flow will be so fast that responding to the inevitable changes in expected vs actual customer demand will allow faster changes in the actual material flow.

Fast access to relevant supply chain information can pay-off handsomely at a lower cost, less inventory, higher quality decision-making, shorter cycle times and better customer service. One of the biggest cost savings is in the overheads associated with lots of paperwork and its inherent redundancies. The non-value added time of manual transaction processing could instead be focussed on higher revenue creation activities without proportional increases in expense. For example, a customer's purchase order instantly becomes the supplier's sales order, which then results in packing, shipping and subsequently, an invoice.

The result in cycle time compression, lower inventories, decision-making quality, reduced overhead costs among other benefits, makes e-chain processing a highly desirable Web application. Supply chain processes can now be more streamlined and efficient than was even thought of just a few years ago. For many companies, more effective supply chain management is where the profit and competitive advantages will emerge.

Federal Express (*http://www.fedex.com*) and UPS (*http://www.ups.com*) offer product tracking information to customers. The "business-to-business" space includes the myriad upstream and downstream transactions that can enhance channel coordination and customer relationships. JC Penny (*www.jcpenny.com*) shares packing, shipping, inventory and product movement with suppliers. Philips Petroleum (*www.phillipsbb.com*) shares product movement trends and forecasts with pipeline partners. In this case, the "marketspace" involves the company, its partners and its customers, and provides the opportunities for supplier customer. The Web enables all suppliers in a supply chain to identify and coordinate data transfers with each other. Research laboratories, pharmaceutical distributors and end-users, for example, can all swap information on new product developments, specific diseases and treatments within these settings.

It is proposed that, with marketspace reconfiguring the traditional value proposition, Supply Chain Management needs to manage the organizational complexity of adopting a dynamic mix and emphasis between content, context and infrastructure. This ability to focus on one layer of value creation has enabled organizations, such as AOL and *lastminute.com* to be far more innovative. Shifts towards virtual organizational architecture focusses on the importance of knowledge and intellect in creating value. By the creation of organizational integration mechanisms on the Internet, such as discussion groups, Web forums and video conferencing, virtual multi-functional teams become enablers of the three independent vectors. The process of innovation, with the adoption of an integrated approach throughout the supply chain, requires a trade-off between autonomy and control, of which the balance decided upon is unique to partner relationships.

The organizational challenge of reaching an acceptable balance between autonomy and control is probably best achieved by the idea of subtle control. The "players" must have access to a wide range of external technological services, such as the Internet and other complementary online networks, in order to operate effectively. They must have access to electronic capabilities using fibre optics, high-speed digital switches, satellite downlinks and compatible EDI ensuring reliable, efficient information flows among suppliers, manufacturers, and distributors while protecting proprietary data. Shared resources, such as harmonised electronic transfer across transportation modes and onsite education and training facilities will also help companies improve their SCM in the emerging marketspace. Even small and medium-sized enterprises now increasingly rely on international networks of suppliers, distributors and customers, frequently via the Internet, to improve their global competitiveness by reducing fixed and operating costs.

Individualization of both product and process driven innovation requires high levels of organizational integration in being able to respond to market demands. Integration along the supply chain in the virtual market can be viewed as being a mix of both formal and loose integration mechanisms, similar to the Internet infrastructure. A common theme which is identified as important to organizations in the development of creativity and innovation, is the relevance of both technological and organizational integration.

Three types of 'Nets' are used to support the e-supply chain. One of them is the Intranet. An Intranet is an internal network maintained within the boundaries of a company. The second type of Net is the Extranet, which connects participating companies, be they customers or suppliers. Here, a customer could have access to the ERP system to know, for instance, his order status, while the supplier could access inventory data to support the automatic replenishment process. The third type of Net is the Internet, which is open to the general public. Using the Internet, a company could publicize its products/services and also accept online orders from its customers.

SCM systems will be substantially altered in terms of strategy, process, and system. Mistakes here could prove very costly in the near and longer terms. E-commerce has and will continue to redefine how companies will compete for customers. While e-commerce offers some exciting opportunities to improve SCM effectiveness by lowering the costs and increasing the speed of order-to-delivery, it is by no means the first stop on the right path to having highly competitive e-supply chain capabilities.

Before taking a big leap into the e-supply chain, companies need to know why they are taking the leap. They need to fulfil the objectives of SCM as illustrated in Figure 8.4. By no means should any company perform the common leap into the latest technology without getting thorough and appropriate answers to questions such as the following:

1. What business opportunities are available for us to improve market presence, sales, cost of operation, service, communication, cycle time, supply-base management, and so on?

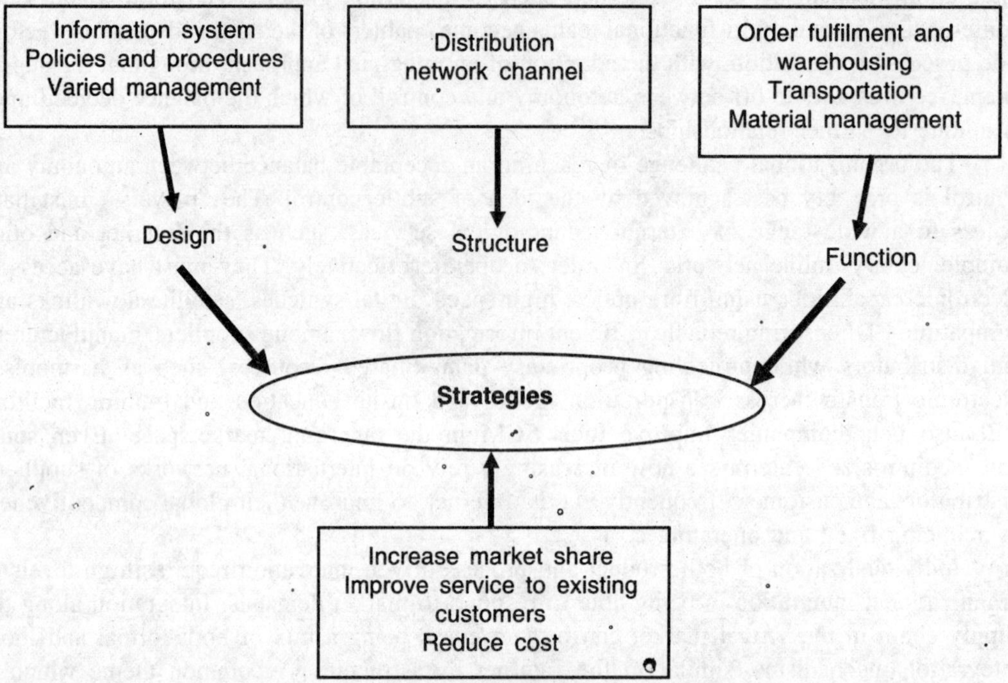

Figure 8.4 Objectives of supply chain management.

2. Do we know and understand our supply chain priorities?
3. How should we structure Web-enabled linkages with our customers and suppliers for pre-eminent supply chain performance?
4. What e-supply chain approaches can we appropriately invest in for near and longer-term business performance gains?
5. Do we have an executive-level champion providing the necessary linkage to top management for effective implementation of e-supply chain management?
6. Have we carefully defined an action plan for pre-implementation preparation activities?
7. What are the missing technical links in our current system or our choice of software?
8. What planning and implementation tasks will be accomplished and when?
9. Do we understand the real benefits of an e-supply chain versus the cost to develop?
10. What e-supply chain strategy will give us the leverage to transform ourselves into marketplace leaders?

Undoubtedly, spending time in the upfront strategy development to improve order-to-delivery cycle and supply chain management will pay big dividends. The hard part is the prerequisite tasks of discovering and thinking through supply chain opportunities and then developing a strategy and plan for an e-supply chain that will improve a company's performance more than its competitors. But without an e-supply chain roadmap, the direction taken may not take the company to its desired destination. The biggest loss of missing the target can never be regained. It is essential to do it right the first time.

In these days of ERP, information technology and other high-tech systems, the tips presented here may seem too simple. These things are simpler to talk about than to actually execute. But put into effect, their pay off can be tremendous.

e-logistics of UPS

United Parcel Service has introduced UPS e-logistics, a provider of integrated, end-to-end supply chain management packages for e-business. UPS e-logistics is marrying the expertise of its partners Oracle, PriceWaterhouseCoopers and EXE Technologies with its global fulfilment and distribution network, information technology infrastructure and logistics expertise of the UPS Logistics Group, to offer a complete range of services to manage the back-end of the e-business supply chain.

The company's services include warehousing and inventory management, order fulfilment, inbound and outbound transportation, returns management, customer call centre and management reporting. UPS e-logistics said that the pre-built services are standardized, can be bundled and configured, and are scalable for future growth.

UPS e-logistics serve both business-to-business and business-to-consumer e-commerce clients, ranging from e-business start-ups to the dot-com divisions of established corporations. Nearly a year in the making, it is the first business to be launched by the UPS e-ventures incubator.

Partners PriceWaterhouseCoopers provides overall systems integration consulting and project management services; software maker Oracle Corp. offers full enterprise resource planning with integral order management and advanced planning and scheduling functionality. EXE Technologies, a leading provider of multi-channel fulfilment, warehouse and distribution software, provides warehouse management systems at all UPS e-logistics distribution centres. United Parcel Service is extending its reach to services traditionally performed by distributors and integrators: logistics fulfilment, call centre support and website development and implementation. And the delivery giant's move could pave the way for other carriers, such as Federal Express, DHL and Airborne Express, to enter or boost their presence in this space down the road.

Supply Chain Management—It is all about Fulfilling Customers' Needs

Supply Chain Management covers all aspects of a business. From the stage of raw material to the end user, each and every aspect of the cycle is covered by the management system—be it sourcing, product design, production planning, order processing, inventory management, transportation and warehousing, and customer service. This complex sequence of steps used to be very difficult to manage efficiently and in the days when organizations have to fight hard to maintain their bottom-line, optimizing these steps become a necessity.

While you enter a store to buy a certain material, just try to imagine the sequence of steps that had brought the material where you see it. On the material, you will find a price tag with all the details of its date of manufacture, date of expiry, lot number, etc. The shop that you have entered has carefully placed it on the shelf after procuring it from a distributor and noting all these details for billing and tracking future complaints. The store also maintains an inventory of this material and hundreds of similar materials that are available in the store and along with this a minimum stock level and a reorder level. This product, like all other products in the store, has been sourced from a distributor who sourced it from the manufacturer. The manufacturer had procured the raw materials required for the production from one or many of his suppliers. A third-party transport and warehousing infrastructure was utilized to ship the material from the manufacturer to the distributor and from the distributor to the store that you have just entered.

After your purchase is complete, the point-of-sale updates this information at various places—the stock level comes down and revenue increases. The information of decrease in stock level should reach the distributor who has to replenish the stock before it becomes zero and the distributor is also to be paid his due amount. This chain is again pushed backwards to the lowest level of the supplier who has to supply the material in time. So, there is a constant flow of money and material between these establishments in order to satisfy the needs of the customer.

The Supply Chain Management manages the flow between different stages to maximize productivity and minimize stock-outs or overstocking. The solution spans across the different companies involved, and the system used by these companies should be able to talk to each other and understand each other's requirement. An SCM system is a combination of many applications—demand, inventory and transportation planning—covering the stages of the supply chain. The increase in product variety and demand for customized products increases demand uncertainty, making it difficult to forecast demand, which is further aggravated by the ever-shortening life cycle of products—this has made supply chain management an inseparable part of today's business.

Smart Chains, Smarter Gains

An efficient supply chain management can bring down the prices of commodities by as high as 40 per cent. This is not with the help of a budget sop, but by reducing average inventory levels, lowering transport costs, lowering warehousing costs—among others.

Industry estimates show that a company spends between 17 per cent and 50 per cent of the price for just moving the goods from their manufacturing plant to shop shelves. This includes the margin of the retailer and of the distributors. Most of it is taken up by logistics and holding inventory, and these costs can be controlled, optimized and reduced, thus reducing price or increasing profit.

Now if we can practically apply this model on a ₹ 50,000 crores FMCG company with thousands of wholesalers and retailers, the result will be mind boggling. This will not only give the company a cost benefit but will also result in improved customer service levels, improved competitiveness and an overall gain in profitability for the organization.

Managing logistics is a nightmare for all company executives in the sales and purchase departments. Handling logistics not only adds cost to the business but also increases the number of business processes and involves lot of resources. The logistics chain starts from the supplier end, and continues to the customer end involving members in surface, air, sea express couriers, brokers, customs, excise, etc. This is for the sales part. Later it will also include similar contacts for the after sales support, repair and maintenance. Many of the companies cannot take up this load and outsource these activities to experts, and many companies manage this efficiently and make huge profits.

Technology in logistics has been advancing in three phases. The first phase is to monitor the logistics chain. Herein, technology helps companies monitor orders, inventory and shipments with all parties. Since logistics is a business a process at the most basic level, IT is used to automate the process to gain visibility. This is primarily done through an enterprise-wide software developed in-house or procured from the solutions already available. Companies like Blue Dart, an integrated air express carrier, use an in-house developed package called COSMAT-II (Computerized Online System for Monitoring and Tracking). They started using this software way back in 1989 when very few standard solutions were available, and have improved it all through these years with the changing needs of business.

Gati, another Indian pioneer multimodal express cargo company, also uses an in-house system that links their various processes in the logistics chain. Over the years, they have included features like vehicle monitoring system, Web-enabled access to various applications, etc. The Lemuir group has further included warehousing, transportation and distribution system with full visibility of the processes. They found it very useful as they could adapt to any internal or external changes or requirements within hours.

The second phase of maturing technology adoption focusses on management capabilities in which the technology must provide the data and intelligence gathering tools necessary to manage the flow of goods and establish business rules to manage exceptions. More evolved technology backbones like GeoVista of the Geo-Logistics group are capable of handling high levels of sophistication.

The final phase of technology in logistics is that of optimization, wherein discrete parts of the chain as well as the entire chain is mathematically optimized to suggest actions which will lead to achievement of preset objectives within constraints. Specialized SCM tools like i2 and Manugistics help in achieving this.

The Indian logistics industries are still immature and yet to adopt the full potential brought about by the supply chain management solutions, as most of the companies have trucking and transportation background plus these are quite expensive taking into consideration the multi-locational setup. Developing software in-house is also a resource-intensive work that involves lot of time. The Internet has helped companies to adopt an SCM solution by lowering communication cost, creating VPNs, intranets and making applications available through Web-enablement. It has also simplified the technical complexity of spreading IT across the multiple-entity of the logistics chain.

Many companies have further improved their SCM by partnering with high-traffic e-commerce sites to fulfil their delivery chain. Blue Dart, for example, will help Fabmart customers to view their order status by providing a link on the Fabmart site and taking him to the Blue Dart site where the dispatch information is located. Customers are more informed now than ever about where their shipment is lying.

AFL effectively uses a Personal Digital Assistant (PDA)—based airway bill scanning and data capturing system for pick-up and delivery, that has reduced the data entry, resulting in cutting down customer response time and improved customer services. The location master is downloaded from the desktop computer to a PDA integrated with a barcode scanner everyday. This contains a setup of the route with relevant customer information for delivery. For the pickup process, the airway bill is scanned and the customer's signature is captured on the PDA. The airway bill is scanned at each stage—handover, arrival and final delivery. All this is then downloaded on to the desktop, which synchronizes with the enterprise system. Use of GPS (Global Positioning System) is also increasing. Global positioning systems help pinpoint the location of a moving target and then with the help of a GSM network, transmit the information to the required location.

It is no surprise that some top FMCG companies like Nestle, P&G have tied up with logistics companies like TCIL, Concor in an initiative called an Efficient Customer Response (ECR), with a one-point mission to clean-up India's supply chain.

Supply Chain Management in Wal-Mart World

Wal-Mart is an ultimate example of Supply Chain Management implementation. Here, vendors have joined hands with Wal-Mart to establish a strong supply chain management that would maximize Wal-Mart's internal profits.

Wal-Mart, starting with P&G, has incorporated vendor-managed inventory, category management, and other inter-company innovations. In order to build this strong SCM infrastructure, Wal-Mart entered into an alliance with P&G and in return got a dedicated account team representing key P&G functions of sales/marketing, distribution/supply chain management, IT and Finance. P&G had one Vice President dedicated for this project, who made the CFO of Wal-Mart as his customer. Customer value maximization was their only drive. Over the past decade, Wal-Mart has invited more of its major suppliers to jointly develop powerful supply chain partnerships. These are designed to increase product flow efficiency and, consequently, Wal-Mart's profitability.

Top managers have learned how to integrate their supply chains with major customers like Wal-Mart. What most companies have not sorted through, however, is what to do with all of their other customers. A common answer to the question of how to structure relationships with other customers is to try to apply the Wal-Mart relationship to all customers. This approach is implicit in commonly shown PowerPoint slides that offer a view of a company's evolving supply chain role. In one version of this view, the company starts as a stable supplier, evolves into a reactive supplier, then an efficient reactive supplier, then an efficient proactive supplier, and finally becomes a revenue and margin driver. This seems logical, with the company's supply chain capabilities inexorably increasing in sophistication over time, enabling the company to develop even more effective integration with its customers.

The problem, however, is that developing Wal-Mart-like supply chain partnerships requires a lot of resources and management attention. It also requires willing, innovative partners. Pursuing this approach too widely would be both costly and frustrating. In the past, suppliers to the retail trade typically had rather monolithic supply chains. The order fulfilment process was designed with a "one size fits all" approach. Customers generally received the same list price, regardless of ordering efficiency. There was very little effective forecasting. Some inventory priority was given to major customers in the event of allocations. Products were delivered in the manner that customers requested, regardless of the inefficiency entailed.

But today, the retailers themselves are changing dramatically. There is very visible consolidation, with the top ten retailers expected to comprise about half of the industry's revenues in a few years. Retailers have very different degrees of willingness to innovate, and the innovators are growing fast. Most retailers were used to having significant buyer power, and many are still very focussed on exerting price pressure on their suppliers rather than seeking increased profitability through process innovations. At the same time, the leading retailers are consolidating their supplier bases. They are looking more and more to major suppliers for supply chain innovations and prioritization, and in return, they are giving them increasing shelf space.

As a result of this history, major retail suppliers find themselves stretched. They are forced to meet the increasing needs of their largest customers while they are devoting disproportionate resources to their smaller customers. This untenable situation is forcing major suppliers to rethink their account relationships and extended supply chains. The key to providing excellent, consistent service at a reasonable cost is service differentiation. This concept can be adapted to guide the development of an appropriate set of broader supply chain policies. It is essential for successful profitability management, because it enables a supplier to match its cost structure and innovation initiatives to account potential. Service differentiation is also good for the customers. It enables them to plan their operations around a very high and consistent level of service. However, it does require that customers establish well-disciplined operations, as the supplier should adhere to a specific set of agreed-upon processes.

What Happens at Dell?

An outstanding example of e-supply chain is the one in force at Dell Computers, the US-based PC manufacturer. The company publicizes its products through the Internet. Any customer can order a PC of a configuration of his choice and pay for it online, using his credit card. Once the order is registered, the e-supply chain takes control of the execution. The system triggers three actions simultaneously—one to Dell's suppliers in Taiwan for providing parts, second to its assembly shop in Singapore, and third to its courier company, with all the data being transferred through the extranet. The intranet takes care of internal transactions relating to realization of collections from customers and effecting payments to the suppliers/service providers. Dell's success lies in reducing costs and improving customer satisfaction. Figures 8.5 and 8.6 explain how the model for supply chain operates.

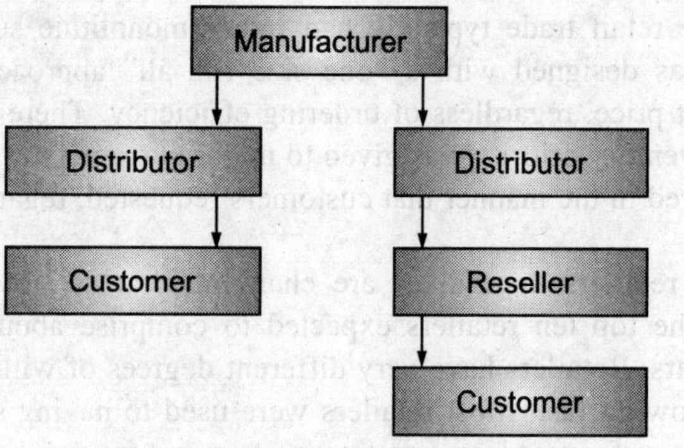

Figure 8.5 Industry model for supply chain.

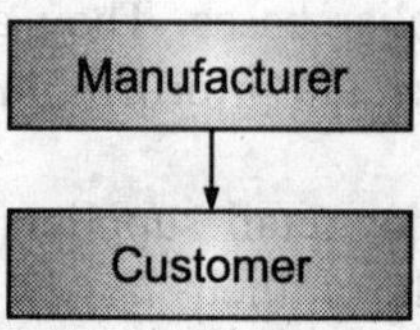

Figure 8.6 Dell model for supply chain management.

The Pay-off

Every company aims at reducing costs and cycle time and increasing revenue. E-supply chain supports these objectives. Companies find that enterprise integration leads to a new level of relationship, be it with its customers or suppliers. Customers can quite literally check the status of their orders, and suppliers can gain access to inventory levels to find out whether they need to replenish stock, all through the extranet. The benefits of reduced cycle time provide measurable competitive advantage in terms of both cost and performance. When we speak of cycle time, we refer to the time it takes to react to a new demand from the customers. The faster we move a critical data through the Internet, the quicker we can react and deliver the end product to the customer. This leads to enhanced customer satisfaction and promotes revenue growth.

Seven Ways to Reduce Inventory

How much inventory does he need to run a business effectively, is a perpetual concern of every manager. If he has too much, he may find himself confronted with cash-flow problems; if too little, he runs the risk of customers accusing him of poor service. So what is the way out? Here are seven tips that can help him strike the right balance.

1. ***Improve data accuracy.*** Introduce a well-designed cycle counting system. It will help you know how much of inventory to have and where you are. A well-designed and implemented cycle counting system pays for itself within a short time.

2. ***Cut your lead-time.*** If lead-time is long, you cannot but have more inventories in your system. Think of a 'rush' order in one week for a valued customer. The rush order does not wait in the long queue of WIP (Work-in-Progress) inventory for something to happen.

3. ***Increase the velocity of your operation.*** The amount of inventory you have has a lot to do with how fast you can replace it. If for instance, you can replace the same item in one day, a two-day supply will be more than enough to fill any order and, a stock out—if it occurs—will be for only one day, not until the next batch is produced. On the other hand, if it takes six weeks to replace an item, you will need to re-order with at least six weeks (plus safety stock and 'Just in Case' inventory) supply or be at the risk of a stock out.

4. ***Eliminate misalignment from your process.*** It is not unusual for companies to buy raw material in thousands, produce product in hundreds, and sell in units. The result is the piling up of inventory that runs the risk of slow movement, obsolescence and damage, and tie up of valuable cash. 'Just in time' techniques are aimed at eliminating such misalignments.

5. ***Clean your attic.*** There are companies, which carry an item that typically may be ordered once a year, if at all. Some companies may keep an item in the fond hope that someone will buy it some day or other, or hold on to an item because too much of money was spent on it. The answer to all this is simple: liquidate, donate or have a sale.

6. ***Eliminate variation.*** Erratic vendors may have product quality related problems on the shop floor, which can cause unnecessary inventory to pile up. The typical way of dealing with such situations is to order early, order more than needed, and increase safety stocks throughout the system.

7. ***Replenish based on market demand.*** Forecasts may seem advantageous but it must be remembered that many are no more than informed guesses. Using market demand as reference for replenishing finished goods is a better approach to keep your inventory level aligned with what customers are actually buying.

e-SCM Provides "Real-time" Benefits

E-SCM is being transformed by the rapid growth of Internet-based communications. The movement to Internet-based communications represents a paradigm shift from the client/server model. The power of Web-based applications is their ability to allow people to communicate mission-critical, real-time information anywhere in the world instantaneously. This migration has precipitated the widespread adoption of Internet software applications utilizing the latest technology to fulfil these new and complex communication needs. As these applications emerge, their immediate and measurable benefit make them essential business tools. With the increasingly competitive business landscape, it has become a strategic necessity to optimize a company's supply chain in a fashion that leverages the potential of the Internet. Some of these are:

- Global trading capabilities
- Mass personalization and customization
- Global knowledge exchange
- Global communities
- Collaborative workflow
- Industry specific (vertical) marketplaces
- Horizontal marketplaces
- Enterprise-to-Enterprise connectivity
- E-marketplace-to-E-marketplace connectivity

e-SCM—The Strategic Advantage

Rapid Deployment and Scalability

The e-SCM suite of applications is based on an "open" Internet Application Architecture that provides enterprise-wide scalability and rapid deployment to numerous end-users.

Real-time Processing

E-SCM creates an open, integrated system that addresses the complex e-business and supply chain management needs and requirements by allowing the exchange of "real-time" information to take place with employees and their trading partners (customers, suppliers, distributors, manufacturers) regarding product configuration, order status, pricing, and inventory availability. Such functions improve order accuracy and provide 100 per cent order fulfilment through accurate inventory information. This "real-time" data enables users to make informed ordering, purchasing and inventory decisions, and thereby enhances the quality and scope of customer service.

Return on Investment

In addition to increasing productivity and reducing overall operating expenses, e-SCM maximizes selling opportunities by capturing valuable customer information—buying patterns, frequency of visits, preferences, order history—and then uses this information for up-selling, cross-selling and promotional opportunities. E-SCM provides the tool sets to achieve new business by reaching out to customers that you never could before.

Benefits

Some of the benefits of e-SCM are enumerated below:

1. It is Web-based (client and server), not Web-enabled;
2. It incorporates broadcast and active messaging to proactively notify an individual of a condition that requires attention;

3. It supports the exchange of "real-time" information through trading communities such as employees, customers, suppliers, distributors and manufacturers;
4. It has open Internet Application Architecture which allows for rapid deployment and scalability, combining unlimited internal/external users in a "real-time" environment;
5. It has an interface capability with any third party software;
6. It is platform independent;
7. It is a fully integrated system;
8. It has Web visibility and processing capability—24 × 7;
9. It is rules-based.

e-Supply Chain Components[1]

The components of e-supply chain are as follows:

Advanced Scheduling and Manufacturing Planning Programme

This automated programme provides detailed coordination of all manufacturing and supply efforts based on individual customer orders. Scheduling is based on real-time analysis of changing constraints throughout the process, from equipment malfunctioning to supply interruptions. Scheduling creates job schedules for managing the manufacturing process as well as logistics.

Demand Forecasting Programme

This module supports a range of statistical tools and business forecasting techniques. It constantly takes into account changing market scenarios and economic factors while making decisions.

Transportation Logistics Programme

This programme facilitates resource allocation and execution to ensure that materials and finished goods are delivered at the right time and at the right place, according to the planning schedule, at minimal cost. It considers such variables as transportation mode and availability of each mode such as airlines, trains, and trucks.

Distribution Planning Programme

This is integrated with demand forecasting, manufacturing schedules and transportation logistics to reach the customer.

Order Commitment

Order commitment is linked to all the other modules so that accurate delivery of goods and services can be guaranteed. These are illustrated in Figure 8.7.

1. Kalakota R. and Robinson M., *e-business*, Addison-Wesley, NJ, USA, 1999, p. 206.

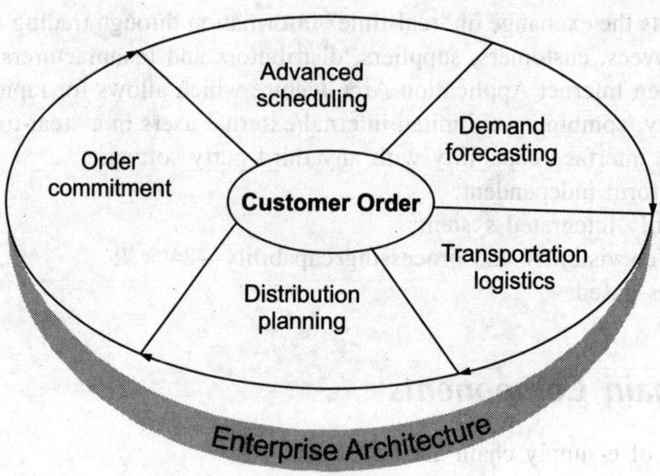

Figure 8.7 e-SCM components.

e-Supply Chain Architecture[2]

Historically, the elements in the supply chain have consisted largely of separate legacy applications at the headquarters, factory, store and distribution levels. These applications have targeted only distinct levels of supply chain and not the entire supply chain levels. So this three-tier architecture as found in Figure 8.8, shows a bottom-up view of the entire supply chain management.

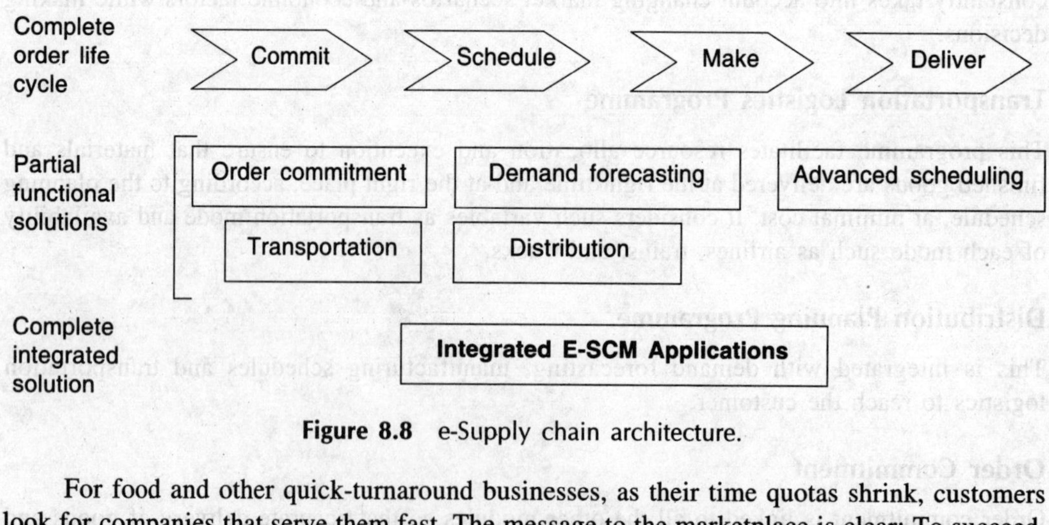

Figure 8.8 e-Supply chain architecture.

For food and other quick-turnaround businesses, as their time quotas shrink, customers look for companies that serve them fast. The message to the marketplace is clear: To succeed, companies must reduce the processing time between search, selection, order entry, and order fulfilment. Delays at any step of the process are unacceptable!

2. Kalakota R. and Robinson M., *e-business*, Addison-Wesley, NJ, USA, 1999, p. 211.

There are two main types of SCM software:

Planning applications: Planning applications use advanced algorithms to determine the best way to fill an order.

Execution applications: Execution applications track the physical status of goods, the management of materials, and financial information involving all parties.

Some SCM applications are based on open data models that support the sharing of data both inside and outside the enterprise (this is called the extended enterprise, and includes key suppliers, manufacturers, and end customers of a specific company). This shared data may reside in diverse database systems, or data warehouses, at several different sites and companies. By sharing this data "upstream" (with a company's suppliers) and "downstream" (with a company's clients), SCM applications have the potential to improve the time-to-market of products, reduce costs, and allow all parties in the supply chain to better manage current resources and plan for future needs.

Major Trends in e-SCM

What does e-SCM trend mean for e-business? When one considers the challenge of meeting the demands of busy, time-starved, dissatisfied consumers in an environment of hostile competition, low margins and countless sales outlets selling similar products, it becomes clear that changing the entire business model is the only plausible strategy (see Table 8.1). E-business applications must cut the time customers wait for service. Customers now penalize

TABLE 8.1 Major Trends in e-SCM

Trends	*Characteristics*
Consumer trends	Speed of service.
	Self-service.
	Integrated solutions, not piecemeal products.
Service/Process trends	Convergence of sales and services: Customization and integration.
	Ease of use: Making service consistent and reliable.
	Flexible and convenient service delivery.
	Streamlining the supply chain.
Organizational trends	Contract manufacturing: Becoming brand-intensive, not capital-intensive.
	Business process outsourcing: retain the core, outsource the rest.
	Increasing process transparency and visibility.
	Constant innovation and employee retention.
Enterprise technology trends	Enterprise applications: Connect the corporations.
	Infrastructure convergence: Increase melding of voice, data, and video.
	Multichannel integration: Computer telephony integration and voice recognition wireless applications.
	Leveraging legacy investments: The rise of middleware for application integration.

companies that infringe on their time through delays, mistakes, or inconveniences. If companies do not expedite processes, customers will go to someone who does it faster. If one company does not make it easy for the customer to do business, another will.

It is very important that managers understand and diagnose the cause behind service delays. They need to analyze if an integrated system can speed-up service. If so, they need to strategize, design and implement such systems as soon as possible. Unfortunately for some companies, their managers may wake up too late to heed the sound of their customers' fists pounding on the counters for faster service. These companies will not be in business for long.

In the e-business world, innovation is derived from spotting the trend well before any one else does and from the sophisticated exploitation of information and technologies to create value. It is the senior managers in particular who will be called on to lead the innovation charge. Today, every manager is wondering how the Internet can remake his or her business. In a concerted search for growth, corporations are intent on mastering the art of trend spotting in order to discover new products and services, design new business processes and structures, even to create completely new businesses.

An Internet-enabled supply chain helps companies to:

- Avoid costly disasters
- Reduce administrative overhead
- Reduce unnecessary inventory
- Decrease the number of hands that touch goods on their way to the end customer
- Eliminate obsolete business processes
- Reap cost-cutting and revenue-producing benefits
- Speed up production and responsiveness to consumers and garner higher profit margins on finished goods.

Effective integration of an organization's supply chain can save millions, improve customer service and reduce inventories.

New Trends in Supply Chain Management

1. ***Back to basics.*** Companies have strayed from the traditional 'blocking and tackling' needed to achieve superior results in an effort to cut corners and save money. Company executives will return to the value of "doing the right things, right" once again to meet customer demand.

2. ***Cost reductions and process improvements.*** Most company executives will turn to smaller, more agile, and highly skilled consultancies who are focused on reducing costs by changing behaviour through real PROCESS improvements.

3. ***There era of big software is over.*** People now understand that 90 per cent of the cost savings from any major implementation comes from process improvements, not software. Companies will also see the fallacy in SaaS when they start calculating the Total Utility as the key variable in Total Cost of Ownership. With this in mind, they will turn to smaller, cost efficient, and value laden new products, like Babbleware

and other thought leaders, to maximize their existing investment and reduce the risk of technology.

4. ***The supply chain is the business.*** Executives are becoming painfully aware that the "supply chain" is not just purchasing and logistics anymore...if it ever was. Company supply chain activities touch every aspect of a business in significant ways, from supplier management, customer service, and operations to finance, inventory, and profitability. It is widely reported that 65 per cent to 85 per cent of all company cost within any organization that makes, moves, or manages products and services is within the supply chain. This means that a small improvement, as little as 2 per cent to 5 per cent, will deliver savings at orders of magnitude greater than any other area. CEOs, CFOs, and COOs will realize the "hidden value" of supply chain management and make significant investments in improving their business through the power of supply chain management.

Supply Chain Management at Marico Industries Limited

Marico Industries Limited is a leading consumer goods company of India, with sales of ₹ 6.96 billion. It has six factories and about 1000 employees. Marico offers a range of products to the local and export markets (primarily South Asia and the Middle East), including refined edible oils, food products such as jams and sauces, niche fabric care products, and hair oils. Marico's distribution network is key to ensuring that its product reaches about 100 million people throughout India each month. Marico produces 125 SKUs at its own factories and through 15 subcontracting manufacturers. It stores products at 32 warehouses and sells to 3500 distributors. These distributors in turn provide products to 1.6 million retail outlets. Marico's peer companies in other countries recognize its strength in distribution; consequently, Marico has secured a distribution alliance/agreement with Nissin Foods and Procter & Gamble.

Strategic Goals

- Enhance long-term value of company brands by achieving excellence in distribution performance.
- Maintain market share growth in a competitive environment with much larger, offshore rivals.
- Scale supply chain operations to sustain customer service as the business grows.
- Reduce total delivery cost.

Results

- Decreased stock-outs associated with distributor sales to retailers by 33 per cent.
- Reduced lost sales due to stock-outs by 28 per cent, thereby improving total revenue by 1.5 per cent.
- Lowered excess distributor inventory by 33 per cent.
- Reduced late deliveries to distributors by 37.5 per cent.

- Reduced costs associated to supply chain exceptions by 25 per cent (for example, intracompany stock transfers, truck detention costs).
- Positioned the company for a vendor-managed inventory implementation and further performance improvements.

Approach

Marico shortened its planning cycle from 30 days to about 15 days; revised its demand planning process to forecast "sales out" (shipment from distributors to retailers); and implemented and improved process to replenish its distributors. The company focussed on achieving relatively even shipment levels throughout each month and developed internal collaborative processes to support planning. This approach was enabled by *mySAP.com* Supply Chain Management Software, which includes demand planning and supply network planning capabilities coupled with SAP Business Information Warehouse.

Supply Chain Management at Mahindra & Mahindra Ltd.

Mahindra & Mahindra Limited (M&M) is a ₹ 39.2 billion company, employing 12,000 people. It is a flagship of the Mahindra Group, one of the top-ranking private sector companies in India. The company has been the market leader in farm equipment machinery in the highly competitive Indian market since 1986. M&M has about 400 dealers and 800 suppliers who interact daily with the sales and procurement divisions.

Strategic Goals

- Link all plants and decide which plant should make what, when and for which global market.
- Enable a pull-based replenishment system to optimize logistics and manufacturing operations.
- Reduce inventory by 30 per cent and bring down replenishment lead times to 19 days.

Results

- Dealer stock of 12,000 and company stock of 7000 units of tractors reduced to 6000 and 3500 respectively on implementation of pull-based replenishment system.
- Anticipated additional inventory reduced by 30 per cent.
- Ability to measure crucial metrics of the as the supply chain operates, e.g. the company will measure the production schedule adherence across daily and weekly buckets, inventory at each node of the supply chain.
- Units actually supplied against what was required to be supplied as per demand from the central stockyard or area stockyard or from the supplier, and cost per tractor.

M&M articulated clear objectives for this global competitiveness initiative enabled by mySAP SCM: reduce inventories across the supply chain by aligning the company's business processes for IT-enabled supply chain management and ensure availability of tractors as per sales requirement—right model, right place, right time—at minimum cost. In 2002–2003, they reduced supply chain inventory by more than 50 per cent. In the current year, they expect to reduce inventory by another 30 per cent. Replenishment lead times, which include planning and execution lead times, were around 52 days before the implementation of SCM. These times have been reduced considerably, and it is expected to reduce to 19 days or lower with the full mySAP SCM implementation. Private websites for our 400 dealers were developed to collect sales information and for 800 suppliers to post mySAP SCM planning information and material requirements planning (MRP) schedules. With the full implementation of mySAP SCM, it will be possible to further reduce dealer inventory from 6000 to 4000 tractors and company stock from 3500 to 2000 units, while maintaining excellent customer delivery response times. M&M is experimenting with mounting of global positioning systems (GPS) on the trucks that carry raw material/components and interfacing them with mySAP SCM. This way they will be able to plan their production schedule based on actual material in transit rather than vendor commitment.

Supply Chain Management at Amul Dairy

It was started in December 1946, with a group of farmers keen to free themselves from intermediaries, gain access to markets and thereby ensure maximum returns for their efforts.

Based in the village of Anand, the Kaira District Milk Cooperative Union (better known as Amul) expanded exponentially. It joined hands with other milk cooperatives, and the Gujarat network now covers 2.12 million farmers, 10,411 village level milk collection centers and fourteen district level plants (unions) under the overall supervision of GCMMF.

Amul and GCMMF acknowledged that development and growth could not be left to market forces and that proactive intervention was required.

Two Key Requirements were Identified

The first, that sustained growth for the long term would depend on matching supply and demand. It would need heavy investment in the simultaneous development of suppliers and consumers.

Second, that effective management of the network and commercial viability would require professional managers and technocrats.

To implement their vision while retaining their focus on farmers, a hierarchical network of cooperatives was developed, which today forms the robust supply chain behind GCMMF's endeavours. The vast and complex supply chain stretches from small suppliers to large fragmented markets. Management of this network is made more complex by the fact that GCMMF is directly responsible only for a small part of the chain, with a number of third party players (distributors, retailers and logistics support providers) playing large roles.

Managing this supply chain efficiently is critical as GCMMF's competitive position is driven by low consumer prices supported by a low cost system.

Developing demand. At the time Amul was formed, consumers had limited purchasing power, and modest consumption levels of milk and other dairy products. Thus, Amul adopted a low-cost price strategy to make its products affordable and attractive to consumers by guaranteeing them value for money.

Introducing higher value products. Beginning with liquid milk, GCMMF enhanced the product mix through the progressive addition of higher value products while maintaining the desired growth in existing products.

Despite competition in the high value dairy product segments from firms such as Hindustan Lever, Nestle and Britannia, GCMMF ensures that the product mix and the sequence in which Amul introduces its products is consistent with the core philosophy of providing milk at a basic, affordable price.

The distribution network. Amul products are available in over 500,000 retail outlets across India through its network of over 3,500 distributors. There are 47 depots with dry and cold warehouses to buffer inventory of the entire range of products. GCMMF transacts on an advance demand draft basis from its wholesale dealers instead of the cheque system adopted by other major FMCG companies. This practice is consistent with GCMMF's philosophy of maintaining cash transactions throughout the supply chain and it also minimizes dumping.

Wholesale dealers carry inventory that is just adequate to take care of the transit time from the branch warehouse to their premises. This just-in-time inventory strategy improves dealers' return on investment (ROI). All GCMMF branches engage in route scheduling and have dedicated vehicle operations.

Umbrella brand. The network follows an umbrella branding strategy. Amul is the common brand for most product categories produced by various unions: liquid milk, milk powders, butter, ghee, cheese, cocoa products, sweets, ice-cream and condensed milk. Amul's sub-brands include variants such as Amulspray, Amulspree, Amulya and Nutramul. The edible oil products are grouped around Dhara and Lokdhara, mineral water is sold under the Jal Dhara brand while fruit drinks bear the Safal name. By insisting on an umbrella brand, GCMMF not only skillfully avoided inter-union conflicts but also created an opportunity for the union members to cooperate in developing products.

Managing the supply chain. Even though the cooperative was formed to bring together farmers, it was recognized that professional managers and technocrats would be required to manage the network effectively and make it commercially viable.

Coordination

Given the large number of organizations and entities in the supply chain and decentralized responsibility for various activities, effective coordination is critical for efficiency and cost control. GCMMF and the unions play a major role in this process and jointly achieve the desired degree of control. Buy-in from the unions is assured as the plans are approved by GCMMF's board. The board is drawn from the heads of all the unions, and the boards of the unions comprise farmers elected through village societies, thereby creating a situation of interlocking control.

The federation handles the distribution of end products and coordination with retailers and the dealers. The unions coordinate the supply side activities. These include monitoring milk collection contractors, the supply of animal feed and other supplies, provision of veterinary services, and educational activities.

Managing third party service providers. From the beginning, it was recognized that the unions' core activity lay in milk processing and the production of dairy products. Accordingly, marketing efforts (including brand development) were assumed by GCMMF. All other activities were entrusted to third parties. These include logistics of milk collection, distribution of dairy products, sale of products through dealers and retail stores, provision of animal feed, and veterinary services. It is worth noting that a number of these third parties are not in the organized sector, and many are not professionally managed with little regard for quality and service. This is a particularly critical issue in the logistics and transport of a perishable commodity where there are already weaknesses in the basic infrastructure.

Establishing best practices. A key source of competitive advantage has been the enterprise's ability to continuously implement best practices across all elements of the network: the federation, the unions, the village societies and the distribution channel.In developing these practices, the federation and the unions have adapted successful models from around the world. It could be the implementation of small group activities or quality circles at the federation. Or a TQM program at the unions. Or housekeeping and good accounting practices at the village society level.

Each meeting has its pre-set format in terms of Purpose, Agenda and Limit (PAL) with a process check at the end to record how the meeting was conducted. Similar processes are in place at the village societies, the unions and even at the wholesaler and C&F agent levels as well.

Examples of benefits from recent initiatives include reduction in transportation time from the depots to the wholesale dealers, improvement in ROI of wholesale dealers, implementation of Zero Stock Out through improved availability of products at depots and also the implementation of Just-in-Time in finance to reduce the float.

Kaizens at the unions have helped improve the quality of milk in terms of acidity and sour milk. (Undertaken by multi-disciplined teams, Kaizens are highly focussed projects, reliant on a structured approach based on data gathering and analysis.) For example, Sabar Union's records show a reduction from 2.0 per cent to 0.5 per cent in the amount of sour milk/curd received at the union.

The most impressive aspect of this large-scale roll out is that improvement processes are turning the village societies into individual improvement centres.

Technology and e-initiatives

GCMMF's technology strategy is characterized by four distinct components: new products, process technology, and complementary assets to enhance milk production and e-commerce.

Few dairies of the world have the wide variety of products produced by the GCMMF network. Village societies are encouraged through subsidies to install chilling units. Automation in processing and packaging areas is common, as is HACCP certification. Amul actively pursues developments in embryo transfer and cattle breeding in order to improve cattle quality and increases in milk yields.

GCMMF was one of the first FMCG (fast-moving consumer goods) firms in India to employ Internet technologies to implement B2C commerce. Today, customers can order a variety of products through the Internet and be assured of timely delivery with cash payment upon receipt.

Another e-initiative underway is to provide farmers access to information relating to markets, technology and best practices in the dairy industry through net enabled kiosks in the villages.

GCMMF has also implemented a Geographical Information System (GIS) at both ends of the supply chain, i.e. milk collection and the marketing process. Farmers now have better access to information on the output as well as support services while providing a better planning tool to marketing personnel.

EXERCISES

1. Explain how FedEx meets the quick delivery requirement using the Internet.
2. What should be the architecture that will assure JIT delivery at the time of ordering?
3. Analyze the workflow in DHL. A short description is given here.
   DHL can now access the DHL global Web page (*http://dhl.com*) and locate their freight, book a package to be picked up, calculate freight costs, and check delivery times, just to name a few. The global website allows customers to open an account, track international and domestic shipments, calculate freight costs and the projected time of delivery, and print out forms such as customs declarations. International customers have hotlinks to the DHL website so that they can track their purchases. The Web has been fundamental to DHL for developing new supply chain forms through far faster communication on the Internet. The information captured contains details on customers at various stages of the customer relationship—suspects, prospects, current, and old customers. For each customer, information like the key contacts in the organization, decision makers and their buying cycles, as well as information on each contact is maintained. Basically, all case histories should be easily available. There are many customized solutions that help you automate CRM and the associated workflow.
4. Analyze the supply chain management of a company like TELCO (Chapter 1) with regard to CRM and SCM, based on the workflow.
5. Visit *www.ups.com* and find their recent e-commerce initiatives. Compare them with those of www.fedex.com.

CHAPTER 9

e-Strategy and Knowledge Management

LEARNING OBJECTIVES

After reading this chapter, you should be able to:

- Understand how knowledge becomes an asset in an organization.
- Understand how the various types of business information systems relate to or operate in a corporate business context.
- Learn about the role of strategy in the business context.
- Understand the seven dimensions of e-commerce strategy.
- Describe the value chain and e-strategy.
- Explain e-business strategy and the use of data warehousing and data mining.

Knowledge Management at Tata Steel

Tata Steel pioneered **"Knowledge Management"** to shift the basis of growth from natural resources and physical assets to intellectual capital, which has become the source of innovation, growth and value in modern competitive scenario. The essence of knowledge management is to create and capture the abundant knowledge assets available either tacit (experience, thumb rules, etc.) or explicit (literature, reports, failures analysis, etc.) and then share and utilize it again at right place and in right time.

Since there is no accepted standard framework for KM, Tata Steel has evolved a framework in accordance with its needs, to achieve its business vision. Tata Steel has conceived, developed and deployed internally, an elaborate architecture for KM that aims to take the company to a Learn Once, Use Anywhere paradigm. It was initiated with building up of a "Knowledge Repository" with all the officers actively participating in it. There are basically two broad strategies that are being followed.

There are broadly two strategies for KM, viz., Personalization and Codification (Figure 9.1). Looking at a wide variety of employees that Tata Steel has, both the strategies are implemented in a different way for different cross-section of employees. Steel making and its related maintenance practices require a lot of tacit knowledge. It also needs a lot of new products and new experiments, which may result because of internalization of the new explicit knowledge. Therefore, it is important to have both the strategies.

While the Personalization strategy has a big advantage in that the knowledge sharing is very rich and there is almost no distortion, it has one big disadvantage: It is imperative that both the interested parties should be present at the same time to ensure that knowledge transfer takes place. Since knowledge is not captured in the form of documents, the organization loses it when the person leaves the organization.

The Codification strategy, on the other hand, does not require that both the parties should be present at the same time. It is independent of time and space. The only problem is that knowledge transfer is not rich and can get distorted.

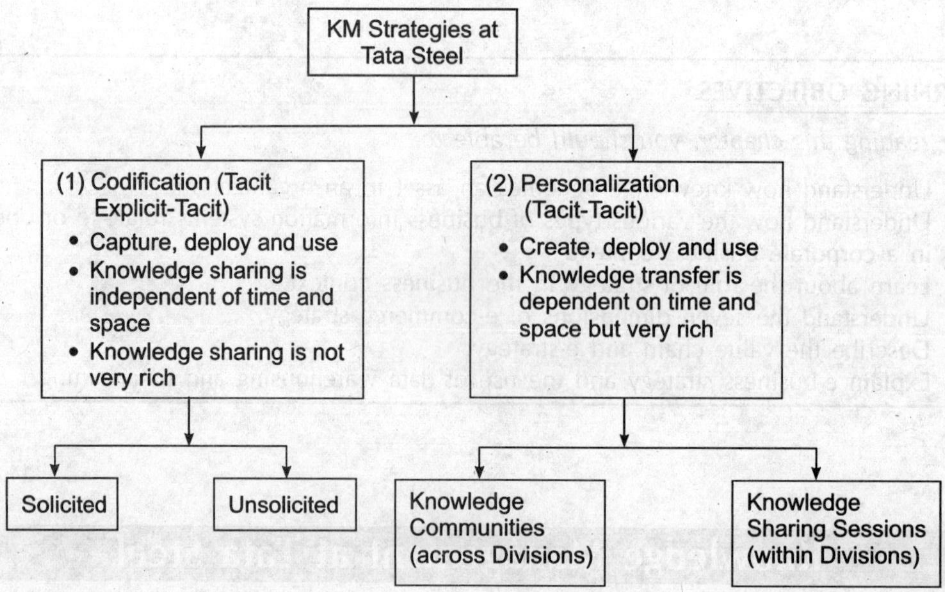

Figure 9.1 Knowledge management at Tata Steel.

1. *Codification Strategy (Unsolicited):* Knowledge database includes best practices, learning from failures, improved and new practices adopted, competitive intelligence, customer and supplier knowledge, and benchmarks of different parameters. These captured knowledge assets are being deployed and used instantaneously in respective work area to give benefits. The challenge in the knowledge repository process is to keep database updated and useful. With increasing number and size of knowledge database, it will be more challenging to store and offer a range of contents to a variety of users.

Figure 9.2 explains the knowledge repository process that how the knowledge is being captured, evaluated by experts and then used by users.

Some new features in the codification strategy that were added are:

- **Ask expert (solicited):** In today's economy, the most challenging job is to initiate conversation especially between the knowledge seeker and the knowledge provider, i.e., expert. The fact that the organization is big, actually makes this more difficult

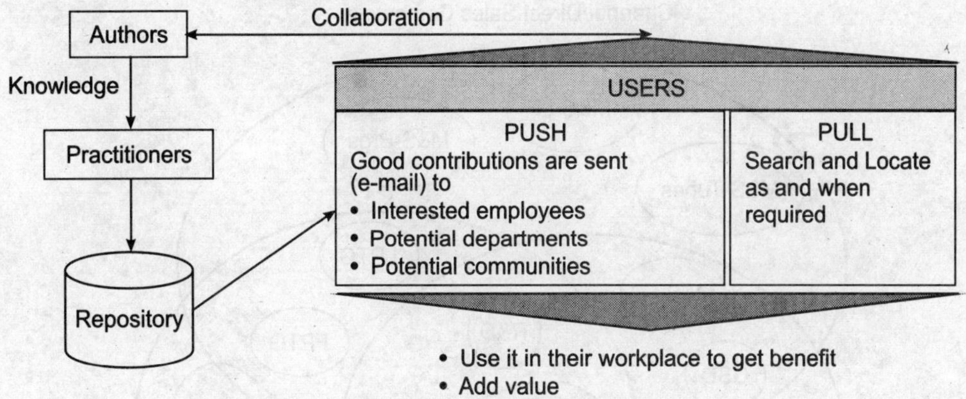

Figure 9.2 Knowledge repository process.

because an individual actually does not know that there may be others in the organization whom he does not know, who can provide solutions to his problems. Tata Steel is trying to do it through their "Ask Expert" feature. In "Ask Expert" system, employees are free to log on their work related problem online and there are more than 100 experts involved in providing instant solutions to them. These solutions are stored for future use.

- **Integration of different databases and product catalogue:** A detailed analysis of the failures of products at the customer end is also available on the KM portal. Customer's knowledge is also available on the KM portal. Indian standards (IS) are also made available on the KM portal.
- **Treasured jewels:** Details of retired employees are also available with complete profile (Name, Phone No., Address, e-mail id, expertise). Tata steel intends to involve them in their KM process at a later date.

2. *Personalization strategy:* To encourage knowledge transfer across divisions and departments, a few Knowledge Communities have been formed, which are actually groups of like–minded people who came together to share what they know, and to learn from one another regarding some aspects of their work. They are an investment towards the future of the organization and not expected to yield a short-term gain. It is more of a knowledge creating and sharing platform rather than a task force to solve a problem.

Figure 9.3 shows complexity of Knowledge Communities. Four Knowledge Communities are being shown with participation from various divisions.

Communities play a very important role in capturing experts' tacit knowledge, improving the quality of knowledge repository and encouraging usage of the repository. In Tata Steel, the knowledge community comprises distinct roles, viz. Champions, Convener, Practice Leader, lead experts and practitioners. These communities exist not only on core business but also on functions like HR, Town, and Community development.

Beside the responsibility of keeping the knowledge repository current, communities have various knowledge deliverables as follows:

- Innovation: Plan, conduct and learn from new experiments.
- Identify Best Practices, Update regularly.
- Identify new Bench Marks, Update regularly.

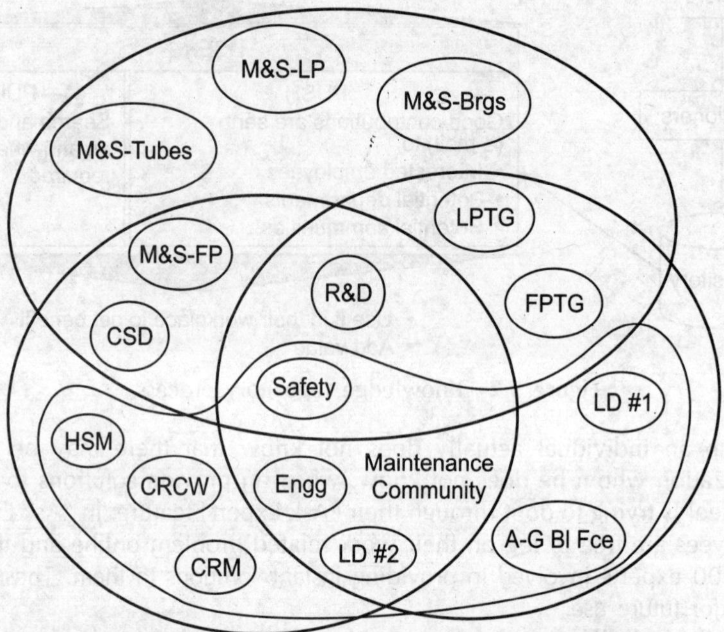

Figure 9.3 Complexity of knowledge communities.

Deployment of KM Strategies

An index called "KM Index" has been also developed to measure the performance of KM system. This KM Index is an item in the Balanced Scorecard of CEO, which has been cascaded down at lower levels. Both the above strategies are in place at almost all the locations of Tata Steel. Almost 80 per cent of officers are involved in the above-explained KM system.

Rewards and Recognition

Knowledge Management forms a part of the Performance Management system. Rewards and recognition are given to those who perform well in the Knowledge Management systems. There are individual rewards for the codification strategy and team rewards for the personalization strategy. Figure 9.4 explains the interface between K-communities and divisions.

Measurements

Figure 9.5 shows the measurements in various phases in Tata Steel.

It is evident from the figure that as the KM enters into a new phase or matures to a certain level, the type of measures changes. Knowledge Communities in Tata Steel are quite matured and they help the organization to:

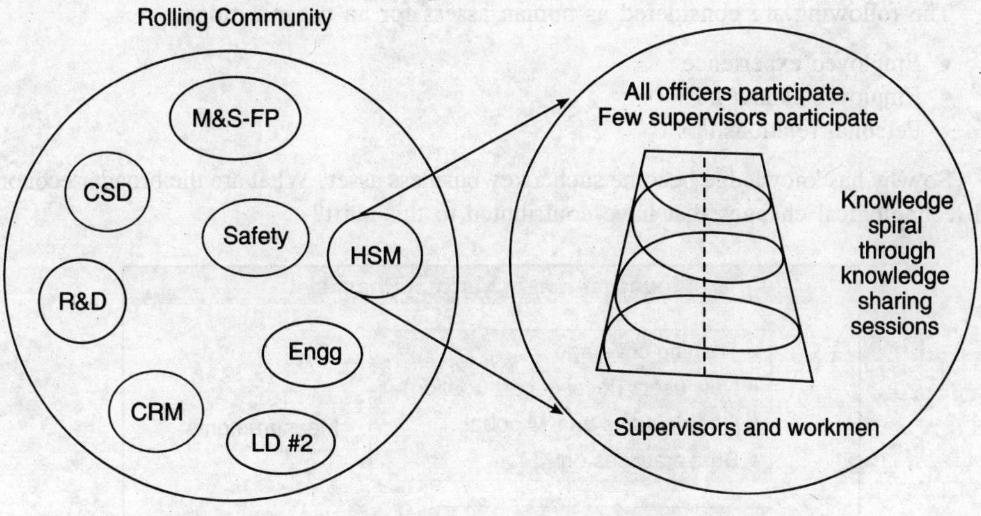

Figure 9.4 Interface between K-communities and divisions.

- Solve problems quickly.
- Transfer best practices.
- Develop professional skills.

Case Discussion

1. How is knowledge codified at Tata Steel?
2. What is the need for knowledge management?
3. What structures are needed in the organization for knowledge gathering?
4. Why knowledge can be lost in an organization?

Knowledge as a Key Business Asset

We are living in the information age where knowledge is now considered the key strategic business asset. *'How do we leverage the knowledge in our business?'* is a fundamental question being raised by senior business leaders, in all business sectors. The Chief Executive of Hewlett-Packard has been quoted as saying *'if HP knew what HP knows, it would be three times as profitable.'*

The following are considered as knowledge assets for an organization:

- Structural assets
- Brands
- Customer relationships
- Patents
- Products
- Operational processes

The following are considered as human assess for an organization:

- Employee experience
- Employee 'know-how'
- Personal relationships

So why has knowledge become such a key business asset? What are the broader economic and technological changes that have contributed to this shift?

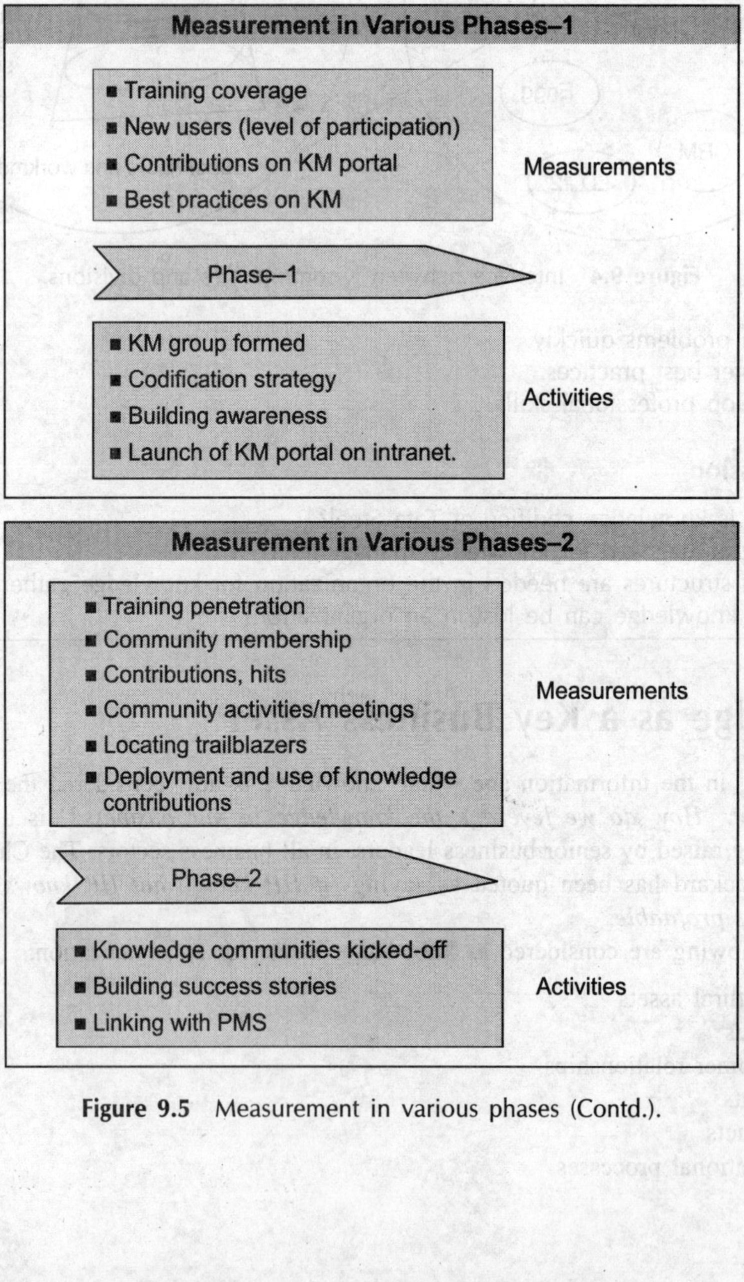

Figure 9.5 Measurement in various phases (Contd.).

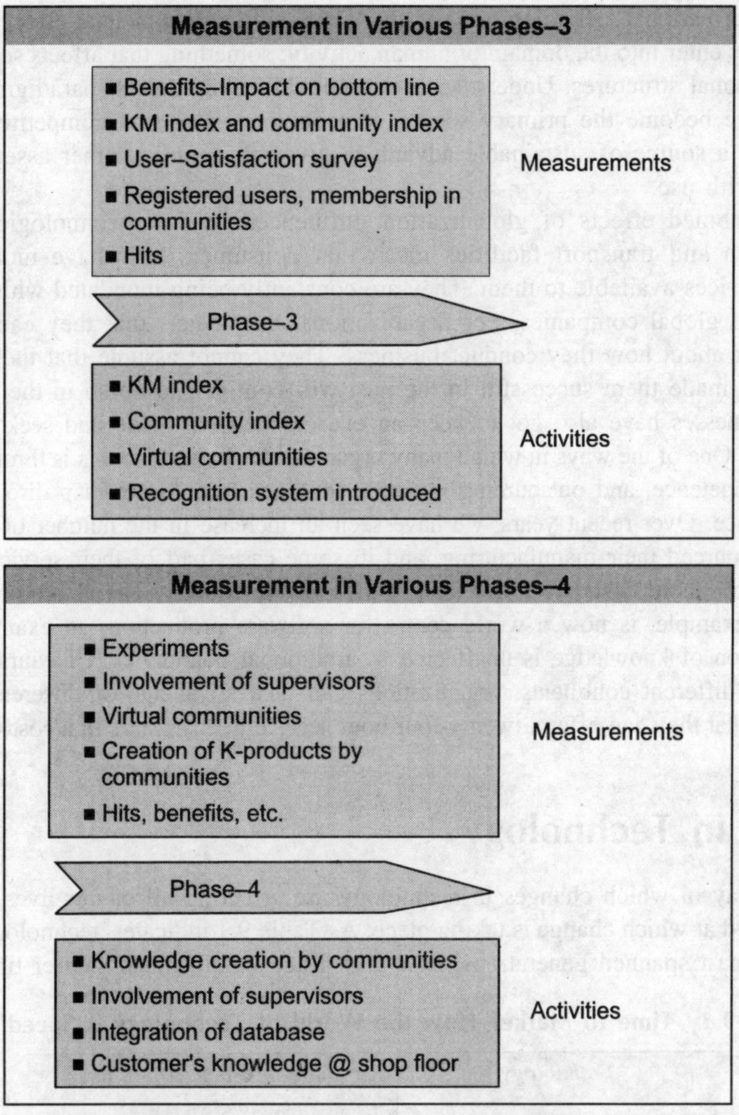

Figure 9.5 Measurement in various phases.

Changes in the Global Business Economy

A number of significant changes have occurred in the global business economy, and in society more generally over the past couple of decades points out how a '..... sense of economic transformation within the western industrial economies has been present for some time, at least since the 1970s.' While there are differing views as to what type of economy we are moving from there seem to be some converging views that information and knowledge are becoming the primary source of economic value.

The 'informational technological' paradigm is having a fundamental effect on businesses since processes enter into the domain of human activity; something that affects social structures and organizational structures. Under the 'informational technological' paradigm, information and knowledge become the primary source of economic value and competitive advantage. Knowledge is a source of sustainable advantage given that, unlike other assets, knowledge assets grow with use.

The combined effects of globalization, influenced by new technologies, and better communication and transport facilities mean that consumers now have more choice for goods and services available to them. They are constantly being inundated with new product offerings from global companies. For organizations, this means that they cannot afford to be complacent about how they conduct business. They cannot assume that the products and processes that made them successful in the past will continue to do so in the future.

But businesses have also got to keep an eye on their cost base and seek new ways of managing this. One of the ways in which many organizations have done this is through reviewing their core competence, and outsourcing business activities that do not map directly onto their core competence. Over recent years, we have seen an increase in the number of organizations that have outsourced their manufacturing, and in some cases part of their service function, to countries where labour costs are lower than in their native country. The area around Bangalore in India, for example, is now a world centre for software production; an example of where the globalization of knowledge is unaffected by traditional boundaries. Of course, by shifting production to different continents, organizations can take advantage of different time zones, which means that they can offer a twenty-four hour service to customers in a cost-effective way.

Changes in Technology

Despite the way in which changes in technology are affecting all of our lives, it is easy to forget the speed at which change is taking place. As Table 9.1 indicates, technological changes, which in the past spanned generations, now take place within much shorter time frame.

TABLE 9.1 Time to Market–How the World of Technology is Speeding Up

Technology	*Time to reach 10 million customers (years)*
Pager	41
Telephone	38
Table TV	25
Fax machine	22
VCR	9
Cellular telephone	9
Personal computer	7
CD-ROM drive	6
Netscape Internet browser	0.5 (i.e. six months)

Over the past couple of decades, we have seen significant and rapid changes in Information and Communications Technologies. Two important technologies evolved during the 1980s and 1990s. One was a change in telecommunications technologies providing a hundred-fold increase in the amount of data that can be transmitted over computer networks. Another was the growth in the number of networked computers enabling more open communications systems and new ways of working.

These technological changes have enabled new organizational forms to develop, for example networked organizations, virtual organizations and e-businesses—all of which are based on a different set of assumptions about the way business should be organized and managed. In these new business environments, hierarchical structures have been found to be less effective as they get in the way of providing a differentiated and responsive service to customers. In addition, they are based on a different set of assumptions about the way business should be organized and managed.

These combined technological changes have also led to a number of observable changes in the way that work is structured and organized. First, information that in the past would have been restricted to individuals in certain job roles, can now be made more accessible both vertically and horizontally, within and across organizations; such a change can affect how and where business decisions are made. Second, these new technologies have enabled work to be location-independent, thus transcending traditional geographical boundaries. With the relevant technologies, work, as pointed out above, can be distributed around the world in order to minimize production costs. Finally, these new technologies have opened up the possibilities for individuals to work from home, thus bringing about a return to a way of living and working that existed in the pre-industrial era, in which work, family and community life were closely intertwined.

Knowledge-based businesses apart, more and more jobs now involve the use of Information and Communications Technologies (ICT). ICT skills are seen as being essential in the modern workplace. However, as more and more organizations opt to have their IT systems developed and serviced by third party suppliers, this will have implications for the skills mix within organizations. What will be required is IT literate employees who understand the business, but IT literacy will come to mean knowing how to use computers more so than knowing how to manage them.

What are the implications of these continuous changes in technology for HR? First, HR professionals will need to become more IT literate themselves, sufficient enough to be able to enter into meaningful discussions with their IT counterparts. Second, they will need to consider the implications for the organizations' future resources, skills and capabilities. Third, they will need to help prepare employees for new roles and opportunities that are likely to emerge from emerging technologies.

The introduction of flexible working practices has organizational benefits too. These include: the ability to provide a more responsive service to customers; the ability to attract employees from diverse backgrounds, who otherwise might be excluded from traditional employment models; attracting and retaining skilled professionals; and retaining employees looking to have a balance between their work and home lives.

However, when considering structural change, such as the introduction of flexible working practices, organizations also need to consider and plan for the impact that this might have on their ability to manage their knowledge. While having more mobile and flexible workers may make it easier to deliver a more responsive service to customers, unless properly managed, this could have an adverse affect on an organization's knowledge capabilities. In addition, organizations will need to plan for the fact they may have less time to capitalize on their employees' 'know-how'.

The combined effects of structural change, i.e. the shift from manufacturing to service-based businesses (which are more information and knowledge dependent) and technology are having an effect on the skills needed within the workplace. Today's businesses are more knowledge intensive.

The pace of change in the modern business world means that the life span of certain knowledge is getting shorter and shorter. Individuals in all employment sectors, not just those working in knowledge-intensive businesses, need constantly to update their skills and knowledge in order to maintain their employability. In the modern workplace, continuous learning is becoming the norm. But there is an issue here with regard to who should pay for this learning—should it be businesses, individuals themselves, or should the Government be expected to contribute some funding too?

In order to be able to work any place, any time, anywhere, individuals need to be provided with the right technological infrastructure (laptop, mobile phone) and they also need to have access to up-to-date centralized information systems that can be accessed from any location. One of the difficulties, however, of having a global and mobile workforce is that it can be difficult to ensure certain types of knowledge sharing. Creating a sense of community can be difficult in organizations in which the majority of employees are mobile, leaving them feeling isolated and lacking a sense of belonging.

Definitions of Knowledge

The term 'knowledge' is in itself a difficult concept. Unlike many other assets, knowledge is not something that you can touch, or feel, hence the reason why it is often described as the invisible, or intangible asset. Some knowledge exists outside the individual, in text format, but a large percentage of knowledge resides within people. One of its other elusive characteristics is that the value of knowledge is highly contextual, i.e. you only know what you need to know, at the time when you need to know it; something that many organizations have discovered far too late.

While many knowledge management practitioners argue that we should not get too hung-up on definitions, it is important to ensure that there is some common understanding about what knowledge the organization is trying to manage. Tom Boyde, a leading writer on learning organizations, has developed a framework for thinking about knowledge. This consists of four types of knowledge and three knowledge levels. The four types of knowledge include:

(a) Knowing about things
(b) Knowing how to do things
(c) Knowing how to become yourself
(d) Knowing how to achieve things with others

The three knowledge levels are:

1. Knowing how to implement
2. Knowing how to improve
3. Knowing how to integrate

Knowledge is different from information, since information only becomes knowledge when transformed by one or more of the following processes:

- Comparison—How does information about this situation compare to that of others?
- Consequences—What implications do this information have for decisions and actions?
- Connections—How does this bit of knowledge relate to other pieces of knowledge?
- Conversation—What do others think about this information? It is this particular activity that emphasizes the importance of social interaction for the knowledge creation process.

Know of, or Know about

This is often referred to as 'operational level' knowledge, i.e. knowledge that is used as part of individuals' day-to-day work. In a retail environment, operational level knowledge might include awareness of the current week's special offers, new promotions, store layout changes, etc. In a legal environment, operational level knowledge might include changes in legislation relating to employment law.

This type of knowledge lends itself to being codified and hence more readily accessible through intranet systems, or transmitted, via mass communication techniques (e.g. through e-mail, memos).

Know how

This again is often referred to as operational level knowledge. However, the type of knowledge here is tacit knowledge, i.e. our accumulated experience of how things work and also how things get done. It is the type of knowledge that gets called upon when problem-solving and decision-making sets the context within which knowledge gets applied. It is for this reason that tacit knowledge is more difficult to codify.

Accessing 'know how' is not something that can always easily be extracted through the use of interviewing techniques. This was an important discovery made by the Xerox corporation when researching how to design information systems to support the way people really work. The initial stage of the Xerox research involved interviewing certain groups of employees about how they went about their day-to-day jobs. When clerks working in the organization's accounts department were interviewed about their jobs, what they described in the interviews pretty much matched the information in their job description.

However, when these same clerks were observed at work by anthropologists, a very different picture of their jobs emerged. The anthropologists observed how although the clerks referred to formal procedures as they went about their day-to-day work, they also had to adapt many of their day-to-day work activities in order to get the job done. What was concluded from this study was that employees use formal procedures as a way of understanding what needs to be done, rather than to identify the actual steps that need to be taken to get from A to B. Instead the clerks draw on 'workarounds', i.e. informal steps, which are undocumented, and which managers are often unaware of. Given these findings, it is clear why induction and initial on-the-job training for new members of the team become so important. Without this an organization is likely to find that new employees follow documented procedures that do not deliver the intended results. The result: dissatisfied customers and disheartened employees.

Know why

In the complex and ever-changing business world that we operate today, employees need to be more strategically aware. They need to know where their organization is going and why. They also need to know about the organization's value system and how this links to the organization's strategic direction. This is important for two reasons. One is to ensure that the decisions that individuals make as part of their day-to-day jobs are consistent with the organization's overall strategic direction. The second reason is that individuals can understand how they can best contribute to the organization's strategic goals.

If individuals are clearer about where and how they can contribute to the organization's future, then this will help them feel more connected. Robert B. Reich, Professor of Economic and Social Research at Brandeis University, argues that in the modern workplace, employers need to work at creating 'social glue'. Reich suggests that 'collaboration and mutual advantage are the essence of the organization. They can create flexibility, resiliency, speed and creativity—the fundamental qualities of the 21st century.' To help build 'social glue', individuals, according to Reich, need to be given opportunities to work on projects which make a real difference and where the organizational goal is aligned with the individual's own personal goals and values.

In today's ever-changing business world, individuals also need to be aware of the economic, social and political changes taking place around them, so that they can have intelligent discussions about the likely implications for the business, as well as their own careers. Building this external perspective can help individuals spot emerging trends, as well as see existing landscapes through a new pair of lenses.

Some of the ways in which organizations are helping individuals build their 'know why' are discussed in later chapters in this book.

Know who

As much of an organization's knowledge resides within individuals' heads, knowledge of who is who, both within and outside the organization, and what knowledge can be unlocked through networking is critical. The ability to build and maintain social networks, as we shall see later, has become one of the critical knowledge-building competencies.

In any organization, it is important to have this taxonomy of knowledge in mind when developing policies and practices for managing knowledge. Without this, organizations may focus their energies and other resources on developing one particular type of knowledge, leaving themselves vulnerable in other areas.

Other KM practitioners have adopted other methods for categorising the types of knowledge that organizations need to focus on managing (Knight, 2001). The 'knowledge types' method pioneered by Knight and his colleagues in ICL, for example, include knowledge types such as:

- Product and service knowledge—the business 'content' relating to the customer experience.
- Process knowledge—how to get things done.
- Customer and supplier knowledge—knowledge about relationships.
- Project knowledge—focused on organizational memory and learning.
- Technical, or expert knowledge—supporting people with know how.

Defining Knowledge Management

Just as there are difficulties coming up with a single definition of knowledge, so it is with identifying a single definition of the term 'knowledge management'. Some practitioners feel it is important not to get too hung up on definitions, or indeed get embroiled in a lengthy debate about the differences between data, information and knowledge. However, if individuals are to engage in a dialogue about knowledge management, then they at least need to have a working definition of what knowledge management is, within the context of their own organization.

Knowledge can be defined as ***processed and meaningful inferences derived from available information.*** Knowledge can be of two types—**tacit and explicit knowledge.** Explicit knowledge can be expressed in words and numbers, and easily communicated and shared in the form of hard data, scientific formulae, codified procedures or universal principles. However, knowledge so expressed represents only the tip of the iceberg. Knowledge is primarily *tacit*—something not easily visible and expressible. It is highly personal and hard to formalise, making it difficult to communicate and share it with others. Subjective insights, intuitions fall into this category. Furthermore, tacit knowledge is deeply rooted in an individual's action and experience, as well as in the ideals, values or emotions that he or she embraces. Different stages in Knowledge Management are shown in Figure 9.6

The objective of knowledge management is to make the process of knowledge sharing more effective. This means that corporate knowledge be made available in forms which are readily accessible. This could take the form of knowledge document, process and rules. This could be done in the form of information technology. The various technologies used to do this are:

- Data Warehouses
- Groupware
- Workflow Management Systems
- Distribution via Internet/Intranet
- Web Mining

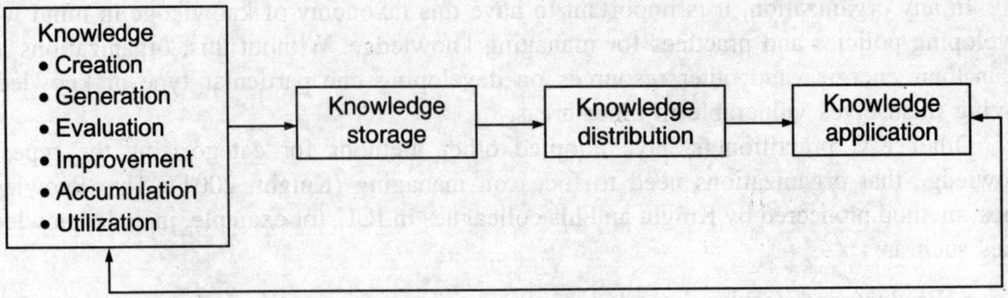

Figure 9.6 Stages of creation of knowledge management.

The general objectives while designing a knowledge management system are the following:

- Improve learning and foster innovation by streamlining information access and retrieval, putting content in context.
- Enhance information organization, thus allowing enterprises to maximize the value of information, deliver products and services faster, and provide users a rich knowledge discovery.
- Protect knowledge assets to reduce the duplication of work and to enable organizations to identify knowledge gaps.
- Automate the knowledge management.

Importance of Knowledge Management

- The marketplace is increasingly competitive and the rate of innovation is rising, so that knowledge must evolve and be assimilated at an ever-faster rate.
- Corporations are organizing their businesses to be focused on creating customer value. Staff functions are being reduced, and management structures are being pruned to bring in greater flexibility.
- Competitive pressures are reducing the size of the workforce, which holds this knowledge.
- Knowledge takes time to acquire and mature. Employees have less and less time for this.
- There are chances that experts may leave the organization or retire, leading to loss of knowledge.
- There is a need to manage increasing complexity, as more and more companies are becoming trans-national in nature.
- Loss due to high employee turnover in knowledge industries can be minimized.
- Reduction in training cost for new employees.
- Avoid duplication of efforts and reduction in repetition of mistakes.

A change in strategic direction may result in the loss of knowledge in a specific area. A subsequent reversal in policy may then lead to a renewed requirement for this knowledge, but the employees with that knowledge may no longer be there.

The components of knowledge management can be summarized as follows:

- Learning
- Sharing
- Having people in the right place at the right time
- Effective decision-making
- Creativity
- Making people's jobs easier
- Generating new business and business value

For these things to happen requires a culture where individuals are motivated enough to want to share their knowledge with others, such that they themselves grow, as well as enabling the business to grow and survive too.

The organic knowledge management approach is felt to be more fruitful for the development of tacit knowledge. It requires an approach whereby knowledge is created through volunteering, encouraging self-organized communities, building an open environment where the motivation for knowledge sharing comes from the desire to leave some form of legacy. In this way, knowledge sharing becomes a self-reinforcing activity.

Where is your organization on its knowledge management journey?

Table 9.2 provides the stages through which an organization needs to progress to become knowledge-centric. The first step is to become aware of the current stage of the organization from the five stages as shown. Once an audit is done, then it is possible to set a goal to achieve it.

TABLE 9.2 Stages in an Organization's Knowledge Management Journey

Stage	*Name*	*Characteristics*
1	Knowledge-chaotic	unaware of concept
		no information processes
		no information sharing
2	Knowledge-aware	awareness of KM need
		some KM processes
		technology in place
		sharing information an issue
3	Knowledge-enabled	benefits of KM clear
		standards adopted
		issues relating to culture and technology
4	Knowledge-managed	integrated frameworks
		benefits case realised
		issues in previous stages overcome
5	Knowledge-centric	KM part of mission
		Knowledge-value recognized in
		market capitalization
		KM integrated into culture

If you feel that your organization is at the knowledge-chaotic stage, then perhaps a first step for HR would be to conduct its own internal audit. Questions that you might include are:

For the organization as a whole:

- Where does knowledge management fit within the organization's strategic plans?
- What do people in different parts of the organization understand by the term knowledge management?
- Where do they think responsibilities for managing knowledge should rest?
- What do people see as the blocks and enablers to managing knowledge within your organization?
- What do they think could be done to minimize the blocks and strengthen the enablers?
- What practices already exist that could be considered as helping to build the organization's knowledge capabilities?
- What do people know about the practices that exist within other organizations?

For teams

- What are the things that get in the way of them performing at their best, e.g. certain types of information, tools, processes, certain organizational practices or rituals?
- How much is known about the skills, expertise and interests of team members? Where is this information held? How is it kept up-to-date?
- What practices are in place to enhance knowledge transfer within and across teams?
- How receptive are teams to learning from the experiences of others outside the team? How is this facilitated?
- What practices are in place to capitalise on individuals' knowledge as they join, grow and move on from the team?
- What is the psychological contract between team members for developing and sharing knowledge?

For individuals

- Where does managing knowledge fit with individuals' concept of a career?
- How are individuals investing in themselves in order to keep their own knowledge up-to-date and in demand?
- What support/resources do individuals find most useful in developing their knowledge?
- How do individuals help others develop their knowledge?

These same questions could also be used and/or adapted when carrying out periodic evaluations of how well the organization is managing its knowledge.

Need for a Strategic Approach to Managing Knowledge

The knowledge management journey in many organizations often begins in a piecemeal way with a local initiative, kicked off by a group of like-minded forward-thinking individuals.

This was the experience within ICL, for example, where a group of colleagues got together to address the question of 'How can we add true organizational learning to the existing emphasis on training and developing people?

Knowledge Management Drivers and the Link with Organisational Strategy

What are the pressures that the organization is facing? Why is managing knowledge important to us as a business?

Knowledge management strategy. Where do we need to be? What are the key levers for change? These might be a focus on people, processes, leadership, or technology. Some of the common strategic levers for knowledge management include: customer knowledge; knowledge in products and service; knowledge in people; knowledge in processes; organizational memory; knowledge in relationships and knowledge assets.

Implementation. How do we move forward? Here consideration needs to be given to implementation from a top-down, lateral and bottom-up approach.

Measuring the results. How are we doing? Here consideration could be given to adopting a balanced scorecard approach, focusing on the four elements of financial, customer, process and future.

As other writers point out, it is important that wherever an organization starts on its knowledge management journey, or wherever the initial focus is placed, it is important to adopt a holistic approach (Probst, Raub and Romhard, 2000). Probst *et al.* see the core building blocks of knowledge management as:

Knowledge identification. How do we ensure that there is sufficient transparency of external and internal knowledge? How do we help employees to locate the information that they need?

Knowledge acquisition. What forms of expertise should we buy in from outside? Are we making full use of the expertise embedded in the external relationships that we have?

Knowledge development. How can we build new expertise and capabilities?

Knowledge sharing and distribution. How do we get the knowledge to the right places?

Knowledge utilization. How do we ensure that the knowledge that we have is applied productively for the benefits of the organization?

Knowledge retention. How do we ensure that we retain the knowledge that we have? How knowledge enabled is the organization?

Evaluation. How well are we doing on our knowledge management journey? What have been our key successes and failures? Where should we focus our energy going forward?

The ability to learn to do new things (i.e. products, services, processes) and then deliver more quickly than competitors is crucial. To do this, organizations and individuals need to become better at information management, as well as managing different types of knowledge: 'know how', 'know who' and 'know why'.

In many organizations there is still confusion about what managing knowledge is really about. This has caused confusion regarding responsibilities for managing an organization's knowledge. For organizations to move forward on their knowledge management journey, there needs to be greater acknowledgement that:

- Knowledge resides in people, not in systems, although systems contain valuable data and information that can help the knowledge process.
- Knowledge creation is fundamentally a social process, it is created through the interactions between individuals as they go about their daily lives.

Stages in Developing Knowledge Management Systems

Systems analysis and design have proved to be of great importance in developing successful business information systems. They have an equally important role in Knowledge Management system development. A business Knowledge Management system is a computerized decision tool. When the size and strategic significance of Knowledge Management system are great, its analysis and design play crucial roles in its successful development.

Business information systems and business Knowledge Management system share common features. Both have the ultimate goal of improving the quality of the decision and control process within the business. Their applications alter the business environment, and change the day-to-day operation. In turn, they are greatly affected by the business culture and the business environment for which they are designed. Their development requires a commitment of resources and time by top managers and users. The similarities between business information systems and Knowledge Management system indicate that the development of business Knowledge Management system could greatly benefit from the use of systems analysis and design techniques. In practice, this indeed has proven to be the case.

In analysing and designing Knowledge Management system, one must be aware of the major differences between Knowledge Management system and information systems. Differences that impact the choice of methods in analysing Knowledge Management system are:

- Knowledge Management system is new and less established than Information systems. The top managers, experts, and users need more extensive communication and discussions to define the objectives of the Knowledge Management system and grasp its capabilities and limitations. This demands an extra degree of interaction among those involved in the development of an expert system, as discussed in a later section in this chapter.
- While information systems computerize mostly the structured aspects of business processes, Knowledge Management system is designed for solving unstructured and semi structured decision problems. The developer of Knowledge Management

system must impose a structure for solving such problems. This requires development approaches that allow for many iterations and trial and error, before the final product is produced. One such method is prototyping, which is discussed in the next section.

- Knowledge Management system contains domain knowledge, which must be attained through the arduous process of knowledge acquisition and knowledge modelling. Information systems need data, whose methods of collection and storage are well established. The underlying data models in information systems are easier to attain.
- Knowledge Management system normally comes up with an *answer,* such as categorizing an object (for example, a loan application), diagnosing a problem (for example, the reason for a machine failure) or taking an action (for example, opening a valve). Information systems give input to the user, normally without producing a definite recommendation. This means that a Knowledge Management system requires the added steps of validation and verification for establishing the correctness or, at least, the acceptability of its answers.

System Development Life Cycle

In organizing the development of a relatively large expert system, one must use the system development stages common to those in information systems:

These stages are shown in Figure 9.7, where the arrows indicate the iterative nature of the development stages.

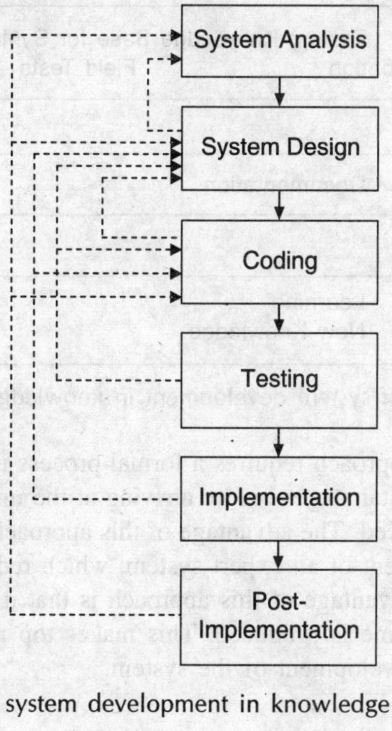

Figure 9.7 Stages of system development in knowledge management system.

Each stage, however, has features unique to Knowledge Management system, as shown in Figure 9.8. In the following sections of this chapter, each one of these stages is discussed in more detail.

System Analysis

Problem Identification	Domain Analysis	Goal Identification
Modularization	Communication	Expert Identification

System Design

Logical Design:	Knowledge Acquision
Physical Design:	Software Selection Hardware Interface Design User Interface Design Physical Design of Knowledge Base

Coding

Coding or Buying Software	Coding the Knowledge Base	Coding the User Interface
	Coding Hooks to Other Systems	

Testing

Software Testing	Testing Knowledge Base for Syntax Erros		
Verification	Validation	Field Tests	System Reliability

Implementation

User Training	Documentation	Field Support

Post-implementation

Collection Field Reports and Statistics	Learning New Knowledge	Discarding Obsolete Knowledge

Figure 9.8 Features of system development in knowledge management system.

The *system life cycle* approach requires a formal process in which the system developer goes through the developmental stages before arriving at the implementation phase, in which the finished product is produced. The advantage of this approach is that it provides an orderly framework for the development of an expert system, which reduces the probability of major errors and pitfalls. The disadvantage of this approach is that it takes a long time before any product with a visible outcome is produced. This makes top managers reluctant to commit financial resources to the development of the system.

Some Applications of Knowledge Management

Wipro: Wipro Infotech, which offers a comprehensive suite of IT infrastructure solutions, professional services, communication services, and business solutions.

Knowledge Management in Wipro Infotech has three objectives:

- Mature the organization to a competency based and knowledge driven organization.
- Enable new technology/practices adoption for diversification and growth.
- Develop competency extension framework to create new business opportunities.

The Wipro Infotech KM frame has three main frameworks which enable the organization. They are:

- Learning.
- KEEP (Knowledge Enhancement, Extraction and Practice)
- CARE (Competency Augmentation With Research Excellence)

***Learning*:** This ensures that people build their competency using a mix of tools and processes like E-learning, competency assessment and competency development through specialised training and personalised instruction. Learning is based on the competency model.

KEEP: Through the KEEP (Knowledge Enhancement, Extraction and Practice) initiative, Wipro ensures collection of desparate knowledge and expertise within the organization into a central repository. The knowledge is supplemented by gathering additional information from various external resources. The four pillars of KEEP are taxonomy (a uniform structure through which knowledge can be stored and accessed) IT enablers, practice based offering and knowledge channels.

CARE: Through CARE (Competency Augmentation With Research Excellence), they leverage on the expertise and knowledge built up in the organization to come up with innovative products and services and inculcate creative thinking within Wipro Infotech that capitalizes on people competency and expertise, supplementing it with a technology tracking activity, resulting in higher intellectual property.

Also, the company has a system to maintain the KM progress reports.

HLL: HLL has formed Communities of Practice (COP) around their key function, Like Branding, Packaging etc. Packaging is their one of the most successful COP. Here is in brief explained about formation, functioning and key activities, which this knowledge community is doing.

Packaging in HLL is very important for providing protection to the product in transit and storage as well as its contribution to pack presentation/brand image. Total packaging cost is very significant. Packaging professionals work very closely with different product categories. The challenge is to deliver packaging and operational excellence right across all categories. The task is to ensure that the collective knowledge of the packaging community irrespective of the category, to which they are linked, is fully leveraged for maximum, collective value addition.

The packaging team formed a knowledge community consisting of the packaging developing managers and officers and packaging buyers of various businesses in the company. Some of the key suppliers were also invited to be part of the community. This community developed a charter. The charter included areas for improving speed and quality of innovations, identifying opportunities for technology-led cost effectiveness and creating processes for achieving packaging synergy through harmonization, exchange of best proven practices and cross-category transfer of key insights obtained.

The community is very focussed on learning, sharing and effective implementation of its charter. Knowledge is shared in a structured way with each team member wearing two 'hats'—one of the business/category unit and the other of packaging. The community meets periodically to share knowledge in a structured way and monitors progress on implementation of the charter. This has enabled systematic implementation of packing innovation projects and preparation of best practice documents. The following approaches have been adopted:

- Clarification of business objectives from the business team, understanding the packaging skills chain and improving appreciation of consumer needs through participation in 'consumer clinics'.
- The team identifies well-defined knowledge blocks in the packaging area and appoints sub-teams to specialise/lead in each of the knowledge blocks.
- The packaging community organizes 'knowledge workshop' to generate new ideas and opportunities. It focuses on capability building through continuous skill-mapping, gap analysis and need based training.
- The team has developed an intranet application with collaboration tools.

The case of the packaging community demonstrates that KM is essentially a process to increase the capacity for energetic and focussed action, by connecting people to people and people to knowledge; that KM facilitates capability building; it raises the floor, raises the ceiling; that it promotes a culture of faster transfer of best proven practices and insights; and that an organised KM process reduces the scope for 'reinventing the wheel'

Knowledge Management and Data Warehousing and Data Mining

A data warehouse is a **structured extensible environment** designed for the analysis of **non-volatile data**, **logically and physically transformed** from multiple source applications to align with business structure, updated and maintained for a long time period, expressed in simple business terms, and summarized for **quick analysis**.

Importance of Data Warehouse for an Organization

1. ***Immediate information delivery.*** Data warehouses decrease the length of time between business events occurrence and executive alert. Using a data warehouse, daily, weekly, and monthly sales reports are available on a daily basis. Given this data delivery time compression, business decision makers can exploit opportunities that they would otherwise miss.

2. ***Data integration from across and even outside the organization.*** To provide a complete picture, Data warehouses typically combine data from multiple sources such as a company's order entry and warranty systems. Thus, with a warehouse, it may be possible to track all interactions a company has with each customer—from that customer's first inquiry, through the terms of their purchase all the way through any warranty or service interactions.

3. ***Future vision from historical trends.*** Effective business analysis frequently includes trend and seasonality analysis. To support this, warehouses typically contain multiple years of data.

4. ***Tools for looking at data in new ways.*** Instead of paper reports, warehouses give users tools for looking at data differently. They also allow those users to manipulate their data. An interactive table that allows the user to drill down into detail data with the click of a mouse can answer questions that might take months to answer in a traditional system.

Characteristics of a Data Warehouse

The main features of a data warehouse are:

- ***Subject oriented:*** Data warehouses are designed to analyse the data. Suppose a sales executive wants to learn more about top 10 customers, a data warehouse is built with a focus on sales, thus imparting itself subject orientation.
- ***Integrated:*** Integration is closely related to subject orientation. Data warehouses must put together data from desparate form into consistent format. They must resolve the naming conflicts and inconsistencies among units of measure, in order to be integrated.
- ***Non-Volatile:*** This means that once data has been entered into the data warehouse, it cannot be changed.
- ***Time Variant:*** In order to find business trends, management needs to analyze a large amount of data quickly in contrast to OLTP (On Line Transaction Processing) where performance requirements lead to archival of history data.

Functions of a Data Warehouse

The principal functions of a data warehouse are:

1. **Extracting:** Chucking out of data from desparate sources.
2. **Integrating:** Putting together the extracted into a consistent format.
3. **Filtering:** Process of extracting the data from the OLTP or external data sources. For example, the user may be interested in only the last five years' sales data.
4. **Standardizing:** As the data will be moved from different OLTP database or flat file system, to one target, data need to be standardized.

5. **Transforming:** Data is extracted from OLTP databases and external data source data. Data transformation will have to be carried out on the extracted data before data is carried to the warehouse.
6. **Cleaning:** To ensure data quality, accuracy.

Data Warehouse Architecture

A Data Warehouse Architecture (DWA) is a way of representing the overall structure of data, communication, processing and presentation that exists for end-user computing within the enterprise. The architecture is made up of a number of interconnected parts:

- Operational Database/External Database Layer
- Information Access Layer
- Data Access Layer
- Data Directory (Metadata) Layer
- Process Management Layer
- Application Messaging Layer
- Data Warehouse Layer
- Data Staging Layer

Business Use of a Data Warehouse

No discussion of the data warehousing systems is complete without review of the type of activity supported by a data warehouse. Some of the activity against today's data warehouses is predefined and not much different from traditional analysis activity. Other processes such as multi-dimensional analysis and information visualization were not available with traditional analysis tools and methods.

Standard Reports and Queries

Many users of the data warehouse need to access a set of standard reports and queries. It is desirable to periodically automatically produce a set of standard reports that are required by many different users. When these users need a particular report, they can just view the report that has already been run by the data warehouse system rather than running it themselves. This facility can be particularly useful for reports that take a long time to run.

Such a facility would require report server software. It is likely that these reports can be accessed only using the client program for that system. This facility would need to work with or be part of the preferred data warehouse access tool previously mentioned. Many end user query and analysis tools now include server software that can be run with the data warehouse to serve reports and query results. These tools are now providing a web interface to the reports. In many data warehouse systems, this report and query server becomes an essential facility. The data warehouse users and administrators constantly need to consider any reports that are candidates to become standard reports for the data warehouse. Frequently, individual users may develop reports that can be used by other users.

Data Mining

Data mining, in simple terms, can be called the extraction of hidden predictive information from large databases or data warehouses. The growth of data warehousing has created huge chunks of data. These chunks represent a valuable resource to the enterprise. But to extract value from these data chunks, we must "mine" for high-grade "nuggets" of precious metal, i.e. the gold in data warehouses and data marts.

Data mining tools predict future trends and behaviours, allowing businesses to make proactive, knowledge-driven decisions. The automated, prospective analyses offered by data mining move beyond the analyses of past events provided by retrospective tools typical of decision support systems. Data mining tools can answer business questions that traditionally were too time consuming to resolve. They scour databases for hidden patterns, finding predictive information that experts may miss because it lies outside their expectations.

Most companies already collect and refine massive quantities of data. Data mining techniques can be implemented rapidly on existing software and hardware platforms to enhance the value of existing information resources, and can be integrated with new products and systems as they are brought on-line. When implemented on high performance client/server or parallel processing computers, data mining tools can analyse massive databases to deliver answers to questions such as, "Which clients are most likely to respond to next promotional mailing, why?"

Data mining software allows users to analyse large databases to solve business decision problems. Data mining is, in some ways, an extension of statistics, with a few artificial intelligence and machine learning twists thrown in. Like statistics, data mining is not a business solution, it is just a technology. Consider a catalogue retailer who needs to decide who should receive information about a new product. The information operated on by the data mining process is contained in a historical database of previous interactions with customers and the features associated with the customers, such as age, zip code, and their responses. The data mining software would use this historical information to build a model of customer behaviour that could be used to predict which customers would be likely to respond to the new product. By using this information, a marketing manager can select only the customers who are most likely to respond. The operational business software can then feed the results of the decision to appropriate touch point systems (call centres, web servers, email systems, etc.) so that the right customers receive the right offers.

The Scope and the Techniques Used

Given databases of sufficient size and quality, data mining technology can generate new business opportunities by providing these capabilities:

- ***Automated prediction of trends and behaviours.*** Data mining automates the process of finding predictive information in large databases. Questions that traditionally required extensive hands-on analysis can now be answered directly from the data—quickly. A typical example of a predictive problem is "targeted marketing". Data mining uses data on past promotional mailings to identify the targets most likely to maximize return on investment in future mailings. Other predictive problems include forecasting bankruptcy and other forms of default, and identifying segments of a population likely to respond similarly to given events.
- ***Automated discovery of previously unknown patterns.*** Data mining tools sweep through databases and identify previously hidden patterns in one step. An example of "pattern discovery" is the analysis of retail sales data to identify seemingly unrelated products that are often purchased together. Other pattern discovery problems include detecting fraudulent credit card transactions and identifying anomalous data that could represent data entry keying errors.

Data mining techniques can yield the benefits of automation on existing software and hardware platforms, and can be implemented on new systems as existing platforms are upgraded and new products developed. When data mining tools are implemented on high performance parallel processing systems, they can analyse massive databases in minutes. Faster processing means that users can automatically experiment with more models to understand complex data. High speed makes it practical for users to analyse huge quantities of data. Larger databases (larger in depth as well as breadth), in turn, yield improved predictions.

The following techniques are used in data mining:

- ***Artificial neural networks.*** Non-linear predictive models that learn through training and resemble biological neural networks in structure.
- ***Decision trees.*** Tree-shaped structures that represent sets of decisions. These decisions generate rules for the classification of a dataset. Specific decision tree methods include Classification and Regression Trees (CART) and Chi Square Automatic Interaction Detection (CHAID).
- ***Genetic algorithms.*** Optimization techniques that use processes such as genetic combination, mutation, and natural selection in a design based on the concepts of evolution.
- ***Nearest neighbour method.*** A technique that classifies each record in a dataset based on a combination of the classes of the k record(s) most similar to it in a historical dataset (where $k^3 = 1$). Sometimes called the k-nearest neighbour technique.
- ***Rule induction.*** The extraction of useful if-then rules from data based on statistical significance.

Many of these technologies have been in use for more than a decade in specialized analysis tools that work with relatively small volumes of data. These capabilities are now evolving to integrate directly with industry-standard data warehouse and OLAP (Online Analytical Processing) platforms.

Business Applications

A wide range of companies have deployed successful applications of data mining, early adopters being industries such as financial services and direct mail marketing. The technology is applicable to any company looking to leverage a large data warehouse to better manage their customer relationships. Two critical factors for success with data mining are: a large, well-integrated data warehouse and a well-defined understanding of the business process within which data mining is to be applied such as customer prospecting, retention, and campaign management.

Some of the applications of data mining in business are as follows:

- A pharmaceutical company can analyse its recent sales force activity and their results to improve targeting of high-value physicians and determine which marketing activities will have the greatest impact in the next few months. The data needs to include competitor market activity as well as information about the local health care systems. The results can be distributed to the sales force via a wide-area network that enables the representatives to review the recommendations from the perspective of the key attributes in the decision process. The ongoing, dynamic analysis of the data warehouse allows best practices from throughout the organization to be applied in specific sales situations.
- A credit card company can leverage its vast warehouse of customer transaction data to identify customers most likely to be interested in a new credit product. Using a small test mailing, the attributes of customers with an affinity for the product can be identified.
- A diversified transportation company with a large direct sales force can apply data mining to identify the best prospects for its services. Using data mining to analyse its own customer experience, this company can build a unique segmentation identifying the attributes of high-value prospects.
- A large FMCG company can apply data mining to improve its sales process to retailers. Data from consumer panels, shipments, and competitor activity can be applied to understand the reasons for brand and store switching. Through this analysis, the manufacturer can select promotional strategies that best reach their target customer segments.

Whether they call it "the post-industrial society", "the third wave" or "the knowledge era", most policy makers, academics and business leaders would agree that we have recently entered a new era. Undoubtedly, some of the defining characteristics of this era—which shall here be referred to as "the information age"—are still to emerge and develop. However, we now recognize that the information age differs markedly from the industrial age in several important respects. These differences can be summarized as in Figure 9.9.

Over the past 40 years or so, many business analysts have tried to determine what has been driving these changes. The consensus has shifted over time. At first, it was thought to be the automating power of computers and computation. Then, it was the ability to collapse time and space through telecommunications. More recently, it is found to be the value-creating power of information, a resource which can be reused, shared, distributed or exchanged

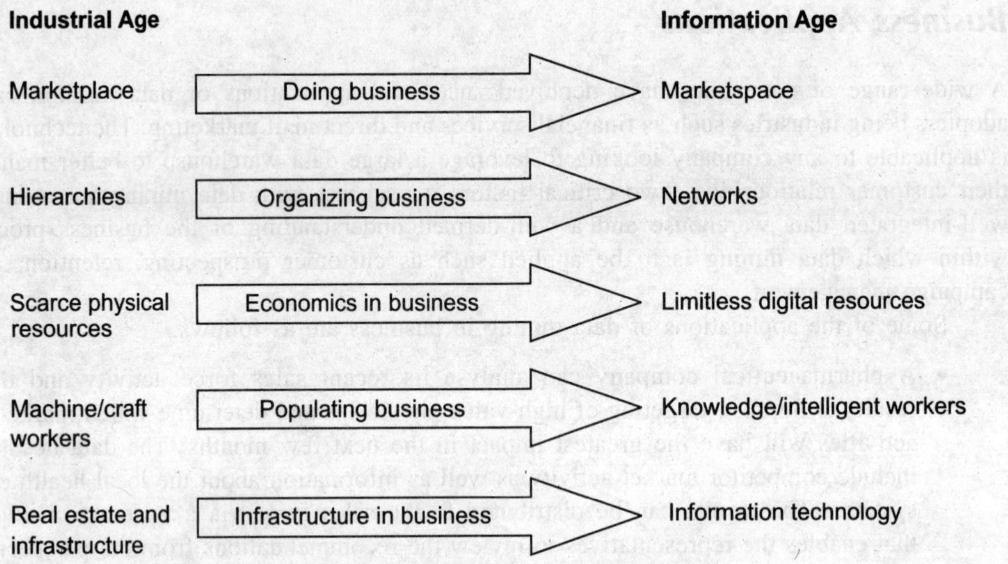

Figure 9.9 Industrial age vs. information age.

without any inevitable loss of value; indeed, value is sometimes multiplied. And today's fascination with competing on invisible assets means that people now see knowledge and its relationship with intellectual capital as a critical resource, because it undermines innovation and renewal.

Information and Strategy

All these claims are valid in some ways and therefore, there are diminishing returns to arguing which is the critical motive force. But we can recognize that today every business is an information business. Let us first take the perspective of industrial structure. We see battles in the marketplace all the time, as "content" companies try to acquire related content businesses, not only because of their thirst for information but also because of the opportunities for synergy created by repackaging, reuse and navigation. More significantly perhaps, content companies acquire or build alliances with communication companies, and vice versa. Both sides recognize that to command the airwaves is to command the distribution channels of the information age, and that the high value added opportunities are likely to rely on selling content and repackaging and reusing it in manifold ways. Sometimes, novels are made into television films. That is an example of repackaging opportunity.

It is not just the obviously information-intensive companies that are trying out these new strategies. More and more "traditional" companies follow some of the same logic. So, when SmithKline Beecham acquired Diversified Pharmaceutical Services in 1994, the purchase was as much about buying the data embedded in prescriptions and healthcare administration processes—which could then guide research and development programmes and sales management—as about more conventional synergies.

When Indiaworld was bought by Satyam Online, the sale soon turned out to have a similar information thread. So, we need to rewrite, or at least re-examine, the industrial economic rules of vertical integration and diversification.

Indeed, it becomes difficult in the world of intangible assets and electronic distribution channels to be clear to define vertical or horizontal integration. Microsoft takes stakes in software, communications and information-providing businesses, and America Online acquires Netscape. Are these "horizontal" or "vertical" manoeuvres?

If you choose to take an information perspective, businesses converge, partly because of the integrated e-strategy, exemplified in Figure 9.10. In other words, brand, technology, market and service are the four aspects of e-strategy. In some cases this happens because the product is information-based, as in the case of Disney and ABC. In other cases, it is because processes are information-based, such as in our pharmaceuticals examples. In still other cases, it is simply because market understanding or decision-making is information-based. So retailers, financial services, organizations and airlines will form alliances because of the information (and sales) potential of customer cards.

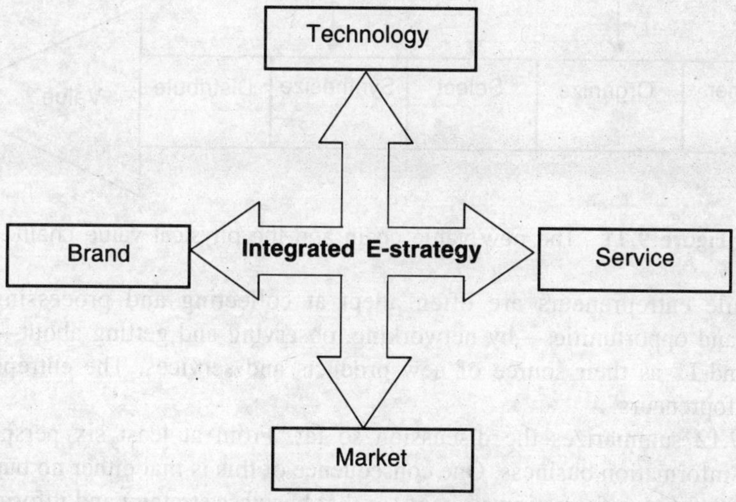

Figure 9.10 Convergence.

While the price-system coordinates the economy, managers integrate activity inside the firm. Increasingly, strategic advantage requires the integration of external activities and technologies. So, an integrated e-strategy implies integration of technology, brand standing, customer-service and meeting the needs of the market.

The Virtual Value Chain

Information can be captured at all stages of the physical value chain. Such information can be used to improve performance at each stage of the physical value chain and to coordinate across it. However, it can also be analyzed and repackaged to build content-based products or to create new lines of business. Thus, insurance companies, for example, are becoming adept at analyzing customer and claims information and then tele-selling both financial and physical products. A company can also use its information to reach out to other companies' customers or operations, thereby rearranging the value system of an industry; if you like, sectors become "value jigsaws" which can be rearranged so that traditional sector boundaries disappear.

As digital technologies converge, the whole concept of physical value chain undergoes a change. Today the focus is on the virtual value chain, which can be seen in Figure 9.11.

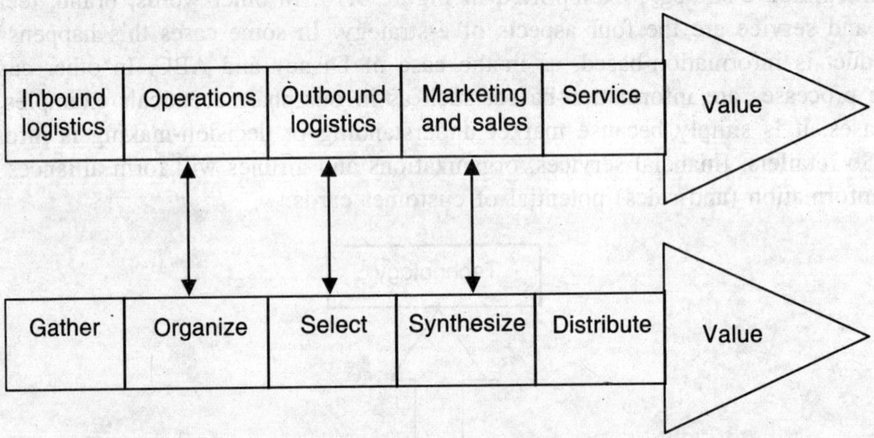

Figure 9.11 The new value chain and the physical value chain.

And while entrepreneurs are often adept at collecting and processing information about threats and opportunities—by networking, observing and getting about—many look to information and IT as their source of new products and services. The entrepreneurs of the future are "infopreneurs".

Figure 9.12 summarizes the discussion. so far. From at least six perspectives, every business is an information business. One consequence of this is that either no business strategy is complete without an information strategy, or that business strategy and information strategy need to be integrated. IT, information systems and information as a resource no longer just support business strategy; they indeed help to determine it. But what does an information strategy look like?

Figure 9.13 is a conceptual framework which distinguishes Information Systems (IS) strategy from IT strategy. IT, which was about the "how"—the technology infrastructure or platform—often seemed to distract attention from IS, which was the "what"—the identification and prioritization of systems or applications for development.

Then comes information management strategy, which was about the "who"—the all important question of roles and responsibilities in the delivery, support and strategic development of IS and IT. All of these were influenced by the business or organizational strategy, which was concerned with strategic intent ("why") and organizational architecture. In a perfect world, corporations strove for a good fit between these four domains.

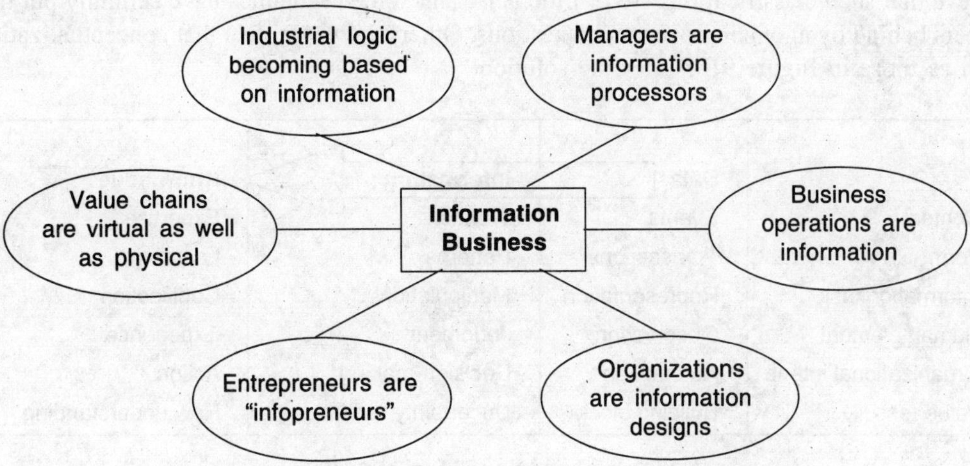

Figure 9.12 Every business is an information business.

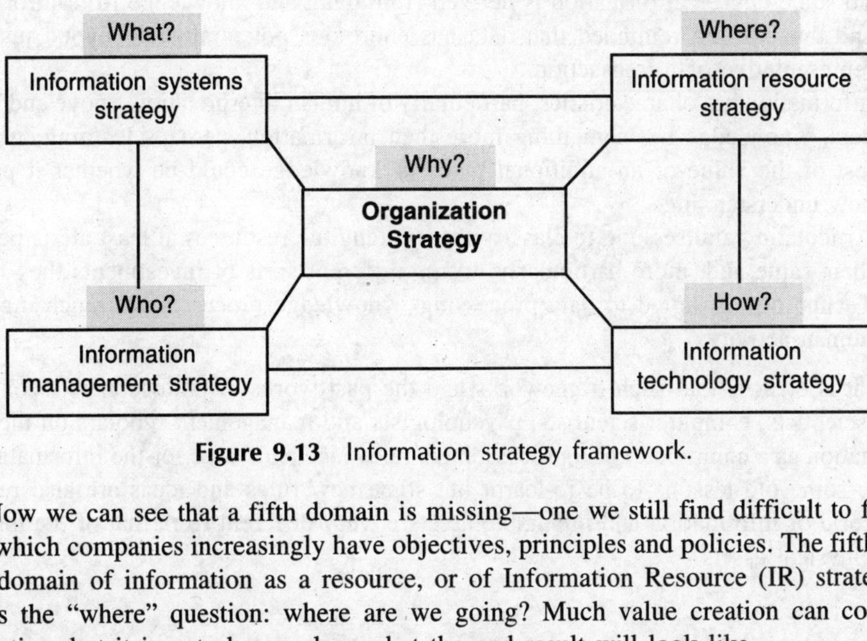

Figure 9.13 Information strategy framework.

Now we can see that a fifth domain is missing—one we still find difficult to formalize but in which companies increasingly have objectives, principles and policies. The fifth domain is the domain of information as a resource, or of Information Resource (IR) strategy. It is perhaps the "where" question: where are we going? Much value creation can come from information, but it is not always clear what the end result will look like.

In more traditional content companies, such as advertising agencies, broadcasters and movie companies, you will find policies about not giving away or even releasing content that others could reuse. And in financial services companies, you will find executives scratching their heads as to 'Why they never collected critical data such as date of birth when their customers registered with them?' and 'Why information resellers make money out of their transaction data'.

One aspect of IR strategy is the increasing interest in the distinction among data, information and knowledge. Some chief information officers and chief knowledge officers believe that such classifications are of little help, and some academics have certainly put their careers behind by agonizing over such questions. Others, however, feel that conceptualizations such as those in Figure 9.14 offer the solution.

	Data	**Information**	**Knowledge**
Content	Events	Trends	Expertise
Form	Transactions	Patterns	Learnings
Information task	Representation	Manipulation	Codification
Human element	Observation	Judgment	Experience
Organizational intent	Automation	Decision-making	Action
Value test	Building block	Uncertainty reduction	New understanding

Figure 9.14 From data to knowledge.

5. To some degree, information is derived from data, and knowledge from information, and thus we are reminded that data has enormous potential—far beyond just being representative of a transaction.
6. Information has characteristics, particularly of human interpretation, above and beyond data. Knowledge has something more than information, perhaps learning. A logical test of the value of an additional piece of knowledge could be whether it provides new understanding.
7. Articulating and seeking to classify these intangible resources at least alerts people to their value and, more particularly, to the different sorts of investments they require. Technology is suited to data processing. Knowledge processing is much more of a human activity.

What is clear is that such frameworks and the past works of philosophers, economists, political scientists, computer scientists, psychologists and management scholars on the nature of information as a commodity or a process, have relevance and value for the information age. There are some old lessons to be re-learnt but some new rules and ideas are also required, for the world of information and intangible assets is very different from that of the industrial age and physical assets.

Seven Dimensions of e-Commerce Strategy[1]

In order to understand the process of e-commerce strategy, systematic examination of the strategic factors involved has to be considered. Looking at the most successful e-commerce companies, we see a strategy emerging, which is modelled in Figure 9.15.

It can be argued that this model can be applied to all forms of organizations in the traditional sectors. However, this model is specially applicable to assisting the needs of

1. Plant R., *E-commerce Strategy*, Prentice-Hall PTR, Upper Saddle River, New Jersey, 2000, p. 32.

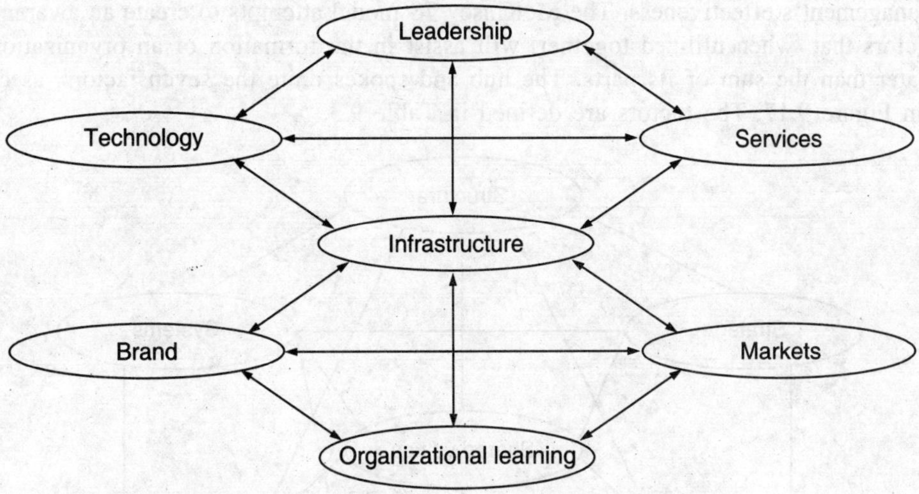

Figure 9.15 The seven dimensions of e-strategy.

e-commerce strategies. The bonds of an e-strategy lie in the preparation of the ground before the functional issues are addressed. Leadership, organizational learning, and infrastructure form the bonds as shown in Figure 9.16. Clearly, there is a strong interaction among these three components.

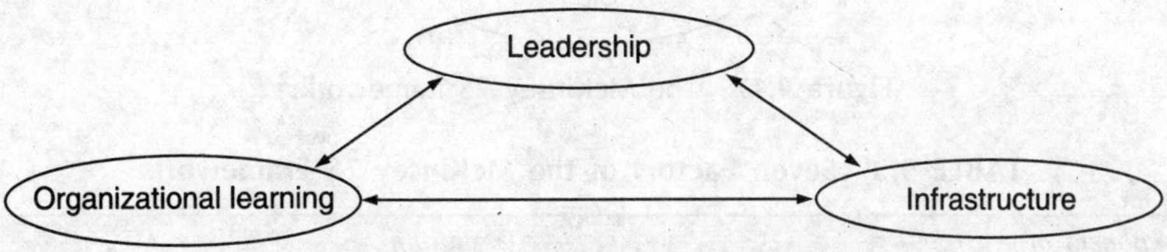

Figure 9.16 The bonds of e-strategy.

The primary drivers and the creators of strategic vision in an organization are the CEO and the senior executives. The market for intellectual capital in the form of experienced, proven, and successful leadership has never been more extreme. Once the need to develop e-strategy is identified, the single most important issue facing the executives is the IT infrastructure. This spans the technology spectrum from a single Internet file server connected to an ISP to the information-intense online transaction processing. Leadership with vision facilitates, encourages and allows an environment to develop within the organization, where institutional learning and memory thrive.

Internal Technology Leadership: The 7S Framework

The essence of the McKinsey's 7S model is that a firm is the comprehensive sum of its parts, and the internal dynamics of an organization clearly determine that organization's ability to compete, the premise being that both the strategy and the structure of the organization determine the management's effectiveness. The McKinsey 7S model attempts to create an awareness of the factors that, when utilized together, will assist in the formation of an organization that is greater than the sum of its parts. The hub and spokes unite the seven factors, as can be seen in Figure 9.17. The factors are defined in Table 9.3.

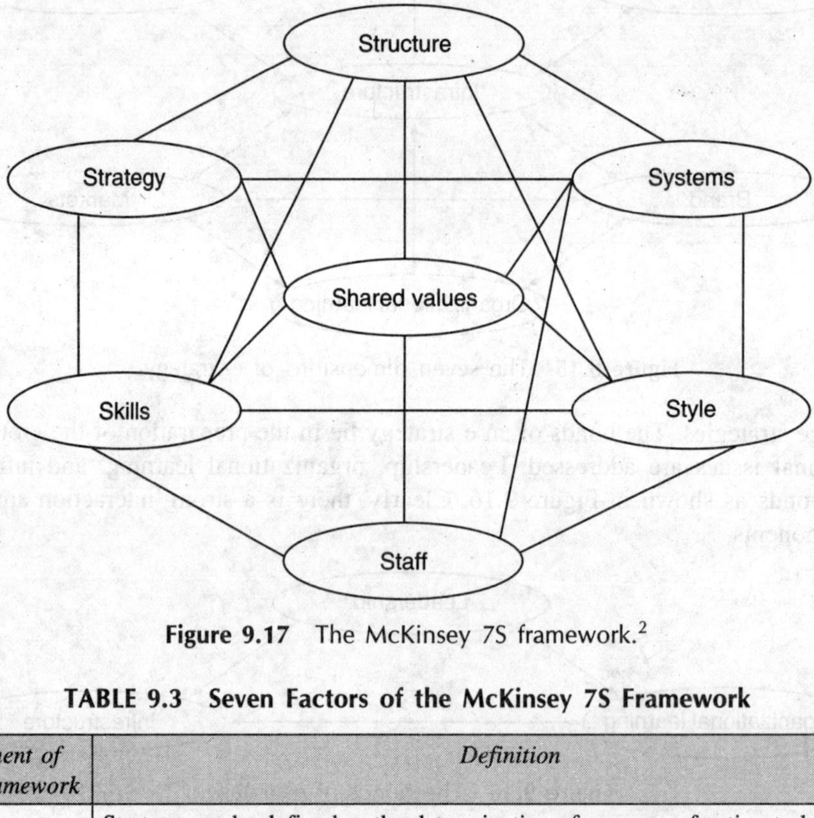

Figure 9.17 The McKinsey 7S framework.[2]

TABLE 9.3 Seven Factors of the McKinsey 7S Framework

Component of the 7S framework	*Definition*
Strategy	Strategy can be defined as the determination of a course of action to be followed in order to achieve a desired goal, position or vision.
Structure	An organization's structure is the interrelationship of processes and human capital in order to fulfil the enterprise's strategic objectives.
Systems	The organization's information systems and infrastructure.
Staff	Human resources management.
Style	Corporate style is a synthesis of the leadership philosophy of executive management, the internal corporate culture generated, and the orien-tation the organization adopts to its markets, customers, and competitors.
Skills	The unique or distinctive characteristics associated with an organi-zation's human capital.
Shared values	The concepts that an organization utilizes to drive towards a common goal through common objectives and a common value set.

2. Waterman R.H., Peters T.J., Philips J.R., "Structure is not Organization", *The McKinsey Quarterly*, Summer 1980, p. 7.

The Alignment of Technology and Corporate Planning

The whole basis of technology formulation is the ability of the organization's executive to achieve alignment between the technology strategy and the strategy of the enterprise as a whole.

Structure

The second key issue that organizations need to address in leveraging technology towards reaching a position of marketspace leadership is their ability to manage their internal structural dimensions, generally characterized by a company's organizational chart. Organizations must ensure that their structural characteristics facilitate their ability to be flexible and agile enough to effectively and efficiently meet the needs of their markets as they change.

Systems

This is the nervous system through which the organization communicates to its environment. In developing an e-strategy, one of the hidden strength an organization can create is a flexible systems infrastructure. The three major dimensions of technology infrastructure are:

- Enterprise Resource Planning (ERP) systems
- Data warehousing
- Knowledge management

ERP systems can help cut costs across the value chain by re-engineering their processes. For this, the ERP systems should incorporate flexibility without complexity. And to improve their relationships with customers, organizations need to generate information and content that add value from the processes themselves.

Data warehousing can be seen as the basis of a knowledge repository that, when used effectively, enables cost reduction strategies to be identified, added-value services to be achieved at a manageable cost, and the delivery of an improved data effectiveness within the organization.

The third dimension of an organization's e-commerce infrastructure is that of knowledge management, an area that can be defined as the formal management of an organization's knowledge resources.

Staffing

Human capital is the bedrock of any organization. As organizations evolve towards becoming knowledge-based, the value of an organization's intellectual assets cannot be overstated and magnified by a scarcity of IT skills. So, outsourcing has been a trend in many organizations.

Skills

The two skills that form the pillars between which the Information Systems structure is supported are the technical skills and relationship management skills.

Style

Style can be defined as 'characterization of how key managers behave in achieving the organization's goals, and also the cultural style of the organization'. Managers succeed and fail in inspiring peak performance, not only according to their ability to appreciate the values and motives of those they direct, but also according to their willingness to align their own managerial styles to the personal, situational and organizational environment. The bottom line for every effective manager is to deliver results. Since management is also an art, every manager has a personalized way of doing things.

Shared Values

Shared values can be defined as the significant meanings or concepts that an organization utilizes to drive towards a common goal through common objectives and a common value set. Key to achieve these are the driver for flexibility in process, for lower transaction costs, and for achieving mass customization for the customers.

Value Chain and e-Strategy

The intensity of information in the value chain and in the product offers some clues to the role of e-commerce in an industry. Industries that have high information intensity are much more likely to develop quickly into e-commerce than those that do not. An industry with high information intensity, like the computer business, is much more likely to depend on e-commerce than one with low information intensity, like the sand and gravel business.

To determine the intensity of information in one's industry, he has to look at his value activities and value chain. These concepts will help in figuring out what may happen in the future.

Value Activities

Value chain activities are the things that the company does to design, produce, sell, and service products. Typical value activities for a manufacturing firm would be things like:

- Gathering customer needs
- Designing products
- Purchasing materials
- Producing products
- Promoting products
- Selling products
- Servicing products
- Servicing customers

Assessment of Information Intensity

Assessment of the intensity of information in the value chain and value activities takes the next priority. The industry that has high information intensity in the value chain would have characteristics like those listed below:

- A large number of direct suppliers or customers
- A complex product line
- A product that needs a lot of information to sell
- A product composed of many parts
- Many steps in the production process
- A long order fulfilment cycle time.

Next, if there is high information intensity in the products of your industry, it is reasonable to adopt e-commerce. Characteristics of high information intensity in the product would be a product that:

1. Provides information
2. Involves information processing
3. Requires the buyer to process a lot of information
4. Has high user training costs
5. Has many alternatives uses.

The Validity of This Technique

Most of the early adopters of e-commerce have come from industries that would score highly if rated on the information intensity scale; those with low scores have not participated so far.

Software business embraced the Web from the beginning and today, much of the business is conducted online. Products are promoted on the Web and sales leads are generated. Product information is supplied to prospective customers on the Internet—not just online brochures but rich, interactive information via demonstrations. Sales transactions are initiated electronically by buyers, orders are fulfilled in some cases by immediate download, payment is quickly made electronically via credit card, and customer service is delivered by e-mail and Web-based tools.

How do software companies rate on the information intensity scale? They typically need a large customer base to survive. Their products are complex and customers expect a lot of information before they buy. The products have many components and features, and they take a long time to create. The product mainly provides information and information processing. It typically has a high learning curve and many uses.

As shown in Figure 9.18, we have a very general value chain for Internet commerce. This value chain[3] is focussed on the interactions of a business with its customers. The details will certainly be different for different businesses (and for some different business models), but we have found this general approach to be very effective in organizing an approach to do business online. The components of this general value chain are the following:

3. Porter M., "How Information Gives You Competitive Advantage", *Harvard Business Review*, July/August 1985.

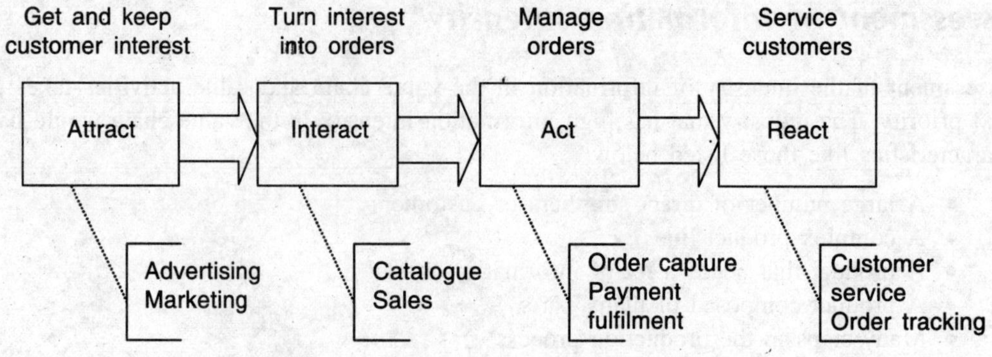

Figure 9.18 The commerce value chain.

1. Attract customers by means of advertising and marketing; invite and retain the interests of the customers;
2. Interact with customers by means of sales, and convert their interests into 'orders';
3. Act on customer instructions and manage orders such as order capture, payment and fulfilment;
4. React to customer requests and involve in customer service and offer technical support.

Looking at the value chain for a business helps to define areas of focus such as what the business is best at, or where the most emphasis should be given. Even in businesses that may appear to be very similar, differences in emphasis can have major effects, both for Internet commerce and for more traditional forms.

Components of the Commerce Value Chain

The key components of the value chain can be very different for different industries, and even among different businesses within a particular industry, such as in the following example. In this section, we will look at a generic value chain for Internet commerce. In part it serves as an example of how one might break down a value chain to analyze it more closely, and in part it exemplifies some of the most important components of business on the Internet. Throughout this section, we use catalogues for consumer retail purchases as examples. In the next chapter, we will look at several different kinds of businesses and how the commerce value chain applies to them.

Attract Customers

The first component of the generic Internet commerce value chain is to attract customers. By this we mean, whatever steps we take to draw customers into the primary site, whether by paid advertisements on other websites, e-mail, television, print, or other forms of advertising and marketing. The point here is to make an impression on customers and draw them into the detailed catalogue or other information about products and services for sale. Instead of attract, the catchword today is **'addict'** the customers.

Interact with Customers

The second component is interaction. By this we mean, turning customer interest into orders. This phase is generally content oriented and includes the catalogue, publication, or other information available to the customer on the Internet. The content may be distributed by many different mechanisms, such as the World Wide Web or e-mail. In some cases, there may be links between Internet commerce and contents distributed by other media, such as CD-ROMs.

Editorially, contents may change infrequently or frequently. Technically, content may be static or dynamic. Static content typically consists of prepared pages, such as those from a catalogue, that are sent to a client upon request. These pages must be recreated and updated whenever the information on them changes. Dynamic content, on the other hand, is generated at the time of the request, drawing upon one or more information sources to produce an appropriate page of information for the client. Some sources of information for dynamic content include databases, such as a parts database with pricing information, the capabilities of client software, such as what graphic formats can be used or even who the clients are, or what organizations they are with. Dynamic content is often used when the editorial content changes frequently, or when the natural storage medium for the information is a database, or when the information is used for multiple purposes.

Act on Customer Instructions

The next component in the commerce value chain is to act. Once a buyer has searched through a catalogue and wishes to make a purchase, there must be a way to capture the order, process payment, handle fulfilment and other aspects of order management.

Order processing. Often a buyer wishes to purchase several items at the same time, so the order processing must include the ability to group items together for later purchase. This capability, sometimes called a shopping cart in the case of retail transactions, usually includes the ability to modify the contents of the shopping cart at any time. Thus, the buyer is able to discard items, add new ones, change the quantities, and so on. When the buyer is ready to complete the purchase, it is often necessary to compute additional charges, such as sales tax and shipping costs. The order processing system then presents the buyer with an itemized order form including all charges, so that the buyer can pay for the items.

Payment. Depending on the terms of the order, the buyer may pay for it (or provide payment instructions) as part of the order capture. Once an order is finalized, the buyer can make the payment. As in the real world, there may be many ways to pay for an item. Some of the methods may be online analogues of those found in the real world: credit cards, purchase orders and the like. Other methods of payment may exist only on Internet commerce, using new technologies developed especially for a networked system. For example, in an online publishing system, it may be feasible to charge a small amount for a single magazine article, rather than requiring someone to purchase the entire magazine.

The most important property of an online payment system is that the seller can use it to collect payment from the buyer. That is, no matter which payment mechanisms each one may be capable of, there must be at least one they can agree on. This property has several implications. First, the seller's system must be able to handle the kinds of payment important to the seller's business. For example, credit cards are commonly used for consumer retail transactions, but businesses often buy from each other using purchase orders. There may also be non-technical constraints on what payment methods can be used. To accept credit cards, a merchant must have an account with an acquiring bank that handles the transactions. Without such an account, creating the technical infrastructure to allow for credit card payment is useless.

Second, the seller must be careful about imposing requirements on the buyer's system. If the buyer must have a particular software package to handle a particular kind of payment system, the universe of possible buyers is likely to be much smaller than it would be otherwise. In some cases, of course, all of the desired customers will have such software, or be willing to obtain it. Again, the key point is to keep the customer and the business in mind when selecting the technology.

Note also that completing this stage does not necessarily mean that funds have been transferred into the seller's bank account. Some payment instruments, including both credit cards and purchase orders, extend credit to the buyer who will make the actual payment later. In such cases, it is common for the seller's system to authorize the transaction, whether by requesting such authorization from a third party (such as the bank that issued a credit card) or its own internal rules (such as whether a purchase order relationship has been established). As such, final settlement of a transaction may not take place until the item has been shipped.

Fulfilment. Now the order has been placed and the payment made (or at least a satisfactory promise of payment). The next step is fulfiling the order How that happens depends on the type of thing purchased. If the item ordered is a physical good (sometimes called a hard good), it will be delivered to the buyer. The order is usually forwarded to a traditional order processing system, with the result that someone picks up the object, packs it, and ships it. In this case, the online commerce system must have a method for forwarding orders. This step could be as simple as printing out or faxing an order form for a person to handle, or it may use a more complicated interface, such as EDI, with another computer system. The precise mechanism, of course, depends on how orders are handled by the rest of the business.

A second kind of order is a request for a service to be performed in the real world. For example, one might order a singing telegram online. Although the fulfilment happens in the physical world, this is a service, not a physical good. For our purposes, however, we can think of these as being handled like physical goods. The order is passed on to a system or a person who fulfils it.

The third kind of order is more closely tied to the Internet commerce system. We call this category, digital goods. Digital goods include a wide variety of online delivery, including software that is delivered online, magazine or news articles, reports, access to a database for a period of time, and so on.

React to Customer Inquiries

Finally, after a sale is complete, the customer may have some questions or difficulties that require service. Although many questions require a person to answer, others can be answered with the appropriate information system. For example, a transaction system that keeps track of all of a customer's purchases, can generate a statement summarizing them. Customers who wonder whether or not their orders have been shipped, might check back with the system. A more complicated example is how the system handles a failure when delivering a digital good.

Suppose that a customer buys a software package online. While the software is being downloaded to the customer's computer, an error in the network causes the download to fail. What can the customer do? Clearly they should not buy the item again, so they need some "proof of purchase"—such as a receipt—that the fulfilment server will accept in order to allow the customer to attempt another download.

Using people to answer customer service calls can be very expensive, so it is worth investing in systems that eliminate questions that do not require the capabilities of a person. As noted previously, these systems often provide routine (or even exceptional) information in response to simple queries. But it is very important to design the system to cater to the needs of the customer in solving any problem that may arise in the process of transaction.

The Quantitative Approach for e-Strategy

Speed, round-the-clock availability, and security are the most common indicators of quality of service of an e-business site. Management faces a two-fold challenge. On the one hand, companies must meet customer expectations in terms of quality of service. On the other hand, companies have to keep site costs under control to stay competitive. Therefore, capacity, reliability, scalability, and security are key issues to e-business site managers. E-business sites are complex computer-system architectures, with multiple interconnected layers of software and hardware components, such as networks, caching proxies, routers, high speed links, and mainframes with large databases. The nature of e-business workload is also complex due to its transactional nature, secure requirements, payment protocols, and the unpredictable characteristics of service requests over the Internet. Planning the capacity of e-business sites requires more than just adding extra hardware. It requires more than intuition, ad hoc procedures, and rules of thumb. There are many possible alternative architectures and one has to be able to determine the most cost-effective architecture. This is where the quantitative approach of this book and capacity planning techniques for e-businesses come into play.

Planning the e-Commerce Project

A successful business plan for an e-commerce initiative should include the following activities.

1. Identifying the initiative's specific objectives
2. Linking objectives to business strategies
3. Managing the implementation of business strategies
4. Overseeing the continuing operations of the initiative, once it is launched.

In setting the objectives for an e-commerce initiative, managers should consider the strategic role of the project, its intended scope, and the resources available for executing it.

Identifying Objectives

Businesses undertake e-commerce initiatives for a wide variety of reasons. Common objectives that a business might hope to accomplish through e-commerce could include increasing sales in existing markets, opening new markets, serving existing customers better, identifying new vendors, coordinating more efficiently with existing vendors, or recruiting employees more effectively.

Resource decisions for e-commerce initiatives should consider the expected benefits and expected costs of meeting the objectives. These decisions should also consider the risks inherent in the e-commerce initiative and compare them to the risks of inaction—a failure to act could concede a strategic advantage to competitors.

Linking Objectives to Business Strategies

Businesses can use downstream strategies, which are tactics that improve the value that the business provides to its customers. Alternatively, businesses can pursue upstream strategies that focus on reducing costs or generating value by working with suppliers or inbound logistics.

You have already learnt about the different things that companies do on the Web. Although the Web is a tremendously attractive sales channel for many firms, companies can use e-commerce in a variety of ways to do much more than selling: they can use the Web to improve their business strategies and their competitive positions. As described in earlier chapters of this book, e-commerce opportunities can inspire businesses to undertake activities such as:

- Building brands
- Enhancing existing marketing programs
- Selling products and services
- Selling advertising
- Improving after-sale service and support
- Purchasing products and services
- Managing supply chains
- Operating auctions
- Creating virtual communities and web portals.

Although the success of each of these activities is measurable to some degree, many companies have undertaken these activities on the Web without setting specific, measurable goals. In the mid 1990s—the early days of e-commerce—businesses that had good ideas could start a business activity on the Web and not face competition. Successes and failures were measured in broad strokes. A company would either become the *amazon.com* or the *eBay* of its industry, or it would disappear, either slipping into bankruptcy or be acquired by another company.

As e-commerce is now beginning to mature, more companies are taking a closer look at the benefits and costs of their e-commerce projects. Measuring both benefits and costs is becoming more important. A good business plan will set specific objectives for benefits to be achieved and costs to be incurred. In many cases, a company will create a pilot website to test an e-commerce idea, and then release a production version of the site when it works well. These companies must specify clear goals for the pilot test, so that they know when the site is ready to scale up.

Measuring Benefit Objectives

Many companies create websites to build their brands or enhance existing marketing programs. These companies can set goals in terms of increased brand awareness, as measured by market research surveys and opinion polls. Companies that sell goods or services on their sites can measure sales volume in units or dollars. A complication that occurs in measuring either brand awareness or sales is that the increases can be caused by other things that the company is doing at the same time or by a general improvement in the economy. A good marketing staff or outside consulting firm can help a company sort out the specific causes and effects of marketing and sales programs. Firms may need these groups to help set and evaluate these kinds of goals for e-commerce initiatives.

Companies that want to use their websites to improve customer service or after-sale support might set goals of increased customer satisfaction or reduced costs of providing customer service or support. For example, Philips Lighting wanted to use the Web to provide an ordering system for its smaller customers, that did not use EDI. The primary goal for this initiative was to reduce the cost of processing smaller orders. Philips had identified that over half the cost of processing smaller orders was towards handling inventory availability and order status requests. Customers who placed small orders often called or sent faxes asking for this information. In 1999, Philips built a pilot website and invited a number of its smaller customers to try it. The company found that customer service phone calls from the test group of customers dropped by 80 per cent. Based on that measurable increase in efficiency, Philips decided to invest in additional hardware and personnel to staff a version of the website that could handle virtually all its smaller customers. The reduction in the cost of handling small orders justified the additional investment.

Companies can handle a variety of similar measures to assess the benefits of other electronic commerce initiatives. Supply chain managers can measure supply cost reductions, quality improvements, or faster deliveries of ordered goods. Auction sites can set goals for the number of auctions, the number of bidders and sellers, the dollar volume of items sold, the number of items sold, or the number of registered participants. The ability to track such numbers is usually built into auction site software. Virtual communities and Web portals measure the number of visitors and try to measure the quality of their visitors' experiences. Some sites use online surveys to gather these data. However, most settle for approximations provided by measuring the length of time that each visitor remains on the site and the frequency of his visits. A summary of benefits and measurements that companies can make to assess the value of those benefits is found in Table 9.4.

TABLE 9.4 Measuring the Benefits of e-commerce Initiatives

E-commerce initiatives	*Common measurements of benefits provided*
Build brands	Surveys or opinion polls that measure brand awareness.
Enhance existing marketing programs	Change in per unit sales volume.
Improve customer service	Customer satisfaction surveys, the number of customer complaints.
Reduce cost of after-sale support	Quantity and type (telephone, fax, e-mail) of support activities.
Improve supply chain operation	Cost, quality, and on-time delivery of materials or services purchased.
Hold auctions	Quantity of auctions, bidders, sellers, items sold, registered participants; dollar volume of items sold.
Provide portals and virtual communities	Number of visitors, number of return visits per visitor, and duration of an average visit.

No matter how a company measures the benefits provided by its website, it usually tries to convert the raw activity measurements to dollars. Having the benefits measured in dollars lets the company compare benefits to costs and compare the net benefit (benefits minus costs) of a particular initiative to the net benefits provided by other projects. Although each activity provides some value to the company, it is often difficult to measure that value in dollars. Usually, even the best attempts to convert benefits to dollars yield only rough approximations.

Measuring Cost Objectives

At the first glance, the task of identifying and estimating costs may seem much easier than the task of setting benefits objectives. However, many managers have found that information technology project costs can be as difficult to estimate and control as the benefits of those projects. Since Web development uses relatively new hardware and software technologies, managers have little experience on which they can make estimates. Most changes in the cost of hardware are on the decline, but the increasing sophistication of software provides an ever-increasing demand for newer, cheaper hardware. This often yields a net increase in overall hardware costs. Even though e-commerce initiatives tend to be completed within a shorter time frame than many other information technology projects, the rapid changes in web technology can destroy a manager's best-laid plans very quickly.

In addition to hardware and software costs, the project budget must include the costs of hiring, training, and paying the personnel who will design the website, write or customize the software, create the content, and operate and maintain the site. As more companies build e-commerce sites, people who have the skills necessary to do the work are demanding increasingly higher compensation.

The initial cost of building an electronic commerce site is not the whole story, unfortunately. Since Web technology continues to evolve at a rapid pace, most businesses will want to take advantage of what that technology offers, to remain competitive. Most experts agree that the annual cost to maintain and improve a site once it is up and running, whether it is a small site or a large site, will be between 50 per cent to 100 per cent of its initial cost.

As an increasing number of traditional businesses create Web versions of their physical stores, the cost to build an online business that is a true differentiator—a site that stands out and offers something new to customers—will continue to increase. Much of the cost in such a website is for elements that make a major difference in how well the site works, but are not readily apparent to a site visitor. For example, Kmart's Web business site *BlueLight.com*, costed more than $140 million to create. The site's home page is certainly well-designed and highly functional, but the typical visitor would never guess how much this company spent to build its site. Much of the site's cost was incurred in building connections to Kmart's vast inventory and logistics databases.

Comparing Benefits to Costs

Most companies have procedures that call for an evaluation of any major expenditure of funds. These major investments in equipment, personnel, and other assets are called capital projects or capital investments. The techniques that companies use to evaluate proposed capital projects range from very simple calculations to complex computer simulation models. However, no matter how complex the technique is, it always reduces to a comparison of benefits and costs. If the benefits exceed the cost of a project by a comfortable margin, the company invests in the project.

A key factor in creating a business plan for e-commerce initiatives is the process of identifying potential benefits (including intangibles such as employee satisfaction and company reputation), identifying the costs required to generate those benefits, and evaluating whether the benefits exceed the costs. Companies should evaluate each element of their e-commerce strategies using this cost/benefit approach. A simplified representation of the cost/benefit approach appears in Figure 9.19.

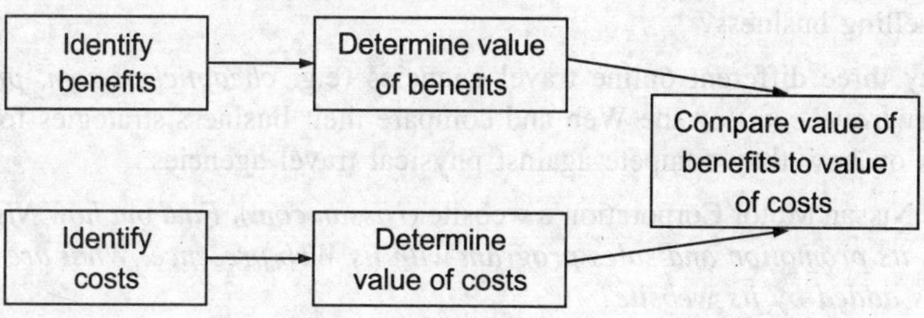

Figure 9.19 Cost/benefit evaluation of e-commerce strategy elements.

You might have learned techniques for capital project evaluation, such as the payback method or the net present value method, in your accounting or finance courses. These evaluation approaches provide a quantitative expression of a comfortable benefit-to-cost margin for a specific company. They can also mathematically adjust for the reduced value of benefits that the investment will return in future years (benefits received in future years are worth less than those received in the current year). Managers often use the term Return on Investment (ROI) to describe any capital investment evaluation technique, even though ROI is the name of only one of these techniques.

Although most companies evaluate the anticipated value of e-commerce initiatives in some way before approving them, many companies see these projects as absolutely necessary investments. Thus, they might not subject them to the same close examination as they do to other capital projects. These companies fear being left behind as competitors stake their claims in the online marketspace. The value of early positioning in a new market is so great that many companies are willing to invest very large amounts of money with no near-term prospects of profit.

Newspaper websites are a very good example of this desire to establish a foothold in the online marketspace. Gannet's *USA Today* and Dow Jones' *Wall Street Journal Interactive Edition* sites are a few profitable electronic commerce initiatives in the newspaper business. *Editor & Publisher* magazine estimated that online news websites lost a total of $80 million in 1998 alone. Despite the losses, most newspaper companies believe that they cannot afford to ignore the long-term potential of the Web, and feel compelled to make whatever investment is required to move into the online world.

EXERCISES

1. What are the difficulties in designing a knowledge management system?
2. Describe the value chain of e-commerce.
3. Describe the procedures for implementing e-commerce.
4. How would you start performing the industry analysis for a small business that wants to launch an e-commerce project?
5. What might be the typical competitive strategy for a company trying to launch a bookselling business?
6. Survey three different online travel agencies (e.g. *cheaptickets.com, priceline.com, previewtravel.com*) on the Web and compare their business strategies for customers. Focus on how they compete against physical travel agencies.
7. Go to Nissan Motor Corporation's website (*Nissan.com). Find out how Nissan complements its promotion and sales program with its Web presence. What are the business values added by its website*?

CHAPTER 10

Information Systems for Mobile Commerce

LEARNING OBJECTIVES

After reading this chapter, you should be able to:

- ➠ Understand the importance of mobile communications for business transactions.
- ➠ Know the areas where mobile commerce is growing.
- ➠ Describe the wireless spectrum used for mobile communications.
- ➠ Understand the wireless application protocol.
- ➠ Understand the difference between GSM and CDMA.
- ➠ Assimilate more information about mobile commerce in India.

The Story of Smartphones

With more than 2.5 billion users worldwide in 2019 and 2.5 million apps available, smartphones are transforming our day-to-day life in some surprising ways. In a span of 30 years since its invention, smartphones have impacted human life all over the world. They have brought out a massive change in the lives of people in most cultures. Smartphones play a vital role in this regard offering users a great platform for communication and access to a wide range of applications. Some of these roles are:

- Better means of communication
- Learning options to users
- Great exposure to the latest things
- Ways to personality development
- Simple ways to access applications
- Ideas to succeed in business
- Platform to grow along with technology

The main thing people do with smartphones is to have entertainment and get connected to the people all over the world through social media. Entering into social networking platforms gives them a better avenue to get exposed and also improve in all facets of life.

By combining many gadgets into one, smartphones have brought in convenience to everyone using them. Today, some of the uses of smartphones are as follows:

- Sending and receiving e-mails
- Registering contacts
- Calculator
- Currency converter
- Watches and alarm clock
- Video chatting
- Point-of-sale terminal when paying for goods or services
- Barcode scanning
- Determining user's exact location utilizing GPS
- Document scanner
- Digital camera
- Audio recorder
- Video recorder
- Multimedia messaging
- Web client
- Gaming platform
- Documents viewer
- Computer adjunct
- Music player
- TV
- Electronic wallet
- Calendars
- Maps, navigation, and travel accessory
- Online banking and finance medium
- Flashlight/Torch
- News, sports, and live events viewer
- Crime prevention and evidence gathering support
- Learning and research support
- Remote working support
- Emergencies support
- Notes and reminders
- Texting device

History of Smartphones

DynaTac was the world's first handheld mobile phone. It weighed about a kilogram, took 10 hours to charge, and offered 30 minutes of talk time. In 1984, the phone cost $3,995. In 1992, IBM revealed a revolutionary device that had more capabilities than its preceding cell phones. This prototype smartphone was known as the *Simon Personal Communicator*.

It allowed a person to make landline calls instead of being at the mercy of expensive carrier rates. Unfortunately, at $1,100 retail price, it only sold 50,000 units in 6 months. But, Simon created a great launching pad for others to innovate.

From Keypad to Alphanumeric Keyboard

Text messaging was the first, widespread data application for cell phones introduced in the Global System for Mobile communications (GSM) standard in the early 1990s. However, the challenge was using a phone's keypad to type text messages. Pressing a key several times enabled a single key to represent several letters. For example, the number 5 key pressed once represented the letter 'J', twice for the letter 'K', and thrice for the letter 'L'. Although this design provided a solution, it was a very slow and tedious way of entering a text message.

The next brilliant stroke of genius in the evolution of smartphone design was the introduction of the touchscreen. This design allows the graphics display to encompass nearly the entire footprint of the smartphone itself, leaving some room on the surface and along the edge, perhaps, for a few buttons, like a power switch and menu selection. When Apple® launched the iPhone®, they incorporated a 'finger-friendly' design approach. The 'finger-friendly' touchscreens have now become state-of-the-art for smartphones.

First Phase of Growth of Smartphones (1994–2006)

The first phase was purely meant for enterprises. During this phase, all the smartphones were targeting the corporations, and the features and functions were as per the corporate requirements.

BlackBerry is considered as the revolutionary device of this era; it introduced many features, including e-mail, Internet, fax, Web browsing, and camera. This phase was totally based on smartphones targeting enterprises. BlackBerry primarily targeted business professionals. It kept releasing more and more advanced devices, and became the market leader in smartphones until the iPhone gained steam.

Second Phase of Growth of Smartphones (2006–2008)

Apple had already introduced portable technology with the iPod, and the stage was set for it to unveil its latest device in 2007. The iPhone was one of the most advanced consumer smartphones the market had ever seen. Priced at $499 for the 4 GB RAM, users flocked to the device. At the end of 2007, Google unveiled its Android Operating System, with the intention of approaching the consumer Smartphone market. It introduced features that the general consumer requires, and at the same time, kept the cost at lower side to attract more and more customers. Features like e-mail, social website integration, audio/video, Internet access, chatting along were part of these phones. Google Android is the most popular operating system on mobile phones now. Most Android phones are customized by their manufacturers.

Third phase of Growth of Smartphones (2008 till date)

Improvement of the display quality, display technology and stable mobile operating system, more powerful batteries and the enhanced user interface were some of the many features introduced during this period. This phase started in 2008 and continues till now.

Impacts of Smartphones on Human Life

Smartphones have impacted almost all aspects of human life. However, some effects are positive, some are negative.

Positive Impacts

1. ***Impact on business.*** Smartphones are creating new dimensions for business. Smartphone vendors and manufacturers are constantly coming out with newer versions and better amenities, and making money. Internet services providers utilize the smartphone to gain competitive advantages. There has been a drastic growth in broadband and Internet service providers business in past ten years and one of the main reasons for this drastic increase in their business is the ever-increasing use of smartphones. The presence of a large number of smartphone users provided an opportunity to businesses to invest in mobile application development and allowed to introduce new business dimensions in market space. Different mobile operating system vendors have their own mobile application technology, hence having a different market for mobile applications.

2. ***Impact on education.*** The use of the Internet has become a part of life for every student. Internet, together with smartphones, provide an alternative channel to deliver education services and distance education.
   - Students learn the way they are comfortable.
   - They can get answers quickly.
   - Audio and video can bring learning to life.
   - Access to educational applications takes learning up a notch.
   - Smartphones allow for social learning.

   Smartphones are really helpful for the students enrolled in distance learning courses. As we know, distance education liberates students from limitations of time and location while offering flexible opportunities for education. It enables students to utilize their time such that they can continue their education without impacting their work and family life. The smartphone with the capability of always connected makes it much easier for the students to avail this type of education facility and makes the smartphone a perfect fit device for distance learning. The smartphones within and without a classroom make it easier for students and teachers to collaborate and provide access to a massive amount of educational and learning resources. Smartphones enable students to text, cooperate on social networking sites, check e-mails, play online games, and even watch TV channels. In this age of mobilism, affordable mobile technologies enable students all over the world to be hyperconnected.

3. ***Impact on social connectivity and community.*** Social connectivity is a part of being human and there has never been a time in human history when people have been able to connect to one another with such an ease. Social connections are no longer restricted to the people in our immediate surroundings, instead electronic media such as smartphones, e-mails, and online social networks have enabled us to connect with those both near and far. The notion of community is at the

heart of the World Wide Web. The psychological need for connectedness could, therefore, explain the popularity of social networks such as Facebook. Social media and online communities offer increased possibilities for connection, interaction and participation, and also, new media with tools for self-presentation and identity management. Social media such as Twitter, Facebook, MySpace, YouTube, Flickr, and others have been growing at a tremendous rate and the adoption rate of such media has been skyrocketing which, in turn, has delivered astronomical numbers of users in less than 15 years.

Originating from the Internet, different online communities pervade the public and private life. Being part of a community or group fulfils one of the basic human needs, that of *belonging*. Nowadays, the use of the Internet to build different Interest-based and self-identified communities evidently stresses that communities do not necessarily need to interact face-to-face. The development of the Internet has resulted in the increase in different online communities since information and communication technologies have enabled geographically disperse groups and individuals to connect.

4. ***Impact on marketing.*** With over 1.2 billion active users, Facebook provides a virtual reality in cyberspace, where users can enact identities for their friends, acquaintances, and a larger passing public. The social media revolution has given consumers around the world the most powerful voice they have ever had. Facebook's Like button, introduced in April 2010, has already been added by more than three million distinct websites. The Like button allows Facebook's more than one billion users, with one click, to express approval of companies, organizations, articles, or ideas.

5. ***Impact on health.*** Users of smartphones, with simple touch of finger, can access the health and related services anytime and anywhere. There are several apps to manage prescriptions, promote alternative treatment options, provide price comparison, and validate prescriptions. There are also several apps available to track exercise, diet and blood pressure. These apps assist healthcare workers to access specific information in areas of radiology, neurology, neonatology, pediatrics, and continuing education activities.

Negative Impacts

1. ***Impact on elections.*** Barack Obama's 2008 US presidential campaign has often been described as the first electoral campaign in which the use of social media had a decisive impact. The 2008 US presidential campaign had a huge presence on social networking sites. Barack Obama, a virtually unknown Democratic candidate, utilized 15 different social media websites to form relationships with the millions of American citizens who utilize those networks.

   The 'Arab Spring' uprisings in Tunisia, Egypt, and Libya have proven that social media can be used to transform society and politics on a global scale. These uprisings used social media to organize protests, highlight injustices and government crackdowns, and sway public opinion at home and abroad. The effects spread to other nations, as even now, several nations in the Middle East find the status quo challenged by youths and social activists who use social media to rally others to their cause.

Now, that social media sites let people from all over the world share their story through videos and images; it has changed the way people get their news and think about news in general. It has become a big issue for governments or organizations that want to hide the truth behind the veil of official secrets.

2. ***Impact on psychology.*** Smartphones can be used to reduce stress in busy work life by providing a means to interact with friends and families as and when they get time. Interacting with friends and families, while traveling or waiting on bus stop enables users to utilize such time to promote their social life. It enables the users to interact and stay up-to-date with the latest news and development in the political and social circles, resulting in reducing work stress. Besides social connectivity, it can be used for entertainment like watching movies and sports and these may have an impact on the psychological well-being of people.
3. On the other hand, addiction to smartphone is increasing rapidly. The addiction to smartphone can be described as wanting to be in constant communication with people even though when there is no real need for communication.

Case Discussion

1. List the uses of smartphones in modern society.
2. What are the ways in which smartphones are affecting business?
3. List some of the business models spawned by smartphone usage.

What is Mobile Commerce?

Mobile commerce, also known as *m-commerce*, is defined as the process of performing business transactions using handheld mobile devices which are connected through wireless networks. The business transactions may range from buying and selling goods, making mobile payments, downloading audio/video contents, playing online games, using numerous software applications or getting mobile tickets. The mobile devices include cellular phones, handheld computers such as palmtops or laptops, pagers, smart phones and Personal Digital Assistants (PDAs). The mobile users can access Internet through these devices without any wired connection or a computer. Powered with the emerging technology based on Wireless Application Protocol (WAP), m-commerce employs web-ready micro-browsers in these mobile devices to surf through the Internet anytime, anywhere on the Earth.

Mobility is one of the key factors which help business thrive. Businesses that embrace the idea of Mobile Information Society will reinvent themselves as real-time organizations, where access and interaction can be instant. New brands, partnerships and customer loyalties are on the raise, thanks to the growing number of mobile terminals. Three major segments that can substantially benefit from anywhere and have anytime access to information and services from the use of mobile phones are, financial service providers, health care industry and corporations with a mobile workforce.

Mobile Commerce is about the explosion of applications and services, which are accessible from Internet-enabled mobile devices. It is incubating new technologies, services and business models. Smartphones impose very different constraints than desktop computers. But they also open the door to a variety of new applications and services. Smartphones follow you wherever you go, making it possible to access the Internet while walking down the street with friends and family or while driving, looking for a nearby restaurant or a gas station.

Banks and other financial institutions are exploring the use of m-Commerce to broaden/retain their business by allowing their customers to not only access account information, e.g. bank balances, stock quotes and financial advice, from anywhere, but also the possibility to make transactions, e.g. purchasing stocks, remitting money, via mobile phones. This service is often referred to as Mobile Banking or M-Banking. The stock market services offered via mobile devices have also become more popular and are known as Mobile Brokerage. They allow the subscriber to react to market developments in a timely fashion and irrespective of their physical location.

For financial services providers, the mobile phone has introduced a new channel to reach customers—one that is personal, easy-to-use, secure, location and time independent. Bank branches are increasingly expensive to operate, and the established self-service solutions, such as ATMs and Internet banking, cannot provide competitive efficiency or satisfy the needs of the new generation of customers who want to do business when it is most convenient for them.

Mobile commerce (M-commerce) can be broadly divided into three categories:

1. ***Mobile banking:*** It is the state-of-the-art process that has been introduced in the banks to make sure that the customers are better equipped with all the systems and process. This helps to carry out the transaction quickly and the account holders can check their account balance and the newly available schemes from the mobile web itself. Mobile banking can be accessed through mobile and people can use it for their benefit and they do not have to be physically present at the banks for checking the account balance. Mobile banking has made life a lot easier and this is a programme that is being used by the younger generation a lot more, but if you are a middle-aged or senior person, you can certainly avail it because it is genuinely user friendly.
2. ***M-payment (mobile payment):*** It is a point-of-sale payment made through a mobile device, such as a cellular telephone, a smartphone, or a personal digital assistant (PDA). Using m-payment, a person with a wireless device could pay for items in a store or settle a restaurant bill without interacting with any staff member.
3. ***Mobile money:*** A facility that allows people to use their cell phones and other hand-held devices to handle financial transactions.

PDA's and smart phones have become so popular that many businesses are beginning to use mobile-commerce (m-commerce) as a more efficient method of reaching the demands of their customers. Banks and other financial institutions are exploring the use of m-Commerce to broaden/retain their business by allowing their customers to not only access account information, e.g. bank balances, stock quotes and financial advice, from anywhere, but also the possibility to make transactions, e.g. purchasing stocks, remitting money, via mobile phones. This service is often referred to as Mobile Banking or M-Banking. The stock market services offered via mobile devices have also become more popular and are known as Mobile

Brokerage, as they allow the subscriber to react to market developments in a timely fashion and irrespective of their physical location.

News information is also becoming more popular with subscriptions to daily headlines from anywhere in the world being transmitted to mobile devices. Sports and entertainment are areas that have also grown with the demand for mobile related services. Shopping and reservation services are now more accessible when using mobile devices. Multinational companies are now using m-commerce to expand everything from services to marketing and advertisement. With the increased use of m-commerce comes increased need for security. Cell phone companies are now spending more money to protect their customers and their information from online intrusions and hackers.

M-commerce versus E-commerce

Between e-commerce and m-commerce, the latter is the newer concept, seeing as **mobile technology** had not exploded until about two decades after the Internet was able to be used to conduct commercial transactions using electronic systems.

While e-commerce mainly makes use of computers, and requires Internet connectivity, m-commerce uses mobile devices such as smartphones, PDAs, tablets and it relies mainly on an Internet connection provided by wireless telecommunication networks.

One of the major advantages of m-commerce over e-commerce is **portability** and **flexibility**. While Internet connectivity is required in e-commerce, that is not the case in mobile commerce since these devices come with their own connection to the Internet using telecommunication networks. Since the mobile devices are also smaller and more portable, users can literally conduct commercial activities anywhere, even in places with no electricity. This means that usage of m-commerce is also broader, thanks to this portability feature.

The rise of m-commerce has certainly boosted e-commerce as a whole, since users are given **more options on the platform and tools**, and a majority of the limitations that they have encountered in e-commerce do not exist in m-commerce.

Unique Features of M-commerce

In order to fully understand what sets mobile commerce apart from e-commerce and m-business, it is a good idea to take a look at its unique features, which can be clearly seen as its advantages.

1. ***Mobility and availability:*** Mobile commerce involves the use of portable mobile or cellular devices such as mobile phones, smartphones and tablets. Portability results in close proximity between businesses and their consumers, meaning it is now possible for businesses to reach their target audience faster. The parties are not restricted by physical or geographical locations when doing commerce, be it purchasing a product, completing a bank transaction, or even bidding on an auction. In addition, the technology and devices that power mobile commerce are also available and readily accessible. As such, the probability of the businesses making a sale is also higher.

2. ***Savings on electricity:*** In e-commerce, a constant connection to an electric outlet is mandatory to power the devices. Thanks to the increased usage and flexibility of mobile devices which come with their own batteries, shopping via mobile devices is possible even without electricity.
3. ***Comfort, convenience and spontaneity:*** Many people prefer making their purchases over their desktop or laptop computers, in the comfort of their own homes or offices, instead of making a trip to the physical store or location of the goods or services that they want to buy. However, there are even more people who find it more convenient to do their shopping on their mobile phones, and they can do this while sipping some latte at a coffee shop or even in a bus or train as they travel. There is no need to rush home or to the office to access the computer in order to buy something. All users have to do is whip out their tablets of phones and do their shopping from there.
4. ***Speed:*** Consumers who are normally shopping on mobile phones are engaged in some or the other activity while doing it. They need their online shopping experience to be as quick as possible. In fact, researches recommend that 57% of mobile users will leave your site if they have to wait 3 seconds for it to load. If m-commerce site is not delivering at a certain time, you might miss out an important transaction. Hence, maintaining speed and consistency of performance at the same time is crucial to have repeated business.
5. ***Surreal user experience:*** For years, many people have stepped back from buying products online, due to its inability to provide user the experience of how the products is. However, with m-commerce backed by augmented reality, trying and testing the product of your choice is not far away. Soon, technologies will let its user to see and try the product, on the go, giving a reliability of any retail shop. It is a cross device solution and offers virtual try on experience; it exclusively provides real-time augmented reality try on services for mobile phones and tablets.
6. ***Smart CRMs:*** Wherever there is commerce, there is a software to record, boost and grow the company. The traditional customer management systems like CRM will see a drastic change in their core offerings and will be built to suit the new age requirements.

Uses of Mobile Commerce

The most common products and services on mobile commerce that are seen today are given below:

- ***Mobile banking:*** It involves making inquires about your bank balance, managing your bank accounts, remitting money and transacting with your bank through your mobile phone.
- ***Mobile browsing and purchase:*** Shopping can now be done on your mobile device and if something catches your eye, you can immediately purchase it while browsing.

This is made faster and easier if the merchant has an app, instead of browsing their website on your phone.

- ***Mobile content purchase and delivery:*** This is no longer a new concept, since this is one of the earliest forms of mobile commerce. You can purchase mobile content such as music, games, movies, ringtones, wallpapers and even apps, and they will send it directly to your mobile phone.
- ***Mobile money transfers:*** Now, money can be transferred through the use of mobile devices.
- ***Information and location-based services:*** Sometimes, users may not necessarily want to purchase anything, but they would still be interested in receiving information such as news, local weather, stock and financial quotes, movie and TV programming schedules, traffic reports and even sports scores.
- ***Mobile advertising:*** People check their mobile phones more often than they do their desktop computers. So, marketers and advertisers believe that they will be able to catch the attention of their target consumers better if they send the promotional and marketing materials directly to them on their mobile devices.
- ***Mobile ticketing, vouchers and coupons:*** Tickets, vouchers, coupons and even loyalty cards are now sent to users on their mobile phones. Since they are in digital form, all that is required would be to present these tickets, vouchers or cards, in order to get the service or benefits that they entail.

There are a number of reasons why more users prefer using mobile devices in transactions and commercial activities.

- ***Mobile devices improve efficiency:*** The use of mobile devices will reduce the costs usually associated with the delivery of goods and services such as warehousing and storage costs and the cost of maintaining physical locations and stores of businesses.
- ***Mobile devices promote timeliness:*** If you have a mobile device, transactions may be done in real-time, and this also spurs the businesses to get right away to fulfill their end of the transaction.
- ***Mobile devices improve communications and relationships between the parties involved:*** The instant connection made through mobile devices results in better relations between businesses and their suppliers, sellers, customers and distributors. It also cuts through the time (and costs) that would have been used or spent on dealing with middlemen, since communication is done directly. Customer loyalty and retention are also strengthened.
- ***Mobile devices offer a wider 'reach':*** From the looks of things, the use of mobile devices is not a passing trend. In fact, we can see it playing an even bigger role in business in the future, and so, we expect more businesses to adopt mobile commerce, if they want to be able to enter bigger markets and reach a wider target audience.

By 2021, mobile e-commerce sales are expected to account for 54% of the total e-commerce sales. More importantly, our use of mobile is influencing our buying decisions even when we are in a physical brick-and-mortar store. It is estimated that one-third of our decision to purchase is influenced by looking up additional information on a product via our mobile device.

It has also served as a trigger for new industries and services, or helped the existing ones grow, including:

- Mobile money transfers
- Electronic tickets and boarding passes
- Digital content purchases and delivery
- Mobile banking
- Contactless payments and in-app payments
- Location-based services
- Mobile marketing, coupons, and loyalty cards

In Figure 10.1, a list of mobile services has been depicted.

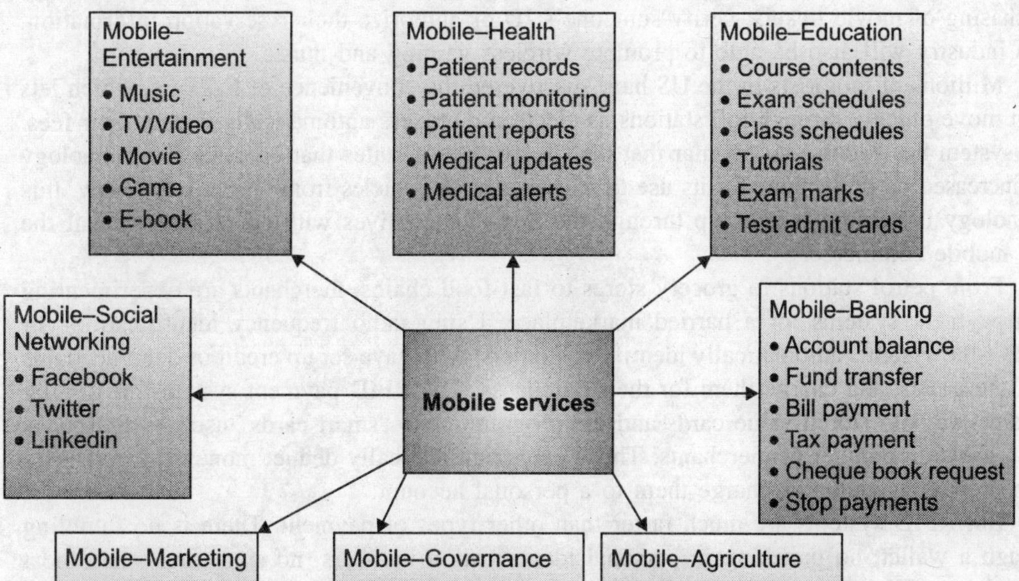

Figure 10.1 A list of mobile services.

Ideal M-commerce Market Characteristics

Financial Institutions such as Banks see mobile commerce as offering new channels of service to customers as well as offering them new and innovative products. These financial institutions are working to design and implement new applications that will offer mobile payment (i.e. being able to pay for groceries) and mobile brokering. The travel industry, in realizing the possible benefits of m-commerce, is working on technologies that will take care of travel arrangements, update customers on flight status, notify them when this information changes and will offer to make new arrangements based on preset user preferences requiring no input from the user. Therefore, a customer's entire trip can be scheduled and maintained using only their mobile device. The retail sector is also looking into the possibility of using mobile commerce for making the purchase of merchandize easier. Customers will be able to browse and order products while using a cheaper more secure payment method. An example of this is; instead of using paper catalogues, retailers can send customers a list of products that the customer would be interested in, directly to their mobile device. Additionally, retailers will also be able to track customers at all times and notify them of discounts at local stores in which that customer would be interested in. Shopping will also be easier[1]. Soon, phones will be equipped with "bar-code scanners" and shoppers could scan an item and find out its pricing and availability. In the entertainment industry, m-commerce could be used for the purchasing of movie tickets, verify someone's ID or authorize their reservation information. This industry will also be able to promote wireless gaming and music.

Millions of motorists in the US have discovered the convenience of E-ZPass, which lets them move quickly through toll stations as electronic readers automatically deduct their fees. The system has become so popular that the consortium of states that operates the technology has increased its projections for its use to 53 per cent of vehicles from 35 per cent. Now, this technology is helping people zip through the rest of their lives with equal ease. Call it the new mobile commerce.

From petrol stations to grocery stores to fast-food chains, merchants are experimenting with payment systems for a harried marketplace. Using radio frequency identification—or RFID—the systems automatically identify customers, who have set up credit or debit accounts with the issuer, and charge them for their purchases. The RFID payment systems are similar in some ways to stored-value cards and the programmable "smart cards" used by Starbucks and a growing number of merchants. Those cards automatically deduct money for purchases from prepaid accounts or charge them to a personal account.

But RFID systems are much faster than other types of payment. There is no fumbling through a wallet, no punching in personal identification numbers, no signatures—and most certainly, no Web browsing. All that is needed is a tiny device called a transponder that might hang on a customer's key chain and is waved in front of an electronic reader like a magic wand.

As more phones and other small-form handheld devices get "smarter", so does the potential for people to use them more often, and for many varied and different purposes. The number of mobile cell phone subscribers worldwide surpassed 4 billion, and technological innovation continues apace as time to market for new products continues to shrink.

Telecom providers continue looking for ways to add premium data and value-added products and services to their networks. As with light and heat, they are attracting a bigger and broader cross section of media, Internet technology and telecoms companies to the space—increasingly powerful mobile handsets and devices come equipped with Internet access, GPS, digital cameras, streaming audio and video, and other capabilities. The mobile

1. http://www.booz.com/media/uploads/BoozCo-Shopper-Strategies-Mobile-Commerce.pdf

entertainment market is opening wide, while at the same time, it offers artists more avenues to reach their audiences directly.

Table 10.1 shows the applications of m-commerce.

TABLE 10.1 M-Commerce Applications

Class of Applications	*Details*	*Examples*
Mobile financial applications (B2B, B2C)	Application where mobile device becomes a powerful financial medium	Banking, brokerage and payments for mobile users
Mobile advertising (B2C)	Application turning the wireless infrastructure and devices into a powerful marketing medium	User specific and loc-sensitive advertisements
Mobile inventory management (B2B, B2C)	Application attempting to reduce the amount of inventory needed by managing-in-house and inventory-in-move	Locaction tracking of goods, boxes, troops and people
Product location and shopping (B2B, B2C)	Application helping to find the location of product and services that are needed	Finding the location of a new/used car of certain model, colour and features
Proactive service management (B2B, B2C)	Applications attempting to provide users information on services they will need in future	Transmission of information related to aging (automobile) components to vendors
Wireless re-engineering (B2B, B2C)	Applications that focus on improving the quality of business services using mobile devices and wireless infrastructure	Instant claim-payments by insurance companies
Mobile auction or reverse auction (B2B, B2C)	Applications allowing users to buy or sell certain items using multicast support of wireless infrastructure	Airlines competing to buy a landing time slot during run-way congestion (a proposed solution to air-traffic congestion problem)
Mobile entertainment services and games (B2C)	Applications providing the entertainment services to users on per event or subscription basis	Video-on-demand,audio-on-demand, and interactive games
Mobile office (B2C)	Applications providing the complete office environment to mobile users anywhere, anytime	Working from traffic jams, airports and conferences
Mobile distance education (B2C)	Applications extending distance/virtual education support for mobile users everywhere	Taking a class using streaming and video
Wireless data centre (B2B, B2C)	Applications supporting large amount of stored data to be made available to mobile users for making "intelligent" decisions	Detailed information on one or more products can be downloaded by vendors

M-commerce Business Models

When mobile phones became smartphones, suddenly many dedicated software for specific functions, known as apps, began to take the world by storm. Some are for personalizing one's device, some are for entertainment purposes, and some are for more educational or work-related tasks. Businesses came up with apps of their own so that their products and services could be accessed with a few taps on the smartphone. Mobile apps are being used by a wide range of businesses.

Widespread Use of Mobile Apps

Although dominated by the gaming and entertainment industries, the world of apps is now open for various functionalities. There are apps for social networking sites and there are apps for controlling certain gadgets. The following are some reasons why mobile apps are popular:

- **Apps are dedicated** and make it easier for users to do what they need to do as compared to doing it on a desktop.
- **Apps can easily utilize the features** of the device it is on. This includes the camera, GPS and Bluetooth. With mobile apps, a lot of processes have been made automatic, especially with checkout and payments. You can also simply scan your credit card with your phone's camera instead of having to key in the numbers.
- **Some apps can be used offline.** Some resources like space for storage are used up, these apps can be operated offline and it is far more convenient this way rather than having to connect to the Internet for everything.
- **Apps load quickly** and users do not have to go through the arduous process of opening the Web browser, typing in the URL, and waiting for the page to load. It is definitely easier to just click the app's icon.
- There really is an **app for almost anything**, and e-commerce is not one to get left behind.
- More and more e-commerce **businesses are creating apps** of their own and it seems that this is one good step for the industry.

Some of the **advantages of mobile apps** for merchants are as follows:

1. ***Provide relevant information:*** The thing about apps is that they are often viewed as a smaller versions of mobile websites. But, all the information that websites have might not be available on mobile apps, so in order to make apps a better alternative for mobile apps, one must provide the essential details on your apps. Product descriptions should be the top priority. Shoppers cannot see the products physically; so, providing accurate and detailed product information is a must.
2. ***Provide discounts, offers and rewards:*** Shoppers love a good deal, so, regularly provide your shoppers with deals that entice them to buy. It is discovered in a survey that 71% of their respondents bought or purchased something via mobile app because of the availability of coupons and discounts. Mobile coupons can be created instantly, making them convenient and cost effective.

According to Koupon Media[2],
39 per cent of customers spend more if they receive a personalized coupon; 42 per cent of mobile users have used a mobile coupon; and 60 per cent of customers would adopt a mobile payment.

3. ***Use of mobile app as a marketing channel:*** Mobiles can be used as a channel for marketing campaigns. If users are required to sign up with an app, then a subscriber list can be made which can be used for marketing campaigns. Another way to market a product or service is through push notifications. Push notifications have a 97 per cent read rate and 90 per cent of them are read within three minutes of receipt. Because mobile phones are also capable of identifying geographic location, in comes location-based targeting. Combining efforts via push notifications and segmenting users according to location translate into more business.

Consumer Decision Journey with Smartphones

Over two-thirds of smartphone users say they check their phone within 15 minutes of waking up in the morning[3], and 30 per cent admit they actually get 'anxious' when they do not have their phone with them. 87 per cent of young people always have their smartphones at their side, day and night. In many countries, including the US, more searches take place on mobile devices than on computers. Consider that 82 per cent of smartphone users say they consult their phones on purchases they are about to make in a store, and 91 per cent of them turn to their phones for ideas in the middle of a task[4]. These micro-moments are critical touch-points within today's consumer journey, and when added together, they ultimately determine how that journey ends. According to some surveys, mobile sessions that average a mere one minute and 10 seconds long, dozens and dozens of times per day are influencing buying decisions. In many ways, micro-moments have become the footsteps that lead people to purchase products of services.

Since we can take action on any need or curiosity at any time, the consumer decision journey has been fractured into hundreds of tiny decision-making moments at every stage. Today, one has to earn the customer's consideration and action, moment after moment. Why? Because people are more loyal to their need in the moment than to any particular brand. That makes micro-moments the new battleground for brands. Consumers may not be visiting stores as often as they used to. Yet consumers are spending more when they do visit because they have done their research and made decisions before ever walking in. In many ways, micro-moments have become the footsteps that lead people to your store or desktop site. 65 per cent of smartphone users agree that when conducting a search on their smartphones, they look for the most relevant information regardless of the company providing the information.

2. http://cdn2.hubspot.net/hubfs/414273/Koupon_State_of_Mobile_Coupons_2016-1.pdf
3. Google Consumer Surveys, August 2015, smartphone users, n=729
4. https://www.thinkwithgoogle.com/marketing-resources/micro-moments/win-every-micromoment-with-better-mobile-strategy/

Mobile Business Models

Mobile has fundamentally transformed consumer behavior and expectations. We do not go online anymore; we live online. We act on our needs in micro-moments. This shift in consumer behavior affects not only mobile marketing strategies but also how organizations think about their marketing strategies at large.

A business model determines the path or process through which a business organization can realize some profit. It shows the way by which an organization can make some investment, add some value to the investment, get a finished product or service and generate some revenue through sales of the product or service. The revenue generated through sales must exceed the operating cost, so that the company gets some profit. Business models specify the mechanism for generating profit margins and to sustain in the value chain. Thus, business models help managers in strategic planning and formulating an overall business strategy of the organization. Electronic commerce has some traditional business models that are widely followed by all major e-commerce vendors worldwide. These include merchant model, broker model, service provider model, advertiser model and the apps model. Mobile commerce business models differ from those of electronic commerce due to their intrinsic difference in operations and technology. As mobile commerce imparts extra mobility to the users, the business models also reflect the mobility in their nature. The four major services offered by mobile commerce are the payment services, mobile advertisements, mobile shopping and mobile entertainment. However, mobile commerce business models also revolve around five applications. The five major mobile commerce business models are described below:

1. ***Payment model:*** In this model, mobile payment service providers offer mobile payment services that allow users to make cashless payment transactions including banking transactions, share trading, tax/bill payments and ticket or other retail purchases using credit/debit card or bank PIN. The payment service providers have collaboration with banks (or other financial institutions) and/or mobile network operators, and accordingly, get bank-controlled mobile payment model or operator-controlled mobile payment model. The payment service provider charges a certain percentage fee for each payment transaction made through the payment application. Alternatively, the user can pay a nominal monthly subscription fee to the payment service provider and can use the service as and when required.

2. ***Advertiser model:*** This model is an extension of traditional e-commerce advertiser model and provides mobile websites which can be viewed by mobile users in their handheld mobile devices. Advertising companies can display their advertising messages in the website and pay a rental fee to the hosting website for displaying their messages. These mobile advertising websites usually offer some basic services such as e-mail service, search engines, news service or social networking service to the users and post advertising messages in these sites to enjoy greater coverage. The advertisements often come with purchase buttons that allow users to purchase the product directly from their mobile devices. The mobile payment service is also provided to facilitate mobile purchase directly from the advertising websites. The

advertiser companies pay a fixed fee to the advertising website for displaying their advertising messages. Additional revenue is generated for each purchase transaction made by the user through the website.

3. ***Shopping model:*** This model is similar to e-commerce merchant model where retailers create mobile websites to display their range of products to the mobile devices of the customers. The mobile users can browse the mobile websites in their WAP-enabled mobile screens and select and purchase any product of their choice. Mobile payment option is also provided in the website so that the users can make mobile payment for the purchased product and complete the deal even while in transit or far away from the actual store location. Thus, shopping model allows retailers to generate additional revenues through mobile shopping and can improve their profit margins.

4. ***Content provider model:*** In this model, mobile service providers offer a host of entertainment contents such as breaking news, weather forecast, traffic updates, music, mobile games, TV shows, video content, movies, etc. that could be downloaded to users' mobile devices. Network operators have tie-ups with various content providers and offer both subscription-based services as well as pay-per-use services to the customers. Location-based services such as map-based navigational services, discount coupons offered in local retail stores or restaurants, news of local events, etc. are also delivered in customers' mobile devices. The revenue is generated through subscription fees (for news, traffic/weather updates, movies, games), usage fees (TV shows, videos, games, etc.) or data download fees (for e-mails, e-books, etc.). Various media houses, press agencies or content aggregators follow this model for generating extra revenue through mobile channel.

5. ***Apps business model:*** Nowadays, mobile apps present a variety of ways of making money and at times, this will make it difficult to rectify which business model one should go for. Whether it is a mobile game or a shopping/photo editing app, the mobile market is pretty huge. There are various ways one can go for monetizing one's app. Let us take a look at some of the mobile application models that one can choose from:

(i) *Selling mobile applications model:* This is the most obvious and the one that is most widely leveraged today—build an app that everyone will want and sell millions of licenses and reap the rewards.

(ii) *Freemium:* The goal of freemium is to get the app in as many hands as possible, and once it reaches, try to generate revenue from one of the following ways:
The first is essentially giving away a limited version of the product in hopes that one can attract enough people to download it and then convert a percentage of those into paying customers.
The second most popular approach to freemium is selling advertising in the app. Once an application is installed on millions of devices, one can now start offering content packs, additional functionality or even have people who pay to remove the in-app advertisements.

(iii) *Extend an existing business into the mobile world:* There are many options for extending an existing business into the mobile world, but it can be summarized into two main business goals—first, it helps in enhancing an existing line of business. This is about finding the one key area of an existing business one is currently involved in and extending it to the mobile world. Second, it extends the reach to the new customers. One of the greatest potentials of mobile is to extend the reach of the product, say from TV, Web or bricks and mortar, to new customers that would not normally consume what is being advertised through the traditional mediums.

(iv) *Build an application as a service:* Ubercab app service allows a customer to quickly book and pay for a car service with one button. This is great example of the future of productive mobile business models, filling a need that is best-suited for our mobile lives.

(v) *Build an app as a subscription:* When 'Wired' launched its iPad app version of the magazine, it surpassed sales of its print version in the first month it went live—that is disruptive[5].

(vi) *Mobilize an existing technology:* Most companies are looking for mobile versions of enterprise software they have already implemented internally—things like CRM applications, HR application or business operations applications. For some, mobile is the natural extension for these services and there is opportunity to fill a very specific niche here.

(vii) *Build an app that extends a Web business:* The most amazing thing to emerge since the dot com bust has been the open Application Programming Interface (API). Many companies currently offering a legitimate Web service have adopted the open API in hopes that their service will find developers, who will create the next layer of service on top of theirs. The mobile area is ripe for entrepreneurs to bring a service into the mobile world as a new level of value.

(viii) *Sell affiliate products through an app:* This requires a very popular application in order to generate substantial revenue from the referral fees, but it could compliment another stream from one of the other business models mentioned above.

Limitations of Mobile Commerce

Although mobile commerce has some distinctive advantages such as instant connectivity and location and time independence over electronic commerce and offers low-cost personalized services to the mobile users, it suffers from some serious limitations, which restrict its use in the mainstream business world. The mobile device limitations such as small screen size, small memory capacity and lower processor speed make it unsuitable for high-quality Internet graphics applications. The limited availability of bandwidth to various mobile operators imposes a limitation on the speed of operation of different mobile commerce applications. The wireless networks used in mobile commerce are more vulnerable to external hacker attacks

5. https://www.wired.com/magazine/

compared to wired networks, and stringent security arrangements in the form of encryption and authentication should be adopted to prevent unwanted intrusions. However, newer mobiles with larger memory sizes and 5G bandwidth may overcome some of these limitations.

The main disadvantages of mobile commerce are explained in detail below:

1. ***Small screen size:*** Mobile devices have smaller screen size and poor resolution, which make them inconvenient for browsing applications. Data entry can be quite difficult using small combinational keypad that comes with most of the mobile handheld devices. The wide and high resolution screens in conventional desktops or laptops used in e-commerce applications offer ease of use in data entry operations as well as viewing Web pages.

2. ***Low speed processor:*** Most mobile devices come with low-powered processors with much lower processing speed compared to sophisticated processors used in desktops or laptops. Such low speed processors restrict the download speed in most mobile commerce applications. The applications requiring too much processing power should be avoided as they may become irritably slow due to low speed processors. Also, keeping the low processor speed in mind, the mobile websites must be optimized to ensure customer satisfaction. Unnecessary plug-ins, flash images and animations should be removed to ensure speed of delivery.

3. ***Small memory capacity:*** The mobile devices do not have large storage space as compared to desktop computers.

4. ***Wireless network limitations:*** Mobile commerce depends on wireless networks which are usually of lower speed compared to wired networks. In many cases, wireless networks offer one-fourth speed of standard wired network. So, online mobile services may become unavailable in some rural areas, and thus, the popularity of mobile services may be suffered. Atmospheric interference and fading of signals transmitted through wireless networks sometimes cause severe data errors and may even lead to disconnections.

5. ***Bandwidth restrictions:*** A major disadvantage of mobile commerce is the bandwidth limitation, which imposes a limitation on speed of operation in various m-commerce applications. Wireless networks use frequency spectrum to transmit information across the network. Regulatory bodies control the use of available frequency spectrum and allocate the spectrum to various mobile operators.

6. ***Security issues:*** Another concern that is often raised in connection with mobile commerce is the security issue. Mobile devices are more vulnerable to theft, loss and mishandling. Special care must be taken to ensure that the security and privacy of the mobile customer are not compromised at the event of loss of a mobile device. Mobile commerce employs public wireless networks for transmission of signals, which can be easily intercepted by hackers for capturing/altering stream of data travelling through the wireless medium. In wired networks, in order to gain access, the intruder has to gain physical access to the wired infrastructure. In wireless networks, anyone, with the ability to receive signal in a mobile device, can gain access to the network.

In order to protect the wireless network from unwanted users, various encryption and authentication techniques should be employed. As the handheld devices have limited computing power and storage capacity, it is difficult to employ 256-bit encryption technique that requires enough computing power. However, the SIM cards inside a cell phone can include the digital signatures of PKI system. Thus, the PKI system of digital signatures can be integrated in a mobile device, which adds to the security of the mobile application. Authentication of mobile devices prior to carrying out any financial transaction is another important issue. The Subscriber Identity Module (SIM) stores the subscriber's identity in the form of cryptographic keys. The authentication server of the wireless network stores the matching keys and verifies the user identity prior to any transaction. Though it is far easier to intercept signals over wireless networks, the encryption and authentication mechanism makes it harder to decipher by the unwanted user.

Trends of M-commerce

New trends in the world of m-commerce are driving changes in the market place. Some of those trends are given below:

1. ***Chatbots:*** Many users prefer chatting service than calling or writing e-mails, and so, chatbot service use is becoming more common. The success of 'Alexa' of Amazon or 'Siri' of Apple heralded the use of chatbots. Chatbots provide customers with round-the-clock service. Besides, artificial intelligence makes it possible to gather data about customers and analyze it. It allows chatbots to predict the next question and prepare a reply, and also, chatbots are able to offer personalized experience according to the customers' preferences.
2. ***Augmented reality:*** Augmented reality (AR) technology is only a few years old, but it has already become very popular and different types of business apply this tech.
3. ***Geofencing:*** Geofencing is the use of GPS or RFID technology to create a virtual geographic boundary, and this enables software to trigger a response when a mobile device enters or leaves a particular area. It is a very novel trend since it allows businesses to offer people products and services that are more popular in their specific region. Using GPS, when a customer enters an online market, it can start monitoring that customer's location immediately. The app can offer appropriate products and it will also help users find nearby shopping centers to buy something.
4. ***Purchase via one click:*** M-commerce apps are created to trigger spontaneous purchases. If with one click, purchases can be done, some customers will be happy. So, instead of putting something in the shopping cart and then paying, one-click purchase is a trend that helps make such purchases fast.
5. ***Personalization:*** Today, many e-commerce businesses collect data about users in social networks to know about customers as much as possible. As a result, they send

personalized offers to a customer. The use of artificial intelligence to analyze and predict what a customer will prefer buying next helps them to send the appropriate message. And customers are happy when they receive information about what they want to buy.

6. ***Big data:*** When a business has many customers, it can collect a huge amount of data. To handle huge amounts of data, special programs are needed. Today, such tools are available to analyze the sentiments of customers or their buying habits according to seasons. That is where big data processing comes to the rescue. It allows you to find the best price among other ones suggested by competitors and you can offer the best price to your customers. Also, big data helps collect information about the latest trends and all up-to-date information from the e-commerce world.
7. ***Increased trust:*** More consumers feel comfortable shopping on mobile than ever before. Security issues have diminished as the age of m-commerce has increased. Additionally, consumers are more and more of the 'digital native' age, meaning they have grown up with computers and the Internet in their entire lives. These generations are more likely to use mobile commerce than older generations.
8. ***Faster checkouts:*** One-page checkouts and digital wallets (Amazon Pay, Apple Pay, PayPal One Touch) have improved mobile conversion. And there is no surprise, as more consumers are comfortable in shopping on mobile and more convenient mobile checkout experiences have surged in popularity.
9. ***Easier to use sites:*** More and more sites are now optimized for mobile use. M-commerce is the next new trend. It is a staple of modern retail. As a result, e-commerce platforms and businesses alike have moved into near 100 per cent responsive site builds, meaning most sites today are easy to use on mobile.

What is more though is that many brands are moving to mobile-first, or mobile-unique experience. In this instance, a mobile site is created specifically for the mobile user—different than what the desktop version looks like.

Cellular Networks

A cellular network is a radio network made up of a number of **radio cells** (or just **cells**) each served by a fixed transmitter, known as a cell site or base station. These cells are used to cover different areas in order to provide radio coverage over a wider area than the area of one cell. Cellular networks are inherently asymmetric with a set of fixed main transceivers each serving a cell and a set of distributed (generally, but not always, mobile) transceivers which provide services to the network's users.

Cellular networks offer a number of advantages over alternative solutions:

- increased capacity
- reduced power usage
- better coverage

Communication channels are expensive. Communication services providers must engage multiple paid users over limited resources to make money. Access methods allow many users to share these limited channels to provide the economy of scale necessary for a successful communication business. There are five basic access or multiplexing methods—frequency division multiple access (FDMA), time division multiple access (TDMA), code division multiple access (CDMA), orthogonal frequency division multiple access (OFDMA), and spatial division multiple access (SDMA). Of these, CDMA and FDMA are the most widely used methods.

Broadcast Messages and Paging

Practically every cellular system has some kind of broadcast mechanism. This can be used directly for distributing information to multiple mobiles, commonly, for example in mobile telephony systems, the most important use of broadcast information is to set up channels for one to one communication between the mobile transreceiver and the base station. This is called **paging**.

The details of the process of paging vary somewhat from network to network, but normally we know a limited number of cells where the phone is located (this group of cells is called a Location Area in the GSM or UMTS system, or Routing Area if a data packet session is involved). Paging takes place by sending the broadcast message to all of those cells. Paging messages can be used for information transfer. This happens in pagers, in CDMA systems for sending SMS messages, and in the UMTS system where it allows for low downlink latency in packet-based connections.

Frequency Reuse

The increased capacity in a cellular network, compared with a network with a single transmitter, comes from the fact that the same radio frequency can be reused in a different area for a completely different transmission. If there is a single plain transmitter, only one transmission can be used on any given frequency. Unfortunately, there is inevitably some level of interference from the signal from the other cells which use the same frequency. This means that, in a standard FDMA system, there must be at least a one cell gap between cells which reuse the same frequency.

The frequency reuse factor is the rate at which the same frequency can be used in the network. It is 1/K where K is the number of cells which cannot use the same frequencies for transmission. Common values for the frequency reuse factor are 1/3, 1/4, 1/7, 1/9 and 1/12.

In case of N sector antennas on the same base station site, each with different direction, the base station site can serve N different cells. N is typically 3. A **reuse pattern** of N/K denotes N sector antennas per site. Common reuse patterns are 3/3, 3/9 and 3/12.

If the total available bandwidth is B, each cell can only utilize a number of frequency channels corresponding to a bandwidth of B/K, and each base station site can use a bandwidth of BN/K.

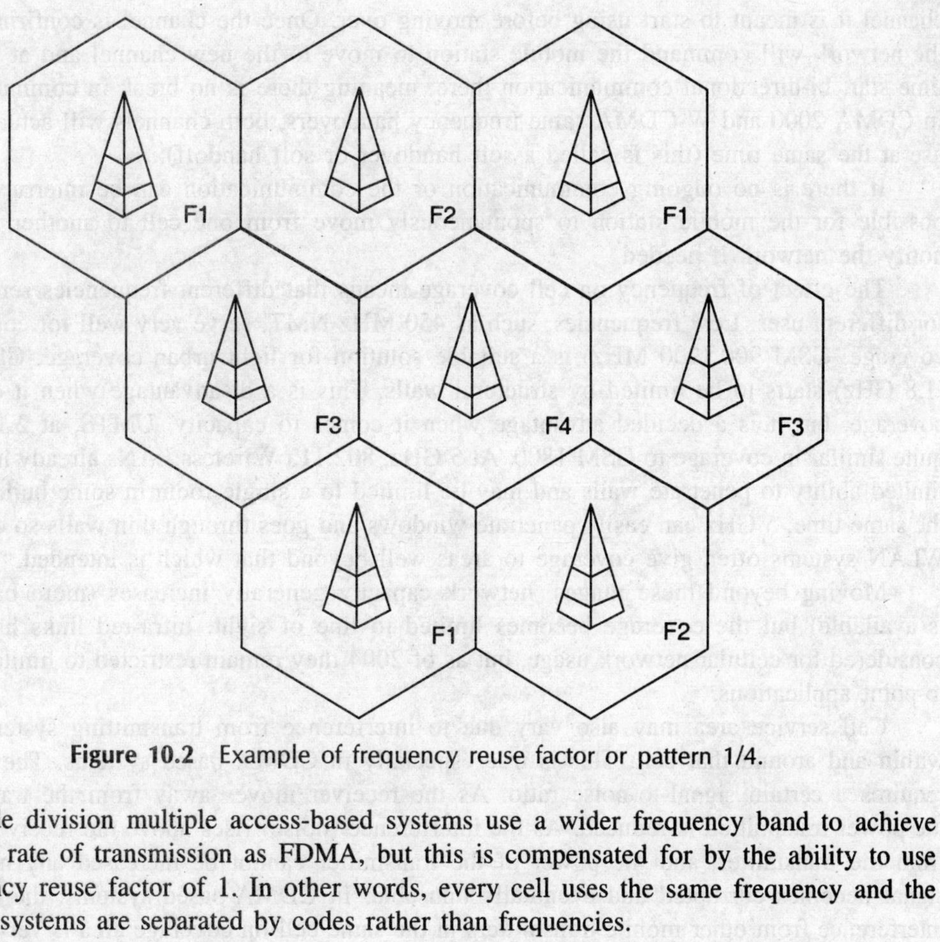

Figure 10.2 Example of frequency reuse factor or pattern 1/4.

Code division multiple access-based systems use a wider frequency band to achieve the same rate of transmission as FDMA, but this is compensated for by the ability to use a frequency reuse factor of 1. In other words, every cell uses the same frequency and the different systems are separated by codes rather than frequencies.

Movement from Cell to Cell and Handover

The use of multiple cells means that, if the distributed transceivers are mobile and moving from place to place, they also have to change from cell to cell. The mechanism for this differs depending on the type of network and the circumstances of the change. For example, if there is an ongoing continuous communication and we don't want to interrupt it, then great care must be taken to avoid interruption. In this case there must be clear coordination between the base station and the mobile station. Typically such systems use some kind of multiple access independently in each cell, so an early stage of such a handover (handoff) is to reserve a new channel for the mobile station on the new base station which will serve it. The mobile then moves from the channel on its current base station to the new channel and from that point on communication takes place. The exact details of the mobile system's move from one base station to the other varies considerably from system to system. For example, in all GSM handovers and W-CDMA inter-frequency handovers the mobile station will measure the channel it is meant to start using before moving over. Once the channel is confirmed okay, the network will command the mobile station to move to the new channel and at the same time start bi-directional communication there, meaning there is no break in communication. In CDMA 2000 and W-CDMA same-frequency handovers, both channels will actually be in use at the same time (this is called a soft handover or soft handoff).

If there is no ongoing communication or the communication can be interrupted, it is possible for the mobile station to spontaneously move from one cell to another and then notify the network if needed.

The effect of frequency on cell coverage means that different frequencies serve better for different uses. Low frequencies, such as 450 MHz NMT, serve very well for countryside coverage. GSM 900 (900 MHz) is a suitable solution for light urban coverage. GSM 1800 (1.8 GHz) starts to be limited by structural walls. This is a disadvantage when it comes to coverage, but it is a decided advantage when it comes to capacity. UMTS, at 2.1 GHz is quite similar in coverage to GSM 1800. At 5 GHz, 802.11a Wireless LANs already have very limited ability to penetrate walls and may be limited to a single room in some buildings. At the same time, 5 GHz can easily penetrate windows and goes through thin walls so corporate WLAN systems often give coverage to areas well beyond that which is intended.

Moving beyond these ranges, network capacity generally increases (more bandwidth is available) but the coverage becomes limited to line of sight. Infra-red links have been considered for cellular network usage, but as of 2004 they remain restricted to limited point-to-point applications.

Cell service area may also vary due to interference from transmitting systems, both within and around that cell. This is true especially in CDMA based systems. The receiver requires a certain signal-to-noise ratio. As the receiver moves away from the transmitter, the power transmitted is reduced. As the interference (noise) rises above the received power from the transmitter, and the power of the transmitter cannot be increased any more, the signal becomes corrupted and eventually unusable. In CDMA-based systems, the effect of interference from other mobile transmitters in the same cell on coverage area is very marked and has a special name, *cell breathing*.

To see real examples of cell coverage look at some of the coverage maps provided by real operators on their websites; in certain cases they may mark the site of the transmitter, in others it can be located by working out the point of strongest coverage.

Cellular Telephony

A mobile phone is a portable telephone which receives or makes calls through a cell site (base station), or transmitting tower. Radio waves are used to transfer signals to and from the cell phone. Large geographic areas are split up into smaller cells to deal with line-of-sight signal loss and the large number of active phones in an area. In cities, ½ mile is the norm for range for each cell site. In rural areas, the range is approximately 5 miles. All of the cell sites are connected to cellular telephone exchanges "switches", which in turn connect to the public telephone network or another switch of the cellular company.

As the phone user moves from one cell area to another, the switch automatically commands the handset and a cell site with a stronger signal to go to a new radio channel (frequency). When the handset responds through the new cell site, the exchange switches the connection to the new cell site.

Figure 10.3 Cell site.

Since almost all mobile phones use cellular technology, including GSM, CDMA, and AMPS (analog), the term "cell phone" is used interchangeably with "mobile phone"; however, an exception of mobile phones not using cellular technology is satellite phones.

Wireless Spectrum

The electromagnetic spectrum is the entire range of energy waves over which communicating devices transmit. Over the airwaves, TV, radio, cell phones, or any wireless Internet devices communicate with a transceiver. Each kind of transceiver uses dedicated frequency ranges that are measured in Hertz (Hz); 1 Hz is one cycle per second.

An interesting property of the spectrum is that higher frequencies travel shorter distances. Higher frequencies can be modulated to carry more bits per second than longer waves, but they are subject to atmospheric interference. Broadcasters generally prefer owning a lower frequency because it costs less to transmit a signal, it carries farther, and it is generally "safer".

The US Federal Communications Commission (FCC) and similar agencies around the world break up the spectrum and assign bands for specific purposes. Bands are ranges of frequency with common names. Worldwide bodies such as the International Telecommunications Union (ITU) also make frequency agreements, so that devices will operate clearly worldwide.

Regulating radio interference is necessary so that wireless devices do not interfere with one another. To prohibit interference from a neighbouring transmitter, the FCC restricts bands of coverage.

GSM-900 and GSM-1800

GSM-900 and GSM–1800 are used in most parts of the world: Europe, Middle East, Africa and most of Asia.

GSM-900 uses 890–915 MHz to send information from the Mobile Station to the Base Transceiver Station (uplink) and 935–960 MHz for the other direction (downlink), providing 124 RF channels (channel numbers 1 to 124) spaced at 200 kHz.

Most of the GSM operators in India use the 900 MHz band. Operators like, Airtel, Idea, and some others, use 900 MHz in rural areas as well as in urban areas whereas hutch uses 1800 MHz everywhere except in its bpl network.

GSM-850

GSM-850 and GSM-1900 are used in the United States, Canada, and many other countries in the Americas.

GSM-850 uses 824–849 MHz to send information from the Mobile Station to the Base Transceiver Station (uplink) and 869–894 MHz for the other direction (downlink). Channel numbers 128 to 251.

Multi-band and Multi-mode Phones

Today, most telephones support multiple frequencies used in different countries. These are typically referred to as multi-band phones. Dual-band phones can cover GSM networks in pairs such as 900 and 1800 MHz frequencies (Europe, Asia, Australia and Brazil) or 850 and 1900 (North America). European tri-band phones typically cover the 900, 1800 and 1900 bands giving good coverage in Europe and allowing limited use in North America, while North American tri-band phones utilize 850, 1800 and 1900 for widespread North American service but limited worldwide use. A new addition has been the quad band phone, supporting all four major GSM frequency groups, allowing for widespread usage globally, including in North America.

There are also multi-mode phones which can operate on GSM systems as well as on mobile-phone systems using other technical standards.

AMPS and European Analog Cellular

Advanced Mobile Phone Service or AMPS, is the analog cellular transport used throughout North America and in other parts of the world, notably Central and South America, New Zealand, and Australia. It has the best coverage of all North American systems.

AMPS operates at 800 MHz. It is a voice-only analog transport. You can also use it with a cellular modem for circuit-switched data communications. AMPS is slowly being replaced with various competing digital networks. For the foreseeable future however, it will be the most readily available cellular network in North America.

At the same time, AMPS systems were being built in the United States, a variety of incompatible analog systems were when being promoted in Europe and the rest of the world. Although, they all operated in the 900 MHz frequency range, the European systems did not work well with each other. These 900 MHz European analog systems, which we do not identify individually, are rapidly being phased out in favour of all-digital systems.

TDMA

Time Division Multiple Access (TDMA) is a digital transport that divides the frequency range allotted to it into a series of channels. Each channel is then divided into time slots. Each conversation within that channel gets a time slot; hence the term "division" in the name.

TDMA has been in use for quite sometime in Europe as the basis for the GSM (Global System for Mobile Communications). More recently, it is being adopted in North America, in some PCS systems.

It is possible to overlay TDMA on top of an AMPS transport, converting an analog network to a hybrid analog/digital network. Some AMPS carriers in North America have been doing this to add security, capacity, and data capabilities to their older voice systems. This type of network has several names, such as Digital AMPS (D-AMPS) and North American TDMA (NA-TDMA).

CDMA

Code Division Multiple Access (CDMA) is a digital transport that has been in use by the US military since the 1940s. However, as a commercial wireless transport, it is the new kid on the block compared to TDMA and AMPS.

Pioneered by US-based QUALCOMM, a CDMA transmitter assigns a unique code to each wireless connection and then broadcasts its data out on the channel simultaneously with all other connections. The receiver is able to decode each conversation by knowing the unique code assigned to each connection.

CDMA is often described as a party in a room where everyone speaks a different language. If everyone speaks at approximately the same volume, you should be able to hear all the conversations. If you know the unique code (language) used by each speaker, you can hear and understand all the conversations.

CDMA advocates the claim that it has some definite advantages over TDMA. First and foremost, CDMA enables simultaneous usage: approximately 10–20 times AMPS, and three times TDMA. It uses less power, giving you much better phone battery life. It is also more secure, because it hops from one frequency to another during a conversation, making it less prone to eavesdropping and phone fraud. Other benefits include fewer dropped calls and better voice quality.

CDMA is being widely deployed in North America in new PCS systems, but less widely throughout the world. Like TDMA, it can also be overlaid on top of AMPS systems to create hybrid analog/digital networks.

For more information about CDMA, visit QUALCOMM's website at *www.qualcomm.com.*

GSM

In the late 1980s, noting the wide disparity of analog cellular systems in Europe, various European political, trade, and academic interests started collaborating on an all-digital cellular communications network. Eventually called GSM, it has gone on to be the most widely deployed digital network in the world to date. It is used by millions of people in more than 200 countries.

Using an all-digital, TDMA-based network, every GSM phone has access to a variety of data functions at speeds limited to 9600 bps (the effective throughput is typically about half that speed). These services include direct-connect Internet access (both circuit-switched and packet data) without requiring a modem, mobile fax capabilities, and short message service.

GSM started operating in the 900 MHz frequency range in all European countries. Additional networks are being deployed in the 1800 MHz frequency range. An alternate name for GSM is PCN (Personal Communication Network), the European equivalent of PCS (Personal Communication Services). For more information about GSM, visit www.gsmdata.com.

Different Generations in Wireless Communication

First Generation (1G)

The first generation of cellular phones can be traced to the early eighties, and is marked by the use of **Analog** technology. The bandwidths used then were confined to a maximum of 30 kHz. The most widely used analog cellphone standard in this generation was the **Advanced Mobile Phone System** (AMPS). In 1983, AMPS was approved by the FCC and first used in Chicago. AMPS is the analog cellular transport used throughout North America and other parts of the world, notably Central and South America, New Zealand, and Australia. The AMPS system uses 832 full-duplex channels, each consisting of a pair of simplex channels. AMPS uses a range of frequencies between 824 MHz and 894 MHz. Each simplex channel is 30 kHz wide, and AMPS uses Frequency Division Multiplexing (FDM) to separate the channels. The 832 channels can be divided into four categories:

(a) *Control* (base to mobile) to manage the system,
(b) *Paging* (base to mobile) to alert mobile users to calls for them,
(c) *Access* (bidirectional) for call set up and channel assignment, and
(d) *Data* (bidirectional) for voice, fax, or data.

The problem with AMPS is that in the 800 MHz band, radio waves are 40 cm long and travel in straight lines. Hence, they are absorbed by trees and plants, and bounce off buildings, leading to a high level of echo and signal distortion. Hence, AMPS is slowly being replaced by various competing digital networks.

Second Generation (2G)

The first generation of mobile phones was analog; the second generation was **digital**. Just as there was no worldwide standardization during the first generation, there was none in the second either. Four 2G systems are in use now, namely, D-AMPS, GSM, CDMA, and PDC. We will look at two of the more popular technologies: **GSM** and **CDMA**.

Group System Mobile (GSM)

GSM was the first European digital standard, developed to establish cellular compatibility throughout Europe. It is the first digital cellular system to be used commercially, and its success has spread to all parts of the world, including countries in Asia, Middle East, Africa, North, Central and South America, and Australia. Over 80 GSM networks are now operational, making it the most widely deployed digital network in the world to date, used by millions of people in more than 200 countries.

Communication using GSM is based on the **Time Division Multiple Access** (TDMA) digital standard. See Table 10.2. TDMA is a digital transport scheme, wherein multiple users are granted access to the same radio frequency source by limiting the subscribers' transmitted and received signals to time slots.

TABLE 10.2 Technical Specifications of Standard (GSM)

Mobile Frequency Range	Rx: 925–960 MHz; Tx: 880–915 MHz
Multiple Access Method	TDMA/FDM
Duplex Method	FDD
Number of Channels	124 (8 users per channel)
Channel Spacing	200 kHz
Modulation	GMSK (0.3 Gaussian Filter)
Channel Bit Rate	270.833 kilobits

GSM operates at 900 MHz. A GSM system supports 124 pairs of simplex channels. Each simplex channel is 200 kHz wide, and supports eight separate connections on it using TDM.

GSM cell phones require SIM (Subscriber Identity Module) cards for their operation. The SIM is a smart card that identifies the user terminal. By inserting the SIM card into the terminal, the user can have access to all the subscribed services. Without the SIM card, the terminal is not operational. To connect to the specific service providers in these different countries, GSM users simply switch Subscriber Identification Module (SIM) cards.

Code Division Multiple Access (CDMA)

Over 35 countries have either commercial or trial activity ongoing in the field of CDMA. These include countries in the regions of North America, Caribbean, Africa, Latin America, Europe, and Russia. However, CDMA is most popular in the Asia Pacific region, with around

84,000,000 users. There are already 43 Wireless Local Loop (WLL) systems in 22 countries using CDMA technology, and the number of global users of CDMA has surpassed 202 million.

CDMA is an air link interface coding scheme, wherein multiple subscribers are granted access to the same radio frequency source by assigning subscribers' transmitted and received signals a spectrum-spreading code. Developed originally by QUALCOMM, CDMA is characterized by its high capacity and its small cell radius, and the fact that it employs spread spectrum technology and a special scheme. It was adopted by the Telecommunication Industry Association (TIA) in 1993. IS-95 is a standard for CDMA (Code Division Multiple Access) digital cellular (See Table 10.3).

TABLE 10.3 Technical Specifications of Standard CDMA or IS-95

Mobile Frequency Range	Rx: 869-894 MHz; Tx: 824-849 MHz
Multiple Access Method	CDMA/FDM
Duplex Method	FDD
Number of Channels	20 (798 users per channel)
Channel Spacing	1250 kHz
Modulation	QPSK/OQPSK
Channel Bit Rate	1.2288 megabits

A CDMA transmitter assigns a unique code to each wireless connection and then broadcasts its data out on the channel simultaneously with all other connections. The receiver is able to decode each conversation by deciphering the unique code assigned to each connection. Basically, instead of dividing the allowed frequency range into a few hundred channels, CDMA allows each station to transmit over the entire frequency spectrum all the time.

CDMA normally operates in a band of 1.25 MHz (versus 200 kHz for GSM), but it supports many more users in that band than any of the other systems. In practice, the bandwidth available to each user is at least as good as GSM, if not better.

Third Generation (3G)

The most recent generation of cellular radio systems for mobile telephony are referred to as third generation (3G) technologies, and generally refer to those that promise to provide very high transmission speeds and performance. The technical framework for 3G has been defined by the International Telecommunications Union (ITU) as part of its International Mobile Telecommunications 2000 (IMT-2000) program. The third generation will be the first cellular radio technology designed from the outset to support wideband data communications at the same level of its voice communications.

CDMA 2000 and WCDMA

The two 3G models of CDMA are Wideband CDMA (WCDMA) and CDMA 2000, and both use the direct spread spectrum type of modulation.

WCDMA is a third-generation technology proposed by Ericsson that increases data transmission rates in GSM systems using CDMA instead of TDMA. CDMA 2000 has been proposed by QUALCOMM. It is basically an extension of IS-95 and backward compatible with it.

With the onset of the third generation, an urgent need is being felt to have a common standard across the telecom spectrum, so that there are no compatibility problems and technical differences. Efforts are now being made towards this integration.

Fourth Generation Wireless (4G)

4G is the short name for fourth-generation wireless, the stage of broadband mobile communications. According to the ITU, a 4G network requires a mobile device to be able to exchange data at 100 Mbit/sec.

Table 10.4 is a basic list of the specifications of both technologies, 3G and 4G. The table compares and contrasts the two from a technical standpoints.

TABLE 10.4 Specifications for 3G and 4G

	3G	4G
Frequency	1.8–2.5 GHz	2–8 GHz
Bandwidth	5–20 MHz	5–20 MHz
Data Rate	Up to 2 Mbps	100 Mbps Mobile, 1 Gps Stationary
Access	W-CDMA	VSF-OFCDM and VSF-CDMA
Switching	Circuit/Packet	Packet

Fifth Generation (5G)

Wireless networks are composed of cell sites divided into sectors that send data through radio waves. Fourth generation (4G) Long-Term Evolution (LTE) wireless technology provides the foundation for 5G. Unlike 4G, which requires large, high-power cell towers to radiate signals over longer distances, 5G wireless signals will be transmitted via a large number of small cell stations located in places like light poles or building roofs. The use of multiple small cells is necessary because the millimeter wave spectrum—the band of spectrum between 30 GHz and 300 GHz that 5G relies on to generate high speeds—can only travel over short distances and is subject to interference from weather and physical obstacles like buildings.

Previous generations of wireless technology have used lower frequency bands of spectrum. To offset millimetre wave challenges relating to distance and interference, the wireless industry is also considering the use of lower frequency spectrum for 5G networks, so that network operators could use spectrum they already own to build out their new networks. Lower frequency spectrum reaches greater distances, but has lower speed and capacity than millimeter wave.

5G fixed wireless broadband services deliver Internet access to homes and businesses without a wired connection to the premises. To do that, network operators deploy NRs in small cell sites near buildings to beam a signal to a receiver on a rooftop or a windowsill that is amplified within the premises. Fixed broadband services are expected to make it less expensive for operators to deliver broadband services to homes and businesses because this approach eliminates the need to roll out fiber optic lines to every residence. Instead, operators need only install fiber optics to cell sites, and customers receive broadband services through wireless modems located in their residences or businesses.

5G technology is driven by eight specification requirements, which are as follows:

1. Up to 10 Gbps data rate — > 10 to 100 × improvement over 4G and 4.5G networks
2. 1 ms latency
3. 1000 × bandwidth per unit area
4. Up to 100 × number of connected devices per unit area (compared with 4G LTE)
5. 99.999 per cent availability
6. 100 per cent coverage
7. 90 per cent reduction in network energy usage
8. Up to 10-year battery life for low power IoT devices

EXERCISES

1. Visit *www.ericsson.com* and look at all the business opportunities that they offer with regard to GPRS, EDGE, PDC, GSM, and TDMA. Comment on one of the case studies.
2. What is bluetooth? Get the information from *www.bluetooth.com.*
3. Study the 3G technologies by visiting the sites of ericsson, mpegtv, nokia, and mobile wireless Internet forum.
4. What does the future hold for mobile commerce? Look at the UMTS Market forecast study (*www.analysis.co.uk/news/umts/default.htm*).
5. Compare and contrast the wired business scenario in India with the wireless business scenario.
6. Compare and contrast CDMA and GSM in the Indian context. Why is the Reliance company betting on CDMA?
7. Prepare a write-up describing evolution of mobile communication services.
8. Give an example of wireless system each from 1G, 2G, 2.5G and 3G.
9. Compare analog and digital signal.

CHAPTER

11

Portals for E-commerce Analytics

LEARNING OBJECTIVES

After reading this chapter, you should be able to:

- Understand the customer interface elements of a portal.
- Learn about the requirements of intelligent websites.
- Understand the website goals and objectives.
- Describe the web development tools.
- Know the use of portals for ERP and intranets.

Goldcorp and Mass Collaboration

Rob McEwen owned an underperforming gold mine in northwestern Ontario, and he needed new ideas about where to dig. So he broke new ground—and made data on the mine available online to anyone who wanted to help.

Goldcorp, a small Toronto-based gold-mining firm, was struggling, besieged by strikes, lingering debts, and an exceedingly high cost of production, which had caused them to cease mining operations. Most analysts assumed that the company's fifty-year-old mine in Red Lake, Ontario, was dying. Without evidence of substantial new gold deposits, the mine seemed destined for closure, and Goldcorp was likely to go down with it.

In 1999, with the future still uncertain, McEwen took some time out for personal development. He wound up at an MTT conference for young presidents when coincidentally the subject of Linux came up. Perched in the lecture hall, McEwen listened intently to the remarkable story of how Linus Torvalds and a loose volunteer brigade of software developers had assembled the world-class computer operating system over the Internet. The lecturer explained how Torvalds revealed his code to the world, allowing thousands of anonymous programmers to vet it and make contributions of their own.

McEwen had a deep insight. If Goldcorp employees could not find the Red Lake gold, maybe someone else could. And maybe the key to finding those people was to open up the exploration process in the same way Torvalds "open sourced" Linux.

McEwen raced back to Toronto to present the idea to his head geologist. "I'd like to take all of our geology, all the data we have that goes back to 1948, and put it into a file and share it with the world," he said. "Then we'll ask the world to tell us where we're going to find the next six million ounces of gold." McEwen saw this as an opportunity to harness some of the best minds in the industry. Perhaps understandably, the in-house geologists were just a little skeptical.

Mining is an intensely secretive industry, and apart from the minerals themselves, geological data is the most precious and carefully guarded resource. It is like the Cadbury secret—it is just not something companies go around sharing. Goldcorp employees wondered whether the global community of geologists would respond to Goldcorp's call in the same way that software developers rallied around Linus Torvalds. Moreover, they worried about how the con rest would reflect on them and their inability to find the illusive gold deposits.

In March 2000, the "Goldcorp Challenge" was launched with a total of $575,000 in prize money available to participants with the best methods and estimates. Every scrap of information (some four hundred megabytes worth) about the 55,000 acre property was revealed on Goldcorp's Web site. News of the contest spread quickly around the Internet, as more than one thousand virtual prospectors from fifty countries got busy crunching the data.

Within weeks, submissions from around the world came flooding in to Goldcorp headquarters. As expected, geologists got involved. But entries came from surprising sources, including graduate students, consultants, mathematicians, and military officers, all seeking a piece of the action. "We had applied math, advanced physics, intelligent systems, computer graphics, and organic solutions to inorganic problems. There were capabilities I had never seen before in the industry," says McEwen. The contestants had identified 110 targets on the Red Lake property, 50 per cent of which had not been previously identified by the company. Over 80 per cent of the new targets yielded substantial quantities of gold. In fact, since the challenge was initiated an astounding eight million ounces of gold have been found. McEwen estimates the collaborative process shaved two to three years off their exploration time.

Today, Goldcorp is reaping the fruits of its open source approach to exploration. Not only did the contest yield copious quantities of gold, it catapulted his under performing $100 million company into a $9 billion juggernaut while transforming a backward mining site in Northern Ontario into one of the most innovative and profitable properties in the industry. In 2010, the revenue of the company was 3737 million Dollars[1].

Perhaps the most lasting legacy of the Goldcorp Challenge is the validation of an ingenious approach to exploration in what remains a conservative and highly secretive industry. Rob McEwen bucked an industry trend by sharing the company's proprietary data and simultaneously transformed a lumbering exploration process into a modern distributed gold discovery engine that harnessed some of the most talented minds in the field.

1. http://www.goldcorp.com/investors/financials/

Case Discussion

1. How are portals helping mass collaboration today? Give some examples.
2. What is the impact of Facebook and Twitter and such sites in bringing people together?

Portals

The term "Portal" means different things to different people. To many, a simple website aimed at employees is a portal. A portal may be defined as a point of access to and interaction with relevant information, applications and business processes, by select targeted audiences, in a highly personalized manner.

Different Types of Portals

Portals can be broadly classified into different categories as shown in Figure 11.1.

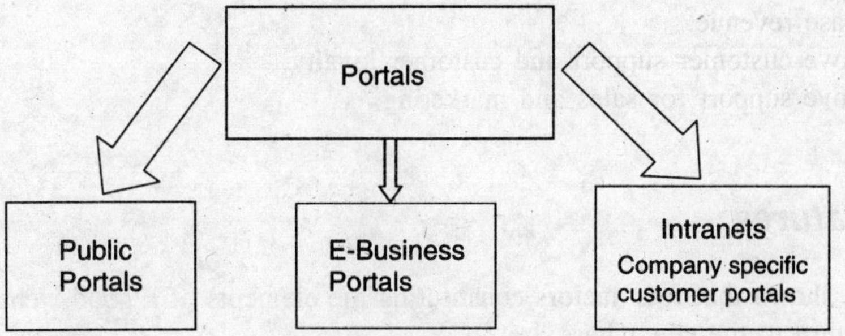

Figure 11.1 Types of portals.

1. **Public portals.** Most internet users are aware of portals like Yahoo or Google. Indian Railways is another example.
2. **e-Business portals.** These portals support business transactions (i.e. buying, selling, order booking, payments, etc.) online. These can be classified into three categories:

2(a) **B2C portals.** These portals extend the reach of the business to its customers for the purpose of ordering, billing, customer service, self-service, etc. Some of the successful B2C portals are: Amazon, eBay, Dell, etc. where people browse products, buy, order and pay online. Indian Rail site (IRCTC) is one of the successful B2C sites in India where thousands of people book train tickets and pay online daily.

2(b) **B2C.** Those portals are quite popular for airline ticket booking, hotel booking, etc. The basic idea of such portals is to attract and keep the attention of buyers as well as to collect information about buyers that can be used to enhance and personalize the customer relationship and thus, drive future sales. More personalized relationships can result in increased customer loyalty.

2(c) **B2B portals.** This extends the enterprise to its suppliers and partners. This helps to build better relationships between the company and its suppliers, customers and partners (via extranets) and this improved relationship can lead to increased trading partner loyalty. Generally, these portals are made by individual companies for their own suppliers and customers.

3. **Intranets.** These are normally portals aimed at customers of an organization. Employee portals, University portals, etc. are some of the examples.

Portal Benefits

Portals can bring benefits in a number of areas:

- Unify the enterprise.
- Give visibility for the enterprise all over the world.
- Reduce cost.
- Improve productivity.
- Reduce administration overhead.
- Increase revenue.
- Improve customer support and customer loyalty.
- Improve support for sales and marketing.

Portal Features

Surveys have shown that four factors constituting the elements of a good website encourage viewers to return to the site. These are:

- ***High quality content.*** Having the right information at the right place and right time.
- ***Ease of use.*** The structure of the side should not be overcomplicated or too big. You never get lost in a good site, since it is always clearly signposted.
- ***Quick to download.*** Good sites also download quickly. Bad sites are cumbersome and slow. Visitors would not wait.
- ***Frequently updated.*** Good sites put up new information which is useful, relevant and timely for their audience, which takes money, time and energy to maintain.

Figure 11.2 shows the customer interface elements that are needed in a website.

The Web gives the customer unlimited choice, with millions of sites to select from. In order to make the customer visit, stay and revisit your site, the site must have a unique proposition for the visitor. This is called an Internet Value Proposition (IVP).

Ideally, a good website needs to find a proposition that explains how and what their organization is offering. For example:

- Is different from its competitors

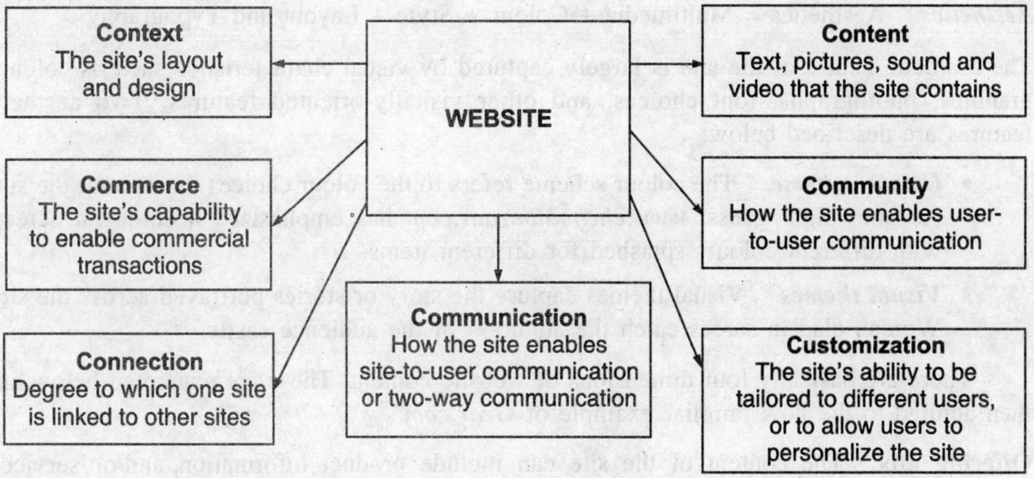

Figure 11.2 Interface elements in a website.

- Is not available in the real world
- Makes a difference to the customer's life

At the very least the proposition should clearly show the offered services and the credibility to deliver. Once a proposition has been finalized, the following steps need to be taken:

1. First we need to leverage the proposition in traffic-building by combining it with the URL or Web address and advertising it.
2. We need to clearly state the proposition on-site.
3. We need to deliver on the proposition through all interactions a customer has, including online and offline fulfilment and service.

The two basic aspects of site context are *function* and *aesthetics*.

Function. The vast amount of information displayed on a website must be presented to the customer in a coherent manner, and the customer must be able to move freely throughout the website. Three factors are critical in the layout of the site:

1. ***Section breakdown.*** This describes the way that the site is organized into subcomponents. For example, *www.chennaibazaar.com* is an online retail store whose site structure includes search, different kinds of merchandise, gift ideas, and help. There are also categories of goods—men's, women's, kid's clothes.
2. ***Linking structure.*** Linking structure describes the way in which alternative sections of the site are linked. Clicking on sarees on the homepage of *www.chennaibazaar.com* takes you to the sarees section, with lots of choices. This linking structure enables the users to easily move back and forward between the sections of the site.
3. ***Navigation tools.*** Navigation tools refer to the site tools that facilitate the movement of the user throughout the site. Navigation tools for *www.chennaibazaar.com* include sarees search for all occasions.

Aesthetics. Aesthetics = Multimedia + Colour + Style + Layout and Typography

The aesthetic nature of the site is largely captured by visual characteristics such as colours, graphics, photographs, font choices, and other visually-oriented features. Two aesthetic features are described below:

- ***Colour scheme.*** The colour scheme refers to the colour choices throughout the site. As one might guess, *www.chennaibazaar.com* has emphasized a colourful screen, with different colours splashed for different items.
- ***Visual themes.*** Visual themes capture the story or stories portrayed across the site. Women clad in sarees catch the attention of the audience easily.

There are basically four dimensions of website content. These are examined below and then applied to the now familiar example of *Gear.com.*

Offering mix. The content of the site can include product information and/or services. Frequently, sites include a mixture of these three elements. *www.chennaibazaar.com* focuses almost exclusively on product content, with significantly less emphasis on information or services.

Appeal mix. This refers to the promotional and communications messaging projected by the company. Academic literature has identified two broad types of appeal: cognitive and emotional. *Cognitive appeals* focus on the functional aspects of the offering, like low price, reliability, availability, customer support, and degree of personalization. *Emotional appeals* focus on emotionally resonant ties to the brand or product—humour, novelty, warmth, or stories.

Multimedia mix. This term refers to the variety of media—text, audio, image, video, and graphics—incorporated into the site. There is very limited use of product photographs.

Content type. Current content on a website is highly time-sensitive, whereas reference content is less time-sensitive and has a longer shelf life. *www.timesofindia.com*, the online version of *The Times of India*, offers an archive of articles published in the past.

Personalization plays an important role in making a website customer-effective. Internet- based personalization delivers customized content and services for the individual, either through Web pages, e-mail, or through push-technology. Personalization contributes to a website in the four following ways:

- ***Sell.*** Personalization can make it easier for customers to select their products. Customers of an online supermarket do not want to select a new shopping basket of goods each time they shop.
- ***Serve.*** Customers who uses an online travel booking service do not want to have to key in the same journey details if it is a common itinerary. Instead, personalization helps them to save their itinerary.
- ***Speak.*** Through personalization, customers can select the type of communication they want to receive from a company as part of permission marketing.
- ***Sizzle.*** All the above can help add value, strengthen the brand, and develop the relationship.

To attract users and make them return, some sites provide a variety of features. Some of them are described below:

- ***Login registration.*** Having previously registered on a site, the user returns and enters the requisite information through the site interface. The site recognizes the returning user, and configures itself to the user's preset preferences.
- ***Cookies.*** Most sites, to identify visitors, attempt to track and gather data on returning user's behaviour by quietly saving, identifying and tracking information on the user's local disk storage in temporary files called cookies.
- ***Personalized e-mail accounts.*** Many sites provide free e-mail accounts to send and receive e-mails from the site, using a unique e-mail address.
- ***Content and layout configuration.*** Users can select screen layouts and content sources based on their interests.

Requirements of Intelligent Websites

Building an intelligent website that optimally leverages all sources of information for an online company does not happen overnight. It takes several iterations, a significant investment in technology, and an accumulation of knowledge that comes only with experimentation, trial and error. Companies that are new to the online game usually are at stage zero and use almost no data at all, whereas companies more advanced in e-business intelligence are able to integrate data coming from transactions, clickstream, and other sources to build powerful consumer relationships and market leadership.

There are four primary types of customer information that are leveraged through e-business intelligence:

1. ***Demographics.*** This describes the basic attributes of the customers—who they are, what neighbourhood they live in, what their income bracket is, their marital status, and so on.
2. ***Expressed preferences.*** This describes what topics customers have expressed an interest in (e.g. types of books or music they like, stocks they track, sports teams they follow). The preferences are usually captured through form-based questionnaires when the consumer registers for a site or service.
3. ***Past transactions.*** These are the records of past transactions that the consumers have had with the company (e.g. what books they have purchased, what auctions they have conducted). These are recorded when the consumer actually conducts his or her purchases.
4. ***Observed behaviours.*** This information is derived from observing the navigation the customer follows in using the website, as well as where he came from and where he went afterwards. This data, called *clickstream information,* comes from every single click throughout the consumer online experience, and it is collected in large log files.

As the e-commerce company gets more and more sophisticated in building an intelligent e-business, it should progressively leverage these different types of information in an efficient way. Let us now look at the steps e-commerce companies typically follow in leveraging their information, in the order in which they typically evolve as they get more and more skilled in exploiting the power of e-business intelligence.

Step 1: Basic Web traffic analysis. The very first type of analysis of any Web activity is the measure of Web traffic. In the early days of the Web, hit counters were the rage. Hits and page views are the lowest level of clickstream data—the sequential record of pages visited. This data provides a record of entry and exit points into a website, pages that were visited, links that were followed, the duration for which a person viewed a particular page, the precise day and time, the browser type, the visitor's IP address, and other information. This type of information is often used to help secure advertising dollars. It can also point to problems in a site—a problematic page, for example, where people drop off because response time is too slow. It can help a website establish its quality and systems maintenance practice to ensure that the site is able to absorb high traffic times.

Step 2: Customer interaction analysis. The next step is to go into more details about customer interactions with the website. The first type of measure is the conversion rate from a browser to a customer. Conversion rates have been viewed as a key indicator of a website's effectiveness.

Registered users are the people who have had to register for site usage, often by filling out a survey form. *The New York Times,* for instance, is a free site, but requires the user to fill in a registration form. Depending on the questions asked, this data could allow a website to size up its visitors and customers by profession, education, age, gender, race, leisure activities, merchandise purchasing, and so forth. Through the registration process, the site is able to get the demographic as well as the preference information. Recorded e-mail addresses provide a way for the site to communicate with these registered visitors.

This data may then be used to help inform personalization engines to serve the contents according to the visitor's interests. It enables the site to display the person's name when he visits, in a bid to build intimacy. A visitor with an expressed affinity for golf or gardening, may then be served advertisements or contents, specific to those interests. Combined with clickstream data on the visitor's site usage, the website is able to develop a fuller picture of both individual visitors and its visitors population as a whole. Once users have become customers, the site is able to analyze the historical transactions to identify their most loyal customers and their purchasing patterns, as well as the segments they fall into with respect to interests, frequency, or profitability.

A 'dotcom' company should start by producing a series of standard reports that can be executed automatically on a regular basis, in order to provide business users with answers to the basic questions such as the following about the business:

- Who are my top 20 per cent customers? What percentage of my total revenue do they generate?
- What is the trend in the buy/view ratio—how effective was our site redesign?
- Which portals referred the greatest number of visitors?

- How many orders did we get this week?
- What was the average order size?
- What is our weekly sales volume?
- Can the production volume of my suppliers support sales fulfilment?
- How much ad revenue are we generating with the new site design compared with the old one?

Step 3: Real-time personalization. Personalization is the ultimate realization of the one-to-one marketing dream. Customers are recognized when they come in, can tailor the way they interact with the merchant, and receive promotions and marketing programs that perfectly fit their personal requirements and preferences.

The four primary ways of performing personalization are greetings, customization, narrowcasting, and recommendation.

Greetings are the most basic form of personalization. The customer is greeted by name and welcomed back when he or she comes on the site. Personalization engines recognize a visitor's Internet protocol address or cookies stored on his personal computer, and correlate that information with past visits in order to recognize the visitor.

Customization allows a customer to tailor the service he is receiving from an e-commerce site, or to configure the products he wants to buy. As an example, any Yahoo! user can customize his use of the popular search by creating a '*MyYahoo!*' environment which is more adapted to his needs. The '*MyYahoo!*' page will, for instance, show only stock quotes for your portfolio, and the particular news subjects you are interested in.

One great example of customization is the American Airlines website. Once logged into the site, customers are welcomed by name, and they are shown the number of frequent flyer miles they have on their account, as well as customized information and special offers based on their profile and previous choice of preferences, including home airport, preferred destination, hotel and car rental companies, and preferred seating choices.

Narrowcasting is the delivery of time-sensitive information, personalized to each consumer. Instead of sending messages to a large numbers of customers, they can be intimated about particular events they want to be alerted about. These kinds of personalized messages can be sent through e-mail, phone, or pagers which enable the customer to be informed without having to connect to the site. *Yahoo!Finance*, for example, enables a customer to define an alert that will be delivered if a stock price fluctuates more than a certain percentage. United Airlines also provides flight-paging services via various wireless devices. Flight paging provides customers automatic notification of flight delays or cancellations so that they can remain informed of any changes in the status of United Airlines flights.

Recommendation enables a site to propose products that are tailored to the customers' requirements, whether they have been explicitly expressed by the consumer or implicitly calculated by the e-commerce engine. Recommendation technology has evolved dramatically in the past few years. It used to be based only on the preferences that a customer would have explicitly expressed at registration time. Now it can be done in real time and predicted automatically by the personalization engine using different types of information such as observed real-time behaviour, purchase histories, and expressed preferences. Finally, it can match that data with information regarding other consumers who share similar interests, using a technique known as *collaborative filtering*. The system is then able to make recommendations that are quite accurate.

Step 4: Getting to fine-grained segmentation. Personalization technologies are not very adaptive to drive a massive marketing campaign, nor are they particularly suitable for many types of purchasing decisions with complex sales cycles and multiple decision-makers. The next step, therefore, is to enhance the site's marketing power by using an e-business intelligence system performing customer segmentation. We start with products that are at a hand's reach through coarse segmentation, and we continue on to fine-grained segmentation.

The harvesting of Web generates large, complex data volumes. Companies are gathering data that is more finely grained than in the past. By integrating data from various systems, they are able to go beyond the basic profile of a customer who is a 35 year old male who buys a piece of electronics equipment on the average of once a year. Website activity, information on cookies, household and demographic information, online surveys, customer support calls, consumer credit reports and other sources enable the company to collect additional details. The number of attributes associated with one single piece of data can grow by several factors.

The mounting quantity and complexity of this data often beg for data mining. Data mining goes beyond reporting, query, and multidimensional analysis to automatically sift through large data sets to discern patterns that might otherwise be difficult to detect. It uses artificial intelligence technologies to conduct knowledge discovery—that is, it can look for patterns in large data sets and identify common elements.

Step 5: Going through the streams of clicks. Every move on a website, every ad banner clicked through, every page request from every visitor is recorded by the website owners into massive log files; this is the clickstream information.

The clickstream data contains details on customer behaviour that are richer than what can be achieved in traditional channels. It moves a step beyond the department store practice of using video surveillance cameras to track customer movement throughout the store to improve merchandising.

Savvy online merchants are squeezing into the clickstream to answer some key business questions, such as:

- Which pages are drawing traffic that results in a purchase?
- Which ads are most frequently followed?
- What do our most profitable customers do on our website?
- What path is followed by those who buy our most profitable products?
- How can one predict when someone will be at the best point to propose a cross-sell or upsell?
- What navigation do customers follow before abandoning their shopping?

Answering these questions enables a website to take informed actions like the following:

- Optimize placement of the page and the link to it
- Increase advertising rates
- Segment those customers' characteristics and provide a special site for gold customers
- Encourage more customers down the most profitable path

- Propose cross-selling at the right time
- Examine the shopping process for weakness or obstacles that prompt customers to turn away.

Step 6: Enrich content with external data. Once a customer has made several purchases, the website is able to further enhance the customer profile. Demographic data from third- party providers may be appended to the profile to provide a richer view of the customer base. Analyzing that enriched data might show, for instance, that a customer who buys history books falls into a demographic segment inclined to also buy classical music. Marketing pitches in the form of e-mails and personalized content may then be delivered to cross-sell classical music CDs.

This data is critical in building profitable repeat business. It enables refinements in one-to-one marketing in the form of e-mails, snail mail, and personalized content served during site visits. The overall customer base may be segmented by a host of characteristics to better understand who is buying what. The data may be analyzed to determine an overall customer score that provides the website with a roadmap on which customers are their best bets for marketing efforts.

The simple fact to be realized is, the more data you have about your customers, the more sophisticated data mining and segmentation models you will be able to build. Using third-party data to enrich your database will help you find segments that were otherwise undetectable. Sometimes this data must be purchased. Sometimes, you can devise business arrangements or partnerships that provide it. American Airlines and United Airlines, for example, have recognized that a great source of information that helps in their marketing efforts is the data coming from the affinity credit card businesses they have associated with their name, and their frequent flying programs.

Step 7: Reaching optimal intelligence. A company can reach optimal intelligence once it is able to combine historical transaction records, observed behaviour via clickstream data, and preferences expressed in online surveys.

Setting Website Goals and Objectives

The first thing that an e-business entrepreneur should do before any Web page is created, is to determine the goals, objectives, and overall purpose of the e-business website. Without these the website may not have the focus it needs to be successful. To help determine the goals and objectives, you should ask and answer questions such as the following. Will the website:

1. Allow customers to order products and services online?
2. Provide technical support for products and services?
3. Advertise products and services?
4. Build the e-business's image and brand?
5. Collect information about current and potential customers?
6. Provide links to related web pages?
7. Provide general or industry information? and
8. Recruit employees?

A quick look at this list of sample questions clearly indicates that most e-business websites have multiple goals and objectives. The answers to these and similar questions are used to determine the website's overall purpose.

Considering the Website's Target Audience

After you establish the website's goals, objectives, and overall purpose, the next step is to consider the website's target audience. In too many instances, e-businesses design websites around the needs of the e-business rather than the needs of the target audience. It is critical to consider both the information the target audience wants and the tools it uses to access the Web. Again, a series of questions such as the following, should be asked and answered:

1. Is the audience composed of experienced internet users, novice users, or a mix of both? Experienced internet users are likely to be able to handle a more sophisticated level of website complexity than novice users.
2. What type of browser will the audience be using—Netscape, Internet Explorer, WebTV, or other specialized browsers? Some design techniques that are supported by later Web browser versions, such as animations and frames, may not be supported by earlier versions of the same browser or by other browsers.
3. At what speed does the audience connect to the internet—at 56 Kbps over a modem or over a high-speed dedicated connection? A website designed to be viewed successfully over a high-speed dedicated connection may be problematic for viewers using a slow modem connection.
4. At what screen resolution does the target audience view Web pages—640 × 480, 800 × 600, or higher? Websites designed to be viewed at 800 × 600 resolution without horizontal scrolling will greatly annoy those who view the site using a monitor with 640 × 480 resolution.

Answers to each of these questions will determine how the Web page design can enhance or detract from a visitor's viewing experience and, ultimately, the ability or failure of the website to meet its goals.

Analyzing the Website's Structure

An e-business must carefully organize the information used as the website's content. A website must show visitors what information is available at the site, how to quickly find the information they want and need, and how to get additional information, if necessary. That information may include, but is not limited to the following:

- Name of the e-business
- Slogan, logo, or trademark
- Statement on mission or purpose
- Information on products or services

- Press releases and testimonials
- Employment information
- Contact information
- Maps to physical locations
- Website map
- Customer support information
- Purchase or customer information forms.

Designing the website to make it both attractive and well organized is the best way to give customers what they want from the site. Before considering the website content, you must design the site structure. Some website designs consist of a single level of separate and unrelated pages to which viewers have links directly from a home page. Although easy to use, this flat structure can be somewhat boring. Some websites have multiple layers of linked pages, creating a complicated structure that requires viewers to click through several pages to find the information they need. Viewing such unnecessarily complex websites can frustrate potential customers who want to find information quickly. One way to achieve balance in the structure of a website is to limit the number of linked pages and include important information as much as possible in the first three levels of linked pages.

Once this is done, you can draw connection links between the pages. This presents a good picture of how a viewer would click through the site from page to page. It also helps identify potential navigation problems a viewer might experience. Sometimes, when a website structure is 10 levels deep, a viewer might have to click 10 times through those 10 levels of pages to find useful information. Most users want to find information within three to five mouse clicks. The best suggestion to have a website with ten levels is to organize the site into a flat structure with fewer levels, and include a search tool that allows viewers quick access to pages below the third to fifth levels. After you have determined the website structure, the next step is to plan the design of each page on the site.

Another very effective way to help viewers with navigation is to use a **hierarchical navigational outline** showing all the levels of links between the home page or another major page and the page currently being viewed. Viewers using this outline can quickly move up or down in the hierarchy and easily understand the relationship of the page being currently viewed to the page on which they started. Hierarchical navigational outlines are great visual cues to the linking relationships among pages, and should be used in addition to other navigational hyperlinks such as navigation bars.

Good website design should enhance an e-business website's message and objectives without diverting the visitor's attention. For example, if viewers are thinking or talking about the design of an e-business website instead of its contents, the design is distracting from the website's message. Website design techniques include the use of the text, colour, graphics, sound, video, and Web technology such as animation, to convey the website's message.

Using Navigation Elements

Navigation elements are important because a viewer may not always enter a website from its home page. He or she may enter the website through any page of the site, using a search engine or a hyperlink from a different website. When this happens, the viewer must have a way to get to the site's home page or other major pages. Navigation elements like hyperlinks are important to assist the viewer in finding information about other pages of the website.

An internal hyperlink is a connection between two pages of the same website. A well-designed website should have a logical navigation scheme, based on internal hyperlinks, that is easy for viewers to understand and to use. That navigation scheme should include an easy way for the viewers to interconnect all the major pages of the website, including the home page. Since viewers do not necessarily begin viewing a website from its home page, all pages should contain an internal hyperlink back to the home page.

A navigation bar is a series of icon or text hyperlinks to major pages of a website. Navigation bars using icons are often positioned at the top of a page, while navigation bars using text are often positioned on the left side or at the bottom of a Web page. The position of navigational bars should be consistent in all the pages of the website.

Another important navigational technique is the inclusion of 'top-of-page' hyperlinks at the bottom of each Web page. A top-of-page hyperlink can be a text or a graphic image that is linked to a position at the top of the current page. This hyperlink enables a viewer to quickly return to the top of the same page after having scrolled down.

Other Web design considerations include whether to use text or graphics or a combination of both to convey the website message; what typeface, colour combinations, background colours or images, and page layouts to be used? and whether or not the site should use flumes, animations, and multimedia. A startup e-business may want to get advice from a professional web designer when resolving these design issues.

Maintaining Consistency

It is important that the Web design emphasizes consistency in its presentation. For example, there are certain elements that should necessarily appear on every page on a website. They are:

- Name of the e-business
- Contact information
- About the business
- Products and services offered
- Copyright information
- Navigation elements

The e-business name and contact information are important because customers may print a hard copy of individual pages (not necessarily the home page) from a website, and may want the e-business name and contact information available on the printout. Next in importance are the details about the business and the products and services offered online by them. If an e-business website has copyright protection, it is better to post a copyright notice on the site to remind viewers of that protection. Typeface and colours should also be consistent throughout the website.

Using Text and Icon Hyperlinks

Text and icon hyperlinks can also be positioned in the body of a Web page to help viewers navigate a website, or to allow viewers to access Web pages on different websites. Traditionally, text hyperlinks have been underlined and formatted with a dark colour, generally blue. Today, many websites do not use underlining for text hyperlinks, but use different accent colours to indicate text hyperlinks. Some websites use animated hyperlinks that appear or disappear as the viewer moves the mouse pointer over the hyperlink. When designing a website, remember that the whole point of hyperlinks is for viewers to have a quick access to information they want, which may be located elsewhere. Hyperlinks that are animated and appealing, but hard to locate and use, may frustrate viewers and drive them to the competitors' websites.

Often, websites use graphic hyperlinks instead of text hyperlinks. Certain graphic images can effectively communicate the purpose of a hyperlink, especially to global viewers who speak different languages. For example, an e-tailer might use a shopping cart icon in addition to the text *Shopping Cart* to indicate that it is a hyperlink to the shopping cart. Also, an envelope icon is often used to indicate a hyperlink viewers can click to send an e-mail message. However, graphic hyperlink can be confusing if the graphic image does not clearly indicate where the hyperlink takes the viewer. A well-designed website uses a combination of text and graphic hyperlinks.

Using Colour

Choosing the right colours for a website can be critical, because colour is one of the first things a viewer sees as a Web page loads in his or her browser. In general, bright colours such as blue, red, yellow, orange, and green are used on conservative corporate websites. However, bright colours such as red can be used effectively to call attention to specific Web page elements. Pastel colours (colours that contain a large proportion of white) are more relaxing and undemanding. Earth tones (brown, beige, tan) are unobtrusive and tend to contrast well with primary colours. A good rule to be followed while designing an e-business website is not to use too many different colours in the colour scheme. Also, the background colour should either be a very light and neutral colour (possibly white, which evokes a no-nonsense businesslike attitude) or black.

Colour choices should reflect the values of the website's audience. Since Internet is global, remember that people around the world respond differently to colours. For example, in the US, blue is a colour that represents trust; however, in Korea, the idea of trust is enforced with pastel colours, especially pink. Understanding the emotional effect of different colours on a website's audience can enhance the website's design.

Also important in selecting a colour scheme for a website, is the issue of available colours. Web pages use the RGB (red, green, blue) colour model that uses different numbers from 0 to 256 to represent each of the three colours. Web browsers are capable of displaying only a small set of the 16 million possible RGB colour combinations, and substitute a different colour if the one used on a Web page is not available in its recognizable RGB colour set. Therefore, most Web designers use a browser-safe palette of colours when designing a colour scheme. There are a number of websites that illustrate and discuss browser-safe colours.

Using Text

There are important differences between writing for the Web and writing for the printed page. Although the same basic grammar and spelling rules apply, the way a viewer reads the text online is different. Online readers scan the text instead of reading it word by word. They try to pick out a few words or phrases to get the information they want. Instead of long, scrollable pages with dense text, online readers prefer Web pages which are short and to the point. Finally, online readers prefer concise, factual information to marketing 'fluff' in an overtly hyped language. Online readers like to scan text quickly; so, use frequent paragraph breaks, headings, bulleted lists, and ample blank space in Web page text. Online readers also prefer to read narrow columns rather than lines of text that go from margin to margin.

A **font** is a collection of characters that have the same appearance. A serif is the small tail at the end of a line in characters such as "I", "M", and "N". A serif leads the viewer's eyes smoothly to the next character. Fonts containing characters without a serif are called sans serif fonts. For the sake of consistency and easy reading, some Web designers suggest that Web page text should use only one or possibly two different fonts. A common combination in both print media and Web pages is to use a sans serif font, such as Arial, for headings and a serif font, such as Times New Roman, for body text. Web browsers display text in a font that a viewer has on his or her computer system. If a Web page contains fonts not available on the viewer's system, the Web browser will substitute a different font. For this reason, it is usually preferable to use common fonts such as Arial or Times New Roman for web page text.

Font styles or attributes, such as bold or italic, can be used to draw attention to a word or a phrase in a Web page body text. Underlining is often used for emphasis on a printed page, but underlining is generally not appropriate for emphasis on a Web page because most viewers associate underlining with hyperlinks. Finally, it is critical that all the text on a website be checked for spelling errors and professionally proofread and edited for grammatical and stylistic errors. Next comes a careful consideration of the use of background images on the pages of the site.

Background Images

Images and other multimedia options can, if used carefully, effectively communicate a website's message. Large background images that fill the whole screen can cause problems for viewers using different monitor resolutions. A small image that repeats over and over, called a tiled image, is preferable. Also, a background image may obscure the text on a Web page, making it difficult for viewers to read the text. Many Web designers therefore think that it is better not to use a background image, and instead go for a light-coloured background. Others suggest using only a white or a black background colour.

Using Images and Multimedia

Almost every website uses images to enhance the site's design and to effectively communicate information. Some websites also make use of animation, sound, or video. All multimedia used should support the purpose of the website, and should not be included simply because it looks or sounds great.

Image file size is important when designing Web pages because the larger the image file size, the longer a Web page takes to upload. To minimize the upload time, Web page image files should be compressed. There are two primary types of compressed images used on Web pages: GIF images (usually pronounced "jif", as in "jiffy") and JPEG images (pronounced "jay-peg"), each with their own properties and uses. GIFs are often used for simpler images such as logos and icons, but are usually not used for photographs because photographs compress better as JPEG files. GIFs have some interesting features that JPEGs do not have. GIFs can be animated, like a very short movie or flipbook animation showing a sequence of frames rapidly. GIFs can also allow a transparent colour—a colour that will appear transparent on a Web page, allowing the background to show through. In order to reduce the loading time, it may be necessary to optimize the Web page image file sizes. There are several e-businesses such as Spinwave, GIF Wizard and *xat.com* that offer image optimization software packages.

There are some techniques that make Web pages containing images load faster. For example, a small version of an image, called a thumbnail, can be used to link to the larger version of the image. When the viewer loads a Web page, the small thumbnail images load faster. The viewer can click a thumbnail image to see the larger version of the image. Thumbnail images are often used by e-businesses to illustrate their product catalogues.

Sounds can also be added to play in the background as a page is viewed, or they can be used to respond to an event, such as clicking an icon. Sound files come in three formats: audio recordings (such as WAV files or AU files), which are like a digital tape recording of sounds; MIDI files, which describe the sequence of musical notes and how they are played; and streaming audio, which is like a radio broadcast over the internet. In general, there are few situations in which sound supports the purpose of an e-business website, except when the e-business is selling sound or creative design services. Also, many viewers get annoyed by the additional time required to download a page containing sound, and by the continuous sound playing in the background as they view a Web page.

Video is becoming more common as internet access becomes faster and compression methods improve. There are two methods of providing video: downloadable video, which can be downloaded and saved on the hard disk; and streaming video, which is like a radio broadcast. Advances in Web-browser technology now allow different kinds of animation of text, images, and hyperlinks. Unfortunately, many websites include sound, video, and animation without considering how these features affect the website's effectiveness and usability from a viewer's perspective. Most Web designers agree that sound, video, and animation should be used only as a necessary tool to support an e-business site's purpose and message. Another feature that should be used sparingly is, frames.

Using Frames

A Web browser's display area can be divided into separate sections called frames. For example, the home page of a website might consist of two frames: a top frame containing navigational links, and a main frame containing scrollable content.

Unfortunately, frames may make a page look cramped and cluttered, and may, if not correctly designed, cause navigation problems for the viewer. Additionally, frames may cause problems for search engine robot or spider programs trying to index the website pages, and may make it difficult for a viewer to add the Web page URL to his or her 'bookmarks' or 'favourites' folder. Because of these potential problems, many Web designers suggest avoiding frames in website design.

An important component of any website is its use of online forms.

Using Forms

Another Web page element that should not be overlooked is, use of forms. Forms, consisting of text labels and the related input boxes, option buttons, drop-down lists, or check boxes, are used to collect information from viewers. Forms allow a viewer to enter specific information on the Web page and then send that information to the e-business's e-mail address or website database. Forms are used for many things. Collecting site feedback, registering for approval to use website functions, and ordering products online are just three examples.

Sometimes a viewer is required to complete a paper form. Creating downloadable forms, as well as other documents, is a way to provide these paper forms without having to mail them or fax them to the user. A model form, or form template, is created in a software application such as Microsoft Word. Then either the Word file itself is made available for download (which would require users to have Word installed on their own computers), or the file is converted into a format that any computer can read, such as plain text, rich text (RTF), or Adobe's PDF format. A PDF reader named Adobe Acrobat, which can be freely downloaded from the Adobe website, is used to read and print PDF documents. The advantage of a PDF file is that it displays and prints on any computer the way it was designed, regardless of the word-processing programs or fonts on a viewer's computer.

Designing a Website for a Variety of Displays

One of the most complex aspects of Web design is knowing that your page is at the mercy of the software and hardware configuration of each individual user. A page that looks great on your machine may look radically different, or perhaps even ghastly, when viewed on another user's set-up. This is partly due to the browser's functionality and the individual user's preferences (font size, colours), but the display device itself also plays a large part in the success of the page's design.

For the majority of your audience, the variation in displays is a function of the monitor and its size (or, more accurately, its resolution) and colour capabilities. However, it is important to keep in mind that the diversity does not end there. Some users may be watching your Web page on TV. Still others may be viewing it in the palm of their hand on a Personal Digital Assistant (PDA), also referred to as a palmtop, or a cell phone. Sight-impaired users may be listening to your page, not viewing it.

Selecting a Hosting Service

For larger website implementations, the team will want to obtain the advice of consultants or other firms that rate ISPs and CSPS, such as Keynote Systems and the Directory of Internet Service Providers published by *Boardwatch Magazine*. The most important factors to evaluate when selecting a hosting service include:

- Functionality
- Reliability, bandwidth and server scalability
- Security
- Back-up and disaster recovery
- Cost

Companies that sell hosting services provide different features and different levels of service. The functionality offered by a service provider can include credit card processing and the ability to link to existing databases that store customer and product information. Some tracking software provides much more detailed information and easy-to-use report generators than other tracking software. You should determine the functionality offered by a hosting service and carefully evaluate whether that functionality will be sufficient to meet the needs of your website.

The service should offer a guarantee that limits possible down time. E-commerce buyers expect hosting services to be up and running 24 hours a day, every day. Of course, no hosting service can promise never-to-fail service, but some can provide staffing and back-up hardware that minimizes reliability problems. Coordination of this function with the service provider can be very important. Usually, a business must have some round-the-clock staff available or on-call to work with the service provider when an interruption occurs.

The bandwidth of the service's connection to the Internet must be sufficient to handle the peak transaction loads that its customers require. Sometimes a service provider will sign up new accounts faster than it can expand the bandwidth of its connections, resulting in access bottlenecks. A guarantee that specifies bandwidth availability or server response times is worth negotiating into a service provider contract. If you expect your site's traffic to increase rapidly, it is important that your service provider increases rapidly the server capacity and the bandwidth provided. In general, larger hosting services can scale up more easily than smaller hosting services. Again, it is worth negotiating some scalability into the service provider contract in such situations.

Since the company's information on customers, products, pricing, and other data will be placed in the hands of the service provider, the vendor's security policies and practices are very important. The service provider should specify the types of security it provides and how it implements security. No matter what security guarantees the service provider offers, the company should monitor the security of the e-commerce operation through its own personnel or by hiring a security consulting firm. Security consultants can periodically test the system and launch attacks on the security features used by the service provider to determine whether they are easily breached.

The hosting service should be able to guarantee close to 100 per cent reliability by having a workable disaster recovery plan in place. In addition to having off-site data back-up or mirroring, the hosting service should have a way to restore your site very quickly in the case of a natural disaster. Service providers offer many different pricing plans for different levels of service. Knowing what types of server hardware and software your site will require, and having a good estimate of the range of transaction loads the site is likely to generate, can help in negotiating a price for the hosting service.

E-commerce Analytics

Netflix and Data Analytics[2]

In 1997, Reed Hastings and Marc Randolph started Netflix. Originally a DVD-rental service Netflix innovated from its mail order service. Netflix started a subscription model which allowed customers to rent as many DVDs as they wanted, without adding any additional costs. Netflix was focused on recommendation algorithms and unique experiences through its website. In 2006, Netflix launched the $1 million Netflix Prize contest to see if anyone could improve by 10 per cent its recommendation system, an algorithm for predicting an individual's movie preferences based on previous rental data. Three years later the prize was awarded to BellKor's Pragmatic Chaos[3]. In 2007, it rolled out its video streaming service, which differentiated Netflix from Blockbuster and many of the other DVD-rental services. It took a few years for the streaming service to make a difference. Netflix pivoted to a platform only approach, canning the DVD-rental service and launching Netflix worldwide.[4]

In 2007, Netflix began offering subscribers the option to stream some of its movies and television shows directly to their homes through the Internet. For most subscription plans, the streaming service was unlimited. Netflix subsequently partnered with manufacturers of various consumer electronics products, including video game consoles and Blu-ray Disc players, in order to enable its videos to be streamed over an Internet connection to those devices. In 2010, Netflix introduced a streaming—only plan that offered unlimited streaming service but no DVDs.

In 2013, with the episodic drama series *House of Cards*, was started. Netlix offered video content produced specifically for its streaming service. By the end of 2021, it had offered more than 2,400 original titles.[5]

With more than 222 million subscribers worldwide, Netflix is reigning as the top streaming content platform. Netflix achieved it using advanced data analytics.

Netflix is able to:

- Provide users with personalized movie and TV show recommendations
- Predict the popularity of original content before it is streamed
- Personalize marketing content such as trailers and thumbnail images

Netflix makes use of collected data, transforms it into information, translates them into insights, results and then recommends TV shows and movies according to customers' preferences and interests. Netflix claims that viewer activity depends on personalized recommendations and the results are true for most of subscribers. Making use of all the collected data, a detailed profile of each subscriber will be generated. The profiles created by Netflix is much more detailed than the information provided by the subscriber at the

2. https://netflixtechblog.com/analytics-at-netflix-who-we-are-and-what-we-do-7d9c08fe6965
3. https://www.britannica.com/topic/Netflix-Inc
4. https://www.businessofapps.com/data/netflix-statistics/
5. https://www.britannica.com/topic/Netflix-Inc

beginning of their Netflix usage. If you're watching any TV show or movie on Netflix, it knows the following:

- date, location, and the device being used to watch
- the time of your watching
- how and when you pause and resume your shows and movies
- if the customer is completing the show or not, how many hours, days, or weeks to complete the episode or a season or a movie.
- Ultimately, it tracks every action taken by the user on Netflix and considers it as a data point.
- habit of watching their favorite scenes repeatedly.

Netflix will implement the 'recommendation algorithms' using all the available information. Netflix's ability to collect and use the data is the reason behind its success. It results in better customer retention per year.

If someone watches movies of certain directors only or certain actors or actresses only then Netflix already knows the interests and sensitive likes or dislikes of their subscribers.

Netflix takes feedbacks from subscribers. The feedback is then converted into a rating and then the team works on system improvement or recommendations.

Case Discussion

1. What is the innovation that Netflix introduced to bring success to the company?
2. What factors are taken into consideration for Netlix's recommendation system?
3. Compare and contrast Netflix's business model with that of Blockbuster and HBO.

Data Analytics

To merge data from multiple sources about customers, products, and markets is a common problem for today's businesses. Analysts struggle to productively analyze the datasets available to them.

The primary aim of an E-Commerce platform is to make user experience on their website delightful. Other than that they are simply a platform between sellers and buyers. With such focus on user experience, analytics itself becomes a product. An e-Commerce platform provides customers to compare prices across various sellers and analyse customer reviews before making buying decisions. The most effective way to determine what attracts customers to a platform is to collect data on their behavior. This is where **e-Commerce Analytics becomes relevant**.

E-commerce analytics is the process of accumulating data from all avenues that can affect the e-commerce platform. This data can be used to comprehend shifts in customer behavior and online shopping trends. E-commerce analytics can include many metrics, such as discovery, acquisition, conversion, retention and advocacy.

Consumer demand, combined with technological innovations, will continue to drive growth in global e-commerce sales. The key drivers of success over the next years will be centered on building a deep understanding of the consumer and establishing connection to the consumer, and the only way to understand consumer behavior is to measure and analyze.

It would be easy to gather the necessary information on customer requirements and act on it if you are dealing with only one customer, but a company may have thousands or millions of customers. Because of that most companies are collecting huge volumes of data in its raw form. This data will not make any sense unless it is analyzed and transformed into meaningful information. The ability to derive key performance indicators (KPIs) from data can be difficult. With data scattered throughout an organization, getting integrated information in a timely manner can be difficult. Often, getting the desired information or insights for the business needs to compete takes too long and requires too much effort.

Data analytics is used in almost every sector of business. Some examples are given below:

1. **Retail:** To understand their customer needs and buying habits to predict trends and recommend new products, retailers use Data Analytics. Thus, they can optimize the supply chain, and retail operations at every step of the customer journey.
2. **Healthcare:** To analyze patient data to provide lifesaving diagnoses and treatment options, data analytics can help. Also, it helps in discovering new drug development methods.
3. **Manufacturing:** To discover new cost-saving opportunities in manufacturing, analytics can be used. They can solve complex supply chain issues, labor constraints, and equipment breakdowns.
4. **Banking sector:** To find out probable loan defaulters and customer churn out rate banking sector, Analytics will be useful. It also helps in detecting fraudulent transactions immediately.
5. **Logistics:** To develop new business models and optimize routes analytics is used by Logistics companies. This, in turn, ensures that the delivery reaches on time in a cost-efficient manner.

A data analyst will extract raw data, organize it, and then analyze it, transforming it from incomprehensible numbers into coherent, intelligible information. Having interpreted the data, the data analyst will then pass on their findings in the form of suggestions or recommendations about what the company's next steps should be.

Below are the steps that you can take to solve your problems.

1. **Understand the problem:** E-commerce companies often encounter issues such as predicting the return of items, giving relevant product recommendations, cancellation of orders, identifying frauds, optimizing vehicle routing, etc. These business problems can be understood through analysis and pinpoint the source of the problem.
2. **Data collection:** Past data plays a crucial role in shaping the future of a business. So, collecting transactional business data and customer-related information from the past few years or months can be used to address the problems the business is facing.

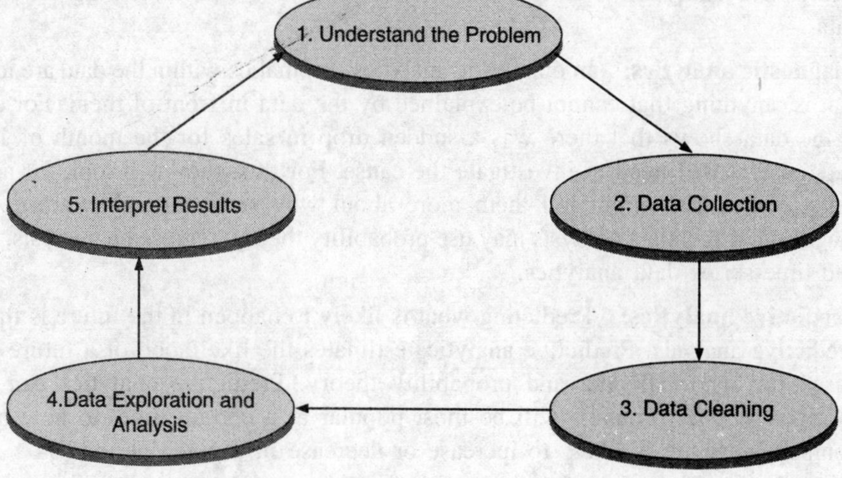

Figure 11.3 Data Analytics process steps.

3. **Data cleaning:** There is a need to clean the data to remove unwanted, redundant, and missing values to make it ready for analysis. Very often, collected data will often be disorderly, messy, and contain unwanted or missing values.
4. **Data exploration and analysis:** After gathering the data, the next step is to do an exploratory data analysis. One can use data visualization and business intelligence tools, data mining techniques, and predictive modeling to analyze, visualize, and predict future outcomes from this data. Applying these methods can tell us the impact and relationship of a certain feature as compared to other variables.
5. **Interpret the results:** The final step is to interpret the results and validate if the outcomes meet your expectations. One can find out hidden patterns and future trends. This will help you gain insights that will support you with appropriate data-driven decision making.

The above analysis will yield the following results:

- Predict when a customer purchases the next product.
- Understand how long it took to deliver the product.
- Get a better insight into the kind of items a customer looks for, product returns, etc.
- Predict the sales and profit for the next quarter.
- Minimize order cancellation by dispatching only relevant products.
- Able to figure out the shortest route to deliver the product, etc.

Different Types of Data Analytics

There are four main types of data analytics:

1. **Descriptive analytics:** Data aggregation and data mining are the two main techniques used in descriptive analytics. Aggregation is when the data analyst gathers the data and presents it in a summarized format. After that, mining is done to discover patterns.

Descriptive analytics is simply a case of determining and describing the "what" of data.

2. **Diagnostic analytics:** In diagnostic analytics, anomalies within the data are identified, that is, anything that cannot be explained by the data in front of them. For example: If the data shows that there was a sudden drop in sales for the month of Julyl, the data analyst will need to investigate the cause. For this, they will look for additional data sources that might tell them more about why such anomalies arose. For this diagnostic stage, data analysts may use probability theory, regression analysis, filtering, and time-series data analytics.
3. **Predictive analytics:** Predicting what is likely to happen in the future is the role of predictive analysis. Predictive analytics estimates the likelihood of a future outcome based on historical data and probability theory. Predictive analytics can be used to forecast what products will be most popular at a certain time, to how much the company revenue is likely to increase or decrease in a given period.
4. **Prescriptive analytics:** Prescriptive analytics demonstrates how to take advantage of the outcomes that have been predicted. It may involve working with algorithms, machine learning, and computational modeling procedures. The effective use of prescriptive analytics can have a huge impact on the company's decision-making process and its finances.

Tools for Data Analytics

1. **Regression analysis:** Regression analysis is a set of statistical processes used to estimate the relationships between variables to determine how changes to one or more variables might affect another. For example, how might social media spending affect sales?
2. **Monte carlo simulation:** Monte Carlo simulations are used to model the probability of different outcomes in a process that cannot easily be predicted due to the intervention of random variables. It is frequently used for risk analysis.
3. **Factor analysis:** Factor analysis is a statistical method for taking a massive data set and reducing it to a smaller, more manageable one. This has the added benefit of discovering hidden patterns. Factor analysis is often used to explore things like customer loyalty.
4. **Cohort analysis:** Cohort analysis is used to break a dataset down into groups that share common characteristics, or cohorts, for analysis. This is often used to understand customer segments.
5. **Cluster analysis:** Cluster analysis is a group of techniques that are used to classify objects or cases into relative groups called clusters. It can be used to reveal structures in data—insurance companies might use cluster analysis to investigate why certain locations are associated with particular insurance claims, for instance.

6. **Time series analysis:** Time series analysis is a statistical technique that deals with trend analysis. Time series analysis can be used to identify trends and cycles over time. It is frequently used for sales forecasting.
7. **Sentiment analysis:** Sentiment analysis uses tools such as natural language processing, text analysis, computational linguistics, and so on, to understand the feelings expressed in the data. While the previous six methods seek to analyze quantitative data, sentiment analysis seeks to interpret and classify qualitative data by organizing it into themes. It is often used to understand how customers feel about a brand, product, or service.

Benefits of E-commerce Analytics

(a) ***Helps to build a robust supply chain:*** Customers shop online for two reasons—convenience and better prices. So, supply chain needs to be robust. Are the products being advertised available in adequate quantities? If not, it will result in slower delivery and the level of customer satisfaction is bound to drop and the customer lifetime value will be negatively affected. On the flip side, having too many units in stock will take up space and increase costs. Striking this balance, between supply and demand is tricky, and this is why using analytics to forecast future sales is vital.

(b) ***Analyze information to detect fraud:*** Analytics plays a key role in the detection of fraud. Since analytics can detect patterns based on customer behavior, it can warn the owner when an aberrant transaction is detected. As an e-commerce business, you can send a notification to the customer asking them if it is really them who are trying to conduct a particular transaction and await their express approval before processing the transaction.

(c) ***Predicts what's going to happen:*** Analytics for e-commerce merchants helps them determine future trends based on several factors including the size of transactions, the season, category of products and so on. Such analysis is useful in determining what future sales will look like and helps the merchant in determining what products they need to focus on, whether they need to readjust their inventory, what marketing tactics they need to deploy to promote certain products and what promotions to offer on different products.

(d) ***Personalize recommendations for your customers:*** Selling to the same customer is much easier than acquiring a new one—any sales person will attest to that. This is why when you can sell to the same customer more than once, you are optimizing the value you can get from them. Personalized recommendations are a great way to do that.

Every time someone clicks on a product, if they see what other products are recommended, there is a chance they will want to explore and buy something in addition to their original purchase. Recommender systems are also great because when the same customer returns to the retailer's website, they can see upfront what's new and relevant for them, based on their previous shopping history.

(e) ***Forecast inventory for the next season:*** As a retailer, you need to know whether having a particular product on your virtual shelf is worth the cost of maintaining it in your inventory. E-commerce Analytics helps you determine the volume of sales of a particular product, what sales are predicted for the future, what has been the customer satisfaction rate, among other factors.

E-commerce analytics helpful in determining which products you need to continue stocking and which might need to be reconsidered for sale in the next season.

(f) ***Measure your marketing:*** Information related to online marketing analytics is very important to a retailer. You may pour in hundreds or thousands of dollars in online marketing campaigns, but if you are not able to determine its effectiveness, you will never be able to figure out whether or not your marketing strategy is working.

Analytics takes care of this by measuring ad clicks, engagement time of the visitors on your site, channel data and promotion effectiveness. By measuring these metrics, you can determine your return on investment and fine-tune your marketing strategy for the future.

(g) ***Personalize the customer's shopping experience:*** Different customers engage with an ecommerce website differently. Some love to constantly check out the "deal of the day" while others are only looking to shop for books and dive straight into that section, ignoring even the home page. When a particular customer visits your site, what is the first thing you would like to show him/her?

E-commerce analytics helps retailers study the users' behavior and determine how the site should be structured based on a customer's preferences, the product landing page most likely to engage the customer and convert them by getting them to make a purchase.

(h) ***Lets to know your customers better:*** Retailers need to understand the types of customers, their demographics, their behavior as well as the churn cases. All such analysis is useful in determining the product strategy and any realignment needed in order to meet revenue and business goals. Such analysis can also help you in deciding what promotions to launch in order to maximize conversions of visitors who are visiting your website.

(i) ***Optimize pricing of the products:*** In the e-commerce industry, the price of a product is determined based on the demand for a product, its availability in the market and how competitors are pricing the same product. You can use predictive analytics to analyze pricing trends and determine what the optimum price for a product should be in order to maximize profit. Amazon is a classic example of an online retailer that uses predictive pricing.

The use of analytics to drive business is on the rise, across industries. The senior management through the e-commerce dashboard gets the insights on the business objectives, product managers get the insights on the product sales and whether the sales are drawing an optimum profit, e-commerce analytics find favor across the entire organization.

Google Analytics[6]

Google offers Google Analytics which is a web analytics service offered by Google that tracks and reports website traffic, currently as a platform inside the Google Marketing Platform brand. Google launched the service in November 2005 after acquiring Urchin. Google Analytics is a free website analytics platform that offers a wealth of insights that improve the understanding of your website audience, their acquisition, behavior, and profitability.

Types of E-commerce Analytics

1. **Audience:** In-depth analysis regarding the demographics of the audience, such as their gender, age, income, occupation, devices they use, where they are based and what language they speak can provide useful information to promote the business. Audience data gives e-commerce company owners the ability to adapt how they conduct their shipping options and how they advertise based on the locations of their audience.
2. **Acquisition:** Data relating to the acquisition of customers is highly valuable because that will provide how customers visitors ended up on the website. Using acquisition data, will provide online marketing channels that are bringing the most visitors to the website. You will also discover what channels are driving the greatest sales or conversions from the following:
   - From social media posts
   - From email campaigns
   - From blog posts
   - From paid ads?

   This data will be crucial in helping one to understand which marketing channels are the most profitable to the business so that one can focus more that.
3. **Behavior:** Once consumers land on a website, how do they behave?
   - What products do customers end up buying?
   - How many viewers end up leaving your website straight away rather than exploring?
   - What page do people click on first?
   - What marketing content do viewers click on?
   - Which products generate a lot of interest but very few sales?
   - How long do viewers spend on your website on average?

   These sorts of questions can help one to understand how the website is being used at the moment, so that improvements can be made.

   All in all, behavior analytics are going to enable the owner to discover the parts of the store that can be enhanced in order to boost the engagement rates and conversion level.

6 https://analytics.google.com › analytics › web

4. Conversions

- When do online users convert into actual customers?
- How do online users convert into actual customers?

These are the two questions we are looking at when it comes to conversion analytics. For marketing strategy, the owner simply cannot ignore this part of it.

When the owner starts digging deeper, there are many different things that they can find out.

- How long does it take a typical user to convert into a paying customer?
- Do customers tend to convert once a year or at multiple times?
- Do customers tend to buy items after one visit to your e-store or do they need to make several visits before they buy?
- Do customers tend to make repeat purchases?
- How many customers abandon their shopping cart rather than converting?

Knowing the above specifics can help to impact the marketing messaging, to effectively engage with users and potential customers.

EXERCISES

1. Compare and contrast the website of Pepsi cola with that of Coca-cola.
2. Visit Harvard University website and comment on its animation graphics.
3. Compare the navigational bar of www.cdnow.com with www.boo.com.
4. Design a website for the following case using the techniques that you have learned. Specify the following before undertaking the actual design:

   (a) Site structure
   (b) Navigational bar
   (c) Hyperlink structure
   (d) Colour schemes
   (e) Graphics and animation that you plan to use.

CHAPTER

12

Legal and Ethical Issues

LEARNING OBJECTIVES

After reading this chapter, you should be able to:

- Understand how Information Technology is being misused to violate ethical principles.
- Describe how computers act as targets of crime.
- Know how IT is being misused to violate privacy issues.
- Explain how IT is being misused to perpetuate crimes against children.

Doubleclick's Collecting Information about Webusage

Doubleclick is an internet advertising agency that encountered a firestorm of complaints after its acquisition of Abacus Direct in 1999. AbacusDirect had a repository of names, addresses, and buying habits collected from almost 1800 merchants and about 90 million households.

Doubleclick's business is based on capabilities related to banner advertisements a web user often sees at the top and on the sides of weba pages. Doubleclick controls the banner advertisements in the following manner across its network that links 1500 sites. If BMW wanted to place a banner ad on a luxury car website, that website would provide a link that allows Doubleclick to display the BMW ad whenever a particular web page is viewed. If the user clicks on the ad, Doubleclick sends the user to the appropriate BMW web page and also deposits or updaes a Doubleclick cookie on the user's computer. If a Doubleclick cookie already existed on the user's computer, Doubleclick would therefore know at least one other site that the user had visited. Since Doubleclick places banner ads for over 1000 web merchants, it can use its database to generagte anonymous profiles that show correlations between visiting one site and visiting other sites. Doubleclick aggregates these profiles in a variety of ways to help specific companies understand their customers and markets.

These anonymous profiles generally were not considered a major threat to individual privacy because the basic identifier in the cookies linked to each profile refers to the computer rather than the individual user. Doubleclicks's purchase of Abacus was considered a much greater threat to privacy because Abacus had a large database that included names and addresses taken from magazine subscriptions and other sales activities. This database would give Doubleclick a way to link many of its profiles to information about specific individuals. Now it could have a single database containing a person's name, address, details of all the gardening supplies or sweaters they have bought from catalogues, and a log of every website they have visited that's part of Doubleclick's network. This would have great commercial value because the personal information plus the web usage information could be used to direct highly targeted promotions and advertisements at people whose past purchases and web activity revealed interests in particular type of products.

Privacy advocates complained and the US Federal Trade Commission began a probe into the matter. As a result, Doubleclick lost some of its business. By October 2000, Doubleclicks stock price had plummeted to $12 from $135.

Case Discussion

1. Look at google and yahoo sites and read their privacy statements.
2. Discuss priacy issues raised by the use of cookies.

Ethical Issues in the Digital Economy

The opening up of the Indian economy in 1991 coincided with the spurt in Information Technology that was pervading all over the world. Indian software companies used that opportunity to transform India into a software powerhouse and improving the GDP of India.

Technology can be a double-edged sword. It can be the source of many benefits. One great achievement of contemporary computer system is the ease with which digital information can be transmitted and shared among many people. But at the same time, this powerful capability creates new opportunities for breaking the law or taking benefits away from others. Balancing the convenience and privacy implications of providing personal data on-line is one of the compelling ethical issues raised by contemporary information systems.

Ethics refers to the principles of right and wrong that can be used by individuals acting as free moral agents to make choices to guide their behaviour. Information technology and information systems raise new ethical questions for both individuals and societies because they create opportunities for intense social change, and thus threaten existing distributions of power, money, rights and obligations.

Five moral dimensions of the information age are:

1. ***Information rights and obligations.*** What information rights do individuals and organization possess with respect to information about themselves? What can they protect?
2. ***Property rights.*** How will traditional intellectual property rights be protected in a digital society in which tracing and accounting for ownership is difficult, and ignoring such property rights is so easy?

3. ***Accountability and control.*** Who can and will be held accountable and liable for the harm done to individual and collective information and property rights?
4. ***System quality.*** What standards of data and system quality should we demand to protect individual rights and the safety of society?
5. ***Quality of life.*** What values should be preserved in an information and knowledge-based society? What institutions should we protect from violation? What cultural values and practices are supported by the new information technology?

Internet is a medium of communication, and as such, it has three special features:

1. It offers many-to-many communication on a global scale.
2. It facilitates a certain kind of anonymity.
3. Certain programs on the Internet have the ability to replicate themselves.

The many-to-many communication on a global scale can be misused as a source of diabolic power to disrupt computer functioning by unleashing a computer virus. And as in the case of Melissa virus, it can cause huge losses to many organizations. The Internet has created a new kind of environment in which individuals who want to wreak havoc can do so with relatively little effort.

The widespread desire to be wired should make us reflect on what awaits us as the computer revolution explodes around the world. The digital genie is out of the bottle on worldwide scale. The prospect of a global village in which everyone on the planet is connected to everyone else with regard to computing power and communication, is breathtaking. What is difficult to comprehend is what impact this will have on human life. Surely, some of the effects will be quite positive and others quite negative. The question is to what extent can we bring ethics to bear on the computer revolution in order to guide us to a better world or at least prevent us from falling into a worse world. Although almost everyone would agree that computing is having a significant impact on the world, and that ethical issues about applications of this surging technology should be raised, there is disagreement about the nature of computer ethics.

In the recent past, we have witnessed several technological revolutions, which have transformed the way we communicate, learn, and do business with each other using technologies such as the cell phones, computers and the Internet. They are transforming our communication styles as seen in social media such as Facebook and Twitter. Education is undergoing immense changes due to the changes brought about by the online courses. Business has been undergoing a paradigm shift due to the online platforms where people can buy and sell goods and services. As the Internet's potential to provide immense benefits to the society continues to multiply, there has been a disproportionate increase in unlawful and criminal acts. Most of us take technology for granted that we choose to ignore the detrimental effects it will bring to society rising from these ethical issues. Three characteristics of the Internet challenge the ability of nations and courts to deal with breach of law in matters of privacy, copyright and criminal activities, etc. to online activities. These three characteristics are as follows:

1. High speed
2. Lack of geographical boundaries
3. The ability of crimials to remain anonymous

Actually, these same characteristics have allowed the Internet to bring about a transformation in the world.

Importance of Ethics in Information Technology

Ethics deals with what is good and bad, and also, with moral duty and obligation. While it is important to live an ethical life, it is also important to practise the same everywhere, even in the computing field, where sooner or later, we would face new ethical dilemmas. Information technology ethics analyzes the moral and social acceptability of actions that happen online and offline. Software piracy, pornography, spamming, unauthorized access to somebody else's computer, hacking, and Ransomware are some of the challenges faced by computer ethics. Information technology ethics raises new and unique issues in society. Ethics are the moral values that stop you from doing anything that is not legal and that does not harm or damage anyone else's work, or interests. Information technology ethics can be defined as the analysis of the nature and social impact of computer technology and the corresponding formulation and justification of policies for the ethical use of such technology. Information technology ethics is a special field of ethical research and application. Computer ethics has two parts—(i) the analysis of the nature and social impact of computer technology, and (ii) the corresponding formulation and justification of policies for the ethical use of such technology.

The Computer Ethics Institute has defined the following 10 commandments of computer use[1]:

1. Thou shalt not use a computer to harm other people.
2. Thou shalt not interfere with other people's computer work.
3. Thou shalt not snoop around in other people's files.
4. Thou shalt not use a computer to steal.
5. Thou shalt not use a computer to bear false witness.
6. Thou shalt not use or copy software for which you have not paid.
7. Thou shalt not use other people's computer resources without authorization.
8. Thou shalt not appropriate other people's intellectual output.
9. Thou shalt think about the social consequences of the program you write.
10. Thou shalt use a computer in ways that show consideration and respect.

Information Technology as Targets for Crime

When the confidentiality, integrity, or availability of a computer's information or services is attacked, then there is unlawful conduct. Hackers gain control of the computer system by unethical means, and then, they can steal information or alter the data in the computer or deny services. Military computers are a tempting target to many people, terrorist organizations, and foreign intelligence operatives.

1. https://computerethicsinstitute.org/home.html

A hacker might gain access to a hotel reservation system to steal credit card numbers. Hackers may break into computer system to steal trade secrets, or get access to copyrighted material, which they may duplicate and sell causing loss to the companies involved. Other cases may involve a perpetrator, who seeks private information about another individual, as a means to extort money or to embarrass the victim through public disclosure. Systems containing medical records, telephone customer records, or consumer credit report information are easy targets. An offender may use his computer to break into a telephone switching system to steal long-distance calling services which is called *phone phreaking*.

In the category of attacks collectively known as *denial of service*, the objective is to disable the target system without necessarily gaining access to it. One technically straightforward method of accomplishing this objective is *mailbombing*, the practice of sending large volumes of e-mail to a single site (or user account) to clog the mail server or even to cause the target host to crash. Other methods—ranging from simply tying up incoming phone lines to more sophisticated attacks using low-level data transmission protocols—may also be used to achieve the same end of rendering the target system unavailable for normal use.

Cybercrime is the greatest threat to every company in the world, and one of the biggest problems with mankind. The impact on society is reflected in the numbers.

Last year, Cybersecurity Ventures predicted that cybercrime would cost the world \$6 trillion annually by 2021. This represents the greatest transfer of economic wealth in history, risks the incentives for innovation and investment, and will be more profitable than the global trade of all major illegal drugs combined.

The cybercrime prediction stands, and over the past year, it has been corroborated by hundreds of major media outlets, universities and colleges, senior government officials, associations, industry experts, the largest technology and cybersecurity companies, and cybercrime fighters globally.

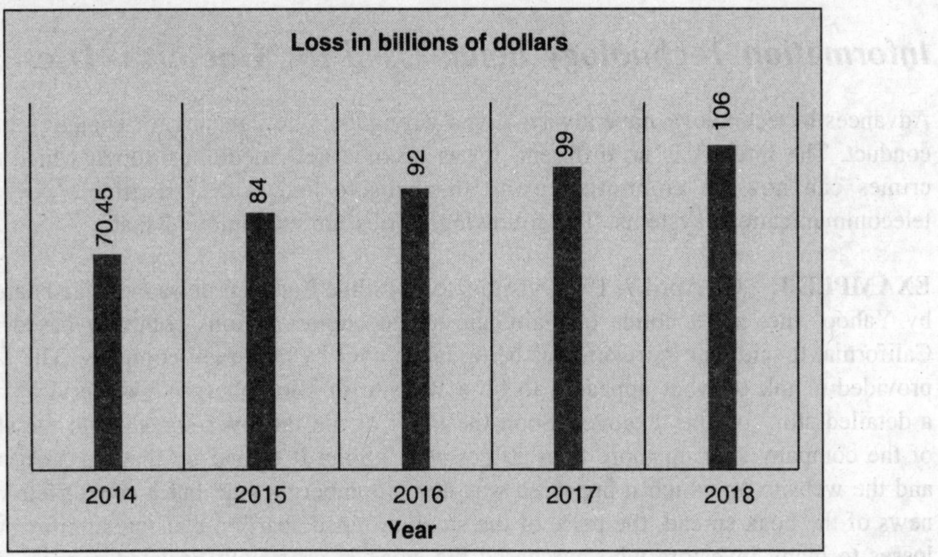

Figure 12.1 Cyber crime losses to business.

The damage cost projections are based on historical cybercrime figures in recent years, which saw a dramatic increase in hostile state sponsored, or organized crime by hacking activities by criminals which are escalating day by day.

Cybercrime costs include damage and destruction of data, stolen money, lost productivity, theft of intellectual property, theft of personal and financial data, embezzlement, fraud, post-attack disruption to the normal course of business, forensic investigation, restoration and deletion of hacked data and systems, and reputational harm.

The Dark Web

More than half of the Web remains non-indexed because it cannot be accessed by standard search engines such as Google. We call this the dark Web. The most significant feature of this world is that the identity of its users is hidden and cannot be tracked. Accessing the dark Web requires the use of a browser called Tor. The Tor browser routes your Web page requests through a series of proxy servers operated by thousands of volunteers around the globe. It makes sure that the incoming IP address remains unidentifiable and untraceable. Dark Web sites have different naming structures. They do not end in '.com' or '.co'. They may end in '.onion' or such words. This is a special-use top level domain suffix linking an anonymous hidden service reachable via the Tor network. They also use a scrambled naming structure that creates URLs that are often impossible to remember. For example, take the case of a site called 'Dream Market'. It goes by the unintelligible address of "eajwlvm3z2lcca76.onion". The dark Web is anonymous and not open to the public. It has been a space for groups wanting to stay hidden online from governments and law enforcement agencies. Frequently, it has been used by paedophile groups, terrorists and criminals to keep their dealings secret.

Information Technology being Used for Unethical Uses

Advances in technology have always given wrongdoers new means for engaging in unlawful conduct. The Internet is no different. It has become new medium through which traditional crimes can now be committed using inexpensive and widely available computer and telecommunications systems. The following stories are examples of that.

EXAMPLE 1: On April 7, 1999, visitors to an online financial news message board operated by Yahoo! Inc. got a notice on PairGain, a telecommunications company based in Tustin, California. It said that PairGain was being taken over by an Israeli company. The e-mail also provided a link to what appeared to be a website of Bloomberg News Service, containing a detailed story on the takeover. Soon the news of the takeover spread, and the stock price of the company shot up more than 30 per cent. Soon it turned up that the story was false, and the website on which it appeared was not Bloomberg's site, but a counterfeit site. When news of the hoax spread, the price of the stock dropped sharply, causing significant financial losses to many investors who purchased the stock at artificially inflated prices.

EXAMPLE 2: In 1999, Bloomberg provided database services to Kazkommerts located in Almaty, Kazakhstan. As a result, Kazkommerts was provided with Bloomberg's software needed to gain access to Bloomberg's services over the Internet. Those services were cancelled by Bloomberg in 1999 because Kazkommerts did not pay its bill. Zezev, an employee of Kazkommerts, manipulated Bloomberg's software to bypass Bloomberg's security system in order to gain unauthorized access to Bloomberg's computer system so that he could pose as a legitimate customer. On 11 separate occasions Zezev illegally entered Bloomberg's computer system and accessed various accounts, including Michael Bloomberg's personal account. He copied various information from these accounts including e-mails, Michael Bloomberg's credit card numbers, and screens relating to internal functions of Bloomberg. He sent an e-mail on April 17, 2000 to Michael Bloomberg, threatening that if Michael Bloomberg did not send him $200,000 he would disclose to the media and Bloomberg's customers that he was able to gain unauthorized access to Bloomberg's computer system. Michael Bloomberg, acting in conjunction with FBI agents, then sent Zezev e-mails saying that if Zezev wanted the money he would have to meet with Michael Bloomberg and some of Bloomberg's computer specialists in London and explain to them how he was able to break into Bloomberg's computer system. Zezev travelled to London and was trapped and arrested.

EXAMPLE 3: The Melissa virus first appeared on the Internet in March of 1999. It spread rapidly throughout computer systems in the United States and Europe. It is estimated that the virus caused $80 million in damages to computers worldwide. In the United States alone, the virus made its way through 1.2 million computers in one-fifth of the country's largest businesses. David Smith pleaded guilty on December 9, 1999 to state and federal charges associated with his creation of the Melissa virus.

In March 1999, David Smith created a "computer virus", known as the "Melissa" virus, designed to evade anti-virus software and to infect computers that used certain word processing computer software programs. On March 26, 1999, after accessing an Internet account that he was not authorized to use, David Smith posted on the newsgroup "Alt.Sex" a message with an attachment infected with the "Melissa" virus, indicating, in substance and in part, that the attachment purportedly contained a list of passcodes to pornographic websites. Upon infecting a computer, the "Melissa" virus did the following:

(a) Lowered security components of certain word processing programs, making the infected computer more vulnerable to computer virus infection;
(b) Altered certain word processing programs such that any document created using the program would be infected with the "Melissa" virus; and
(c) Caused certain computers to send electronic mail with an attachment infected with the "Melissa" virus to the first fifty addresses in the computer user's address book. If the infected attachment was opened on a computer using certain word processing programs, then that computer was infected with the "Melissa" virus.

"Melissa" virus infected word processing programs in over one million computers that were used in interstate and foreign commerce, and caused over $80,000,000 in damage.

Cyberstalking

Cyberstalking refers to the use of the Internet, e-mail, or other electronic communications devices to "stalk" another person. In cyberstalking, the victim is repeatedly harassed or threatened (such as following a person, appearing at a person's home or workplace, making harassing telephone calls, or leaving written messages or objects) that places the victim in reasonable fear of death or bodily injury. The Internet provides novel ways for would-be stalkers to pursue their victims.

EXAMPLE 1: In April 1999, a 50 year old former security guard pleaded guilty to one count of stalking in California. The defendant impersonated the victim in various Internet chat rooms and online bulletin boards, where he posted, along with her telephone number and address, messages that she fantasized about being raped. Several men knocked on the victim's door saying they wanted to rape her.

EXAMPLE 2: A person was arrested by the New Delhi Police in India's first case of cyberstalking. He was stalking a lady by illegally chatting on the Web site MIRC using her name. He used obscene and obnoxious language, and distributed her residence telephone number, inviting people to chat with her on the phone. As a result of which, she kept getting obscene calls from everywhere, and people promptly talked dirty with her. In a state of shock, she called the Delhi police and reported the matter. For once, the police department did not waste time swinging into action, and a case has been registered under Section 509 of the Indian Penal Code for outraging the modesty of that lady.

Cybersquatting

Cybersquatting is registering, trafficking in, or using a domain name with bad faith–intent to profit from the goodwill of a trademark belonging to someone else. The terms derive from squatting, the practice of inhabiting someone else's property without their permission.

EXAMPLE 1: When Domain Active Pty Limited, an Australian entity, floated a website on the domain name, www.sbicards.com, and even 'tricked' financial big-time entities like Chase Manhattan into advertising on the site, the SBI arm, which had already registered the domain name with Fabulous.Com Pty. Ltd, lodged a complaint. The WIPO Administrative Panel found that the Australian entity's website could have attracted potential attention from the public because of its affiliation with SBI Cards' products and services. At the same time, it created a risk of confusion with the products/services and trademark as to the source, sponsorship, affiliation or endorsement of its website. The panel's independent verification showed that the current use of the Australian firm's website, www.sbicards.com, was practically the same. The panel held that the respondent (Domain Active Pty Limited) "has registered the disputed domain name in bad faith". And SBI Card and Payment Services won the case.

EXAMPLE 2: Global steel giant ArcelorMittal has won a cybersquatting case against a Mumbai-based firm that was using some websites, similar to the trademark of the NRI billionaire LN Mittal-led company.

A Mumbai-based firm, known as Taj Group of Companies, had registered five websites—arcelorcement.com, arcelorlabs.com, arcelorlaboratories.com, arcelorchemicals.net and arcelorchemicals.com. To restrain this entity for using trademark, the Luxembourg-based steel major had to approach the UN's World Intellectual Property Organisation (WIPO).

The company contended that the disputed Internet sites were identical in part and confusingly similar as a whole to the 'Arcelor' trademark, for which it owns the rights. ArcelorMittal won the case.

Phishing

Phishing is used to steal user data, including login credentials and credit card numbers. It occurs when an attacker, masquerading as a trusted entity, dupes a victim into opening an e-mail, instant message, or text message. The recipient is then tricked into clicking a malicious link, which can lead to the installation of malware, the freezing of the system as part of a ransomware attack or the revealing of sensitive information. An attack can lead to unauthorized purchases, the stealing of funds, or identify theft.

Recently many banks all over the world encountered a variety of frauds and scams committed by hackers, swindlers, and inside bank officials. Swindlers try to trick consumers into giving up credit card information by posing as mail from regulators like RBI, Government, Income Tax department, etc. The phishing e-mails typically have subject headings of 'Official information' or 'Urgent information to all credit card holders!' and claim that recent changes in the law require that Internet users identify themselves to the federal government to create a secure and safer Internet community.' The e-mail includes a link to a bogus website, which in this case closely resembles an official government website. Once there, users are asked to enter private and personal financial information, including credit card numbers.

Application Fraud

Application fraud is one specific version of what is broadly referred to as "identity theft." As the name implies, it essentially involves a criminal using someone else's name and credentials to fill out a credit card application without their permission. Often, the thief sets the stage for application fraud by stealing supporting documents from the victim, such as utility bills or bank statements, which are then used to substantiate the thief's fraudulent credit card application. If and when they are approved for a card in the victim's name, thieves face few restraints in the damage they are capable of inflicting. FICO scores and payment histories can be ruined in a heartbeat by determined thieves in possession of a fraudulently granted credit card.

Skimming

Skimming is an electronic method of capturing a victim's personal information used by identity thieves. The skimmer is a small device that scans a credit card and stores the information contained in the magnetic strip. Skimming can take place during a legitimate transaction at a business. ATM skimming is like identity theft for debit cards. Thieves use hidden electronics to steal the personal information stored on your card and record your PIN number to access cash in your account. Skimming can occur easily in a restaurant because your card is taken away when the bill is being settled. If your server is a skimming identity thief, he or she will, before giving the card back to you, scan the credit card with a hand-held electronic device, which takes only seconds. The electronically captured information is then used by the thief or sold to other criminals.

Copyright Violations

In general terms, copyright provides an author with a tool to protect a work from being taken, used, and exploited by others without permission. The owner of a copyrighted work has the exclusive right to reproduce it, prepare derivative works based upon it, distribute copies by sale or other transfer of ownership, to perform and display it publicly, and to authorize others to do so.

For a company that depends upon intellectual property for its livelihood, such as a software company or an Internet-based publisher, copyright law provides a framework that ensures that the company can compete in the marketplace. The importance of copyright is illustrated by comparing what happens to an appliance company when a refrigerator is stolen with what happens to a software company when its source code is stolen. The refrigerator company will simply have one less item of merchandise to sell and a loss reflected by the refrigerator's price. The software company, however, will suddenly be faced with the prospect of a market flooded with exact copies of its product—sold or given away by another. Without the ability to prevent unauthorized copying, sale, and distribution of its product, the software company will not be able to survive.

Copyright law protects "original works of authorship". Sheer hard work alone will not suffice—a modicum of creativity is required. The work does not have to be the first of its kind, or novel—it just has to be the independent product of the author, not copied from another source. Copyright, in fact, does not protect against independent creation of similar or identical works.

Certain items are excluded from copyright protection. Registering a work with the Copyright Office is a critical step to be taken in protecting a work under copyright law. While time and money costs are involved, significant benefits are gained by completing the registration process in a timely manner. To protect a work from the date of first publication, it must be registered within three months of that time. The work may be registered by the owner or an exclusive licensee. There is a "mandatory" deposit requirement, but it is not a condition of copyright protection.

A copyright is infringed when one of the exclusive rights of the copyright holder is violated. These include the right to reproduce a copyrighted work, prepare derivative works based upon it, distribute copies by sale or other transfer of ownership, to perform and display it publicly, and to authorize others to do so.

Internet Gambling

The Internet and other emerging technologies, such as interactive television, have made possible certain types of gambling that were not feasible a few years ago. For example, an Indian citizen can now, from his home at any hour of the day or night, participate in an interactive Internet poker game operated by a computer located in the Caribbean. Indeed, a tech-savvy gambler can route his bets through computers located in other countries throughout the world, thereby obscuring the fact that he is placing his bet from India.

Online gambling also makes it far more difficult to prevent minors from gambling. Gambling websites cannot look at their customers to assess their age and request photo identification as is possible in traditional physical casinos and off-track-betting parlours. Currently, Internet gambling businesses have no reliable way of confirming that the gamblers are not minors who have gained access to a credit card and are gambling on their website. Although some companies are developing software to try to detect whether a player is old enough to gamble or whether that player is from a legal jurisdiction, such software has not been perfected and would, of course, be subject to the same types of flaws and vulnerabilities that could be exploited by hackers.

Unlike on-site gambling, online gambling is readily available to all at all hours, and it permits the user to gamble, in many cases, anonymously. This presents a greater danger for compulsive gambling and can cause severe financial consequences for an unsuccessful player. Internet gambling, unlike many other forms of gambling activity, is a solitary activity, which makes it even more dangerous; people can gamble uninterrupted and undetected for unlimited periods of time. Indeed, the problems associated with pathological and problem gamblers, a frighteningly large percentage of which are young people, are well-established and can be measured in the ruined lives of both the gamblers themselves and their families.

Although there are certainly legitimate companies who are either operating or who want to operate online casinos in an honest manner, the potential for fraud connected with casinos and bookmaking operations in the virtual world is far greater than in the physical realm. Start-up costs are relatively low and cheap servers and unsophisticated software are readily available. Online casinos and bookmaking establishments operate in many countries where effective regulation and law enforcement is minimal or non-existent. Like scam telemarketing operations, online gambling establishments appear and disappear with regularity, collecting from losers and not paying winners, and with little fear of being apprehended and prosecuted.

Through slight alterations of the software, unscrupulous gambling operations can manipulate the odds in their favour, make unauthorized credit card charges to the accounts of unsuspecting gamblers, or alter their own accounts to skim money. There is also a danger that hackers can manipulate the online games in their favour, or can steal credit card or other information about other gamblers using the site.

Traditionally, gambling has been one of the staple activities in which organized crime has been involved. Indeed, many of the recent indictments brought against members of organized crime groups have included gambling charges. We have now seen evidence that organized crime is moving into Internet gambling.

Another major concern about online gambling is that Internet gambling businesses provide criminals with an easy and excellent vehicle for money laundering, in large part due to the volume, speed, and international reach of Internet transactions and the offshore locations of most Internet gambling sites, as well as the fact that the industry itself is already cash intensive.

It is a fact that money launderers have to go to financial institutions either to conceal their illegal funds or recycle those funds back into the economy for their use. Because criminals are aware that banks have been subjected to greater scrutiny and regulation, they have turned to other non-bank financial institutions, such as casinos, to launder their money. Online casinos are a particularly inviting target because, in addition to using the gambling that casinos offer as a way to hide or transfer money, casinos offer a broad array of financial services to their customers, such as providing credit accounts, fund transmittal services, check cashing services, and currency exchange services.

Individuals wanting to launder ill-gotten gains through an online casino can do so in a variety of ways. For example, a customer could establish an account with a casino using illegally-derived proceeds, conduct a minimal amount of betting or engage in offsetting bets with an overseas confederate, and then request repayment from the casino, thereby providing a new "source" of funds. If a gambler wants to transfer money to an inside source in the casino, who may be located in another country, he can just play until he loses the requisite amount. Similarly, if an insider wants to transfer money to the gambler, perhaps as payment for some illicit activity, he can rig the game so the bettor wins.

The anonymous nature of the Internet and the use of encryption makes it difficult to trace the transactions. The gambling business may also not maintain the transaction records, in which case tracing may be impossible. While regulators in the United States can visit physical casinos, observe their operations, and examine their books and records to ensure compliance with regulations, this is far more difficult, if not impossible, with virtual casinos.

Threats to Children

With the growing number of classrooms connected to the Internet and the rising number of personal computers used in the home, more and more children are now able to access the Internet. One of the greatest benefits of the Internet is that it provides children with access to such things as educational materials, subject matter experts, online friendships, and penpals. Nevertheless, like many other pursuits that children engage in without adequate parental supervision, the Internet should also be approached with careful consideration of risks and benefits. One concern of course is that the Internet may allow children unrestricted access to inappropriate materials. Such materials may contain sexually explicit images or descriptions, advocate hate or bigotry, contain graphic violence, or promote drug use or other illegal activities. In the worst instances, children have become victims of physical molestation and harassment by providing personal information about themselves over the Internet and making contact with strangers.

To protect children from such risks, parents and teachers therefore need to empower themselves with the tools, knowledge, and resources to supervise and guide children's online experience and to teach children how to use the Internet responsibly.

Technology provides tools that may assist in preventing children from accessing inappropriate materials on the Internet or divulging personal information about themselves or their families online. The most common technological tools are "blocking" and "filtering" software.

Content filtering usually works by specifying character strings, which if matched, indicate undesirable content that is to be screened out. Content is typically screened for pornographic content, and sometimes, also for violence- or hate-oriented content. Critics of content filtering programs point out that it is not difficult to unintentionally exclude desirable content.

Loss of Privacy

As consumers, all our financial transactions are monitored by financial institutions to detect fraud and our preferences are monitored by loyalty programs to enable future marketing campaigns to target us. As mobile phone users, our movements and communications can be tracked for use by the emergency services. As social media users, we are tracked for our usage of social media. As users of google search, we are tracked for what we search. Surveillance is something which can confer access, entitlement and benefit as well as something which is dangerous, oppressive and discriminatory. As data travels silently on Internet across international boundaries, between nations and within multi-national corporations, the impact of surveillance becomes even harder to identify, regulate and debate. Surveillance is embedded within systems and structures. Its application becomes taken for granted and its consequences go unnoticed. The power based on the oversight of activities and of personal data should be wielded fairly, responsibly, and with due respect to human rights, civil liberties and the law. Sifting through consumer records to create a profitable clientele means that certain groups obtain special treatment based on ability to pay, whereas others fall by the wayside.

Restrictions of anonymity in communication have an evident chilling effect on victims of all forms of violence and abuse, who may be reluctant to report for fear of victimization. The harmful effects of surveillance on expression and association are undeniably linked—the right to organise is imperative for political expression and the advancement of ideas.

Along with the explosion of information technology, calls for greater protectionn of privacy rights have increased. Two general and connected understandings of privacy can be found in the legal and philosophical literature:

1. Privacy as a right to be left alone within a personal zone of solitude
2. Privacy as the right to control information about oneself

Privacy is not just about hiding things. It is about self-possession, autonomy, and integrity.

To understand privacy, we need to rethink what privacy really means today.

- It is about the NGO which is afraid to use the Internet to organize its community against antisocial developments affecting the community.
- It is about lovers who will take less joy in walking around city streets or visiting stores because they know they are being photographed by surveillance cameras everywhere they step.
- It is not about the searches and metal detectors, which have become a routine part of our daily lives at airports. It is about a society that views law-abiding citizens as potential terrorists, yet does little to effectively protect its citizens from the real threats to their safety.

Today, more than ever before, we are witnessing the daily erosion of personal privacy and freedom. We are victims of a war on privacy that is being waged by governments, businesses, and computer data thefts. Today's war on privacy is intimately related to the dramatic advances in technology. Video cameras observe personal moments. Computers store personal facts. Communications networks make personal information widely available throughout the world. Privacy is fundamentally about the power of the individual. In many ways, the story of technology's attack on privacy is really the story of how institutions and the people who run them use technology to gain control over human beings, for good and bad. That is because technology by itself does not violate our privacy or anything else, it is the people using this technology and the policies they carry out that create violations.

One group of people say that in order to enjoy the benefits of modern society, we must necessarily relinquish some degree of privacy. If we want the convenience of paying for a book by credit card, then we must accept the routine collection of our purchases in a large databases over which we have no control. Systems are not normally designed to crush privacy and autonomy. What happens more often is that the privacy implications of a new technology go unnoticed; and if the privacy implications are considered, they are misunderstood; if they are understood correctly, errors are made in implementation. In practice, just a few mistakes can turn a system designed to protect personal information into one that destroys our secrets. The large-scale thefts of data that happened recently in credit card companies or social media companies are good examples of that.

Cookies and Privacy

All material on the Web is formatted in a uniform format called Hypertext Markup Language (HTML), and all information requests and responses conform to a similar standard protocol. When someone accesses a server on the Web such as the Railway Reservation System, the user's Web browser sends an information request to the Railway Reservation System computer. The Web server responds to the request by transmitting the desired information to the user's computer. Then, the user's browser displays the received information on the user's screen.

When you visit Internet sites, cookies (pieces of information) are generated by a Web server and stored in the user's computer. Your browser stores each message in a small file, called *cookie.txt*. Cookies are embedded in the HTML information flowing back and forth between the user's computer and the servers. When you request another page from the same server, your browser sends the cookie back to the server. These files typically contain information about your visit to the Web page, as well as any information you have volunteered such as your name and interests. Cookies are used to personalize Web search engines, to allow users to participate in WWW-wide contests, and to store shopping lists of items a user has selected while browsing through a virtual shopping mall.

Cookies are based on a two-stage process. First, the cookie is stored in the user's computer without his/her consent or knowledge. As a result, personal information is formatted by the Web server, transmitted, and saved by the user's computer. During the second stage, the cookie is automatically transferred from the user's machine to a Web server. Internet cookies are incredibly simple, but they are one of those things that have taken on a life of their own. On the other hand, cookies provide capabilities that make the Web much easier to navigate. The designers of almost every major site use them because they provide a better user experience and make it much easier to gather accurate information about the site's visitors. Only the website that creates a cookie can read it, so other servers do not have access to your information. Additionally, Web servers can use only information that you provide or choices that you make while visiting the website as content in cookies.

EXERCISES

1. What is meant by cyberstalking?
2. Identify several types of disputes that have arisen over domain names.
3. Identify the provision of the IT Act, 2000 for the legal transactions of e-commerce in India.
4. List the important attributes of digital signatures.
5. Why privacy issue is important when dealing with e-commerce?
6. Why cookies can compromise privacy?
7. Describe how one can protect oneself against cookies?
8. What is spamming?
9. What is phishing?
10. What are the major kinds of computer crimes?
11. Why is the copyright issue on the Internet so unique?

CHAPTER 13

e-Commerce Laws and Taxation Issues

LEARNING OBJECTIVES

After reading this chapter, you should be able to:

- Learn about Information Technology Act, 2000 of India and its implications.
- Understand the controversies about e-commerce taxation.
- Know about Laws that govern electronic commerce activities.
- Know about Laws that govern the use of intellectual property by online businesses.

E-commerce Taxation in Karnataka State

Are online e-commerce companies retailers, service providers, commission agents or mere facilitators of transactions between buyers and sellers? The answer to this question has suddenly assumed importance after the Karnataka government recently charged third-party sellers on Amazon India with violation of tax laws.

Back in 2012, the marketplace model—in which the e-company facilitates the coming together of buyers and sellers—helped Flipkart, Myntra, Jabong, and others deflect the Enforcement Directorate's allegation that they had violated the foreign direct investment norm, given that FDI is not allowed in direct online retail in India. The companies, most of whom earlier stocked inventory, had restructured themselves into, and defined themselves as, 'technology platforms'. They, therefore, claim that they are not retailers, only facilitators between buyers and sellers.

On September 15, 2014, the Karnataka government issued notices to around 100 sellers, mostly using Amazon's platform, but also present on Flipkart and Snapdeal, asking them to desist from stocking goods at company's fulfillment centers. As an industry insider points out, "The larger question raised by the state government is about how far the word 'marketplace model' can be stretched to define the current business models of e-commerce companies."

Officials point out that the receipts in most e-commerce transactions are generated by the e-commerce companies, while the products are sent to consumers by the third-party seller. This is what a tax expert says:"According to the existing rules, these activities constitute the status of a commission agent rather than a service provider."

The state authorities also argue that any registered additional place of business constitutes a branch of the business and is presumed to be under the control of the supplier. Since, third-party merchants register an e-company's warehouse as their 'additional place of business', it can be assumed that the warehouse-owning e-companies constitute a part of the retail set-up, further qualifying them as commission agents.

Another point of contention is the invoice issued by the e-companies. The state says they are void under the existing law as the Information Technology Act, 2000, requires a digital signature on invoices, not mere digital images.

Experts say that the entire controversy has arisen because of ambiguities both in the FDI policy as well as the undefined nature of the marketplace model. The confusion affects not only the companies, but also the government. Extending the current tax laws against the e-commerce players could prove a dampener for investor sentiment and yet easing FDI norms could alienate the conventional traders who have been lobbying against such a move.

While the industry awaits the Goods and Service Tax regime, the e-commerce business, which is expected to reach $32 billion by 2020, demands more clarity on the taxation policy. Till then, the e-commerce players will probably continue to be bullish on growth even as the government clumsily tries to implement the existing laws.

Case Discussion

1. Discuss the implications of IT Act (2000) on e-commerce.
2. For tax laws to be applied to e-commerce, can you differentiate how e-commerce is different from traditional commerce.
3. What are the business models under which business organizations like Flipkart, eBay, Snapdeal, and Amazon operate?

The Legal Environment of Electronic Commerce

The same laws and regulations that govern the operations of all businesses must apply to business that operate on the Web. If they do not, they will face the same penalties like fines, reparation payments, court-imposed dissolution, and even jail time for officers and owners. Web businesses face two additional complicating factors as they try to comply with the law. First, the Internet extends a company's reach beyond traditional boundaries. A business that uses the Internet immediately becomes an international business. Thus, a company can become subject to many more laws more quickly than a traditional brick-and-mortar business based in one country. Second, the Web increases the speed and efficiency of business communications.

Physical territorial boundaries in the physical world serve a useful purpose in traditional commerce: They specify the range of culture and the kind of laws that will apply very clearly. Normally, when a person travels across international borders, transitions are made very rigid and there are so many norms to be followed like showing the passport or other travel documents, for example, exiting the country and entering another usually requires a formal examination of documents, such as passports and visas. These experiences, and countless others, are manifestations of the differences in legal rules and cultural customs in the two countries. In the physical world, geographic boundaries almost always coincide with legal and cultural boundaries. The limits of acceptable ethical behaviour and the laws that are adopted in a geographic area are the result of the influences of the area's dominant culture.

Usually, laws in the physical world do not apply to people who are not located in that territory or do not own assets in the geographic area that created those particular laws. For example, the United States cannot enforce its copyright laws on a citizen of India who is doing business in India and owns no assets in the United States. Any assertion of power by the United States over such an Indian citizen would conflict with the Indian government's recognized authority over its citizens. Indian citizens who bring goods into the United States to sell, however, are subject to applicable U.S. copyright laws. Laws in the physical world are rooted in the relationship between physical location and the effects of a person's behaviour. Personal or corporate actions have stronger effects on people and things that are within the boundaries than on those that are far away. Government-provided trademark protection is a good example of this. For instance, the Indian government can provide and enforce trademark protection for a business named Taj Hotel in Mumbai. The effects of another restaurant using the same name are strongest in Mumbai, somewhat less in Lucknow, and even less in other parts of India. That is, the effects diminish as geographic distance increases. If someone were to open a restaurant in London and call it Taj Hotel, the Hotel in Mumbai would experience few, if any, negative effects from the use of its trademarked name in London because it would be so far away and because so few people would be potential customers of both hotels. Thus, the effects of the trademark infringement would be controlled by the Indian law because of the limited range within which such an infringement has an effect.

Most people agree that the legitimate right to create and enforce laws derives from the mandate of those who are subject to those laws. In 1970, the United Nations passed a resolution that affirmed this idea of governmental legitimacy. The resolution made clear that the people residing within a set of recognized geographic boundaries are the ultimate source of legitimate legal authority for people and actions within those boundaries. Thus, legitimacy is the idea that those subject to laws should have some role in formulating them.

The levels of authority and autonomy with which governments of various countries operate varies significantly from one country to another. Online businesses must be ready to deal with a wide variety of regulations and levels of enforcement of those regulations as they expand their businesses to other countries. This can be difficult for smaller businesses that operate on the Web.

Territorial boundaries are an efficient way to announce the ending of one legal or cultural system and the beginning of another. Crossing the physical boundary provides warning that one set of rules has been replaced by a different set of rules. Notice is the announcement of such a change in rules. People can obey and perceive a law or cultural norm as fair only if they are notified of its existence. Borders provide this notice in the physical world. The legal systems of most countries include a concept called *constructive notice*. People receive constructive notice to a new set of rules and regulations have come into effect when they cross an international border, even if they are not specifically warned of the changed laws and norms by a sign or a border guard's statement. Thus, ignorance of the law is not a sustainable defence, even in a new and unfamiliar jurisdiction. This concept presents particular problems for online businesses, because they may not know that customers from another country are accessing their Web sites. Thus, the concept of notice—even constructive notice—does not translate very well to online business.

Information Technology Act, 2000

The Parliament of India passed its first **Cyber law** on the 17th of October 2000, the **Information Technology (IT) Act, 2000** which provides the legal infrastructure for e-commerce in India. The purpose of the IT Act, 2000, as mentioned in the language of the Act, is:

> *to provide legal recognition for transactions carried out by means of electronic data interchange and other means of electronic communication, commonly referred to as "electronic commerce" which involve the use of alternatives to paper-based methods of communication and storage of information, to facilitate electronic filing of documents with the Government agencies and further to amend the Indian Penal Code, the Indian Evidence Act, 1872, the Banker's Book Evidence Act, 1891 and the Reserve Bank of India Act, 1934 and for matters connected therewith or incidental thereto.*

By its resolution A/RES/51/162 dated 30th January, 1997, has adopted the Model Law on Electronic Commerce adopted by the United Nations Commission on International Trade Law. The same resolution recommends *inter alia* that all States give favourable consideration to this Model Law when they enact or revise their laws, keeping in mind the need for uniformity of law pertaining to alternatives to paper-based methods of communication and storage of information. The Indian Information Technology Act, 2000, accordingly draws upon the Model Law.

The implementation of this Act has kick started a new era of e-governance and will have a lot of impact on the way people do business in India and will also open up new opportunities for e-business, as people would be less apprehensive about the legal hassles and issues not under the jurisdiction of law, e.g., authenticity of digital documents, hacking, digital signatures, and so on.

Therefore, it is essential for us to understand the IT Act, 2000 offers and what its various perspectives are.

Highlights of the IT Act, 2000

For a basic understanding of the IT Act for the layman, the salient features of the Act and its relevant portions to e-business are stated as:

- Electronic contracts are legally valid—EDI accorded legal recognition.
- Legal recognition accorded to digital signatures.
- Digital signature to be effected by use of asymmetric crypto system and hash function.

- Security procedure for electronic records and digital signature.
- Appointment of Certifying Authorities (CAs) and Controller of Certifying Authorities (CCA) including recognition of foreign Certifying Authorities.
- Controller to be appointed, who will act as repository of all digital signature certificates.
- Certifying Authorities require to get license to issue digital signature certificates.
- Various types of computer crimes defined and stringent penalties provided under the Act.
- Appointment of Adjudicating Officer for holding inquiries under the Act.
- Establishment of Cyber Appellate Tribunal under the Act.
- Appeal from order of Adjudicating Officer to Cyber Appellate Tribunal and not to any Civil Court.
- Appeal from order of Cyber Appellate Tribunal to High Court.
- Act to apply for offenses or contraventions committed outside India.
- Network service providers not to be liable in certain cases.
- Power of Police officers and other officers to enter into any public place and search and arrest without warrant.
- Constitution of Cyber Regulations Advisory Committee to advice the Central Government and Controller.
- Amendments effected in:
  (a) Indian Penal Code
  (b) Indian Evidence Act
  (c) Banker's Books Evidence Act
  (d) Reserve Bank of India Act

Important Concepts Introduced In the IT Act, 2000

Some of the important concepts introduced in the IT Act, 2000 are:

- Electronic record
- Secure electronic record
- Digital signature
- Secure digital signature
- Certifying authority
- Digital signature certificate

The concept of electronic record, as envisaged by the Act has already been described. A secure electronic record has been defined in the Act as follows:

> *Where any security procedure has been applied to an electronic record at a specific point of time, then such record shall be deemed to be a secure electronic record from such point of time to the time of verification.*

The security procedures envisaged are not prescribed by the Act. The Act specifies that the central government shall prescribe the security procedure. Thus, in so far as the Act is concerned, the secure electronic record is a purely legal concept and not a technological one. The application of the prescribed procedure will create a presumption, in the eyes of the law, relating to the authenticity and integrity of the record. Therefore, not only must the security of the procedure be such that it indeed offers adequate security, but it must also be demonstrated that the correct procedure has in fact been applied.

The IT Act, 2000 prescribes that electronic records are to be authenticated by means of affixing a digital signature. This digital signature must be effected by the use of an asymmetric crypto system and hash function. In contrast, the European Electronic Signature Standardization Initiative (EESSI) is technology neutral in its prescription of how an electronic signature may be effected.

This point needs a little elaboration. Until fairly recently (about 1997) it was believed that the use of asymmetric crypto systems would be the foundation for all electronic authentication. However, there is an increasing awareness that other technologies, such as *biometrics,* also offer the promise of electronic authentication. Consequently, there is greater interest in technology-neutral legislation. This type of technology-neutral specification tends to be called *electronic signature* as opposed to digital signature, which is just one type of electronic signature, as the Act put it, is:

The concept of a secure digital signature, as the Act puts it, is:

> *If, by application of a security procedure agreed to by the parties concerned, it can be verified that a digital signature, at the time it was affixed, was*
>
> (a) *unique to the subscriber affixing it;*
>
> (b) *capable of identifying such a subscriber;*
>
> (c) *created in a manner or using a means under the exclusive control of the subscriber and is linked to the electronic record to which it relates in such a manner that if the electronic record was altered the digital signature would be invalidated, then such digital signature shall be deemed to be a secure digital signature.*

It can be seen that the concept of secure digital signature is a purely legal concept rather than a technical one. The parties concerned must agree on a security procedure, and once it is demonstrated that the security procedure was indeed applied, then the digital signature will be deemed secure, and all the legal presumptions that stem from this consideration, will then be applicable.

The technical requirements for effecting digital signatures by use of an asymmetric crypto system with hash function are a private key to effect a digital signature and a public key to verify such a signature. The private key must be kept secret, as its name implies. The public key must be made available to any individual that needs to verify a signature created with the private key. The Act stipulates that the association between a subscriber's name and his public key should be made available by a duly licensed certifying authority in the form of a *digital signature certificate.*

The Act provides for a Controller of Certifying Authorities to be appointed by the central government. The functions of the Controller include the licensing and regulation of operations of organizations that may act as certifying authorities.

A certifying authority provides a subscriber, for a fee, a digital signature certificate and a private key. The private key is known only to the subscriber. The certifying authority is obliged to:

1. Make use of hardware, software, and procedures that are secure from intrusion and misuse.
2. Provide a reasonable level of reliability in its services which are best suited to the performance of intended functions.
3. Adhere to security procedures to ensure that the secrecy and privacy of the digital signatures are assured.
4. Observe such other standards as may be specified by regulations.

The digital signature certificate of any subscriber is used by anyone who wishes to verify a digital signature purported to be affixed by that subscriber. Thus, the basic role of a certifying authority is to establish trust in the name—public key association that is contained in the digital signature certificate.

Positive Aspects for Corporate Sector

From the perspective of the corporate sector, the IT Act, 2000 and its provisions contain the following positive aspects:

1. The implications of these provisions for the corporate sector would be that e-mail will now be a valid and legal form of communication in our country, which can be duly produced and approved in the court of law.
2. Companies shall now be able to carry out electronic commerce using the legal infrastructure provided by the Act. Till now, the growth of e-commerce was impeded in our country basically because there was no legal infrastructure to regulate commercial transactions online.
3. Corporates will now be able to use digital signatures to carry out their transactions online. These digital signatures have been given legal validity and sanction in the Act.
4. The Act also throws open the doors for the entry of corporates in the business of being certifying authorities for issuing digital signatures certificates. The Act does not make any distinction between any legal entity for being appointed as a certifying authority so long as the norms stipulated by the government have been followed.
5. The Act also enables the companies to file any form, application or any other document with any office, authority, body or agency owned or controlled by the appropriate government in the electronic form as may be prescribed by the appropriate government.
6. Corporates are mandated by different laws of the country to keep and retain valuable and corporate information. The IT Act enables companies legally to retain the said information in the electronic form, if the:
   (a) information contained therein remains accessible so as to be usable for further reference,
   (b) electronic record is retained in the format in which it was originally generated, sent or received or in a format which can be demonstrated to represent accurately the information originally generated, sent or received,
   (c) details which will facilitate the identification of the origin, destination, date and time of dispatch or receipt of such electronic record are available in the electronic record.

7. The IT Act also addresses the important issues of security which are so critical to the success of electronic transactions. The Act has also given a legal definition to the concept of secure digital signatures which would be required to have been passed through a system of a security procedure, as stipulated by the government at a later date. In the times to come, secure digital signatures shall play a big role in the New Economy particularly from the perspective of the corporate sector as it will enable a more secure transaction online.
8. IT Act has defined various cyber crimes and has declared them penal offences punishable with imprisonment and fine. These include hacking and damage to computer source code. Often, corporates face hacking into their systems and information. Till date, the corporates were in a helpless condition as there was no legal redress to such issues, but the IT Act changes the scene altogether.

However, despite the overwhelming positive features of the IT Act, 2000 for the corporate sector, some more steps need to be enacted by the government in related areas.

Unresolved Issues in IT Act, 2000

The IT Act, 2000 does not cover the following legal issues:

- Taxation Issues that arise out of e-commerce, Internet and m-commerce, and transactions.
- Intellectual Property Rights such as Digital Copyright Issues, Trade Marks, and Patents.
- Domain Name Registration Policy, Domain Name Disputes, and Cybersquatting.
- Privacy and Data Protection Issues.
- Rights to e-consumers, i.e. no provision for cover under COPRA.

IT (Amended) Act, 2008

The IT (Amendment) Bill, 2006, was introduced in the Lok Sabha (Lower House of the Parliament) on December 15, 2006. It was passed in 2008. According to the 'Statement of Objects and Reasons' of the bill, the purpose of the legislation was (1) harmonization of electronic communication and services with the Information Technology Act (2) protection of Critical Information Infrastructure (3) to suggest penal provisions in the IT Act, Indian Penal Code, Indian Evidence Act, and the Code of Criminal Procedure to prevent the publication of sexually explicit material, video voyeurism, breach of confidentiality and leakage of data by intermediaries, e-commerce fraud like personation (phishing), identity theft, and transmission of offensive materials through communication services. The bill also seeks to enable the government to authorize service providers to collect service charges from customers as specified by the government.

Issue of Taxing Electronic Commerce

In just a decade of astounding growth, the Internet has reached a critical mass that is now attracting millions of consumers, and billions of their dollars, into a gigantic, ever-expanding virtual shopping mall. Tax systems, and particularly international taxation arrangements, can struggle to keep pace with globalization and market liberalization. Most of today's tax arrangements were developed in an era when tax authorities could rely upon exchange controls, highly regulated capital markets and technological constraints to protect them from the negative fiscal effects of global activities. These barriers to cross-border activities protected tax authorities from the full implications of the interaction between national tax systems. While corporations globalized, tax authorities remained constrained by national frontiers.

The existence of 193 different member states to the United Nations Organization (as of January, 20, 2015), creates a significant obstacle for compliance. The Internet is inherently susceptible to multiple and discriminatory taxation in a way that commerce conducted in more traditional ways is not. Double taxation would be inevitable because the borderless nature of the Internet makes taxation very tricky.

Since, Internet commerce is still quite new, it can be quite difficult to figure out what the basic business model will look like in a few years. How can we know how to tax it? There are possibly many adverse unintended and unanticipated consequences lurking in the future.

How would the taxes be collected? One of the main benefits of Web-based businesses is that the availability to reach such a large potential universe of customers cheaply provides an opportunity for small one- and two-person companies to thrive without a tremendous amount of start-up capital. The cost of compliance and tax collection alone for these small businesses could be enough of a deterrent to keep them from participating in the marketplace. Clearly, compelling retailers to collect tax under existing jurisdictional regimes would place a significant burden on merchants; and such a burden would likely not be uniformly felt across all the retailers.

Another major enforcement issue is identifying the state, country or countries that have tax jurisdiction over income generated by electronic transactions. Electronic commerce permits a foreign person to engage in multiple business transactions with customers in several countries without ever having to enter one of them. This is important; since the supplier has no presence at all in the jurisdiction of the customer. Self-assessment by individuals is never a great way to secure this sort of tax—but looking to the supplier to collect the tax, as is the norm for VAT type taxes, is not so easy either because the supplier is in another country.

Furthermore, is it desirable to have a taxation scheme that, to be effectively implemented would systematically undermine our privacy by amassing a comprehensive database on our online purchases so that some government agency can be certain that we paid our relevant taxes?

Webservers are computer systems attached to the Internet, which host many websites and the databases required for their effective functioning. These servers may exist in any place or country, without affecting the operation and effectiveness of the websites they may be hosting. In order to be able to tax the commerce generated on the websites hosted on its webservers, hosting companies must have a "permanent establishment" (the rule which determines the right of a state to tax the profits on an enterprise of another state) status. From a business point of view, websites, which comprise of databases and software do not constitute "real property" and hence, do not constitute permanent establishments on their own.

For an Internet-based business to be liable for taxes, it must either posses ownership or lease of the webserver containing its website. However, the ability to quickly transfer a website and its database to another webserver in another country does not allow for governments to easily track and force Internet businesses to pay most of their taxes.

Still, conclusions can be drawn taking into account of the "Permanent Establishment" criteria and the nature of services provided over the Internet by on-line companies. These are:

1. Irrespective of their geographical location, computers utilized for introducing and promoting goods and services cannot constitute a 'Permanent Establishment' for a company.
2. There is much debate as to whether computers that collect user data and credit card details, in addition to promoting goods and services, can constitute a 'Permanent Establishment' for an on-line company.
3. However, the possession of a computer that introduces and promotes digital goods that can be delivered on-line following collection of user and credit card details should constitute a 'Permanent Establishment' for an on-line company, in the country where that computer is located.

Basic Principles of Taxing e-Commerce

Among the many bodies exploring Internet taxation and other issues are OECD (Organisation for Economic Co-operation and Development). Technical Advisory Group on Monitoring the Application of Existing Treaty Norms for Taxing Business Profits, set up by the Committee on Fiscal Affairs in January 1999 with the general mandate to "examine how the current treaty rules for the taxation of business profits apply in the context of electronic commerce and examine proposals for alternative rules", the U.S. 'Advisory Commission on E-Commerce', established in 1998 under the Internet Tax Freedom Act, and the WTO, which has been carrying out a work programme in accordance with the 'Declaration on Global Electronic Commerce', adopted in 1998. Although, differences among these bodies in approaching e-commerce taxation still prevail, convergences on some basic ideas do exist, namely;

- the non-discriminatory treatment of e-commerce;
- the application of existing rules and concepts;
- the importance of a fair sharing of the tax base internationally; and
- a commitment to pursuing these ends through intensified dialogue with businesses and all international actors.

Jurisdiction on the Internet

The tasks of defining, establishing, and asserting jurisdiction are much more difficult on the Internet than they are in the physical world, mainly because traditional geographic boundaries do not exist. For example, a Chinese company that engages in electronic commerce could have a website that is entirely in English and a URL that ends in ".com," thus not indicating to customers that it is a Chinese firm. The server that hosts this company's Web page could be in Canada, and the people who maintain the website might work from their homes in Australia. If a Mexican citizen buys a product from the Chinese firm and is unhappy with the goods received, that person might want to file a lawsuit against the seller firm. However, the world's physical border-based systems of law and jurisdiction do not help this Mexican citizen determine where to file the lawsuit. The Internet does not provide anything like the obvious international boundary lines in the physical world. Governments that want to enforce laws regarding business conduct on the Internet must establish jurisdiction over that conduct. A contract is a promise or set of promises between two or more legal entities—people or corporations—that provides for an exchange of value (goods, services, or money) between or among them. If either party to a contract does not comply with the terms of the contract, the other party can sue for failure to comply, which is called *breach of contract*. Persons and corporations that engage in business are also expected to exercise due care and not violate laws that prohibit specific actions (such as trespassing, libel, or professional malpractice). A tort is an intentional or negligent action (other than breach of contract) taken by a legal entity that causes harm to another legal entity. People or corporations that wish to enforce their rights based on either contract or tort law must file their claims in courts with jurisdiction to hear their cases. A court has sufficient jurisdiction to hear a matter if it has both subject-matter jurisdiction and personal jurisdiction.

The difficulties of operating in multiple countries are faced by many large companies that do business online. For example, eBay, which had struggled to compete in China for many years, finally closed its operations in the country in 2006. eBay entered China in 2003 with a $30 million investment. In subsequent years, it poured another $250 million into acquisitions and advertising in China. But many others noted that the Chinese government made it difficult for eBay to operate in China by passing laws that favored companies that were majority-owned by Chinese entities and that blocked eBay's PayPal unit from operating in China. Because eBay was a foreign company, it was at a considerable disadvantage regarding government regulation and many have argued that this disadvantage was a larger factor in its failure than cultural issues.

Requirements for Creating a Valid e-Commerce Contracts

In general, contracts are valid even if they are not in writing or signed. However, certain categories of contracts are not enforceable unless the terms are put into writing and signed by both parties. In 1677, the British Parliament enacted a law that specified the types of contracts that had to be in writing and signed. Most courts will hold that a writing exists when the terms of a contract have been reduced to some tangible form. An early court decision in the 1800s held that a telegraph transmission was a writing. Later, courts have held that tape recordings of spoken words, computer files on disks, and faxes are writings. Thus, the parties to an electronic commerce contract should find it relatively easy to satisfy the writing requirement. Courts have been similarly generous in determining what constitutes a signature. A signature is any symbol executed or adopted for the purpose of authenticating a writing. Courts have held names on telegrams, telexes, faxes, and Western Union Mailgrams to be signatures. Even typed names or names printed as part of a letterhead have served as signatures. It is reasonable to assume that a symbol or code included in an electronic file would constitute a signature.

A contract is formed when an offer is accepted for consideration. Problems can arise when the acceptance is issued by an imposter or someone who does not have the authority to bind the company to a contract. In electronic commerce, the online nature of acceptances can make it relatively easy for identity forgers to pose as others. Fortunately, the Internet technology that makes forged identities so easy to create also provides the means to avoid being deceived by a forged identity. If the contract is for any significant amount, the parties should require each other to use digital signatures to avoid identity problems. In general, courts will not hold a person or corporation whose identity has been forged to the terms of the contract; however, if negligence on the part of the person or corporation contributed to the forgery, a court may hold the negligent party to the terms of the contract. For example, if a company was careless about protecting passwords and allowed an imposter to enter the company's system and accept an offer, the court might hold that the company is responsible for fulfilling the terms of that contract.

Determining whether an individual has the authority to commit a company to an online contract is a greater problem than forged identities in electronic commerce. This issue, called *authority to bind*, can arise when an employee of a company accepts a contract and the company later asserts that the employee did not have authority to do so. For large transactions in the physical world, businesses check public information on file with the state of incorporation, or ask for copies of corporate certificates or resolutions, to establish the authority of persons to make contracts for their employers. These methods are available to parties engaged in online transactions; however, they can be time consuming and awkward.

Firms conducting international electronic commerce do not need to worry about the signed writing requirement in most cases. The main treaty that governs international sales of goods, Article 11 of the United Nations Convention on Contracts for the International Sale of Goods (CISG), requires neither a writing nor a signature to create a legally binding acceptance.

Transactions performed via the internet and are only applicable in instances where a person has communicated their consent, through either an expressed or implied contractual agreement. But how are electronic contracts formed? Are the traditional contractual elements still applicable in e-commerce transactions?

It's important to be aware, that just because a transaction has been performed online, still does not negate the fact that all of the required elements of contract law are still applicable, such as:

- offer and acceptance,
- consideration and,
- capacity to enter into a contract.

Online transactions usually fall into three types of e-commerce contracts, and they are:

- click-through
- shrink-wrap, or,
- browse-wrap agreements.

Each form of e-commerce contract requires that a customer undergo different steps in order to validate a transaction. However, it is perhaps the click-through version of the electronic contract which would be most familiar to the online shoppers.

The click-through contract generally requires a person to scroll through the terms and conditions of the agreement, and to then validate their acceptance of their wish to be bound by the enforceable contract, by clicking on a button or ticking a box at the end of the agreement.

If a small business owner wishes to create an enforceable contract, there are certain general requirements which must be present in creating an agreement with a customer:

- unambiguous notice to the customer that the online transaction is governed by the terms of contract law,
- an opportunity for the customer to review the terms and conditions of the agreement before being bound by the contract, and
- a clear statement of what constitutes acceptance of the agreement.

When establishing the validity of a transaction performed online, a requirement of either producing a document or record in writing, or recording or retaining of all the necessary information in electronic form, are the two ways in which a documentary record can be established that a transaction has taken place between the consumer and the business.

Click-Wrap and Web-Wrap Agreements

A **click-wrap** agreement (also known as a *click-through agreement* or *click-wrap license*) is a common type of agreement often used in connection with software licenses. Such forms of agreement are mostly found on the Internet, as part of the installation process of many software packages, or in other circumstances where agreement is sought using electronic media. The name "click-wrap" came from the use of "shrink-wrap contracts" commonly used in boxed software purchases, which "contain a notice that by tearing open the shrink-wrap, the user assents to the software terms enclosed within".

The content and form of click-wrap agreements vary widely. Most click-wrap agreements require the end-user to manifest his or her assent by clicking an "ok" or "agree" button on a dialog box or pop-up window. A user indicates rejection by clicking cancel or closing the window. Upon rejection, the user cannot use or purchase the product or service. Classically, such a take-it-or-leave-it contract was described as a "contract of adhesion, which is a contract that lacks bargaining power, forcing one party to be favoured over the other".

The terms of service or license may not always appear on the same Webpage or window, but are always available before acceptance through a hyperlink embedded in the product's Webpage or through a pop-up screen prior to installation. The purchaser must be put on notice that certain terms of service may apply in order to be deemed to have accepted the terms of service. If the terms of service are not visible and/or accessible, courts have found fault with the notice requirement and as such, the purchaser may not be bound to the terms of the agreement. Many websites frequently contain clauses that impede consumer rights in substantial and often unexpected ways if proper analysis is done.

A **Web-wrap** agreement is an agreement to abide by the terms of a license agreement signified by downloading the software, data or content to which the license agreement applies. Such agreements generally do not provide for any means by which the user can acknowledge acceptance of the terms of the agreement, separate from the act of downloading itself.

The validity and enforceability of Web-Wrap Agreements, which are also known as *on-line Click-Wrap Agreements*, is one of a host of new legal issues that has arisen as a result of the growth in the area of Electronic Commerce. An important related question is whether there is a need for legislation to regulate the use of Web-Wrap Agreements in Canada.

A Web-Wrap Agreement sets forth contractual terms in an on-line environment and is a form of Standard Form Agreement since one party drafts the terms of the agreement without consultation or negotiation of such terms with the other party or parties. A Web-Wrap Agreement usually appears as a dialogue box on a customer's screen when the customer attempts to download software or order goods or services on-line. The dialogue box contains the terms and conditions of the license or sale which the consumer is instructed to review before assenting thereto by clicking a button at the bottom of the dialogue box.

The central legal issues with respect to Web-Wrap Agreements are: (i) whether they are valid contracts and, if so, (ii) whether they are, in all instances, enforceable.

Web-Wrap Agreements are most often compared to Shrink-Wrap Agreements since the requirement of clicking on the "I accept" or "I confirm" button(s) in a Web-Wrap Agreement scenario is similar to the requirement in a Shrink-Wrap Agreement that the customer break the seal to the envelope containing the software media. In both cases, the customer is required to perform a physical act to indicate assent to the contractual terms. In fact, it has become common practice for software vendors to present a licensee with, in addition to a Shrink-Wrap Agreement, a Click-Wrap Agreement prior to the launch of the software for the first time. There is, however, a notable distinction between Web-Wrap Agreements and Shrink-Wrap Agreements, that the latter tend to be used exclusively in the licensing of software, while the former are also used for other transactions such as the purchase of goods and services.

Assuming that a Web-Wrap Agreement is valid, it may nevertheless be unenforceable if the terms of a contract are unfair and give an undue advantage to the drafting party. While any form of agreement is subject to the same qualification, the fact that there is no opportunity for negotiation of the terms of the offer makes this concern more acute in the case of all Standard Form Agreements including Web-Wrap Agreements.

Implied Warranties and Warranty Disclaimers on the Web

To fulfil the requirements needed to create enforceable, legally binding contracts on the Web is easy for most companies. One area that should be noted is the issue of warranties.

All contracts for the sale of goods includes implied warranties. An implied warranty is a promise to which the seller can be held even though the seller did not make an explicit statement of that promise. The law establishes these basic elements of a transaction in any contract to sell goods or services. For example, a seller is deemed to implicitly warrant that the goods it offers for sale are fit for the purposes for which they are normally used. If the seller knows specific information about the buyer's requirements, acceptance of an offer from that buyer may result in an additional implied warranty of fitness, which suggests that the goods are suitable for the specific uses of that buyer. Sellers can also create explicit warranties by providing a specific description of the additional warranty terms. It is also possible for a seller to create explicit warranties, often unintentionally, by making general statements in brochures or other advertising materials about product performance or suitability for particular tasks. Sellers can bypass some implied warranty liability by making an explicit warranty disclaimer. A warranty disclaimer is a statement declaring that the seller will not honour some or all implied warranties. Any warranty disclaimer must be conspicuously made in writing, which means it must be easily noticed in the body of the written agreement. On a Web page, sellers can meet this requirement by putting the warranty disclaimer in larger type, a bold font, or a contrasting colour. To be legally effective, the warranty disclaimer must be stated obviously and must be easy for a buyer to find on the Web site.

Realizing that uniformity and certainty would make interstate transactions easier and more profitable, the Uniform Commercial Code (U.C.C.) was drafted in the U.S.A.

Merchantability implies that the goods must be at least of average quality, properly packaged and labelled, and fit for the ordinary purposes they are intended to serve. For example, a mobile would have to be at least of average quality as compared to other mobiles in the same price range, it must function. The application of the implied warranty of merchantability is limited to a seller of "goods of that kind," meaning the kind of goods the seller usually sells in the marketplace. A seller does not make an implied warranty of merchantability when he sells goods of a kind that he does not normally sell. For example, a mobile store selling mobiles and accessories impliedly warrants that the mobiles and accessories are merchantable because mobiles and accessories are the kind of goods a mobile store typically sells. On the other hand, if the store sells to the store next door an extra display case it no longer needs, the display case is not subject to an implied warranty of merchantability because mobiles and accessories stores generally do not sell display cases. Of course, if the seller makes an express warranty regarding the display case, it will be held to any such warranty, but none will be implied unless the goods being sold are goods of a kind the seller normally sells.

The implied warranty of fitness for a particular purpose is applicable if the seller knows or has reason to know that the buyer will be using the goods he is buying for the same purpose. If the seller knows the purpose for which the goods are to be used, the seller impliedly warrants that the goods being sold are suitable for that specific purpose. For example, a salesman selling a car may sell a car that is perfectly suitable for everyday driving, and therefore is merchantable. But if the salesman knows the buyer wants to use the car as a race car, the salesman also impliedly warrants that the car is suitable to use for racing.

Buyers typically rely on the seller's skill and expertise to help them find the specific goods that meet their specific need. The rationale behind the implied warranty of fitness for a particular purpose is that a buyer who goes to an appliance store may know he wants a washing machine, but he relies on the appliance salesman to find the specific washing machine that fits his house, is big enough for his family, and meets any other specific requirements he might have. Accordingly, it is unfair for a seller to sell something they know will not do the job and later tell the buyer it is not his or her fault if it did not work.

Warranties typically become an issue when a buyer is dissatisfied, a prudent seller tries to limit the scope of the warranties he makes before a problem arises. The U.C.C. specifically allows sellers to disclaim both express and implied warranties on goods they sell, within certain limits. Interestingly, the U.C.C. does not provide many specific rules regarding how warranties are disclaimed.

Terms of Service Agreements

Many websites have stated rules that site visitors must follow, although most visitors are not aware of these rules. If you examine the home page of a website, you will often find a link to a page titled "Terms of Service," "Conditions of Use," "User Agreement," or something similar.

If you follow that link, you find a page full of detailed rules and regulations, most of which are intended to limit the website owner's liability for what you might do with information you obtain from the site. These contracts are often called *Terms of Service* (ToS) agreements even when they appear under a different title. In most cases, a site visitor is held to the terms of service even if that visitor has not read the text or clicked a button to indicate agreement with the terms. The visitor is bound to the agreement by simply using the site, which is an example of the Web-wrap (or browser-wrap) acceptance.

Use and Protection of Intellectual Property (IP) in Online Business

Intellectual Property (IP) is a legal term that refers to industrial property and to **copyright and related rights**. Industrial property comprises the protection of **patents, trademarks, industrial designs,** and **geographical indications**. It also includes the protection of **utility models, trade dress** and **layout-designs or topographies of integrated circuits**, where such protection exists, and **protection against unfair competition including/or protection of undisclosed information/trade secrets**. IP is really a type of property or **asset**, just as valuable (or more valuable) than physical or real property, even though it may be intangible, like knowledge. The value of IP assets relative to physical assets has increased because of the importance of technology and creative works in the modern economy. IP consists of new ideas, original expressions, distinctive names, and appearance that make products unique and valuable. IP is often traded (or "**licensed**") in its own right without trading in the value of an underlying product or service, by means of patent or other IP licenses from a rights owner to another.

Intellectual property law protects against disclosure of trade secrets and, as a result, against unfair competition. That makes intellectual property an asset that is perhaps worth more than any tangible asset. This can be seen most clearly in relation to technology and the digital economy.

Without intellectual property practices and laws, hard work is stolen and spread around the globe without paying the creator for their labour. Who, then, wants to create new works? Technical security is necessary to deter the less proficient thief and intellectual property laws are required to deal with the more serious criminal.

Violating Someone else's Intellectual Property

Many e-commerce Website contains product descriptions and images. Do they have the legal right to publish those descriptions and images? What about all those logos, videos, photos, clip art, icons, sound effects, and background music? They sure make the site more engaging. But, once again, do they have the right to be using them?

E-commerce, more than other business systems, often involves selling products and services that are based on IP and its licensing. Music, pictures, photos, software, designs, training modules, systems, etc. can all be traded through e-commerce, in which case, IP is the main component of value in the transaction. IP is important because the things of value that are traded on the Internet must be protected, using technological security systems and IP laws, or else they can be stolen or pirated and whole businesses can be destroyed.

Also, IP is involved in making e-commerce work. The systems that allow the Internet to function—software, networks, designs, chips, routers and switches, the user interface, and so on—are forms of IP and often protected by IP rights. Trademarks are an essential part of e-commerce business, as branding, customer recognition and goodwill, essential elements of Web-based business, are protected by trademarks and unfair competition law.

E-commerce businesses and internet related businesses are based on product or patent licensing. This is because so many different technologies are required to create a product that companies often outsource the development of some component of products, or share technologies through licensing arrangements. If every company had to develop and produce all technological aspects of every product independently, development of high technology products would be impossible. The economics of e-commerce depends on companies working together to share, through licensing, the opportunities and risks of business. Many of these companies are SMEs.

Finally, e-commerce-based businesses usually hold a great deal of their value in IP; so the valuation of your e-commerce business will be affected by whether you have protected your IP. Many e-commerce companies, like other technology companies, have **patent portfolios** and trademarks that **enhance the value of their business**.

IP Issues When You Design and Build Your Web Site

One of the basic elements of e-commerce business is the design and function of the company's website. In designing and building your web site, the first thing to be aware of is whether you own the website presentation and content and every aspect of IP in it. If you are using a consultant or company to design your website, check out the provisions in the agreement concerning ownership and IP rights. Who owns the website design and text? Check out what obligations the company has to make sure that it doesn't use any IP that belongs to a third party in the course of its work.

If you are using a database, e-commerce system, or search engine or other technical Internet tools licensed to you by another company, check the terms in the license agreement to see who owns the system. Make sure that you do have a written agreement, and get it checked over by a lawyer before you sign it and before any design, custom work or installation of the site begins.

You will need written permission (also referred to as a license, a consent, or an agreement) to use any photos, videos, music, voices, art work, or software, etc. that belong to someone else. Just because you get material on the Internet does not mean that it is in the public domain. You may have to pay for permission to use these materials. In many countries, you will need to communicate with a collecting society or association of artists in order to get permission.

You will need to make sure that, if your country's law requires it, that you have permission to show trademarks owned by other companies that you refer to on your website and that you recognize them. Do not distribute or download any content or music on your website that does not belong to you unless you have obtained written permission from the owner to distribute it on the Internet. Be careful in linking to other websites. Links are a great e-commerce tool, and a useful service to your customers, but in many countries there is no clear law on when and how you can use links. The most careful practice is to seek and obtain permission from the other site before putting in the link.

Framing is a practice that is more controversial that linking. This means including large parts of another Web site in yours in a way that makes it look as though it is part of your Web site. Always get written permission before doing this.

E-commerce and Patents

A patent is an exclusive right granted for an invention by a government. The invention may be a product or a process that provides a new way of doing something, or offers a new technical solution to a problem. There are various kinds of patents. The most well-known type is the utility patent, which protects inventions. Design patents protect new, original and ornamental designs of articles of manufacture. Some countries also have plant patents, which are granted to anyone who invents or discovers and asexually reproduces any distinct and new variety of plants. Utility patent is the most popular patent.

Utility patents seek to protect new machines, systems, and other useful inventions. A utility patent is among the most valuable forms of intellectual property. A utility patent gives a 20-year right to stop anyone from copying the invention. This is not necessarily the same as having a monopoly on practicing the invention. There may be patents held by others that also cover some aspect of the invention. For example, the necessary components to build a car are an engine, a transmission and wheels. Each of these could be protected by one or more patents held by different entities or persons. This would mean that none of them could build a car without the permission of the others. However, any of them could stop an outsider from building a car.

Creations that can be copyrighted include virtually all forms of artistic or intellectual expression—books, music, artworks, recordings (audio and video), architectural drawings, choreographic works, product packaging, and computer software. In the United States, works created after 1977 are protected for the life of the author plus 70 years. Works copyrighted by corporations or not-for-profit organizations are protected for 95 years from the date of publication or 120 years from the date of creation, whichever is earlier.

The original purpose of the patent system was to encourage the development of new inventions, and to encourage the disclosure of those new inventions. Inventors are often hesitant to reveal the details of their invention fearing that someone else might copy it. This forces them to keep their inventions secret, which does not contribute to innovation.

This fear can be overcome by a government-granted temporary monopoly on the commercial use of their invention. This acts as an incentive to disclose the details of the invention. After the monopoly period (usually 20 years) expires, everyone else is free to practice the invention. And because of the disclosure made by the inventor, it is very easy to use the invention.

This 20-year monopoly also gives the inventor a chance to recover his investments for the invention. He could use the patent to monopolize the market with no fear of competitors by enforcing his patent. He could also make a profit. Moreover, he could also demand money from others in return for a license to practice the invention. The licensing income then provides extra income. Licensing a patent can be very lucrative business.

Today, there are an increasing number of software and business methods which are protected by patents in the United States[1]. Under the European Patent Convention and the patent laws of a number of countries members of the European Patent Organization, computer programs and business methods *as such* are still expressly excluded from patent protection. In practice, however, the approach has changed in recent years as the result of long-lasting intensive and controversial discussions and many decisions. The vast majority of applications are today considered not to claim abstract programs or business methods but to describe technical means like, for example, computer networks, for carrying out these programs or methods. In order to be inventive, the programs or methods have to overcome a technical problem in a non-obvious way; in other words, it is not the commercial ingenuity which makes them patentable. In a number of other countries, computer programs and business methods are not yet patentable.

1. http://www.uspto.gov/Web/menu/pbmethod

Some examples of business methods are: patents on using a single click to order goods in an on-line transaction, on an on-line system of accounting, and on-line rewards incentive system. In most countries, patents are available for a wide range of inventions. In e-commerce business, it is prudent to get legal advice about whether any new business methods developed by your company may be patentable.

IP Issues in the Distribution of Content on the Internet

In recent years, there has been much publicity about the unlawful distribution of intellectual property-protected music, films, art, photos, scripts, and software ("content") on the Internet. These unauthorized downloads often violate national laws of copyright. Because of the ease with which digital files can be downloaded, unauthorized copying of content has been a major problem causing the loss of millions of dollars in revenue for the owners of these rights.

As an e-commerce business, it is important to protect your IP rights on the Internet. This can be done in a number of ways. Always clearly identify your content, either with a copyright notice or some other indication of ownership. You may wish to simply tell users what they can and cannot do with your content. Never distribute or permit downloads of third party content that does not belong to your company and put in place programs to make sure that your employees understand your company policies in this regard.

The Napster case in the United States put an international spotlight on unauthorized downloading of music files. The case, which resulted in the court issuing a permanent injunction preventing Napster from operating its file sharing system, was a "contributory infringement" case because the claim was that Napster facilitated illegal copying by users of the system, not that Napster copied the files itself. Other cases will continue to test the law in this area, and there may be different issues and different results in different jurisdictions, but the lesson of Napster is that it is important for an e-commerce company to make sure it has a clear policy against unauthorized copying of files, or any actions that encourage or facilitate such copying.

It is also important for e-commerce companies to make sure that employees do not gain access to or keep in their possession or on their systems any unauthorized copies of software or other content. Your company should have a system of prevention, education and monitoring to make sure that employees are not knowingly or unknowingly using illegal copies of software.

All employees should know about the company's policies against misuse of IP, and senior management should be responsible for reviewing company business practices on a regular basis to make sure that the policy is being followed. It is wise to assess situations in which a policy violation is found, to see if disciplinary action should be taken. Increasingly, some companies are utilizing technical means to protect content on the Internet by **watermarking, encrypting** or otherwise creating identification and tracking systems. **Electronic Copyright Management Systems** are being proposed by business consortia and individual companies who see these systems as a way to use technical means to control use of content.

Trademark Issues

A **trademark** is a distinctive insignia, device, motto, phrase or symbol that a company affixes to the goods it produces for identification purposes. It exclusively identifies a product as belonging to a specific company and recognizes the company's ownership of the brand. The name (or a part of that name) that a business uses to identify itself is called a **trade name**. Trade names are not protected by trademark laws unless the business name is the same as the product (or service) name. They are protected, however, under common law. **Common law** is the part of British and U.S. law established by the history of court decisions that has accumulated over many years. The other main part of British and U.S. law, called **statutory law**, arises when elected legislative bodies pass laws, which are also called *statutes*.

The owners of registered trademarks have often invested a considerable amount of money in the development and promotion of their trademarks. Web site designers must be very careful not to use any trademarked name, logo, or other identifying mark without the express permission of the trademark owner.

Domain Names

Considerable controversy has arisen about intellectual property rights and Internet domain names. Cybersquatting is the misuse of registering a domain name that is the trademark of another person or company in the hopes that the owner will pay huge amounts of money to acquire the URL. Added to it, successful cybersquatters can attract many visitors and, thereby charge high advertising rates.

Registering a generic name such as Wine.com is not cybersquatting. Registering a generic name is speculation that the name might one day become valuable and is completely legal. Disputes that arise when one person has registered a domain name that is an existing trademark or company name are settled by the World Intellectual Property Organization (WIPO). WIPO began settling domain name disputes in 1999 under its Uniform Domain Name Dispute Resolution Policy (UDRP).

The problems of international jurisdiction made enforcement by the courts of individual countries cumbersome and ineffective. As an international organization, WIPO can transcend borders and provide rulings that will be effective in a global online business environment.

Defamation

The crux of a defamation claim is falsity. It is a legal claim involving injury to one's reputation caused by a false statement of fact and includes both libel and slander. A defamatory statement injures the reputation of a product or service instead of a person, it is called *product disparagement*. In some cases, difference between justifiable criticism and defamation can be hard to determine, and so commercial websites should consider the specific laws in their jurisdiction before making negative, evaluative statements about other persons or products.

Web site designers should be especially careful to avoid potential defamation liability by altering a photo or image of a person in a way that depicts the person unfavorably. In most cases, a person must establish that the defamatory statement caused injury. However, most states recognize a legal cause of action, called *per se defamation*, in which a court deems some types of statements to be so negative that injury is assumed. For example, the court will hold inaccurate statements alleging conduct potentially injurious to a person's business, trade, profession, or office as defamatory per se—the complaining party need not prove injury to recover damages. Thus, online statements about competitors should always be carefully reviewed before posting to determine whether they contain any elements of defamation.

Advertising Regulation

In the last few years advertising has become big business because of the proliferation of TV and social media. The advertising business is growing fast. There are several legislations that control the content of advertising. Some of the principal legislations are:

1. Cable Television Networks (Regulation) Act, 1955[2]
2. Press Council of India Act, 1978[3]
3. Cable Television Networks (Amendment) Rules, 2006[4]

There are important legal provisions that regulate advertising. In 1985, the Advertising Standards Council of India (ASCI), a non-statutory tribunal, was established that created a self-regulatory mechanism of ensuring ethical advertising practices. ASCI is a voluntary self-regulation council. The members comprise Advertiser's, Media, Advertising Agencies and other Professional/Ancillary services connected with advertising practice. ASCI entertained and disposed of complaints based on its Code of Advertising Practice (ASCI Code). This Code applies to advertisements read, heard or viewed in India even if they originate or are published abroad so long as they are directed to consumers in India or are exposed to significant number of consumers in India.

In the United States, advertising is regulated primarily by the Federal Trade Commission (FTC). The FTC publishes regulations and investigates claims of false advertising. Its Web site includes a number of information releases that are useful to businesses and consumers. The FTC provides policy statements that can be helpful guides for designers creating electronic commerce Web sites. These policies include information on what is permitted in advertisements and cover specific areas such as these:

- Bait advertising
- Consumer lending and leasing
- Endorsements and testimonials
- Energy consumption statements for home appliances
- Guarantees and warranties
- Prices

2. www.trai.gov.in › Acts & Policies
3. www.presscouncil.nic.in/OldWebsite/act.htm
4. india.gov.in/cable-television-networks-amendment-rules-2006?page=2

Online Crime, Terrorism and Warfare

Internet crime is any illegal online activity committed on the Internet, through the Internet or using the Internet. The Internet crime phenomenon encompasses multiple global levels of legislation. In the continuously changing IT field, security experts are committed to combating Internet crime through preventative technologies, such as intrusion detection networks and packet sniffers.

Because Internet crimes usually engage people from various geographic areas, finding and penalizing guilty participants is complicated.

Types of Internet crime include:

- Cyberbullying and harassment
- Financial extortion
- Internet bomb threats
- Classified global security data theft
- Password trafficking
- Enterprise trade secret theft
- Personally data hacking
- Copyright violations, such as software piracy
- Counterfeit trademarks
- Illegal weapon trafficking
- Online child pornography
- Credit card theft and fraud
- Email phishing
- Domain name hijacking
- Virus spreading

The Internet has opened up new channels for people to connect with each other across the globe and get to know each other better. It has also opened doors for businesses to reach new markets and create opportunities for economic growth. On the other hand, some people have found it as a means for perpetrating crimes, conducting terrorism, and even waging war.

Crime on the Web includes theft, stalking, distribution of pornography, and gambling. Other crimes, such as commandeering one computer to launch attacks on other computers, are new. Law enforcement agencies have difficulty combating many types of online crimes. The first obstacle they face is the issue of jurisdiction.

Cyber Terrorism

In the summer of 1999, hackers thought to be working for Russian intelligence were found to have broken into the systems of the Pentagon. It is said that several nations have developed cyber-warfare capabilities. Among the trends noted recently by computer security officials have been an illegal trade in ageing Cray super-computers which are ideal for cracking complex encrypted passwords used to guard major installations and companies. In the hands of a terrorist organisation, such computers could substantially assist a cyber attack on a country or company.

E-commerce Taxation Norms in Different Countries

E-commerce Law of India—GST

Goods and Services Tax (GST) is a new legislation that came into effect on 1st July 2017. It has replaced many Indirect taxes in India. GST is a comprehensive, multi-stage, destination-based tax on value addition. It has very clear rules and regulations for specific segments, which make it more powerful and applicable, specifically in the field of e-commerce.

E-commerce takes place electronically over the Internet. E-commerce has been flourishing during the last decade. Till recently, there were no specifically dedicated laws to govern the taxation of these online transactions in India. Whereas under the GST regime, this problem has been solved. The new laws encompass all e-commerce transactions. The cascading effect has been removed such as double taxation, tax on tax, etc. It has expanded the horizon of e-commerce operators. In simple language, e-commerce has become easier because of GST.

In the previous tax system, it was complicated to sell products across different state boundaries. Every time you sold something, you had to deal with a variety of different taxes and the complicated paperwork that went with them. For small businesses that did not have the budget to pay a tax professional, the possibility of extra sales was simply not worth the hassle. That limited the ability to expand their business. The new tax system has eliminated all of the confusing interstate taxes and replaced them with a single tax. With GST, you can sell to customers in your own state and in other states, all without worrying about multiple taxes. As a result, you have the opportunity to sell products to customers across India or around the world. It also gives you the chance to compete with big corporations.

GST is a destination-based tax, i.e., the goods/services will be taxed at the place where they are consumed/used and not at the origin. So, the state where they are consumed will have the right to collect GST. This makes the concept of the place of supply crucial under GST as all the provisions of GST revolves around it.

Place of supply of goods under GST defines whether the transaction is counted as intra-state or inter-state, and accordingly levy of SGST, CGST and IGST is determined. CGST is a tax levied on intra-state supplies of both goods and services by the Central Government and is governed by the CGST Act. SGST is also levied on the same intra-state supply, but is governed by the State Government. IGST is a tax levied on all inter-state supplies of goods and/or services and is governed by the IGST Act. IGST is applicable on any supply of goods and/or services in both cases of import into India and export from India.

Wrong determination of place of supply results in tax collection by the wrong state. For example, inter-state supply is wrongly treated as intra-state supply and CGST and SGST filled instead of IGST. The only option is to pay IGST separately and claim a refund of CGST and SGST.

GST depends on the type of online business you run. There are two main types of online businesses.

The first uses a direct-sales method, where you buy or make products and sell them to customers through your website. If that is how you operate, you can simply follow standard GST filing rules.

The second type of online business is an e-commerce aggregator. An aggregator like Flipkart, connects buyers and sellers and takes a commission on each sale. Since they do not always sell the products directly to customers, they handle GST differently. This is done with a Tax Collected at Source (TCS). When your website facilitates a sale between a buyer and a seller, GST law requires you to deduct 2 per cent of the sale before you send payment to the seller. You must pay that amount to the government. Then, your sellers can claim that tax as a deduction on their own GST filings. If you are an aggregator, both you and your sellers must report all sales to the government. Your reports and their reports must match exactly. If they do not match, your sellers are responsible for the outstanding GST. The TCS requirement helps you spot and remove sellers who aren't reporting sales accurately.

Tax Collection at Source (TCS). It is mandatory for all e-commerce operators to collect tax at the rate of one percent as TCS on the net value of sales made by suppliers through e-commerce operators. But this has been put off for the time being. The key purpose of this provision is to encourage compliances under GST and provide a mechanism for the government to track suppliers who sell through e-commerce operators.

Section 43B(e) of the law defines an Electronic Commerce Operator (Operator) as every person who, directly or indirectly, owns, operates or manages an electronic platform which is engaged in facilitating the supply of any goods and/or services. Also, a person providing any information or any other services incidental to or in connection with such supply of goods and services through electronic platform would be considered as an Operator.

One of the most important things the GST law did was reduction in taxes on very small businesses. Companies that bring in less than ₹20 lakh, or ₹10 lakh in northeastern states, do not need to pay GST. As an e-commerce business owner, this threshold does not apply to you. Under GST, all online sellers must register and pay GST. This means that even if you only bring in ₹1 lakh, you must go online and get a GSTIN. In addition, you are required to file monthly returns and pay taxes on all qualified sales.

Challenges of GST for E-commerce Operators. The e-commerce operators should report all supplies made by the seller and the TCS collected thereof on a monthly basis. The sales reported will have to match with the sales declared by the supplier himself at the end of every month, and any difference will be added to the turnover of the supplier and consequently be liable to discharge GST on such additional turnover. The e-commerce operator has to report the product/service code and the applicable rates for each item level individually. This requires them to map every sale done by the dealer and ensure TCS is deducted at the right value. The implementation of compliance is cumbersome for both e-commerce operator and the supplier. Also, the e-commerce operators will have to register in each state and file the reports separately on a monthly basis. This process increases the challenges in compliance and costs of running the business.

Benefits of GST in E-commerce

GST's Implementation have Two Major Benefits to E-commerce Players:

1. The GST model will facilitate seamless credit across supply chains, with tax set offs available across the production value-chain, both for goods and services. This will result in reduction of cascading effect of taxes, therefore bringing down the overall cost of supplies.
2. Consolidated tax rates: Earlier, there were differential rates of VAT for the same goods in different States. There are a lot of classification disputes in current scenario. However, GST rates at both the Central and State level are expected to be uniform and harmonised which would drastically reduce disputes among tax authorities and e-commerce players.

E-commerce Law in the European Union

The directives of the European Parliament and the Council are not directly applicable in the jurisdiction of the member states, but their national laws should be harmonized with the directives. Although, the EU legal acts related to electronic commerce are determined by the member states, the most important provisions of commercial law are laid down in the directives of the European Parliament and the Council (which may be ratified by the Parliaments of the member states) in order to simplify the movement of money and goods in the internal market.

In the attempt to improve its legal acts, including the acts on electronic commerce, Lithuania is using EU commercial law as a model. Reference to the most important documents and their main provisions the reader will find in the following pages.

Directive on Distance Transactions

The Directive on Distance Transactions, adopted in 1997, regulates the principles of consumer protection in respect of transactions made without a physical contact of the parties: by telephone, post, and electronic means. The main provisions of the directive are the following:

1. **Confirmation of the transaction.** After the conclusion of the transaction, the consumer should receive a confirmation in the medium acceptable to both parties (e.g. by e-mail or on paper).
2. **Right of revocation.** The consumer is entitled to withdraw from the transaction within 7 business days without any penalty or requirement to produce reasons.
3. **Full information.** The seller must inform the buyer beforehand of the exact prices for the goods and services offered (as well as any other charges), their validity date, delivery costs and their precise qualities.
4. **Prohibition on inert transactions.** Transactions which are not sanctioned by the consumer are prohibited even if the consumer has been informed of the ways how he may withdraw from the transaction.

Directive on Electronic Commerce

This latest legal act specially designed for digital business lays down, among other things, the requirements for the provider of Information Society Services (ISS) and the regulatory principles of his business:

1. **Identification.** The parties must ensure that information on the ISS provider's, established on their territory, name, postal and e-mail addresses, registration and VAT code should be easily accessible to consumers and competent institutions.
2. **Commercial correspondence.** If the IVP consists, in part or in whole, of material of advertising nature, the service provider must identify it explicitly as such and indicate the natural person or legal entity represented by it. The same is applicable to rebates, games, special offers, gifts, etc. The Directive requires that member states should control the unapproved sources of commercial correspondence distributed via e-mail within their legal framework.
3. **Electronic transactions.** Member States must ensure that their laws should provide for the validity of electronic commercial transactions. The service provider must inform, clearly and unambiguously, the service recipient of all the technical steps necessary to make the transaction. After the conclusion of the transaction, the service provider must issue the confirmation/receipt of the transaction. Throughout this process, up to the last stage, the recipient of the service must have the possibility of withdrawing from the transaction or correct any mistakes.
4. **The responsibility of the communications intermediary.** Electronic communications intermediaries, i.e. the providers of services of Internet communications and telecommunications operators, are not responsible for the content transmitted or placed by using their services or for the transactions made. The electronic communications intermediaries are not obliged to monitor the transmitted or saved information for possible illegal activities.

Directive on the Harmonization of Copyright and Related Rights in the Information Society (draft)

So far, the vast possibilities for the distribution of music and video works on the Internet have been hampered by the equally vast digital pirating wave. This document, which is under deliberation in the European Parliament, meets the requirement of the amusement industry to guarantee copyright and the protection of technologies used to assure the copyright. However, the directive still permits to make copies exclusively for personal use, but only by analogue technology (i.e. copying from a CD to MP3 would be illegal). In addition, illegal are programs and means designed to "break" the anti-pirate protection.

Other Acts

In addition to the documents mentioned above, there are several other EU legal acts which affect the environment of the Internet business.

- Directive on electronic monetary institutions, draft
- Recommendation on electronic payment instruments
- Directive on electronic signatures

Law on Electronic Signature

The only effective legal document specifically designed for electronic data communications is the Law on Electronic Signature, adopted in 2000. Its text is very similar to the EU Directive on electronic signatures, however, it also includes some new provisions.

The electronic signature is a special supplement, formed by a cryptographic algorithm, to a digital document. It is inseparable from the content of the document and the electronic certificate of its author. The purpose of the electronic signature, just as that of a conventional signature, is to ensure the authenticity of the document's author and contents. The recipient of the document uses another algorithm which compares the digital signature to the document and its author's public certificate. This algorithm recognizes if the text of the document has been modified without using the original certificate.

The Law regulates the procedure for the formation of the electronic signature, equipment and the activities of institutions responsible for the issuance of electronic certificates. For example, any natural person or legal entity may issue electronic certificates for its own needs or the needs of its clients, but only the qualified certificates have the legal validity of a written signature. "A secure electronic signature, created by a secure equipment used for the formation of the signature, and certified by a valid qualified certificate, shall have the same legal validity as a signature on written documents, and shall be admissible as a evidence before court" (8.1.a Article). However, subparagraph 2 of the same Article says that the instruments and procedure for the formation of an electronic signature as such may not be pleaded as grounds for doubting the power of proof—other objective criteria must be submitted to the court.

The State Electronic Signature Supervisory Authority is responsible, among other things, for the accreditation of the service providers and the determination of the main procedural and technical requirements for qualified certificates.

The Law does not regulate the rules as to when the electronic form of the documents is admissible or for what purposes. This is left for the regulation by further statutory and regulatory acts, but we can predict that the provisions of this Law will be important for the realization of EDI and business-to-business electronic commerce, i.e. for the area where the documents signed electronically may be used.

Documents under Development or Deliberation

1. **Amendments to the Civil Code provisions related to contract law.** Articles 41–45 of the existing Civil Code of the Republic of Lithuania defines the written and oral forms of contracts between persons. In the electronic market this choice is limited, therefore the new draft of paragraph 2 Article 1.73 of the First Book of the Civil Code 1, says that "Document in written form shall be equated to a document signed by the party and transmitted by telegraph, fax or other instant communication means provided that the protection of the text is ensured and it is possible to identify the

signature." The formulation of this provision provides a basis for the application of the provisions of the Law on Electronic Signature in respect of civil transactions.

2. **The Law on Electronic commerce.** A draft of this law is being developed by the Department of Information and Informatics of the Ministry of Public Administration Reforms and Local Authorities on the basis of the EU directive on electronic commerce and the UNCITRAL model law. The Law, when adopted, will define the legal validity and scope of application of any electronic transaction; it will also determine common requirements for commerce on the Internet.

Legislation Problems

In order to adapt the Lithuanian legal framework to the needs of the Internet business, it is necessary to establish what kind of legal acts are missing and which existing legal acts contradict the fundamental principles of electronic commerce.

Here are some of the most important issues.

Liability of the parties to the electronic settlement

Electronic payments date back much earlier than electronic commerce. They have their roots in banking technologies and the EDI systems of the '80s. Since then, the relations between the parties of the settlement have been regulated by direct agreements or bilateral agreements between a company and the network operator (e.g. S.W.I.F.T.). Such legal environment is still satisfactory to many EDI parties.

There is no infrastructure for direct electronic payments in Lithuania, except for banks, public institutions and financial service companies. However, there are two new factors which require a better definition of the norms applicable to electronic settlements. First, electronic settlements have become a consumption commodity therefore it requires an appropriate program for consumer protection. Second, settlements have moved to the Internet where there is no single operator or mandatory rules. In the rectangle "Purchaser—the purchaser's bank—the seller's bank—the seller" liabilities of each party must be defined in respect to possible damages through its own or a third party's fault. If the national legal acts do not provide for such liabilities, it is quite likely that mass consumers will become the most vulnerable link in these multilateral relations. The EU recommendation on electronic payment instruments is a model for the state to follow in attempts to ensure the protection of the consumer from unrestrained civil sanctions.

Internet domain names

A lot of experts agree that the names of Internet domains are a form of property similar to a trade mark. Therefore, this fact should not be neglected in trade mark law. On the other hand, the territory-related and specificity principles of trade mark law contradict the procedure of the formation and use of domain names. So, strictly speaking, a domain name as such may not get the same protection as is applied to trade marks.

Ownership disputes over domain names and attempts at selling prestigious domain names have become a reality in Lithuania. So far, the status of a domain name as property and its legal protection has not been regulated, while domain names are often provided by organisations whose activities are not regulated by any legal act, except for the internal rules of the register.

Accounting documents

Subject to the EU directives, the receipt/confirmation of a transaction is an essential instrument of electronic commerce. However, taking into consideration the peculiarities of the Internet, the Directive on Distance Transactions permits any "reliable" form of the receipt, i.e. it can be presented by e-mail, on a diskette or on paper.

Article 9 of the Law on the Fundamentals of Financial Accounting of the Republic of Lithuania provides for a strictly defined form of confirmation. It is emphasized that "companies shall support their business transactions, except for telecommunications services for mass consumption, with accounting documents." However, "transactions, including the telecommunications services delivered for mass consumption, which, under the procedures established by the Government of the Republic of Lithuania, are not required to use special accounting documents, and shall be supported by documents drawn up in the model or free form.

The Government has established a procedure for the exemption of certain sales groups from special accounting documents, but the list of such groups does not include electronic sellers. At present, businessmen engaged in electronic commerce deliver the invoice to the buyer together with the purchased product, while for ISS providers and users, who do not communicate in any other way except electronic communication (e.g. paid information services on the Internet), this method is too complicated. A proposal has been submitted to the Government to define the same accounting rules for ISS providers which are applicable to the providers to telecommunications services.

E-commerce Laws in the US

The Federal Trade Commission (FTC) is the primary federal agency regulating e-commerce activities, including use of commercial emails, online advertising and consumer privacy. FTC's e-commerce Guide provides an overview of e-commerce rules and regulations.

In the U.S., each of the 50 states has its own substantive commercial laws and court systems. Each state has a law called a *long-arm statute* which defines the persons and the entities over which the local courts have jurisdiction. In the context of interstate commerce, a corporation from another state that sells products directly within another state is "purposefully availing" itself of the laws of the other state, which is sufficient contact to justify jurisdiction. However, a state cannot exercise jurisdiction over an out-of-state corporation that sells goods that unforeseeably end up in the state.

In the context of the Internet, a Website operator will not normally limit its viewers or customers to those residing in a certain state.

Personal data is not the only thing protected on the Internet. Digital works, including text, movies, music and art are copyrighted and protected via the Digital Millennium Copyright Act (DMCA)[5]. The DMCA offers a number of protections for information published to the Internet, as well as other forms of electronic information. Among its many provisions, the DMCA:

- Limits Internet service providers from copyright infringement liability for simply transmitting information over the Internet. However, service providers, are expected

5. www.copyright.gov/legislation/dmca.pdf

to, upon notification, remove material from their Web sites that appear to constitute copyright infringement.

- Limits liability of nonprofit education institutions for copyright infringement by faculty members or graduate students.
- Makes it a crime to circumvent anti-piracy measures built into most commercial software. However, reverse engineering of copyright protection devices, is permitted to conduct encryption research, assess product interoperability, and test computer security systems.
- Provides exemptions from anti-circumvention provisions for non-profit libraries, archives, and educational institutions solely for the purpose of making a good faith determination as to whether they wish to obtain authorized access to the work.
- Outlaws the manufacture, sale, or distribution of devices used to illegally copy software.
- Requires that "Webcasters" pay licensing fees to record companies.

EXERCISES

1. Discuss the advantages and disadvantages of IT Act, 2000.
2. Why taxation is an issue in e-commerce?
3. What are the possible solutions for e-commerce taxation?
4. Compare e-commerce laws of India, US and European Union.
5. Intellectual property rights has become an issue in E-commerce—Discuss.
6. Discuss Web-wrap and Click-wrap contracts and their legal validity.

Glossary

ACL (Agent Communication Language) A key requirement for interoperation amongst heterogeneous agents.

Ad view A website visitor page request that contains an advertisement.

AES (Advanced Encryption Standard) Software encryption algorithm.

Affiliate marketing An advertising technique in which one site ("affiliate") includes descriptions, reviews, ratings, or other information about products that are sold on another site. The affiliate site includes links to the selling site, which pays the affiliate a commission on the sales made to visitors who arrived from a link at the affiliate site.

Aggregation The gathering of products from multiple suppliers so that the consumer can have more choices on one location.

AMPS (Advanced Mobile Phone Service) First analogue cellular phone WAN standard used in North America.

ASP (Application Service Provider) Allows businesses to outsource value chain functions to separate providers.

Attachment A data file that is appended to an e-mail message.

B2B (Business-to-Business) The marketing of products to business for use in the business operations as components in the business products, or for resale.

B2C (Business-to-Consumer) The marketing of products to the end consumer.

BAM (Brick and Mortar) A traditional, offline firm.

Banner ad A rectangular space appearing on a website, paid for by an advertiser, which allows the user to click through to the advertiser's website.

Bit vendor A type of e-tailer that sells digital products such as media, software and music, and delivers them via the Internet.

Broadband High bandwidth required for the delivery of multimedia content over the Internet.

Browser Software that lets users read HTML documents and move from one document to another using hyperlinks.

Buffer An area of the computer's memory that is set aside to hold data read from a file or database.

C2C (Consumer-to-Consumer) Business transaction from one consumer to another.

Cable modem Allows transmission of Internet traffic over the cable TV wire connected to a point, at speeds between 0.5 and 2.5 Mbps.

Cache A high-speed memory area set aside to store pages.

Catalogue aggregator Brings together many catalogue companies, creating a new searchable database of products for buyers.

Cause marketing An affiliate marketing program that benefits a charitable organization.

CDMA (Code Division Multiple Access) WAN technology for the spread spectrum sharing of a common RF channel for voice and data used by cellular devices; developed by QUALCOMM.

CDPD (Cellular Digital Packet Data) A system overlay for transmitting and receiving data over older AMPS cellular networks.

Chat room Virtual space where Internet users can communicate in real time, using special software.

Cipher text Text that comprises a seemingly random assemblage of bits, the result of encrypting a message.

Circuit switching A way of connecting computers or other devices that use a centrally controlled single connection. In this method which is used by telephone companies to provide voice telephone service, the connection is made, data are transferred, and the connection is terminated.

CISS (Common Internet Scheme Syntax) A common syntax for URL schemes that involve the direct use of IP-based protocols.

Click and mortar Store with offline and online selling.

Clickstream A user's Web surfing pattern.

Clickstream data Data recorded by software on the user PC or a Web server. Includes every page that user visits and the frequency with which the user returns to a page.

Click through Determined when a surfer clicks on a banner or other ad that is hyperlinked to the advertiser's site.

Client/server model A network in which each computer on the network is either a client or a server.

Collaborative filtering This software collects opinions of like-minded users online, and returns the same to the individual in real time.

Conversion rate The percentage of recipient that respond to an ad or promotion.

Cookie A persistent piece of information stored on the user's hard drive, which is keyed to a specific server, and is passed back to the server as part of the transaction that takes place when the user's browser again crosses the specific server/path combination.

CPM (cost per thousand impressions) The cost to deliver 1000 impressions.

CRM (Customer Relationship Management) A holistic process of identifying, attracting, and retaining customers.

Cryptography The science of encryption.

CSD (Circuit Switched Data) A data overlay service available from GSM operators.

Customization The third step in the CRM process. Here, firms tailor their marketing mixes to meet the needs of small target segments, using electronic marketing tools.

Cybersquatting A trademark violation that involves the registration of domains that resemble or duplicate the names of existing corporations or other entities.

Data mining Extracting hidden predictive information from the warehouse via statistical analysis to find patterns and other information in databases.

Data warehouse Repository for an organization's historical data.

Digital signature An encryption message digest.

Disintermediation The process of eliminating traditional intermediaries. This reduces costs.

DNS (Domain Name Service) Internet service that maps names to IP addresses of Internet domain servers.

DoS (Denial of Service) attack A relentless transmission of requests—deliberately intended—to slow down or 'crash' the network or server.

Dutch auction An open auction in which the bidding begins at a high price and drops until a bidder accepts the price.

E-business (Electronic business) Includes all electronic activity conducted by organizations, such as business intelligence, CRM, SCM, e-commerce, and ERP.

E-commerce (Electronic commerce) Includes buying/selling online, digital value creation, virtual marketplaces and storefronts, and new distribution channel intermediaries.

EFT (Electronic Fund Transfer) Electronic transfer of account exchange information over secure private communications networks.

E-marketing (Electronic marketing) The use of electronic data and applications for planning and executing the conception, distribution, promotion, and pricing of ideas, goods, and services to create exchanges that satisfy individual and organizational objectives.

English auction An auction where bidders publicly announce their successively high bids, until no higher bid is forthcoming.

ERP (Enterprise Resourse Planning) Back-office operations such as order entry, purchasing, invoicing, and inventory control. ERP systems allow organizations to optimize business processes while lowering costs.

Escrow service A third party who holds an auction buyer's payment until the buyer receives the purchased item and is satisfied that it is what the seller represented it to be.

E-tailer An 'electronic retailer', an intermediary firm that buys products and sells them online.

GPRS (General Packet Radio Service) A new packet-based bearer that is being introduced on many GSM and TDMA mobile networks from the year 2000 onwards.

GSM (Group System Mobile) European cellular WAN interface. It originated in 1990 based on TDMA technology; implemented largely over 1800 MHz in Europe and 1900 MHz in the US. Also translated as Global System for Mobile Communications.

Hash algorithm A security utility that mathematically combines every character in a message to create a fixed length number that is a 'fingerprint' of the original message.

Hash coding The process used to calculate a number from a message.

Hash value The number that results when a message is hash-coded.

HDML (Handheld Device Markup Language) Cellular phone markup language designed by Unwired Planet in 1997.

HDTP (Handheld Device Transport Protocol) The protocol that enables a hand-held device such as wireless phone, to access the Internet.

Hyperlink A pointer in an HTML document to another location within the same document or to another HTML document.

Hypertext A system of navigating between HTML pages, using links.

ICANN (Internet Corporation for Assigned Names and Numbers) Responsible for the administration of the Internet name and address system.

ICQ ('I Seek You') A program that finds friends, colleagues, and people with similar interests across the globe; services offered include instant messaging.

Infomediary An online organization that aggregates and distributes information.

Internet telephony Use of the Internet to carry simultaneous digitized voice transmission.

InterNIC One of the primary official World Wide Web domain name registration services.

Interstitials Java-based ads that appear while the publisher's content is loading.

IP address The 32-bit number that represents the address of a particular location (computer) on the Internet.

ITTP (Intelligent Terminal Transfer Protocol) WAP protocol introduced by Ericsson.

JIT (Just-in-Time inventory/delivery) A goal of value chain management, in which carrying excessive amounts of inventory is avoided.

LISTSERV A program that provides automatic processing of many functions involved with mailing lists. E-mailing appropriate messages to it will automatically subscribe the e-mailer to a discussion list or unsubscribe the person. LISTSERV will also answer requests for indexes, FAQs, archives of the previous discussions and other files.

Log file In Internet server software, a feature that records every file sent by the server along with the destination address and time sent.

Mailing list An e-mail address that forwards messages to certain users who are subscribers.

Metamediary An agent that represents a cluster of manufacturers, e-tailers and content providers organized around a live event or major asset purchase.

MRO (Maintenance, Repair and Operating) Commodity supplies that are used in a variety of industries.

NAPs (Network Access Points) The four primary connection points for access to the Internet backbone in the US.

Narrowcast Electronic media term referring primarily to cable channels because they contain focussed electronic content that appeals to special interest markets.

NCSA (National Center for Supercomputing Applications) NCSA is one of the five original centres in the National Science Foundation's Supercomputer Centres Program. Mosaic—the first Internet browser program—was invented at NCSA.

Network access providers The four companies that are primary providers of Internet access rights; they sell these rights to smaller Internet service providers.

Newsgroup Communities of interest that post e-mails on electronic bulletin boards.

Non-repudiation Verification that a particular transaction actually occurred; this prevents parties from denying a transaction's validity or its existence.

Online auctions Auction-style sale of merchandise over the Internet.

Online community Users who are widely distributed geographically but come together in cyberspace based on similar interests.

Online exchange Electronic forum in which buyers and sellers meet to make transactions.

Outsource To contract services from external firms in order to accomplish internal tasks.

Packet switched networks Networks designed to transmit data packets without regard to an established circuit. Internet is based on TCP/IP packet switching.

Page An HTML document that may contain text, images, and other online elements such as Java applets and multimedia files. Multiple pages together make up a site.

Page view The number of times a page is downloaded by users, often measured as a function of time.

Permission marketing Allows advertisers to send marketing communication messages to consumers who agree to receive them.

Personalization Ways that marketers personalize in an impersonal computer networked environment.

Personalized web page Page created with cookies that can be saved on the user's hard disk.

Private key A single key that is used to encrypt and decrypt messages.

Private key encryption The encoding of a message using a single numeric key to encode and decode data; it requires both the sender and the receiver of the message to know the key, which must be guarded from public disclosure.

Public key One of a pair of mathematically related numeric keys used to encrypt messages; freely distributed to the public.

Public key encryption The encoding of messages using two mathematically related but distinct numeric keys.

Reverse auction Allows individual buyers to enter the price they will pay for particular items at the purchasing agent's website; sellers may agree or not.

RFM (Recency/Frequency/Monetary) analysis Scans the database for three criteria: recency, frequency, and monetary value. This process allows firms to target offers to the customers who are most responsive, thus saving promotional costs and increasing sales.

ROI (Return-on-Investment) A method of evaluating the potential costs and benefits of a proposed capital investment.

Router A computer that determines the best for data packets to move forward to their destination.

RSA The encryption algorithm invented by Rivest, Shamir and Adleman in 1976.

SCM (Supply Chain Management) The behind-the-scenes coordination of the distribution channel to deliver products effectively and efficiently to customers.

SET (Secure Electronic Transaction) A secure protocol that provides security for card payments as they traverse the Internet between merchant sites and processing banks.

Shopping cart An e-commerce utility that keeps track of selected items for purchase, and automates the purchasing process.

SIM (Subscriber Identity Module) A chip found in a GSM phone that holds customer billing information and data.

Site stickiness A measure of the length of time spent at a site.

SMS (Short Message Service) A 2G-network service first made popular in GSM.

Sniffer program A program that taps into the Internet and records information that passes through a router from the data's source to its destination.

Spider The first part of a search engine, it automatically and frequently searches the Web to find pages and updates its database of information about old websites.

Spoofing Pretending to be someone you are not, or representing a website as an original when it is an imposter.

TDCC (Transportation Data Coordinating Committee) A grouping formed in 1968 by a number of freight and shipping companies to reduce their paperwork burden.

TDMA (Time Division Multiple Access) A radio technology that divides cellular bandwidth among subscribers; each caller is given a time slot and only allowed to transmit during that time.

Trojan horse A destructive program hidden inside another program or utility or sometimes, a game.

Usenet (User's News Network) One of the first mailing lists; it allows subscribers to read and post articles within topic areas.

USSD (Unstructured Supplementary Services Data) A means of transmitting information or instructions over a GSM network.

VAN An independent company that provides connection and EDI transaction forwarding services to businesses engaged in EDI.

Viral marketing Tactics that rely on existing customers to tell others—the company's prospective customers—about the products or services they have enjoyed using.

Virtual mall A model, similar to a shopping mall, in which multiple online merchants are hosted on a website.

Virus Software that attaches itself to another program and can cause damage when the host program is activated.

W3C (World Wide Web Consortium) Organization that develops high-level Internet protocols for the World Wide Web. The W3C was founded in October 1994.

WAE (Wireless Application Environment) It encompasses the devices, the content development languages (WML and WMLScript), the telephony APIs for accessing telephony functionality from within WAE programs, and some well-defined content formats for phone book records, calendar information, and graphics.

WAN (Wide Area Network) A geographically distributed network.

WAP (Wireless Application Protocol) Protocol that governs WAP phones, gateways, and servers; defined by the WAP Forum.

WAP gateway A junction between the cellular network and the Internet.

Web form A Web page where users can enter information.

Web page Another name for an HTML document.

Web server A system capable of continuous access to the Internet through retrieving and displaying documents and files via HTTP.

WML (Wireless Markup Language) An XML defined markup language defined by the WAP Forum. Rather than a Web page, it uses a deck of cards as its publishing model.

WMLScript It is the wireless scripting language. Similar to JavaScript, it provides some programming logic for performing calculations within an application.

Worm A virus that replicates itself on other machines.

WSP (Wireless Session Protocol) The session layer of the wireless OSI model along with the WTLS. This layer provides a consistent interface to WAE for two types of session services: a connection mode, and a connectionless service.

WTAI (Wireless Telephony Application Interface) Allows network operators to access the telephony features of a WAP device.

WTLS (Wireless Transport Layer Security) Part of the session layer of the wireless OSI model along with the WSP. It provides services to protect data, including data integrity, privacy, authentication, and denial-of-service protection.

WTP (Wireless Transaction Protocol) The transport layer of the wireless OSI model. It provides connection-oriented service to the upper layer, transaction-oriented service suitable for web browsing, and datagram service.

XML (Extensible Markup Language) The next generation of HTML that allows browsers to pull information from databases on the fly, and display in pages. In other words, it is an object-based model for exchanging program data across the Internet.

Index